CAPITAL MARKET EXPECTATIONS, MARKET VALUATION, AND ASSET ALLOCATION

CFA® PROGRAM CURRICULUM
2013 • Level III • Volume 3

WILEY
John Wiley & Sons, Inc.

Cover photographs courtesy of Hector Emanuel and Justin Runquist.

Copyright © 2012, 2011, 2010, 2009, 2008, 2007, 2006 by CFA Institute
All rights reserved.

This copyright covers material written expressly for this volume by the editor/s as well as the compilation itself. It does not cover the individual selections herein that first appeared elsewhere. Permission to reprint these has been obtained by CFA Institute for this edition only. Further reproduction by any means, electronic or mechanical, including photocopying and recording, or by any information storage or retrieval system, must be arranged with the individual copyright holders noted.

CFA®, Charter Financial Analyst®, AIMR-PPS®, and GIPS® are just a few of the trademarks owned by CFA Institute. To view a list of CFA Institute trademarks and the Guide for Use of CFA Institute Marks, please visit our website at www.cfainstitute.org.

This publication is designed to provide accurate and authoritative information in regard to the subject matter covered. It is sold with the understanding that the publisher is not engaged in rendering legal, accounting, or other professional service. If legal advise or other expert assistance is required, the services of a competent professional should be sought.

All trademarks, service marks, registered trademarks, and registered service marks are the property of their respective owners and are used herein for identification purposes only.

ISBN 978-1-937537-14-2 (paper)
ISBN 978-1-937537-35-7 (ebk)

10 9 8 7 6 5 4 3 2 1

Please visit our website at
www.WileyGlobalFinance.com

Contents

Portfolio Management

Study Session 6		**Capital Market Expectations in Portfolio Management**	3
Reading 18		**Capital Market Expectations**	5
		Introduction	6
		Organizing the Task: Framework and Challenges	7
		A Framework for Developing Capital Market Expectations	7
		Challenges in Forecasting	13
		Tools for Formulating Capital Market Expectations	23
		Formal Tools	23
		Survey and Panel Methods	47
		Judgment	48
		Economic Analysis	49
		Business Cycle Analysis	49
		Economic Growth Trends	65
		Exogenous Shocks	71
		International Interactions	72
		Economic Forecasting	77
		Using Economic Information in Forecasting Asset Class Returns	86
		Information Sources for Economic Data and Forecasts	100
		Summary	102
		Practice Problems for Reading 18	104
		Solutions for Reading 18	111
Study Session 7		**Economic Concepts for Asset Valuation in Portfolio Management**	121
Reading 19		**Equity Market Valuation**	123
		Introduction	123
		Estimating a Justified P/E Ratio	124
		Neoclassical Approach to Growth Accounting	124
		The China Economic Experience	125
		Quantifying China's Future Economic Growth	128
		Equity Market Valuation	129
		Top-Down and Bottom-Up Forecasting	137
		Portfolio Suitability of Each Forecasting Type	139
		Using Both Forecasting Types	140
		Top-Down and Bottom-Up Forecasting of Market Earnings per Share	141
		Relative Value Models	144

indicates an optional segment

	Earnings-Based Models	**144**
	Asset-Based Models	**153**
	Summary	**158**
	References	**159**
	Practice Problems for Reading 19	**161**
	Solutions for Reading 19	**167**

Reading 20 **Dreaming with BRICs: The Path to 2050** **171**

Introduction	**171**
A Dramatically Different World	**173**
Economic Size	**173**
Economic Growth	**173**
Incomes and Demographics	**173**
Global Demand Patterns	**177**
Currency Movements	**177**
How Countries Get Richer	**177**
Breaking Down Growth	**179**
A More Detailed Look at The BRICs' Potential	**180**
Are The Results Plausible?	**186**
A Look Back in Time—What Would We Have Said in 1960?	**187**
Ensuring The Conditions for Growth	**189**
How Different Assumptions Would Change Things	**191**
Implications of the BRICs' Ascendancy	**192**
Summary	**194**
Appendix 20A	**195**
Appendix 20B	**196**
Appendix 20C	**201**

Study Session 8 **Asset Allocation** **203**

Reading 21 **Asset Allocation** **205**

Introduction	**206**
What Is Asset Allocation?	**206**
The Role of Strategic Asset Allocation in Relation to Systematic Risk	**207**
Strategic versus Tactical Asset Allocation	**209**
The Empirical Debate on the Importance of Asset Allocation	**210**
Asset Allocation and The Investor's Risk and Return Objectives	**212**
Asset-Only and Asset/Liability Management Approaches to Strategic Asset Allocation	**212**
Return Objectives and Strategic Asset Allocation	**214**
Risk Objectives and Strategic Asset Allocation	**216**
Behavioral Influences on Asset Allocation	**220**
The Selection of Asset Classes	**222**
Criteria for Specifying Asset Classes	**223**
The Inclusion of International Assets (Developed and Emerging Markets)	**226**
Alternative Investments	**228**
The Steps In Asset Allocation	**229**

◘ indicates an optional segment

Contents

Optimization	231
The Mean–Variance Approach	232
The Resampled Efficient Frontier	249
The Black–Litterman Approach	250
Monte Carlo Simulation	257
Asset/Liability Management	260
Experience-Based Approaches	268
Implementing the Strategic Asset Allocation	270
Implementation Choices	270
Currency Risk Management Decisions	271
Rebalancing to the Strategic Asset Allocation	271
Strategic Asset Allocation for Individual Investors	272
Human Capital	272
Other Considerations in Asset Allocation for Individual Investors	278
Strategic Asset Allocation for Institutional Investors	280
Defined-Benefit Plans	281
Foundations and Endowments	285
Insurance Companies	289
Banks	292
Tactical Asset Allocation	294
Summary	300
Practice Problems for Reading 21	303
Solutions for Reading 21	313

Reading 22

The Case for International Diversification	**321**
The Traditional Case For International Diversification	323
Risk Reduction through Attractive Correlations	323
Portfolio Return Performance	333
Currency Risk Not a Barrier to International Investment	339
The Case Against International Diversification	340
Increase in Correlations	341
Past Performance Is a Good Indicator of Future Performance	343
Barriers to International Investments	344
The Case For International Diversification Revisited	347
Pitfalls in Estimating Correlation During Volatile Periods	348
Expanded Investment Universe and Performance Opportunities	349
Global Investing Rather than International Diversification	349
The Case For Emerging Markets	352
The Basic Case	352
Volatility, Correlations, and Currency Risk	353
Portfolio Return Performance	355
Investability of Emerging Markets	355
Segmentation versus Integration Issue	356
Summary	356
Practice Problems for Reading 22	359
Solutions for Reading 22	363
Glossary	**G-1**
Index	**I-1**

◉ indicates an optional segment

How to Use the CFA Program Curriculum

Congratulations on passing Level II of the Chartered Financial Analyst (CFA®) Program. This exciting and rewarding program of study reflects your desire to become a serious investment professional. You are embarking on a program noted for its high ethical standards and the breadth of knowledge, skills, and abilities it develops. Your commitment to the CFA Program should be educationally and professionally rewarding.

The credential you seek is respected around the world as a mark of accomplishment and dedication. Each level of the program represents a distinct achievement in professional development. Successful completion of the program is rewarded with membership in a prestigious global community of investment professionals. CFA charterholders are dedicated to life-long learning and maintaining currency with the ever-changing dynamics of a challenging profession. The CFA Program represents the first step towards a career-long commitment to professional education.

The CFA examination measures your mastery of the core skills required to succeed as an investment professional. These core skills are the basis for the Candidate Body of Knowledge (CBOK™). The CBOK consists of four components:

- A broad topic outline that lists the major top-level topic areas (CBOK Topic Outline)
- Topic area weights that indicate the relative exam weightings of the top-level topic areas
- Learning outcome statements (LOS) that advise candidates about the specific knowledge, skills, and abilities they should acquire from readings covering a topic area (LOS are provided in candidate study sessions and at the beginning of each reading)
- The CFA Program curriculum, readings, and end-of-reading questions, which candidates receive upon exam registration

Therefore, the keys to your success on the CFA exam is studying and understanding the CBOK™. The following sections provide background on the CBOK, the organization of the curriculum, and tips for developing an effective study program.

CURRICULUM DEVELOPMENT PROCESS

The CFA Program is grounded in the practice of the investment profession. Using the Global Body of Investment Knowledge (GBIK) collaborative website, CFA Institute performs a continuous practice analysis with investment professionals around the world to determine the knowledge, skills, and abilities (competencies) that are relevant to the profession. Regional expert panels and targeted surveys are conducted annually to verify and reinforce the continuous feedback from the GBIK collaborative website. The practice analysis process ultimately defines the CBOK. The CBOK contains the competencies that are generally accepted and applied by investment professionals. These competencies are used in practice in a generalist context and are expected to be demonstrated by a recently qualified CFA charterholder.

Copyright © CFA Institute.

A committee consisting of practicing charterholders, in conjunction with CFA Institute staff, designs the CFA Program curriculum in order to deliver the CBOK to candidates. The examinations, also written by practicing charterholders, are designed to allow you to demonstrate your mastery of the CBOK as set forth in the CFA Program curriculum. As you structure your personal study program, you should emphasize mastery of the CBOK and the practical application of that knowledge. For more information on the practice analysis, CBOK, and development of the CFA Program curriculum, please visit www.cfainstitute.org.

ORGANIZATION OF THE CURRICULUM

The Level III CFA Program curriculum is organized into 10 topic areas. Each topic area begins with a brief statement of the material and the depth of knowledge expected.

Each topic area is then divided into one or more study sessions. These study sessions—18 sessions in the Level III curriculum—should form the basic structure of your reading and preparation.

Each study session includes a statement of its structure and objective, and is further divided into specific reading assignments. An outline illustrating the organization of these 18 study sessions can be found at the front of each volume.

The reading assignments are the basis for all examination questions, and are selected or developed specifically to teach the knowledge, skills, and abilities reflected in the CBOK. These readings are drawn from CFA Institute-commissioned content, textbook chapters, professional journal articles, research analyst reports, and cases. All readings include problems and solutions to help you understand and master the topic areas.

Reading-specific Learning Outcome Statements (LOS) are listed at the beginning of each reading. These LOS indicate what you should be able to accomplish after studying the reading. The LOS, the reading, and the end-of-reading questions are dependent on each other, with the reading and questions providing context for understanding the scope of the LOS.

You should use the LOS to guide and focus your study, as each examination question is based on an assigned reading and one or more LOS. The readings provide context for the LOS and enable you to apply a principle or concept in a variety of scenarios. The candidate is responsible for the entirety of all of the required material in a study session, the assigned readings as well as the end-of-reading questions and problems.

We encourage you to review the material on LOS (http://www.cfainstitute.org/cfaprogram/courseofstudy/Pages/cfa_los.aspx), including the descriptions of LOS "command words," (www.cfainstitute.org/Documents/cfa_and_cipm_los_command_words.pdf).

FEATURES OF THE CURRICULUM

- **Required vs. Optional Segments** - You should read all of an assigned reading. In some cases, however, we have reprinted an entire chapter or article and marked certain parts of the reading as "optional." The CFA examination is based only on the required segments, and the optional segments are included only when they might help you to better understand the required segments (by seeing the required material in its full context). When an optional segment begins, you will see text and a dashed vertical bar in the outside margin that will continue until the optional segment ends, accompanied by another icon. *Unless the material is specifically marked as optional, you should assume it is required.* You should rely on the required segments and the reading-specific LOS in preparing for the examination.

How to Use the CFA Program Curriculum

- **Problems/Solutions** - *All questions and problems in the readings as well as their solutions (which are provided directly following the problems) are part of the curriculum and are required material for the exam.* When appropriate, we have included problems within and after the readings to demonstrate practical application and reinforce your understanding of the concepts presented. The questions and problems are designed to help you learn these concepts and may serve as a basis for exam questions. Many of these questions are adapted from past CFA examinations.
- **Margins** - The wide margins in each volume provide space for your note-taking.
- **Six-Volume Structure** - For portability of the curriculum, the material is spread over six volumes.
- **Glossary and Index** - For your convenience, we have printed a comprehensive glossary and index in each volume. Throughout the curriculum, a **bolded blue** word in a reading denotes a term defined in the glossary.
- **Source Material** - The authorship, publisher, and copyright owners are given for each reading for your reference. We recommend that you use this CFA Institute curriculum rather than the original source materials because the curriculum may include only selected pages from outside readings, updated sections within the readings, and contains problems and solutions tailored to the CFA Program.
- **LOS Self-Check** - We have inserted checkboxes next to each LOS that you can use to track your progress in mastering the concepts in each reading.

DESIGNING YOUR PERSONAL STUDY PROGRAM

Create a Schedule - An orderly, systematic approach to examination preparation is critical. You should dedicate a consistent block of time every week to reading and studying. Complete all reading assignments and the associated problems and solutions in each study session. Review the LOS both before and after you study each reading to ensure that you have mastered the applicable content and can demonstrate the knowledge, skill, or ability described by the LOS and the assigned reading. Use the LOS self-check to track your progress and highlight areas of weakness for later review.

As you prepare for your exam, we will e-mail you important exam updates, testing policies, and study tips. Be sure to read these carefully. Curriculum errata are periodically updated and posted on the study session page at www.cfainstitute.org. You may also sign up for an RSS feed to alert you to the latest errata update.

Successful candidates report an average of over 300 hours preparing for each exam. Your preparation time will vary based on your prior education and experience. For each level of the curriculum, there are 18 study sessions, so a good plan is to devote 15–20 hours per week, for 18 weeks, to studying the material. Use the final four to six weeks before the exam to review what you've learned and practice with sample and mock exams. This recommendation, however, may underestimate the hours needed for appropriate examination preparation depending on your individual circumstances, relevant experience, and academic background. You will undoubtedly adjust your study time to conform to your own strengths and weaknesses, and your educational and professional background.

You will probably spend more time on some study sessions than on others, but on average you should plan on devoting 15-20 hours per study session. You should allow ample time for both in-depth study of all topic areas and additional concentration on those topic areas for which you feel least prepared.

Online Sample Examinations - CFA Institute online sample examinations are intended to assess your exam preparation as you progress toward the end of your study. After each question, you will receive immediate feedback noting the correct response and indicating the relevant assigned reading, so you will be able to identify areas of weakness for further study. The 120-minute sample examinations reflect the question formats, topics, and level of difficulty of the actual CFA examinations. Aggregate data indicate that the CFA examination pass rate was higher among candidates who took one or more online sample examinations than among candidates who did not take the online sample examinations. For more information on the online sample examinations, please visit www.cfainstitute.org.

Online Mock Examinations - In response to candidate requests, CFA Institute has developed mock examinations that mimic the actual CFA examinations not only in question format and level of difficulty, but also in length and topic weight. The three-hour online mock exams simulate the morning and afternoon sessions of the actual CFA exam, and are intended to be taken after you complete your study of the full curriculum, so you can test your understanding of the CBOK and your readiness for the exam. The mock exams are available in a printable PDF format with feedback provided at the end of the exam, rather than after each question as with the sample exams. CFA Institute recommends that you take these mock exams at the final stage of your preparation toward the actual CFA examination. For more information on the online mock examinations, please visit www.cfainstitute.org.

Preparatory Providers - After you enroll in the CFA Program, you may receive numerous solicitations for preparatory courses and review materials. When considering a prep course make sure the provider is in compliance with the CFA Institute Prep Provider Guidelines Program (www.cfainstitute.org/partners/examprep/Pages/cfa_prep_provider_guidelines.aspx). Just remember, there are no shortcuts to success on the CFA examinations; reading and studying the CFA curriculum is the key to success on the examination. The CFA examinations reference only the CFA Institute assigned curriculum—no preparatory course or review course materials are consulted or referenced.

SUMMARY

Every question on the CFA examination is based on the content contained in the required readings and on one or more LOS. Frequently, an examination question is based on a specific example highlighted within a reading or on a specific end-of-reading question and/or problem and its solution. To make effective use of the CFA Program curriculum, please remember these key points:

1. All pages printed in the curriculum are required reading for the examination except for occasional sections marked as optional. You may read optional pages as background, but you will not be tested on them.

2. All questions, problems, and their solutions - printed at the end of readings - are part of the curriculum and are required study material for the examination.

3. You should make appropriate use of the online sample/mock examinations and other resources available at www.cfainstitute.org.

4. You should schedule and commit sufficient study time to cover the 18 study sessions, review the materials, and take sample/mock examinations.

5. **Note:** Some of the concepts in the study sessions may be superseded by updated rulings and/or pronouncements issued after a reading was published. Candidates are expected to be familiar with the overall analytical framework contained in the assigned readings. Candidates are not responsible for changes that occur after the material was written.

FEEDBACK

At CFA Institute, we are committed to delivering a comprehensive and rigorous curriculum for the development of competent, ethically grounded investment professionals. We rely on candidate and member feedback as we work to incorporate content, design, and packaging improvements. You can be assured that we will continue to listen to your suggestions. Please send any comments or feedback to curriculum@cfainstitute.org. Ongoing improvements in the curriculum will help you prepare for success on the upcoming examinations, and for a lifetime of learning as a serious investment professional.

Portfolio Management

STUDY SESSIONS

- **Study Session 3** Behavioral Finance
- **Study Session 4** Private Wealth Management
- **Study Session 5** Portfolio Management for Institutional Investors
- **Study Session 6** Capital Market Expectations in Portfolio Management
- **Study Session 7** Economic Concepts for Asset Valuation in Portfolio Management
- **Study Session 8** Asset Allocation
- **Study Session 9** Management of Passive and Active Fixed-Income Portfolios
- **Study Session 10** Portfolio Management of Global Bonds and Fixed-Income Derivatives
- **Study Session 11** Equity Portfolio Management
- **Study Session 12** Equity Portfolio Management
- **Study Session 13** Alternative Investments for Portfolio Management
- **Study Session 14** Risk Management
- **Study Session 15** Risk Management Applications of Derivatives
- **Study Session 16** Execution of Portfolio Decisions; Monitoring and Rebalancing
- **Study Session 17** Performance Evaluation and Attribution
- **Study Session 18** Global Investment Performance Standards

This volume includes Study Sessions 6–8.

TOPIC LEVEL LEARNING OUTCOME

The candidate should be able to prepare an appropriate investment policy statement and asset allocation; formulate strategies for managing, monitoring, and rebalancing investment portfolios; evaluate portfolio performance; and analyze a presentation of investment returns for consistency with Global Investment Performance Standards (GIPS®).

PORTFOLIO MANAGEMENT
STUDY SESSION

6

Capital Market Expectations in Portfolio Management

After identifying the client's objectives and constraints and creating an investment policy statement, the manager's next task in the investment management process is to formulate capital market expectations. These forecasts of risk and return characteristics for various asset classes form the basis for constructing portfolios that maximize expected return for given levels of risk. This reading examines the process of setting capital market expectations and covers the major tools of economic analysis.

READING ASSIGNMENT

Reading 18 *Capital Market Expectations*
Managing Investment Portfolios: A Dynamic Process, Third Edition, John L. Maginn, CFA, Donald L. Tuttle, CFA, Jerald E. Pinto, CFA, and Dennis W. McLeavey, CFA, editors

READING 18

Capital Market Expectations

by John P. Calverley, Alan M. Meder, CFA, Brian D. Singer, CFA, and Renato Staub

LEARNING OUTCOMES

Mastery	The candidate should be able to:
☐	**a** discuss the role of, and a framework for, capital market expectations in the portfolio management process;
☐	**b** discuss, in relation to capital market expectations, the limitations of economic data, data measurement errors and biases, the limitations of historical estimates, *ex post* risk as a biased measure of *ex ante* risk, biases in analysts' methods, the failure to account for conditioning information, the misinterpretation of correlations, psychological traps, and model uncertainty;
☐	**c** demonstrate the application of formal tools for setting capital market expectations, including statistical tools, discounted cash flow models, the risk premium approach, and financial equilibrium models;
☐	**d** explain the use of survey and panel methods and judgment in setting capital market expectations;
☐	**e** discuss the inventory and business cycles, the impact of consumer and business spending, and monetary and fiscal policy on the business cycle;
☐	**f** discuss the impact that the phases of the business cycle have on short-term/long-term capital market returns;
☐	**g** explain the relationship of inflation to the business cycle and the implications of inflation for cash, bonds, equity, and real estate returns;
☐	**h** demonstrate the use of the Taylor rule to predict central bank behavior;
☐	**i** evaluate 1) the shape of the yield curve as an economic predictor and 2) the relationship between the yield curve and fiscal and monetary policy;
☐	**j** identify and interpret the components of economic growth trends and demonstrate the application of economic growth trend analysis to the formulation of capital market expectations;
☐	**k** explain how exogenous shocks may affect economic growth trends;
☐	**l** identify and interpret macroeconomic, interest rate, and exchange rate linkages between economies;

Managing Investment Portfolios: A Dynamic Process, Third Edition, John L. Maginn, CFA, Donald L. Tuttle, CFA, Dennis W. McLeavey, CFA, and Jerald E. Pinto, CFA, editors. Copyright © 2007 by CFA Institute.

Mastery	The candidate should be able to:
☐	m discuss the risks faced by investors in emerging-market securities and the country risk analysis techniques used to evaluate emerging market economies;
☐	n compare the major approaches to economic forecasting;
☐	o demonstrate the use of economic information in forecasting asset class returns;
☐	p evaluate how economic and competitive factors affect investment markets, sectors, and specific securities;
☐	q discuss the relative advantages and limitations of the major approaches to forecasting exchange rates;
☐	r recommend and justify changes in the component weights of a global investment portfolio based on trends and expected changes in macroeconomic factors.

1 INTRODUCTION

A noted investment authority has written that the "fundamental law of investing is the uncertainty of the future."[1] Yet investors have no choice but to forecast at least elements of the future because nearly all investment decisions look toward it. Specifically, investment decisions incorporate the decision maker's expectations concerning factors and events believed to affect investment values. The decision maker finally integrates these views into expectations about the risk and return prospects of individual assets and groups of assets.

The particular concern of this reading is **capital market expectations** (CME): the investor's expectations concerning the risk and return prospects of asset classes, however broadly or narrowly the investor defines those asset classes. Capital market expectations are an essential input to formulating a strategic asset allocation. For example, if an investor's investment policy statement specifies and defines eight permissible asset classes, the investor will need to have formulated long-term expectations concerning those asset classes to develop a strategic asset allocation. The investor may also act on short-term expectations. Capital market expectations are expectations about classes of assets, or **macro expectations**. By contrast, **micro expectations** are expectations concerning individual assets. Micro expectations are key ingredients in security selection and valuation. Insights into capital markets gleaned during CME setting should help in formulating accurate micro expectations in security selection and valuation.

One theme of this reading is that a disciplined approach to expectations setting will be rewarded. Therefore, much of the reading is devoted to explaining a widely applicable expectations-setting process. A second theme of this reading is that skillful economic analysis can contribute to expectations setting. That theme is supported by the observation that securities markets trade claims on the cash flows of the business sector and that other markets reflect the macro economy too.

The reading is organized as follows: Section 2 presents a general framework for developing capital market expectations and alerts the reader to the range of problems and pitfalls that await the investor or analyst in this arena. Section 3 then turns to describing the range of tools, both formal and judgmental, that an analyst may use in expectations setting. Section 4 covers economic analysis as applied to formulating capital market expectations, and we then summarize the reading.

---
[1] Peter L. Bernstein in the foreword to Rapaport and Mauboussin (2001), p. xiii.

ORGANIZING THE TASK: FRAMEWORK AND CHALLENGES

In this section, we provide a guide to collecting, organizing, combining, and interpreting information. After illustrating the process, we turn to a discussion of typical problems and challenges to formulating the most informed judgments possible.

2.1 A Framework for Developing Capital Market Expectations

The following is a framework for a disciplined approach to setting CME.

1. *Specify the final set of expectations that are needed, including the time horizon to which they apply.* The analyst needs to understand the specific objectives of the analysis in order to work efficiently toward them. To make this step even more concrete, the analyst should write the questions that need to be answered. Accomplishing this step requires the analyst to formulate his or her specific needs in terms of a relevant set of asset classes that are of concern, giving appropriate regard to the constraints of the client. In many cases, the investor's investment policy statement may provide guidance in this task. For example, for a taxable investor with a 10-year time horizon, the portfolio manager would develop long-term after-tax expectations for use in developing a strategic asset allocation.

2. *Research the historical record.* Most forecasts have some connection to the past. For many markets, the historical record contains useful information on the investment characteristics of the asset, suggesting at least some possible ranges for future results. Beyond the raw historical facts, the analyst should seek to identify the factors that affect asset class returns and to understand the what, when, where, why, and how of these return drivers. The analyst will then have a better sense of the information mosaic that he or she will need to piece together to arrive at wellin-formed conclusions.

3. *Specify the method(s) and/or model(s) that will be used and their information requirements.* The investor, capital market analyst, or unit responsible for developing capital market expectations (as the case may be) should be explicit about the method(s) and/or model(s) that will be used and should be able to justify the selection. Information requirements (economic and financial market data needs, for example) depend on the decision about method(s).

4. *Determine the best sources for information needs.*

5. *Interpret the current investment environment using the selected data and methods, applying experience and judgment.* The analyst should be sure that he or she is working from a common set of assumptions in interpreting different elements of the investment and economic scene so that the analyst's conclusions are mutually consistent. The analyst often needs to apply judgment and experience to interpret apparently conflicting signals within the data.

6. *Provide the set of expectations that are needed, documenting conclusions.* These are the analyst's answers to the questions set out in Step 1. The answers should be accompanied by the reasoning and assumptions behind them.

7. *Monitor actual outcomes and compare them to expectations, providing feedback to improve the expectations-setting process.*

Disciplined capital market expectations setting requires experience and expertise in investments and economics. Large asset managers may have a research unit—for example, an economics unit—with responsibility for developing capital market expectations. Through superior forecasts, such asset managers seek to better control risk and improve the results of actively managed accounts in particular. The development of capital market expectations is **beta research** (research related to systematic risk and returns to systematic risk). As such, it is usually centralized so that the CME inputs used across all equity and fixed-income products are consistent. On the other hand, **alpha research** (research related to capturing excess risk-adjusted returns by a particular strategy) is typically conducted within particular product groups with the requisite investment-specific expertise. For institutional investors, professional consultants are a resource for systematically developed capital market expectations. Consultants' assistance may be given in the course of asset allocation reviews or asset–liability planning studies. Institutional investors may develop capital market expectations in-house, although they will usually be aware of the perspectives of professional consultants and peers. Most individual investors rely on their investment adviser or other external source for guidance in setting capital market expectations, as they often do not have expertise in this area. Yet an adviser may incorporate the client's perspectives on capital markets prospects, as the portfolio is run on the client's behalf and the client must be comfortable with the inputs to constructing the portfolio.

The first step in the framework for developing CME requires that analysts set boundaries to focus their attention on the expectations most relevant for their investment situation. Otherwise, effort is wasted. Even pared down to the minimum needs, the scope of the expectations-setting process can be quite challenging. As Example 1 illustrates, there is a direct relationship between the number and variety of permissible asset class alternatives and the scope of the expectations-setting task facing the manager.

Example 1

Capital Market Expectations Setting: Information Requirements (1)

Consider the tasks facing two investment managers, John Pearson and Michael Wu.

Pearson runs U.S. balanced separately managed accounts (SMAs) for high-net-worth individuals within a bank trust department. The mandates of these accounts restrict investments to U.S. equities, U.S. investment-grade fixed-income instruments, and prime U.S. money market instruments. These balanced accounts have an investment objective of long-term capital growth and income. In contrast, Wu is the chief investment officer of a large Hong Kong–based, internationally focused asset manager that uses the following types of assets within its investment process:

Equities	Fixed Income	Alternative Investments
Hong Kong equities	Eurozone sovereign debt	Eastern Europe venture capital
Eurozone equities*	U.S. government debt	New Zealand timber assets
U.S. large-cap equities		U.S. apartment properties
U.S. small-cap equities		
Canadian large-cap equities		

---

*The **Eurozone** is the region of countries using the euro as a currency. As of the end of 2011, the Eurozone consisted of Austria, Belgium, Cyprus, Estonia, Finland, France, Germany, Greece, Ireland, Italy, Luxembourg, Malta, the Netherlands, Portugal, Slovakia, Slovenia, and Spain.

Note: Venture capital is equity investment in private companies.

Organizing the Task: Framework and Challenges

> Wu runs SMAs with generally long-term time horizons and global tactical asset allocation (GTAA) programs. Compare and contrast the information and knowledge requirements of Pearson and Wu.
>
> **Solution:**
>
> Pearson's in-depth information requirements relate to U.S. equity and fixed-income markets. By contrast, Wu's information requirements relate not only to U.S. and non-U.S. equity and fixed-income markets, but also to three alternative investment types with nonpublic markets, located on three different continents. Wu's need to be current on political, social, economic, and even trading-oriented operational details worldwide is more urgent than Pearson's. Given their respective investment time horizons, Pearson's focus is on the long term while Wu needs to focus not only on the long term but also on near-term disequilibria among markets (as he runs GTAA programs). One challenge that Pearson has in U.S. fixed-income markets that Wu does not face is the need to cover corporate as well as government debt securities. Nevertheless, Wu's overall information and knowledge requirements are clearly more demanding than Pearson's.

In the next example, the balanced fund manager from Example 1 specifies the final set of expectations needed and the time frame for those expectations.

Example 2

Capital Market Expectations Setting: Information Requirements (2)

Following the practice of his employer, Pearson uses the results of constrained mean–variance optimization (MVO) and information from clients' investment policy statements to develop strategic asset allocations for the balanced accounts.

Pearson is now addressing the first step in the framework given in the text for a client whose investment time horizon is five years. What set of final expectational data does Pearson need?

Solution:

Pearson needs the following final set of expectations:

- the expected U.S. broad market annual equity total return over a five-year horizon;
- the expected U.S. investment-grade bond annual total return over a five-year horizon;
- the standard deviation of annual returns of U.S. broad market equities;
- the standard deviation of annual returns of U.S. investment-grade bonds; and
- the correlation of annual U.S. stock and U.S. bond returns.

In total, Pearson needs two expected returns, two standard deviations, and one correlation for the MVO.

Steps 2 and 3 in the expectations-setting process involve understanding the historical performance of the asset classes and researching their return drivers. The analyst can approach these tasks by collecting macroeconomic and market information (e.g., asset returns) by:

- geographic area (e.g., domestic, nondomestic, or some subset—for example, a single international area), or
- broad asset class (e.g., equity, fixed-income, or real estate).

The finer classifications depend on the characteristics of the task and the orientation of the investor. For equities, one approach would be to further classify by economic sector, possibly making style-related (e.g., market-capitalization) distinctions. A fixed-income investor might distinguish between governmental and corporate sectors and make further credit distinctions. For example, an industry rotation equity strategist might formulate expectations on domestic equities as follows:

Economic Sector (e.g., technology manufacturers)
    Industry (e.g., computer equipment manufacturers)
        Subindustry (e.g., microchip component manufacturers)

Example 3

Historical Analysis

As Peter L. Bernstein (2004) has written, forecasters who make predictions without regard to past experience have no benchmarks to distinguish between what is new about their expectations and what may be a continuation of past experience. Dimson, Marsh, and Staunton (2011), in a rigorous study covering the 111-year period from 1900 to 2010, found that equities achieved higher annualized geometric mean real returns than did bonds or bills in seventeen major national markets. It would be appropriate for an analyst forecasting that bonds would outperform equities over some (probably shorter-term) horizon to supply supporting analysis that recognizes the tension between the forecast and past long-term experience.

In Step 3, the analyst also needs to be sensitive to the fact that the effectiveness of forecasting approaches and relationships among variables may be related to the investor's time horizon. As an example, a discounted cash flow approach to developing equity market expectations is usually considered to be most appropriate to long-range forecasting.

The fourth step involves determining the best sources for information needs. Executing this step well requires that the analyst research the quality of alternative data sources. Factors such as data collection principles and definitions, error rates in collection, calculation formulas, and for asset class indices, qualities such as investability, correction for free float, turnover in index constituents, and biases in the data are relevant. The cost of data may also be relevant. In short, analysts must understand everything they can about the data they will use for analysis. Using flawed or misunderstood data is a recipe for faulty analysis. Furthermore, analysts should constantly be alert to new, superior sources for their data needs.

Besides taking care with data sources, the analyst must select the appropriate data frequency. For instance, long-term data series should not be used for setting short-term trading expectations or evaluating short-term volatility. Daily series are of more use for setting shorter-term capital market expectations. Quarterly or annual data series are useful for setting long-term capital market expectations.

The fifth step involves interpreting the current investment environment using the selected data and methods, applying experience and judgment. In the sixth step, we take all of our analyses of the economic and market environment into forward-looking views on capital markets, developing any required quantitative forecasts. In other words, the questions formulated in Step 1 are answered in Step 6. Economic analysis may work itself into quantitative forecasts in a variety of ways depending on the investor's selection of methodology. Top-down investment approaches often use economic analysis more intensively than bottom-up approaches. Example 4 illustrates several ways an analyst's relative optimism or pessimism concerning a market might be reflected in quantitative forecasts.

Example 4

Incorporating Economic Analysis into Expected Return Estimates

Michael Wu has gathered information on consensus expectations in equity and fixed-income markets. On the basis of his economic analysis, Wu is optimistic relative to the consensus on the prospects for Hong Kong equities. On the other hand, Wu is pessimistic relative to the consensus on the prospects for U.S. large-cap equities. Depending on the model chosen, Wu's views might be reflected in his quantitative expectations in several ways, including the following:

- **Historical mean return with adjustments**. If Wu takes a historical mean return as his baseline for each asset class, he may make an upward adjustment to that mean for Hong Kong equities and a downward adjustment for U.S. large-cap equities.

- **Risk premium approach**. Wu may frame his analysis in terms of the equity risk premium (the expected return on equities in excess of the long bond expected return). After translating his views into equity risk premium estimates for Hong Kong and U.S. large-cap equities, his return expectation for each asset class is the expected equity risk premium in each market plus the long bond expected return in each market (which he can estimate directly from the term structure of interest rates).

- **Discounted cash flow (DCF) model estimates**. Wu may use his economic analysis to forecast the growth rates of corporate profits for the United States and Hong Kong and input those forecasts into a DCF model solved for the required return on equities in each country.

- **Implied market estimates of expected return with adjustment**. Making use of a world market benchmark and a methodology known as the Black–Litterman model, Wu may infer the equilibrium expected returns on asset classes as reflected by their values in the allocated world market benchmark. Wu can then incorporate his own views on Hong Kong and U.S. large-cap equities using a procedure specified by Black–Litterman.[2]

For a Hong Kong–based client, Hong Kong dollar returns are relevant, so Wu will also need to make exchange rate forecasts to arrive at his conclusions.

---

[2] The Black–Litterman model is discussed further in the reading on asset allocation.

Finally, we want to use experience to improve the expectations-setting process. We measure our previously formed expectations against actual results to assess the level of accuracy that the expectations-setting process is delivering. Generally, good forecasts are:

- unbiased, objective, and well researched;
- efficient, in the sense of reducing the magnitude of forecast errors to a minimum; and
- internally consistent.

Internal inconsistency can take a number of forms. For example, domestic bond and domestic equity expectations developed by different analysts using different inflation projections would not be internally consistent. A restructuring of a portfolio based on those expectations would, at least in part, merely reflect an unresolved difference in assumptions. In some cases, inconsistent forecasts may result in conclusions that are implausible or impossible. Example 5 illustrates inconsistent statistical forecasts.

Example 5

Inconsistency of Correlation Estimates: An Illustration

Frequently, the expected correlations between asset classes form part of the final expectational data that an analyst needs. If the number of asset classes is n, the analyst will need to estimate $(n^2 - n)/2$ distinct correlations (or the same number of distinct covariances). In doing so, the analyst must be sure that his or her estimates are consistent. For example, consider the correlation matrix for three assets shown in Exhibit 1.

Exhibit 1	Inconsistent Correlations		
	Market 1	Market 2	Market 3
Market 1	1	−1	−1
Market 2	−1	1	−1
Market 3	−1	−1	1

According to Exhibit 1, the estimated correlation between each asset and each other asset is −1. These estimates are internally inconsistent but, in fact, not possible. If Markets 1 and 2 are perfectly negatively correlated and Markets 2 and 3 are as well, then Markets 1 and 3 should be perfectly positively correlated rather than perfectly negatively correlated.

Other cases of an inconsistent correlation matrix are not so obvious.[3]

As a result of the final feedback step, we may be able to identify and correct weaknesses in our expectations-setting process or methods.

---

[3] What may look like a viable correlation matrix at first inspection is not necessarily feasible. In a three-asset case, it is feasible for all pairwise correlations to be −0.50; however, it can be shown that correlations that are all equal to −0.51 are not feasible (i.e., are inconsistent). Correlations must be consistent for variances to be nonnegative.

2.2 Challenges in Forecasting

A range of problems can frustrate analysts' expectations-setting efforts. Expectations reflecting faulty analysis or assumptions may cause a portfolio manager to construct a portfolio that is inappropriate for the client. At the least, the portfolio manager may incur the costs of changing portfolio composition without any offsetting benefits. On the principle that forewarned is forearmed, the following sections provide guidance on the points where special caution is warranted. The discussion focuses on problems in the use of data and on analyst mistakes and biases.

2.2.1 *Limitations of Economic Data*

The analyst needs to understand the definition, construction, timeliness, and accuracy of any data used, including any biases. The time lag with which economic data are collected, processed, and disseminated can be an impediment to their use. Although in some highly developed markets some economic data may be reported with a lag as short as one week, other important data may be reported with a lag of more than a quarter. The International Monetary Fund sometimes reports macroeconomic data for developing economies with a lag of two years or more. Older data for a variable increase the uncertainty concerning the current state of the economy with respect to that variable.

Furthermore, one or more official revisions to the initial values are common. In effect, measurements are made with error, but the direction and magnitude of the error are not known at the time the data are initially publicized.

Definitions and calculation methods change too. For example, the sampling procedures and calculation methods for the U.S. Consumer Price Index for All Urban Consumers (CPI-U) used by the Bureau of Labor Statistics (BLS) have changed in significant ways since the series was first published. In 1983, for example, the BLS shifted to a flow-of-services model for pricing owner-occupied housing, based on the costs that would be associated with renting such housing. In 1991, the BLS began the introduction of hedonic or regression-based quality adjustments to prices to reflect any increases in quality and features of various consumption items.

Example 6

A Change in Focus from GNP to GDP

In the late 1980s, expanding international trade caused economists to favor the use of Gross Domestic Product (GDP) over Gross National Product (GNP). Basically, GDP measures production within national borders regardless of whether the labor and property inputs are domestically or foreign owned. In contrast, GNP makes an adjustment to GDP equal to the receipts of factor income from the rest of the world to the country, less the payments of factor income from a country to the rest of the world. This change in preference reflected the fact that product subcomponents, such as automobile parts, were being created in various regions of the world. Thus, measuring economic activity according to what nation was responsible for activities in various regions of the world was becoming more difficult and less useful than being able to measure what was being made within a nation or particular region. Consistent with this observation, the United Nations System of National Accounts (known as UNSNA, or SNA for short) emphasizes GDP.

An analyst must realize that suppliers of indices of economic and financial data periodically **re-base** these indices, meaning that the specific time period used as the base of the index is changed. A re-basing is not a substantive change in the composition of an index. It is more of a mathematical change. Analysts constructing a data series should take care that data relating to different bases are not inadvertently mixed together.

2.2.2 Data Measurement Errors and Biases

Analysts need to be aware of possible biases in data measurement of series such as asset class returns. Errors in data series include the following:

- **Transcription errors**. These are errors in gathering and recording data. Such errors are most serious if they reflect a bias.

- **Survivorship bias**. Survivorship bias arises when a data series reflects only entities that have survived to the end of the period. For example, a share index may be based on companies that trade on an exchange. Such companies are often delisted (removed from trading on the exchange) after events such as bankruptcy filings and mergers. Shares of bankrupt companies may trade elsewhere after delisting. Do reported returns on a share index reflect post-delisting returns? If not, the return series will probably convey an overly optimistic picture of the real-time investment returns from owning all listed shares. Without correction, statistics derived from series subject to survivorship bias can be misleading in the forward-looking context of expectations setting.[4]

- **Appraisal (smoothed) data**. For certain assets without liquid public markets, appraisal data are used in lieu of market price transaction data. Appraised values tend to be less volatile than market-determined values for the identical asset would be. The consequences are 1) the calculated correlations with other assets tend to be smaller in absolute value than the true correlations, and 2) the true standard deviation of the asset is biased downward. This concern has been raised particularly with respect to alternative investments such as real estate.

Example 7

Smoothed Data: The Case of Alternative Investments (1)

The perception of alternative investments is that they yield high returns with low risk and that they barely correlate with traditional asset classes. At least in some cases, this perception results from the uncritical use of flawed historical statistics because alternative assets are not traded on exchanges with continuously observable markets. First, risk is underestimated. Consider the following analogy: A bat is flying through a dark tunnel. While it is in the tunnel, you cannot see it. The bat may exit from the tunnel at about the same height it entered the tunnel, as shown.

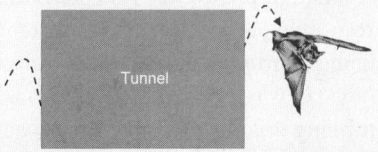

Source: UBS Global Asset Management White Paper Series – "Global Investment Solutions – Capital Market Assumptions," February 2005 © UBS 2005. All rights reserved. Reproduced with permission.

---

4 See Brown, Goetzmann, and Ross (1995).

Organizing the Task: Framework and Challenges

However, the bat's flight within the tunnel, if it could be viewed, would be seen to go up and down:

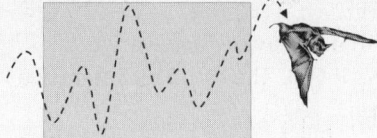

Source: UBS Global Asset Management White Paper Series – "Global Investment Solutions – Capital Market Assumptions," February 2005 © UBS 2005. All rights reserved. Reproduced with permission.

In this analogy, the time in the tunnel corresponds to the time between trades (or fund valuations) and the bat's height of flight corresponds to the true price of the asset. In measuring the bat's height only at the points of entry and exit from the tunnel, we would underestimate the real volatility of price. Asset liquidity corresponds to the end of the tunnel, when the true price is first clearly visible. In the context of venture capital, for instance, the end of the tunnel is analogous to the initial public offering date.

Data for alternative investments tend to overly smooth return variation because they are often appraisal-based rather than transaction-based. Many indices, such as those for real estate, private equity, and natural resources, were created with a focus on measuring return rather than risk. Unfortunately, these indices have been used to derive risk and correlation estimates that are biased downward. For alternative investments, the issue is not only whether the past is a good indicator of the future, but also whether the past is even correctly recorded.

As an illustration, consider the quarterly returns on the S&P 500 between 1981 and 1999, which include the crash of 1987. The period contains 18 negative quarters and has an annual standard deviation of returns of 16.1 percent. Venture capital also represents equity claims, but on less seasoned and riskier companies. Nevertheless, based on venture economics data, the index-based quarterly venture capital returns over the same period are considerably smoother. Venture capital also seems unaffected by the crash, with a reported 5.2 percent return in the fourth quarter of 1987. Only six negative quarters are reported. The reported annual standard deviation of returns is 9.1 percent, and correlation with the S&P 500 is 0.28.

The analyst can attempt to correct for the biases in datasets (when a bias-free dataset is not available). For example, one heuristic approach to correcting for smoothed data is to rescale the data in such a way that their dispersion is increased but the mean of the data is unchanged. Example 8 illustrates this idea.

Example 8

Smoothed Data: The Case of Alternative Investments (2)

How might an analyst address the biases resulting from smoothed data? To continue with the case of venture capital return data, one approach would be to rescale the reported data so that dispersion is increased but the mean is unchanged. The point is that the larger the rescaling, the larger the number of negative quarterly returns, because the frequency distribution is centered in the same place but there is more probability in the tails as dispersion is larger. For example:

> - The venture returns rescaled by a factor of 1.4 provide 18 negative quarters—that is, as many as the S&P 500. The estimated standard deviation of the rescaled data is 13 percent.
> - The venture returns rescaled by a factor of 4.1 provide 36 negative quarters, which is twice as many as the S&P 500. The estimated standard deviation of the rescaled data is 37 percent.
> - The venture returns rescaled by a factor of 4.4 provide 38 negative quarters, 2.1 times as many as the S&P 500. The estimated standard deviation of the rescaled data is 40 percent.
>
> Using these data in conjunction with other analyses, one might propose risks of 43 percent for early-stage venture capital, 34 percent for late-stage venture capital, 29 percent for leveraged buyouts (largely debt-financed purchases of established companies), and 20 percent for distressed debt (the debt of companies that are under financial distress or in or near bankruptcy).[5]
>
> The key is to model the risks of alternative investments as if they were frequently traded, focusing not on statistical observations but on the underlying fundamental and economic drivers of returns.

2.2.3 *The Limitations of Historical Estimates*

With justification, analysts frequently look to history for information in developing capital market forecasts. But although history is usually a guide to what we may expect in the future, the past cannot be simply extrapolated to produce future results uncritically. A historical estimate should be considered a starting point for analysis. The analysis should include a discussion of what may be different from past average results going forward. If we do not see any such differences, we may want to project the historical estimates into the future (perhaps after making certain technical adjustments). However, making such projections without raising the question of differences is questionable. Changes in the technological, political, legal, and regulatory environments, as well as disruptions such as wars and other calamities, can alter risk–return relationships. Such shifts are known as changes in **regime** (the governing set of relationships) and give rise to the statistical problem of **nonstationarity** (meaning, informally, that different parts of a data series reflect different underlying statistical properties). For example, the shifts in U.S. central bank policy in 1980 began a period of declining and subsequently stable inflation that is widely recognized as representing a break with the past. Also, disruptive events in a particular time period may boost volatilities in a manner that is simply not relevant for the future. However, extending a dataset to the distant past increases the chance of including irrelevant data. The well-informed analyst tracks the range of events that can indicate an important change in a time series. Statistical tools are available to help identify such changes or turning points.[6]

When many variables are considered, a long data series may be a statistical necessity. (For example, to calculate a historical covariance matrix, the number of observations must exceed the number of variables.) If we could be assured of stationarity, going back farther in time to capture a larger sample should increase the precision with which population parameters of a return distribution are estimated.[7] Related to

---

[5] See the reading on alternative investments portfolio management for a discussion of these alternative investments.
[6] See Hamilton (1994).
[7] According to sampling theory, the precision of the estimate of the population mean is proportional to $1/\sqrt{\text{(number of observations)}}$.

Organizing the Task: Framework and Challenges

that point, using larger samples may reduce the sensitivity of parameter estimates to the starting and ending dates of the sample. In practice, using a long data series may involve a variety of problems. For instance:

- The risk that the data cover multiple regimes increases.
- Time series of the required length may not be available.
- In order to get data series of the required length, the temptation is to use high-frequency data (weekly or even daily). Data of high frequency are more sensitive to asynchronism across variables.[8] As a result, high-frequency data tend to produce lower correlation estimates.

Researchers have concluded that the underlying mean returns on volatile asset classes such as equities are particularly difficult to estimate from historical data.[9] Using high-frequency data is of no help in increasing the accuracy of mean return estimates.

A practical approach to deciding whether one should use the whole of a long data series is to answer two questions. The first question is: Is there is any fundamental reason to believe that the entirety of the series' time period is no longer relevant? If there is, the next question to answer is: Do the data support that hypothesis? Texts on time-series and regression analysis offer a variety of means to assess objectively whether there is a break in a time series. If the answers to both questions are yes, one should use only that part of the time series that appears to be relevant to the present.

Example 9

Using Regression Analysis to Identify a Change in Regime

The effects of specific events on a time series (e.g., the announcement by a central bank of a new monetary policy) can be most simply modeled in a regression framework using a dummy explanatory variable $z(t)$, where $z(t) = 0$ for t before the intervention (change) date and $z(t) = 1$ for t at and subsequent to the intervention date. This dummy variable approach models a simple shift in the mean of the dependent variable.

2.2.4 Ex Post Risk Can Be a Biased Measure of Ex Ante Risk

In interpreting historical prices and returns over a given sample period for their relevance to current decision making, we need to evaluate whether asset prices in the period reflected the possibility of a very negative event that did not materialize during the period. Looking backward, we are likely to underestimate *ex ante* risk and overestimate *ex ante* anticipated returns.[10] For example, suppose that bond prices reflect an anticipation of a small chance of a central bank policy change that would be very negative for inflation and bond returns. When investors become aware that the risk has passed, bond prices should show strong gains. *Ex post* realized bond returns are high although *ex ante* they were lower. Because the bank policy change did not occur, it may be overlooked as a risk that was faced by bond investors at the time. An analyst reviewing the record might conclude that bonds earn high returns in excess of the

---

8 **Asynchronism** is a discrepancy in the dating of observations that occurs because stale (out-of-date) data may be used in the absence of current data.
9 See Luenberger (1998).
10 That situation of biased measurement has been called the "generalized peso problem" or the "peso problem." The name comes from an explanation for the fact that forward markets for the Mexican peso in the mid-1970s consistently underpredicted the U.S. dollar/peso exchange rate. The explanation is that traders feared that the Mexican government would devalue the peso from its peg.

short-term interest rate.[11] Similarly, a high *ex post* U.S. equity risk premium may reflect fears of adverse events that did not materialize and may be a poor estimate of the *ex ante* risk premium.[12] Only the *ex ante* risk premium is important in decision making.

2.2.5 Biases in Analysts' Methods

Analysts naturally search for relationships that will help in developing better capital market expectations. Among the preventable biases that the analyst may introduce in such work are the following:

- **Data-mining bias**. Data-mining bias is introduced by repeatedly "drilling" or searching a dataset until the analyst finds some statistically significant pattern. Such patterns cannot be expected to be of predictive value. It is almost inevitable that the analyst will find some statistically significant relationship by mining the data: Using a given sample, if we examine 50 different variables as predictors of the equity risk premium and set a 10 percent significance level in our tests, we would expect 5 variables to appear significant by random chance alone. The absence of an explicit economic rationale for a variable's usefulness is one warning sign of a data-mining problem: no story, no future.[13]

- **Time-period bias**. Time-period bias relates to results that are time period specific. Research findings are often found to be sensitive to the selection of starting and/or ending dates. As one example, the small-cap stock effect in U.S. stock returns has been found to be largely concentrated in the nine-year period 1975 to 1983, when as a group, small-cap stocks outperformed large-cap equities by 19.6 percent per year. Excluding the 1975–1983 period, a given investment in large-cap equities in 1926 would have grown by the end of 2001 to an amount that was 20 percent greater than the amount resulting from an equal initial investment in small-cap equities.[14]

How might the analyst avoid the mistake of using a variable in a forecasting mode that historical analysis has suggested as useful but which is actually irrelevant? The analyst should scrutinize the variable selection process for data-mining bias and be able to provide an economic rationale for the variable's usefulness in a forecasting mode. A further practical check is to examine the forecasting relationship out of sample (i.e., on data other than those used to estimate the relationship). For example, the available data period could be split into two subperiods. If the forecasting relationship estimated from the first period does not hold similarly when tested using data from the second subperiod, the variable may not be useful as a forecaster.

2.2.6 The Failure to Account for Conditioning Information

We observed above that the analyst should ask whether there are relevant new facts in the present when forecasting the future. Where such information exists, the analyst should condition his or her expectations on it.

We can take the case of estimating mean returns. Long-run mean returns and risk involve an averaging over many different economic and market conditions. Prospective returns and risk for an asset as of today are conditional on the specific characteristics of the current marketplace and prospects looking forward. That fact explains the role of economic analysis in expectations setting: We should not ignore any relevant information or analysis in formulating expectations. Indeed, the use of unconditional expectations can lead to misperceptions of risk, return, and risk-adjusted return.

---

11 This explanation has been offered by Bekaert, Hodrick, and Marshall (2001) along with time-varying term premiums for anomalies in the term structure of interest rates noted by Campbell and Shiller (1991).
12 See Goetzmann and Jorion (1999) and references therein.
13 See McQueen and Thorley (1999).
14 See Siegel (2002), pp. 134–135.

Consider an asset class that has a beta of 0.80 in economic expansions and 1.2 in recessions (with respect to a world market portfolio). If we make the assumptions in Exhibit 2 on the market return and the risk-free rate, the asset class's expected return is 10 percent in an expansion versus 4.4 percent in a recession and its true unconditional expected return is 0.5(10%) + 0.5(4.4%) = 7.2%. The asset class fairly rewards risk in both expansions and recessions [alpha = 0.5(0%) + 0.5(0%) = 0%]. The asset class would appear to have a beta of 0.5(0.8) + 0.5(1.2) = 1.0 in a regression. Given this unconditional beta, the expected return according to the CAPM would be 8 percent.

Exhibit 2   Misvaluation from Using an Unconditional Benchmark

	Expansion	Recession	Unconditional Expectation
Risk-free rate	2%	2%	2%
Exp. return on market	12%	4%	8%
β_i	0.80	1.20	1.0
$E(R_i)$	2% + 0.8 (12% − 2%) = 10%	2% + 1.2 (4% − 2%) = 4.4%	True: 7.2% Using β_i = 1.0: 2% + 1.0 (8% − 2%) = 8%
α_i	0%	0%	7.2% − 8% = −0.8%

Note: An expansion and a recession are assumed to be equally likely.

Comparing the unconditional expected return using the unconditional beta of 1.0, the asset class appears to inadequately reward risk (alpha = −0.8 percent) although we know from the analysis presented that the asset class fairly rewards risk.[15] How would an analyst avoid drawing the wrong conclusion? The analyst would need to uncover through research that the asset class's systematic risk varies with the business cycle. The analyst would then condition his or her forecasts on the state of the economy to formulate the most accurate expectations.

2.2.7 Misinterpretation of Correlations

In financial and economic research, the analyst should take care in interpreting correlations. When a variable A is found to be significantly correlated with a variable B, there are at least three possible explanations:

- A predicts B;
- B predicts A;
- a third variable C predicts A and B.

Without the investigation and modeling of underlying linkages, relationships of correlation cannot be used in a predictive model. For example, suppose A relates to natural disasters in quarter t and B represents property insurer claims in quarter $t + 1$. One can discern on the basis of simple economic reasoning a cause-and-effect link from A to B. Supporting that conclusion, no plausible feedback linkage exists from B to A: A is truly an exogenous variable (an **exogenous variable** is determined outside the system, in contrast to an **endogenous variable**, which is determined within the system). One might consider using A as one predictor of B, but the reverse—using claims in $t + 1$ to predict natural disasters in $t + 2$—would not be fruitful (although the observed correlation by itself would not tell you that).

---

15 Note that Ferson and Schadt (1996) developed a method to estimate conditional alpha.

As the third bullet point represents, there may be no predictive relationship between A and B; the relationship between A and B is conditional on the presence of the variable C, and the correlation between A and B is spurious.

Another surprise that might be in store: A and B could have a strong but *nonlinear* relationship but have a low or zero correlation.[16]

Suppose that one has a plausible model of an underlying causal link to support the use of a variable as a predictor. Are there any more powerful tools to apply to establish the variable's usefulness than simple correlation? Multiple-regression analysis may be one such tool. For example, suppose we have a model that suggests B predicts A but we need to eliminate C as mediating the relationship between A and B (as in the third bullet point above). We can estimate the following regression:

$$A = \beta_0 + \beta_1 B + \beta_2 C + \varepsilon$$

The variable C in this regression is a control variable. The coefficient β_1 represents the effect of B on A after accounting for the effect of the control variable C on A. The coefficient β_1 reflects the **partial correlation** between A and B. If the estimated value of β_1 is significantly different from 0 but β_2 is not significantly different from 0 (based on *t*-tests), we have a piece of evidence in support of the proposition that B predicts A. The multiple-regression framework supports the introduction of multiple control variables. The analyst may also use time-series analysis. For example, with sufficiently long time series, we can regress A on lagged values of itself, lagged values of B, and lagged values of control variables, and test the null hypothesis that all the coefficients on the lagged values of B jointly equal 0. If we can reject the null hypothesis, the variable B may be useful in predicting A.[17]

Example 10

Causality Relationships

That one event follows another is not sufficient to show that the first event caused the second. For example, a decrease in the number of new accountants following an increase in tax rates would be association without cause-and-effect relationship. But seasonal incoming tax receipts probably bear a direct cause-and-effect relationship to the needs of governments to borrow funds in some months versus others. If an increase in income tax rates causes individuals to be more concerned with minimizing taxes, one might discern an indirect cause-and-effect relationship between the tax rate increase and a subsequent jump in sales of tax preparation software.

2.2.8 Psychological Traps

Hammond, Keeney, and Raiffa (1998) formulated several psychological traps that are relevant to our discussion because they can undermine the analyst's ability to make accurate and unbiased forecasts.

The **anchoring trap** is the tendency of the mind to give disproportionate weight to the first information it receives on a topic. In other words, initial impressions, estimates, or data anchor subsequent thoughts and judgments. For instance, in an investment committee in which several different perspectives on capital market returns

---

[16] For example, consider $B = A^2$ (A raised to the second power indicates a nonlinear association). The variable B increases with increasing values of A when A is above 0. But consider negative values of A. As A increases from –100 to 0, B decreases. The correlation between A and B is zero, although the relationship between them is so precise that it can be expressed in a mathematical equation.

[17] This would be a test of "predictive causality," known as Granger causation. See Granger (1969) and Diebold (2004).

are presented, the first presentation may tend to function as an anchor for discussion and its lead-off position might give it an edge in being adopted. The analyst can try to address this trap by consciously attempting to avoid premature conclusions.

The **status quo trap** is the tendency for forecasts to perpetuate recent observations—that is, to predict no change from the recent past. If inflation has been rising at a double-digit rate for several recent periods, it is a natural tendency to forecast a similar increase in the next period. In a decision-making context, because doing something other than maintaining the status quo (risking an error of commission) may lead to increased work and regret if the decision is wrong, doing nothing (risking an error of omission) becomes the easy and oft-preferred alternative. The status quo trap may be overcome with rational analysis used within a decision-making process.

The **confirming evidence trap** is the bias that leads individuals to give greater weight to information that supports an existing or preferred point of view than to evidence that contradicts it. The tendency to seek out information that supports an existing point of view also reflects this bias. Several steps may be taken to help ensure objectivity:

- Examine all evidence with equal rigor.
- Enlist an independent-minded person to argue against your preferred conclusion or decision.
- Be honest about your motives.

The **overconfidence trap** is the tendency of individuals to overestimate the accuracy of their forecasts. Many people do not admit or attempt to measure the possibility of failure in predicting uncertain events. In similar fashion, we tend to believe that most people share our particular views. The overconfidence trap would be reflected in admitting too narrow a range of possibilities or scenarios in forecasting. A good practice to prevent this trap from undermining the forecasting endeavor is to widen the range of possibilities around the primary target forecast.

The **prudence trap** is the tendency to temper forecasts so that they do not appear extreme, or the tendency to be overly cautious in forecasting. In a decision-making context, it is the tendency to be cautious when making decisions that could be potentially expensive or damaging to the decision maker's career. To avoid the prudence trap, an analyst is again wise to widen the range of possibilities around the target forecast. In addition, the most sensitive estimates affecting a forecast should be carefully reviewed in light of the supporting analysis.

The **recallability trap** is the tendency of forecasts to be overly influenced by events that have left a strong impression on a person's memory. Often, forecasts are overly influenced by the memory of catastrophic or dramatic past events. For example, investors' memory of the stock market crash of 1929 has sometimes been cited as a depressing influence on equity valuation levels for as long as three decades following the crash. To minimize the distortions of the recallability trap, analysts should ground their conclusions on objective data and procedures rather than on personal emotions and memories.

Example 11

Traps in Forecasting

Cynthia Casey is a Canada-based investment adviser with a clientele of ultra-high-net-worth individuals. The Canadian equity allocation of client Philip Lasky's portfolio had favorable risk-adjusted performance from 2006 to 2008 but nevertheless lost 20 percent of its year-end 2007 value by the end of 2008. In a phone call prior to a quarterly portfolio review at the end of 2008, Lasky

> expressed the thought that the pain of the recent and continuing bear market had made him very cautious about investing in the stock market. Although his equity allocation results with Casey showed healthy appreciation over the entire period he had invested with her, his conversation dwelled mostly on the experience of the past year. Lasky told Casey that he had read a variety of financial reports containing predictions by investment notables on the equity risk premium ranging from near zero to 6 percent. During the call, he repeated to Casey, sometimes inaccurately, the arguments of the most bearish prognosticator. At the time of the call, Casey was preparing to share with clients relatively optimistic forecasts for Canadian equities, developed with an assistant who was well grounded in capital market analysis. Perceiving that Lasky and many of her other clients held more pessimistic viewpoints and that she might lose their trust if her own viewpoint turned out to be wrong, after the phone call, Casey decided to revise downward some of the economic growth assumptions she had previously made.
>
> Critique the forecasts of A) Lasky and B) Casey with respect to psychological traps in forecasting.
>
> **Solution to A:**
>
> In focusing on the most recent period only and predicting a continuation of the most recent trend, Lasky may have fallen into the status quo trap. The pain of the bear market may have overly influenced his thinking about the present (recallability trap). Furthermore, in sharing the viewpoint of the most bearish prognosticator, Lasky may be falling into the confirming evidence trap.
>
> **Solution to B:**
>
> By trimming her assumptions to be more conservative without real supporting analysis, Casey may have fallen into the prudence trap.

2.2.9 Model Uncertainty

The analyst usually encounters at least two kinds of uncertainty in conducting an analysis: **model uncertainty** (uncertainty concerning whether a selected model is correct) and **input uncertainty** (uncertainty concerning whether the inputs are correct). For example, suppose an analyst takes the equity risk premium of U.K. equities to be the realized value of the return of U.K. equities over U.K. bonds over the past 50 years. The analyst's model might be described as follows: "The *ex ante* U.K. equity risk premium was, is, and will be equal to some constant number μ." If the model is far off the true state of affairs, the analyst's forecast will also be off. (The sampling error in the estimate of μ using 50 years of data would constitute the input error in this approach.) To take another example, if the analyst uses a monetarist model for forecasting future inflation, the analyst faces uncertainty concerning whether that model is correct. In some cases, the analyst may gauge model uncertainty by observing the variation in results that comes from shifting between the several most promising models.

Input uncertainty and model uncertainty in particular often make it hard to confirm the existence of capital market anomalies (inefficiencies); some valuation model usually underlies the identification of an inefficiency. **Behavioral finance** (the theory that psychological variables affect and often distort individuals' investment decision making) has offered explanations for many perceived capital market anomalies. Kurz, Jin, and Motolese (2005) argue that many of these apparent anomalies could represent equilibria resulting from the actions of investors who use competing models but process and act on information rationally.[18]

---

[18] That is, apparent anomalies could represent a *rational belief equilibrium* in the sense of Kurz (1994).

TOOLS FOR FORMULATING CAPITAL MARKET EXPECTATIONS

The following sections introduce a range of tools that have been used in professional forecasting of capital market returns. Although an analyst may have distinct preferences among these approaches, familiarity with all these major tools will be helpful in addressing the widest variety of forecasting problems according to their particular characteristics.

3.1 Formal Tools

Formal tools are established research methods amenable to precise definition and independent replication of results. The information provided by well-chosen formal tools applied to sound data can help the analyst produce accurate forecasts.

3.1.1 Statistical Methods

Statistical methods relevant to expectations setting include **descriptive statistics** (methods for effectively summarizing data to describe important aspects of a dataset) and **inferential statistics** (methods for making estimates or forecasts about a larger group from a smaller group actually observed).

The simplest approach to forecasting is to use past data to directly forecast future outcomes of a variable of interest.

3.1.1.1 Historical Statistical Approach: Sample Estimators[19]

Suppose an investor uses the FTSE 100 as his benchmark for UK large-cap equity allocations. The investor could use the mean return on the FTSE 100 over some selected sample period as his forecast of the long-run expected return on UK large-cap equities. If future returns over the selected time horizon reflect the same probability distribution as past returns (because the time series is **stationary**—that is, the parameters that describe the return-generating process are unchanged), the resulting estimate will be useful. For example, in a mean–variance framework, the analyst might use:

- the sample arithmetic mean total return or sample geometric mean total return as an estimate of the expected return;
- the sample variance as an estimate of the variance; and
- sample correlations as estimates of correlations.

One decision point relates to the choice between an arithmetic mean and a geometric mean. The arithmetic mean return (which is always used in the calculation of the sample standard deviation) best represents the mean return in a single period. The geometric mean return of a sample represents the compound rate of growth that equates the beginning value to the ending value of a data series. The geometric mean return represents multiperiod growth more accurately than the arithmetic mean return. The geometric mean return is always lower than the arithmetic mean return for a risky variable. The differences between the arithmetic mean and the geometric mean in historical estimates of the equity risk premium can be substantial.[20] Both approaches are used in current practice.

---

19 A **sample estimator** is a formula for assigning a unique value (a **point estimate**) to a population parameter.

20 Looking forward to later discussion, the arithmetic historical equity risk premium would be calculated as the difference between the arithmetic mean return on the proxy for equities and the arithmetic mean return on long-term bonds. The geometric mean can be approximated as the difference between the geometric mean return on the proxy on equities ($R_{G,e}$) and the geometric mean return on long-term bonds ($R_{G,b}$), or more precisely, as $(1 + R_{G,e})/(1 + R_{G,b})$. In practice, the geometric mean calculation produces a lower estimate for the equity risk premium than does the arithmetic mean calculation.

Dimson, Marsh, and Staunton (2011) presented authoritative evidence on asset returns in 17 countries for the 111 years 1900–2010. Exhibit 3 excerpts their findings.

An analyst using a historical statistical approach would use historical data such as those given in Exhibit 3 as the basis for forecasts. Alternatively, using a historical statistical approach for the equity risk premium and a current term-structure estimate for the expected return on bonds (e.g., a yield to maturity on a zero-coupon government bond), the expected return on equities could be estimated as their sum.

Exhibit 3 Real (Inflation-Adjusted) Equity and Bond Returns: Seventeen Major Markets, 1900–2010

	Equities		Bonds	
Country	Arithmetic Mean Equity Return	Standard Deviation of Return	Arithmetic Mean Bond Return	Standard Deviation
Australia	9.1%	18.2%	2.3%	13.2%
Belgium	5.1	23.61	1.1	12.0
Canada	7.3	17.2	2.6	10.4
Denmark	6.9	20.9	3.7	11.7
France	5.7	23.5	0.8	13.0
Germany	8.1	32.2	0.8	15.7
Ireland	6.4	23.21	1.9	14.9
Italy	6.1	29.0	−0.4	14.1
Japan	8.5	29.8	1.6	20.1
Netherlands	7.1	21.8	1.8	9.4
Norway	7.2	27.4	2.4	12.2
South Africa	9.5	22.6	2.3	10.4
Spain	5.8	22.3	1.9	12.4
Sweden	8.7	22.9	3.2	11.8
Switzerland	6.1	19.8	2.5	9.3
United Kingdom	7.2	20.0	2.2	13.7
United States	8.3	20.3	2.3	10.2

Source: Dimson, Marsh, and Staunton (2011), Tables 2 and 5. German data exclude 1922–1923.

3.1.1.2 Shrinkage Estimators **Shrinkage estimation** involves taking a weighted average of a historical estimate of a parameter and some other parameter estimate, where the weights reflect the analyst's relative belief in the estimates. This "two-estimates-are-better-than-one" approach has desirable statistical properties that have given it a place in professional investment practice. The term "shrinkage" refers to the approach's ability to reduce the impact of extreme values in historical estimates. The procedure has been applied to covariances and mean returns.

A **shrinkage estimator** of the covariance matrix is a weighted average of the historical covariance matrix and another, alternative estimator of the covariance matrix, where the analyst places the larger weight on the covariance matrix he or she believes more strongly in.[21] Why are analysts often not satisfied with using the historical sample

---

[21] This method is usually presented in terms of covariances rather than correlations for technical reasons. Either covariance or correlation can be used in MVO. Stein (1956) introduced shrinkage estimates.

Tools for Formulating Capital Market Expectations

covariance matrix? Basically, because investment data series are relatively short and samples often reflect the nonrecurring peculiarities of a historical period. The sample covariance matrix is perfectly well suited for *summarizing* an observed dataset and has the desirable (large-sample) property of unbiasedness. Nevertheless, a shrinkage estimator is a superior approach for estimating the population covariance matrix for the medium- and smaller-size datasets that are typical in finance.

A shrinkage estimator approach involves selecting an alternative estimator of the covariance matrix, called a **target covariance matrix**. For example, an analyst might believe that a particular model relating asset class returns to a particular set of return drivers or systematic risk factors has some validity. The asset classes' estimated betas or factor sensitivities in such a model can be used to estimate the asset classes' covariances. To consider one number in the covariance matrix, suppose that the estimated covariance between domestic shares and bonds is 48 using the factor model and 80 using a historical estimate, and assume further that the optimal weights on the model and historical estimates are 0.75 and 0.25, respectively. The shrinkage estimate of the covariance would be 0.75(48) + 0.25(80) = 56. There is a systematic way to determine the optimal weights on the two estimates that the analyst can obtain from the investment literature on this topic.[22]

A surprising fact concerning the shrinkage estimator approach is that any choice for the target covariance matrix will lead to an increase (or at least not a decrease) in the efficiency of the covariance estimates versus the historical estimate. The improvement will be greater if a plausible target covariance matrix is selected. If the target covariance matrix is useless in improving the accuracy of the estimate of covariance, the optimal weight on the historical estimate would be calculated as 1. One reasonable choice for the target covariance matrix would be a factor-model-based estimate of the covariance matrix, following the lead of Ledoit and Wolf (2003). Another choice for the target covariance matrix would be a covariance matrix based on assuming each pairwise covariance is equal to the overall average covariance.[23]

Example 12

Adjusting a Historical Covariance

Cynthia Casey has estimated the covariance between Canadian equities and U.S. equities as 230 using historical data. Using a factor model approach based on a proxy for the world market portfolio, she estimates the covariance as 190. Casey takes a shrinkage estimator approach to estimating covariances and determines that the optimal weight on the historical estimate is 0.30.

1. Calculate the shrinkage estimate of the covariance between U.S. and Canadian equities.
2. Describe the theoretical advantage of a shrinkage estimate of covariance compared to a raw historical estimate.

Solution to 1:

0.30(230) + 0.70(190) = 202.

Solution to 2:

The shrinkage estimate should be more accurate, given that the weights are chosen appropriately.

---

[22] Ledoit and Wolf (2003) give a simple formula for the optimal weights. The criterion their formula satisfies is that the weights minimize the mean square error in the resulting estimate.
[23] An identity matrix or a scalar multiple of it is considered a serviceable choice when the researcher has no insight into an intuitive target for the covariance matrix.

A shrinkage estimator of mean returns involves taking a weighted average of each historical mean return and some other target constant—for example, the overall (grand) mean historical return across assets. Given five assets with sample mean returns of 4 percent, 6 percent, 7 percent, 8 percent, and 10 percent, respectively, and a weight of 80 percent on the sample mean, we would calculate the overall mean return as 7 percent and the shrinkage estimate of the first asset's return as 0.8(4%) + 0.2(7%) = 4.6%.

3.1.1.3 Time-Series Estimators **Time-series estimators** involve forecasting a variable on the basis of lagged values of the variable being forecast and often lagged values of other selected variables.

Time-series methods have been found useful in developing particularly short-term forecasts for financial and economic variables. Time-series methods have been notably applied to estimating near-term volatility, given persuasive evidence of variance clustering (particularly at high frequencies, such as daily and weekly) in a number of different markets, including equity, currency, and futures markets.[24] **Volatility clustering** is the tendency for large (small) swings in prices to be followed by large (small) swings of random direction. Volatility clustering captures the idea that some markets represent periods of notably high or low volatility. Robert F. Engle shared the 2003 Nobel Prize in Economics in part for the development of time-series models that can accurately capture the property of volatility clustering.[25]

One of the simplest specifications in this broad class of models was developed within a division at JPMorgan that was later established as the RiskMetrics Group. This model specifies that the volatility in period t, σ_t^2, is a weighted average of the volatility in the previous period, σ_{t-1}^2, and the squared value of a random "noise" term, ε_t^2. The expression is

$$\sigma_t^2 = \beta \sigma_{t-1}^2 + (1 - \beta)\varepsilon_t^2 \qquad (1)$$

with $0 < \beta < 1$. The coefficient β measures the rate of decay of the influence of the value of volatility in one period on future volatility, and the rate of decay is exponential. The higher β is, the more volatility in one period "remembers" what happened in the past and the more it clusters.

To illustrate using $\beta = 0.94$, we will suppose that the standard deviation of returns in $t = 11$ is 10 percent, so $\sigma_{11}^2 = 0.10^2 = 0.01$. The noise term is $\varepsilon_{12} = 0.05$, so $\varepsilon_{12}^2 = 0.05^2 = 0.0025$. The prediction for $t = 12$ is therefore

$$\begin{aligned}\sigma_{12}^2 &= 0.94\sigma_{11}^2 + 0.06\varepsilon_{12}^2 \\ &= 0.94(0.01) + 0.06(0.0025) \\ &= 0.00955\end{aligned}$$

implying that $\sigma_{12} = \sqrt{0.00955} = 0.0977$, or 9.77 percent. Intuitively, the high weight on σ_{11}^2 means that it had a strong effect on σ_{12}^2. However, on occasion, the noise term will take on an extreme value and cause volatility to shift quite a bit. In a similar vein to this approach to variance estimation, the correlation matrix has also been estimated with some success using exponentially weighted historical observations.[26]

3.1.1.4 Multifactor Models A **multifactor model** is a model that explains the returns to an asset in terms of the values of a set of return drivers or risk factors.

---

[24] See Drost and Nijman (1993) and references therein.
[25] Such models are called autoregressive conditional heteroskedasticity (ARCH) time-series models. The Nobel Prize was shared with Clive W. J. Granger, who developed methods for analyzing cointegrated time series (informally, time series with common trends).
[26] For more details on models of volatility clustering, see Bollerslev, Engle, and Nelson (1994).

The structure of a multifactor model, if the analyst believes that K factors drive asset returns, is as follows:

$$R_i = a_i + b_{i1}F_1 + b_{i2}F_2 + \ldots + b_{iK}F_K + \varepsilon_i \tag{2}$$

where

R_i = the return to asset i
a_i = an intercept term in the equation for asset i
F_k = the return to factor k, $k = 1, 2, \ldots, K$
b_{ik} = the sensitivity of the return to asset i to the return to factor k, $k = 1, 2, \ldots, K$
ε_i = an error term with a zero mean that represents the portion of the return to asset i not explained by the factor model. The error term is assumed to be uncorrelated with each of the K factors and to be uncorrelated with the error terms in the equations for other assets.

This structure has been found useful for modeling asset returns and covariances among asset returns. Multifactor models are useful for estimating covariances for the following reasons:

- By relating the returns on all assets to a common set of return drivers, a multifactor model simplifies the task of estimating covariances: estimates of covariances between asset returns can be derived using the assets' factor sensitivities.
- When the factors are well chosen, a multifactor model approach may filter out noise (i.e., random variation in the data specific to the sample period).
- Such models make it relatively easy to verify the consistency of the covariance matrix, because if the smaller factor covariance matrix is consistent, so are any covariances computed on the basis of it.

In the balance of this section, we illustrate a top-down structured approach to using factor models in estimating the covariance matrix. In this approach, we model factors as portfolios of securities and start from a simple two-factor model at the most aggregated level.

Assume that two factors, a global equity factor and a global bonds factor, drive the returns of all assets in the investable universe. In this case, we start the modeling process with a covariance matrix for global equity and global bonds (we will refer to it in this discussion as the *equity–bonds covariance matrix*). A standard deviation of 14 percent for global equity and 4 percent for global bonds and a correlation between them of 0.30 imply the covariance matrix shown in Exhibit 4. In Exhibit 4, 0.0196 is the variance for global equity, 0.0016 is the variance for global bonds, and 0.0017 is the covariance between global equity and global bonds. The covariance between global equity and global bonds is the product of their standard deviations times the correlation between them, or $(0.14)(0.04)(0.30) = 0.0017$ to four decimal places; for global equity variance, $0.0196 = (0.14)^2$; for global bonds variance, $0.0016 = (0.04)^2$.

Exhibit 4   Factor Covariance Matrix

	Global Equity	Global Bonds
Global Equity	0.0196	0.0017
Global Bonds	0.0017	0.0016

This is a **factor covariance matrix**, as it contains the covariances for the factors assumed to drive returns. In order to derive the **asset covariance matrix** (the covariance matrix for the asset classes or markets under consideration), we need to know how each of the markets responds to factor movements. We measure the responsiveness of markets to factor movements by the markets' **factor sensitivities** (also known as factor betas or factor loadings), represented by the quantities b_{ik} in Equation 2. If Market 1 moves by 110 basis points in response to a 100 basis point move of global equities, the corresponding factor sensitivity is 1.10. In addition, every market has some risk that is not explained by the factors. This is called the market's idiosyncratic or residual risk and is represented by the residual variance, $Var(\varepsilon_i)$ for market i. It is assumed that the residuals are uncorrelated.

Exhibit 5 shows hypothetical statistics for five securities markets.

Exhibit 5   Hypothetical Statistics for Five Markets

	Sensitivities		
	Global Equity	Global Bonds	Residual Risk (%)
Market A	1.10	0	10.0
Market B	1.05	0	8.0
Market C	0.90	0	7.0
Market D	0	1.03	1.2
Market E	0	0.99	0.9

Source: Staub (2006).

Judged by its factor sensitivities, Market A is an equity market, with zero sensitivity to global bonds and a positive sensitivity to global equity. The zero sensitivity to global bonds does not mean that Market A is uncorrelated with global bonds, although it does mean that its partial correlation with bonds (the correlation after removing the influence of the other markets) is zero and that global bonds are not one of Market A's return drivers.[27]

In the case we are examining, we are assuming that the return of market i, M_i, is as follows:

$$M_i = a_i + b_{i1}F_1 + b_{i2}F_2 + \varepsilon_i, \quad i = 1 \text{ to } 5$$

We compute the markets' variances and covariance using Equations 3a and 3b, respectively:

$$M_{ii} = b_{i1}^2 \text{Var}(F_1) + b_{i2}^2 \text{Var}(F_2) + 2b_{i1}b_{i2}\text{Cov}(F_1, F_2) + \text{Var}(\varepsilon_i), \quad \text{(3a)}$$
for $i = 1$ to 5

where M_{ii} is the variance of market i;

$$M_{ij} = b_{i1}b_{j1}\text{Var}(F_1) + b_{i2}b_{j2}\text{Var}(F_2) + (b_{i1}b_{j2} + b_{i2}b_{j1})\text{Cov}(F_1, F_2) \quad \text{(3b)}$$
for $i = 1$ to $5, j = 1$ to 5, and $i \neq j$

where M_{ij} is the covariance of market i with market j.

---

[27] Through the positive covariance (and correlation) between global equity and global bonds, Market A is still positively correlated with global bonds, although moderately.

Tools for Formulating Capital Market Expectations

For example, suppose we want to compute the covariance between Markets A and B. Using Equation 3b (with $i = 1$ for Market A and $j = 2$ for Market B), we calculate that

$$M_{12} = (1.1)(1.05)(0.0196) + (0)(0)(0.0016)$$
$$+ \big[(1.10)(0) + (0)(1.05)\big](0.0017) = 0.0226$$

Because both Market A and Market B have zero sensitivity to the global bonds factor, their correlation is explained only through their sensitivities to the global equity factor. Equations 3a and 3b are basic formulas for using multifactor models to estimate asset class covariance.

Note that establishing the consistency of the equity–bonds covariance matrix would not be a challenge, because it has only four entries. If the equity–bonds covariance matrix is consistent, then the covariance matrix for the markets calculated using Equations 3a and 3b will be consistent, even if many markets are involved so that consistency might be hard to check directly. The ability to establish consistency efficiently is a significant advantage of a multifactor model approach.

Exhibit 6   A Two-Layer Factor Approach

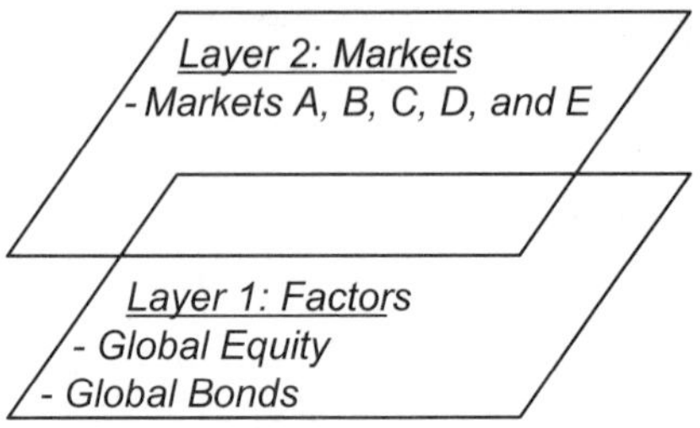

Layer 2: Markets
- Markets A, B, C, D, and E

Layer 1: Factors
- Global Equity
- Global Bonds

Source: Staub (2006). © 2006 UBS Global Asset Management (Americas) Inc. All rights reserved.

The above example, illustrated in Exhibit 6, is a two-layer structure with the factors on the first layer and the markets to be modeled on the second and final layer.[28]

In practice, a two-layer approach is not sufficient to accurately model interrelationships with the level of detail needed. Consider expanding the set of markets from securities markets to real estate markets, including U.S. real estate sectors—apartment, industry, office, and retail. These are mutually fairly highly correlated but have moderate or weak correlations with most other markets.

In the case of these real estate sectors, we would require new factor layers to model co-movements that are unrelated to the movement of factors in the prior layer. To meet our needs, the two-layer approach must be replaced by a multilayer approach, as illustrated in Exhibit 7.

In a layer immediately below the U.S. real estate sectors, we would introduce U.S. real estate as a whole as a factor. The total number of layers would depend on the final set of markets whose covariance structure we wanted to model.[29]

---

[28] The two-layer concept goes back to Grinold and Kahn (1995), who employ it for stock modeling. For more details, see p. 58f.
[29] See Staub (2006) for more details.

Exhibit 7   A Multilayer Factor Approach

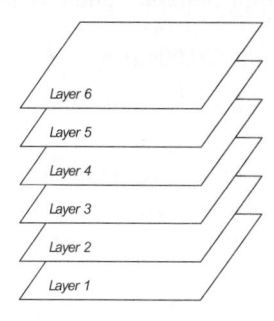

```
                Layer 6
              Layer 5
            Layer 4
          Layer 3
        Layer 2
      Layer 1
```

Source: Staub (2006). © 2006 UBS Global Asset Management (Americas) Inc. All rights reserved.

3.1.2 Discounted Cash Flow Models

Discounted cash flow models (DCF models) express the idea that an asset's value is the present value of its (expected) cash flows. Formally, the value of an asset using a DCF approach is as follows:[30]

$$V_0 = \sum_{t=1}^{\infty} \frac{CF_t}{(1+r)^t} \quad (4)$$

where

V_0 = the value of the asset at time $t = 0$ (today)
CF_t = the cash flow (or the expected cash flow, for risky cash flows) at time t
r = the discount rate or required rate of return

For simplicity, we represent the discount rate in Equation 4 as the same for all time periods—a flat term structure of discount rates.

Analysts use DCF models in expectations setting both for traditional securities markets and for alternative investment markets where the investment (e.g., private equity or real estate) generates cash flows.

DCF models are a basic tool for establishing the intrinsic value of an asset based on fundamentals (e.g., its projected cash flows) and its fair required rate of return. DCF models have the advantage of being forward-looking. They do not address short-run factors such as current supply-and-demand conditions, so practitioners view them as more appropriate for setting long-term rather than short-term expectations. That said, asset prices that are disconnected from fundamentals may reflect conditions of speculative excess that can reverse abruptly.[31]

3.1.2.1 Equity Markets
Analysts have frequently used the **Gordon (constant) growth model** form of the dividend discount model, solved for the required rate of return, to formulate the long-term expected return of equity markets. The Gordon growth model assumes that there is a long-term trend in dividends and corporate earnings, which is a reasonable approximation for many developed country economies.[32] The expression for the Gordon growth model solved for $E(R_e)$, the expected rate of return on equity, is

$$E(R_e) = \frac{D_0(1+g)}{P_0} + g = \frac{D_1}{P_0} + g \quad (5)$$

---

[30] If the asset trades in an integrated market, the future cash flows of the asset are to be translated into the home currencies of investors.
[31] See Calverley (2004) for a discussion of **bubbles** (episodes in which asset market prices move to extremely high levels in relation to estimated intrinsic value).
[32] See Jagannathan, McGrattan, and Scherbina (2000).

where

D_0 = the most recent annual dividend per share
g = the long-term growth rate in dividends, assumed equal to the long-term earnings growth rate
P_0 = the current share price

According to the Gordon growth model, share price should appreciate at a rate equal to the dividend growth rate. Therefore, in Equation 5, the expected rate of return is composed of two parts: the dividend yield (D_1/P_0) and the capital gains (or appreciation) yield (g).

The quantity g can be estimated most simply as the growth rate in **nominal gross domestic product** (nominal GDP), a money measure of the goods and services produced within a country's borders.[33] Nominal GDP growth can be estimated as the sum of the estimated real growth rate in GDP plus the expected long-run inflation rate. A more advanced analysis can take account of any perceived differences between the expected growth of the overall economy and that of the constituent companies of the particular equity index that the analyst has chosen to represent equities. The analyst can use

Earnings growth rate = GDP growth rate + Excess corporate growth
(for the index companies)

where the term *excess corporate growth* may be positive or negative depending on whether the sectoral composition of the index companies is viewed as higher or lower growth than that of the overall economy.[34] If the analyst has chosen a broad-based equity index, the excess corporate growth adjustment, if any, should be small. Exhibit 8 presents the real GDP growth rates for selected countries.

Exhibit 8 Average Annual Real GDP Growth Rates: 1980–2009 (in Percent)

	Time Period		
Country	1980–89	1990–99	2000–09
Australia	3.4%	3.3%	3.2%
Canada	3.0	2.4	2.1
Denmark	2.2	2.3	0.8
France	2.1	1.8	1.3
Germany	1.9	1.3	0.8
Italy	2.4	1.5	0.5
Japan	3.9	1.7	0.6
Netherlands	2.0	3.0	1.6
Sweden	2.4	1.8	1.9
Switzerland	1.8	1.1	1.7
United Kingdom	2.4	2.1	1.7
United States	3.1	3.1	1.8

Source: OECD, Datastream, Bloomberg, World Bank.

---

[33] See Diermeier (1990) and Singer and Terhaar (1997) for a theoretical analysis of this relationship.
[34] See Grinold and Kroner (2002), p. 12.

In the United States and other major markets, share repurchases have become an important means for companies to distribute cash to shareholders. Grinold and Kroner (2002) provided a restatement of the Gordon growth model that takes explicit account of repurchases. Their model also provides a means for analysts to incorporate expectations of valuation levels through the familiar P/E ratio. The **Grinold–Kroner model**, which is based on elaborating the expression for the expected single-period return on a share, is[35]

$$E(R_e) \approx \frac{D}{P} - \Delta S + i + g + \Delta PE \qquad (6)$$

where

$E(R_e)$ = the expected rate of return on equity
D/P = the expected dividend yield
ΔS = the expected percent change in number of shares outstanding
i = the expected inflation rate
g = the expected real total earnings growth rate (not identical to the EPS growth rate in general, with changes in shares outstanding)
ΔPE = the per period percent change in the P/E multiple

The term ΔS is negative in the case of net positive share repurchases, so $-\Delta S$ is a positive **repurchase yield** in such cases.

Equation 6 consists of three components: an expected income return, an expected nominal earnings growth return, and an expected repricing return (from expected P/E ratio expansion or contraction).

- Expected income return: $D/P - \Delta S$.
- Expected nominal earnings growth return: $i + g$.
- Expected repricing return: ΔPE.

The expected nominal earnings growth return and the expected repricing return constitute the expected capital gains.

The Grinold–Kroner model can be used not only in expectations setting, but also as a tool to analyze the sources of historical returns. For example, the S&P 500 achieved a compound growth rate of 10.7 percent per year over the 76-year period 1926–2001 (corresponding to an equity premium of 5.3 percent).[36] Following the Grinold–Kroner analysis, the sources of this return were as follows:

- 4.4 percent from income;
- 4.8 percent from nominal earnings growth (consisting of 1.7 percent real earnings growth and 3.1 percent annual inflation); and
- 1.5 percent from repricing.

As a check, 4.4% + 4.8% + 1.5% = 10.7%. Repricing return was a volatile contributor to total return. The growth of the P/E ratio from 10.2 in 1926 to 30.6 in 2001 represented a compound annual growth rate of 1.5 percent. However, the P/E of 10.2 in 1926 was actually somewhat above the P/E in 1981: Most of the repricing return was concentrated in the 20 years leading up to the ending date of 2001.

---

[35] See Grinold and Kroner (2002) for a derivation. Ibbotson and Chen (2003) presented a broadly similar analysis of the sources of equity returns but did not model stock repurchases.
[36] The equity risk premium was defined by the authors as the mean return on the S&P 500 less the mean 10-year U.S. Treasury bond return over this period.

Example 13

The Grinold–Kroner Forecast of the U.S. Equity Risk Premium

The details of the Grinold–Kroner (GK) forecast of the U.S. equity risk premium (as of early 2002) are instructive. Their forecast horizon was 10 years.

Expected Income Return

The forecast dividend yield was 1.75 percent (somewhat above the then-current yield of 1.4 percent but below the historical mean of over 4 percent for 1926–2001). The repurchase yield was forecast to be 0.5 percent, down from the 1–2 percent rate of the 1990s, which was viewed as an unusual period. The expected income return was therefore 1.75% + 0.5% = 2.25%.

Expected Nominal Earnings Growth Return

Economic theory suggests that the real GDP growth rate is the sum of labor productivity growth and labor supply growth. GK took the historical 2 percent per year U.S. labor productivity growth rate as their forecast. Using a U.S. population growth forecast of 0.8 percent and assuming a 0.2 percentage point increase in the labor force participation rate, the forecast of the labor supply growth rate was 1 percent per year. The overall real GDP growth estimate of 2% + 1% = 3% was within the 2.7 percent to 3.6 percent range of forecasts by economists. Viewing the S&P 500 companies as having a slightly higher growth profile than the overall economy, GK added a 0.5 percent excess corporate growth return for a 3.5 percent real earnings growth return estimate. GK expected an inflation rate of 2.5 percent, 0.3 percentage points above the contemporaneous consensus estimate of economists (viewed by GK as slightly optimistic). Thus, the expected nominal earnings growth return was 3.5% + 2.5% = 6%.

Expected Repricing Return

This component was perhaps the hardest to forecast. Viewing the contemporaneous P/E of 28 as a slight overreaction to the positive factors of decreased inflation, technological advances (positive productivity shocks), and an expected increase in growth rates from globalization, over a 10-year horizon, GK forecast downward repricing equal to –0.75 percent per year.

The GK forecast of the expected return on U.S. equities was therefore 2.25% + 6% – 0.75% = 7.5%. Subtracting the 10-year government bond yield of 5 percent, the GK forecast of the U.S. equity risk premium was 2.5 percent.

The 2.5 percent estimate put GK in a middle position between the predictions of the "risk premium is dead" and the "rational exuberance" camps.

Example 14

Forecasting the Return on Equities Using the Grinold–Kroner Model

Cynthia Casey employs the Grinold–Kroner model in forecasting long-term developed market equity returns. Casey makes the following forecasts:

- a 2.25 percent dividend yield on Canadian equities, based on the S&P/TSE Composite Index;
- a repurchase yield of 1 percent for Canadian equities;

> - a long-term inflation rate of 2 percent per year;
> - long-term corporate real earnings growth at 4 percent per year, based on a 1 percentage point premium for corporate growth over her expected Canadian GDP growth rate of 3.0 percent; and
> - an expansion rate for P/E multiples of 0.25 percent per year.
>
> Based only on the information given, determine the expected rate of return on Canadian equities consistent with Casey's assumptions.
>
> **Solution:**
>
> Using Casey's assumptions and Equation 6, the expected rate of return on Canadian equities should be 9.5 percent, calculated as
>
> $$E(R_e) \approx 2.25\% - (-1.0\%) + 2.0\% + 4.0\% + 0.25\% = 9.5\%$$

DCF model thinking has provided various methods for evaluating stock market levels. The best known of these is the Fed model, which asserts that the stock market is overvalued if the market's current earnings yield (earnings divided by price) is less than the 10-year Treasury bond yield.[37] The earnings yield is the required rate of return for no-growth equities and is thus a conservative estimate of the expected return for equities. The intuition of the Fed model is that when the yield of T-bonds is greater than the earnings yield of stocks (a riskier investment than T-bonds), stocks are overvalued.

3.1.2.2 Fixed-Income Markets The DCF model is a standard tool in the pricing of fixed-income instruments. In many such markets, bonds are quoted in terms of the single discount rate (the yield to maturity, or YTM) that equates the present value of the instrument's promised cash flows to its market price. The yield to maturity of a bellwether (reference) instrument for a bond market segment is a readily available first approximation of the market expected return for the asset segment at a time horizon equal to the maturity of the instrument.[38] The YTM calculation makes the strong assumption that as interest payments are received, they can be reinvested at an interest rate that always equals the YTM. Therefore, the YTM of a bond with intermediate cash flows is an estimate of the expected rate of return on the bond that is more or less plausible depending on the level of the YTM. If a representative zero-coupon bond is available at the chosen time horizon, its YTM would be a superior estimate.

3.1.3 The Risk Premium Approach

The **risk premium approach** expresses the expected return on a risky asset as the sum of the risk-free rate of interest and one or more risk premiums that compensate investors for the risky asset's exposure to sources of **priced risk** (risk for which investors demand compensation). Investors would avoid purchasing assets offering inadequate expected compensation for priced risk; the lower demand should lead to lower asset prices until the point is reached at which the compensation for risk is adequate. The risk premium approach (sometimes called the **build-up approach**) is

---

[37] This model was developed by the U.S. Federal Reserve System (the Fed), the central bank of the United States.

[38] If the bond is callable, a downward adjustment would generally need to be made. **Yield to worst** (the yield assuming the bond is called at the earliest opportunity) is sometimes used as a conservative estimate in such cases.

Tools for Formulating Capital Market Expectations

most often applied to estimating the required return in equity and bond markets.[39] In the following discussion, we assume that assets are fairly priced so that an asset's required return is also an investor's expected return.[40]

3.1.3.1 A General Expression Following our verbal definition of the risk premium approach, a formal expression for the expected return on a risky asset is

$$E(R_i) = R_F + (\text{Risk premium})_1 + (\text{Risk premium})_2 + \ldots + (\text{Risk premium})_K \qquad (7)$$

where $E(R_i)$ is the asset's expected return and R_F denotes the risk-free rate of interest.

3.1.3.2 Fixed-Income Premiums The expected bond return, $E(R_b)$, can be built up as the real rate of interest plus a set of premiums:

$$E(R_b) = \text{Real risk-free interest rate} + \text{Inflation premium} \\ + \text{Default risk premium} + \text{Illiquidity premium} \\ + \text{Maturity premium} + \text{Tax premium}$$

- The **real risk-free interest rate** is the single-period interest rate for a completely risk-free security if no inflation were expected. In economic theory, the real risk-free rate reflects the time preferences of individuals for current versus future real consumption.

- The **inflation premium** compensates investors for expected inflation and reflects the average inflation rate expected over the maturity of the debt plus a premium (or discount) for the probability attached to higher inflation than expected (or greater disinflation). The sum of the real risk-free interest rate and the inflation premium is the **nominal risk-free interest rate**, often represented by a governmental Treasury bill YTM.[41]

- The **default risk premium** compensates investors for the possibility that the borrower will fail to make a promised payment at the contracted time and in the contracted amount. This itself may be analyzed as the sum of the expected default loss in yield terms plus a premium for the nondiversifiable risk of default.[42]

- The **illiquidity premium** compensates investors for the risk of loss relative to an investment's fair value if the investment needs to be converted to cash quickly.[43]

- The **maturity premium** compensates investors for the increased sensitivity, in general, of the market value of debt to a change in market interest rates as maturity is extended, holding all else equal. The difference between the interest rate on longer-maturity, liquid Treasury debt and that on short-term Treasury debt reflects a positive maturity premium for the longer-term debt (and possibly different inflation premiums as well).

---

[39] For more discussion on equity risk premiums, see Arnott and Bernstein (2002), Grinold and Kroner (2002), and Ilmanen (2003).
[40] If there is a mispricing, then the expected return would differ from the required return by a capital appreciation or depreciation component reflecting the convergence to fair value over some time frame.
[41] Technically, 1 plus the nominal rate equals the product of 1 plus the real rate and 1 plus the inflation rate. As a quick approximation, however, the nominal rate is equal to the real rate plus an inflation premium. In this discussion, we focus on approximate additive relationships to highlight the underlying concepts.
[42] See Elton, Gruber, Agrawal, and Mann (2001) for empirical support for such an analysis.
[43] Some writers refer to the "illiquidity premium" as the "liquidity" premium (where "lack of liquidity" is understood).

- A **tax premium** may also be applicable to certain classes of bonds in some tax jurisdictions.[44]

For example, consider the expected return on a five-year Treasury instrument traded in a developed market when the real risk-free interest rate is 1.5 percent per year, the expected inflation rate over that horizon is 2.5 percent per year, and a one-year Treasury instrument has a yield to maturity of 4 percent per year. Suppose that the five-year Treasury instrument is priced to yield 5 percent. What is the source of the 5 percent to 4 percent spread? As government debt does not have default risk, the longer-term instrument does not bear a default risk premium. Nor does it have an illiquidity premium or differ in taxation from the one-year instrument. The spread would be accounted for as a 1 percent maturity premium.

Example 15

The Long-Term Real Risk-Free Rate

The real risk-free rate is compensation for forgoing current consumption in exchange for certain future consumption. Historical real cash rates exhibit high volatility and differ through time and between countries. We distinguish between the current real rate (driven by cyclical factors) and the long-term real rate assumption (based on sustainable equilibrium conditions). In a free economy, the real rate equilibrates the productivity of the economy and society's time preference for consumption. On a forward-looking basis, we can form opinions about the size of the real rate by analyzing societal consumption time preferences and studying the economy's productivity. For developed countries, a range for the long-term real risk-free rate is 2.0 percent to 2.8 percent. Obviously, variation around this estimate has been and is likely to be substantial, but 2.4 percent is an indication of central tendency over the long term.

Example 16

The Real Interest Rate and Inflation Premium in Equilibrium

The expected return to any asset or asset class has at least three components: the real risk-free rate, the inflation premium, and the risk premium. In equilibrium and assuming fully integrated markets, the real risk-free rate should be identical for all assets globally. Similarly, from the frame of reference of any individual investor, the inflation premium should be the same for all assets. For investors with different base currency consumption baskets, different inflation premiums are required to compensate for different rates of depreciation of investment capital.

The inflation premium is the compensation for the depreciation of invested principal because of *expected* price inflation. In equilibrium, we use the inflation rate that each market is using to compensate it for the loss of purchasing power.

---

[44] For example, in the United States, bonds issued by private corporations are generally tax disadvantaged relative to bonds issued by the federal government, and a tax premium would compensate corporate bondholders. See Elton, Gruber, Agrawal, and Mann (2001) for evidence on the tax premium.

> **Example 17**
>
> ### The Risk Premium: Some Facts
>
> The term "risk premium" is often used to refer to the total premium above the nominal default-risk-free interest rate. Some points to keep in mind:
>
> - In comparing risk premium estimates, the analyst should make sure that a common benchmark for the risk-free rate is being used; if not, the estimates should be adjusted to a common risk-free-rate reference point.
>
> - Some analysts do not view illiquidity as a kind of risk and may refer to an illiquidity premium in addition to the risk premium when estimating the required return on an illiquid asset.
>
> - Modeling any risk premium requires an assessment of the degree of capital market integration. Capital market integration will be discussed in Section 3.1.4.

Examples 15, 16, and 17 provide some information on the real risk-free interest rate, including long-term levels. The inflation premium is typically a more volatile element of the yield of bonds. In standard discussions of term-structure theory, the term structure of interest rates for default-free government bonds can provide an estimate of inflation expectations. Furthermore, in markets with active issuance of inflation-indexed bonds, the yield spread at a given maturity of conventional government bonds over inflation-indexed bonds of the same maturity may be able to provide a market-based estimate of the inflation premium at that horizon. The analyst can use market yield data and credit ratings (or other credit models) to estimate the default risk premium by comparing the yields on bonds matched along other dimensions but differing in default risk. An analogous approach may be applied to estimating the other premiums.

3.1.3.3 The Equity Risk Premium

The **equity risk premium** is the compensation required by investors for the additional risk of equity compared with debt (debt has a prior claim on the cash flows of the company). An estimate of the equity risk premium directly supplies an estimate of the expected return on equities through the following expression:

$$E(R_e) = \text{YTM on a long-term government bond} + \text{Equity risk premium} \quad (8)$$

where "long-term" has usually been interpreted as 10 or 20 years. (In many markets, bonds with maturities longer than 10 years are not available or actively traded.) As long as one is consistent with the choice of maturity in defining the equity risk premium, either choice is feasible. Equation 8 has been called the **bond-yield-plus-risk-premium method** of estimating the expected return on equity. From Equation 8, we also see that the *equity risk premium in practice is specifically defined as the expected excess return over and above a long-term government bond yield*.

A historical analysis has often been used as a point of departure in estimating the equity risk premium. Exhibit 9 gives the *ex post* data for the 111 years from 1900 to 2010. The standard deviation column represents the volatility in the difference between equity returns and bond returns on a year-by-year basis.

Exhibit 9: Historical Equity Risk Premiums around the World: 1900–2010

Annual Realized Equity Risk Premium Relative to Long Bond Returns

Country	Geometric Mean	Arithmetic Mean	Standard Error	Standard Deviation
Australia	5.9%	7.8%	1.9%	19.8%
Belgium	2.6	4.9	2.0	21.4
Canada	3.7	5.3	1.7	18.2
Denmark	2.0	3.4	1.6	17.2
France	3.2	5.6	2.2	22.9
Germany (ex-1922/23)	5.4	8.8	2.7	28.4
Ireland	2.9	4.9	1.9	19.8
Italy	3.7	7.2	2.8	29.6
Japan	5.0	9.1	3.1	32.8
Netherlands	3.5	5.8	2.1	22.2
Norway	2.5	5.5	2.7	28.0
South Africa	5.5	7.0	1.9	19.6
Spain	2.3	4.3	2.0	20.8
Sweden	3.8	6.1	2.1	22.3
Switzerland	2.1	3.6	1.7	17.6
United Kingdom	3.9	5.2	1.6	17.0
United States	4.4	6.4	1.9	20.5
World average	3.8	5.0	1.5	15.5

Source: Dimson, Marsh, and Staunton (2011), Table 10. See this source for the details of the equity and bond series used. Note that the world average is based on more markets than are shown in this exhibit.

From Exhibit 9, we can draw the following conclusions:

- The geometric mean historical equity risk premium ranged from a low of 2.0 percent (Denmark) to a high of 5.9 percent (Australia) with an average of 3.8 percent.

- The arithmetic mean historical equity risk premium ranged from a low of 3.4 percent (Denmark) to a high of 9.1 percent (Japan) with an average of 5.0 percent.

- As measured by the standard error (which applies to the arithmetic mean), for most markets there is considerable sampling error in the sample mean estimate of the (presumed unchanging) population mean equity risk premium. Consider the United States, with a standard error of 1.9 percent. Under a normality assumption, one could be only 68 percent confident that the population mean is between 4.5 percent (6.4 percent − 1.9 percent) and 8.3 percent (6.4 percent + 1.9 percent).

- The standard deviation column shows that there is a great amount of variation in the annual return difference between equities and bonds.

The size of *ex ante* equity risk premiums in international markets and the interpretation of the historical record for the purposes of estimating them have been the source of a lively, continuing, and unresolved debate. Grinold and Kroner (2002) and Dimson, Marsh, and Staunton (2002, 2006 and 2011) provide useful observations on the issues raised.

Tools for Formulating Capital Market Expectations

3.1.4 Financial Market Equilibrium Models

Financial equilibrium models describe relationships between expected return and risk in which supply and demand are in balance. In that sense, equilibrium prices or equilibrium returns are fair if the equilibrium model is correct.

Equilibrium approaches to setting capital market expectations include the Black–Litterman approach and the international CAPM–based approach presented in Singer and Terhaar (1997). The Black–Litterman approach reverse-engineers the expected returns implicit in a diversified market portfolio, combining them with the investor's own views in a systematic way that takes account of the investor's confidence in his or her views.[45] This approach is discussed at greater length in the reading on asset allocation.

Singer and Terhaar (1997) proposed an equilibrium approach to developing capital market expectations that involves calculating the expected return on each asset class based on the international capital asset pricing model (ICAPM),[46] taking account of market imperfections that are not considered by the ICAPM.[47]

Assuming that the risk premium on any currency equals zero—as it would be if purchasing power parity relationships hold—the ICAPM gives the expected return on any asset as the sum of:

- the (domestic) risk-free rate, and
- a risk premium based on the asset's sensitivity to the world market portfolio and expected return on the world market portfolio in excess of the risk-free rate.

Equation 9 is the formal expression for the ICAPM:

$$E(R_i) = R_F + \beta_i \left[E(R_M) - R_F \right] \tag{9}$$

where

$E(R_i)$ = the expected return on asset i given its beta
R_F = the risk-free rate of return
$E(R_M)$ = the expected return on the world market portfolio
β_i = the asset's sensitivity to returns on the world market portfolio, equal to $\text{Cov}(R_i, R_M)/\text{Var}(R_M)$

An important question concerns the identification of an appropriate proxy for the world market portfolio. Based on the criteria of Brinson, Diermeier, and Schlarbaum (1986, p. 17), the analyst can define and use the **global investable market** (GIM). The GIM is a practical proxy for the world market portfolio consisting of traditional and alternative asset classes with sufficient capacity to absorb meaningful investment.[48]

Equation 9 implies that an asset class risk premium, RP_i, equal to $E(R_i) - R_F$, is a simple function of the world market risk premium, RP_M, equal to $E(R_M) - R_F$:[49]

$$RP_i = \frac{\sigma_i}{\sigma_m} \rho_{i,M} \left(RP_M \right)$$

---

[45] See Black and Litterman (1991, 1992). The notion of using reverse optimization to infer expected returns was first described in Sharpe (1974).

[46] ICAPM has also been used as an acronym for the intertemporal capital asset pricing modeleveloped by Merton (1973). In this reading, ICAPM refers to the international capital asset pricing model.

[47] See also Terhaar, Staub, and Singer (2003). The specific suggestion of this approach is to use the factor-model-based estimate of the covariance matrix presented in Section 3.1.1.4.

[48] See Brinson, Diermeier, and Schlarbaum (1986) for more details.

[49] The expression is derived as follows: $RP_i = \beta_i (RP_M) = \left[\text{Cov}(R_i, R_M)/\sigma_M^2 \right](RP_M) = \left(\sigma_i \sigma_M \rho_{iM}/\sigma_M^2 \right)(RP_M) = \sigma_i \rho_{iM} (RP_M/\sigma_M)$, where we have used the fact that $\text{Cov}(R_i, R_M) = \sigma_i \sigma_M \rho_{iM}$.

Moving the market standard deviation of returns term within the parentheses, we find that an asset class's risk premium equals the product of the Sharpe ratio (RP_M/σ_M) of the world market portfolio, the asset's own volatility, and the asset class's correlation with the world market portfolio:

$$RP_i = \sigma_i \rho_{i,M} \left(\frac{RP_M}{\sigma_M} \right) \tag{10}$$

Equation 10 is one of two key equations in the Singer–Terhaar approach. The Sharpe ratio in Equation 10 (i.e., RP_M/σ_M) is the expected excess return per unit of standard deviation of the world market portfolio. The world market portfolio's standard deviation represents a kind of risk (systematic risk) that cannot be avoided through diversification and that should therefore command a return in excess of the risk-free rate. An asset class's risk premium is therefore the expected excess return accruing to the asset class given its global systematic risk (i.e., its beta relative to the world market portfolio).

Equation 10 requires a market Sharpe ratio estimate. Singer and Terhaar (1997, pp. 44–52) describe a complete analysis for estimating it. As of the date of their analysis, 1997, they recommended a value of 0.30 (a 0.30 percent return per 1 percent of compensated risk). Goodall, Manzini, and Rose (1999, pp. 4–10) revisited this issue on the basis of different macro models and recommended a value of 0.28. For this exposition, we adopt a value of 0.28. In fact, the Sharpe ratio of the global market could change over time with changing global economic fundamentals.

To illustrate Equation 10, suppose that an investor predicts that the standard deviation of Canadian bonds will be 7.0 percent per year and that their correlation with the GIM is 0.54. Then, with our estimate of the market Sharpe ratio, we would estimate the risk premium as

7% × 0.54 × 0.28 = 1.06%

For Canadian equities, with a standard deviation of 17 percent and a 0.70 correlation with the GIM, we would estimate the equity risk premium as

17% × 0.70 × 0.28 = 3.33%

The Singer–Terhaar approach recognizes the need to account for market imperfections that are not considered by the ICAPM. We will consider two market imperfections: illiquidity and market segmentation.

In the discussion of bonds, we defined the illiquidity premium as compensation for the risk of loss relative to an investment's fair value if the investment needs to be converted to cash quickly. The ICAPM assumes **perfect markets** (markets without any frictional costs, where all assets trade in liquid markets). Thus, we need to add an estimated illiquidity premium to an ICAPM expected return estimate as appropriate. The ICAPM was formulated with developed securities markets such as the Canadian bond and equity markets in mind, and the Singer–Terhaar approach would not add an illiquidity premium to ICAPM expected return estimates for Canadian stocks and bonds.

However, the illustrated risk premium estimates for Canadian bonds and equities (1.06 percent and 3.33 percent, respectively) are those that would hold if Canadian bond and equity markets were perfectly integrated with other world asset markets. **Market integration** means that there are no impediments or barriers to capital mobility across markets. Barriers include not only legal barriers, such as restrictions a national emerging market might place on foreign investment, but also cultural predilections and other investor preferences. If markets are perfectly integrated, all investors worldwide participate equally in setting prices in any individual national market. Market integration implies that two assets in different markets with identical risk characteristics must have the same expected return. **Market segmentation** means that there are some meaningful impediments to capital movement across markets.

Tools for Formulating Capital Market Expectations

Although many barriers to international capital flows have come down, some do persist and a number of asset markets are in practice at least partially segmented across national borders. The more a market is segmented, the more it is dominated by *local* investors. When markets are segmented, two assets in different markets with identical risk characteristics may have different expected returns. If an asset in a segmented market appears undervalued to a nondomestic investor *not* considering barriers to capital mobility, *after* such barriers are considered, the investor may not actually be able to exploit the opportunity.

Most markets lie between the extremes of perfect market integration and complete market segmentation. A home-biased perspective or partial segmentation is perhaps the best representation of most markets in the world today. We need first to develop an estimate of the risk premium for the case of complete market segmentation. With such an estimate in hand, the estimate of the risk premium for the common case of partial segmentation is just a weighted average of the risk premium assuming perfect market integration and the risk premium assuming complete segmentation, where the weights reflect the analyst's view of the degree of integration of the given asset market.

To address the task of estimating the risk premium for the case of complete market segmentation, we must first recognize that if a market is completely segmented, the market portfolio in Equations 9 and 10 must be identified as the *individual local market*. Because the individual market and the reference market portfolio are identical, $\rho_{i,M}$ in Equation 10 equals 1. (For example, if Canadian equities were a completely segmented market, the reference market portfolio and the individual market portfolio would each be a broad-based index for Canadian equities, and the correlation of such an index with itself would of course be 1.) The value of 1 for correlation is the maximum value, so all else being equal, the risk premium for the completely segmented markets case is higher than that for the perfectly integrated markets case and equal to the amount shown in Equation 11:

$$RP_i = \sigma_i \left(\frac{RP_M}{\sigma_M} \right) \quad (11)$$

This is the second key equation in the Singer–Terhaar approach. Assuming that Canadian bonds and equities trade in completely segmented markets, we would calculate respective risk premiums of[50]

$$7\% \times 0.28 = 1.96\%$$

and

$$17\% \times 0.28 = 4.76\%$$

Taking the degree of integration as 0.8 for both Canadian equities and bonds, our final risk premium estimates would be as follows:

- $RP_{Cdn\ FI} = (0.8 \times 1.06\%) + (0.2 \times 1.96\%) = 1.24\%$
- $RP_{Cdn\ equities} = (0.8 \times 3.33\%) + (0.2 \times 4.76\%) = 3.62\%$

Thus, assuming a risk-free rate of 4 percent, we would estimate the expected returns on Canadian bonds and equities as the sum of the risk-free rate and the relevant risk premium, as follows:

- Canadian bonds: $E(R_{Cdn\ FI}) = 4\% + 1.24\% = 5.24\%$
- Canadian equities: $E(R_{Cdn\ equities}) = 4\% + 3.62\% = 7.62\%$

---

[50] For simplicity, we are assuming that the Sharpe ratios of the GIM and the local market portfolio (used in Equation 11) are the same.

To summarize, to arrive at an expected return estimate using the Singer–Terhaar approach, we take the following steps:

- Estimate the perfectly integrated and the completely segmented risk premiums for the asset class using the ICAPM.
- Add the applicable illiquidity premium, if any, to the estimates from the prior step.
- Estimate the degree to which the asset market is perfectly integrated.
- Take a weighted average of the perfectly integrated and the completely segmented risk premiums using the estimate of market integration from the prior step.[51]

The analyst needs to develop estimates of the degree of integration of an asset market, but as a starting point, research has suggested that developed market equities and bonds are approximately 80 percent integrated. To give a flavor of the variation that might be expected, research has also indicated that U.S. and U.K. real estate is approximately 70 percent integrated; real estate in France, Germany, the Netherlands, and Switzerland is 60 percent integrated; emerging market equities and bonds are about 65 percent integrated; and at the low end of integration are assets such as timber at 50 percent (United States, Australia) or 40 percent (Argentina, Brazil, Chile, Uruguay). Currency and cash markets are 100 percent integrated.[52]

Another task for the analyst is estimating the illiquidity premium for an asset class. Estimating this premium for alternative investments presents a great challenge. Many such investments cannot be traded at all for some time (i.e., are **locked up**, as might be the case for early-stage venture capital). Rebalancing to a target allocation is not feasible during the lockup period and is relatively costly afterward.

Example 18

Justifying Capital Market Forecasts

Samuel Breed, CIO of a university endowment, is presenting the capital market expectations shown in Exhibit 10 to the endowment's board of trustees.

Exhibit 10 Capital Market Projections

Asset Class	Proxy	Projected 5-Year Annual Return (%)	Projected Standard Deviation (%)
Equities			
1. Large-cap U.S. equity	S&P 500	8.8	16.5
2. Small/mid-cap U.S. equity	Russell 2500	9.8	22.0
3. Ex-U.S. equity	MSCI EAFE	9.2	20.0
Fixed Income			
4. Domestic fixed income	LB Aggregate	4.7	4.5
5. Non-U.S. fixed income	Citi Non-U.S. Govt.	4.6	9.5

---

[51] Alternatively, we can substitute the Sharpe ratio of the "typical" local investor's investment portfolio for the GIM portfolio in Equation 10 and use the correlation of the asset class under consideration with that typical local portfolio.
[52] See Staub (2005).

Tools for Formulating Capital Market Expectations

Exhibit 10 Continued

Asset Class	Proxy	Projected 5-Year Annual Return (%)	Projected Standard Deviation (%)
Other Assets			
6. U.S. real estate	NCREIF	7.6	14.0
7. Private equity	VE Post Venture Cap.	12.0	34.0
8. Cash equivalents	90-day T-bill	3.3	1.0
Inflation	CPI-U	2.6	1.4

Correlations:	1	2	3	4	5	6	7	8
1. Large-cap U.S. equity	1.0							
2. Small/mid-cap U.S. equity	0.85	1.0						
3. Ex-U.S. equity	0.74	0.61	1.0					
4. Domestic fixed income	0.27	0.20	0.21	1.0				
5. Non-U.S. fixed income	0.03	−0.03	0.22	0.32	1.0			
6. U.S. real estate	0.64	0.52	0.47	0.20	0.03	1.0		
7. Private equity	0.63	0.57	0.63	0.20	0.10	0.45	1.0	
8. Cash equivalents	−0.10	−0.15	−0.25	0.30	−0.05	−0.06	0.07	1.0

Assume the following:

- The Sharpe ratio of the global investable market portfolio (GIM) is 0.28, and its standard deviation is 7 percent.
- The beta of private equity with respect to the GIM is 3.3, and the beta of small/mid-cap U.S. equity is 2.06.

William Smyth, a trustee, questions various projections for private equity, as follows:

A. "I have seen volatility estimates for private equity based on appraisal data that are much smaller than the one you are presenting, in which the volatility of private equity is much larger than that of small/mid-cap U.S. equity. Your volatility estimate for private equity must be wrong."

B. "The premium of private equity over small/mid-cap U.S. equity is not justifiable because they both represent ownership interests in U.S. business."

C. "Using the ICAPM, the forecast correlation between private equity returns and small/mid-cap U.S. equity returns is lower than your estimate indicates."

1. Evaluate whether Smyth's Comment A is accurate.
2. Evaluate whether Smyth's Comment B is accurate.
3. Evaluate whether Smyth's Comment C is accurate.

Solution to 1:

Smyth's Comment A is not accurate. Although private equity and small-cap stocks both represent ownership interests, private equity is not traded and appraisal data will tend to underestimate volatility.

> **Solution to 2:**
>
> Smyth's Comment B is not accurate. One justification for a higher expected return for private equity is that it has a lockup period and should therefore bear an illiquidity premium.
>
> **Solution to 3:**
>
> Smyth's Comment C is accurate. According to elementary portfolio theory, the correlation between two assets is given by $\beta_1\beta_2\sigma_M^2/\sigma_1\sigma_2$. Thus, the correlation between private equity and small/mid-cap U.S. equity is equal to $(3.3)(2.06)(7\%)^2/(34\%)(22\%) = 0.45$, which is lower than the estimate of 0.57 given in Exhibit 10.

The illiquidity premium for an alternative investment should be positively related to the length of the investment's lockup period or illiquidity horizon. How can the amount of the illiquidity premium be estimated? One estimation approach uses the investment's **multiperiod Sharpe ratio** (MPSR), which is based on the investment's multiperiod wealth in excess of the wealth generated by the risk-free investment (i.e., compounded return over compounded cash return). The relevant MPSR is one calculated over a holding period equal to the investment's lockup period. There would be no incentive to invest in an illiquid alternative investment unless its MPSR—its risk-adjusted wealth—were at least as high as the MPSR of the market portfolio at the end of the lockup period. Suppose that an alternative investment has a lockup period of eight years and its ICAPM-given required rate of return is 12 percent but its MPSR is below that of the GIM—say, 0.67—at an eight-year horizon. If increasing its expected return to 20 percent makes the alternative investment's MSPR equal 0.67 at the eight-year horizon, then the estimate of the illiquidity premium is 20% − 12% = 8%.[53]

Example 19 illustrates the Singer–Terhaar approach. In the example, for simplicity's sake, the ICAPM betas are used to develop covariance estimates.

> **Example 19**
>
> ### Setting CME Using the Singer–Terhaar Approach
>
> Zimmerman Capital Management (ZCM) is developing a strategic asset allocation for a small U.S. foundation that has approved investment in the following five asset classes: U.S. equities, U.S. fixed income, non-U.S. equities, non-U.S. fixed income, and U.S. real estate. The foundation limits nondomestic assets to no more than 12 percent of invested assets.
>
> - The final set of expectations needed consists of the expected returns, standard deviations, and all distinct pairwise covariances of U.S. equities, U.S. fixed income, non-U.S. equities, non-U.S. fixed income, and U.S. real estate. The investment time horizon is 10 years.
> - A risk premium approach will be taken to developing expected return estimates following the methodology of Singer and Terhaar. Historical estimates of standard deviations will be used, and ICAPM betas will be used to develop estimates of covariances.
> - Exhibit 11 supplies the standard deviation estimates and gives relevant inputs for other quantities needed. In addition, ZCM has gathered the following facts and estimates:

---

[53] See Staub and Diermeier (2003) for more details.

Tools for Formulating Capital Market Expectations

- The Sharpe ratio of the GIM is estimated to be 0.28.
- The standard deviation of the GIM is estimated to be 7 percent.
- The risk-free rate of interest is 3 percent.

■ Equities and bonds are assumed to be 80 percent integrated, and U.S. real estate is assumed to be 70 percent integrated.

Exhibit 11   Equilibrium Approach to Risk Premium Estimation

Asset Class	Standard Deviation	Correlation with GIM	Premium to Equate Sharpe Ratio at Illiquidity Horizon
U.S. equities	15.7%	0.85	0%
U.S. fixed income	3.8	0.75	0
Non-U.S. equities	15.6	0.80	0
Non-U.S. fixed income	9.1	0.70	0
U.S. real estate	11.5	0.50	0.30

Based on the information given, address the following problems:

1. Calculate the expected returns on U.S. equities, U.S. fixed income, non-U.S. equities, non-U.S. fixed income, and U.S. real estate. Make any needed adjustments for illiquidity.

2. Show the calculation of the covariance between U.S. equities and U.S. fixed income.

3. Critique the following statement: "The ZCM risk premium estimates are low, given that the foundation has a very strong home-country bias, reflected in its limitation of nondomestic assets to no more than 12 percent of the portfolio."

Solution to 1:

To calculate the expected return for an asset class, we take the following steps. First, we calculate the risk premium of the asset class for two distinct cases: full integration and complete segmentation. In the calculation for either case, we take care to add any applicable illiquidity premium. Second, we average the two estimates of the risk premium for an asset class by weighting the full integration estimate by the assumed degree of integration and the complete segmentation estimate by (1 − assumed degree of integration). The result of this step is our informed estimate of the asset class's risk premium. Finally, adding the risk premium estimate to the risk-free rate yields our estimate of the expected return on the asset class.

Step 1

Using Equation 10, we find that in the fully integrated case,

$RP_{\text{U.S. equities}} = 15.7\% \times 0.85 \times 0.28 = 3.74\%$

$RP_{\text{U.S. FI}} = 3.8\% \times 0.75 \times 0.28 = 0.80\%$

$RP_{\text{non-U.S. equities}} = 15.6\% \times 0.80 \times 0.28 = 3.49\%$

$RP_{\text{non-U.S. FI}} = 9.1\% \times 0.70 \times 0.28 = 1.78\%$

$RP_{\text{U.S. RE}} = (11.5\% \times 0.50 \times 0.28) + 0.30\% = 1.61\% + 0.30\% = 1.91\%$.

Using Equation 11, we find that in the fully segmented case,

$$RP_{\text{U.S. equities}} = 15.7\% \times 0.28 = 4.4\%$$
$$RP_{\text{U.S. FI}} = 3.8\% \times 0.28 = 1.06\%$$
$$RP_{\text{non-U.S. equities}} = 15.6\% \times 0.28 = 4.37\%$$
$$RP_{\text{non-U.S. FI}} = 9.1\% \times 0.28 = 2.55\%$$
$$RP_{\text{U.S. RE}} = (11.5\% \times 0.28) + 0.30\% = 3.22\% + 0.30\% = 3.52\%.$$

Note that we added an illiquidity premium of 0.3 percent to the ICAPM derived premium estimates for real estate.

Step 2

We now weight each asset class's fully integrated and segmented premiums according to the assumed degree of integration.

$$RP_{\text{U.S. equities}} = (0.8 \times 3.74\%) + (0.2 \times 4.4\%) = 3.87\%$$
$$RP_{\text{U.S. FI}} = (0.8 \times 0.80\%) + (0.2 \times 1.06\%) = 0.85\%$$
$$RP_{\text{non-U.S. equities}} = (0.8 \times 3.49\%) + (0.2 \times 4.37\%) = 3.67\%$$
$$RP_{\text{non-U.S. FI}} = (0.8 \times 1.78\%) + (0.2 \times 2.55\%) = 1.93\%$$
$$RP_{\text{U.S. RE}} = (0.7 \times 1.91\%) + (0.3 \times 3.52\%) = 2.39\%$$

Step 3

The expected return estimates are as follows:

$$E(R_{\text{U.S. equities}}) = 3\% + 3.87\% = 6.87\%$$
$$E(R_{\text{U.S. FI}}) = 3\% + 0.85\% = 3.85\%$$
$$E(R_{\text{non-U.S. equities}}) = 3\% + 3.67\% = 6.67\%$$
$$E(R_{\text{non-U.S. FI}}) = 3\% + 1.93\% = 4.93\%$$
$$E(R_{\text{U.S. RE}}) = 3\% + 2.39\% = 5.39\%.$$

Solution to 2:

Based on Equation 3b with one factor, the covariance between any two assets in a one-beta model (such as the ICAPM) is equal to the product of each asset's beta with respect to the market times the variance of the market. The needed betas can be calculated as

$$\beta_{\text{U.S. equities}} = (15.7\% \times 0.85)/7\% = 1.91$$
$$\beta_{\text{U.S. FI}} = (3.8\% \times 0.75)/7\% = 0.41$$

and the covariance between U.S. equities and U.S. fixed income returns as

$$\text{Cov}(\text{U.S. equities}, \text{U.S. FI}) = 1.91 \times 0.41 \times (7\%)^2 =$$
$$38.37 \text{(in units of percent squared)}$$

Solution to 3:

Although the client is correct about the foundation's home-country bias, the point being made is not correct. The equilibrium risk premium is determined by all investors, reflected in the overall degree of integration estimates.

Tools for Formulating Capital Market Expectations

3.2 Survey and Panel Methods

The **survey method** of expectations setting involves asking a group of experts for their expectations and using the responses in capital market formulation. If the group queried and providing responses is fairly stable, the analyst in effect has a panel of experts and the approach can be called a **panel method**. These approaches are based on the straightforward idea that a direct way to uncover a person's expectations is to ask the person what they are.

The oldest continuous survey of expectations is the so-called Livingston Survey, initiated in 1946 by Joseph Livingston, a Philadelphia journalist, and managed since 1990 by the Federal Reserve Bank of Philadelphia, part of the U.S. Federal Reserve System. The survey covers real U.S. GDP growth, CPI and PPI inflation, the unemployment rate, and 3-month T-bill and 10-year T-bond yields. In the United States, Welch surveyed financial economists for their views about the short- and long-term (30-year) equity risk premium in 1998, 2001, and 2009.[54] The results of the three Welch surveys for the 30-year equity risk premium are summarized in Exhibit 12.

Exhibit 12 Consensus Expectations of U.S. Financial Economists of the Long-term (30-Year) U.S. Equity Risk Premium

	2009 Survey	2001 Survey	1998 Survey
Mean	6.2%	5.5%	7.1%
Median	6.0	5.0	7.0
Interquartile range	5%–7%	4%–7%	6%–8.4%

Source: Welch (2000, 2001, 2009).

A 2002 survey of global bond investors by Schroder Salomon Smith Barney found an average equity risk premium in the range of 2–2.5 percent, while a Goldman Sachs survey of global clients recorded a mean long-run equity risk premium of 3.9 percent.[55] Such surveys may be sensitive to the professional identity of the respondents. Lally, Roush, and Van Zijl (2004) found the predictions of practitioners for the New Zealand equity risk premium significantly higher than those of academics.[56] Besides direct questions on capital market expectations, for certain equity markets, there are commercial surveys of analysts' forecasts of long-term earnings growth rates that implicitly contain an equity market forecast given a DCF valuation model.

Example 20

Short-Term Consumer Spending in the United Kingdom

Bryan Smith is researching the 6- to 12-month expectations for consumer spending in the United Kingdom as of the middle of 2012. One piece of evidence he gathers is changes in consumer sentiment in the United Kingdom as measured by the Economic Optimism Index, shown in Exhibit 13.

---

[54] See Welch (2000) and Welch (2001). The 1998 survey had 226 respondents, while the 2001 survey had 510. Graham and Harvey (2001) report a survey of 10-year forecasts of the U.S. equity risk premium by chief financial officers, but their survey question was not specific about whether an arithmetic or geometric mean estimate was sought.
[55] See Ilmanen, Byrne, Gunasekera, and Minikin (2002) and O'Neill, Wilson, and Masih (2002).
[56] The median forecast was 7.0 percent for practitioners and 5.5 percent for academics.

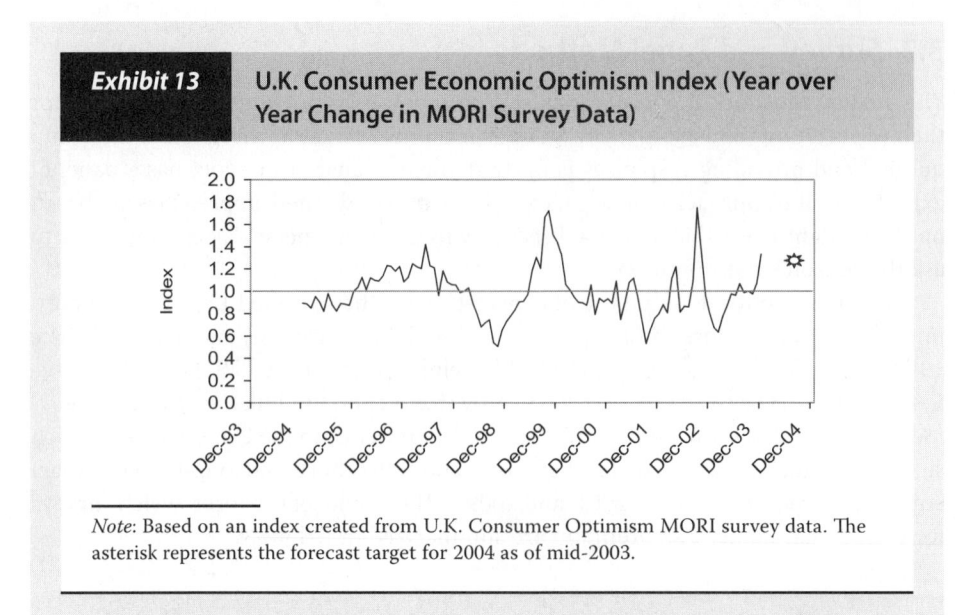

Exhibit 13 U.K. Consumer Economic Optimism Index (Year over Year Change in MORI Survey Data)

Note: Based on an index created from U.K. Consumer Optimism MORI survey data. The asterisk represents the forecast target for 2004 as of mid-2003.

Interpret Exhibit 13 as it relates to the probable path of consumer spending.

Solution:

Based on the reading at December 2003 of the U.K. Consumer Optimism Index, it appears that consumers are considerably more optimistic than in December 2002. Rising consumer optimism is a reflection of consumers feeling secure about their income stream and future. Rising consumer optimism suggests that near-term consumer spending will increase.

3.3 Judgment

In a disciplined expectations-setting process, the analyst should be able to factually explain the basis and rationale for forecasts. Quantitative models such as equilibrium models offer the prospect of providing a non-emotional, objective rationale for a forecast. The expectations-setting process nevertheless can give wide scope to applying judgment—in particular, economic and psychological insight—to improve forecasts. In forecasting, numbers, including those produced by elaborate quantitative models, must be evaluated.

Example 21

Judgment Applied to Correlation Estimation

William Chew's firm uses a multifactor model to develop initial correlation forecasts that are then challenged by professionals within the capital markets unit. Based on U.S. historical data including periods of high inflation, Chew finds that the model forecasts a correlation between U.S. equity and U.S. bonds in the range of 0.40 to 0.45. Based on empirical evidence, Chew believes that the correlation between equity and bond returns is higher in high-inflation periods than in low-inflation periods. His firm's chief economist forecasts that in the medium term, U.S. inflation will be low, averaging less than 3 percent per annum. In light of that forecast, Chew has decided that he will recommend a judgmental downward adjustment of the correlation to 0.30.

Other investors who rely on judgment in setting capital market expectations may discipline the process by the use of devices such as checklists. In any case, investment experience, the study of capital markets, and intelligence are requisites for the development of judgment in setting capital market expectations.

ECONOMIC ANALYSIS

History has shown that there is a direct yet fluid relationship between actual realized asset returns, expectations for future asset returns, and economic activity. The linkages are consistent with asset-pricing theory, which predicts that the risk premium of an asset is related to the correlation of its payoffs with the marginal utility of consumption in future periods. Assets with low expected payoffs in periods of weak consumption (e.g., business cycle troughs) should bear higher risk premiums than assets with high expected payoffs in such periods. Because investors expect assets of the second type to provide good payoffs when their income may be depressed, they should be willing to pay relatively high prices for them (implying lower risk premiums).[57]

Analysts need to be familiar with the historical relationships that empirical research has uncovered concerning the direction, strength, and lead-lag relationships between economic variables and capital market returns.

The analyst who understands which economic variables may be most relevant to the current economic environment has a competitive advantage, as does the analyst who can discern or forecast a change in trend or point of inflection in economic activity. Inflection points often present unique investment opportunities at the same time that they are sources of latent risk. Questions that may help the analyst assess points of inflection include the following:

- What is driving the economy in its current expansion or contraction phase?
- What is helping to maintain economic growth, demand, supply, and/or inflation rates within their current ranges?
- What may trigger the end of a particular trend?

The economic output of many economies has been found to have cyclical and trend growth components. Trend growth is of obvious relevance for setting long-term return expectations for asset classes such as equities. Cyclical variation affects variables such as corporate profits and interest rates, which are directly related to asset class returns and risk. In the following sections, we address business cycles and trend growth.

4.1 Business Cycle Analysis

In business cycle analysis, two cycles are generally recognized: a short-term **inventory cycle**, typically lasting 2–4 years, and a longer-term **business cycle**, usually lasting 9–11 years. Evidence for both these cycles goes back two centuries or more, but they are very far from working like clockwork. In particular, they can be disrupted by major shocks, including wars and shifts in government policy. Also, both the duration and amplitude of each phase of the cycle, as well as the duration of the cycle as a whole, vary considerably and are hard to predict.

---

[57] See Cochrane (1999a, 1999b).

Cycles mark variation in economic activity, so we should be clear on how that variation is measured. The chief measurements of economic activity are as follows:

- **Gross domestic product (GDP)**: GDP is a calculation of the total value of final goods and services produced in the economy during a year. The main expenditure components are Consumption, Investment, Change in Inventories, Government Spending, and Exports less Imports. The total value of goods and services can change because the quantities of goods and services change and/or because their prices change. To focus on increases in the quantity (output) of goods and services produced—which are directly associated with increases in the standard of living—rather than on price-driven increases in the value of output, economists focus on real GDP (reflecting an adjustment for changes in prices during the period). For brevity's sake in our discussion, "GDP" is understood as referring to "real GDP" unless otherwise stated.

- **Output gap**: The **output gap** is the difference between the value of GDP estimated as if the economy were on its trend growth path (sometimes referred to as **potential output**) and the actual value of GDP. A positive output gap opens in times of recession or slow growth. When a positive output gap is open, inflation tends to decline. Once the gap closes, inflation tends to rise. When GDP is above its trend value, the economy is under inflationary pressure. Many macroeconomists consider the output gap as the key measure of real activity for policy making because it provides information about future inflationary pressures as well as an output objective. However, because changing demographics and technology affect the economy's trend path, real-time estimates of the output gap can sometimes be quite inaccurate.

- **Recession**: In general terms, a **recession** is a broad-based economic downturn. More formally, a recession occurs when there are two successive quarterly declines in GDP.

The following sections discuss the inventory cycle and the business cycle in more detail.

4.1.1 The Inventory Cycle

Economists have found evidence of a short-term inventory cycle, lasting 2–4 years. The **inventory cycle** is a cycle measured in terms of fluctuations in inventories. The inventory cycle is caused by companies trying to keep inventories at desired levels as the expected level of sales changes.

In the up phase of the inventory cycle, businesses are confident about future sales and are increasing production. The increase in production generates more overtime pay and employment, which tends to boost the economy and bring further sales. At some point, there is a disappointment in sales or a change in expectations of future sales, so that businesses start to view inventories as too high. In the recent past, a tightening of monetary policy has often caused this inflection point. It could also be caused by a shock such as higher oil prices. Then, business cuts back production to try to reduce inventories and hires more slowly (or institutes layoffs). The result is a slowdown in growth.

It usually takes a year or two for business to correct inventory levels after an inflection point. A good indicator of the inventory position is the inventory/sales ratio. Exhibit 14 shows the inventory/sales ratio for the United States over the period 1992–2011. When the inventory/sales ratio has moved down, the economy is likely to be strong in the next few quarters as businesses try to rebuild inventory, as in early 2004. Conversely, when the ratio has moved sharply up, as in 2008-09, a period of economic weakness can be expected. Note that while this indicator has been trending down because of improved techniques such as "just in time" inventory management, the 2- to 4-year inventory cycle is still evident.

Economic Analysis

Exhibit 14 U.S. Inventory/Sales Ratios

Source: FRED, Federal Reserve Economic Data, Federal Reserve Bank of St. Louis: Inventory to Sales Ratio: Total Business (ISRATIO); U.S. Department of Commerce: Census Bureau. http://research.stlouisfed.org/fred2/series/ISRATIO; accessed 21 December 2011.

In the late 1990s, it was argued that improved and computerized techniques of inventory control would make the inventory cycle obsolete. In fact, the 2001 and 2008–09 recessions saw one of the steepest inventory corrections on record. The reason seems to have been that excess inventories were more visible more quickly than in the past, and businesses rapidly cut back production.

4.1.2 The Business Cycle

In addition to the inventory cycle, there is evidence of a longer cycle, often lasting 9–11 years, called the business cycle. The **business cycle** represents fluctuations in GDP in relation to long-term trend growth. A typical business cycle has five phases: initial recovery, early upswing, late upswing, slowdown, and recession.

1. **Initial Recovery** This is usually a short phase of a few months in which the economy picks up from its slowdown or recession. Generally, confidence is rising among businesses, although consumer confidence may still be at low levels since unemployment is still high. In the initial recovery phase, there are often stimulatory economic policies from the government in the form of lower interest rates or a budgetary deficit. The business cycle recovery is usually supported by a simultaneous upswing in the inventory cycle, which is sometimes the main cause of the recovery. Inflation will still be falling in the initial recovery phase. The output gap is still large.

    Capital market effects: Government bond yields may continue to come down through this phase in anticipation of a further decline in inflation but are likely to be bottoming. Stock markets may rise strongly at this point because fears of a longer recession (or even a depression) dissipate. Cyclical assets—and riskier assets, such as small stocks, higher-yield corporate bonds, and emerging market equities and bonds—attract investors and perform well.

2. **Early Upswing** After the initial recovery period, confidence is up and the economy is gaining some momentum. This is the healthiest period of the cycle, in a sense, because economic growth can be robust without any signs of overheating or sharply higher inflation. Typically, there is increasing confidence, with consumers prepared to borrow and spend more as unemployment starts to fall. Concurrently, businesses build inventories and step up investment in the face of strong sales and increased capacity use. Higher operating levels allow many businesses to enjoy lower unit costs, so that profits rise rapidly.

    Capital market effects: A key question is how long it will take before inflation starts to become a problem. Short rates are moving up at this time as the central bank starts to withdraw the stimulus put in place during the recession. Longer bond yields are likely to be stable or rising slightly. Stocks are still trending up. This phase usually lasts at least a year and often several years if growth is not too strong and the output gap closes slowly.

3. **Late Upswing** At this stage of the cycle, the output gap has closed and the economy is in danger of overheating. Confidence is high; unemployment is low. The economy may grow rapidly. Inflation starts to pick up, with wages accelerating as shortages of labor develop.

    Capital market effects: Typically, interest rates are rising as the monetary authorities become restrictive. Any heavy borrowing puts pressure on the credit markets. Central banks may aim for a "soft landing," meaning a period of slower growth to cool the economy but not a major downturn. Bond markets anxiously watch this behavior, and bond yields will usually be rising as a result of changed expectations. Stock markets will often rise but may be nervous too, depending on the strength of the boom. Nervous investors mean that equities are volatile.

4. **Slowdown** At this point, the economy is slowing, usually under the impact of rising interest rates. The economy is especially vulnerable at this juncture to a shock, which can turn a "soft landing" into a recession. Business confidence starts to waver. Despite the slowdown, inflation often continues to rise. The slowdown is exacerbated by the inventory correction as companies try to reduce their inventory levels. This phase may last just a few months, as in the United States in 2000, or it may last a year or more, as in the United States in 1989–1990 and 2009–2011.

    Capital market effects: Short-term interest rates are high and rising at first but then may peak. Bonds top out at the first sign of a slowing economy and then rally sharply (yields fall). The yield curve often inverts. The stock market may fall, with interest-sensitive stocks such as utilities and financial services performing best.

5. **Recession** A recession is conventionally defined as two successive quarterly declines in GDP. There is often a large inventory pullback and sometimes a large decline in business investment. Consumer spending on big-ticket items such as cars usually declines (although the U.S. 2001 recession was an exception). Once the recession is confirmed, central banks ease monetary policy, but only cautiously at first. Recessions typically last six months to a year. Both consumer and business confidence decline. Profits drop sharply. In a severe recession, the financial system may be stressed by bad debts, making lenders extremely cautious. Often, recessions are punctuated by major bankruptcies, incidents of uncovered fraud, or a financial crisis. Unemployment can rise quickly, putting downward pressure on inflation.

    Capital market effects: Short-term interest rates drop during this phase, as do bond yields. The stock market usually starts to rise in the later stages of the recession, well before the recovery emerges.

Economic Analysis

Exhibit 15 summarizes the characteristics of the five phases of the business cycle. The description given of business cycles is a stylized one. Each cycle is different because of specific events and trends that fall outside the stylized business cycle framework. Trends that have affected the business cycle from the 1990s through the late 2000s include the growing importance of China in world markets, the aging of populations, and the deregulation of markets. Events such as a petroleum or financial crisis can abruptly take the economy to the next phase of the business cycle or intensify the current phase.

Exhibit 15   Five Phases of the Business Cycle

Phase	Economy	Fiscal and Monetary Policy	Confidence	Capital Markets
1. Initial recovery	Inflation still declining	Stimulatory fiscal policies	Confidence starts to rebound	Short rates low or declining; bond yields bottoming; stock prices strongly rising
2. Early upswing	Healthy economic growth; inflation remains low		Increasing confidence	Short rates moving up; bond yields stable to up slightly; stock prices trending upward
3. Late upswing	Inflation gradually picks up	Policy becomes restrictive	Boom mentality	Short rates rising; bond yields rising; stocks topping out, often volatile
4. Slowdown	Inflation continues to accelerate; inventory correction begins		Confidence drops	Short-term interest rates peaking; bond yields topping out and starting to decline; stocks declining
5. Recession	Production declines; inflation peaks		Confidence weak	Short rates declining; bond yields dropping; stocks bottoming and then starting to rise

Example 22

The Yield Curve, Recessions, and Bond Maturity

The yield spread between the 10-year T-bond rate and the 3-month T-bill rate has been found internationally to be a predictor of future growth in output.[58] The observed tendency is for the yield spread to narrow or become negative prior to recessions. Another way of saying the same thing is that the yield curve tends to flatten or become inverted prior to a recession. Effects that may explain a declining yield spread include the following: 1) Future short-term rates are expected to fall, and/or 2) investors' required premium for holding long-term bonds rather than short-term bonds has fallen. At least, the link between an expected decline in short-term rates from expected lower loan demand and declining output growth is economically somewhat intuitive.

When the yield spread is expected to narrow (the yield curve is moving toward inversion), long-duration bonds should outperform short-duration bonds. On the other hand, a widening yield spread (for example, an inverted yield curve moving to an upward-sloping yield curve) favors short-duration bonds.

---

[58] See Estrella and Mishkin (1998).

4.1.3 Inflation and Deflation in the Business Cycle

Inflation simply means rising prices, while **deflation** means falling prices. At any given time, some prices are rising and others are falling. Thus, investors look at indices of prices to discern the overall trend. Consumer price indices, calculated from a basket of goods and services based on consumers' spending patterns, are commonly watched. Another set of price indices which are closely watched are the GDP and consumer expenditure deflators, which are inflation indices used to adjust or deflate the nominal series for inflation.

Inflation is linked to the business cycle, tending to rise in the late stages of a business cycle and to decline during recessions and the early stages of recovery. However, the analyst also needs to note any long-term trends in inflation in formulating capital market expectations.

> **Example 23**
>
> ### Inflation, Disinflation, and Deflation
>
> Today, people expect prices of goods and services and of investment assets to trend up over time. However, during most of the 19th century and through the 20th century prior to the 1960s, price inflation was negligible. Indeed, the price level in the United Kingdom fell for a large part of the 19th century. In the United States, the main period of inflation occurred during the Civil War (1861–65). Prices dropped for long periods otherwise. However, from the late 1950s until the late 1970s, inflation gradually accelerated almost everywhere, reaching over 10 percent in the United States and over 30 percent in the United Kingdom for brief periods. Then from about 1979, a period of disinflation set in as inflation gradually retreated back toward zero. Exhibit 16 illustrates the inflation rates in the United States and the United Kingdom since the 1950s.
>
> **Exhibit 16 U.S. and U.K. Inflation over the Long Term**
>
> *Source*: Bloomberg.

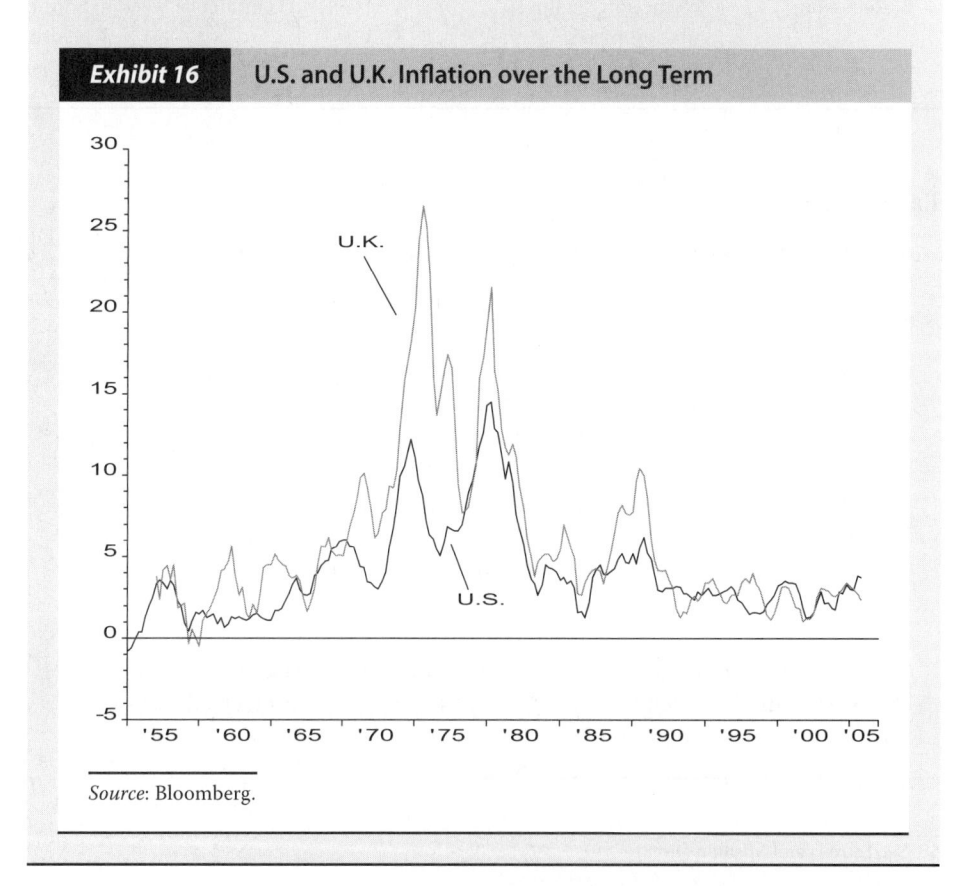

Economic Analysis

Central bank orthodoxy for dealing with inflation rests on three principles:

- Central banks' policy-making decisions must be independent of political influence. If political pressure is brought to bear on central banks, they may be too loose in their monetary policy and allow inflation to gradually accelerate.
- Central banks should have an inflation target, both as a discipline for themselves and as a signal to the markets of their intentions. An inflation target also serves to anchor market expectations.
- Central banks should use monetary policy (primarily interest rates) to control the economy and prevent it from either overheating or languishing in a recession for too long.

By the end of the 20th century, inflation had been defeated almost everywhere. All the major countries enjoyed inflation below 3 percent, and only a handful of emerging countries suffered from double-digit inflation. The challenge is to keep inflation low without succumbing to deflation.

Deflation is a threat to the economy for two main reasons. First, it tends to undermine debt-financed investments. If the price of a debt-financed asset (e.g., new equipment or a house) declines in value, the value of the "equity" in the asset (i.e., the difference between the asset's value and the loan balance) declines at a leveraged rate. For example, if the value of a property financed with a 67 percent loan-to-value mortgage then declines by 5 percent, the value of the equity in the property declines by 15 percent. This phenomenon sometimes leads to panic sales to save some part of the equity and can lead to asset deflation of the kind seen in the United States in the 1930s, the United Kingdom in the early 1990s, and many Asian countries in the late 1990s in the aftermath of the Asian crisis.

Second, deflation undermines the power of central banks. In a deflation, interest rates fall to levels close to zero. When interest rates are already very low, the central bank has less leeway to stimulate the economy by lowering interest rates. (Official interest rate targets cannot drop below zero, and zero is generally also a lower bound on the market level of interest rates.)[59] A very low interest rate environment in the late 2000s, accompanied by high unemployment, led central banks in the United States, United Kingdom, and Eurozone to engage in a relatively untested policy measure, **quantitative easing** (in which a central bank buys financial assets to inject a predetermined quantity of money in the financial system).

In today's economies, prolonged deflation is not really likely. In the now distant past, prolonged deflation was caused by the limited money supply provided by the gold standard currency system. (In the **gold standard currency system**, currency could be freely converted into gold at established rates, so that the money supply was constrained by the size of a government's gold reserves.) With governments able to expand the money supply to any desired degree, there is really no reason for deflation to last long. Nevertheless, even today, weak periods within the business cycle can still bring short periods of deflation, even if the upswing phases produce inflation.

Example 24 looks at some of the considerations that might enter into a short-term inflation forecast.

---

[59] In modern times, occurrences of negative nominal interest rates have been transitory and very rare. One case was the period from late 1938 to early 1941 in the United States, when weekly data showed occasional negative nominal yields on U.S. T-bills.

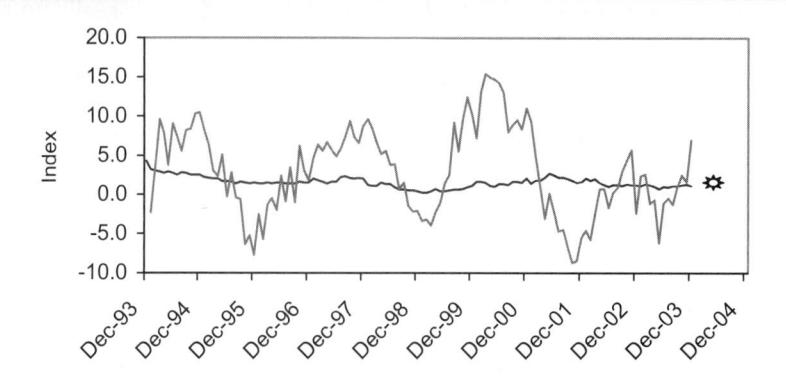

> **Example 24**
>
> ## An Inflation Forecast for Germany
>
> Early in 2011, Hans Vermaelen, a capital market analyst, has the task of making an inflation forecast for Germany over the next 6 to 12 months. Vermaelen gathers the following inputs and outputs:
>
> *Inputs*
>
> 1. A survey of manufacturers, asking them whether they expect to see price declines for the products they sell in order to stay globally competitive in light of a then-strengthening euro.
> 2. Information on German manufacturing orders and consumer price inflation.
> 3. Data inputs for a multifactor model including the following variables:
>   - prices of commodities;
>   - prices for labor;
>   - wholesale and producer price measures.
>
> *Outputs*
>
> 1. The survey of manufacturers indicates that manufacturers are facing challenges passing some price increases to German customers. After initially lowering export product prices to maintain market share in the face of a rising euro, German manufacturers are now passing price increases on to their international customers, thereby restoring their profit margins.
> 2. Current year-over-year annual inflation of 2.6 percent is above the average annual rate of 1.6 percent experienced over the past 10 years and over the past 10 quarters. Manufacturing orders have increased at about a 9 percent average rate over the past year. However, over the past quarter, manufacturing orders have decrease at a 4 percent year-over-year rate. Exhibit 17 graphs inflation and manufacturing orders.
> 3. The multifactor model indicates a positive correlation between the inflation rate and manufacturing orders and a negative correlation between a strengthening local currency (euro) and inflation.
>
> | Exhibit 17 | Inflation Pressure in Germany (Year over Year Consumer Inflation and Change in Manufacturing Orders) |
> |---|---|
>
> *Note*: The asterisk represents a forecast target of 1.5 percent inflation for 2011.

> Based on the above information, Vermaelen forecasts that inflation will decrease to a 1.6 percent rate over the next 6–12 months. Critique Vermaelen's forecast.
>
> ### Solution:
>
> The manufacturing orders have been decreasing recently at a 4 percent year-over-year rate versus a 9 percent average rate over the past year. This fact suggests that the German economy may be weakening. At the same time, the survey of manufacturers indicates that they are having difficulty passing along price increases to customers. These factors suggest a decrease in inflation from the recent 2.6 percent rate. Overall, it is reasonable to forecast a return to the recent average trend inflation rate of 1.6 percent.

Inflation tends to accelerate in the later stages of the business cycle, when the output gap has been closed. Inflation decelerates when, during a recession or in the early years afterward, there is a large output gap putting downward pressure on prices. As a result, the rate of inflation will decelerate to a low level and **deflation** (an increase in the purchasing power of a unit of currency) becomes possible.[60] Resistance to reduction in wages is a counterweight to deflationary pressures. Except in the worst circumstances, such as in the United States in the early 1930s, the rate of annual deflation is likely to be limited to about 2 percent, with wages holding steady.

During a recession, with falling inflation and interest rates, bonds generally post capital gains (for some bonds, deteriorating credit can offset such gains). In a strong upswing, bond yields will rise as investors fear that central banks will not hold inflation on target, resulting in capital losses to bondholders.

The impact of the inflation cycle on equities is more complex. In theory, as long as inflation stays near its expected or equilibrium level, the inflation rate is not very important. Higher inflation should be reflected in higher profits, so stocks will rise to compensate. However, signs that inflation is moving out of equilibrium indicate a potential threat because rising inflation could mean that the central banks need to act to slow the economy. Falling inflation, or possible deflation, is a problem because it threatens a recession and a decline in asset prices.

Exhibit 18 shows how changes in the inflation (deflation) rate affect the relative attractiveness of asset classes.

Exhibit 18 Inflation/Deflation Effects on Asset Classes

	Cash	Bonds	Equity	Real Estate/Other Real Assets
Inflation at or below expectations	Short-term yields steady or declining. [**Neutral**]	Yield levels maintained; market in equilibrium. [**Neutral**]	Bullish while market in equilibrium state. [**Positive**]	Cash flow steady to rising slightly. Returns equate to long-term average. Market in general equilibrium. [**Neutral**]
Inflation above expectations	Bias toward rising rates. [**Positive**]	Bias toward higher yields due to a higher inflation premium. [**Negative**]	High inflation a negative for financial assets. Less negative for companies/industries able to pass on inflated costs. [**Negative**]	Asset values increasing; increased cash flows and higher expected returns. [**Positive**]

(continued)

---

[60] The most extreme instances of deflation in the past hundred years occurred in the years surrounding the Great Depression (in particular, in the period 1926–1933).

Exhibit 18   Continued

	Cash	Bonds	Equity	Real Estate/Other Real Assets
Deflation	Bias toward 0% short-term rates. **[Negative]**	Purchasing power increasing. Bias toward steady to lower rates (may be offset by increased risk of potential defaults due to falling asset prices). **[Positive]**	Negative wealth effect slows demand. Especially affects asset-intensive, commodity-producing (as opposed to commodity-using), and highly levered companies. **[Negative]**	Cash flows steady to falling. Asset prices face downward pressure. **[Negative]**

4.1.4 Market Expectations and the Business Cycle

The description of a typical business cycle may suggest that forming capital market expectations for the short and medium terms is relatively straightforward. If the investor can identify the current phase of the cycle and correctly predict when the next phase will begin, he or she should be able to make money easily. Unfortunately, it is not that simple for several interrelated reasons.

First, the phases of the business cycle vary in length and amplitude. Recessions can be steep, and downturns (such as in the 1930s and, to a lesser extent, the early 1980s) can be frightening. Recessions can be short-lived affairs with only a small decline in output and only a modest rise in unemployment. Sometimes, the weak phase of the cycle does not even involve a recession but merely a period of slower economic growth or a "growth recession." A period of economic growth below trend will open up the output gap. A mild downturn, or growth recession, is most likely if the trend rate of growth of the economy is relatively rapid. For example, China—with a trend rate of annual growth of about 8 percent as of the early 2000s—will see unemployment rise and inflation decline if growth is only 5–6 percent. For the main industrial economies, with trend rates of annual growth of 2–4 percent, a mild downturn is more likely than a recession if some or all of the following conditions hold:

- The upswing was relatively short or mild.
- There was no bubble or severe overheating in the stock market or property market.
- Inflation is relatively low, so the central bank is willing to cut interest rates quickly.
- The world economic and political environments are positive.

> **Example 25**
>
> ### The 1980–1982, 2001, and 2008–09 U.S. Recessions
>
> The U.S. downturn in 1980–1982 was particularly severe. Inflation had reached 12–14 percent in early 1980, partly due to a rise in oil prices. The Board of Governors of the Federal Reserve System under its new chairman, Paul Volcker, was determined to eradicate inflation. The Fed kept interest rates high in 1982. In contrast, the 2001 recession was relatively mild. There had been a stock market bubble, but commercial property prices were not inflated and banks were in good shape. Because inflation was low, the Fed was willing to cut interest rates very rapidly.

Economic Analysis

> The 2001 recession is instructive on the limitations of economic data, which are backward looking and often revised. After the terrorist attack of 11 September 2001 on the World Trade Center, much commentary focused on the risk that it would lead to a recession. In fact, the revised GDP data show that the economy had been in a recession since early in 2001 and began to come out of it starting in October 2001. At the time, it was clear that the economy was weak and therefore growing at less than the trend rate, so bond yields fell and the stock market declined.
>
> In the late 2000s, the collapse of a bubble (speculative run-up) in housing prices, along with a crisis in subprime mortgages, led to a global financial crisis and recessions in most developed countries. The U.S. recession saw a peak-to-trough decline in GDP of 5.1 percent, marking the most severe of post World War II U.S. recessions. A low inflationary environment permitted the Fed to purse expansionary monetary policy, though with limited impact on economic growth and unemployment.

4.1.5 *Evaluating Factors that Affect the Business Cycle*

For the purposes of setting capital market expectations, we need to focus business cycle analysis on four areas:

- consumers;
- business;
- foreign trade; and
- government activity, both **monetary policy** (concerning interest rates and the money supply) and **fiscal policy** (concerning taxation and governmental spending).

Consumer spending amounts to 60–70 percent of GDP in most large developed economies and is therefore typically the most important business cycle factor.

Business investment has a smaller weight in GDP than consumer spending but is more volatile.

Foreign trade is an important component in many smaller economies, for which trade is often 30–50 percent of GDP. However, for the large economies, such as the United States and Japan, foreign trade is typically only around 10–15 percent of GDP and correspondingly less important. The same range holds true for the European Union (EU) in relation to trade outside the EU (although between countries within the EU, trade generally represents a higher percentage of GDP).

Finally, government policy can influence the business cycle. There are three motivations for government to intervene in the cycle. First, both the government and monetary authorities may try to control the cycle to mitigate severe recessions and also, on occasion, to moderate economic booms. Second, the central bank monetary authorities often have an inflation target and they will consciously try to stimulate or constrain the economy to help meet it. Third, because incumbent politicians prefer to hold elections during economic upswings, they may try to influence fiscal and/or monetary policy to achieve this end.

4.1.5.1 Taking the Pulse of Consumers
The principal sources of data on consumer spending are retail sales, miscellaneous store sales data, and consumer consumption data. Like most data, consumer spending can be erratic from month to month and can be affected by unusual weather or holidays (such as New Year celebrations).

By far the most important factor affecting consumption is consumer income after tax, which depends on wage settlements, inflation, tax changes, and employment growth. Employment growth is often closely watched because data are usually available on a very timely basis. Most countries have some particular series that analysts scrutinize. In the United Kingdom, besides the unemployment rate, the British Retail Consortium (BRC) retail sales survey is closely watched. In the United States, the monthly non-farm payrolls as well as the weekly new unemployment claims are regular market movers when they diverge from expectations.

If the household savings rate remained constant, then changes in income would exactly predict changes in spending. But the savings rate does change over time, influenced generally by consumer confidence in future jobs and income and also by changes in asset prices. Consumer confidence survey data are also watched closely as indicators of whether consumers are likely to raise or lower their savings rates.

4.1.5.2 Taking the Pulse of Business Data on business investment and spending on inventories reveal recent business activity. As already mentioned, both tend to be relatively volatile so that it is not uncommon for business investment to fall by 10–20 percent or more during a recession and to increase by a similar amount during strong economic upswings. Data for inventories need careful interpretation, however. A report of rising inventories may mean that businesses are very confident of sales and are spending on inventories ahead of expected sales. This would normally be the case in the early stages of an inventory cycle upswing and is bullish for economic growth. But at the late stage of the inventory cycle, a rise in inventories may be involuntary because sales are lower than expected. Such news would be negative.

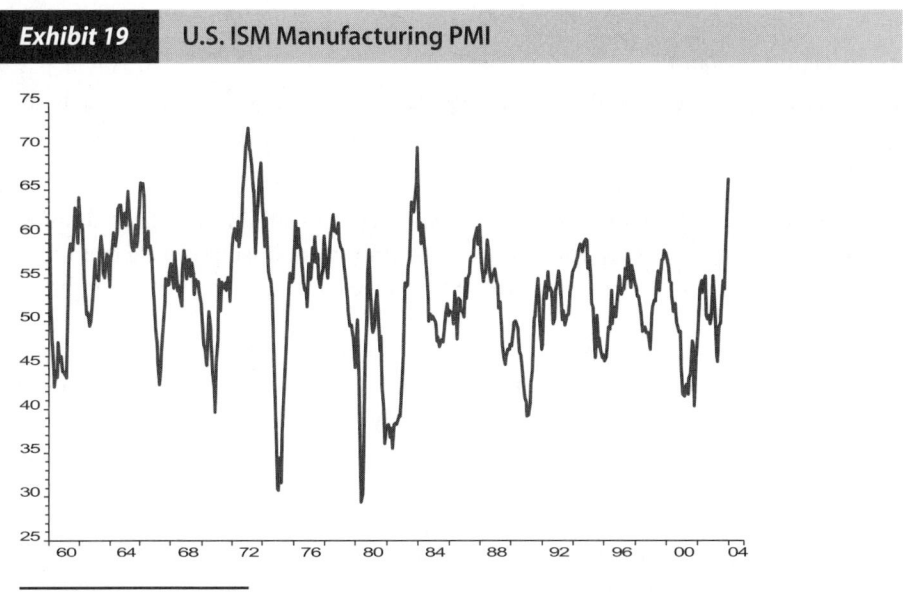

Exhibit 19   U.S. ISM Manufacturing PMI

Source: FRED, Federal Reserve Economic Data, Federal Reserve Bank of St. Louis: ISM Manufacturing: PMI Composite Index (NAPM); Institute for Supply Management. http://research.stlouisfed.org/fred2/series/NAPM ; accessed 21 December 2011.

Some of the most useful data on business are surveys. A particularly useful one is the purchasing managers index (PMI) published for several decades by the Institute of Supply Management (ISM) in the United States (formerly the National Association of Purchasing Managers). The PMI is one of the best indicators of the U.S. economy. In the 1990s, the ISM added a survey of non-manufacturing companies, which is beginning to acquire a useful track record. In recent years, most developed countries have developed PMIs using a similar methodology. Exhibit 19 presents U.S. manufacturing PMI data for the years 1948 to 2011. The lower points on the graph coincide predominantly with shaded areas that indicate recessionary periods, when manufacturing activity declines.

The PMI is based on answers to a series of questions about the company's position, including production plans, inventories, prices paid, prices received, and hiring plans. Each component is reported as well as an overall index. The indices are calibrated so that 50 should be the breakeven point for manufacturing growth. These surveys are particularly useful because of their timeliness.

4.1.5.3 Monetary Policy Monetary policy is sometimes used as a mechanism for intervention in the business cycle. For example, monetary policymakers may switch to stimulative measures (increasing money supply growth and/or lowering short-term interest rates) when the economy is weak and restrictive measures (decreasing money supply growth and/or raising short-term interest rates) when the economy is in danger of overheating. If unemployment is relatively high and there is spare capacity, then a rate of GDP growth higher than the trend rate will be tolerated for a while. This scenario is typical of the recovery and early upswing phases of the business cycle. In the late upswing phase, the economy is threatening to overheat and monetary authorities will restrict money supply to slow growth. If they get it wrong and a recession emerges, then they will cut rates sharply to restore growth. Finally, if a major financial crisis threatens the financial system, they will also cut rates sharply and flood the economy with liquidity, as was seen in the United States in 1987, 1998, and 2001.

The key variables watched by monetary authorities are as follows:

- the pace of economic growth;
- the amount of excess capacity still available (if any);
- the level of unemployment; and
- the rate of inflation.

In recent times, the common means for the largest central banks to effect monetary policy has been setting short-term interest rates to levels that are meant to control inflation without inhibiting economic growth. Central banks often see their role as smoothing out the growth rate of the economy to keep it as near as possible to its long-term sustainable trend rate—in effect, neither too hot nor too cold. A change in short-term interest rates affects the economy through a number of different mechanisms, which vary in their effects at different times.

Lower rates encourage more borrowing by consumers and businesses. Lower interest rates also usually result in higher bond and stock prices. These in turn encourage consumers to spend more and encourage businesses to invest more. From an international trade perspective, lower interest rates usually lower the exchange rate and therefore stimulate exports.

The effect of a cut in interest rates also depends on the absolute level of interest rates, not just the direction of change. For example, suppose that interest rates have been raised from 3 to 6 percent to deal with inflation and then, in response to a recession, are lowered to 4 percent. The lowering of interest rates might stimulate the economy, but interest rates are still higher than where they started. In other words, what matters is not whether interest rates have most recently been moved up or down but where they stand in relation to their average or "neutral" level. It is common to think of this "neutral" level as a point of interest rate equilibrium within the economy. The concept of the neutral level of interest rates is an important one, though in reality, it is impossible to identify precisely. Conceptually, the argument is that a neutral level of short-term interest rates should include a component to cover inflation and a real rate of return component. For example, in the United States, if inflation is targeted at 2 percent and the economy is growing at 2 percent, many economists argue that the neutral level of interest rates is about 4 percent.

The Taylor Rule   One way to assess the central bank's stance and to predict changes is through the so-called **Taylor rule**.[61] In essence, this rule links a central bank's target short-term interest rate to the rate of growth of the economy and inflation. A simple approach to this rule (giving equal weights to GDP growth and inflation) is given by the following Taylor rule equation:

$$R_{optimal} = R_{neutral} + \left[0.5 \times (GDPg_{forecast} - GDPg_{trend}) + 0.5 \times \left(I_{forecast} - I_{target}\right)\right] \quad (12)$$

where

$R_{optimal}$ = the target for the short-term interest rate
$R_{neutral}$ = the short-term interest rate that would be targeted if GDP growth were on trend and inflation on target
$GDPg_{forecast}$ = the GDP forecast growth rate
$GDPg_{trend}$ = the observed GDP trend growth rate
$I_{forecast}$ = the forecast inflation rate
I_{target} = the target inflation rate

The Taylor rule gives the optimal short-term interest rate as the neutral rate plus an amount that is positively related to the excess of the forecasts of GDP and inflation growth rates above their trend or target values. For example, assume that a current short-term rate of 4 percent is the neutral rate. Thus, if the United States is forecast to achieve its 2 percent trend rate of growth and 2 percent inflation target, then the Fed would be happy with the federal funds rate at the neutral rate of 4 percent. At 4 percent, the Fed would expect that the GDP growth and inflation rates would remain at trend or targeted levels. The Taylor rule then states that if the forecast GDP growth rate and/or the forecast inflation rate are above the trend or target level, short-term interest rates need to be raised by *half* the difference between the forecast and the trend or target. Conversely, GDP growth and/or inflation rates below trend or target would motivate the Fed to lower the fed funds rate. (The **federal funds rate**, or fed funds rate for short, is the interest rate on overnight loans of reserves [deposits] at the Fed between Federal Reserve System member banks.)[62] The intuition in this last case is that when GDP forecast growth is below trend, lowering the interest rate will stimulate output by lowering corporations' cost of capital. When forecast inflation is below target, lowering the interest rate will help the inflation rate return to target through its stimulative effect on the money supply.

Example 26

A Taylor Rule Calculation

Assume the following scenario:

- The neutral value of the short-term interest rate is 3.5 percent.
- The inflation target is 2.5 percent.
- The GDP trend rate of growth is 3 percent.

---

61 See Taylor (1993).
62 According to U.S. law, Federal Reserve System member banks are required to hold reserves at the Fed equal to a fraction of the deposits with the banks. In the Eurozone, banks have broadly similar requirements that relate to holding reserves at national central banks.

Economic Analysis

> If the inflation forecast is 4 percent and the forecast for GDP growth is 1 percent, what is the optimal short-term interest rate?
>
> **Solution:**
>
> According to the Taylor rule,
>
> $$\begin{aligned} R_{\text{optimal}} &= R_{\text{neutral}} + \left[0.5 \times \left(\text{GDPg}_{\text{forecast}} - \text{GDPg}_{\text{trend}}\right) + 0.5 \times \left(I_{\text{forecast}} - I_{\text{target}}\right)\right] \\ &= 3.5\% + \left[0.5(1.0\% - 3.0\%) + 0.5(4.0\% - 2.5\%)\right] \\ &= 3.5\% + (-1.0\% + 0.75\%) \\ &= 3.5\% - 0.25\% \\ &= 3.25\% \end{aligned}$$
>
> The GDP growth forecast by itself implies that the short-term interest rate should be lowered by 1 percentage point, because GDP growth is under trend. Partially offsetting the effect of below-trend GDP growth is the interest rate increase implied by above-target inflation. Net, the Taylor rule implies that the central bank should lower short-term rates by 25 bps to 3.25 percent.

Historically, the Taylor rule has provided a reasonably accurate description of central banks' behavior.

Money Supply Trends Trends in the money supply can be a good indicator of monetary conditions and of the trend of the economy. Over the long run, there is a reasonably stable relationship between the growth in money supply and the growth in nominal GDP (inflation plus real growth). If money growth is particularly strong in relation to nominal GDP, chances are that growth will accelerate in the near future and that inflation may eventually accelerate.

What Happens When Interest Rates Reach Zero? All the discussion so far has been about central banks' manipulation of interest rates to affect the economy. But what happens if the economy is weak and interest rates have fallen to zero? This is often the situation in periods of deflation. An important lesson of the Japanese experience in the 1990s is that it is appropriate to cut interest rates aggressively during an economic downturn, if inflation is not at high levels, in order to kick-start an economic recovery before deflation sets in.

Once interest rates are at zero, further monetary stimulus requires new types of measures. First, the central bank can push cash (bank "reserves") directly into the banking system. Japan tried this approach in recent years with limited success because there was still no desire to borrow or lend. A second possibility is to devalue the currency. The third option is to promise to hold short-term interest rates low for an extended period. The United States used this approach in 2003, as did the Bank of Japan. It may not work if the markets think that rates will soon rise, indicating an expected economic recovery. The final option is for the central bank to buy assets directly from the private sector. This option has the effect of putting money directly into people's hands and driving down yields on these assets. The Bank of Japan has been buying government bonds for several years, driving 10-year bond yields below 1 percent at times. It has also bought small amounts of stocks and could buy property or overseas assets.

Given that deflation removes some of the central bank authorities' ability to effect monetary policy, central banks prefer to target a low positive rate of inflation, retaining flexibility in using interest rates to affect the business cycle.

> **Example 27**
>
> **Monetary Policy in the Eurozone Compared with the United States in 2001 and 2010**
>
> Both Europe and the United States saw a sharp economic slowdown in 2001. The Fed responded by cutting the fed funds rate from 6.50 percent to 1.75 percent during 2001. In contrast, the European Central Bank (ECB), the central bank for the Eurozone, cut interest rates from 4.75 percent to 3.50 percent, a much less aggressive move. The reasons for these different responses were twofold:
>
> - In 2001, U.S. CPI inflation stood at 2.6 percent, well within the Fed's likely informal target range of 1–3 percent inflation. Coincidentally, the Eurozone also had inflation of 2.6 percent in mid-2001, but this rate was above the explicit target range of 0–2 percent.
>
> - In the United States, unemployment rose rapidly during 2001 from about 4 percent to nearly 6 percent, opening an output gap in the economy. In contrast, Eurozone unemployment was constant at 8 percent for most of 2001, rising only slightly at the end of the year. Hence, the ECB welcomed the slowdown as a way to put downward pressure on inflation.
>
> - In response to the financial crisis and ensuing recession in the period of 2007–2009, both the ECB and the Fed acted in a coordinated manner by first flooding their respective markets with liquidity and then cutting interest rates to or close to zero. To further address stubborn stagnation in economic growth and high unemployment, the Fed and ECB resorted to such non-traditional measures as implementing bond buying programs which came to be known as Quantitative Easing I and II (QE I and QE II).

4.1.5.4 Fiscal Policy **Fiscal policy** means manipulating the budget deficit to influence the economy. Governments increase spending or cut taxes to stimulate the economy and cut spending or raise taxes to slow the economy. In analyzing fiscal policy, or the so-called "fiscal stance," it is crucial to remember two points. First, an analyst should focus on the *changes* in the government budgetary deficit, not its level. For example, although the Japanese budget deficit has been running at around 8 percent of GDP for many years (as of 2005), it has not been a continuous stimulus to the economy. But if the deficit rose to 10 percent, that increase could represent a stimulus. Conversely, a reduction in the deficit would represent a tighter policy.

Second, it is only changes in the deficit due to *deliberate changes* in government fiscal policy that matter. The budget deficit will constantly change in response to the economy without any change in fiscal policy. During recessions, the deficit tends to rise because tax revenues fall and government spending on unemployment benefits increases. In contrast, when the economy grows strongly, the budget deficit naturally falls.

Linkages with Monetary Policy It is useful to consider the overall mix of fiscal and monetary policy. If fiscal and monetary policies are both tight, then the situation is unambiguous and the economy is certain to slow. Similarly, if both monetary policy and fiscal policy are expansionary, then the economy can be expected to grow. However, monetary and fiscal policies are sometimes at odds with one another. These situations create opportunities for investors as well as risks.

The fiscal/monetary mix usually shows up in the shape of the yield curve. Exhibit 20 illustrates the four possibilities. When both fiscal and monetary policies are loose, the yield curve tends to be steeply upward sloping. When fiscal policy is tightened while monetary policy remains loose, bond yields tend to fall and the yield curve comes back to a more moderate upward slope.

Exhibit 20 Policy Mix and the Yield Curve

		Fiscal Policy	
		Loose	**Tight**
Monetary Policy	**Loose**	Yield curve steep	Yield curve moderately steep
	Tight	Yield curve flat	Yield curve inverted

If monetary and fiscal policies are both tight, the yield curve is typically inverted. Finally, when monetary policy is tight but fiscal policy is loose, the yield curve tends to be flat.

4.2 Economic Growth Trends

The economic growth trend is the long-term growth path of GDP. The long-term growth path reflects the average growth rate around which the economy cycles. The differences between economic trends and cycles need to be understood. Economic trends exist independently of the cycle but are related to it. Business cycles take the economy through an alternating sequence of slow and fast growth, often including recessions and economic booms.

Economists are concerned with a variety of trends besides the economic growth trend, because that trend is determined by other economic trends, such as population growth and demographics, business investment and productivity, government structural policies, inflation/deflation, and the health of banking/lending processes.

Trends are more easily forecast than cycles, but there are always uncertainties. In practice, it is often difficult to know which trends are most important. Moreover, some trends or changes in trends are by definition not open to forecasting. These are often called "shocks." Examples include wars that cause market dislocations, abrupt changes in government tax or trade policies, and the sudden collapse in an asset market or in an exchange rate. Often, these abrupt changes in trend affect the overall paradigm of capital market expectations. One example of a paradigm-changing shock was the revelation of accounting irregularities at Enron and other U.S. companies in 2002. Investors' perceptions both of the reliability of companies' earning statements and of corporate leaders' attitudes profoundly shifted. Changes in regulations reinforced these shifts. In contrast, other trends such as demographics are usually very much in the background because they change only very gradually.

While shocks are not forecastable, investors do try to assess the risk that they will occur. Unrest in the Middle East may push up the price of oil as well as "safe haven" investments such as gold, the Swiss franc, and U.S. government bonds. If a particular tax change is being considered, markets may partially anticipate it in the pricing of such assets. Some events do come unexpectedly, and they are the ones likely to have the greatest impact as investors struggle to understand their implications.

> **Example 28**
>
> ## Cycles and Trends: An Example
>
> Consider the following hypothetical passage describing the German economy in late 2010:
>
> - *After a recession in 2009 and stagnation in the first quarter of 2010, the German economy picked up. Starting in the second quarter of 2010, it grew at 2.1 percent annualized. Exports led the way, and business investment picked up. Consumer spending grew strongly in early 2010.*
> - *Significant progress on labor market reforms and pension reforms by the government, as well as increased sales to India and China, boosted confidence. R & D spending increases led to significant export growth which was further assisted by a weak Euro. In response, the Bundes Bank increased the economic growth forecast from 1.9% to 3.0%, which was above the projected trend growth rate of 2.5%.*
>
> These two statements contain information about the economy. The first refers to the business cycle, while the second describes other economic trends. The final sentence is a mixture of cycle and trend information. It provides the government forecast for economic growth in the following year (cyclical information) but also implies an estimate for the long-term average rate of growth that the German economy is believed capable of achieving (2.5 percent per year).

The expected trend rate of economic growth is a key input in discounted cash flow models of expected return. First, a country with a higher trend rate of growth may offer equity investors a particularly good return. Second, a higher trend rate of growth in the economy allows actual growth to be faster before there is a danger of inflation.

The trend rate of growth of the economy is usually thought not to change much over time. Indeed, for the United Kingdom, historically the first industrial economy, it would appear that GDP has had a 2–2.5 percent trend growth rate for two hundred years with very little variation. However, most countries have had periods of faster and slower trend growth during their development. Emerging countries naturally can more easily have faster growth as they catch up with the leading industrial countries. But the more developed they become, the more likely it is that their growth will slow. This effect has been very obvious in the case of Japan. After Japan's GDP grew at an annual average rate of 11 percent in the 20 years leading up to 1973, growth in the next 17 years averaged only 3.9 percent and then fell to 1.6 percent between 1990 and 2003.

4.2.1 Consumer Impacts: Consumption and Demand

Consumers can be counted upon as the largest source of aggregate economic growth in both developed and developing economies. It is interesting to note that although consumers spend more in response to perceived increases in their wealth due to a "wealth effect," overall consumer consumption is quite stable over the business cycle. Milton Friedman (1957) developed an explanation for this stability in his permanent income hypothesis. The **permanent income hypothesis** asserts that consumers' spending behavior is largely determined by their long-run income expectations. Temporary or unexpected (or one-time) events such as benefiting from an inheritance might temporarily increase an individual's demand for items that might not ordinarily be purchased, but overall spending patterns remain largely determined by long-run expectations. However, if an unexpected event (e.g., winning the lottery) produced an ongoing series of incoming cash flows, it would be expected to permanently alter an individual's spending patterns since the flows would be ongoing and could be depended upon over the long term.

In similar fashion, when temporary events reduce the income flows of consumers, individuals typically reduce the amount they save to maintain their long-term spending patterns. Only when income disruptions occur over the long term may individuals capitulate and reduce their consumption—out of necessity. Thus, consumer trends are usually stable or even countercyclical over a business cycle. When incomes rise the most (during the cyclical expansion phase), spending increases less than income rises. When incomes fall as an economy's growth slows or declines, consumption falls only a fraction and usually only for a relatively short period of time.

4.2.2 A Decomposition of GDP Growth and Its Use in Forecasting

The simplest way to analyze an economy's aggregate trend growth is to split it into

- growth from changes in employment (growth from labor inputs), and
- growth from changes in labor productivity.

For longer-term analysis, growth from changes in employment is broken down further into growth in the size of the potential labor force and growth in the actual labor force participation rate (e.g., more or fewer women or older people working; "growth" can be positive or negative).

For example, annual U.S. GDP growth used to be thought of as likely to average 2.5 percent over the long term. This number results from adding a 1 percent growth in the potential labor force, a 0.5 percent growth in labor force participation, and a 1 percent annual growth in labor productivity.

During the late 1990s, there were signs that productivity had risen perhaps to around 2.5 percent annually, so estimates of trend growth were raised to about 4 percent or somewhat less. In contrast, the figures for many developing countries would be closer to 2 percent potential labor force growth, 1 percent growth in labor force participation, and 3–4 percent growth in labor productivity, suggesting that annual growth could average 6–7 percent over a long period. Exhibit 21 shows the U.S. economic trend growth since 1960.

A more sophisticated approach to economic trend growth estimation breaks down the growth in labor productivity into two components, just as growth from labor inputs was analyzed into two components. Productivity increases come from investment in equipment or new machines (growth from capital inputs) and from **growth in total factor productivity** (TFP growth), known also as technical progress and resulting from increased efficiency in using capital inputs.

To summarize, with this approach, the trend growth in GDP is the sum of the following:

- growth from labor inputs, comprising
  - growth in potential labor force size and
  - growth in actual labor force participation, plus
- growth from labor productivity, comprising
  - growth from capital inputs and
  - TFP growth (i.e., growth from increase in the productivity in using capital inputs).

Exhibit 21 U.S. Business Cycles and Economic Trend Growth

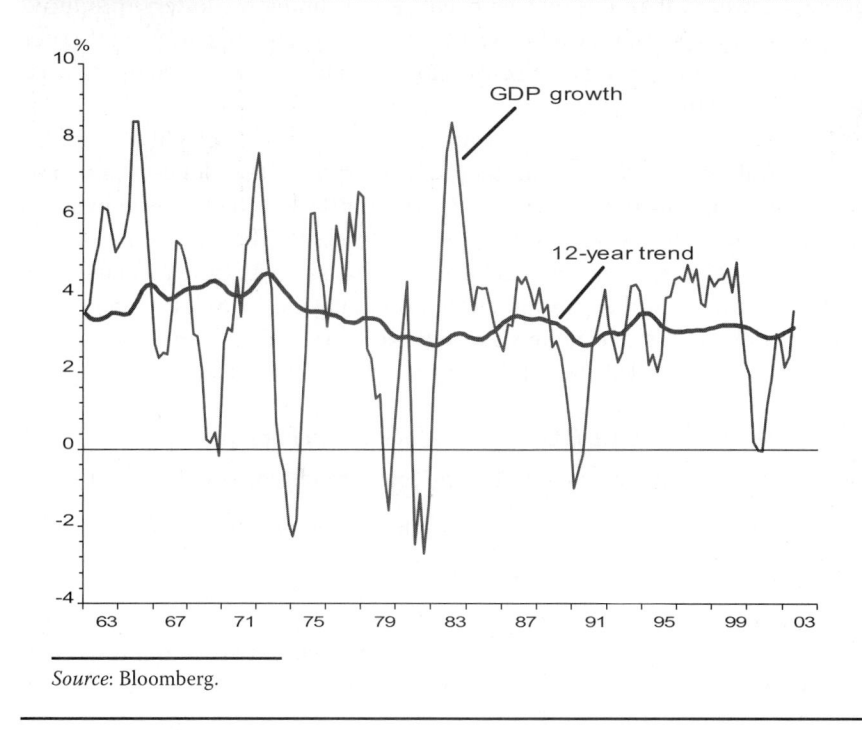

Source: Bloomberg.

The potential sources of TFP growth include technological shocks and shifts in government policies. In historical analyses, TFP is often taken simply as a "residual"—that is, output growth that is not accounted for by the other factors.[63]

Many fast-growing emerging countries are successful because they invest heavily and therefore quickly build capital. In Singapore and China, for example, between 30 percent and 40 percent of GDP is invested annually. Slower-growing countries in South America have typically been able to manage capital investment rates of only 15–20 percent of GDP. It is likely, therefore, that the relatively fast rates of economic growth in Asia owe much to the higher rates of capital investment.

The rapid rate of investment helps explain why stock market returns may not be strong despite the rapid growth in the economy. Ultimately, stock market returns depend on the rate of return on invested capital. If capital is growing fast, returns on invested capital are driven down.

Future economic growth trends can be forecast using the model just given. For example, economic trend growth rates in Japan and many parts of Europe are forecast to be relatively low over the next few decades because labor force growth will be constrained by slow population growth. In contrast, the United States—with its relatively young population and high immigration—should enjoy faster labor force growth. Europe and Japan could, however, change the outlook if they could achieve a higher labor force participation rate. Changes to employment laws, pension entitlements, and child care facilities could encourage more women and older people to enter the workforce.

Trend growth will also be boosted if investment is stronger. For example, the surge in economic growth in the United States in the 1990s was partly linked to higher investment. The combination of an economic boom, higher stock market valuations, and a high level of investment in new opportunities in computers and networking in turn boosted overall productivity. Opinions still differ as to how much of the increase

---
[63] This component is known as the Solow residual estimate of TFP growth.

in productivity was due to "more machines" and how much was due to greater TFP. Part of the problem is how to value the machines, since computer prices have been falling sharply while their power increases.

By 2005, Europe had not seen a comparable surge in productivity. Investment has not been as strong, and various rigidities seem to be in the way of raising TFP. For example, in the United Kingdom, planning (zoning) restrictions on new large shops on the scale of Wal-Mart in the United States may have limited the scope of retailing efficiencies. Continental European labor laws, which restrict redundancies, or layoffs, also may have made companies move relatively slowly in "de-layering" bureaucracies by using the advantages of networking.

Example 29

Forecasting GDP Trend Growth

Cynthia Casey is reviewing a consultant's forecast that Canadian GDP will grow at a long-term 3.5 percent annual rate. According to Casey's own research, a 3.2 percent growth rate is more realistic. Casey and the consultant agree on the following assumptions:

- The size of the Canadian labor force will grow at 1 percent per year based on population projections.
- Labor force participation will grow at 0.25 percent per year.
- Growth from capital inputs will be 1.5 percent per year.

Determine the reason for the discrepancy between Casey's forecast and the consultant's forecast.

Solution:

Casey and the consultant agree on three of the four components of GDP growth, so the reason for the discrepancy in their GDP growth forecasts must be disagreement about the value of the fourth component, total factor productivity growth. For Casey to arrive at a 3.2 percent growth rate estimate, she must be assuming that total factor productivity growth will be 3.2% − (1% + 0.25% + 1.5%) = 0.45%. By contrast, the consultant is predicting that total factor productivity growth will be 3.5% − (1% + 0.25% + 1.5%) = 0.75%. Thus, the consultant is more optimistic than Casey about GDP growth from increases in the productivity in using capital inputs.

4.2.3 Government Structural Policies

Government structural policies refer to government policies that affect the limits of economic growth and incentives within the private sector. Government policies affect economic growth trends in profound ways. In the first three-quarters of the 20th century, governments increasingly intervened in the economy in most countries. This intervention often took the form of outright government ownership of large enterprises, combined with labor market and product market regulation. Starting in the 1980s, the trend to privatization led by former Prime Minister Thatcher in Britain substantially reduced the amount of government ownership in most economies. However, the trend toward heavy government regulation of the economy, other than through direct ownership, remains a powerful one.

The following are elements of a pro-growth government structural policy:

1. **Fiscal policy is sound**. Fiscal policy is sometimes used to influence the business cycle and can play a useful role. For example, decreasing a budget surplus (or increasing a budget deficit) may be a justifiable economic stimulus

during a recession. But countries that regularly run large deficits tend to have one or more of three potential problems. First, a government budget deficit often brings a current account deficit (the so-called "twin deficits" problem), which means that the country must borrow abroad. Eventually, when the level of foreign debt becomes too high, that borrowing must be scaled back. This usually requires a large and potentially destabilizing devaluation of the currency. Second, if the deficit is not financed by borrowing, it will ultimately be financed by printing money, which means higher inflation. Third, the financing of the deficit takes resources away from private sector investment, and private sector investment is usually more productive for the country as a whole. It is for all these reasons that investors prefer to see governments hold the budget deficit close to zero over the long term.

2. **The public sector intrudes minimally on the private sector.** According to economic theory, a completely unfettered competitive market would probably supply too little in the way of public goods, such as national defense, and too much in the way of goods with negative externalities, such as goods whose manufacture pollutes the environment.[64] However, the thrust of economic theory is that the marketplace usually provides the right incentives to individuals and businesses and leads to an efficient allocation of scarce resources. Recognizing this, many countries have privatized government-owned businesses over the last few decades and reduced regulations affecting business. The most damaging regulations for business tend to be labor market rules (e.g., restricting hiring and firing) because such regulations tend to raise the **structural level of unemployment** (the level of unemployment resulting from scarcity of a factor of production); however, such regulations are also the most difficult to lift.

3. **Competition within the private sector is encouraged.** Competition is important for trend growth because it drives companies to be more efficient and therefore boosts productivity growth. In the last several decades, the reduction of trade tariffs and barriers has been very important in increasing competition in the goods sector. Recent advances in networking technologies have spread that competition into the service sector. Another positive government policy is openness to foreign investment. However, note that competition makes it more difficult for companies to earn high returns on capital and thus can work against high stock market valuations.

4. **Infrastructure and human capital development are supported.** Projects supporting these goals may be in partnership with the private sector. Building health and education infrastructure has important economic benefits.

5. **Tax policies are sound.** Governments provide a range of goods, including defense, schools, hospitals, and the legal system. They also engage in a certain amount of redistribution of income directly, through pensions and welfare programs. As a result, developed country governments typically collect between 30 percent and 50 percent of GDP in taxes. According to economic theory, taxes distort economic activity by reducing the equilibrium quantities of goods and services exchanged. A decrease in total societal income and efficiency is the cost of redistributing wealth to the least well-off. As a result, investors often look with skepticism on governments that impose high overall tax burdens. Sound tax policy involves simple, transparent, and rarely altered tax rates; low marginal tax rates; and a very broad tax base.

---

[64] A **public good** is a good that is not divisible and not excludable (a consumer cannot be denied it); because of these properties, a public good cannot be priced or traded. An **externality** is a result of a transaction or process that spills over to the public.

4.3 Exogenous Shocks

Exogenous shocks are events from outside the economic system that affect its course. These could be short-lived political events, changes in government policy, or natural disasters, for example. How do shocks contrast with economic trends? Over time, trends in an economy are likely to stay relatively constant. As such, they should already be discounted in market expectations and prices. Exogenous shocks may have short-lived effects or drive changes in trends. They are typically not built into prices or at most are only partially anticipated.

Most shifts in trends are likely to come from shifts in government policies, which is why investors closely watch both specific measures and the overall direction of government policy (e.g., consumer friendly, business friendly, export friendly).

The biggest impact occurs when there is new government or a major institutional shift. For example, a major fiscal law that prevents the government from borrowing beyond certain limits can be a very effective constraint on excessive spending. A decision to make the central bank more independent or to enter a currency union could have a major impact on the economy. Such government-induced impacts typically are swiftly felt.

Some shocks do not affect trends but are felt in a more immediate or short-term manner. While they are often negative, they are not always so. In 1986, the unexpected breakup of an OPEC meeting without an agreement to cut production led to a sharp decline in oil prices. This event played an important role in keeping inflation low for several years after that. The fall of the Berlin wall triggered German reunification and a "peace dividend" for governments as they cut defense spending.

The creation and assimilation of new products, markets, and technologies provide a positive, longer-term impact on economic trends. Too often, analysts focus on shorter-term benefits, under-appreciating the evolving nature of the technologies and the scope of their effects. For example, the evolution of communication technologies from the telegraph, telephone, phonograph, wireless (cellular and satellite), and internet has been a source of great positive economic impact. These gains show up in TFP growth.

Shocks cannot be forecast in general. But there are two types of economic shock that periodically affect the world economy and often involve a degree of contagion, as problems in one country spread to another. Oil shocks are important because a sharp rise in the price of oil reduces consumer purchasing power and also threatens higher inflation. Financial shocks, which can arise for a variety of reasons, threaten bank lending and therefore economic growth.

4.3.1 Oil Shocks

Crises in the Middle East regularly produce spikes in oil prices. Military conflicts that led to declines in world production of oil occurred in 1973–1974, 1979, 1980, 1990, and 2003–2004. Even though oil is a smaller input to the world economy now than it was in the 1970s, a sudden rise in prices affects consumers' income and reduces spending. Inflation rates also rise, though here the effect is ambiguous. Although inflation moves up initially, the contractionary effect of higher oil prices restricts employment and opens up an output gap so that, after a period, inflation slows to below the level where it otherwise might have been.

There have also been episodes of declining oil prices, most notably in 1986 and again in 1999. These tend to have the effect of extending the economic upswing because they contribute to lower inflation. Low oil prices and low inflation boost economic growth that can contribute to overheating, as was seen in the United States in 1987 and again in 1999–2000. Dependence on Middle East oil remains high, and the sources of political instability in the region remain numerous.

4.3.2 Financial Crises

Periodic financial crises affect growth rates either directly through bank lending or indirectly through their effect on investor confidence. In the last few decades, events in emerging markets have been the cause of several crises. The Latin American debt crisis of 1982, the Mexican currency crisis of 1994, the Asian financial crisis of 1997, and the Russian crisis of 1998 are examples. The last was particularly important because it threatened both financial markets and investment banks with widespread collapse. The reason was a possible domino effect due to the subsequent collapse of Long-Term Capital Management (LTCM), a large U.S. hedge fund. Most of LTCM's positions had been based on expectations of declining risk spreads. When the Russian crisis sent those spreads upward, it triggered a crisis. Among central banks, the U.S. Federal Reserve's response to these emerging market crises was particularly proactive. The Fed injected liquidity into the system, thereby reducing U.S. interest rates and moderating the impact on financial institutions.

There have been other financial crises. Banks are always potentially vulnerable after a major decline in asset prices, particularly property prices, as in the United States in the early 1990s. In that case, the Fed's response was to keep interest rates low for a prolonged period to provide sufficient liquidity to ensure that the payment system could continue. That action would have been more difficult in a world of low inflation or deflation. Financial crises are therefore potentially more dangerous in a low interest rate environment.

4.4 International Interactions

In general, the dependence of any particular country on international interactions is a function of its relative size and its degree of specialization. Large countries with diverse economies, such as the United States, tend to be less influenced by developments elsewhere than small countries, such as Chile, whose production depends significantly on a few commodities like copper. Increasing globalization of trade, capital flows, and direct investment means that practically all countries are increasingly affected by international interactions.

4.4.1 Macroeconomic Linkages

Countries' economies are directly affected by changes in the foreign demand for their exports. This is one way that the business cycle in one country can affect that in others. But there are other international linkages (other than trade) at work, such as those resulting from cross-border direct business investment. The United States has often been the leader in such investment. As a result, an economic slowdown in the United States frequently makes companies worldwide more cautious about investment and hiring.

However, the U.S. economy and the economies of other developed countries are clearly not perfectly integrated. For example, continental Europe did not suffer a recession in 1990 despite the U.S. recession because the stimulative effects of German reunification outweighed the negative effects of the U.S. slowdown. Similarly, while the United States and most other countries suffered a weak economy in the first half of 2003, China's economy boomed under the influence of stimulative monetary and fiscal policies.

4.4.2 Interest Rate/Exchange Rate Linkages

One of the linkages of most concern to investors involves interest rates and exchange rates. Sometimes, short-term interest rates are affected by developments in other countries because one central bank pursues a formal or informal exchange rate link with another currency. Some governments *unilaterally* peg their currencies firmly or loosely to one of the major currencies, usually the U.S. dollar or the euro. This strategy is much less common now than it was before the Asian crisis in 1997, but it is still practiced in Asia (notably Hong Kong) and by members of the Gulf Cooperation Council (Saudi Arabia, Kuwait, Bahrain, Qatar, the United Arab Emirates, and the Sultanate of Oman). Also, various countries in Africa and Eastern and Central Europe peg to the euro.

The countries that follow this strategy find two benefits. First, domestic business has some reassurance that exchange rates are not going to fluctuate wildly. Second, by pegging the exchange rate, a "pegged" country often hopes to control inflation. This consideration was important in Europe under the Exchange Rate Mechanism (an exchange rate regime established in preparation for the introduction of the euro) and was also the reason for Argentina's convertibility plan, which tied the peso to the dollar in the early 1990s but collapsed amidst a severe economic crisis in 2001.

If a country is following such an exchange rate policy, then the level of interest rates will depend on overall market confidence in the peg. A high degree of confidence in the exchange rate peg means the interest rate differential can converge to near zero. For example, the Hong Kong dollar has been pegged to the U.S. dollar. Interest rate differentials were near zero in 2000–2001 after an uncertain period in 1997–1999, when Hong Kong interest rates were periodically much higher than those in the United States because of the handover of sovereignty to China. But if the markets see the peg policy as unsustainable, then investors will demand a substantial interest differential.

If a country is known to be linking its currency to another, then bond yields of the weaker currency are nearly always higher. Hence, in Europe, Polish bond yields bear a spread over euro bond yields. If the expectation were that the zloty/euro exchange rate would remain broadly the same as its current level over the long term, then bond yields in Poland would converge with those in the Eurozone for bonds of equal credit risk. An expectation of a stable exchange rate might be justified by a belief in the Polish government's determination to maintain parity or by a perception that inflation and the competitiveness outlook for Poland obviate the need for a devaluation. If, however, markets anticipate a devaluation at some stage before Poland joins the euro, then a bond yield spread should remain in place.

Even if countries are not trying to link their currencies, bond yields can diverge substantially between countries. For example, if one country's exchange rate is severely undervalued and is expected to rise substantially against another country's, then bond yields in the first country will be lower than they would otherwise be in relation to the other country.

Exchange rates can be over- or undervalued, requiring an offset from bond yields, for a number of reasons, such as government action on *short-term* interest rates. For example, the Exchange Rate Mechanism was maintained as long as it was by using high short-term interest rates to limit speculation against currencies.

Misvaluation can also happen when bond yields reflect a particularly strong economy. In 1984, U.S. bond yields averaged 12.5 percent despite an annual inflation of 4 percent. These high real and nominal rates were due to the combination of the increasing U.S. budget deficit, a strong private sector economy, and a tightening monetary policy. In comparison, Germany had bond yields of 8 percent with an annual inflation of 2.5 percent. Hence, investors in the United States could enjoy real yields 3 percent above those seen by investors in German bonds: 8.5% real U.S. yield – 5.5% real German yield = 3% excess real yield difference in favor of the United States. This yield difference was enough to take the dollar up substantially in 1983–1985, leaving the bond markets in some degree of equilibrium, although the U.S. dollar was then viewed as overvalued.

Obviously, *nominal* bond yields vary between countries according to those countries' different inflation outlooks and other factors. It is sometimes thought that *real* bond yields ought to be similar in different countries because international capital flows will equalize them. However, movements in exchange rates to under- or overvalued levels can compensate for different real bond yields. Although real yields can and often do vary among countries, they tend to move together. In the example above from 1984, bond yields in both the United States and Germany were comparatively high in relation to inflation and overall historical experience.

The key factor linking bond yields (especially real bond yields) is world supply and demand for capital or the perceptions of supply and demand. Take the example of the collapse of world bond markets and the sharp rise in bond yields in 1994. These events seem to have been partly due to a perception that synchronized world growth would force short- and long-term interest rates up as the demand for world savings exceeded the supply. Since in the end, the demand has to equal the supply, interest rates everywhere rose to choke off demand and/or stimulate more supply. Similarly, in 2001, bond yields fell everywhere as private demand for capital dropped off in the face of a world slowdown.

4.4.3 Emerging Markets

There are some special considerations in setting capital market expectations for emerging countries. Here, we outline some of the key differences from major economies and look briefly at country risk analysis techniques and data sources that analysts use in evaluating emerging markets.

4.4.3.1 Essential Differences between Emerging and Major Economies Emerging countries are engaged in a catch-up process. As a result, they need higher rates of investment than developed countries in physical capital and infrastructure and in human capital. But many emerging countries have inadequate domestic savings and therefore rely heavily on foreign capital. Unfortunately, managing the consequent foreign debt often creates periodic crises, dealing a major blow to investors in emerging stocks and bonds.

Very often, emerging countries have a more volatile political and social environment than developed countries. In comparison with developed countries, emerging countries tend to have a relatively large percentage of people with low income and few assets and a relatively small middle class with its typically major stake in political and economic stability.

Most emerging countries need major structural reform to unlock their potential, which can be difficult to achieve in a volatile political environment. The potential for growth is often blocked by governments protecting vested interests. As a result, the International Monetary Fund (the IMF, an international organization entrusted with fostering global monetary and financial stability) and the World Bank (a group of five international organizations responsible for providing finance to developing countries) have often placed conditions on aid both to manage the risk of crises and to promote growth. For countries within an IMF program, analysts often focus closely on a country's progress in meeting the targets.

Even the largest emerging countries are relatively small in world terms, and their economies are often concentrated in a few areas such as particular commodities or in a narrow range of manufactured goods. Others rely heavily on oil imports and are thus vulnerable to fluctuation in oil prices or are dependent on continuing capital inflows.

4.4.3.2 Country Risk Analysis Techniques Investors in emerging bonds focus on the risk of the country being unable to service its debt (make promised payments of interest and principal). Investors in stocks need to assess the growth prospects of emerging countries as well as their vulnerability to surprises. A common approach is to use a checklist of various economic and financial ratios and a series of qualitative questions. Following are six questions that country risk analysis seeks to answer, with suggestions for data to analyze and points to look for.

Economic Analysis

1. *How sound is fiscal and monetary policy?*

    If there is one single ratio that is most watched in all emerging market analysis, it is the ratio of the fiscal deficit to GDP. Most emerging countries have deficits and are engaged in a perpetual struggle to reduce them. Deficits are a major cause of slow growth and frequently a factor in serious crises. A persistent ratio above 4 percent is regarded with concern. The range of 2–4 percent is acceptable but still damaging. Countries with ratios of 2 percent or less are doing well.

    If the fiscal deficit is large for a sustained period, the government is likely to build up significant debt. In developing countries, governments usually borrow in the short term from domestic lenders in local currency and from overseas in foreign currency. The Argentinean crisis in 2001 was essentially the result of too much government debt. For a developing country, the level of debt that would be considered too high is generally lower than for developed countries. Countries with a ratio of debt of more than about 70–80 percent of GDP are extremely vulnerable.

2. *What are the economic growth prospects for the economy?*

    The most successful countries in Asia have been able to grow at annual rates of 6–8 percent on a sustained basis. Others have achieved a respectable rate of 4–6 percent per annum. Annual growth rates of less than 4 percent generally mean that the country is catching up with the industrial countries slowly, if at all. It also means that, given some population growth, per capita income is growing very slowly or even falling, which is likely to bring political stresses.

    Investors usually welcome a wave of reform because it will typically boost economic growth and the stock market. But growth may slow down after that unless there is further reform or new opportunities are opened up. One of the best indicators of the structural health of an economy is the Economic Freedom Index, published by a consortium of research institutes around the world (www.freetheworld.com). This index consists of a range of indicators of the freedoms enjoyed by the private sector, including tax rates, tariff rates, and the cost of setting up companies. Countries such as the United States, Singapore, and Hong Kong have scored well. The index has been found to have a broad positive correlation with economic growth.

3. *Is the currency competitive, and are the external accounts under control?*

    Managing the currency has proven to be one of the most difficult areas for governments. If the exchange rate swings from heavily undervalued to seriously overvalued, there are negative effects on business confidence and investment. Moreover, if the currency is overvalued for a prolonged period, the country is likely to be borrowing too much, creating a large current account deficit and a growing external debt.

    The size of the current account deficit is a key measure of competitiveness and the sustainability of the external accounts.[65] Any country with a deficit persistently greater than 4 percent of GDP is probably uncompetitive to some

---

65 To briefly review accounting for cross-border flows, the **balance of payments** (an accounting of all cash flows between residents and nonresidents of a country) consists of the current account, dominated by the trade balance (reflecting exports and imports), and the financial account, consisting of portfolio flows (from security purchases and sales—e.g., bonds and equities) and foreign direct investment (FDI) by companies (e.g., Toyota Motor Corporation building an automobile assembly plant in the United States), as well as flows such as borrowing from and deposits with foreign banks. The sum of the current account and the financial account, or the **overall trade balance**, should be zero.

degree. Current account deficits need to be financed. If the deficits are financed through debt, servicing the debt may become difficult. A combination of currency depreciation and economic slowdown will likely follow. The slowdown will also usually cut the current account deficit by reducing imports. Note, however, that a small current account deficit on the order of 1–3 percent of GDP is probably sustainable, provided that the economy is growing. A current account deficit is also more sustainable to the extent that it is financed through foreign direct investment rather than debt, because foreign direct investment creates productive assets.

4. *Is external debt under control?*

    External debt means foreign currency debt owed to foreigners by both the government and the private sector. It is perfectly sensible for countries to borrow overseas because such borrowing serves to augment domestic savings. But borrowing needs to be kept within reasonable bounds or lenders will begin to question its sustainability. The resulting reluctance to lend new money may lead to an exodus of capital as money invested in local bonds and stocks flows out.

    Analysts watch several measures of debt burden. The ratio of foreign debt to GDP is one of the best measures. Above 50 percent is dangerous territory, while 25–50 percent is the ambiguous area. Another important ratio is debt to current account receipts. A reading above 200 percent for this ratio puts the country into the danger zone, while a reading below 100 percent does not.

5. *Is liquidity plentiful?*

    By liquidity, we mean foreign exchange reserves in relation to trade flows and short-term debt. Traditionally, reserves were judged adequate when they were equal in value to three months' worth of imports. However, with the vastly greater importance of debt and capital flows, we now relate reserves to other measures. An important ratio is reserves divided by short-term debt (debt maturing in less than 12 months). A safe level is over 200 percent, while a risky level is under 100 percent.

    Excess short-term borrowing is present in most emerging market crises. This is partly a result of the fact that countries often find it more difficult to borrow longer-term in the period leading up to the crisis. But if the country borrows too much, even short-term lending eventually stops and the country is typically in crisis very quickly thereafter.

6. *Is the political situation supportive of the required policies?*

    If the economy of the country is healthy, with fast growth, rapid policy liberalization, low debt, and high reserves, then the answer to this question matters less. Poor political leadership is unlikely to create a crisis. However, if the economic indicators and policy are flashing warning signals, the key issue becomes whether the government will implement the necessary adjustment policies. Cutting the budget deficit, which usually requires some combination of higher taxes and lower spending, is always painfully difficult, especially if the economy is weak already. Other key policy changes are reforms such as privatization and the ending of monopolies.

    In summary, the evaluation of emerging economies uses many of the same tools as the evaluation of developed countries but places a greater emphasis on the balance of payments, debt, liquidity, and politics. The analysis pays off because despite serious risks caused by political instability and periodic crises, many emerging countries grow faster than developed countries and offer good investment opportunities. Since the Asian crisis in 1997, investors are much more conscious of the potential risks, which

Economic Analysis

include market declines, fixed or quasi fixed exchange rates, major recessions, and contagion. The worst losses have been suffered in the countries that turned out to be the weakest politically.

4.5 Economic Forecasting

Having reviewed some practical basics of macroeconomics for the investment analyst with many real-world illustrations, we can now indicate some of the disciplines that the analyst can apply to economic forecasting. Often, analysts consider the implications of a variety of approaches, which will often raise questions that lead to productive analysis and insight. We may distinguish at least three distinct approaches:

- Econometric models, the most formal and mathematical approach to economic forecasting.
- Leading indicators: variables that have been found to lead (precede) turns in the economy.
- Checklists, requiring the subjective integration of the answers to a set of relevant questions.

In the following, we address each of these approaches in turn.

4.5.1 Econometric Modeling

Econometrics is the application of quantitative modeling and analysis grounded in economic theory to the analysis of economic data.[66] Whereas generic data analysis can involve variables of all descriptions (possibly including economic, security characteristic, demographic, and statistical variables), econometric analysis focuses on economic variables, using economic theory to model their relationships.

Econometric models vary from small models with just one equation or perhaps a handful of equations to large, complex models with hundreds of equations. However, they all work in essentially the same way. A model is created of the economy based on variables suggested by economic theory. Optimization (frequently the least-squares criterion from regression analysis) using historical data is used to estimate the parameters of the equations. The estimated system of equations is used to forecast the future values of economic variables, with the forecaster supplying values for the exogenous variables. For example, such a model may require the forecaster to enter an exchange rate, an interest rate, and commodity prices. But the model then uses the estimated past relationships to forecast the future.

A very simple model is presented in the following series of equations:

1. GDP growth = function of (Consumer spending growth and investment growth)
2. Consumer spending growth = function of (Consumer income growth lagged one period and Interest rate*)
3. Investment growth = function of (GDP growth lagged one period and Interest rate*)
4. Consumer income growth lagged one period = Consumer spending growth lagged one period

Here, the asterisk (*) denotes an exogenous variable. So, with this four-equation model estimated on past data and with the actual data for the variables lagged one period, together with the modeler's exogenous forecasts for the interest rate, the model

---

[66] There are also quantitative approaches reflecting **unstructured modeling**—that is, modeling without a theory on the underlying structure—such as vector autoregression (VAR), that may be appropriate for certain types of economic forecasting. See Diebold (2004) for an introduction to VAR.

will solve for GDP growth in time in the current period. Note that the final equation asserting that consumer income growth is always identical to consumer spending growth assumes a static relationship between these two variables.

Additional variables make a model more complex, more realistic, but often more difficult to construct, estimate, and interpret. Most models will incorporate variables such as government spending, employment, the savings rate, money supply, exports, and imports. However, it is by no means certain that larger models are superior to smaller models. Also, different models have different structures, and these structures reflect the views of the modeler both in what variables are included and in how they interrelate with one another. Monetarist models, for example, rely heavily on money-supply-related variables and relationships.

Econometric models are widely regarded as very useful for simulating the effects of changes in certain variables. For example, they can be useful for assessing the impact of a 10 percent rise in oil prices or a rise in income tax rates or a faster growth rate in trading partners on consumer demand.[67] Econometric models have several limitations. First, econometric models require the user to find adequate measures for the real-world activities and relationships to be modeled, and these measures may not be available. Variables may also be measured with error. Relationships among the variables may change over time because of changes in the structure of the economy; as a result, the econometric model of the economy may be misspecified.

In practice, therefore, skillful econometric modelers use a great deal of personal judgment in arriving at forecasts. Very often, the first run of the model will generate a forecast that the modelers do not believe. So, they will go back and change some of the exogenous variables to arrive at a forecast they do believe. The great merit of the econometric approach, however, is that it constrains the forecaster to a certain degree of consistency and also challenges the modeler to reassess prior views based on what the model concludes.

In practice, model-based forecasts rarely forecast recessions well, although they have a better record in anticipating upturns. For example, the U.S. economic upswing that gathered pace in the second half of 2003 was well forecast by econometric models.

4.5.2 Economic Indicators

Economic indicators are economic statistics provided by government and established private organizations that contain information on an economy's recent past activity or its current or future position in the business cycle. **Lagging economic indicators** and coincident indicators are indicators of recent past and current economic activity, respectively. A **leading economic indicator** (LEI) is a variable that varies with the business cycle but at a fairly consistent time interval before a turn in the business cycle. Most analysts' greatest interest is leading indicators because they may provide information about upcoming changes in economic activity, inflation, interest rates, and security prices.

Leading indicator–based analysis is the simplest forecasting approach to use because it requires following only a limited number of variables. The indicators are best thought of as early signs of probable events to come.

Many private sector forecasters try to gain an edge in identifying the factors that best predict the path of the economy and use their own proprietary indicators. Nevertheless, a good place to start for most investors is the leading indicators published by national governments or, in some countries, by established private organizations such as the Conference Board in the United States.

---

[67] Mehra and Peterson (2005) found that in the United States a 10 percent increase in oil prices is associated with the level of consumer spending at the end of six quarters being 0.80 percent to 1.60 percent lower than it otherwise would be.

Analysts may use both individual LEIs and composite LEIs, reflecting a collection of economic data releases that are combined to give an overall reading. Composite LEIs combine these releases using weights based on an analysis of their forecasting usefulness in past cycles. They can also be combined in a so-called **diffusion index**, which measures how many indicators are pointing up and how many down. For example, if 7 out of 10 are pointing upward, then the odds are that the economy is accelerating.

We review a selection of LEIs, both individual and composite, by geographic region:

Worldwide[68]

OECD Composite Leading Indicators (CLI) (www.oecd.org). The Organization for Economic Cooperation and Development (OECD) is a Paris-headquartered organization comprising 23 member countries. The OECD publishes CLI on Friday of the first full week of each month (these releases relate to information on production two months earlier). The indices are based on a range of variables (5 to 11 for each country), such as share prices, industrial production data, building permits, and monetary data that may have predictive value for the course of the business cycle. A Total OECD Composite Leading Indicator is published, as well as indices for the 23 member countries and for seven regions:

- Big Four European countries (France, Germany, Italy, and the United Kingdom);
- Eurozone;
- G–7 (Canada, France, Germany, Italy, Japan, the United Kingdom, and the United States);
- EU–25 (the 25 members of the European Union plus Denmark, Sweden, and the United Kingdom);[69]
- OECD-Europe (the EU–25 countries plus Norway, Switzerland, and Turkey);
- Total OECD countries (OECD-Europe plus Canada, Mexico, the United States, Australia, and Japan); and
- NAFTA (Canada, Mexico, and the United States).

The OECD publishes the six-month rate of change (annualized) in the monthly index numbers. Some analysts follow the six-month rate of change series more closely than the monthly index numbers because it may filter out the meaningless variation (noise) in the monthly numbers.[70]

Europe

Selected indicators include the following:

- **Eurozone Harmonized Index of Consumer Prices** (HICP) (epp.eurostat.ec.eu.int). Eurostat, the statistical office of the EU, publishes a composite index of inflation in the Eurozone. The European Central Bank (ECB) developed this index for use in inflation targeting, and indices standardized on the ECB methodology have been developed for individual EU countries. Inflation indices are not in general viewed as leading indicators. However, because of the ECB's strong focus on inflation containment, an unexpected increase in this index may presage events such as an interest rate increase.

- **German Industrial Production** (www.destatis.de). The Statistisches Bundesamt Deutschland (German Federal Office of Statistics) publishes in the second week of each month an index of German industrial production relating

---

[68] See *Guide to Economic Indicators*, 5th ed. (The Economist, 2003).
[69] As of the beginning of 2012, the European Union has 27 members, subject to national ratification in some cases. The number of countries in the EU may change from time to time.
[70] See Baumohl (2005), p. 328.

to production data two months earlier. Germany is Europe's largest economy and has frequently ranked among the top two exporters in the world. (As of 2009, its largest export partners were France, 10.1 percent; United States, 6.7 percent; United Kingdom, 6.6 percent; Netherlands, 6.6 percent; Italy, 6.3 percent; Austria, 5.7 percent; Belgium, 5.2 percent; China, 4.7 percent; and Switzerland, 4.5 percent.)[71] This series is closely watched as a leading indicator for the German and Eurozone economies.

- The **German IFO Business Survey** (www.ifo.de) and the **French Monthly Business Survey** (www.insee.fr), both released during the fourth week of the month being surveyed, are influential surveys of German and French business executives, respectively. Analysts focus on the answers to the forward-looking component of these series (a six-month-ahead time frame for the German series and a three-month-ahead time frame for the French series) for indications of Eurozone industrial production over the next several months. France is the Eurozone's second-largest economy.

Asia Pacific

Selected indicators include the following:

- The **Tankan Survey** of the Bank of Japan (www.boj.or.jp). Japan's central bank's detailed quarterly survey of business, published at the start of April, July, and October and in mid-December, is a rich source for information on Japanese business conditions and the expectations of business executives. Japan has been ranked among the world's three largest economies and has been the world's largest producer of foreign direct investment. Furthermore, the Japanese yen is one of the world's most important currencies: The Bank of Japan has the world's largest reserves of foreign currency and gold, and the bank has frequently been active in foreign exchange markets. As of the end of 2010, the major export partners of Japan were China, 19.4 percent; United States, 15.7 percent; South Korea, 8.1 percent; Hong Kong, 5.5 percent; and Thailand, 4.4 percent. Japan's largest import partners were China, 22.1 percent; United States, 9.9 percent; Saudi Arabia, 5.2 percent; UAE, 4.2 percent; South Korea, 4.1 percent; and Indonesia, 4.1 percent.

- **China Industrial Production** (www.stats.gov.cn). China's National Bureau of Statistics (NBS) releases monthly data on industrial production usually four weeks after the month being surveyed. These data are measures of the value added by light industry (mainly producing consumer goods) and heavy industry (producing durable goods such as factory equipment and automobiles). Baumohl (2005) provides a critique of the reliability of these data. Valuing the Chinese currency (called the renminbi or yuan) on a purchasing power parity basis (defined in Section 4.6.9.1), as of 2010, China ranked as the world's second-largest economy.

South America

- **Brazil Industrial Production** (www.ibge.gov.br). The Brazilian Institute for Geography and Statistics releases monthly data on industrial production approximately 40 days after the end of the month surveyed. This series is probably the closest watched by analysts. As of the end of 2004, Brazil represented more than 40 percent of South America's total GDP. With an estimated population of over 185 million as of 2005, Brazil is also by far the

---

[71] See "The World Factbook" at www.cia.gov.

most populous South American country. As of 2010, Brazil's major export partners were China, 15.2 percent; United States, 9.6 percent; Argentina, 9.2 percent; Netherlands, 5.4 percent; and Germany, 4.0 percent. Its major import partners were the United States, 15.0 percent; China, 14.1 percent; Argentina, 7.9 percent; Germany, 6.9 percent; and South Korea, 4.6 percent.

North America[72]

- The Conference Board's **Index of Leading Economic Indicators** (www.globalindicators.org). The Conference Board is a private, nonprofit, New York City-headquartered research organization that took over the management of this series from the U.S. Commerce Department in 1995. The Conference Board releases this monthly series three weeks after the end of the month reported upon, as well as coincident and lagging indices. Exhibit 22 shows the 10 components of the U.S. leading indicator index, which is normally quoted as a weighted index but is also available as a diffusion index. The Conference Board also publishes indices for Australia, France, Germany, Japan, Korea, Mexico, Spain, and the United Kingdom, researching the best indicators to use for each country. The United States is the world's largest economy. As of 2010, the United States' largest exporting partners were Canada, 19.4 percent; Mexico, 12.8 percent; China, 7.2 percent; and Japan, 4.7 percent. Its largest importing partners were China, 19.5 percent; Canada, 14.2 percent; Mexico, 11.8 percent; Japan, 6.3 percent; and Germany, 4.3 percent.

Exhibit 22 U.S. Composite Indices: Components and Standardization Factors

Leading Index	Factor
1. Average weekly hours, manufacturing	0.2552
2. Average weekly initial claims for unemployment insurance	0.0307
3. Manufacturers' new orders, consumer goods and materials	0.0773
4. Vendor performance, slower deliveries diffusion index	0.0668
5. Manufacturers' new orders, non-defense capital goods	0.0183
6. Building permits, new private housing units	0.0271
7. Stock prices, 500 common stocks	0.0391
8. Money supply, M2	0.3550
9. Interest rate spread, 10-year Treasury bonds less federal funds	0.1021
10. Index of consumer expectations	0.0284
Coincident Index	
1. Employees on nonagricultural payrolls	0.5426
2. Personal income less transfer payments	0.1890
3. Industrial production	0.1493
4. Manufacturing and trade sales	0.1191

(continued)

---

[72] This example draws on Baumohl (2005).

Exhibit 22	Continued	
Lagging Index		
1. Average duration of unemployment		0.0373
2. Inventory/sales ratio, manufacturing and trade		0.1239
3. Labor cost per unit of output, manufacturing		0.0615
4. Average prime rate		0.2822
5. Commercial and industrial loans		0.1112
6. Consumer installment credit to personal income ratio		0.1880
7. Consumer price index for services		0.1959

Source: Conference Board, www.globalindicators.org.

In a given index, the component factors are inversely related to the standard deviation of the month-to-month changes in each component. They are used to equalize the volatility of the contribution from each component and are "normalized" to sum to 1. When one or more of the components are missing, the other factors are adjusted proportionately to ensure that the total continues to sum to 1.

As Exhibit 22 shows, the Conference Board's LEI index consists of seven non-financial and three financial components (#7, #8, and #9). Of particular note is #5, provided by the Institute of Supply Management (ISM), which is a professional organization of purchasing managers. This release comes out on the first business day of each month and so is one of the earliest pieces of information on the business cycle available in a given month. This release receives more attention than #3, also from the ISM. Because capital goods orders are more sensitive to the business cycle than consumer goods, the release of #5 is often a market-moving event. Another interesting component is #7, the S&P 500 Index, which historically has been a good leading indicator of the stock market.

In contrast with the release of some of its individual components, the release of the LEI index is rarely a market-moving event because some of its components are already public.

Traditionally, the general rule was that three consecutive months of increases, or three consecutive months of decreases, signaled an upturn or downturn in the economy within three to six months. The Conference Board and others have also indicated other rules for interpreting changes in the index.

Exhibit 23 plots the composite LEI against quarterly GDP changes (expressed as a seasonally adjusted annual rate, or SAAR). The left vertical axis represents percentage changes and applies to real GDP changes; the right vertical axis shows index levels and applies to LEI levels.

Economic Analysis

Exhibit 23   U.S.: Leading Indicators and GDP

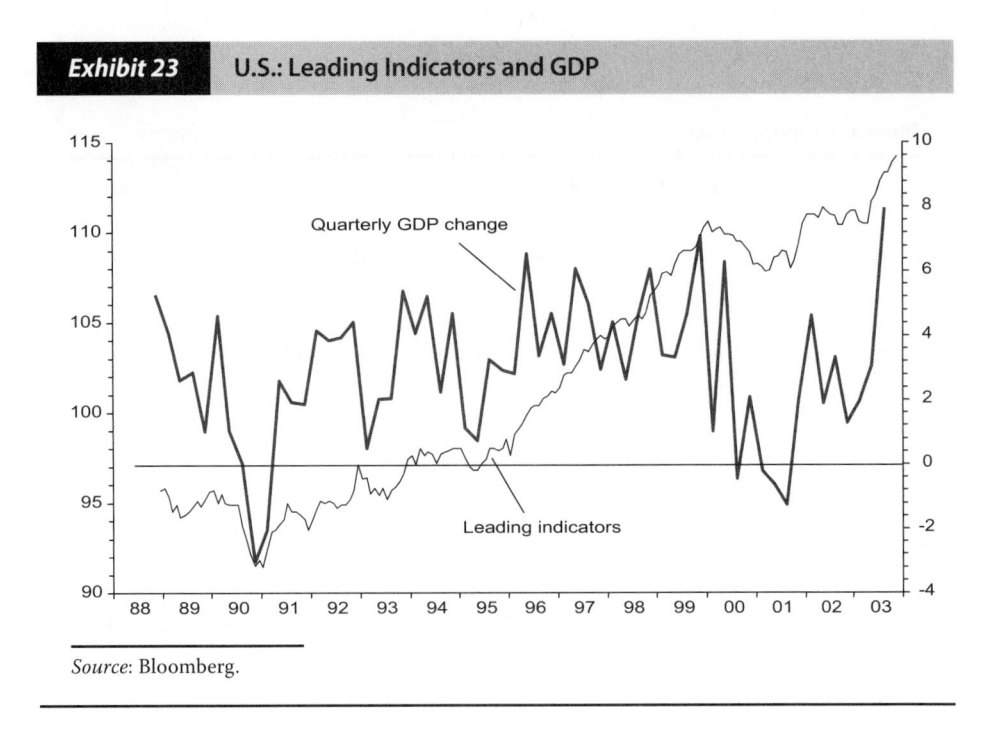

Source: Bloomberg.

The U.S. LEI index gave a somewhat ambiguous signal ahead of the 1990 recession but performed much better in the most recent cycle. In the late 1990s, it correctly showed that the Asian crisis was not threatening a U.S. downturn. Then, in 2000, it peaked in January. By midyear, it was clearly falling, well before there was general agreement that the economy was slowing. In 2003, it picked up strongly in May and continued to rise rapidly, correctly signaling a strong recovery. The strong uptick after the recession of 2008–09 in the face of a tepid U.S. recovery (as indicated by the declining quarter-over-quarter GDP change) is once again an ambiguous signal.

4.5.3 Checklist Approach

Formally or informally, many forecasters consider a whole range of economic data to assess the future position of the economy. Checklist assessments are straightforward but time-consuming because they require looking at the widest possible range of data. The data may then be extrapolated into forecasts via objective statistical methods, such as time-series analysis, or via more subjective or judgmental means. An analyst may then assess whether the measures are in an equilibrium state or nearer to an extreme reading.

Inflation reports provided by many central banks or through the minutes of central bank meetings give an idea of the range of indicators that may be included in checklists related to preparing general economic forecasts.

Exhibit 24 is an example of a checklist for evaluating economic growth. In effect, the forecaster asks a series of questions about likely components of spending and then, aggregating the information gathered, reaches a conclusion about the outlook for the economy. Such an approach involves a substantial amount of subjective judgment as to what is important in the economy.

Exhibit 24   Checklist for Economic Growth

Spending Components	Focus
1. Where in the cycle is the economy now?	Aggregate activity
■ Review previous data on GDP growth and its components (consumer spending, business investment, inventories, net exports, and government spending).	Aggregate activity
■ How high is unemployment relative to estimates of "full employment"?	Consumer
■ Has unemployment been falling?	Consumer
■ How large is the output gap?	Business
■ What is the inventory position?	Business
■ Where is inflation relative to target, and is it threatening to rise?	Inflation
2. How strong will consumer spending be?	Consumer
■ Review wage/income patterns.	Consumer
■ How fast will employment grow?	Consumer
■ How confident are consumers? Consumer confidence indices.	Consumer
3. How strong will business spending be?	Business
■ Review survey data (e.g., purchasing managers indices).	Business
■ Review recent capital goods orders.	Business
■ Assess balance sheet health of companies.	Business
■ Assess cash flow and earnings growth trends.	Business
■ Has the stock market been rising?	Business
■ What is the inventory position? Low inventory/sales ratio implies GDP strength.	Business
4. How strong will import growth be?	Government
■ Exchange rate competitiveness and recent movements.	Government
■ Strength of economic growth elsewhere.	Government
5. What is the government's fiscal stance?	Government
6. What is the monetary stance?	Central bank
■ Review recent changes in interest rates.	Central bank
■ What do real interest rates tell us?	Central bank
■ What does the Taylor rule tell us?	Central bank
■ Monetary conditions indices (i.e., trends in asset prices and exchange rate).	Central bank
■ Money supply indicators.	Central bank
7. Inflation	Inflation
■ How fast is inflation rising, or are prices falling?	Inflation

Economic Analysis

Example 30 is a simple illustration of the checklist approach.

Example 30

An Analyst's Forecasts

As a capital market analyst at a large money management firm, Charles Johnson has developed a list of six broad questions for evaluating the economy. The questions are given below with his responses for his own national market. The current inflation rate is 2 percent per year.

A. Is consumer spending increasing or decreasing? *Johnson*: Consumer spending is increasing at a lackluster rate of 0.75 percent per annum.

B. Are business conditions and fundamentals growing stronger or weakening? *Johnson*: Based on recent values of manufacturers' new orders for consumer goods and materials and non-defense capital goods, business demand is weakening.

C. What is the consensus forecast for the GDP growth rate over the next year? *Johnson*: The median forecast from a survey of economists is that GDP will decline from a 3.5 percent to a 3.0 percent annual growth rate.

D. Are government programs and fiscal policy becoming more restrictive or expansive? *Johnson*: Political support for a stimulative fiscal policy is absent; fiscal policy will be neutral.

E. Is monetary policy neutral, tightening, or loosening? *Johnson*: Monetary policy is neutral.

F. Is inflation in a steady state (state of equilibrium)? *Johnson*: The current inflation rate of 2 percent is close to a steady state value.

Based on the information given, what conclusions will Johnson reach concerning:

1. inflation over the next six months?
2. short-term interest rates?

Solution to 1:

Based on the expected slow growth in consumer demand and weakening business demand, inflation should remain muted over the next six months.

Solution to 2:

Reduced aggregate economic activity and stable inflation should allow for stable to falling interest rates.

The subjectivity of the checklist approach is perhaps its main weakness. The checklist's strength is its flexibility. It allows the forecaster to take changes in the structure of the economy into account quickly by changing the variables or the weights assigned to variables within the analysis. The next section summarizes the three chief approaches.

4.5.4 Economic Forecasting Approaches: Summary of Strengths and Weaknesses

Exhibit 25 summarizes the advantages and disadvantages of forecasting using econometric models, leading indicators, and checklists.

Exhibit 25 Advantages and Disadvantages of Three Approaches to Economic Forecasting

Advantages	Disadvantages
Econometric Models Approach	
■ Models can be quite robust with many factors used that can approximate reality. ■ Once models are built, new data may be collected and consistently used within models to quickly generate output. ■ Provides quantitative estimates of the effects on the economy of changes in exogenous variables.	■ Most complex and time-consuming to formulate. ■ Data inputs and relationships not easy to forecast and not static. ■ Requires careful analysis of output. ■ Rarely forecasts recessions well.
Leading Indicator–Based Approach	
■ Usually intuitive and simple in construction. ■ May be available from third parties. ■ May be tailored for individual needs. ■ A literature exists on the effective use of various third-party indicators.	■ Historically, has not consistently worked, as relationships between inputs are not static. ■ Can provide false signals.
Checklist Approach	
■ Limited complexity. ■ Flexible: allows structural changes to be easily incorporated.	■ Subjective. ■ Time-consuming. ■ Complexity has to be limited due to the manual nature of the process.

4.6 Using Economic Information in Forecasting Asset Class Returns

Movements in economic variables play a key role in forming investors' expectations. Although some investors, such as pure bottom-up stock pickers or fully hedged arbitrage specialists, do not care much about the way that economic developments move markets, it is important for most investors. In this section, we look at how the principal asset classes are moved by different economic variables.

4.6.1 Cash and Equivalents

Cash managers make money through selection of the maturity of the paper in their portfolio or, if permitted by investment policy, by taking credit risk. Longer maturities and lower credit ratings reward the extra risk with higher expected returns. Managers lengthen or shorten maturities according to their expectations of where interest rates will go next. Normally, longer-maturity paper will pay a higher interest rate than shorter-maturity paper, even if overnight interest rates are expected to remain the same, because the risk of loss is greater for the longer-term paper if this expectation is not fulfilled. If further rises in rates are expected over time, then 6- and 12-month paper should offer even higher rates than shorter-term paper.

The overnight interest rate is targeted by the central bank and will normally vary only slightly from the target set. For example, in the United States, the Federal Reserve's target for the fed funds rate along with open market operations usually ensures the overnight interest rate is close to the target. (**Open market operations** are the purchase or sale by a central bank of government securities, which are settled using reserves, to influence interest rates and the supply of credit by banks.) Occasional variations are due normally to liquidity factors, especially close to year-end or during unusual market turbulence. In other countries, the target rate may be the repo rate (repurchase rate), as in the Eurozone, where the European Central Bank conducts open market operations.

At any given time, the yield curve of interest rates of a particular security (e.g., Treasury bills or interest rate futures) reflects the market's expectations of rates over that period. The money manager is trying to be ahead of others in correctly forecasting those levels. In practice, this means forecasting both the behavior of the economy and the reaction of the central bank to that behavior. It also means understanding what the markets currently anticipate and distinguishing between future data surprises and what is already factored into expectations (i.e., likely to have no effect on the market). Money managers therefore spend a great deal of time in so-called "central bank watching."

Example 31

Central Bank Watching and Short-Term Interest Rate Expectations

At the beginning of 2000, the U.S. stock market bubble peaked and the economy was strong. At this point, one-month U.S. interest rates stood at about 5.7 percent per annum, with the six-month yield about 40 basis points higher at 6.1 percent per annum. Interest rates had already moved up in 1999, but the market was expecting the Federal Reserve to announce additional small increases in rates to help slow the economy and avoid rising inflation. A money manager might have been tempted to buy the longer-term paper, given its higher yield. However, the Federal Reserve raised interest rates faster than expected, with the fed funds rate moving up from 5.5 percent to 6.5 percent by June 2000. The best place to be was therefore at the short end of the curve, because by May 2000, one-month paper could be bought to yield 6.5 percent per annum and six-month paper could be bought to yield 6.8 percent per annum. During periods of rising short-term rates, keeping maturities short is a good strategy.

Early summer 2000 turned out to be the peak for U.S. interest rates, and rates were cut sharply in 2001 when the U.S. economy went into recession. In November 2000, shortly before the markets began to expect that the Fed would cut interest rates sharply, six-month rates of 6.7 percent per annum were available, just above one-month rates of 6.5 percent per annum. In the first months of 2001, the Fed cut rates rapidly and one-month yields plummeted to 4 percent per annum by May 2001 with an average yield of only just over 5 percent per annum.

Consider a manager who, during the summer of 2000, correctly anticipated the actions of the Fed in 2001. For such a manager, contrast the appropriateness of the following two strategies:

- An investment strategy of rolling over one-month paper.
- An investment strategy of buying longer-maturity paper (in this case, six-month paper).

Solution:

The second strategy is superior, as it would lock in the higher yields for six months in a declining interest rate environment. By contrast, the first strategy counts on interest rates rising, not declining. The first strategy would produce higher returns only if interest rates rose.

4.6.2 Nominal Default-Free Bonds

Nominal default-free bonds are conventional bonds that have no (or minimal) default risk. Conventional government bonds of developed countries are the best example. Thus, our focus is on the government yield curve. One way to think of the yield on a government bond is that it reflects the expected future short-term Treasury bill yields over the same horizon. Another approach, which is more useful for longer-term bonds, is to break down the yield into at least two components. First, the so-called real bond yield is determined by the growth rate of GDP and the supply and demand for capital. Second, yields are affected by forecast inflation over the investment period. For default-risk-free bonds, the credit spread or default risk premium is zero. Investors may thus assess whether bonds are cheap or expensive according to their view on whether the markets are too optimistic or too pessimistic based on real yields and inflation.

Historically, taking the period 1900–2010, the average annual real return on long-term government bonds above inflation was 2.3 percent for the United States and 2.2 percent for the United Kingdom.[73] However, there is some evidence that investors underestimated inflation during several periods, including the world wars and the peacetime inflation of the 1960s and 1970s. Hence, a better estimate of the *ex ante* expectations for annual returns above inflation (i.e., real yields) is 2–4 percent.

The investor then needs to forecast the inflation rate over the long term. For example, if 10-year bonds yield 5 percent and inflation is forecast at 2 percent, then the investor is hoping to receive approximately a 3 percent real return. If his or her judgment is that annual inflation is likely to be only 0.5 percent or perhaps that deflation will occur, then these bonds will be particularly attractive. Conversely, if inflation is thought likely to accelerate—for example, to 6 percent—then the bonds are very unattractive because they will not compensate for this higher inflation rate and will likely fall below par value during their lifetime as market yields rise.

For investors buying and selling long-term bonds over a shorter time period, the emphasis is on how bond yields will respond to developments in the business cycle and changes in short-term interest rates. News of stronger economic growth usually makes bond yields rise (prices fall) because it implies greater demand for capital and perhaps higher inflation too. Changes in short-term rates have less predictable effects on bond yields. More often than not, a rise in short-term rates will lead to a rise in longer-term bond yields. However, a rise in rates will sometimes be expected to slow the economy, and bond yields could fall as a result. If bond markets expect that central banks will exactly achieve their inflation objectives, then bond yields should not change on inflation expectations but nevertheless could go up and down according to changes in short rates (with higher short rates making bonds less attractive in relative terms).

As bond investors look toward the long-term picture, they must carefully assess the future effects of inflation, which erodes the future purchasing power of the yields earned on their fixed-income investments. In the 1970s, bond investors in the United States and most major countries suffered severe losses in real terms because of unexpected inflation. Yields in the 1960s were at single-digit levels, and yet inflation in the following 15 years moved up into double digits. In the 1980s, after this bad experience, investors were apprehensive of a new surge in inflation and therefore demanded higher yields (a higher inflation premium). Hence, yields were often 4–6 percent above recorded inflation—much higher than normal. As of early 2005, with inflation very low, U.S. bond investors have begun to believe not only that inflation will stay low, but also that there is a risk of deflation. Thus, as inflation fears declined during the 1990s, the inflation premium in bond yields likewise declined, reducing overall nominal yields. In recent years, the inflation premium embedded in bond yields fell further, to unusually low levels in the first half of 2003, when deflation fears reached a high point and bond yields registered as little as 1–2 percent above recorded inflation.

---

[73] See Dimson, Marsh, and Staunton (2011).

Economic Analysis

4.6.3 Defaultable Debt

Defaultable debt is debt with some meaningful amount of credit risk—in particular, most corporate debt. For corporate debt, such as certificates of deposit and bonds, the spread over Treasuries represents at least in part the market's perception of default risk.[74] Individual securities move in response to particular corporate circumstances, but the market as a whole responds primarily to changes in short-term rates and changes in the business cycle. During a business cycle, spreads tend to rise during a recession because companies are under stress from both weak business conditions and, typically, higher interest rates. Sometimes, borrowing from banks or in the commercial paper market becomes more difficult too, so that companies can be severely squeezed. Default rates typically rise during recessions. Investors demand higher rates to pay for the uncertainties and possible surprises, such as fraud. In contrast, during periods of strong economic growth, spreads narrow as fears of default decline.

4.6.4 Emerging Market Bonds

Emerging market debt refers here to the sovereign debt of nondeveloped countries. So far, we have considered only government issues and regarded them as virtually risk-free from a credit point of view. Almost all of the main industrial country governments, the members of the OECD area, are AAA rated by the rating agencies and likely to remain so. Japan is the main exception (rated AA), with its rapidly rising debt/GDP ratio an increasing concern. In practice, even in Japan, rising debt is more likely to lead to a bout of inflation than an outright default, as long as governments can control monetary policy and therefore can ultimately print money to pay off debts. Emerging market bonds, as an asset class, are different in that the country is borrowing in a foreign currency. The government therefore cannot simply inflate its way out of a problem in servicing the debt, and so the risk of default is correspondingly higher. Assessing this risk, using what is known as country risk analysis, involves a large array of economic and political factors. Much of country risk analysis comes down to predicting policy moves and therefore often hinges on politics—that is, whether a government has the power to follow the necessary policies to stabilize the economy. Emerging market bonds are usually analyzed by developed market investors in terms of their spread over domestic Treasuries compared to similarly rated domestic corporate debt.

4.6.5 Inflation-Indexed Bonds

Many governments now issue bonds linked to inflation, so in principle, we can directly observe the market's forecast of inflation by comparing the yield of these indexed bonds with the yield on similarly dated conventional bonds. Examples of this important class of bonds are Treasury Inflation-Protected Securities (TIPS) in the United States and Index-Linked Gilts (ILGs) in the United Kingdom. These provide a fixed coupon (the real portion) plus an adjustment equal to the change in consumer prices. In principle, indexed bonds are the perfect risk-free asset because, unlike conventional bonds, they entail no risk from unexpected inflation. However, the yield on indexed bonds still changes over time, and in practice it varies with three economic factors.

First, the yield goes up and down with the real economy and particularly with the level of short-term interest rates. If real yields generally are high because the economy is strong, then real yields on TIPS and ILGs will be higher. Second, yields fall if inflation accelerates because these securities are more attractive when inflation is volatile. In other words, their value in hedging against inflation risk is higher. Finally, as with all assets, the yield can vary according to institutional supply and demand. In practice, tax effects and the limited size of the market (particularly for TIPS in the United States)

---

[74] Other factors, such as differences in taxation or the presence or absence of a call provision, can also account for part of this spread.

may also distort the real yield; thus, investors usually find it worthwhile to forecast all three components (real yield, inflation, and supply and demand).

The yield-related relationships that affect indexed fixed-income securities can be shown as in Exhibit 26.

Exhibit 26 The Macroeconomy and Real Yields

Economic Observation	Effect on Real Bond Yields
Economic growth rising (falling)	Rise (fall)
Inflation expectations rising (falling)	Fall (rise)
Investor demand rising (falling)	Fall (rise)

4.6.6 Common Shares

To relate economic analysis to common equity valuation, it is useful to think of economic factors, first, in the way that they affect company earnings and, second, in the way that they affect interest rates, bond yields, and liquidity. The two views combined provide a forecast for the equity markets and can lead to new investor ideas and trading activity. Particular economic factors will also affect the outlook for specific companies—for example, the price of oil or the demand for airline travel. Here, we focus on the impact on the overall stock market.

4.6.6.1 Economic Factors Affecting Earnings In the long term, the trend growth in aggregate company earnings is mainly determined by the trend rate of growth of the economy. A faster-growing economy is likely to show faster average earnings growth, while a slower economy is correlated with slower earnings growth. The trend rate of growth of an economy is dependent on labor force growth, the level of investment, and the rate of labor productivity growth. Variations in growth rates among countries are usually due to past overinvestment, government overregulation or political instability, or the bursting of a major asset price bubble.

Example 32

Economic Return Drivers: Energy and Transportation

Willem DeVries is researching the macroeconomic return drivers of the energy and transportation industries. He has gathered the information in Exhibit 27 from a U.S. investment manager's research report.

Exhibit 27 Correlations of GDP, Inflation, and Interest Rates with Industry Sales, Earnings, and Dividends[75]

	Energy Industry			Transportation Industry		
	GDP	Inflation	Interest Rates	GDP	Inflation	Interest Rates
Sales	+0.10	+0.77	+0.78	+0.58	+0.75	+0.74
Earnings	+0.13	+0.66	+0.67	+0.81	+0.26	+0.25
Dividends	+0.16	+0.03	+0.05	+0.65	−0.03	−0.08

---

[75] Analysis excerpted from a Duff & Phelps Investment Management Co. study of the 1,000 largest U.S. companies over 1990–2003, using annual data.

> Using only the information given, compare and contrast the macroeconomic return drivers of the energy and transportation industries.
>
> **Solution:**
>
> The larger positive correlations between GDP and the transportation industry's sales, earnings, and dividends compared to the corresponding correlations for the energy industry are an indication that transportation companies are more procyclical.
>
> Sales for the energy and transportation industries are approximately equally positively related to inflation and interest rates. However, earnings are less positively correlated with inflation and interest rates for the transportation industry. Transportation companies appear to be less able to pass through to customers the increased costs of higher inflation and interest rates. These observations should be helpful when one is using economic factors to draw inferences on future industry fundamentals.

Over the shorter term, the share of profits in GDP varies with the business cycle and is influenced by a variety of factors, including final sales, wages, capacity utilization, and interest rates.

During a recession, earnings are depressed because of reduced sales and a set amount of fixed costs. Capacity utilization is typically low. In severe recessions, earnings can disappear altogether for many companies. Other companies, less affected by the cycle (e.g., food companies), may see very little change in earnings. Companies that can maintain earnings growth through recessions receive high market valuations from investors.

During the early stages of an economic upswing, earnings recover strongly. One reason is the rise in capacity utilization and increasing employment. Many costs stay the same while volume rises, which brings large increases in profits. Wage awards usually remain modest because of continuing relatively high unemployment, so that most of the productivity gains flow straight into profits. A second factor is often the efficiency gains made during the recession that become evident when output rises. A leaner, fitter company emerges from recession as some of the fat built up during the growth years, including both obvious waste and "luxury" projects, is cut out.

Later in the economic upswing, wage growth starts to quickly rise, profits contract, and earnings growth slows. Some companies, generally the ones with large fixed costs and a pronounced sales cycle, are more sensitive to the business cycle than others. These are called **cyclical stocks**. Examples include car manufacturers and chemical producers.

Example 33 shows an analyst methodically organizing the economic analysis to formulate an answer to a client's question on the equity risk premium.

Example 33

Researching U.S. Equity Prospects for a Client

In the beginning of 2004, Michael Wu has one of his regular quarterly meetings with an institutional client for whom he manages a U.S. equity portfolio. The economic forecasts of Wu's firm covering the next 12–18 months are consistent with the client's view that short-term interest rates will be increasing from 3.0 percent to 3.5 percent while long-term government bonds will return 5.5 percent. The client views U.S. equities as currently slightly overvalued. The client is not optimistic about long-term prospects for U.S. equities either and states to Wu that the long-term U.S. equity risk premium fwill be in the range of 1.0 percent to 2.5 percent. The client asks Wu to help him decide, based on economic analysis, whether a 1.0 percent or 2.5 equity risk premium is more likely.

Wu summarizes his firm's research in Exhibit 28.

Exhibit 28 Current and Expected Economic/Market Trends: United States

Category	Expected Economic Trends/Impact Forecast Short-Term (1 Year)	Long-Term (> 1 Year)	Comments on Economic Measures and Categories
Macroeconomy	$E_{(Trend)}$: Slowing GDP growth $E_{(Economic\ Impact)}$: Negative: Growth slowing from 4 percent to a lower rate	Average growth [3.1% annual GDP growth] $E_{(Trend)}$: Stable $E_{(Economic\ Impact)}$: Neutral	High current economic growth rate is due to fiscal and monetary stimuli and is not sustainable. Overall economic growth rate to slow to a lower 3.1% rate beyond 1-year time horizon.
Consumer	$E_{(Trend)}$: Improving consumer spending $E_{(Economic\ Impact)}$: Positive	$E_{(Trend)}$: Stable $E_{(Economic\ Impact)}$: Positive	Looking forward, stabilization in employment patterns and personal income will aid the consumer component of the economy.
Business	$E_{(Trend)}$: Stable $E_{(Economic\ Impact)}$: Neutral	$E_{(Trend)}$: Stable $E_{(Economic\ Impact)}$: Positive	The low base against which current results are being compared has aided profit and sales growth rate comparisons. Productivity growth has been aided by the weak employment (hiring) practices of the past few years. As employment rises, profit and productivity increases will diminish. Export-oriented businesses will be in the best position over the next few years as the U.S. dollar is expected to decline further. Sales and profits showing signs of strength but are being compared to weak prior year results.
Central bank	Economic strength and fiscal deficits likely to put pressure on short-term interest rates; slightly higher inflation $E_{(Trend)}$: Declining stimulation $E_{(Economic\ Impact)}$: Negative	$E_{(Trend)}$: Stable $E_{(Economic\ Impact)}$: Neutral Short-term rates and inflation rate will stabilize near long-term average rates	Monetary stimulus expected to be reduced in light of the increased economic strength. The stronger economy will place upward pressure on short-term interest rates and on the rate of inflation near-term, but short-term interest rates and inflation are expected to quickly stabilize near their long-term average rates.
Government	$E_{(Trend)}$: Stable measures $E_{(Economic\ Impact)}$: Positive	$E_{(Trend)}$: Weakening $E_{(Economic\ Impact)}$: Negative	Fiscal stimulus (i.e., deficit spending and tax cuts) is giving a current boost to GDP. More work must be done to cut the budget deficit and to deal with a declining dollar. The U.S. government needs to deal with the problem of increasing long-term transfer payment costs.

Note: Expected economic trends are denoted by $E_{(Trend)}$, while expected economic impact is denoted by $E_{(Economic\ Impact)}$.

Using only the information in Exhibit 28, address the following problems:

1. State and justify a long-term expected return for equities within the client's guidelines.
2. Comment on whether the economic data support the client's belief that the equity market is overvalued.

Economic Analysis

> **Solution to 1:**
>
> The consumer and business sectors are critical for corporate profits, and the long-term forecast strengths of these sectors are a positive for U.S. equities. The central bank appears to be a neutral factor long-term. Although the government sector is a negative, it is not expected to push inflation and interest rates above their long-term averages. Overall, a 2.5 percent equity risk premium, at the upper end of the client's range, appears to be justified by the positive economic outlook, which would lead to a forecast of an 8.0 percent arithmetic average return on equities. (A long government bond expected return of 5.5% + expected equity risk premium of 2.5% = 8.0% expected equity return over the forecast period.)
>
> **Solution to 2:**
>
> By contrast to the long-term forecasts, the short-term economic forecasts of decelerating growth and increasing interest rates might constitute a negative for short-term equity returns. However, the analyst would need to evaluate whether current market prices incorporate this information before concurring in the client's assessment.

4.6.6.2 The P/E Ratio and the Business Cycle

The price-to-earnings ratio of a stock market is the price that the market is willing to pay for the earnings of that market. During the business cycle, the P/E ratio tends to be high and rising when earnings are expected to rise. For example, the P/E would be high in the early stages of an economic recovery, or when interest rates are low and the return on fixed-rate investments such as cash or bonds is less attractive. Conversely, P/Es are likely to be low and falling if the outlook for earnings worsens (e.g., in an economic slump). Nevertheless, P/Es of cyclical companies may be above their own historical means during economic downturns as investors anticipate a sharp future earnings recovery when the economy turns up (a phenomenon known as the Molodovsky effect).

P/E ratios vary over longer periods too. In general, they are lower for an economy stuck on a slower growth path. During the 1990s, P/E ratios were at relatively high levels (e.g., multiples greater than 20 in the United States). At the time, some saw this situation as reflecting the benign economic influences of falling inflation, relatively low interest rates, fast productivity and profits growth, and a relatively stable economy. Another view was that these valuations were too high and would decline in the future, and this view has been borne out since 2000.

High inflation rates tend to depress P/E ratios. Inflation can distort the economic meaning of reported earnings, leading investors to value a given amount of reported earnings less during inflationary periods, which tends to lower observed P/Es during those periods. Consequently, comparisons of current P/E with past average P/E that do not control for differences in inflation rates may be suspect.[76]

4.6.6.3 Emerging Market Equities

Empirical evidence points to *ex post* equity risk premiums for emerging markets that are on average higher and more volatile than those in developed markets. *Ex post*, emerging market equity risk premiums in U.S. dollar terms appear to be positively correlated with expansion phases in G–7 economies as proxied by industrial production.[77] Transmission channels for G–7 macroeconomic fluctuations to developing economies include trade (demand for many of the goods produced by emerging countries, such as natural resources, is procyclical), finance, and direct sectoral linkages. In addition to evaluating linkages, the analyst needs to do considerable country and often sector-specific research to appraise the prospects for equity investments in a particular emerging country.

---

[76] For more details, see Bodie, Kane, and Marcus (2001).
[77] See Salomons and Grootveld (2003).

4.6.7 Real Estate

Ling and Naranjo (1997, 1998) identify growth in consumption, real interest rates, the term structure of interest rates, and unexpected inflation as systematic determinants of real estate returns. Interest rates are linked with a number of factors that affect the supply and demand for real estate, such as construction financing costs and the costs of mortgage financing. In general, lower interest rates are net positive for real estate valuation, resulting in lower capitalization rates.

In Example 34, an analyst with a one-year horizon applies a checklist approach to economic forecasting in modifying baseline historical capital market forecasts. The set of asset classes includes real estate.

Example 34

Modifying Historical Capital Market Expectations

Cortney Young is an investment analyst in a firm serving an international clientele. Young's firm has developed the baseline forecasts shown in Exhibit 29 for six asset classes that are particularly relevant for U.K.-focused portfolios. The forecasts are based on a recent part of the historical record of the asset classes. Young is currently working on establishing capital market expectations for mean return and standard deviation of returns for these six asset classes based on a one-year horizon; she focuses first on the U.K. equities, U.K. intermediate-term bonds, U.K. long-term bonds, and U.K. real estate.

Exhibit 29 Baseline Forecasts

Asset Class	Mean Annual Returns (%)	Standard Deviation of Returns (%)
U.K. equities	9.72	15.3
Non-U.K. equities	8.94	11.6
U.K. intermediate-term bonds	3.60	6.5
U.K. long-term bonds	4.42	7.7
International bonds	4.81	8.3
U.K. real estate	12.63	8.7

Young's economic analysis leads her to the conclusions on the U.K. economy shown in Exhibit 30.

Exhibit 30 Economic Conclusions

Economic Category	Economic Conclusion
Consumers	Consumer spending is expected to be stronger over the next year with very positive effects for the U.K. economy.
Business	Business spending, revenues, and profits are expected to show solid growth in year-over-year results over the next 12 months.
Government	Tax policies are stable. Government is currently a source of moderate economic stimulation.
Central bank	It is anticipated that the Bank of England (the central bank) will want to hold short-term interest rates steady over the next year. The inflation target is 2 percent.
Inflation rates	The inflation rate is expected to increase to 2.2 percent per year over the next year.
Other/Unique	The U.K. economy is expected to outperform other major economies over the next 12 months. The growth of the real estate sector will moderate.

Economic Analysis

1. Explain the expected impact on U.K. asset classes of each of Young's economic conclusions.
2. Demonstrate and justify the direction of judgmental modifications that Young might make to the baseline forecasts of her firm.

Solution to 1:

Young reaches the conclusions shown in Exhibit 31.

Exhibit 31 Market/Asset Class Conclusions

Economic Conclusion	Market/Asset Class Impact
Consumers	Consumers are creating a positive investment environment for corporate profits and therefore for U.K. equities and credit quality. However, if spending rises much more steeply than anticipated, we might expect upward pressure on both short-term and long-term interest rates that would be a negative for bonds and real estate.
Business	The economic conclusion is a positive for U.K. equities and bonds via improved credit quality. However, predicted business growth may put upward pressure on wages, costs, and inflation rates.
Government	The government sector conclusion is a slight positive for the economy at this time.
Central bank	The expected steady interest rate environment is a positive factor for the U.K. investment market. If the economy expands too quickly, there may be pressure from the central bank for higher interest rates looking out 12 months.
Inflation rates	The current stable inflation picture should have a positive impact on the economy and on the financial assets we are comparing in this analysis.
Other/Unique	Returns to U.K. real estate should moderate from unusually high rates.

Solution to 2:

The arrows in Exhibit 32 indicate the direction of adjustment to the baseline forecasts.

Exhibit 32 Modifications to Capital Market Forecasts for U.K. Asset Classes

Asset Class	Average Annual Returns	Average Annual Standard Deviation
U.K. equities	↑	↓ or →
Intermediate bonds	→	↑
Long-term bonds	→	↑
Real estate	↓	↑

The growth outlook for consumers and businesses is a strong positive for U.K. equities. The steady central bank, government, and inflation outlooks suggest below-average or at least unchanged volatility. The outlook of steady interest rates is neutral for intermediate- and long-term bonds, but the uncertainty about the economy overheating suggests an increase in risk. Real estate's returns should decrease from the high baseline forecast. The break with the past trend growth should translate into higher risk for real estate.

4.6.8 Currencies

The exchange rate between two countries reflects the balance of buyers and sellers. One major reason for buying and selling foreign currencies is to facilitate trade in goods and services (exports and imports). If a country begins to import more, the currency will tend to depreciate (all else being equal). Hence, considerable attention is usually paid to determining a competitive exchange rate at which the trade balance—or, more broadly, the current account balance (which includes services and transfers)—is zero. Governments and central banks are often concerned with maintaining a competitive exchange rate and may try to do so by buying or selling foreign currencies or by raising or lowering interest rates.

However, trade is only one motive for purchases and sales of foreign currency and it has become relatively less important. The other motive is international flows of capital. Companies wishing to invest in a country are likely to be buyers of the currency as they bring in capital to build assets. Strong domestic economic growth and an opening of new industries to foreign ownership are two possible drivers of a rise in foreign direct investment that will likely push up a currency too. The liberalization of capital flows and the increasing trend toward global diversification mean that there may also be inflows to buy local stocks, bonds, or short-term instruments, including deposits. These flows can be volatile and may quickly reverse. The foreign direct investment is likely to be more stable.

Portfolio flows may be influenced by the growth of the economy or by domestic interest rates. When interest rates are high, inflows are likely to be higher and the currency value rises. Conversely, falling interest rates often weaken a currency. However, the link between interest rates and the currency sometimes works the other way. This is because investors may see higher interest rates as slowing the economy. If a currency departs from the level that equilibrates trade for a long time, the resulting deficits or surpluses may eventually become too large for capital flows to finance. Among the major currencies, there are often prolonged over- and undervaluations around a long-term equilibrium level. For this reason, many governments in emerging countries use some combination of capital controls and currency management (pegs, currency boards, managed floats, etc.) to try to keep the currency competitive. This approach tends to lead to stability for extended periods punctuated by periodic sudden, large movements.

Example 35

A Currency Example

Between 1990 and July 1997, the Bank of Thailand managed the Thai baht in a narrow range. Over time, a gradual loss of competitiveness through higher inflation pushed the current account deficit up to 8 percent of GDP, financed by strong capital inflows. In 1996, the economy slowed and capital inflows faltered, prompting speculation that the baht might fall. The central bank intervened heavily to defend the baht in early 1997 but by midyear had exhausted its reserves and was forced to float the currency. Within a few months, the baht halved in value and other currencies in the region were also under pressure. The Asian crisis of 1997 had begun.

Forecasting exchange rate movements is widely viewed as especially difficult. For this reason, some investors try to fully hedge currency exposure. Others see opportunities in currency forecasting because of the volatility of many exchange rates and the highly liquid markets. The following sections review the major approaches to exchange rate forecasting.

4.6.9 Approaches to Forecasting Exchange Rates

There are four broad approaches to forecasting exchange rates, and most forecasters probably use a combination of them all.

4.6.9.1 Purchasing Power Parity

Purchasing power parity (PPP) asserts that movements in an exchange rate should offset any difference in the inflation rates between two countries.[78] PPP reflects the idea that exchange rates should find a level that keeps different countries broadly competitive with each other.

To illustrate PPP, suppose that over a five-year period, Canadian prices are forecast to increase by 10.41 percent (equal to 2 percent annual inflation) while Eurozone prices are forecast to show 15.93 percent growth (equal to 3 percent annual inflation). Over the five-year period, the Canadian–Eurozone inflation differential is 10.41% – 15.93% = –5.52%. PPP would predict that the Canadian dollar will appreciate against the euro by approximately the same percentage. For example, if the exchange rate is C$1.3843 per euro, PPP would predict an exchange rate of approximately (1 – 0.0552) × (C$1.3843 per euro) = C$1.3079 per euro.

PPP in broad terms does seem to be useful in the long run—say, over periods of five years or longer. Furthermore, governments and central banks take PPP very seriously in their approach to exchange rates because periods of under- or overvaluation of a currency may lead to sudden exchange rate instability or be destabilizing for business.

However, with the huge rise in capital flows over the last three decades, exchange rates can depart from PPP levels for long periods of time. PPP is often not a useful guide to the direction of exchange rates in the short or even medium run (up to three years or so). There are also times when factors other than PPP dominate exchange rate movements. This usually happens when a large current account deficit is opening up and the markets question whether a growing deficit can be financed. Markets then focus on what level of the currency is needed to correct the deficit.

4.6.9.2 Relative Economic Strength

The **relative economic strength forecasting approach** focuses on investment flows rather than trade flows. It suggests that a strong pace of economic growth in a country creates attractive investment opportunities, increasing the demand for the country's currency and causing it to appreciate. Sometimes, demand comes from a higher short-term deposit rate in that country combined with an expectation that the currency will stay the same or appreciate. More recently, the focus has been on the pace of economic growth and the existence of attractive investment opportunities in general.

When interest rates are relatively high in a country, capital moves into that country and, as a result, the currency strengthens. Even if investors begin to see the exchange rate as overvalued in some long-term sense, they may still be content if they feel the extra yield compensates for that overvaluation. However, once the exchange rate reaches an excessive level, they will question whether the high yield is enough to justify the likely exchange rate depreciation.

What is the role of short rates? There is little question that short-term interest rates can influence exchange rates but primarily over a short-term time horizon. The level of short-term interest rates influences the extent to which speculators are willing to bet against a currency. If interest rates in a particular country are especially high, speculators are less likely to short that currency because that currency will probably strengthen as a result of the higher interest rates. Similarly, very low interest rates on Japanese yen in recent years have periodically encouraged investors to borrow yen to fund other investments (a so-called carry trade).

It can be helpful to combine the PPP and relative strength approaches. The relative strength approach indicates the response to news on the economy but does not tell us anything about the level of exchange rates. The PPP approach indicates what level of the exchange rate can be regarded as a long-term equilibrium. By combining the two, we can generate a more complete theory.

---

[78] The definition refers to relative PPP, the form of PPP most economists are concerned with. See Solnik and McLeavey (2004) for further details.

4.6.9.3 Capital Flows The **capital flows forecasting approach** focuses on expected capital flows, particularly long-term flows such as equity investment and foreign direct investment (FDI). Inflows of FDI into a country increase the demand for the country's currency, all else being equal.

From 1999 onward, there was considerable focus on this approach because of the surprising strength of the dollar versus the euro. This situation coincided with a clear increase in long-term flows from the Eurozone to the United States, especially FDI and U.S. equities. This capital was being attracted into the United States by the boom in the domestic economy and the attractiveness of equity assets, particularly in the internet and technology sectors, until at least 2001.

Note that long-term capital flows may have the effect of reversing the usual relationship between short-term interest rates and the currency. This is explained by the fact that a cut in short-term rates would be expected to boost economic growth and the stock markets, thereby making long-term investments more attractive. In this environment, central banks face a dilemma. Whereas they might want to raise interest rates to respond to a weak currency that is threatening to stimulate the economy too much and boost inflation, the effect may actually be to push the currency lower. Hence, the effectiveness of monetary policy is much reduced.

This appeared to be a problem for the Eurozone at times during 2001. As the economy slowed, the ECB was reluctant to cut interest rates because of rising inflation and a weak currency. The inaction seemed to make the currency weaker. Similarly, the Fed's aggressive cutting in the first half of 2001 pushed the dollar higher, which attracted capital and thus reduced the impact of lower interest rates in stimulating the economy.

4.6.9.4 Savings–Investment Imbalances The **savings–investment imbalances forecasting approach** explains currency movements in terms of the effects of domestic savings–investment imbalances on the exchange rate. Although it is not easy to use for forecasting, this approach can sometimes help with understanding why currencies depart from equilibrium for long periods. It starts from the fact that the current account deficit of a country is the sum of its government deficit and private sector deficit. For example, in the United States in 2004, the current account deficit was estimated at about 6 percent of GDP, with the government deficit at about 5 percent and the private sector deficit at about 1 percent. In contrast, Japan had a current account surplus of 4 percent of GDP, with a government deficit of 8 percent balanced by a private sector surplus of 12 percent of GDP. So, in Japan, the private sector was financing the government deficit as well as an outflow of capital.

However, if the private sector or government currency-related trends change, then the current account position must change too and the exchange rate moves to help achieve that. Suppose that an economy suddenly begins to expand rapidly, driven by a new government budget deficit or bullish entrepreneurs. If domestic savings do not change, there will be excess demand for capital as investment tries to exceed savings. The only way that investment can exceed savings in reality is for foreign savings to be used, since the accounts have to balance. But this solution requires a deficit on the current account of the balance of payments.

So, where does this deficit on the current account come from? Some of it may arise simply because imports are strong due to the buoyant economy or because exports are weak as companies focus on the domestic market. But if that is not enough, the exchange rate needs to rise. If capital flows are attracted to the country, either due to high interest rates or due to attractive expected returns on investments, then the exchange rate will indeed rise as needed.

Because trade takes time to adjust, the exchange rate will frequently depart far from generally accepted equilibrium rates for prolonged periods, typically two to four years. Eventually, the rising currency will widen the current account deficit sufficiently and the domestic currency may start to decline. Of course, it needs to stay reasonably strong as long as domestic investment exceeds savings.

If the economy becomes weak enough at this point and domestic investments no longer exceed domestic savings, then the currency will also weaken. To return to a current account surplus, the exchange rate may need to drop to a level well below its equilibrium rate. Hence, there is a risk that the currency could swing sharply to an undervalued position.

Example 36

The USD/Euro Exchange Rate, 1999–2004

The euro was first established as a currency at the beginning of 1999. To the surprise of nearly everyone, it started trading weakly, its value against the U.S. dollar falling from about US$1.17 to a low of US$0.82 in late 2000. But beginning in 2001 and accelerating in 2002–2004, the dollar fell. In 2004, the euro reached US$1.37. On a PPP basis, the euro probably lies in the range of US$1.10–US$1.20. So, in the course of five years, the exchange rate cycled around that level. These swings can be considered according to the three explanations below.

Relative economic strength: This approach explains why the dollar rose strongly in 1999–2000, with faster economic growth and consequent higher interest rates in the United States. In 2001, the fact that the U.S. economy was weaker than that of the Eurozone helps to explain why the dollar peaked and went sideways during that year. The explanation breaks down in 2002–2003, however. Despite the superior performance of the U.S. economy over the Eurozone in 2002 and beyond, the dollar retraced its path all the way back to its starting point.

Capital flows: This approach explains more about the dollar's recent moves. The dollar's strength in 1999–2000 was matched by massive long-term inflows into the United States in the form of foreign direct investment and equity purchases. In 2001, these flows fell off rapidly, though there were still large inflows into U.S. bonds. The current account deficit had expanded by then as a result of the strong dollar, so the capital flows were no longer large relative to the necessary inflow to finance the deficit. Hence, the dollar's decline.

Savings–investment imbalances: During 1999–2000, the U.S. economy grew very rapidly with pressure to reduce domestic savings and increase investment. Households reduced savings, encouraged by low and falling unemployment and the rising stock prices. Businesses cut savings because they saw major new investment opportunities. The result was a soaring U.S. dollar opening up the current account deficit, further encouraged by the inflow of capital described above. In 2001–2002, the private sector deficit was slashed drastically as companies cut back on borrowing and spending. The government cut taxes and shifted the government accounts from surplus to deficit. But the dollar still fell back against the euro because the current account deficit needed to be in the 4–6 percent range to balance the internal savings balances. Hence, the dollar fell back from its still-overvalued position and nosed into undervalued territory.

This approach, if correct, suggests that the dollar's weakness (at least in 2004–2005) may be limited by the continued large government borrowing requirement and low private savings. Beyond 2005, however, the dollar could reach past lows if either the government makes a major effort to reduce the budget deficit or an economic slowdown prompts increased private savings.

4.6.10 Government Intervention

Since the developed world moved to floating rates in the early 1970s, periodic attempts have been made to control exchange rates. However, economists and the markets have been skeptical about whether governments really can control exchange rates with market intervention alone because of three factors. First, the total value of foreign exchange trading, in excess of US$1 trillion *daily*, is large relative to the total foreign exchange reserves of the major central banks combined. Second, many people believe that market prices are determined by fundamentals and that government authorities are just another player. Third, experience with trying to control foreign exchange trends is not encouraging in the absence of capital controls. Unless governments are prepared to move interest rates and other policies, they cannot expect to succeed.

4.7 Information Sources for Economic Data and Forecasts

Having presented economic analysis for capital market expectations setting, we can indicate several fruitful sources for gathering economic data. The sources we present link to many other useful resources.

The main sources of leading indicators are the Conference Board and national sources. Most other economic data also come from national statistical sources, such as central banks and government statistical offices. Some survey data come from other organizations, such as the Institute of Supply Management. Useful international sources include the OECD, IMF, and World Bank. A list of websites is provided below.

Forecasts from econometric models are published by governments. The OECD publishes forecasts twice a year in its *Economic Outlook* reports. The IMF publishes forecasts, and various private sector forecasters also publish forecasts, though these are sometimes proprietary. Exhibit 33 summarizes some sources for researching U.S. markets.

Exhibit 33   A Selection of Data Sources for Researching U.S. Markets

Categories of Economic Interest	Factor Measures	Data Use LT	Data Use ST	Data Source
Economic fundamentals	Measures of economic output/growth (e.g., GDP, industrial production)	✓		www.bea.gov Bloomberg
	General price level stability	✓		
Consumers	Employment/unemployment	✓		Bloomberg
	Measures of consumption/income	✓		www.bea.gov
	Measures of savings, investment, and leverage	✓		
	Measures of sentiment	✓		U. of Michigan Survey
Business	Measures of profitability	✓		www.bea.gov
	Measures of productivity	✓		Federal Reserve Bank
	Industry price level stability	✓	✓	Internal or third-party research; Trade pub.
	Capacity utilization rates		✓	
Central bank	Measures of monetary policy	✓	✓	www.stls.frb.org
	General price level stability (inflation)	✓	✓	Bloomberg
	Assessment of central bank independence		✓	Internal analysis

Exhibit 33 Continued

Categories of Economic Interest	Factor Measures	Data Use LT	Data Use ST	Data Source
Government	Fiscal policy	✓	✓	Congressional Budget Office; Bloomberg
	Assessment of exchange rate stability/trends	✓	✓	Internal; www.wto.org
	Measures of political stability	✓		Internal analysis
	Assessment of legal system's ability to protect assets (including intangible assets) and ability to settle disputes (due process)	✓		Internal analysis
Economic technical factors	Capital flows		✓	Internal/third-party research;
	Sector/industry supply and demand		✓	Trade publications
Market fundamentals	Rates of return	✓	✓	Relative (industry) internal research;
	Valuation trends (e.g., equity P/E multiples)	✓	✓	
	Asset class price volatility			Third-party research; Trade publications
	Large-cap equities	✓		
	Corporate bonds vs. overall market	✓	✓	
	Short sovereign debt		✓	
	Exchange rate movements	✓		
Market technical factors	Ratio of advances/declines in equity market		✓	Reuters;
	Corporate bond issuance (market yield)		✓	Internal research
Other: unique; social; political	Demographic influences	✓	✓	Internal; third-party
	Seasonal patterns of consumption	✓	✓	Third-party; Trade pub.
	Current account trends; net exports versus imports	✓	✓	Bloomberg

Some additional useful resources include the following:

- www.imf.org
- www.worldbank.org
- www.oecd.org
- www.federalreserve.gov
- www.ecb.int
- www.bankofengland.co.uk
- www.boj.or.jp/en (the English site for the Bank of Japan)
- www.bis.org
- www.nber.org (the website of the National Bureau of Economic Research, the U.S. organization that dates business cycles; it contains useful data and research on past business cycles)

SUMMARY

In this reading, we have discussed how investment professionals address the setting of capital market expectations.

- Capital market expectations are essential inputs to deciding on a strategic asset allocation. The process of capital market expectations setting involves the following steps:
    1. Specify the final set of expectations that are needed, including the time horizon to which they apply.
    2. Research the historical record.
    3. Specify the method(s) and/or model(s) that will be used and the information needs for developing expectations.
    4. Determine the best sources for information needs.
    5. Interpret the current investment environment using the selected data and methods, applying experience and judgment.
    6. Formulate the set of expectations that are needed, documenting conclusions.
    7. Monitor actual outcomes and compare to expectations, providing feedback to improve the expectations-setting process.

- Among the challenges in setting capital market expectations are *the limitations of economic data* (including lack of timeliness as well as changing definitions and calculations); *data measurement errors and biases* (including transcription errors, survivorship bias, and appraisal [smoothed] data); *the limitations of historical estimates* (including nonstationarity); *ex post risk as a biased risk measure* (historical prices may reflect expectations of a low-probability catastrophe that did not occur); *biases in analysts' methods* (including data-mining bias and time-period bias); *the failure to account for conditioning information*; *the misinterpretation of correlations*; and *psychological traps* (including the anchoring trap, the status quo trap, the confirming evidence trap, the overconfidence trap, the prudence trap, and the recallability trap); and *model uncertainty*.

- The tools for formulating capital market expectations include formal tools, survey and panel methods, and judgment. Formal tools include statistical tools, discounted cash flow models, the risk premium approach, and financial market equilibrium models. Analyst judgment includes economic and psychological insight.

- Economic output has cyclical and growth trend components. The cyclical components include the inventory cycle (measured in terms of fluctuation of inventory) and the business cycle (representing fluctuations in GDP in relation to long-term trend growth). A typical business cycle has five phases: initial recovery, early upswing, late upswing, slowdown, and recession. Each of the two cyclical components has implications for variables such as interest rates and corporate profits, which are important for capital market expectations. The economic trend growth component (the long-term growth path of GDP) is important particularly for setting long-term expectations.

- Consumer spending is typically the most important factor affecting GDP (it often accounts for 60–70 percent of GDP). Retail sales and consumer consumption are closely watched for indications of consumer spending.

Summary

- Business investment has a smaller weight in GDP than consumer spending but is more volatile. Data on business investment and spending on inventories reveal recent real business activity.
- Fiscal policy and monetary policy are means by which governments attempt to influence the business cycle.
- Monetary policymakers often target inflation rates and use the central bank's influence over interest rates to achieve policy goals. The Taylor rule gives the optimal short-term interest rate as the neutral rate plus an amount that is positively related to the excess of the GDP and inflation growth rates above their respective trend and target values.
- If monetary and fiscal policies are both tight, the yield curve is typically inverted. When monetary policy is tight but fiscal policy is loose, the yield curve tends to be flat. An inverted yield curve has often preceded a recession.
- In managing cash and equivalents, central bank actions are closely watched.
- For investors buying and selling nominal default-free bonds for the short term, developments in the business cycle and changes in short-term interest rates must be closely watched. News of stronger economic growth usually makes bond yields rise. For long-term investors, inflation expectations are of great importance. For holders of corporate bonds and other defaultable debt, the spread over Treasuries in relation to the business cycle is an important factor.
- Investing in emerging market debt involves special considerations, such as country risk analysis. Emerging market governments borrow in a foreign currency and so cannot simply inflate their way out of a problem in servicing the debt; this limitation increases the risk of default.
- Inflation-indexed bonds are not exposed to the risk of unexpected inflation. Generally, yields on such instruments rise with real economic growth and the level of short-term interest rates.
- Investors in common shares should analyze economic factors, first, in the way that they affect company earnings and, second, in the way that they affect interest rates, bond yields, and liquidity. The trend growth in the aggregate economy largely determines the trend growth in aggregate corporate earnings.
- During the economic cycle, the P/E ratio tends to be high and rising when earnings are expected to rise but low and falling if the outlook for earnings worsens. P/E ratios are usually lower for an economy stuck on a slower growth path. High inflation often tends to depress P/E ratios.
- Among the systematic factors affecting real estate returns are growth in consumption, real interest rates, the term structure of interest rates, and unexpected inflation.
- Among the factors affecting exchange rate movements are purchasing power parity, relative economic strength, capital flows, and savings–investment imbalances.

PRACTICE PROBLEMS FOR READING 18

1. An analyst is assembling data for use in her firm's expectations-setting process. Several historical measures have been collected and used to set expectations on inflation and consumer consumption trends. Previously, only the most recent 25 years of historical data concerning these measures had been collected and analyzed. Now, an executive has suggested extending the starting point of the data 25 years further back to make the overall analysis more robust. Discuss why the inclusion of the additional data may present problems for the expectations-setting process despite the request's objective of making the analysis more robust.

2. Seth Bildownes is an analyst who has prepared forecasts regarding the current capital market environment. He recently gave his presentation to the managing directors of his firm. Excerpts of his presentation follow:

   > "Noting that year-end holiday sales have been weak over the past several years, I believe that current expectations should be likewise muted. In fact, just last week, I had an occasion to visit Harrods and noticed that the number of shoppers seemed quite low. The last time I saw a retail establishment with so little pedestrian traffic at the beginning of December was in 1990, and that coincided with one of the worst holiday sales periods in the past 50 years. Thus, there will be no overall year-over-year retail sales growth this holiday season."

   A. Identify any psychological traps that may be interfering with the creation of Bildownes' forecasts.

   B. Recommend a way to mitigate the bias caused by any trap identified in Part A.

3. An investor is considering adding three new securities to his internationally focused fixed-income portfolio. The securities under consideration are as follows:

   - 1-year U.S. Treasury note (noncallable);
   - 10-year BBB/Baa rated corporate bond (callable);
   - 10-year mortgage-backed security (MBS) (government-backed collateral).

   The investor will invest equally in all three securities being analyzed or will invest in none of them at this time. He will only make the added investment provided that the expected spread/premium of the equally weighted investment is at least 0.5 percent (50 bps) over the 10-year Treasury bond. The investor has gathered the following information:

Real risk-free interest rate	1.2%
Current inflation rate	2.2%
Spread of 10-year over 1-year Treasury note	1.0%
Long-term inflation expectation	2.6%
10-year MBS prepayment risk spread (over 10-year Treasuries)[a]	95 bps
10-year call risk spread	80 bps
10-year BBB credit risk spread (over 10-year Treasuries)	90 bps

   [a] This spread implicitly includes a maturity premium in relation to the 1-year T-note as well as compensation for prepayment risk.

Practice Problems and Solutions: *Managing Investment Portfolios: A Dynamic Process*, Third Edition, John L. Maginn, CFA, Donald L. Tuttle, CFA, Dennis W. McLeavey, CFA, and Jerald E. Pinto, CFA, editors. Copyright © 2007 by CFA Institute.

Practice Problems for Reading 18

Using only the information given, address the following problems using the risk premium approach:

A. Calculate the expected return that an equal-weighted investment in the three securities could provide.

B. Calculate the expected total risk premium of the three securities, and determine the investor's probable course of action.

4. An Australian investor currently holds a A$240 million equity portfolio. He is considering rebalancing the portfolio based on an assessment of the risk and return prospects facing the Australian economy. Information pertaining to the Australian investment markets and the economy has been collected in the following table:

10-Year Historical	Current	Capital Market Expectations
10-yr avg govt. bond yield: 6.2%	10-yr govt. bond yield: 3.8 %	
Avg annual equity return: 8.2%	Year-over-year equity return: −9.4%	
Avg annual inflation rate: 2.8%	Year-over-year inflation rate: 2.6%	Expected annual inflation: 3.5%
Equity market P/E (beginning of period): 15.0x	Current equity market P/E: 14.5x	Expected equity market P/E: 14.0x
Avg annual income return: 2.0%		Expected annual income return: 1.5%
Avg annual real earnings growth: 6.0%		Expected annual real earnings growth: 5.0%

Using the information in the table, address the following problems:

A. Calculate the historical Australian equity risk premium using the bond-yield-plus-risk-premium method.

B. Calculate the expected annual equity return using the Grinold–Kroner model (assume no change in the number of shares outstanding).

C. Using your answer to Part B, calculate the expected annual equity risk premium.

5. An analyst is reviewing various asset alternatives and is presented with the following information directly pertaining to the broad equity market in Switzerland and various industries within the Swiss market that are of particular investment interest.

Expected risk premium for overall global investable market (GIM) portfolio	3.5%
Expected standard deviation for the GIM portfolio	8.5%
Expected standard deviation for Swiss Health Care Industry equity investments	12.0%
Expected standard deviation for Swiss Watch Industry equity investments	6.0%
Expected standard deviation for Swiss Consumer Products Industry equity investments	7.5%

- Assume that the Swiss market is perfectly integrated with world markets.
- Swiss Health Care has a correlation of 0.7 with the GIM portfolio.

- Swiss Watch has a correlation of 0.8 with the GIM portfolio.
- Swiss Consumer Products has a correlation of 0.8 with the GIM portfolio.

A. Basing your answers only upon the data presented in the table above and using the international capital asset pricing model—in particular, the Singer–Terhaar approach—estimate the expected risk premium for the following:

   i. Swiss Health Care Industry.

   ii. Swiss Watch Industry.

   iii. Swiss Consumer Products Industry.

B. Judge which industry is most attractive from a valuation perspective.

6. Consider the information given in the following table:

Eurodollar Short Rates (as of Start of Month)

Month	1-Month Rates	6-Month Rates	Spread: 6-Mo. vs. 1-Mo.
Jan 20X0	5.71%	6.14%	43 bps
Feb 20X0	5.80	6.26	46
Mar 20X0	5.97	6.35	38
Apr 20X0	6.07	6.48	41
May 20X0	6.47	6.93	46
Jun 20X0	6.58	6.90	32
Jul 20X0	6.54	6.84	30
Aug 20X0	6.53	6.75	22
Sept 20X0	6.54	6.68	14
Oct 20X0	6.53	6.64	11
Nov 20X0	6.54	6.61	07
Dec 20X0	6.58	6.28	−30
Jan 20X1	5.48	5.16	−32
Feb 20X1	5.13	4.82	−31
Mar 20X1	4.98	4.58	−40

A. Determine the implicit economic forecast in the interest rate data given.

B. For a one-year holding period extending from 1 March 20X0 to 1 March 20X1, determine the relative merits of buying a six-month security now and then another one in six months, or purchasing a one-month Eurodollar security and then rolling that security over each month at the then-prevailing yield.

7. A. How might an analyst use the data reflected below to confirm her suspicion that the country is currently experiencing an output gap?

Variable	3/31/2009	3/31/2010	3/31/2011
GDP (index)	129.0	128.5	128.0
Unemployment rate	10.5%	11.0%	11.5%
Capacity utilization rate	80.5%	80.0%	80.0%
Inflation rate	9.0%	8.5%	7.0%

Practice Problems for Reading 18

B. Given your response in Part A, would you expect inflation over the next year to accelerate or decline?

8. Based on the trends that may be calculated from the following economic measures, which of the countries below would be expected to achieve higher economic growth rates over the next year if current trends are sustained? Justify your response.

Economic Measures	Croatia (Millions of Kuna) Qtr 1	Qtr 2	Czech Republic (Millions of Koruna) Qtr 1	Qtr 2
Consumer spending	28	30	350	386
Business capital investment	12	13	205	250
Government investment/fiscal spending	10	11	110	140
Other miscellaneous GDP factors	–1	–2	–58	–111
Total GDP	49	52	607	665

9. A. Based on targets for inflation and overall economic growth rate and on actual observations of inflation and economic growth rates, apply the Taylor rule to estimate what short-term interest rate level should be an appropriate target for monetary authorities.

B. Explain why the monetary action suggested by the Taylor rule output may not actually be taken by central bank authorities.

Economic Measures	GDP Trend/ Inflation Target (%)	Forecast (%)
Year-over-year increase in GDP	3.2	2.6
Inflation rate	2.0	4.0
Short-term interest rate (neutral value)	4.0	

10. Pharmavest is an investment advisory firm that focuses solely on companies within the health care (HC) sector. The firm conducts research and manages several commingled health sector funds. Pharmavest is conducting an analysis of health sector companies that have business exposures to the economies of Europe and the United States. The following tables show current and historical economic data and Pharmavest's forecasts of the most likely economic outcomes for the next year in Europe and the United States. In the tables, "Y/Y" is short for "year-over-year."

Using the economic categories shown in the tables, compare and contrast European and U.S. economic trends and forecasts. Indicate and justify which economic region is expected to provide a relative advantage for the health care sector (Europe or the United States).

Europe

	3-Year Trend	1-Year Trend	Current Measure	1-Year Forecast
Broad economic output measure	Stable	Improving	1.3% Y/Y GDP growth in HC	3.0% Y/Y GDP growth in HC
Economic impact of consumers	Stable	Improving	8.9% consumer spending HC % of GDP	10.0% consumer spending HC % of GDP
Economic impact of businesses	Weakening	Improving	4.0% HC business profits 3.6% HC sales	5.5% HC business profits 8.0% HC sales
Economic impact of central bank	Improving/ stimulative	Stable	2.7% avg. short interest rates 2.6% inflation	2.8% avg. short interest rates 2.7% inflation
Economic impact of government	Stimulative	Stimulative but stable	5.0% government spending % of GDP (fiscal stimulus)	5.0% government spending % of GDP (fiscal stimulus)
Other unique economic factors, population growth, demographics	Stable	Stable	49 average age of aggregate population	49 average age of aggregate population

United States

	3-Year Trend	1-Year Trend	Current Measure	1-Year Forecast
Broad economic output measure	Stable	Improving	3.8% Y/Y GDP growth in HC	2.8% Y/Y growth in HC
Economic impact of consumers	Stable	Improving	9.6% consumer spending HC % of GDP	9.5% consumer spending HC % of GDP
Economic impact of businesses	Stable	Improving	5.2% HC business profits 9.0% HC sales	5.0% HC business profits 9.0% HC sales
Economic impact of central bank	Stimulative	Stable	1.0% avg short interest rates 2.2% inflation	2.2% avg short interest rates 2.5% Inflation
Economic impact of government	Stimulative	Increasingly stimulative	6.0% government spending % of GDP (fiscal stimulus)	6.5% government spending % of GDP (fiscal stimulus)
Other unique economic factors, population growth, demographics	Stable	Stable	44 average age of aggregate population	44 average age of aggregate population

11. Plim Ltd. is a manufacturing company in Finland that is a defined-benefit pension plan sponsor. Plim intends to increase its overall plan diversification by making an investment in Country X. The table below provides data for Country X indices representing various economic variables.

Based only on the data presented, from the perspective of year-end 2011, indicate whether the 1-year trend for each of the economic variables is stronger than, weaker than, or the same as its 3-year and 20-year data trend growth rates.

Practice Problems for Reading 18

Economic Index Data for Country X

Variable	Year-End 2008	Year-End 2009	Year-End 2010	Year-End 2011	20-Yr. L/T Average Annual % Increase
GDP	118.3	121.3	124.3	127.4	4.2
Consumer spending	1,569.2	1,596.2	1,584.3	1,647.7	2.5
Business spending	650.1	632.0	707.8	726.9	2.6
Inflation	2,749.8	2,901.1	3,133.1	3,446.4	14.3
Government spending (% of GDP)	16.2	16.5	16.0	15.8	3.6

12. **A.** List five general elements of a pro-growth government structural policy.

    B. For each of the variables given below, describe the change or changes in the variable that would be pro-growth and determine the element of a pro-growth government structural policy that would best describe the change or changes.

    i. Tax receipts as a percent of GDP.

    ii. Government tariff receipts.

    iii. Number of publicly funded schools.

    iv. Number of state-owned businesses.

    v. Long-term average budget deficit as a percent of GDP.

13. Identify four differences between developed economies and emerging market economies.

14. In late 2011, K.C. Sung is planning an asset allocation strategy but would first like to assess Country M's current economic environment, then make a forecast for the economic conditions expected over the succeeding six- to nine-month period. Sung has learned that the leading indicator measures that he has compiled are quite indicative of current economic activity. However, Sung has seen over time that these specific measures impact many parts of the economy and thus are also predictive of potential longer-term (six- to nine-month) economic impacts as the initial economic activities create jobs and other beneficial output throughout Country M's economy.

Leading Indicators: Component Contributions and Total Index	June 2011	July 2011	August 2011 (Most Current Period)
Consumer orders growth	−0.01	0.02	0.07
Business capital goods orders growth	0.04	0.05	0.04
Central bank money supply growth	0.12	0.15	0.16
Total index value	111	115	116

Using the leading indicator approach to forecasting, draw a conclusion for Country M's economy for the next six to nine months using only the above table.

15. Other than changes in the rate of inflation, specify two factors that impact the yields available on inflation-indexed bonds.

16. J. Wolf is an individual investor who intends to make an additional investment in various South Korean–based assets based on the outcome of your capital market expectations-setting framework analysis. Your analysis should use the data provided in the following table. However, each measure should be analyzed independently of the other measures. While examining the forward-looking one-year forecast relative to the data provided for the recent trends, indicate whether the equity market impact and the corporate fixed-income market impact would be positive or negative. Justify your answer considering the likely risk premium impact that would result if the one-year forecast actually occurred.

Index Data (South Korea)	Current Index Measure	Index 1-Year Forecast	South Korean Equity Market Impact	Corporate Fixed-Income Market Impact
GDP	159	173		
Consumer spending	432	430		
Business profits	115	100		
Central bank money supply	396	455		
Government spending relative to tax receipts	1,385	1,600		

17. Discuss four approaches to forecasting exchange rates.

18. Looking independently at each of the economic observations below, indicate the country where an analyst would expect to see a strengthening currency for each observation.

	Country X	Country Y
Expected inflation over next year	2.0%	3.0%
Real (inflation-adjusted) government 10-year bond rate	4.8%	5.1%
Short-term (1-month) government rate	1.9%	5.0%
Expected (forward-looking) GDP growth over next year	2.0%	3.3%
New national laws have been passed that enable foreign direct investment in real estate/financial companies	Yes	No
Current account surplus (deficit)	8.0%	−1.0%

19. Fap is a small country whose currency is the fip. Ten years ago, the exchange rate with the Swiss franc (CHF) was 3 fips per 1 CHF, the inflation indices were equal to 100 in both Switzerland and Fap, and the exchange rate reflected purchasing power parity (PPP). Now, the exchange rate is 2 fips per 1 CHF. The Swiss inflation index level is at 150, and the Fap inflation index is at 140.

   A. What should the current exchange rate be if PPP prevails?
   B. Are fips over- or undervalued, according to PPP, relative to CHF?

SOLUTIONS FOR READING 18

1. The chief point is that extending the data series further back in time increases the risk of using data representing more than one regime. The analyst also needs to be aware of adjustments or revisions to the data, which can create inconsistencies in the data and make interpretation of those data difficult. The analyst must be sure that any adjustments to the data were made on a consistent and uniform basis. Furthermore, the analyst needs to be aware that variable definitions and calculation methods may have changed over the original and extended periods.

2. **A-B.** Drawing an inference that current sales expectations might be muted due to the weak sales numbers posted over the past several years is an example of the *status quo trap*. An objective assessment of early sales figures, surveys of shoppers, and collecting data about retail order patterns and shipments represent more unbiased bases for a year-end sales forecast.

    The *confirming evidence trap* was evident when Bildownes used the recent observation of the number of customers in a single department store as further support of his forecast for weak year-end retail sales. To help prevent this bias, an analyst could undertake more observations and then honestly and independently assess them with equal rigor before drawing a conclusion.

    Bildownes also seemed to be strongly influenced by his memory of previous weak year-end sales periods being associated with low pedestrian traffic during early December 1990. In assuming that a correlation witnessed in the past will repeat again without further analysis, Bildownes has fallen into the *recallability trap*. To counter this forecast-tainting bias, Bildownes should emphasize objective assessments of data, rather than personal memories, in forecasting.

    In drawing the conclusion that "there will be no overall year-over-year retail sales growth this holiday season," Bildownes has fallen into the *overconfidence trap*. This trap relates to the natural tendency for individuals to be overconfident about the accuracy of their forecasts. The easiest way to help prevent this trap from biasing a forecast is to admit the possibility that the forecast may be inaccurate and to increase the range of possible outcomes around the primary target outcome.

3. **A.**

	Real risk-free rate (%)	+	Expected inflation (%)	+	Spreads or premiums (%)	=	Expected annual fixed-income return (%)
1-year U.S. T-note	1.2	+	2.6	+	0	=	3.8
10-year corp. bond	1.2	+	2.6	+	1.0 + 0.8 + 0.9	=	6.5
10-year MBS	1.2	+	2.6	+	0.95	=	4.75

    Note: We assign the 10-year corporate a 1% maturity premium based on the 10-year over 1-year government spread.

    Estimate of the expected return of an equal-weighted investment in the three securities: (3.8% + 6.5% + 4.75%)/3 = 5.02%

    B. The average spread at issue is [0 + (1.0% + 0.8% + 0.9%) + 0.95%]/3 = 1.22%. As 1.22% − 1% = 0.22% is less than 0.5 percent, the investor will not make the investment.

4. **A.** The historical equity risk premium is 2.0%, calculated as follows:

Historical equity returns	–	Historical 10-Year government bond yield	=	Historical equity risk premium
8.2%	–	6.2%	=	2.0%

B. The Grinold–Kroner model states that the expected return on equity is the sum of the expected income return (1.5%), the expected nominal earnings growth return (8.5% = 3.5% from inflation + 5.0% from real earnings growth), and the expected repricing return (−3.45%). The expected change in market valuation of −3.45% is calculated as the percentage change in the P/E level from the current 14.5x to the expected level of 14.0x: (14 − 14.5)/14.5 = −3.45%.

Thus, the expected return is 1.5% + 8.5% − 3.45% = 6.55%, or approximately 6.6 percent.

C. Using the results from Part B, the expected equity risk premium is 2.8 percent.

Expected equity return	–	Current 10-Year government bond yield	=	Expected equity risk premium
6.6%	–	3.8%	=	2.8%

5. **A.** Using the formula $RP_i = \sigma_i \rho_{iM} \left(\dfrac{RP_M}{\sigma_M} \right)$ we can solve for each expected industry risk premium. The term in brackets is the Sharpe ratio for the GIM, computed as 3.5/8.5 = 0.412.

   i. $RP_{\text{Health Care}} = (12)(0.7)(0.412) = 3.46\%$
   ii. $RP_{\text{Watch}} = (6)(0.8)(0.412) = 1.98\%$
   iii. $RP_{\text{Consumer Products}} = (7.5)(0.8)(0.412) = 2.47\%$

B. Based on the above analysis, the Swiss Health Care Industry would have the highest expected return. However, that return is expected compensation for systematic risk. We cannot conclude which industry is most attractive from a valuation standpoint.

6. **A.** The yield curve is inverting over the time period specified. This is an implicit forecast of an economic slowdown or a recession.

B. Rolling over six-month Eurodollar securities would have provided superior results to rolling over one-month securities during the stated period. Extending the duration of the bond portfolio will be profitable when the yield curve subsequently flattens or inverts.

7. **A.** All of the measures in the table would lead an analyst to conclude that the country is currently experiencing an output gap. The economy, as measured by GDP, has been contracting in each of the past two years. Thus, the economy has produced a higher level of output in the recent past. The unemployment rate has also been increasing steadily over the past two years and is quite high at over 10 percent. Thus, there is an ample supply of labor that could be put to work to increase economic output. Further, while the capacity utilization rate has been holding quite steady near 80 percent, it has declined from the reading posted two years ago. Thus, there is spare capacity that could be used to increase economic output. Finally, the decline in inflation in the latest year confirms that there is an output gap. The decline in inflation is important because otherwise the economic slowdown could be from an extreme overheating position and might not have opened up an output gap as yet.

Solutions for Reading 18

B. Given the conclusion that the country is experiencing an output gap, an analyst would expect a further decline in the rate of inflation in the next year.

8. The changes between Quarter 1 and Quarter 2 will be observed more clearly if we convert the economic measures from currency amounts into absolute percentage changes. The results are shown in the following table.

	Percentage Change: Qtr 1 to Qtr 2	
Economic Variable	Croatia	Czech Republic
Consumer spending	7.1%	10.3%
Business capital investment	8.3	22.0
Government investment/fiscal spending	10.0	27.3
Other miscellaneous GDP factors	100.0	91.4

Aggregate economic activity (including measures such as the components of GDP) is derived from many of the same factors from country to country. However, the proportion of economic activity derived from the multiple factors varies between economic regions and within a single region over time. Other issues that must be confronted when one analyzes across countries are the varying units of currency used and the differing levels of inflation between countries, which require an adjustment of some sort to be made before direct comparisons may be accomplished. Constant or inflation-adjusted measures may be used, and absolute currency measures may also be translated to a base currency to allow for direct comparisons. Alternatively, an analyst can examine the factors contributing to economic growth in proportion to an aggregate measure of activity such as GDP, as is shown in the following table.

	Absolute Currency Amounts Translated into Percentages of GDP			
	Croatia		Czech Republic	
Economic Variable	Qtr 1	Qtr 2	Qtr 1	Qtr 2
Consumer spending	57.1%	57.7%	57.7%	58.0%
Business capital investment	24.5	25.0	33.8	37.6
Government investment/fiscal spending	20.4	21.2	18.1	21.1
Other miscellaneous GDP factors	−2.0	−3.8	−9.6	−16.7

Finally, using the information in the two previous tables allows one to analyze more clearly how meaningful the recent changes in economic output are to a specific economy. If we multiply the percentage change in GDP from Quarter 1 to Quarter 2 by the percentage of GDP that that factor represents in Quarter 2 to a particular economy, we can more clearly gauge the importance of the economic trends in the economic output data that we have collected.

For example, the 7.1 percent increase in consumer spending in Croatia in Quarter 2 versus Quarter 1 is weighted quite heavily since the table above reflects that consumer spending represents about 57.7 percent of Croatia's total GDP as of the end of Quarter 2. Multiplying 7.1 percent by the 57.7 percent weighting that consumer spending represented to the Croatian economy produces a positive 4.1 percent weighted-average percentage change to the overall Croatian economy between Quarter 1 and Quarter 2. Here, we see the combined effect of underlying changes in each component of economic output and the relative importance of each component's change to overall economic output.

Economic Variable	Percentage Change: Qtr 1 to Qtr 2 (Weighted by Each Factor's GDP Percentage)	
	Croatia	Czech Republic
Consumer spending	4.1%	6.0%
Business capital investment	2.1	8.3
Government investment/fiscal spending	2.1	5.8
Other miscellaneous GDP factors	−3.8	−15.3
Sum of weighted percentage change: Qtr 1 to Qtr 2	4.5	4.8

Analyzing the weighted percentage changes in the economic measures reflected in the table above shows that the Czech Republic would be expected to achieve a slightly higher economic growth rate relative to Croatia over the next year if current trends are sustained. However, the large and growing drag (negative absolute values) that other miscellaneous GDP factors are placing on the Czech economy should be explored further. This drag is probably due to factors such as a large amount of imports (relative to exports) of goods and supplies required to maintain the current robust pace of the economy.

9. **A.** The Taylor rule can be used to estimate the direction and magnitude of a short-term interest rate adjustment that could be made by central bank authorities. The calculation follows:

$$R_{optimal} = R_{neutral} + \left[0.5 \times \left(GDPg_{forecast} - GDPg_{trend} \right) + 0.5 \times \left(I_{forecast} - I_{target} \right) \right]$$
$$= 4.0\% + \left[0.5 \times (2.6\% - 3.2\%) + 0.5 \times (4.0\% - 2.0\%) \right]$$
$$= 4.70\%$$

B. The Taylor rule is a simple yet useful tool that an analyst can use to determine from macroeconomic factors when it might be appropriate for central bank authorities to push down short-term interest rates in order to monetarily stimulate an economy that is functioning below potential (i.e., has an output gap). Conversely, if an economy is operating above its long-term average rate (substantial growth) and there are signs of accelerating inflation or rising inflation expectations, the Taylor rule can signal the need for central bank authorities to raise the level of short-term interest rates so that economic activity and increasing inflation expectations may be mitigated.

However, many other economic factors also affect aggregate output, inflation, and interest rates. Beyond economic factors, political and social factors come into the decision-making process when central bank authorities are setting interest rate targets. Central banks also typically take account of fiscal policies, wage behavior, asset prices, and developments in other economies. Periods of deflation would also call for more unorthodox central bank actions due to the fact that the central bank's ability to influence the economy is diminished once short-term interest rates approach zero during deflationary periods.

Solutions for Reading 18

10. Comparing the broad economic output measures for Europe and the United States, the data show that both Europe and the United States have posted similar trends over the past few years and have had improving trends over the past year. The U.S. economy has posted higher absolute levels of GDP health care growth, which is expected to moderate over the next year. However, overall output and health care-related output are expected to continue to increase in Europe over the next year. Advantage: Europe.

    Recent consumer trends for Europe and the United States have also been quite correlated. However, the United States recently has registered higher absolute measures of overall consumer health care spending. Whereas this consumer impact is likely to be stable in the United States over the next year, Europe is expected to continue to show increased growth. Advantage: Europe.

    Regarding the economic impact of businesses, the United States posted better results than Europe over the past three years. However, over the past year, improving conditions have been seen for both regions. Currently, business profits have rebounded more in the United States. Thus, absolute economic measures look stronger in the United States than in Europe in the near term. However, over the next year, business-related economic impacts should be stronger in Europe. Advantage: Europe.

    Monetary authorities have been stimulative in both Europe and the United States over the past several years. However, the stimulation is expected to reverse in the United States over the next year, with short-term rates rising from 1 percent to 2.2 percent. Short-term rates are expected to rise only slightly over the next year in Europe. Thus, monetary policy will be a more neutral factor for both economies over the next year. The United States is expected to have lower overall interest rates and slightly lower inflation. Advantage: United States.

    Fiscal policies for Europe and for the United States have been stimulative over the past few years but have been increasingly stimulative in the United States. Over the next year, the fiscal stimulation in the United States is expected to widen further in comparison to Europe. This trend is favorable to the United States as long as inflation is not an unexpected outcome of this fiscal stimulation and government borrowing caused by the fiscal stimulation does not crowd corporate borrowers out of the health care industry. Advantage: United States.

    The higher average age of the aggregate general population in Europe relative to the United States is a positive factor for the health care industry from the perspective of Pharmavest. Advantage: Europe.

    With more advantages pointing toward Europe's economies over the next year, Europe appears to be the economic region that should provide the stronger economic backdrop for the health care sector over the next year.

Matrix Summarization of Relative Advantages: Europe versus United States

	Recent Trends	Current Measures	1-Year Forecast
Broad economic measures	Similar (in Europe/U.S.)	Similar	Advantage: Europe
Impact of consumers	Similar	Similar	Advantage: Europe
Impact of businesses	Advantage: U.S.	Similar	Advantage: Europe
Impact of central bank	Similar	Similar	Advantage: U.S.
Impact of government	Similar	Advantage: Europe	Advantage: U.S.
Other/unique factors	Similar	Advantage: Europe	Advantage: Europe

11. To address the question, we first convert the data from the table into trend information (1-year, 3-year, and long-term 20-year trend information). The time periods are from the perspective of the end of 2004.

Trend Comparisons	1-Year Trend	3-Year Trend	20-Year Trend
GDP	2.5%	7.7% (2.5% compound average annual growth)	4.2%
Consumer spending	4.0	5.0 (1.6% compound average annual growth)	2.5
Business spending	2.7	11.8 (3.8% compound average annual growth)	2.6
Inflation	10.0	25.3 (7.8% compound average annual growth)	14.3
Gov't. spending (% of GDP)	−1.25	−2.5 (−0.8% compound average annual growth)	3.6

Based on the above comparisons, our conclusions about current trends witnessed over the past year for the economy of Country X relative to longer-term 3-year and 20-year trends are reflected in the table below.

Trend Analysis	1-Year Trend	3-Year Trend	20-Year Trend
GDP	2.5%	1-year trend is the same as the average annual GDP growth 3-year trend of 2.5%.	1-year trend of GDP growth is weaker than the 20-year trends.
Consumer spending	4.0	1-year trend is stronger than average annual consumer spending growth 3-year trend of 1.6%.	1-year trend is stronger than the average annual consumer spending growth 20-year trend of 2.5%.
Business spending	2.7	1-year trend is weaker than the average annual business spending growth 3-year trend of 3.8%.	1-year trend is stronger than the average annual business spending growth 20-year trend of 2.6%.
Inflation	10.0	1-year trend is weaker (higher inflation) than the average annual inflation growth 3-year trend of 7.8%.	1-year trend is stronger (lower inflation) than the average annual inflation growth 20-year trend of 14.3%.
Gov't. spending (% of GDP)	−1.25	1-year trend is weaker than the average annual govt spending growth 3-year trend of −0.8%.	1-year trend is weaker than the average annual govt spending growth 20-year trend of 3.6%.

12. **A.** Five elements of a pro-growth government structural policy are as follows:
    - Fiscal policy is sound. Fiscal policy is sometimes used to control the business cycle.
    - The public sector intrudes minimally on the private sector.
    - Competition within the private sector is encouraged.
    - Infrastructure and human capital development are supported.
    - Tax policies are sound.

    B. **i.** Declines in government tax receipts as a percent of GDP would be pro-growth because the equilibrium level of goods and services would increase. *Associated structural policy element: Tax policies are sound.*

    ii. Declines in government tariff receipts would be pro-growth. Such declines would imply that government is fostering competition. By

Solutions for Reading 18

      contrast, increases in tariff receipts would imply that government is protecting domestic businesses from international competition. *Associated structural policy element: Competition within the private sector is encouraged.*

   iii. Increases in the number of publicly funded schools would be pro-growth because businesses stand to gain from a well-educated workforce. *Associated structural policy element: Infrastructure and human capital development are supported.*

   iv. A negative net change in the number of state-owned businesses (that is, fewer such businesses) would be pro-growth. Such a change would increase the private sector's share of output, which would favor the efficient allocation of scarce resources. *Associated structural policy element: The public sector intrudes minimally on the private sector.*

   v. A decrease in the long-term average budget deficit as a percent of GDP is pro-growth, because it would be a positive for controlling the current account deficit. *Associated structural policy element: Fiscal policy is sound.*

13. Four factors usually associated with emerging market economies are as follows:

    - Emerging market economies require high rates of investment, which is usually in short supply within the emerging economy itself. This situation creates a reliance on foreign capital. Areas of needed investment usually include both physical assets (capital equipment and infrastructure) and human capital (education and skills building).

    - Emerging economies typically have volatile political and social situations. Leaders usually acquire and maintain power using force and other less-than-democratic means. The social environment is usually strained by the fact that a large portion of the population possesses few assets, has little formal education, and is unable to generate income to feed/support family and neighbors.

    - To alleviate the first two factors above, organizations such as the IMF and World Bank provide conduits for external sources of investment and a means to push for structural reforms—political, social, educational, pro-growth, etc. The "conditions" usually prescribed by these institutions are often felt to be draconian.

    - Emerging countries typically have economies that are relatively small and undiversified. Those emerging economies that are dependent on oil imports are especially vulnerable in periods of rising energy prices and can become dependent on ongoing capital inflows.

14. The consumer-oriented aspect of Country M's economy (as measured by consumer orders) has been consistently strengthening over the past several months. The consumer measure had a negative reading in June, a slightly positive reading in July, and an even stronger August reading. From this information, we can state that the consumer-oriented aspect of Country M's economy appears to be improving.

    The business-oriented aspect of Country M's economy (as measured by business capital goods orders) has remained quite flat in the period reviewed. From this information, we can state that the business-oriented aspect of the Country M's economy currently appears to be a positive contributor but is not necessarily showing signs of improvement or weakness. Thus, in recent months, the measure has been a stable but positive contributor.

The central bank-oriented aspect of Country M's economy (as measured by central bank money supply) has also steadily improved over the period being analyzed.

All of the leading indicator components have been positively contributing to the economy, and most have been contributing at an increasingly positive rate (all except business capital goods orders). These components are a sign of current economic activity and also typically create additional economic activity by their very nature. In addition, the total index of leading indicators, which includes all the components, has likewise moved upward steadily over the past few months. Thus, we can conclude from the measures in the table that Country M's economy should show continued growth over the next six to nine months.

15. Two factors that affect the yields available on inflation-indexed bonds (IIBs) are as follows:

- Overall economic growth and its corresponding impact on real interest rates bear a direct impact on IIB yields. A growing economy places upward pressure on all bond yields. Though the impact may be muted due to the nature of the IIB structure, IIBs are not immune to interest rate risk.

- Investor demand for bonds in general and for IIBs in particular has an inverse impact on IIB yields. As with non-IIBs, rising investor demand serves to drive interest rates lower and the lack of investor demand drives up the yields that issuers must pay in order to sell the bonds they need to issue.

16.

Index Data (South Korea)	Current Index Measure	Index 1-Year Forecast	South Korean Equity Market Impact	Corporate Fixed-Income Market Impact
GDP	159	173	Positive	Negative
Consumer spending	432	430	Negative	Positive
Business profits	115	100	Negative	Negative
Central bank money supply	396	455	Positive	Negative
Government spending relative to tax receipts	1,385	1,600	Positive	Negative

Justification:

GDP: A large 9 percent annual increase in GDP would give rise to strong corporate profits and would represent a favorable economic environment for equity investors (positive equity impact). However, such a strong economy would be a negative for corporate bond investors in that such economic growth and aggregate demand would place upward pressure on bond yields. In addition, in time, expectations of rising inflation could also hurt corporate bond investors (negative corporate bond impact).

Consumer Spending: A slight decrease in consumer spending represents an economic drag on overall economic output. This drag serves to reduce real earnings growth (negative equity impact). A slight decrease in consumer spending will not place any upward pressure on corporate bond yields or inflation or generally impact a debt issuer's ability to pay back the bondholders (positive corporate bond impact).

Business Profits: A 13 percent decline in business profits is a negative factor for both the equity market and the corporate bond market. Equity returns ultimately depend on businesses being able to earn a profit on the capital being employed. Thus, a steep decline in corporate profitability also increases the credit risk of corporate bondholders. Falling business profits can lead to corporate bond rating downgrades or insolvency (negative corporate bond impact).

Central Bank Money Supply: A 15 percent increase in money supply represents central bank monetary stimulation. Such stimulation should foster stronger economic growth (positive equity impact). However, bond yields could be expected to increase because monetary stimulation may increase expectations for higher aggregate growth and because of the potential higher inflation that monetary stimulation can cause over time (negative corporate bond impact).

Government Spending Relative to Tax Receipts (government budget deficit spending): A large increase in government spending relative to tax receipts (fiscal budget deficit) also represents stimulation to the economy. This stimulation can create an attractive environment for increasing corporate profits (positive equity impact). However, bond yields could be expected to increase because fiscal stimulation may increase expectations for higher aggregate growth and because of the potential higher inflation that monetary stimulation can cause over time (negative corporate bond impact).

17. Four approaches to forecasting exchange rates are as follows:

   - PPP (or relative inflation rates), as exchange rate movements should offset inflation differentials.
   - Relative economic strength, because a strong pace of economic growth tends to attract investment.
   - Capital flows, as net inflows into a country, such as foreign direct investment, increase the demand for that country's currency.
   - Savings-investment imbalances, through their ultimate effect on the need for foreign savings.

18.

	Country X	Country Y
Expected inflation over next year	2.0% ✓	3.0%
Real (inflation-adjusted) government 10-year bond rate	4.8%	5.1% ✓
Short-term (1-month) government rate	1.9%	5.0% ✓
Expected (forward-looking) GDP growth over next year	2.0%	3.3% ✓
New national laws have been passed that enable foreign direct investment in real estate/financial companies	Yes ✓	No
Current account surplus (deficit)	8.0% ✓	–1.0%

Note: A ✓ represents the comparatively stronger measure, where an analyst could expect to see a strengthening currency based on the factor being independently reviewed.

19. **A.** The Swiss price index has increased by (150 − 100)/100 − 1.0 = 50%. The Fap price index has increased by (140 − 100)/100 − 1.0 = 40%. The inflation differential is therefore 10 percent. According to PPP, to offset higher Swiss inflation, the fip should appreciate against the Swiss franc by approximately the same percentage to 0.90 × (3.0 fips per 1 CHF) = 2.70 fips per 1 CHF.

B. Contrasting the exchange rate of 2.7 fips per 1 CHF implied by PPP and the actual exchange rate of 2 fips per 1 CHF, we see that the fip is overvalued relative to its PPP value: At actual exchange rates, fewer fips are required to purchase 1 CHF than PPP would predict.

PORTFOLIO MANAGEMENT
STUDY SESSION

7

Economic Concepts for Asset Valuation in Portfolio Management

"Equity Market Valuation" illustrates how economic theory can be applied to the valuation of equity markets. "Dreaming with BRICs: The Path to 2050" addresses emerging markets, a dynamic and important subcategory of international investing. It examines the economic conditions under which certain developing countries might become a much stronger force in the world economy and the implications that would have for investors.

READING ASSIGNMENTS

Reading 19 *Equity Market Valuation*
by Peter C. Stimes, CFA and Stephen E. Wilcox, CFA

Reading 20 *Dreaming With BRICs: The Path to 2050*
Global Economics Paper Number 99, by Dominic Wilson and Roopa Purushothaman

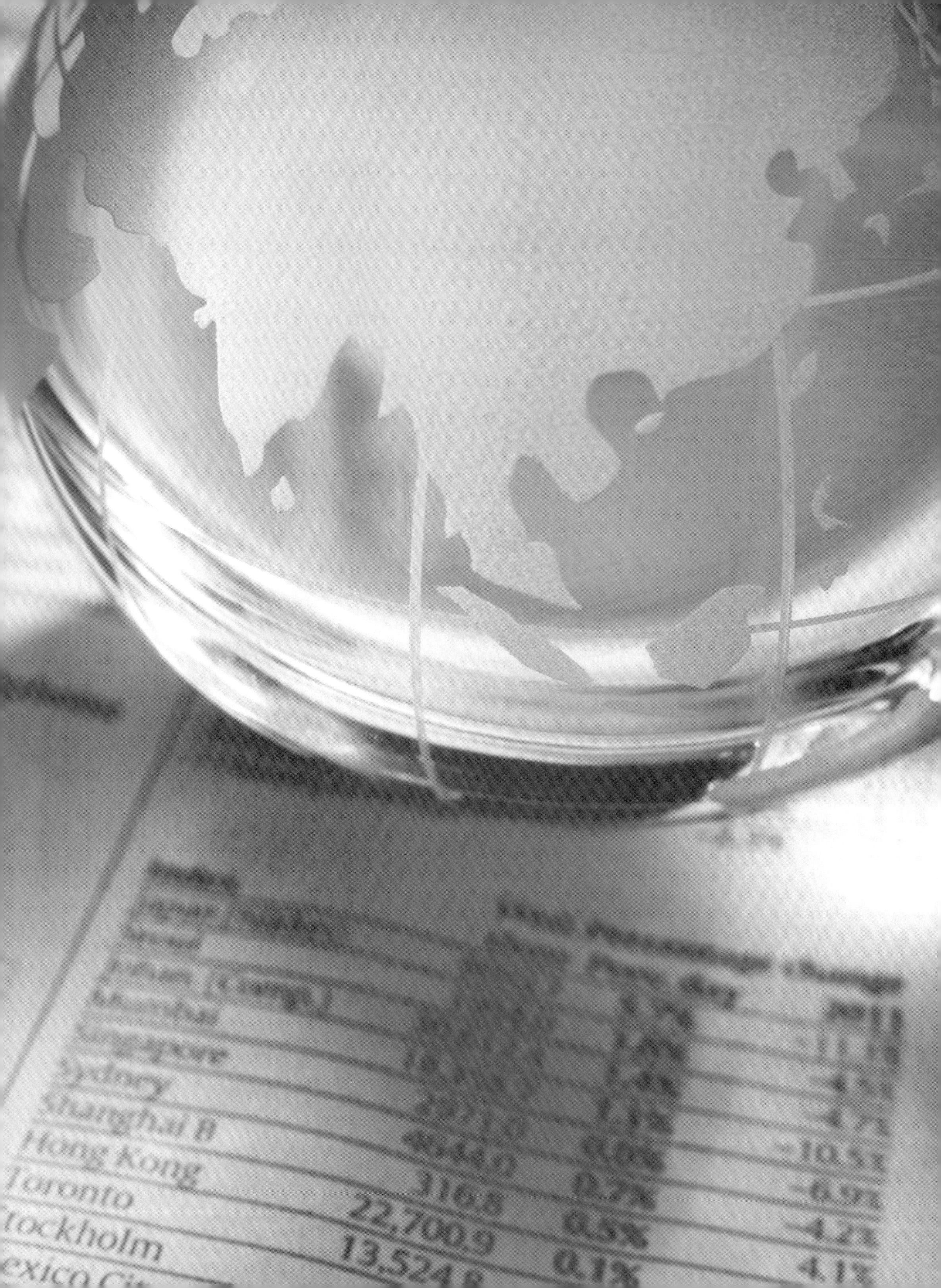

READING
19

Equity Market Valuation

by Peter C. Stimes, CFA and Stephen E. Wilcox, CFA

LEARNING OUTCOMES

Mastery	The candidate should be able to:
☐	**a** explain the terms of the Cobb-Douglas production function and demonstrate how the function can be used to model growth in real output under the assumption of constant returns to scale;
☐	**b** evaluate the relative importance of growth in total factor productivity, in capital stock, and in labor input given relevant historical data;
☐	**c** demonstrate the use of the Cobb-Douglas production function in obtaining a discounted dividend model estimate of the intrinsic value of an equity market;
☐	**d** critique the use of discounted dividend models and macroeconomic forecasts to estimate the intrinsic value of an equity market;
☐	**e** contrast top-down and bottom-up approaches to forecasting the earnings per share of an equity market index;
☐	**f** discuss the strengths and limitations of relative valuation models;
☐	**g** judge whether an equity market is under-, fairly, or over-valued using a relative equity valuation model.

INTRODUCTION

Economic strength or weakness affects equity prices through its effect on risk-free rates, risk premiums, and corporate earnings. These economic drivers of security prices are often considered fundamental because they will affect security returns throughout most investment horizons. It is widely accepted that equity prices are negatively related to risk-free rates and risk premiums and positively related to earnings growth.

There are, of course, other drivers of equity returns and most of these can be considered behavioral. The cognitive and emotional factors experienced by investors can create both positive and negative feedback mechanisms. Market momentum may thus result in both bull market rallies and bear market declines lasting longer than may be justified by fundamental factors. This reading does not deal specifically with such behavioral drivers. Rather, this reading illustrates the application of economic

Copyright © CFA Institute.

forecasts to the valuation of equity markets. While many factors interact to determine whether equity prices are currently rising or falling, economic fundamentals will ultimately dictate secular equity market price trends.

Section 2 uses GDP forecasts for a developing country, China, to develop inputs for a discounted cash flow valuation of that country's equity market.[1] Section 3 contrasts the top-down and bottom-up valuation approaches. Section 4 explains and critiques popular earnings- and asset-based models to relative equity market valuation. Section 5 summarizes the reading, and practice problems in the CFA Institute format follow.

2. ESTIMATING A JUSTIFIED P/E RATIO

Investors commonly use the market's price-to-earnings (P/E) ratio or multiple to gauge the prospects for future equity returns. Sections 2.1 through 2.3 develop the **Cobb–Douglas production function** (also called the **Cobb–Douglas model**) for obtaining growth rates for an economy and, thus, the dividend growth rate trajectories for a corresponding equity market. This model is particularly useful in the case of developing markets such as China where the structure of the underlying economy has experienced, and may experience, fundamental changes (as compared with the relatively stable growth rates of more developed economies).

In Section 2.4 we apply a form of the dividend discount model known as the H-model to the complicated dividend growth trajectory because it is well suited to instances where near-term growth rates can diverge significantly from the ultimately sustainable dividend growth rate. We also standardize the results in justified P/E form. This facilitates inter-temporal and cross-border market value comparisons. The difference between prevailing P/Es and justified P/Es is a measure of potential investment attractiveness.

As will be shown, the Cobb–Douglas and dividend discount models may also be applied to developed economies and equity markets.

2.1 Neoclassical Approach to Growth Accounting

Growth accounting is used in economics to measure the contribution of different factors—usually broadly defined as capital and labor—to economic growth and, indirectly, to compute the rate of an economy's technological progress. The neoclassical approach to growth accounting uses the Cobb–Douglas production function.[2] This approach can be useful to financial analysts because it gives insights into the long-term potential economic growth in individual countries, in larger regions, and for the world as a whole. The Cobb–Douglas estimate of the growth of total production can help to estimate corporate profit growth and develop corporate cash flow projections for stock market composites.

The basic form of the Cobb–Douglas production function is set forth as Equation 1, where Y represents total real economic output, A is total factor productivity, K is capital stock, α is output elasticity of K, L is labor input, and β is the output elasticity of L. **Total factor productivity (TFP)** is a variable which accounts for that part of Y not directly accounted for by the levels of the production factors (K and L).

$$Y = AK^{\alpha}L^{\beta} \quad (1)$$

---

[1] Forecasts and opinions offered in this reading are those of the authors (or the writers cited) and are not positions of CFA Institute.
[2] See Cobb and Douglas (1928).

Estimating a Justified P/E Ratio

If we assume that the production function exhibits **constant returns to scale** (i.e., a given percentage increase in capital stock and labor input results in an equal percentage increase in output), we can substitute β = (1 − α) into Equation 1.[3] Taking the natural logarithm of both sides of the equation gives

$$\ln(Y) = \ln(A) + \alpha\ln(K) + (1-\alpha)\ln(L) \qquad (2)$$

Taking first differences of Equation 2 and utilizing the fact that, for small changes in any variable x, $\ln(x + \Delta x) - \ln(x) = \ln\left(\frac{x + \Delta x}{x}\right) \approx \frac{\Delta x}{x}$, we obtain the expression:

$$\frac{\Delta Y}{Y} \approx \frac{\Delta A}{A} + \alpha\frac{\Delta K}{K} + (1-\alpha)\frac{\Delta L}{L} \qquad (3)$$

Equation 3 is the expression that we will employ in our analysis. In Equation 3, the percentage growth in real output (or gross domestic product, GDP) is shown as $\Delta Y/Y$, and it is decomposed into its components: $\Delta A/A$ is growth in TFP; $\Delta K/K$ is the growth in the capital stock; $\Delta L/L$ is the growth in the labor input; α is the output elasticity of capital; and 1 − α is the output elasticity of labor where 0 < α < 1.

In practice, all the variables in Equation 3, with the exception of the growth in TFP, are directly observable or can be derived from national income and product accounts.[4] However, growth in TFP is determined using the other inputs as noted by Equation 3 and is commonly referred to as the **Solow residual**.[5]

TFP growth means that aggregate output (i.e., GDP) can grow at a faster rate than would be predicted simply from growth in accumulated capital stock and the labor force. Interpreting TFP as a measure of the level of technology, growth in TFP is often described as a measure of "technical progress" and linked to innovation. As examples, such technological advances as the introduction of the steam engine, electricity, the internal combustion engine, telecommunications, microchips, penicillin, and the internet are thought to have contributed to growth in TFP. However, growth in TFP, as a residual in the sense described, can be driven by factors other than improvements in technology. These factors could be particularly significant in economies that are experiencing major changes in political and/or regulatory structures. As examples, liberalization of trade policies, abolition of restrictions on the movement and ownership of capital and labor, the establishment of peace and the predictable rule of law, and even the dismantling of punitive taxation policies would be expected to contribute to growth in TFP. Finally, growth in TFP can benefit from improvements in the division of labor that arise from the growth of the economy itself. By contrast, developments such as the depletion and degradation of natural resources would detract from growth in TFP.

The robustness and simplicity of the approach we have presented can be tested against the complex and important case of valuing the equity markets in mainland China.

2.2 The China Economic Experience

China has been widely regarded as the most influential emerging economy, and its growth performance since reform has been hailed as an economic miracle. Historical growth accounting results, as presented in Zheng, Hu, and Bigsten (2009), are reported in Exhibit 1. Note particularly the comparisons of China's growth in the capital stock,

---

[3] As a result, if both capital and labor change by a percentage x, then the total change in output is $\alpha x + (1-\alpha)x = x$. The use of constant returns to scale is predicated on empirical results from several large economies over various time periods during the 19th and 20th centuries.

[4] Capital, α, and labor, (1 − α), output elasticities may differ across national economies.

[5] See Solow (1957). The Solow residual is thus simply: $\frac{\Delta A}{A} \approx \frac{\Delta Y}{Y} - \alpha\frac{\Delta K}{K} - (1-\alpha)\frac{\Delta L}{L}$

$\Delta K/K$, and growth in the labor input, $\Delta L/L$, to those of the (former) Soviet Union, United States, and European Union. The growth in capital stock stands out particularly for China and is most apparent during the period of economic liberalization that commenced in the early 1990s. According to estimates by the World Bank and other institutions, the gross effective savings in China (loosely defined as investment in plant, property, equipment, and inventories) divided by economic output have been in the neighborhood of 40 percent. This compares with 15 to 20 percent over the comparable periods for the other countries in Exhibit 1.

Exhibit 1 Historical Growth Accounting for China, the (Former) Soviet Union, United States, and European Union

Countries	Time Period	Real GDP Growth $\Delta Y/Y$ (%)	Growth in Total Factor Productivity $\Delta A/A$ (%)	Growth in Capital Stock $\Delta K/K$ (%)	Growth in Labor Input $\Delta L/L$ (%)
China	1978–1995	10.11	3.80	9.12	3.49
	1995–2007	9.25	1.45	12.81	2.78
Soviet Union	1950–1970	5.4	1.6	8.8	1.8
	1970–1985	2.7	−0.4	7.0	1.1
United States	1950–1972	3.9	1.6	2.6	1.4
	1972–1996	3.3	0.6	3.1	1.7
	1996–2004	3.6	1.5	2.6	0.7
European Union	1960–1973	5.1	3.2		4.8
	1973–2003	2.2	1.0	0.5	2.8

Source: Zheng, Hu, and Bigsten (2009). China's output elasticity for capital (α) and output elasticity for labor (1 − α) were both estimated to be 0.5.

Concerns over the sustainability of China's growth have emerged in recent years because, as is evident from Exhibit 1, the growth in TFP has slowed. Zheng, Bigsten, and Hu (2006) studied the Chinese economy and found that reform measures had a significant positive impact on TFP, but this impact should be considered a one-time event. These authors make a case that China should now focus on achieving sustained increases in productivity.

Exhibit 1 also shows that Chinese economic growth has been largely driven by growth in the capital stock. Zheng, Bigsten, and Hu note that government policies in the mid- to late 1990s supported this extraordinary growth in investments. Key input prices were kept low through subsidies, and controlled pricing and a high savings rate allowed for the availability of cheap credit. A huge trade surplus has been another side-effect of both high investment[6] and an unsustainably low fixed exchange-rate policy designed to support exports. China's foreign reserves are currently the world's largest by a considerable amount and have recently surpassed $2 trillion.[7] Because of this, China is facing excessive growth in its money supply, and there are concerns about potential bubbles in both real estate and share prices. (Recent year-over-year growth in the broad M2 measure of the money supply has been over 25 percent.[8])

---

[6] In lieu of higher consumption spending, particularly on imported goods.
[7] Preston (2009).
[8] Xin and Rabinovitch (2009).

A necessary, eventual "course correction" in exchange rate and monetary policies would reduce or reverse the forces that contributed to a de facto subsidization of capital formation.

In addition to the foregoing structural factors, changes in consumer behavior are also likely to cause the Chinese savings/investment rate to moderate. Altogether, government policy changes, structural imbalances, and an increased propensity to consume all point to an eventual reduction from the double-digit growth rates of capital stock. At the same time, while the labor force of China has grown at a much more rapid pace than for European and American economies, this has been attributable both to higher population growth rates and to a rise in labor force participation rates. The Chinese population growth rate has slowed to less than 1.0 percent per year in recent years, according to the World Bank. Furthermore, major changes in labor force participation rates, largely due to more people leaving rural occupations and household/childcare activities, represent one-time changes rather than sustainable trends. In sum, these considerations suggest that Chinese economic growth will eventually moderate, which is consistent with the economic history for the Soviet Union, United States, and European Union presented in Exhibit 1.

Finally, in addition to the factors above, an investment analyst might wish to consider other, more qualitative factors in producing a long-term growth forecast (e.g., China's educational system or pollution side-effects of China's strategy of rapid capital formation). Because adjustments for such factors would typically have a large judgmental element, this reading does not address them.

Example 1

The Neoclassical Approach to Growth

1. The savings rate for a national economy is comparatively stable. The economy faces a sharp uptick in energy prices and at the same time imposes stringent restrictions on environmental pollution. The combined impact of energy and environmental factors renders a large portion of the existing stock of manufacturing equipment and structures economically obsolescent. What is the impact on the economy according to Equation 3?

2. A country experiences a sharp demographic rise in the divorce rate and single-parent households. Using the framework of Equations 1 and 3, what is likely to happen to total national production, total per capita income, and total income per household?

Solution to 1:

The sudden, unexpected obsolescence of a significant portion of the capital stock means that the percentage growth rate in capital stock in that period will be negative, that is, $\Delta K/K < 0$. All other things being equal, this implies a one-time reduction in economic output. Assuming no change in technological innovation, savings rates, and labor force growth trends, the subsequent long-term growth rates should be relatively close to the previously prevailing growth rates, starting from the lower base value for Y.

Solution to 2:

The change in demographics implies an increase in the aggregate labor force as stay-at-home parents and spouses re-enter the workforce. That is, the labor force will grow, for some period of time, at a pace faster than underlying population growth until a new steady-state labor force participation rate is attained. Total economic production (and income) will thus also rise at an above-trend rate

> during this adjustment period. Above-trend growth in national income, holding population trends constant, means that per capita income will also grow above trend during this period of demographic adjustment. Per-household income, by contrast, will grow at a below-trend rate (and may even decline) due to an uptick in new household formation during the shift in divorce and separation rates to ultimately prevailing steady-state levels.

2.3 Quantifying China's Future Economic Growth

Now that we have covered a simple model for estimating an economy's growth rate, the next step is to apply the model using our best estimates of the model inputs. As in any forecasting exercise, the specific forecasts must be based on currently available information. Any forecast has an "as of" date associated with it. Comparing the forecasts to actual outcomes subsequently, some inputs or elements of the forecast may appear to be misjudged or dated. With that caution in mind, we can proceed to develop our economic growth projections for China.

Zheng, Hu, and Bigsten (2009) offer the GDP growth projections presented in Exhibit 2 for China, the United States, and the European Union. The forecast of an 8 percent GDP growth rate for China is consistent with the Chinese government's 8 percent GDP growth target as presented by Premier Wen Jiabao. Zheng, Hu, and Bigsten note their own projections rely heavily on two basic assumptions: 1) growth in the capital stock cannot exceed GDP growth and 2) a TFP growth rate of 2 to 3 percent will prevail for the foreseeable future. These authors believe that the potential for China to absorb new technologies from developed nations is double that for the United States and European Union. Given the history of other developing countries and the record of economic recovery of developed countries after World War II, this does not seem unreasonable.

Exhibit 2 Growth Projections (2009–2030)

Country	Real GDP Growth $\Delta Y/Y$ (%)	Growth in Total Factor Productivity $\Delta A/A$ (%)	Output Elasticity of Capital α	Growth in Capital Stock $\Delta K/K$ (%)	Output Elasticity of Labor $1 - \alpha$	Growth in Labor Input $\Delta L/L$ (%)
China	8.0	2.5	0.5	8.0	0.5	3.0
United States	2.75	1.2	0.3	4.0	0.7	0.5
European Union	2.2	1.0	0.4	3.0	0.6	0.0

Source: Zheng, Hu, and Bigsten (2009).

The neoclassical framework we have presented permits analysts to apply their own forecasts of factors of production, with particular emphasis on how such factor trajectories might change over time. Once the analyst has developed a long-term macro forecast, it can then be used in conjunction with traditional valuation models.

In applying the framework, we modify the Zheng, Hu, and Bigsten ("ZHB") projections by using a lower estimate of the growth rate in the labor force, since World Bank data indicate that population growth in China now appears to have declined to below 1.0 percent annually. At the same time, we are inclined to think that savings and investment rates will only decline gradually from over 35 percent of GDP, thereby keeping the growth rate of capital stock much higher than the 8 percent per annum assumed by ZHB. We have no disagreement with the ZHB projection of 2.5 percent

Estimating a Justified P/E Ratio

per year for TFP growth. If we utilize the labor and capital elasticities from the ZHB study, a reasonable projection for economic growth would therefore be:

Total factor productivity	plus	Growth in capital stock	plus	Labor force growth	
2.5%	+	0.5 × 12%	+	0.5 × 1.5%	= 9.25%

This near-term rate is higher than the ZHB forecast, the official forecast of the Chinese government, and the consensus of many economic forecasters. We note, however, that there are several factors that are consistent with our higher near-term forecast. First, actual real growth has cumulatively exceeded the 8 percent Chinese official growth target of the past several years. Second, and more importantly, our forecast is to be thought of as a normalized forecast of sustainable cash flow growth potential.

While our near-term forecast for economic growth is higher than ZHB and the Chinese government, the reasoning set forth in the preceding section leads us to believe that economic growth will gradually decline to levels lower than the ZHB analysis.[9] This is because, as economies develop and as the stock of accumulated capital per person rises, savings rates tend to decline and TFP trends fall to levels closer to those of more highly developed countries. Finally, although labor force growth can exceed population growth for some time (as labor force participation rates increase), in the long run, labor force growth is constrained by population growth. China appears to be on its way towards zero population growth (much like Japan and Western Europe). With this in mind, an ultimately sustainable economic growth rate might be:

Total factor productivity	plus	Growth in capital stock	plus	Labor force growth	
1.25%	+	0.5 × 6%	+	0.5 × 0.0%	= 4.25%

2.4 Equity Market Valuation

In this section we translate macroeconomic forecasts into corporate cash flow forecasts and combine those corporate forecasts with an appropriate discounted cash flow model to estimate the intrinsic value of an equity market in terms of justified P/E ratios.

The growth rate of corporate earnings and dividend cash flow, adjusted for inflation, should bear a close relationship with real GDP growth over the long term. For purposes of this analysis, we assume that earnings and dividend cash flow for the underlying comprehensive stock composite grow at the same rate as the core growth rate of Chinese GDP.[10]

In theory, we would like to be able to forecast, year by year, each of the underlying factors of production and the change in TFP. In practice, however, we recognize that a less complicated cash flow representation might be more suitable, because it lessens the possibility of compounding forecast errors. Fuller and Hsia (1984) developed a valuation model, known as the **H-model**, in which dividend *growth rates* are expected to decline in a linear fashion, over a finite horizon, towards an ultimately sustainable rate from the end of that horizon into perpetuity. It incorporates a growth rate in dividends that is expected to prevail in the initial period g_S, a period of years, N, where the dividend growth rate declines in a linear fashion, and a long-term dividend

---
9 Our forecast is for a 30-year time period and was made in the summer of 2009. As noted in Exhibit 2, the ZHB forecast was for 2009–2030. We believe the choice of a longer time horizon for our forecast is also supportive of the choice of a lower terminal growth rate.
10 In principle, the sector of publicly traded companies could grow somewhat above or below the overall growth rate of GDP, because it is a subset of the overall economy. However, the approach used in the text should serve as a good approximation for analytical purposes.

growth rate g_L that is expected to prevail to perpetuity beginning at the end of period N. With an initial annualized dividend rate at time zero of D_0 and a discount rate to perpetuity of r, the H-model estimate of value, V_0, is given by Equation 4:

$$V_0 = \frac{D_0}{r - g_L}\left[(1 + g_L) + \frac{N}{2}(g_s - g_L)\right] \tag{4}$$

The H-model provides a convenient means for modeling initially high ("supernormal") dividend growth rates that gradually transition to a lower, long-run growth at a constant mature-stage growth rate. The H-model involves an approximation to the value estimate that would result from period-by-period discounting of cash flows in the phase prior to the mature or terminal phase when a constant growth rate is assumed. The approximation is generally very good in most practical situations and the gain from using an approximation is an easy to evaluate expression.[11] In the case of valuation of mature developed equity markets, the Gordon (constant) growth dividend discount model would be more commonly used than the H-model because supernormal growth would not generally need to be modeled in such cases.

In our valuation analysis, we express the discount rate and both growth factors in real, that is, inflation-adjusted terms. A key to valuation is consistency: stating variables consistently on a nominal basis or consistently on a real basis are both feasible approaches. Economists, however, typically prefer to use real variables as they tend to be more stable and, therefore, easier to predict than their nominal counterparts.

We use our growth rate trajectory and apply the H-model to the S&P China BMI Index. This index underlies the SPDR S&P China ETF, which is an exchange-traded fund designed to track the investment performance of the mainland China and (to a much lesser extent) Hong Kong stock markets. Both the underlying stocks and the ETF itself are avenues in which both Chinese and non-Chinese investors may obtain participation in the Chinese equity markets. The index underlying the ETF and the information provided by the ETF's sponsor (State Street Global Advisors) provide up-to-date information that can enter traditional valuation models.

In evaluating the investment attractiveness of a market index, we utilize a price–earnings ratio or P/E approach. Because of the behavioral factors mentioned in the introduction, prices of equities and equity market composites tend to vary more than underlying normalized earnings and growth prospects. P/E analysis permits us to make useful inter-temporal valuation comparisons and has the additional benefit of providing intuition when making comparisons across international borders. As of 15 July 2009, the forward or prospective P/E ratio for the underlying S&P China BMI Index was 19.1 (this P/E is the level of the S&P China BMI Index divided by year-ahead expected earnings for that index). In the following analysis, we estimate what justified P/E ratios should be under differing inflation-adjusted equity discount rates and for different estimates of the ultimately prevailing terminal inflation-adjusted dividend growth rate to perpetuity.

The (forward) **justified P/E** is the estimated intrinsic value divided by year-ahead expected earnings; in this case we are estimating intrinsic value using the H-model. Reflecting the meaning of *justified* here as *warranted by fundamentals*, price in the justified P/E ratio is assumed in this discussion to equal intrinsic value as estimated by the valuation model, i.e., P_0 (or P) = V_0.[12] In all instances, we assume

---

[11] Valuation differences between the H-Model and a period-by-period approach should be minimal so long as the differences between long-term and interim growth rates are of single-digit magnitude and the "interim" period length is not much longer than 30-40 years. In any event, the possible valuation error from adopting a simpler model is reasonable in comparison with the incremental valuation error that can arise from introducing an excessive number of valuation parameters, i.e., year-by-year cash flows.

[12] Analysts and practitioners may, if desired, proceed directly to forecasting a justified market index *level* based on the H-Model, the current dividend rate, and the growth-factor inputs. (Strictly speaking, the H-Model does not directly utilize earnings per share, although, indirectly, the trajectory of dividend growth is assumed to be supported by growth in EPS.) Under our approach, the relative differences in P/E ratios in Exhibits 3 and 4 translate directly into the relative differences between observed and justified market levels.

Estimating a Justified P/E Ratio

that core inflation-adjusted growth rates decline in a linear fashion over a 30-year time horizon from the 9.25 percent per year we estimate for year one.[13] The 30-year time horizon is selected both because it is a round number and because it is not unlike other historical instances where national economies experienced fundamental changes in political and economic structure, the notable examples being post-World War II European economies and Japan both in the late 19th century and after World War II.

Exhibit 3 Justified P/E Ratios for Chinese Equity Market at Mid-Year 2009

Terminal Real Growth Rate (%)	\multicolumn{7}{c}{Real Equity Discount Rate}
	6.00%	6.50%	7.00%	7.50%	8.00%	8.50%	9.00%	9.50%
3	26.8	23.0	20.1	17.9	16.1	14.6	13.4	12.4
4	37.3	29.9	24.9	21.3	18.7	16.6	14.9	13.6
5	69.0	46.0	34.5	27.6	23.0	19.7	17.2	15.3

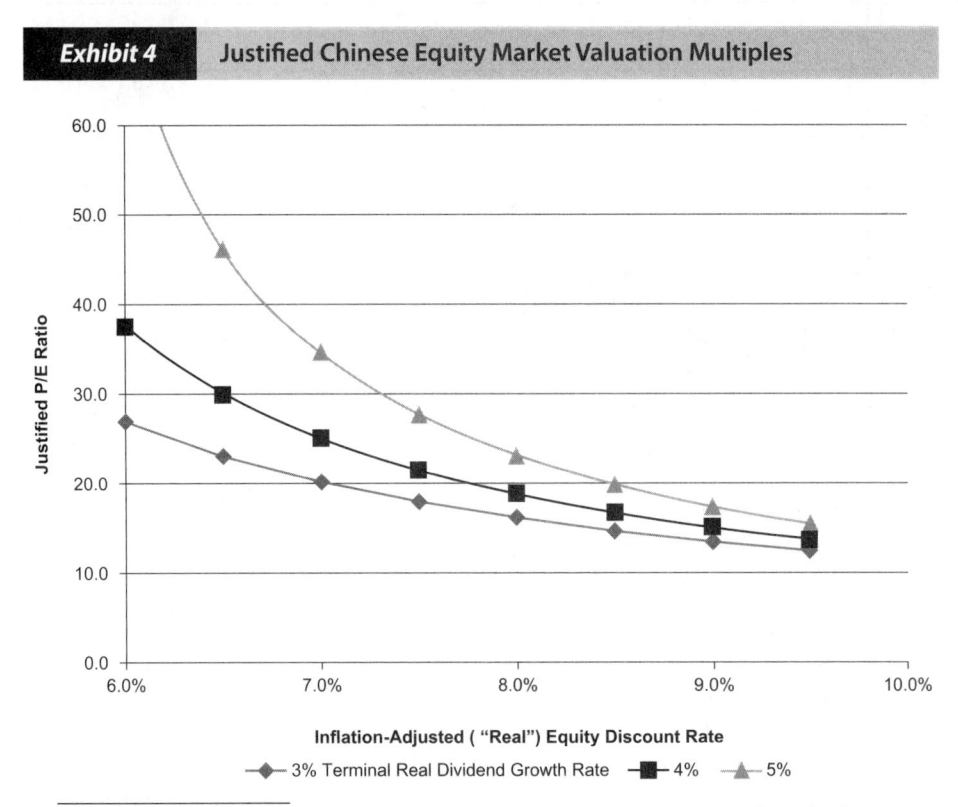

Exhibit 4 Justified Chinese Equity Market Valuation Multiples

Note: Chinese Equity Markets Justified P/Es: 30-Year Transition from 9.25% Real Dividend Growth Rate to Various Terminal Growth Rates to Perpetuity.

---

13 The geometric average growth rate during the 30-year period is around 6.7%. Also of interest, the *average* compound growth rate for the first 20 years is not far off from the ZHB 20-year 8% annual growth rate.

In Exhibit 3 and Exhibit 4, we have presented justified P/E ratios. Interpolating visually, the observed 19.1 P/E ratio on 15 July 2009, assuming a terminal 4.25 percent real dividend growth rate to perpetuity, is consistent with a real equity discount rate just under 8.0 percent.

This leads immediately to the question of what the proper discount rate should be. To answer this we would like to know a little bit about both the volatility of Chinese equity prices and how such return/volatility prospects compare with other world equity markets.

In Exhibit 5, we present cumulative return data for both the S&P China BMI Index and the S&P 500. The data series commence in 2001, the point at which the China BMI Index data are first available, and a point by which mainland Chinese equity markets had become seasoned and widely accessible to non-Chinese investors.[14]

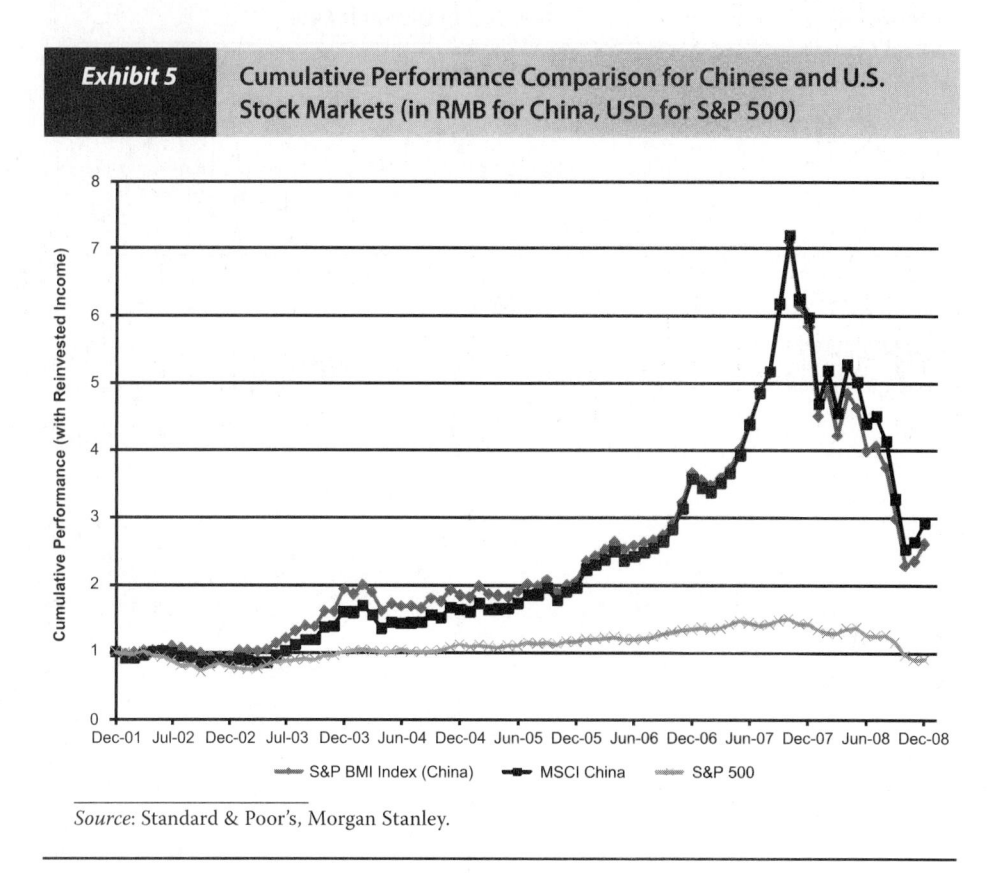

Exhibit 5 Cumulative Performance Comparison for Chinese and U.S. Stock Markets (in RMB for China, USD for S&P 500)

Source: Standard & Poor's, Morgan Stanley.

Over the 7-year period, the cumulative return of Chinese equities far outpaced those of the United States. However, Chinese markets also experienced more of a bubble and subsequent collapse, resulting in a much higher volatility of returns. For China, the annualized return over this time frame approached an inflation-adjusted 13 percent. This outpaced the return one would have expected even from coupling a 2 to 2.5 percent dividend yield with an aggressive core dividend real growth rate of 9 percent. The cumulative return benefited from a positive shift in P/E ratios between the beginning and end of the measurement period. In fact, the P/E expansion and subsequent contraction appear to be the chief cause of the 2007 Chinese bubble and the following collapse.

---

14 To check the reasonableness of the data, we computed the cumulative total returns for the Morgan Stanley Capital International (MSCI) China Index and found them in good accord with the S&P China BMI Index.

Estimating a Justified P/E Ratio

By comparison, the equity markets in the United States were much less volatile, although the cumulative return, particularly net of inflation, was negative. Assuming a 6 percent inflation-adjusted discount rate for the U.S. equity market (in line with long-term historical realized returns), the cumulative nominal return—incorporating the 2.6 percent average inflation rate—would have resulted in an ending cumulative return index value of around 1.80 in December 2008 (compared with the 2.61 achieved by the S&P China BMI Index). The explanation for the poor performance by U.S. equities was largely attributable to a contraction from the high normalized P/E valuation relationships prevailing in 2001 to the below-average levels at the end of the period. Additional evidence is presented in Exhibit 6.

Exhibit 6 Return and Volatility Data

31 December 2001 – 31 December 2008

	S&P China BMI (%)	MSCI China (%)	S&P 500 (%)
Annualized nominal total return[1]	14.7	16.6	−1.5
Annualized standard deviation of total returns[2]	29.4	29.4	14.3
Annualized inflation rate[3]	3.7	3.7	2.6

Notes:
[1] In RMB for Chinese composites, USD for S&P 500.
[2] Based on monthly observations.
[3] Data through 2007, reflects changes in GDP deflator.

Sources: Standard & Poor's, Morgan Stanley, Bloomberg, World Bank.

In establishing a reasonable discount rate to apply to our cash flow forecasts, we should take into account the higher volatility of Chinese markets, which has arisen in part because of structural macroeconomic instabilities (discussed above) and the evolution of their legal and regulatory systems.

The higher observed volatility also has arisen from behavioral shifts in P/E relationships that are more pronounced than those usually seen in U.S. and European markets. Such valuation-induced price volatility is not unusual for any market that is new by historical standards and has been experienced in the past by U.S., European, and Japanese markets in their own long paths to economic maturity. Furthermore, because the bulk of mainland equities are still 75 percent owned (directly or indirectly) by the mainland Chinese government, there is an overhanging risk of intervention or divestiture that might be occasioned by non-economic motives. However, the possibility of denationalization, such as carried out by the United Kingdom in the 1980s, might be viewed more as a market opportunity than as a risk.

The effect of higher volatility on required returns might be somewhat mitigated to the extent 1) market returns are less than perfectly correlated with other international equity markets and 2) cross-border investing and divesting of equities is freely achievable by investors both inside and outside of China.

On balance, the foregoing factors suggest that the required real equity discount rate be higher in China than, for example, in the United States. This naturally leads us to investigate both what the realized real equity discount rate has been in the United States and what real equity discount rates are predicted based on alternative theoretical models. Historical studies have been undertaken[15] which indicate that a prospective

---

[15] Ibbotson and Sinquefield (1989), Siegel (1992), Arnott and Bernstein (2002), Siegel (2005).

inflation-adjusted equity discount rate[16] in the area of 5–7 percent is reasonable. Work based on macroeconomic, corporate finance, and financial market equilibrium[17] suggests that a slightly higher range might be possible in equilibrium. Purely theoretical models have had mixed results. The utility function models,[18] for example, find that real discount rates in the 5–7 percent area are well above what can be justified by underlying market volatility. On the other hand, a theoretical approach[19] simply based on prospective wealth accumulation under different volatility assumptions is consistent with the results actually realized in the U.S. historical record.

In the volatile economic and market conditions at the time this reading is being written (2009), the higher end of the discount rate estimates seem to be in order for the United States. If we place these at 6–7 percent, the additional relative risk considerations for the Chinese market suggest that a required discount rate for that market might be in the range of 7.5–8.5 percent. This is a necessarily judgmental adjustment but should 1) reflect an analyst's view of differential riskiness (in the context of a well-diversified international portfolio) and 2) reflect congruence with historical realized return differentials between markets that were then seasoned and those that were then developing.

Referring back to Exhibit 4 and integrating our view of the real (i.e., inflation-adjusted) equity discount rate with the sustainable dividend growth rates obtained from our macroeconomic framework, we can conclude that the currently observed 19.1 forward P/E ratio for Chinese equities is not unreasonable. As a further check, we note that a 19.1 P/E would be somewhat on the high side for seasoned U.S. and European stock markets. However, reflecting much higher growth prospects over the next several decades, a much higher Chinese P/E ratio would be warranted (although the impact would be somewhat offset by a greater discount rate reflecting higher volatility in China) as compared with U.S. and European markets.

Inherent in our analysis of equity composites is the difficulty of specifying precise price or P/E ratios at which a "buy" or "sell" recommendation is to be made. However, the strength of this kind of relative value approach is that, in a diversified portfolio context, investors can usually make reasonable decisions—at the margin—whether it is then appropriate to raise or lower market exposures relative to the investable universe in the aggregate. The price/value relationships prevailing at the date of the analysis were such that those investing on a fundamental basis should have a weighting in Chinese equities close to their baseline or normal-strategy allocation.[20] Stated differently, only those with a very optimistic long-term dividend growth rate forecast and/or a low required discount rate would find the Chinese market to have substantially better than average current attractiveness.

Example 2

Equity Market Valuation Using Dividend Discount Models

1. The S&P China BMI Index on 30 September 2009 is 358. Forecasted 12-month earnings per share for the composite are 18.00 RMB, and the current annual dividend rate for the composite is 7.90 RMB. Assuming an 8.0 percent inflation-adjusted equity discount rate, a 30-year decline in dividend growth rates from an initial growth rate of 8.25 percent, and a terminal sustainable growth rate to perpetuity of 4.25 percent, compute the composite index price level implied by the H-Model (Equation 4). Next compute the justified P/E ratio implied by such price level.

---

[16] Geometrically compounded.
[17] Ibbotson, Diermeier, and Siegel (1984), Stimes (2008).
[18] Mehra and Prescott (1985), Mehra (2003).
[19] Arnott (2004).
[20] Which could, of course, be zero.

Estimating a Justified P/E Ratio

2. Assuming the same annualized dividend rate of 7.90 RMB, using the Gordon growth model compute the discount rate required to reproduce the prevailing index level of 358 under different growth assumptions, specifically assuming an 8 percent real growth rate of dividends to perpetuity, rather than a gradually slackening rate of growth as in Question 1. Evaluate the result.

3. Assuming the same information in Question 1, what would be the appropriate composite index price level and justified P/E ratio, if the period at which the 4.25 percent growth rate to perpetuity is reached A) at year 20, and B) at year 40?

Solution to 1:

The H-Model states that:

$$V_0 = \frac{D_0}{r - g_L}\left[(1 + g_L) + \frac{N}{2}(g_s - g_L)\right]$$

Inserting the information given, we get

$$V_0 = \frac{7.90}{0.08 - 0.0425}\left[(1 + 0.0425) + \frac{30}{2}(0.0825 - 0.0425)\right] = 346.02$$

Dividing this result by forecasted earnings of 18.00 produces a justified P/E ratio of 19.2.

Solution to 2:

The standard Gordon growth model states that:

$$V_0 = \frac{D_0(1 + g)}{r - g}$$

which can be rearranged as

$$r = \frac{D_0(1 + g)}{V_0} + g$$

Substituting in the given values, we obtain:

$$r = \frac{7.90(1 + 0.08)}{358} + 0.08 = 0.1038 \approx 10.4\%$$

This result, which assumes no slackening in core growth rates, produces an implied discount rate that appears unusually large relative to the prospects of other world equity markets. Given the ability of international portfolio reallocation, even on a constrained basis, capital market equilibrium does not seem consistent with a real equity discount to perpetuity rate almost twice that of mature equity markets. The implication is that Chinese market participants are pricing the index at a lower discount rate, consistent with other worldwide investment opportunities, but also with a more restrained long-term growth outlook relative to those growth rates expected over the next few years.

Solution to 3A:

Assuming an interim period of 20 years, Equation 4 produces:

$$V_0 = \frac{7.90}{0.08 - 0.0425}\left[(1 + 0.0425) + \frac{20}{2}(0.0825 - 0.0425)\right] = 303.89$$

and a P/E = 303.89 ÷ 18 = 16.9.

> **Solution to 3B:**
>
> Assuming an interim period of 40 years, Equation 4 produces:
>
> $$V_0 = \frac{7.90}{0.08 - 0.0425}\left[(1 + 0.0425) + \frac{40}{2}(0.0825 - 0.0425)\right] = 388.15$$
>
> and a justified P/E = 388.15 ÷ 18 = 21.6

The possible criticisms of our approach should not be overlooked. From a practical perspective, there may be severe problems with the accuracy of data inputs. It is difficult enough to obtain macroeconomic data in developed countries with long-established methods and facilities. In developing markets or in economies experiencing profound governmental and structural change, such as the Eastern Bloc after the fall of the Berlin Wall, the problems of obtaining accurate and, more importantly, historically consistent, data are multiplied. The same fluidity in political and demographic fundamentals also calls into question whether companies' growth rates will track GDP growth rates. In certain instances, there can be long departures between growth rates, meaning that for long periods of time the share of corporate profits may be rising or declining relative to GDP.

The analysis in this reading has also focused on inflation-adjusted income, cash flow, and discount rates. In a global economy with reasonably robust currency exchange markets and where monetary growth is targeted to keep inflation at manageable levels, this is probably appropriate. However, hyperinflation, currency instability, and other trade disequilibria have occurred far too frequently from a historical perspective to be overlooked. In the presence of such factors, the confidence of our model's approach could be diminished.

> **Example 3**
>
> ## Applying Valuation Methodology to a Developed Economy
>
> In the following, assume that all growth and discount rates are stated in real terms.
>
> 1. Assume the Eurozone inflation-adjusted average growth in capital stock is 3.0 percent per annum into perpetuity. Long-term labor force growth is expected to remain stable at 0.0 percent, while TFP growth is projected to average 1.0 percent per annum over time. If the output elasticity of capital is 0.4 and the output elasticity of labor is 0.6, calculate the implied growth rate of Eurozone GDP.
>
> 2. The Dow Jones Euro Stoxx 50 Index is comprised of mature, large capital common equities domiciled in the Euro currency zone. At 30 September 2009 the index level stood at 2450. Forecasted 12-month dividends per share for the composite (net of withholding tax) are €125.00. Because of the mature nature of the economy and the particular market composite, you project that growth in both inflation-adjusted earnings and dividends will equal that of GDP. Using the Gordon constant dividend growth rate model solved for the discount rate, estimate the implied inflation-adjusted discount rate to perpetuity.
>
> 3. **A.** Applying the Gordon growth model to value the DJ Euro Stoxx 50 Index, you assume that the appropriate discount rate to perpetuity

Top-Down and Bottom-Up Forecasting

should be 6.0 percent. If this assumption is correct, what is the fair value of the DJ Euro Stoxx 50 Index?

B. As of the end of September 2009, the DJ Euro Stoxx 50 Index was trading almost 30 percent below its high of twelve months earlier. What is the likely major cause for the price decline?

Solution to 1:

In the context of Equation 1 from the text, total growth in GDP is:

$$\frac{\Delta Y}{Y} \approx \frac{\Delta A}{A} + \alpha \frac{\Delta K}{K} + (1-\alpha)\frac{\Delta L}{L}$$

Substituting the information given, the GDP growth rate is 2.2 percent, computed as follows:

$$\frac{\Delta Y}{Y} \approx 1.0\% + 0.4 \times 3.0\% + 0.6 \times 0.0\% = 2.2\%$$

Solution to 2:

The Gordon growth model can be rearranged as

$$r = \frac{D_1}{P_0} + g$$

Substituting in the given values for dividends, the index level, and our forecast for dividend growth, we obtain:

$$r = \frac{125}{2450} + 0.022 = 0.051 + 0.022 = 0.073 = 7.3\%$$

Solution to 3A:

The constant growth model gives us the following estimate of the fair value of the DJ Euro Stoxx 50:

$$V_0 = \frac{D_1}{r-g} = \frac{125}{0.06 - 0.022} = 3289$$

This estimate is more than 34 percent above the level observed at 30 September 2009.

Solution to 3B:

Given the mature nature of the underlying economic region and the companies in the composite, it is unlikely that the estimate of long-term, real dividend growth changed much, if at all. If the actual dividends paid also did not change much, the most likely major cause of the price decline is an increase in the discount rate over the period.

3. TOP-DOWN AND BOTTOM-UP FORECASTING

When it comes to predicting equity returns, analytical approaches can be divided into two major categories: top-down and bottom-up. In top-down forecasting, analysts use *macroeconomic* projections to produce return expectations for large stock market composites, such as the S&P 500, the Nikkei 225, or the FTSE 100. These can then be further refined into return expectations for various market sectors and industry groups within the composites. At the final stage, such information can, if desired, be distilled into projected returns for individual securities.

By contrast, bottom-up forecasting begins with the *microeconomic* outlook for the fundamentals of individual companies. An analyst can use this information to develop predicted investment returns for each security. If desired, the forecasts for individual security returns can be aggregated into expected returns for industry groupings, market sectors, and for the equity market as a whole.

Exhibit 7 sets forth the manner in which top-down and bottom-up approaches are typically implemented. Top-down can be characterized as moving from the general to the specific, while bottom-up forecasting moves from the specific to the general. Depending on the investment strategy and portfolio context, one of the types of forecasting may be more suitable. In other instances, both types of forecasting may be useful. In those cases where both top-down and bottom-up are used, the additional work involved may provide valuable insights.

Exhibit 7 Comparison of Top-Down and Bottom-Up Analyses

Top-Down Analysis

- Market analysis: Examine valuations in different equity markets to identify those with superior expected returns.
  - Compare relative value measures for each equity market to their historical values to identify those markets where equities are relatively cheap or expensive.
  - Examine the trends in relative value measures for each equity market to identify market momentum.
  - Compare the expected returns for those equity markets expected to provide superior performance to the expected returns for other asset classes, such as bonds, real estate, and commodities.
- Industry analysis: Evaluate domestic and global economic cycles to determine those industries expected to be top performers in the best-performing equity markets.
  - Compare relative growth rates and expected profit margins across industries.
  - Identify those industries that will be favorably impacted by expected trends in interest rates, exchange rates, and inflation.
- Company analysis: Identify the best stocks in those industries that are expected to be top-performers in the best-performing equity markets.

Bottom-Up Analysis

- Company analysis: Identify a rationale for why certain stocks should be expected to outperform, without regard to the prevailing macroeconomic conditions.
  - Identify reasons why a company's products, technology, or services should be expected to be successful.
  - Evaluate the company's management, history, business model, and growth prospects.
  - Use discounted cash flow models to determine expected returns for individual securities.
- Industry analysis: Aggregate expected returns for stocks within an industry to identify the industries that are expected to be the best performers.
- Market analysis: Aggregate expected industry returns to identify the expected returns for every equity market.

3.1 Portfolio Suitability of Each Forecasting Type

In theory and practice, it is not necessary for either top-down or bottom-up forecasting to be carried to the final step shown for each method in Exhibit 7. For example, if a portfolio focuses primarily on tactical asset allocation among different market composites (and/or different industry groups within such composites), a top-down forecast may not need to focus all the way down to the relative merits of individual securities.

Likewise, there are instances where either the investment strategy or specific portfolio constraints dictate a focus primarily on individual security returns. In such instances, the unique factors pertaining to particular securities may render the need to study industry and market composite unnecessary. In such cases, the bottom-up method stops well short of the top. The partial application of each method is developed in the following examples.

> **Example 4**
>
> ### Growth Model Questions
>
> Explain whether top-down or bottom-up forecasting is more appropriate for each of the different investors.
>
> 1. The MegaCosmos Mutual Fund has a stated goal of investing in the stock market composites of developed country economies in North America, Western Europe, and Japan. Its return target is expressed in euros. The Fund may or may not hedge individual country currency returns depending on its outlook for foreign exchange rates. Furthermore, the Fund attempts to track individual country stock market composites while minimizing tracking error via the use of index baskets wherever possible.
>
> 2. EMF Advisers is a boutique firm that manages a dedicated portfolio of electric, gas, and water utility companies domiciled in the United States. The portfolio EMF oversees is, in turn, a small part of the American Pipefitters Union Pension Plan.
>
> 3. Bocage International is a hedge fund that actively bets on the relative attractiveness of stocks, interest rates, currencies, and commodities. Its investment in equities is limited to futures and options on exchange-traded equity indexes.
>
> 4. Alpha Bet Partnership is an investment vehicle featuring a U.S. long/short overlay. Specifically, the partnership may keep short positions in U.S. equities in an amount not to exceed 30 percent of the net value of the partnership. All short positions must be invested in U.S. equities to maintain an overall beta of 1.0. The partnership hopes for the stocks it owns to outperform the stocks it has sold short in order to generate a respectable alpha. The partnership specifies that with the objective of minimizing tracking error, every stock sold short must be matched by a stock bought in the same industry.
>
> **Solution to 1:**
>
> MegaCosmos' ability to carry out its strategy will depend on its ability to forecast economic factors at a very "macro" scale. It would employ a top-down approach involving an examination of the economic strength of different international economies, different fiscal and tax policies among the governments involved, and international trade patterns and currency flows. MegaCosmos' desire to track underlying national markets quite closely means that its holdings will not diverge materially from the particular market composites selected. Individual

security selection will not be much of a focus, thereby minimizing the need for continuing the top-down analysis as low as individual market sectors, industry groups, or securities.

Solution to 2:

EMF Advisers' ability to carry out its strategy will depend on its ability to select among different securities within the very specific niche to which it has been assigned by the pension plan sponsor. As a result, bottom-up forecasting is most appropriate and probably no higher than the industry level in any great detail. The plan sponsor, however, will need to be concerned with top-down forecasting to determine the appropriate allocation to EMF's strategy.

Solution to 3:

Bocage's situation is very similar to that of MegaCosmos in Question 1, and top-down forecasting is thus appropriate. In Bocage's case, exposure to individual stocks is not permitted so the analysis need not be carried down to the level of industry groups or market sectors.

Solution to 4:

There are two parts to the answer for Alpha Bet. Because the underlying beta is targeted at 1.0, this portion of the strategy can be considered passive and very little or no top-down forecasting is required. In contrast, the remaining portion of the strategy, the long/short overlay, involves pure security selection on a "matched" or "paired trades" basis. Within each long/short combination, aggregate factors (global, market, industry) cancel each other out, because both long and short candidates must be matched to the same country, market, and industry. Only specific factors affecting each of the two paired companies matter. Therefore, a bottom-up forecast is necessary—and one that likely does not need to go above the level of individual securities.

3.2 Using Both Forecasting Types

When engaged in fundamental securities analysis, it can be wise to use both top-down and bottom-up forecasting. However, when we use both approaches, we often find ourselves in the situation of the person with two clocks, each displaying a different time. They may both be wrong, but they cannot both be right!

It is frequently the case that top-down and bottom-up forecasts provide significantly different results. In such instances, the analyst should investigate the underlying data, assumptions, and forecast methods before employing them as a basis for investment decisions. After all, if forecasts cannot be consistent with each other, at least one of them cannot be consistent with underlying reality.

Because we are fallible human beings, most forecasting discrepancies arise from our own limited knowledge, errors, and incomplete assumptions. Reconciling top-down and bottom-up forecasts is therefore a discipline that can help prevent us from taking inappropriate investment actions. In other words, most of the time, the aggregate market consensus will tend to be more accurate than the individual forecasts that comprise the consensus. The reconciling and revision process is therefore useful in helping us better understand the market consensus.

However, in rare and significant instances, we will find that carefully retracing the steps reveals a gap between the two forecast types that gives rise to significant market opportunities. In such instances, the process of reconciling the two types of forecasts creates instances where we differ significantly and correctly from the consensus.

Top-Down and Bottom-Up Forecasting

Recent years have provided major examples of this. In the early 2000s, top-down forecasts provided much more subdued outlooks compared to bottom-up projections for corporate profits, both in the aggregate and for particular industries. In the tech area, both consumer and capital spending on computer equipment were below the projected sales growth that companies, and the analysts following them, were individually expecting. After all, individual companies were optimistic about their own prospects. However, in the aggregate, many of their technologies and products competed with each other. Thus, the success of some companies meant the failure of others, and this natural, competitive offsetting tendency was correctly reflected in aggregate, top-down sales growth for the industry.

Aggregating the bottom-up forecasts of individual companies, however, produced a wildly inflated forecast of both sales quantities and average prices and profit margins. Thus, the high-tech "bubble" originated from the mistaken principle that *all* the companies could be above average. For those who recognized the inconsistency of the top-down and bottom-up forecasts, and the accuracy of the top-down forecast, much of the carnage of the bubble collapse was avoided.

More recently, the collapse of equity markets in developed countries was a case where bottom-up forecasts proved their superiority over top-down approaches. In both the United States and the United Kingdom, some banking and real estate analysts perceived the excesses in residential real estate in a microeconomic sense. Those who pushed their analyses to a macro conclusion realized that certain large financial institutions were imperiled, particularly the highly levered Fannie Mae and Freddie Mac in the United States. Those who understood the pressure on these and other large financial institutions correctly foresaw that then-prevailing worldwide forecasts of economic activity and equity market returns were dramatically overstated.

3.3 Top-Down and Bottom-Up Forecasting of Market Earnings per Share

Two different methods are employed when estimating earnings for a market index, such as the S&P 500 Index. The first is to add up the individual estimates of the companies in the index. This is referred to as the bottom-up earnings estimate. The top-down estimate relies on forecasts for various macroeconomic variables and a model that fits these forecasts to past trends in aggregate earnings.

Example 5

Comparing and Evaluating Top-Down and Bottom-Up Forecasts

Standard & Poor's July 2009 top-down and bottom-up forecasts for operating earnings per share appear in Exhibit 8. Note that the bottom-up forecasts are more optimistic than the top-down forecasts.

Exhibit 8   Standard & Poor's Forecasts: July 2009

Quarter Ending	Operating Earnings per Share (Estimates Are Bottom-Up)	Operating Earnings per Share (Estimates Are Top-Down)	Difference
31 Dec 2010	$20.39	$12.50	$7.89
30 Sep 2010	19.11	11.42	7.69
30 Jun 2010	18.00	11.18	6.82

(continued)

Exhibit 8	Continued		
Quarter Ending	Operating Earnings per Share (Estimates Are Bottom-Up)	Operating Earnings per Share (Estimates Are Top-Down)	Difference
31 Mar 2010	16.59	10.86	5.73
31 Dec 2009	16.25	11.72	4.53
30 Sep 2009	15.05	11.68	3.37
30 Jun 2009	14.06	11.05	3.01

The bottom-up projection starts from a June 2009 level of earnings that is some 27 percent above the top-down estimate. Furthermore, the annualized growth of estimated earnings over the subsequent 18 months is 28.1 percent for the bottom-up forecast and a much lower 8.6 percent for the top-down projection.

There are several possible reasons for the forecast discrepancies. First, the bottom-up estimates may be influenced by managers believing that their own company's earnings prospects are better than those for the economy as a whole.[21] This is simple human nature as confirmed by survey results, which consistently report that 85 percent of all drivers think they are better than average.

Alternatively, the bottom-up estimates may be correctly detecting signs of a cyclical economic and profit upturn. Most top-down models are of the econometric type and rely on historical relationships to be the basis for assumptions about the future. Thus, top-down models can be slow in detecting cyclical turns. This would be particularly true if the current statistical relationships between economic variables deviate significantly from their historic norms.

In short, the data indicate that we need to investigate both forecasts in greater detail. Without further analysis, we might be unable to distinguish whether the S&P 500 composite is overvalued, undervalued, or somewhere in between due to the disparity in the two earnings forecasts.

Example 6

Earnings Forecast Revisions

The information in Exhibit 9 was collected from the Standard & Poor's website. Note that actual Q2 2008 EPS for the S&P 500 was $17.02. The percentages for the S&P 500 represent how much Q2 2009 EPS were expected to change from the Q2 2008 amount of $17.02 on a particular forecast date. For example, the estimate for Q2 2009 EPS on 30 September 2008 was that the year-over-year change would be an increase of 49.47 percent:

$$\$17.02(1 + 0.4947) \approx \$25.44$$

On 30 June 2009, the estimate for Q2 2009 EPS was that the year-over-year change would be a decrease of 17.38 percent:

$$\$17.02(1 - 0.1738) \approx \$14.06$$

---

[21] For company EPS estimates, Darrough and Russell (2002) showed that bottom-up forecasts are systematically more optimistic than top-down forecasts. The authors contend this occurs because analysts rely heavily on management's assessment of future profitability and such estimates often are overly optimistic.

Similarly, the percentages for the various industry sectors noted in Exhibit 9 reflect how much Q2 2009 EPS were expected to change from the Q2 2008 amount on a particular forecast date. Exhibit 9 shows that earnings forecast revisions can be significant.

Exhibit 9 Revisions to Bottom-Up Estimates of Operating Earnings per Share Standard & Poor's Forecasts: July 2009

Q2 Estimates	9/30/2008	12/31/2008	3/30/2009	6/30/2009	7/7/2009
S&P 500	49.47%	17.04%	−12.82%	−17.38%	−17.42%
Consumer Discretionary	134.52%	72.02%	−40.30%	36.61%	36.61%
Consumer Staples	14.52%	12.88%	6.83%	2.96%	4.12%
Energy	16.91%	−17.06%	−43.35%	−65.11%	−65.11%
Financials	691.43%	450.48%	289.93%	297.10%	293.35%
Health Care	13.56%	10.41%	4.51%	3.06%	3.06%
Industrials	1.17%	−14.07%	−34.53%	−42.89%	−42.89%
Information Technology	24.12%	−5.04%	−28.02%	−26.31%	−26.31%
Materials	9.30%	−26.85%	−51.13%	−69.52%	−69.52%
Telecommunication Services	26.22%	6.67%	−9.77%	−5.64%	−5.44%
Utilities	14.61%	8.99%	−1.10%	−4.80%	−4.80%
S&P 500 EPS	$25.44	$19.92	$14.84	$14.06	$14.06

Example 7

Bottom-Up and Top-Down Market EPS Forecasts

What considerations might encourage a market analyst to rely more on a top-down or bottom-up forecast of S&P 500 operating earnings?

Solution:

Bottom-up forecasts are based on consensus earnings estimates from equity research analysts covering the S&P 500 stocks. Top-down estimates are often based on econometric methods rather than fundamental analysis of the companies comprising the index.

Analysts frequently wait for information from the companies they follow to change their forecasts. Thus, bottom-up estimates may be more optimistic than top-down heading into a recession, and more pessimistic than top-down coming out. If the belief exists that companies are reacting slowly to changes in economic conditions, then a market analyst may prefer a top-down forecast.

However, top-down earnings forecasting models also have limitations. Most such models rely on the extrapolation of past trends in economic data. As a result, the impact of a significant contemporaneous change in a key economic variable or variables on the stock market may not be accurately predicted by the model. If the belief exists that the economy is on the brink of a significant change, then a market analyst may prefer the bottom-up forecast.

4 RELATIVE VALUE MODELS

Relative value investing is consistent with the popular trading maxim that investors should buy what is cheap and sell what is expensive. The relative value models presented in this section can be used to support the tactical asset allocation decision. They can help to identify times when investors would be well served switching from bonds to stocks, or vice-versa. As an investor, it is important to focus on the markets in a comparative fashion.

4.1 Earnings-Based Models

In its 22 July 1997 Humphrey-Hawkins report to Congress, the United States Federal Reserve compared 1982–1997 10-year Treasury note yields to the earnings yield of the S&P 500 and showed a very close correlation between the two. The **Fed model**, so named by Edward Yardeni of (at the time) Prudential Securities, was based primarily on the results of this report. However, use of the term "Fed model" is somewhat misleading as the model has never been formally adopted by the Federal Reserve as a policy-making tool.

The Fed model is a theory of equity valuation that hypothesizes that the yield on long-term U.S. Treasury securities (usually defined as the 10-year T-note yield) should be equal to the S&P 500 earnings yield (usually defined as forward operating earnings divided by the index level) in equilibrium. Differences in these yields identify an overpriced or underpriced equity market. The model predicts:

- U.S. stocks are undervalued if the forward earnings yield on the S&P 500 is greater than the yield on U.S. Treasury bonds.
- U.S. stocks are overvalued if the forward earnings yield on the S&P 500 is less than the yield on U.S. Treasury bonds.

For example, if the S&P 500 forward earnings yield is 5 percent and the 10-year T-note yield is 4.5 percent, stocks would be considered undervalued according to the Fed model.

> **Example 8**
>
> ### Fed Model with U.S. Data
>
> The difference between the S&P 500 earnings yield (based on forward operating earnings estimates) and the 10-year T-note yield for the time period January 1979 through December 2008 is presented in Exhibit 10.
>
> The Fed model predicts that investors will be indifferent between investing in equities and investing in government bonds when the difference between the two yields is zero. Note that the average difference between the two yields was 0.70 percent during this time period. The positive difference between the two yields was at its greatest in December 2008. Thus, the model predicted that equities were significantly undervalued at that time, following the stock market sell-off during the second half of 2008. Similarly, the largest negative differences occurred prior to the collapse of the stock market bubbles in October 1987 and early 2000.

Relative Value Models

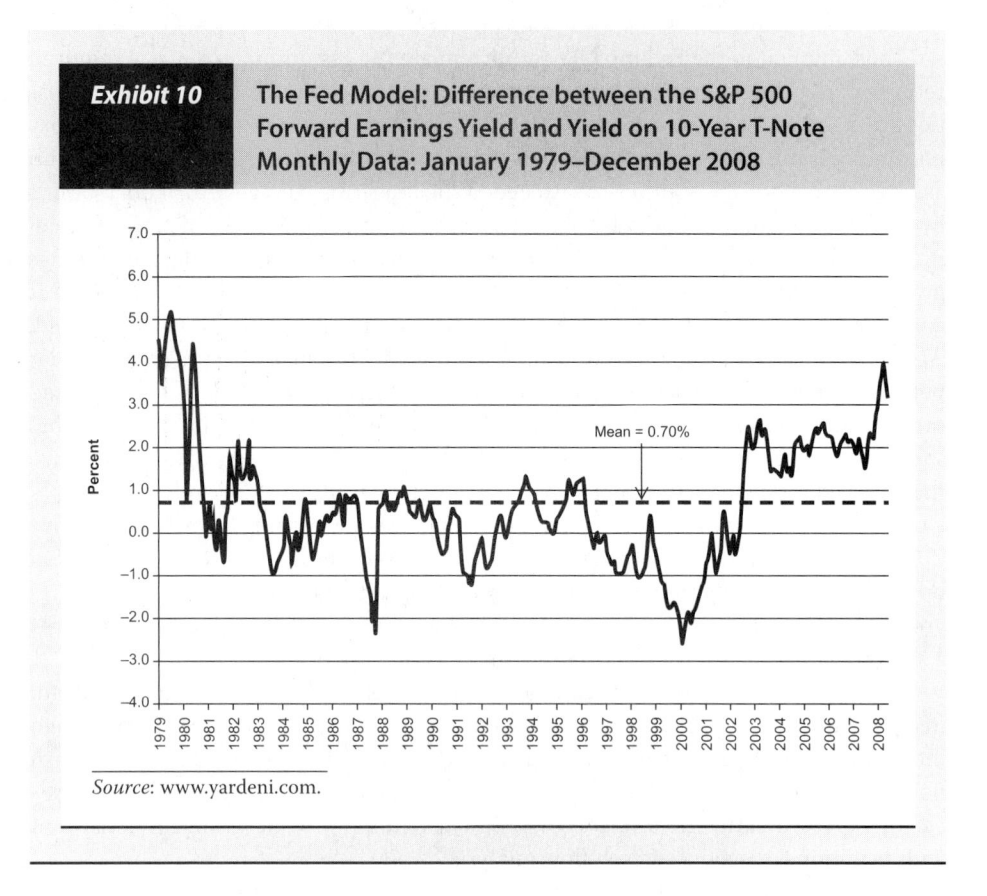

Exhibit 10 The Fed Model: Difference between the S&P 500 Forward Earnings Yield and Yield on 10-Year T-Note Monthly Data: January 1979–December 2008

Source: www.yardeni.com.

The key criticism of the Fed model is that it ignores the equity risk premium. (Informally, the **equity risk premium** is the compensation demanded by investors for the greater risk of investing in equities compared to investing in default-risk-free debt.) The validity of this criticism is apparent if one understands the assumptions necessary to derive the Fed model from the Gordon growth model. Equation 5 presents the Gordon growth model where V_0 is intrinsic value, D_1 is the dividend per share to be received one-year from today, r is the required return, and the constant annual dividend growth rate is g:

$$V_0 = \frac{D_1}{r - g} \tag{5}$$

Assuming markets correctly set price, P_0, equal to intrinsic value, then $P_0 = V_0$. The expected dividend, D_1, can be determined as the payout ratio, p, times expected earnings, E_1. Sustainable growth, g, can be estimated as return on equity, ROE, times the earnings retention rate, $(1 - p)$.

Substituting $D_1 = p E_1$ and $g = \text{ROE}(1 - p)$ into Equation 5 and noting that $P_0 = V_0$ we are able to derive Equation 6. Equation 6 provides a Gordon growth model estimate for the forward earnings yield, E_1/P_0:

$$\frac{E_1}{P_0} = \frac{r - \text{ROE}(1 - p)}{p} \tag{6}$$

The Fed model hypothesizes that the earnings yield, E_1/P_0, and the yield on Treasury bonds, y_T, are equal in equilibrium. One way to produce this equilibrium using Equation 6 is to assume that the required return, r, and the return on equity, ROE, are equal to the Treasury bond yield, y_T. Making these substitutions in Equation 6 shows this result:

$$\frac{E_1}{P_0} = \frac{r - \text{ROE}(1 - p)}{p} = \frac{y_T - y_T(1 - p)}{p} = y_T \tag{7}$$

Thus, implicit in the Fed model equilibrium are the assumptions that the required return, r, and the accounting rate of return on equity, ROE, for risky equity securities are equal to the Treasury bond yield, y_T. Historical evidence and financial theory resoundingly reject the notion that either assumption is true. For example, the long-run average return on U.S. equities has exceeded the long-run average return on T-bonds by a significant amount.[22] Because of this, many analysts consider the Fed model flawed.

Two additional criticisms of the Fed model are that it ignores inflation and earnings growth opportunities. Asness (2003) criticized the Fed model because it compares an arguably real variable, the earnings yield, to a nominal variable, the T-bond yield. According to this argument, the earnings yield is real because it is a ratio of current period prices.[23] The T-bond yield is nominal because it is reflective of the expected rate of inflation as first noted by Fisher (1930). In the presence of inflation, investors should compare the earnings yield with a real interest rate. Asness provides evidence that the Fed model has often been a poor predictor of future equity returns.

Another criticism of the Fed model is that it ignores any earnings growth opportunities available to equity holders beyond those forecasted for the next year (as reflected by expected earnings, E_1). In the United States, long-term compound average earnings growth has been 3–4 percent nominal and 1–2 percent real.[24] Thus, the model ignores a significant portion of total equity return.[25]

In spite of the several criticisms, the Fed model still can provide some useful insights. It does suggest that equities become more attractive as an asset class when interest rates decline. This is consistent with the predictions of any discounted cash flow model and is supported by market evidence. In practice, the model typically makes use of expected earnings (a future cash flow) as an input, which is again consistent with traditional discounted cash flow analysis.

Some analysts find a comparison of the earnings yield and Treasury bond yield to be most useful when the relationship is towards the extremes of its typical range. For example, some analysts compare the current difference between the earnings yield and the Treasury bond yield with the historical average difference. Stocks are viewed as more attractive as an investment when the current period difference significantly exceeds the historical average difference.

Example 9

Fed Model with U.K. Data

The Fed model can be applied to the valuation of non-U.S. equity markets. In early 2009, the Fed model produced a very bullish prediction for British stocks. The forecasted earnings yield on the FTSE 100 was 10.1 percent and the yield on 10-year U.K. government debt was 3.6 percent. The difference between these yields was much greater than the long-term average, according to Citigroup data, of 4.5 percent.

---

[22] Bodie, Kane, and Marcus (2007) show that the geometric average annual return on U.S. large capitalization stocks was 10.23 percent over the 1926 to 2003 time period. The geometric average annual return on long-term Treasury bonds was 5.10 percent during this same time period.

[23] Wilcox (2007) and Palkar and Wilcox (2009) note that accounting and debt adjustments must be made to GAAP-based reported earnings before they can be considered real.

[24] Based on a dataset maintained by Professor Shiller (www.econ.yale.edu/~shiller/data.htm), the compound (geometric mean) annual earnings growth rate was 3.52% from 1872–2008. In the more recent shorter term, the growth rate has been higher: from 1990–2008, the rate was 3.55%, but stopping at 2007 (i.e., from 1990–2007), reflecting an unusually long-period of sustained growth, it was 6.89%. The long-run rate is probably most appropriate here.

[25] The required return on equity for a no-growth company that pays all of its earnings out as dividends is the earnings yield (based on a constant EPS).

Relative Value Models

> Analysts should always question the inputs to any valuation model. Reasonable questions for these results include "Can the government bond yield be expected to rise?" and "Can the forecast for earnings be expected to decline?" Most would likely agree that the latter question was of greater concern in early 2009.

Example 10

Fed Model Questions

1. Assume the S&P 500 forward earnings yield is 5 percent and the 10-year T-note yield is 4.6 percent. Are stocks overvalued or undervalued according to the Fed model?
2. Why might the earnings yield be considered a poor measure for the true worth of equities?

Solution to 1:

According to the Fed model, stocks are undervalued because the forward S&P 500 earnings yield exceeds the 10-year T-note yield. However, recall from Example 1 that the average difference between the S&P 500 earnings yield and the 10-year T-note yield for the time period January 1979–December 2008 was 0.70 percent. In this question, the difference between the two yields is 0.40 percent. Analysts who compare the difference in yields to this average difference would contend that equities are overvalued.

Solution to 2:

The forward earnings yield measure used in the Fed model to assess the worth of equities fails to accurately capture the long-term growth opportunities available to equity investors. Although studies show that the dividend yield has been the major determinant of long-term equity returns, the impact of earnings growth has been significant and arguably should not be ignored.

The **Yardeni model** addresses some of the criticisms of the Fed model. In creating the model, Yardeni (2002) assumed investors valued earnings rather than dividends. With the assumption that markets set price equal to intrinsic value, $P_0 = V_0$, a constant growth valuation model that values earnings is presented in Equation 8. E_1 is an estimate of next year's earnings, r is the required return, and g is the earnings growth rate. Equation 8 shows that, given the assumptions of the model, the earnings yield, E_1/P_0, is equal to the required return, r, minus the growth rate, g.

$$P_0 = \frac{E_1}{r - g} \Rightarrow \frac{E_1}{P_0} = r - g \qquad (8)$$

As a data input for the required return, r, Yardeni used the Moody's A-rated corporate bond yield, y_B, which allowed for risk to be incorporated into the model. The risk premium captured by the model, however, is largely a default risk premium (the credit spread between the A-rated bond, y_B, and the yield on a Treasury bond, y_T), not the unobservable equity risk premium. Thus, while an improvement over the Fed model, the Yardeni model still does not fully capture the risk of equities.

As an input for the growth rate, g, Yardeni used the consensus five-year earnings growth forecast for the S&P 500 from Thomson Financial, LTEG. Note that g is truly a perpetual or sustainable growth rate and that a five-year forecast for growth may not be sustainable.

The Yardeni model introduces an additional variable, the coefficient d. It represents a weighting factor measuring the importance the market assigns to the earnings projections. Yardeni (2000) found that the historical values for d averaged about 0.10.[26] However, depending on market conditions, d can vary considerably from its historical average. Equation 9 presents the Yardeni model stated as the justified (forward) earnings yield on equities.

$$\frac{E_1}{P_0} = y_B - d \times \text{LTEG} \tag{9}$$

A justified forward earnings yield that is below, equal to, or greater than the forward earnings yield value implied by current equity market index values (using consensus forward earnings estimates, for example) would indicate that equities are undervalued, fairly valued, or overvalued in the marketplace. A valuation judgment can also be made by using Equation 9 solved for P_0, which gives the Yardeni model expression for the fair value of the equity market: $E_1/(y_B - d \times \text{LTEG})$. The judgment would be that the equity market is undervalued, fairly valued, or overvalued if the fair value estimate is above, equal to, or below the current equity market level. Example 11 shows such an analysis.

Example 11

The Yardeni Model (1)

Exhibit 11 presents in logarithmic ("log") scale the actual S&P 500 Index and a fair value estimate of the S&P 500 using the Yardeni model assuming $d = 0.10$. The time period is January 1985 to December 2008.

As Exhibit 12 shows, the Yardeni model predicted the S&P 500 was undervalued by 39.25 percent in December 2008. The Yardeni model also did a good job predicting the overvaluation and subsequent pullbacks of October 1987 and the early 2000s. However, the model signaled the equity market was significantly undervalued in 2007 even though U.S. and other world equity markets collapsed dramatically in the wake of a major financial crisis.

---

[26] Note that rearranging the terms in Equation 9 so that they produce a formula for d results in $d = \dfrac{y_B - \dfrac{E_1}{P_0}}{\text{LTEG}}$. Thus, historical values for d can be estimated from market data.

Relative Value Models

Exhibit 11 S&P 500 Index and Fair Value Estimate Using Yardeni Model with $d = 0.10$ (Log Scale) Monthly Data: January 1985–December 2008

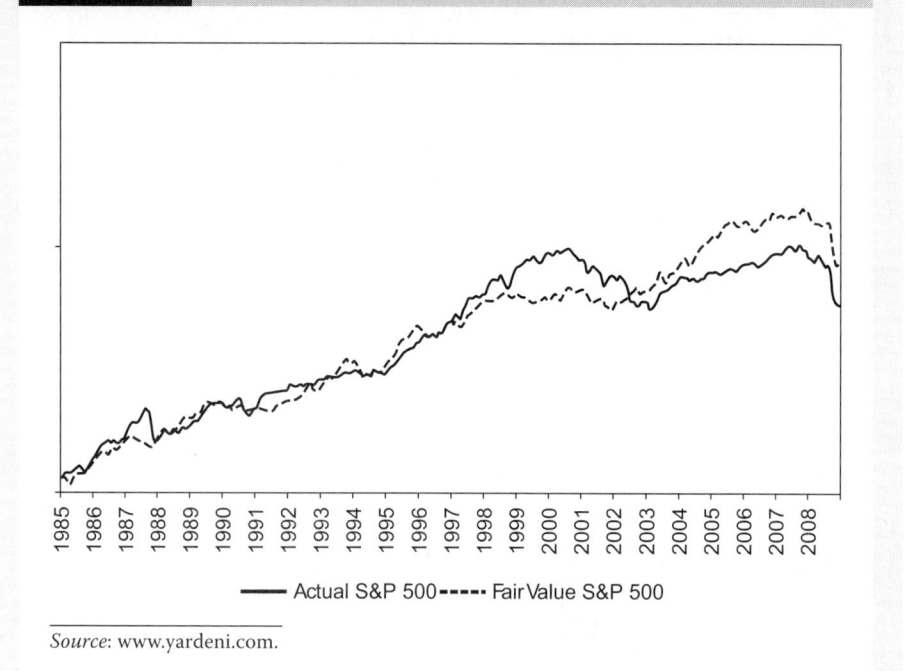

——— Actual S&P 500 ----- Fair Value S&P 500

Source: www.yardeni.com.

Exhibit 12 Overvaluation (+) and Undervaluation (−) of S&P 500 Index versus Fair Value Estimate Using Yardeni Model with $d = 0.10$ Monthly Data: January 1985–December 2008

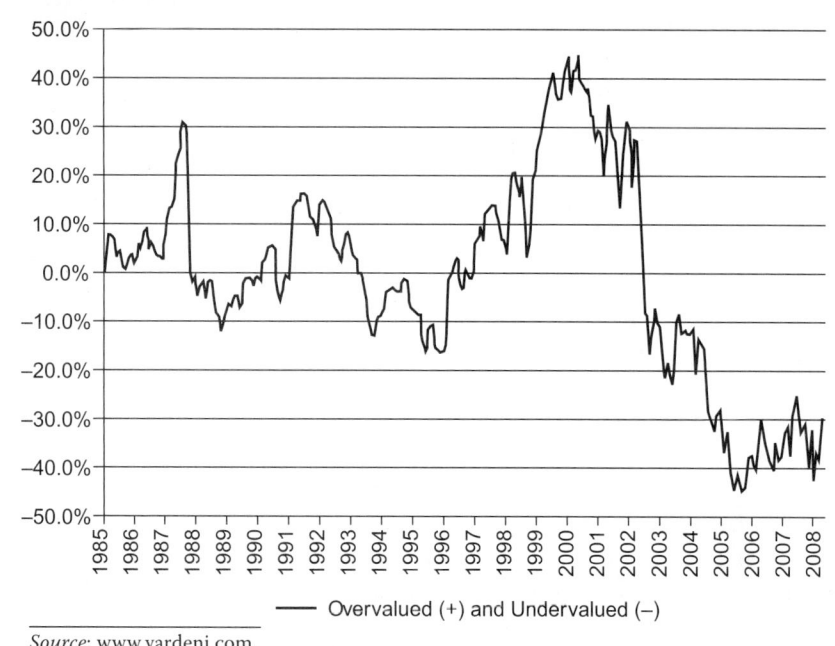

——— Overvalued (+) and Undervalued (−)

Source: www.yardeni.com.

> **Example 12**
>
> ## The Yardeni Model (2)
>
> 1. Assume the Moody's A-rated corporate bond yield is 6.49 percent and the forecast for long-term earnings growth is 11.95 percent. Determine the Yardeni model estimate of the fair value earnings yield assuming $d = 0.05$ and $d = 0.10$. Are equities overvalued or undervalued if the S&P 500 earnings yield is 5.5 percent?
>
> 2. Assume the Moody's A-rated corporate bond yield is 6.32 percent and the forecast for long-term earnings growth is 11.5 percent. Determine the Yardeni model estimate of the fair value price–earnings (P/E) ratio assuming $d = 0.10$. When would equities be undervalued? When would equities be overvalued?
>
> 3. A. Indicate the directional relationship predicted by the Yardeni model between changes in y_B, LTEG, and d and changes in the earnings yield.
>
>   B. Indicate the directional relationship predicted by the Yardeni model between changes in y_B, LTEG, and d and changes in the P/E ratio.
>
> **Solution to 1:**
>
> For $d = 0.05$: $0.0649 - 0.05(0.1195) \approx 0.0589 \approx 5.89\%$ is the Yardeni model estimate. Equities are overvalued as 5.5% < 5.89%.
>
> For $d = 0.10$: $0.0649 - 0.10(0.1195) \approx 0.530 \approx 5.30\%$ is the Yardeni model estimate. Equities are undervalued as 5.5% > 5.30%.
>
> **Solution to 2:**
>
> P/E is the reciprocal of the earnings yield. The Yardeni estimate of the fair value P/E ratio would be $1 \div [0.0632 - 0.10(0.115)]$ or approximately 19.3. Stocks would be undervalued if the actual P/E ratio for the S&P 500 is less than 19.3. Stocks would be overvalued if the actual P/E ratio for the S&P 500 is greater than 19.3.
>
> **Solution to 3A:**
>
> Increases in y_B and decreases in d and LTEG produce higher fair value estimates of the earnings yield.
>
> **Solution to 3B:**
>
> Decreases in y_B and increases in d and LTEG produce higher fair value estimates of the P/E ratio.

Examples 11 and 12 were taken from U.S. equity markets. To date, nearly all analysis using the Yardeni model has been limited to the U.S. equity market. If adequate data are available, especially for forecasted earnings growth, the Yardeni model could be applied in any equity market.

Campbell and Shiller's (1998, 2005) **10-year Moving Average Price/Earnings** [P/10-year MA(E)] has become a popular measure of market valuation. The authors defined the numerator of P/10-year MA(E) as the real S&P 500 price index and the denominator as the moving average of the preceding 10 years of real reported earnings. "Real" denotes that the stock index and earnings are adjusted for inflation using the Consumer Price Index (CPI). The purpose of the 10-year moving average of real reported earnings is to control for business cycle effects on earnings and is based on recommendations from the seminal Graham and Dodd (1934) text.

Relative Value Models

Example 13

Determining P/10-Year MA(E): A Historical Exercise

For the purpose of illustrating the calculation of P/10-year MA(E) one can use data from any period. Exhibit 13 is a historical exercise showing the calculation of P/10-year MA(E) for U.S. equities as of 1881. The real stock price index and real earnings are priced in 2009 U.S. dollars and are determined using the January 2009 CPI value of 211.143. Note that:

$$\text{Real stock price index}_t = \text{Nominal stock price index}_t \times CPI_{2009} \div CPI_t \quad \text{Real earnings}_t = \text{Nominal earnings}_t \times CPI_{2009} \div CPI_{t+1}$$

$$\text{Real stock price index}_{1871} = 4.44 \times 211.143 \div 12.464061 = 75.21424358 \quad \text{Real earnings}_{1871} = 0.4 \times 211.143 \div 12.654392 = 6.674141278$$

The P/10-year MA(E) in 1881 of 18.21479737 is the real stock price index in 1881 of 138.7532563 divided by average real earnings from 1871 to 1880 of 7.617611851.

$$\text{Average real earnings}_{1871 \to 1880} = (6.674141278 + \ldots + 10.9836988) \div 10 = 7.617611851$$
$$\text{P/10-year MA(E)}_{1881} = 138.7532563 \div 7.617611851 = 18.21479737$$

Exhibit 13 Determining P/10-Year MA(E) in 1881[27]

Year	Stock Price Index (January)	Earnings Accruing to Index	Consumer Price Index	Real Stock Price Index	Real Earnings	P/10-Year MA(E)
1871	4.44	0.40	12.464061	75.21424358	6.674141278	
1872	4.86	0.43	12.654392	81.09081653	7.016448545	
1873	5.11	0.46	12.939807	83.38151643	7.852421105	
1874	4.66	0.46	12.368896	79.54843989	8.436439183	
1875	4.54	0.36	11.5126510	83.26398672	7.007878524	
1876	4.46	0.28	10.8465750	86.81982838	5.403166224	
1877	3.55	0.30	10.9417400	68.50442891	6.863396587	
1878	3.25	0.31	9.2290893	74.35346302	7.907328567	
1879	3.58	0.38	8.2776793	91.31689120	8.031199688	
1880	5.11	0.49	9.9903306	107.99850110	10.983698800	
1881	6.19	0.44	9.4194198	138.75325630		18.21479737

Source: www.econ.yale.edu/~shiller/data.htm.

Real earnings in 1880 exceeded the 10-year moving average by a considerable amount, and this is a typical result. This discrepancy undoubtedly reflects the real growth in corporate earnings. If some smoothing for business cycle effects is necessary, the case can be made that it would be better to compute a moving average of the P/E ratio (current period price divided by current period earnings).

Many analysts believe that P/10-year MA(E) should be considered a mean-reverting series. Exhibit 14 presents P/10-year MA(E) from January 1881 to January 2009. The mean value of P/10-year MA(E) for this time period was 16.3 and the January 2009 P/10-year MA(E) was 15.8, suggesting the U.S. equity market was slightly undervalued at that time. The highest value for P/10-year MA(E) was 42.5 in 2000, and the lowest value for P/10-year MA(E) was 5.3 in 1921.

---

[27] The number of decimal places shown reflects the precision given in the Shiller dataset referenced.

Campbell and Shiller (1998, 2005) made the case that the U.S. equity market was extremely overvalued in the late 1990s and provided evidence that future 10-year real price growth was negatively related to P/10-year MA(E). Exhibit 15 updates the Campbell-Shiller results through 2009. Each plotted data point represents an annual observation for real price growth for the next 10 years and P/10-year MA(E) for that same year. A trend line is plotted and shows the ordinary least squares regression relationship between 10-year real price growth and P/10-year MA(E).

The table in the upper right-hand corner of Exhibit 15 shows the predicted 10-year real price growth given some value for the explanatory variable P/10-year MA(E). The regression results predict that 10-year real price growth will be 17.9 percent given the January 2009 P/10-year MA(E) of 15.8. The R-squared for the regression is 0.1488, which indicates that P/10-year MA(E) explains only 14.88 percent of the variation in 10-year real price growth. Furthermore, the traditional regression statistics for this regression are unreliable because of the serial correlation induced by the overlapping time periods used to compute returns.

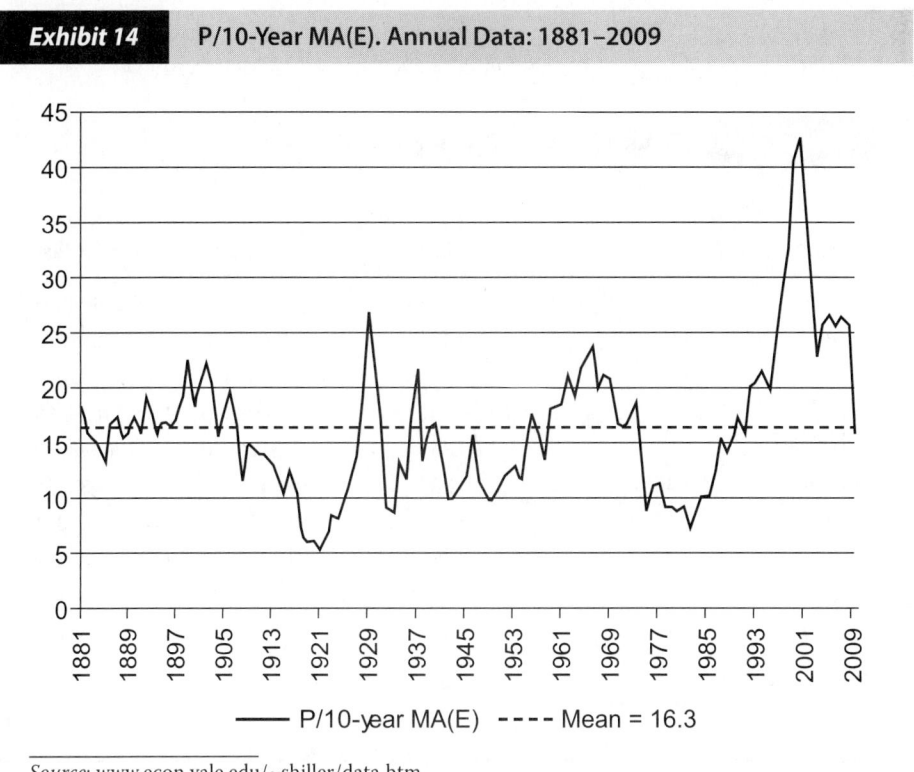

Exhibit 14 P/10-Year MA(E). Annual Data: 1881–2009

Source: www.econ.yale.edu/~shiller/data.htm.

With a 10-year projected real price growth of 17.9 percent, the annualized growth rate is less than 1.7 percent per year. Given a dividend yield of about 2.9 percent and assuming share repurchases effectively add 1 percent to the annual real cash flow to shareholders, the inflation-adjusted expected return would be approximately 5.6 percent, which is below the 6–7 percent compounded average inflation-adjusted return over long periods in the United States (Siegel 2005). Thus, in contrast to the Fed model and the Yardeni model, the Campbell and Shiller model implies below-average prospective returns.

The conflicting signals between and among various valuation models may provide valuable insights, especially if they cause us to rethink how the parameter estimates and the numerical inputs give rise to the different results. For example, assume that changes in accounting rules lead to significant differences in how earnings are reported over

Relative Value Models

time. Thus, the P/10-year MA(E) at some given point in time might not be comparable with other time periods. A high or low P/10-year MA(E) relative to the long-term average at present could be due to differences in prior accounting rules, thereby resulting in stocks actually being more undervalued or overvalued than they currently appear.

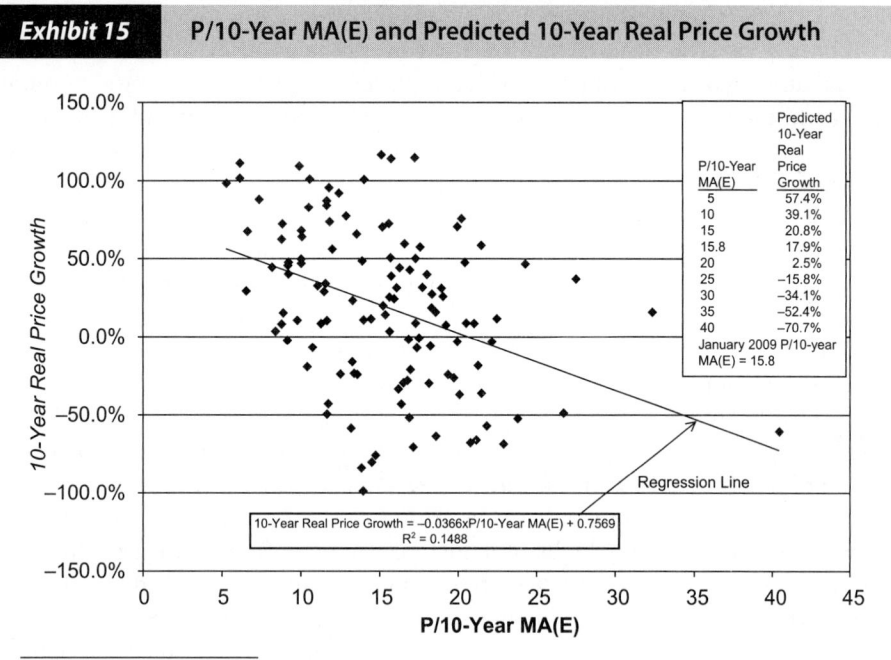

Exhibit 15   P/10-Year MA(E) and Predicted 10-Year Real Price Growth

P/10-Year MA(E)	Predicted 10-Year Real Price Growth
5	57.4%
10	39.1%
15	20.8%
15.8	17.9%
20	2.5%
25	−15.8%
30	−34.1%
35	−52.4%
40	−70.7%

January 2009 P/10-year MA(E) = 15.8

Regression equation: 10-Year Real Price Growth = −0.0366×P/10-Year MA(E) + 0.7569, $R^2 = 0.1488$

Source: www.econ.yale.edu/~shiller/data.htm.

Example 14

P/10-Year MA(E) Questions

1. What adjustments are made to earnings in determining P/10-year MA(E)?
2. Assume P/10-year MA(E) reached an all-time high of 42.5 in 2000. Use the regression results in Exhibit 15 to determine predicted real price growth for the time period 2000–2009.

Solution to 1:

Following Graham and Dodd, Campbell and Shiller averaged earnings over a 10-year time period. Their goal was to normalize earnings by providing an estimate of what earnings would be under mid-cyclical conditions. The implicit assumption is that the typical business cycle lasts 10 years.

Campbell and Shiller also control for inflation by adjusting past earnings to current period dollars using the Consumer Price Index.

Solution to 2:

10-year Real price growth = −0.0366 × 42.5 + 0.7569 = −0.7986 = −79.86%.

4.2 Asset-Based Models

Tobin's *q* ratio, pioneered in Brainard and Tobin (1968) and Tobin (1969), is an asset-based valuation measure. Tobin's *q* has been used for several purposes, including decision-making concerning physical capital investment and equity market valuation. The first application is the simplest: At the company level, Tobin's *q* is calculated as the market value of a company (i.e., the market value of its debt and equity) divided by the replacement cost of its assets. According to economic theory, Tobin's q is approximately equal to 1 in equilibrium. If it is greater than 1 for a company, the marketplace values the company's assets at more than their replacement costs, so additional capital investment should be profitable for the company's suppliers of financing. By contrast, a Tobin's q below 1 indicates that further capital investment is unprofitable.

Tobin's q has also been calculated at an overall market level. In that case, the denominator involves an estimate of the replacement cost of aggregate corporate assets, and the numerator involves estimates of aggregate equity and debt market values. Some analysts have used a market-level Tobin's q to judge whether an equity market is misvalued. This application involves a comparison of the current value of market-level Tobin's q with its presumed equilibrium value of 1 or with its historical mean value. Assuming that Tobin's q will revert to the comparison value, a Tobin's q below, at, or above the comparison values is interpreted as the market being undervalued, fairly valued, or overvalued. Strong economic arguments exist that both Tobin's q and equity q, discussed later, should be mean-reverting series.

The calculation of Tobin's q often poses difficulties. At the company level, it is usually possible to get a fairly accurate estimate of market value (the numerator of Tobin's q) by summing the values of the securities a company has issued, such as its stocks and bonds. It is much more difficult to obtain an accurate estimate of replacement costs of the company's assets (the denominator of Tobin's q). Liquid markets for many assets (e.g., many kinds of industrial equipment) do not exist. Moreover, such items as human capital, trade secrets, copyrights and patents, and brand equity are intangible assets that are often difficult to value. Typically, researchers who try to construct Tobin's q ignore the replacement cost of intangible assets in their calculations.

Smithers and Wright (2000) created an **equity q** that is the ratio of a company's equity market capitalization divided by net worth measured at replacement cost. Their measure differs from the price-to-book value ratio because net worth is based on replacement cost rather than the historic or book value of equity. Based on a market-level equity q, Smithers and Wright made the case that the U.S. equity market was extremely overvalued in the late 1990s. The principles of that application parallel those given for Tobin's q.

To date, much of the market-level analysis using Tobin's q or equity q has been conducted in the U.S. equity market, but analysis based on European and Asian equity markets is increasingly available.

> **Example 15**
>
> ### Market-Level Analysis of Tobin's q and Equity q
>
> Data from which Tobin's q and equity q can be calculated are published in the *Flow of Funds Accounts of the United States-Z.1*, published quarterly by the Federal Reserve.[28] This data source is available from 1952 onwards. Below are data for Nonfarm Nonfinancial Corporate Business for the fourth quarter of 2008 (billions of U.S. dollars). Based on this data, determine Tobin's q and equity q.
>
> | Assets at Market Value or Replacement Cost | Liabilities | Market Value of Equities Outstanding |
> |---|---|---|
> | 28,277.33 | 12,887.51 | 9,554.05 |
>
> *Source*: www.federalreserve.gov/releases/z1/.

---

[28] Specifically, the data currently appear in Table B.102 of that publication.

Relative Value Models

Solution:

$$\text{Tobin's } q = (12{,}877.51 + 9{,}554.05) \div 28{,}277.33 = 0.793623726$$

$$\text{Equity } q = 9{,}554.05 \div (28{,}277.33 - 12{,}877.51) = 0.620803232$$

Using this data, the long-term average for Tobin's q and equity q are both significantly below 1.0. Smithers and Wright suggest this is due to the true economic rate of depreciation being underestimated, which leads to the replacement cost of assets being overstated. Such overstatement means that the denominator in both formulations of the q ratio is too high and that the correctly measured ratios should be much higher.

Exhibit 16 presents quarterly Tobin's q data and quarterly equity q data for the U.S. equity market over the time period 1952 to 2008. Last quarter 2008 values for these two variables relative to their respective means suggest that the U.S. equity market was slightly undervalued at that time. However, both series had declined to significantly lower levels relative to their means in the early 1950s and early 1980s.

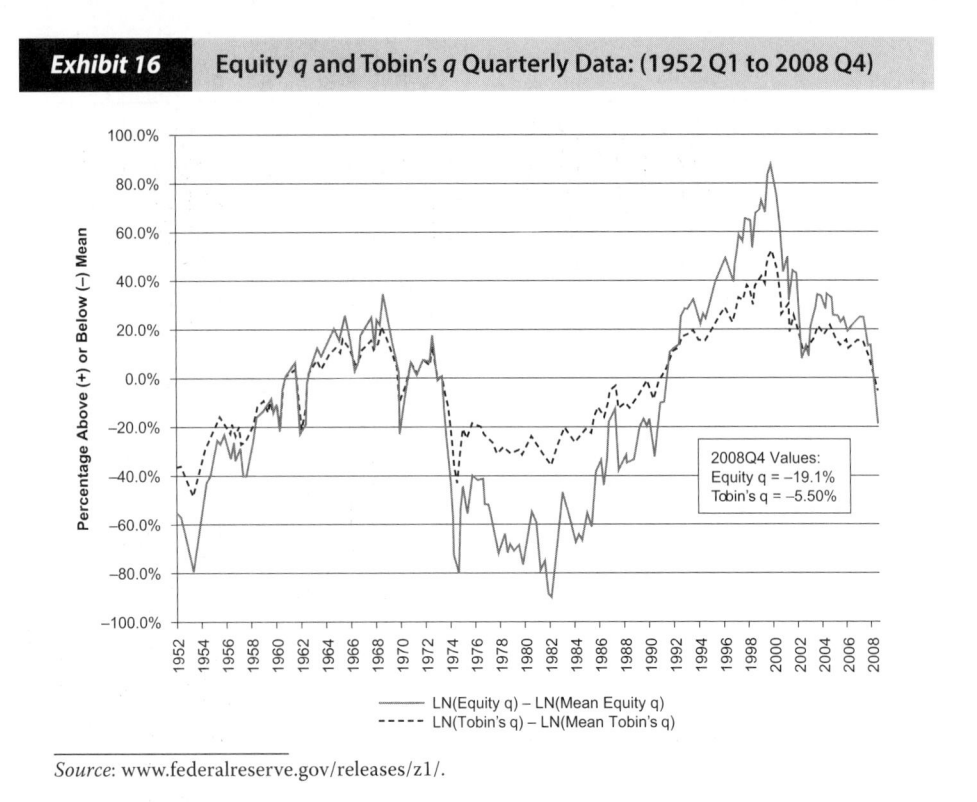

Exhibit 16 Equity q and Tobin's q Quarterly Data: (1952 Q1 to 2008 Q4)

2008Q4 Values:
Equity q = –19.1%
Tobin's q = –5.50%

Legend: LN(Equity q) – LN(Mean Equity q); LN(Tobin's q) – LN(Mean Tobin's q)

Source: www.federalreserve.gov/releases/z1/.

Example 16

Tobin's q and Equity q

1. Why should Tobin's q be expected to mean revert?
2. How does equity q differ from the price-to-book ratio?

> **Solution to 1:**
>
> If Tobin's *q* is greater than 1.0, then the market is valuing a company at more than it costs to replace its assets. Either security prices must fall or the company should continue to invest in new assets until the ratio returns to its equilibrium. If Tobin's *q* is below 1.0, then security prices are undervalued because new businesses cannot be created as cheaply as they can be bought in the open market. Either security prices must rise or the company should sell some of its assets until the ratio returns to its equilibrium.
>
> **Solution to 2:**
>
> Book value in the price-to-book ratio reflects the value of equity that is reported on the company's balance sheet. The denominator of equity *q* reflects the difference between the replacement cost of assets and the market value of liabilities. Most financial reporting standards require the use of acquisition cost as a measure of asset value. Thus, the book value of assets is typically less than their replacement cost, and this is particularly true during periods of rising prices.

A summary of the relative value models appears in Exhibit 17.

Exhibit 17 Summary of Relative Value Models

Model	Predictions of the Model	Strengths	Limitations
Fed model	The equity market is undervalued if its earnings yield exceeds the yield on government securities.	■ Easy to understand and apply. ■ Consistent with discounted cash flow models that show an inverse relationship between value and the discount rate.	■ Ignores the equity risk premium. ■ Compares a real variable to a nominal variable. ■ Ignores earnings growth.
Yardeni model	Equities are overvalued if the fair value estimate of the earnings yield provided by the model exceeds the actual earnings yield for the market index.	■ Improves on the Fed model by including the yield on risky debt and a measure of expected earnings growth as determinants of value.	■ Risk premium captured by the model is largely a default risk premium that does not accurately measure equity risk. ■ The forecast for earnings growth may not be accurate or sustainable. ■ The estimate of fair value assumes the discount factor investors apply to the earnings forecast remains constant over time.
P/10-year MA(E)	Future equity returns will be higher when P/10-year MA(E) is low.	■ Controls for inflation and business cycle effects by using a 10-year moving average of real earnings. ■ Historical data supports an inverse relationship between P/10-year MA(E) and future equity returns.	■ Changes in the accounting methods used to determine reported earnings may lead to comparison problems. ■ Current period or other measures of earnings may provide a better estimate for equity prices than the 10-year moving average of real earnings. ■ Evidence suggests that both low and high levels of P/10-year MA(E) can persist for extended periods of time.

Relative Value Models

Exhibit 17   Continued

Model	Predictions of the Model	Strengths	Limitations
Tobin's q and equity q	Future equity returns will be higher when Tobin's q and equity q are low.	■ Both measures rely on a comparison of security values to asset replacement costs (minus the debt market value, in the case of equity q); economic theory suggests this relationship is mean-reverting. ■ Historical data supports an inverse relationship between both measures and future equity returns.	■ It is difficult to obtain an accurate measure of replacement cost for many assets because liquid markets for these assets do not exist and intangible assets are often difficult to value. ■ Evidence suggests that both low and high levels of Tobin's q and equity q can persist for extended periods of time.

Example 17

Questions Regarding the Relative Value Models

1. Which of the models ignore the current level of market interest rates as determinants of equity market value?
2. Under what conditions might the Fed model and Yardeni model provide a different assessment of the value of the equity market?
3. Which of the models use some measure of earnings as an input? How might this lead to comparison issues?

Solution to 1:

In assessing equity market value, P/10-year MA(E), Tobin's q, and equity q are typically compared to their long-term averages and not to market interest rates. While the Yardeni model compares the fair value earnings yield predicted by the model to the actual earnings yield, the A-rated corporate bond yield is an input to the model.

Solution to 2:

The Fed model compares the earnings yield to the Treasury bond yield. The Yardeni model uses the A-rated corporate bond yield and the consensus 5-year earnings growth forecast to determine a fair value earnings yield. One scenario in which the two models might differ in their predictions would be if the default risk premium on the A-rated corporate bond was currently high, the Treasury bond yield was currently low, and earnings were forecasted to grow at a slow rate. Given these assumptions, the Fed model might indicate that equities are undervalued while the Yardeni model indicates equities are overvalued.

Solution to 3:

The Fed model, Yardeni model, and P/10-year MA(E) all use some measure of earnings as a determinant of value. Time series comparisons will be problematic if the accounting methods used to determine earnings change over time.

SUMMARY

In this reading, we have investigated several ways in which economic theory can be applied to the valuation of equity markets. Among the major points are the following:

- The growth accounting equation allows one to decompose real GDP growth, $\Delta Y/Y$, into components that can be attributed to the observable factors: the growth of the capital stock, $\Delta K/K$, the output elasticity of capital, α, the growth in the labor force, $\Delta L/L$, the output elasticity of labor, $1 - \alpha$, and a residual factor—often called the Solow residual—that is the portion of growth left unaccounted for by increases in the standard factors of production, $\Delta A/A$.

$$\frac{\Delta Y}{Y} \approx \frac{\Delta A}{A} + \alpha \frac{\Delta K}{K} + (1 - \alpha)\frac{\Delta L}{L}$$

- The existence of TFP growth, $\Delta A/A$, means that total output can grow at a faster rate than would be predicted simply from growth in accumulated capital stock and the labor force. TFP is typically linked to innovation and technical progress. However, changes in work organization, government regulation, and the literacy and skills of the workforce, as well as many other factors, also affect TFP.

- The inputs for the H-model include the initial growth rate, g_S, a period of years, N, where the dividend growth rate declines in a linear fashion, and a long-term dividend growth rate, g_L, that is expected to prevail to perpetuity beginning at the end of period N. With an initial annualized dividend rate D_0 and a discount rate to perpetuity of r, the formula for intrinsic value, V_0, according to the H-model is:

$$V_0 = \frac{D_0}{r - g_L}\left[(1 + g_L) + \frac{N}{2}(g_S - g_L)\right]$$

- In top-down forecasting, analysts use macroeconomic forecasts to develop market forecasts and then make industry and security forecasts consistent with the market forecasts. In bottom-up forecasting, individual company forecasts are aggregated to industry forecasts, which in turn are aggregated to produce a market forecast.

- Bottom-up forecasts tend to be more optimistic than top-down forecasts. Top-down models can be slow in detecting cyclical turns if the current statistical relationships between economic variables deviate significantly from their historic norms.

- The Fed model is a theory of equity valuation that hypothesizes that the yield on long-term U.S. Treasury securities (usually defined as the 10-year T-note yield) should be equal to the S&P 500 earnings yield (usually defined as forward operating earnings divided by the index level) in equilibrium.

- A common criticism of the Fed model equilibrium is that it fails to incorporate the equity risk premium. The earnings yield can also be a poor measure of the true value of equities if significant growth opportunities exist. Some authors have also argued that the Fed model comparison is flawed because the earnings yield is real while the Treasury yield is nominal.

- The Yardeni model addresses some of the criticisms of the Fed model. As inputs, Yardeni used the Moody's A-rated corporate bond yield, y_B, the consensus five-year earnings growth forecast for the S&P 500 from Thomson Financial, LTEG, and the coefficient d, which represents a weighting factor measuring the importance the market assigns to the earnings projections.

Yardeni found that the historical values for d averaged about 0.10. The formula for the Yardeni model is:

$$\frac{E_1}{P_0} = y_B - d \times \text{LTEG}$$

- Limitations of the Yardeni model include that the risk premium captured by the model is largely a default risk premium and not the future equity risk premium, which is unobservable. Also, the consensus five-year earnings growth forecast for the S&P 500 from Thomson Financial may not be sustainable, and evidence suggests that the weighting factor varies significantly over time.

- Campbell and Shiller's P/10-year MA(E) has become a popular measure of market valuation. The numerator of P/10-year MA(E) is the real S&P 500 and the denominator is the moving average of the preceding 10 years of real reported earnings. "Real" denotes that the stock index and earnings are adjusted for inflation using the Consumer Price Index (CPI). The purpose of the 10-year moving average of real reported earnings is to control for business cycle effects on earnings and is based on recommendations from the seminal work of Graham and Dodd.

- Tobin's q is calculated at the individual company level as the market value of a company divided by the replacement cost of its assets. Smithers and Wright created an equity q that is the ratio of a company's market capitalization divided by net worth measured at replacement cost. Market-level measures may be computed for Tobin's q and equity q by a process of aggregation; these market-level measures may be used to form a valuation judgment about an equity market. Assuming that Tobin's q will revert to the comparison value, a Tobin's q below, at, or above the comparison value is interpreted as the market being under-, fairly, or overvalued. Strong economic arguments exist that both Tobin's q and equity q should be mean-reverting series.

- In practice, estimating replacement cost can be problematic due to the lack of liquid markets for many assets. Moreover, such items as human capital, trade secrets, copyrights and patents, and brand equity are intangible assets that are difficult to value.

REFERENCES

Arnott, Robert D., and Peter L. Bernstein. 2002. "What Risk Premium is 'Normal'?" *Financial Analysts Journal*, vol. 58, no. 2 : 64–85.

Arnott, Robert D. 2004. "The Meaning of a Slender Risk Premium." *Financial Analysts Journal*, vol. 60, no. 2 : 6–8.

Asness, Clifford S. 2003. "Fight the Fed Model." *Journal of Portfolio Management*, vol. 30, no. 1 : 11–24.

Bodie, Zvi, Alex Kane, and Alan Marcus. 2007. *Essentials of Investments*, 6th Edition. New York: McGraw-Hill Irwin.

Brainard, William C., and James Tobin. 1968. "Pitfalls in Financial Model Building." *American Economic Review*, vol. 58, no. 2 : 99–122.

Campbell, John Y., and Robert J. Shiller. 1998. "Valuation Ratios and the Long-Run Stock Market Outlook." *Journal of Portfolio Management*, vol. 24, no. 2 : 11–26.

Campbell, John Y., and Robert J. Shiller. 2005. "Valuation Ratios and the Long-Run Stock Market Outlook: An Update." *Behavioral Finance II*. Edited by R. Thaler. New York: Russell Sage Foundation.

Cobb, C.W., and Paul H. Douglas. 1928. "A Theory of Production." *American Economic Review*, vol. 18, no. Supplement: 139–165.

Darrough, Masako N., and Thomas Russell. 2002. "A Positive Model of Earnings Forecasts: Top Down versus Bottom Up." *Journal of Business*, vol. 75, no. 1 : 127–152.

Fisher, Irving. 1930. *The Theory of Interest: As Determined by Impatience to Spend Income and Opportunity to Invest It*. New York: Macmillan Company.

Fuller, Russell J., and Chi-Cheng Hsia. 1984. "A Simplified Common Stock Valuation Model." *Financial Analysts Journal*, vol. 40, no. 5 : 49–56.

Graham, Benjamin, and David L. Dodd. 1934. *Security Analysis*. New York: McGraw-Hill.

Ibbotson, Roger G., and Rex A. Sinquefield. 1989. *Stocks, Bonds, Bills, and Inflation: Historical Returns(1926–1987)*. Chicago: Dow-Jones Irwin.

Ibbotson, Roger G., Jeffrey J. Diermeier, and Laurence B. Siegel. 1984. "The Demand for Capital Market Returns: A New

Equilibrium Theory." *Financial Analysts Journal*, vol. 40, no. 1 : 22–33.

Mehra, Rajnish. 2003. "The Equity Premium: Why Is It a Puzzle?" *Financial Analysts Journal*, vol. 59, no. 1 : 54–69.

Mehra, Rajnish, and Edward C. Prescott. 1985. "The Equity Risk Premium: A Puzzle." *Journal of Monetary Economics*, vol. 15, no. 2 : 145–162.

Palkar, Darshana, and Stephen E. Wilcox. 2009. "Adjusted Earnings Yields and Real Rates of Return." *Financial Analysts Journal*, vol. 65, no. 5 : 66–79.

Preston, R. 2009. "China's Foreign Reserves Top $2tn." *BBC News*, 15 July 2009.

Siegel, Jeremy J. 1992. "The Equity Premium: Stock and Bond Returns Since 1802." *Financial Analysts Journal*, vol. 48, no. 1 : 28–38.

Siegel, Jeremy J. 2005. "Perspectives on the Equity Risk Premium." *Financial Analysts Journal*, vol. 61, no. 6 : 61–73.

Smithers, Andrew, and Stephen Wright. 2000. *Valuing Wall Street*. New York: McGraw-Hill.

Solow, Robert. 1957. "Technical Change and the Aggregate Production Function." *The Review of Economics and Statistics*, vol. 39: 312–320.

Stimes, Peter C. 2008. *Equity Valuation, Risk, and Investment: A Practitioner's Roadmap*. Hoboken, NJ: John Wiley & Sons.

Tobin, James. 1969. "A General Equilibrium Approach to Monetary Theory." *Journal of Money, Credit and Banking*, vol. 1, no. 1 : 15–29.

Wilcox, Stephen E. 2007. "The Adjusted Earnings Yield." *Financial Analysts Journal*, vol. 63, no. 5 : 54–68.

Xin, Z., and S. Rabinovitch. 2009. "China Central Bank Taps on Brakes as Money, Supply Surges." *Reuters*, 15 July 2009.

Yardeni, Edward E. 2000. "How to Value Earnings Growth." *Topical Study #49* (Deutsche Banc Alex Brown).

Yardeni, Edward E. 2002. "Stock Valuation Models," Prudential Financial Research, *Topical Study #56* (August 8).

Zheng, Jinghai, Arne Bigsten, and Anagang Hu. 2006. "Can China's Growth be Sustained? A Productivity Perspective." *Working Papers in Economics236*, Göteborg University, Department of Economics.

Zheng, Jinghai, Angan Hu, and Arne Bigsten. 2009. "Potential Output in a Rapidly Developing Economy: The Case of China and a Comparison with the United States and the European Union." *Federal Reserve Bank of St. Louis Review*, vol. 91, no. 4 : 317–348.

PRACTICE PROBLEMS FOR READING 19

1. Elizabeth Villeneuve is a senior economist at Proplus Financial Economics Consulting (Proplus). She is responsible for the valuation of equity markets in developing countries and is reviewing the preliminary report on Emerge Country prepared by one of her analysts, Danielle DeLaroche. Emerge Country is now experiencing stronger economic growth than most developed countries.

   DeLaroche has summarized in Exhibit 1 some of the assumptions contained in the report. In modeling the growth in the country's real output, she has used the Cobb-Douglas production function under the assumption of constant returns to scale and, in valuing the equity market, she has used the standard Gordon growth model with constant dividend growth rate.

   Exhibit 1 Assumptions for the Equity Index of Emerge Country

Annual dividend per share in 2008	450 CU*
Forecasted earnings per share in 2009	750 CU*
Forecasted annual growth in TFP	1.5%
Expected real growth rate of dividends to perpetuity	5.5%
Required real discount rate to perpetuity	7.5%

   *CU = currency unit of Emerge Country

   A. Based on the information in Exhibit 1, calculate the equity index price level of Emerge Country implied by the Gordon growth model, as of 31 December 2008.

   Villeneuve is familiar with the Gordon growth model but not the H-model.

   B. Identify *two* variables that are needed in the H-model and not needed in the Gordon growth model.

   As an illustration of a relative value approach that can be used to support tactical asset allocation, DeLaroche has estimated that the forward operating earnings yield of the equity index in Emerge Country is 6 percent and that the medium-term government bond yield is 7 percent. She then applies the Fed model to the situation in Emerge Country.

   C. Based on the Fed model, determine whether the equity market is undervalued or overvalued and identify three criticisms of the Fed model.

   Because most of Proplus's clients use strategies that require fundamental security analysis, Proplus uses both top-down and bottom-up approaches in all reports dealing with equity return forecasts.

   D. Contrast the two forecasting approaches used by DeLaroche as they relate to industry analysis.

2. Don Murray, an economist, is president of the investment committee of a large U.S. pension plan. He is reviewing the plan's recent investment returns and finds that non-U.S. equity returns have been much higher than U.S. equity returns. Before making any changes to the plan's asset allocation, he has asked to meet with Susan McLean, CFA, who is responsible for the equity portion of the pension plan assets. Murray wants to discuss with McLean the current valuation levels of various equity markets.

End-of-reading problems and solutions copyright © CFA Institute.

Murray develops his own growth projections for the U.S and for a hypothetical country (Hyp Country) that enjoys a well-developed economy but whose population is aging. These projections are shown in Exhibit 2. In addition, Murray projects that output elasticity of capital equals 0.3 and 0.5 for the United States and Hyp Country, respectively.

Exhibit 2   Growth Projections (2010–2029)

Country	Growth in Total Factor Productivity (%)	Growth in Capital Stock (%)	Growth in Labor Input (%)
United States	0.6	3.5	0.4
Hyp Country	1.0	3.3	0.1

A. Based on the information in Exhibit 2, calculate the projected GDP growth for the United States for the period 2010–2029. Use the Cobb-Douglas production function and assume constant returns to scale.

Murray identifies two possible measures that the government of Hyp Country could implement, and he wants to know how these measures would affect projected GDP growth for Hyp Country.

Measure 1   Lower the retirement age from 65 to 63, gradually over the next four-year period.

Measure 2   Reduce subsidies to higher education over the next five years.

B. For each of the growth measures identified by Murray in Exhibit 2, indicate which growth factor is *most* affected. Justify your answers.

Murray is surprised that the bottom-up forecasts produced by McLean for the United States in the last five years have been consistently more optimistic than her top-down forecasts. As a result, he expresses doubt about the validity of either approach.

C. State *one* justification for using both top-down and bottom-up models even when these models produce different forecasts, and state *one* justification for using the bottom-up approach by itself.

Murray suggests replacing earnings-based models with asset-based models in valuing equity markets. In response, McLean recommends using Tobin's q ratio and equity q ratio, although both are subject to estimation errors when applied to valuing a particular company.

D. Identify *two* problems that McLean may have in estimating the Tobin's q ratio and the equity q ratio for the pension plan assets that she manages.

The following information relates to Questions 3–10

Claudia Atkinson, CFA, is chief economist of an investment management firm. In analyzing equity markets, the firm has always used a bottom-up approach, but now Atkinson is in the process of implementing a top-down approach. She is discussing this topic with her assistant, Nicholas Ryan.

At Atkinson's request, Ryan has prepared a memo comparing the top-down approach and the bottom-up approach. Ryan presents three conclusions:

Conclusion 1   The top-down approach is less optimistic when the economy is heading into a recession than the bottom-up approach.

Conclusion 2   The top-down approach is more often based on consensus earnings estimates from equity analysts than the bottom-up approach.

Practice Problems for Reading 19

Conclusion 3   The top-down approach is often more accurate in predicting the effect on the stock market of a contemporaneous change in a key economic variable than is the bottom-up approach.

Atkinson explains to Ryan how the Cobb-Douglas function can be used to model GDP growth under assumptions of constant returns to scale. For illustrative purposes, she uses the data shown in Exhibit 1.

Exhibit 1   Hypothetical Data for a Developing Country

Time Period	Growth in Total Factor Productivity (%)	Output Elasticity of Capital	Growth in Capital Stock (%)	Growth in Labor Input (%)
1970–1989	2.5	0.4	4.8	3.0
1990–2009	2.8	0.4	4.4	4.6

Atkinson wants to use the data shown in Exhibit 1 as an input for estimating justified P/E ratios. Ryan expresses some criticisms about using such historical data:

- "In a context of hyperinflation, the approach may not be appropriate."
- "The companies' growth rates may not match GDP growth for long periods."
- "Government-implemented measures may not be taken into account in any of the growth factors."

Atkinson intends to use relative value models in order to support the firm's asset allocation recommendation. The earnings-based approach that she studies is the Fed model. She asks Ryan to write a summary of the advantages of that model. Ryan's report makes the following assertions about the Fed model:

- "The model can be used for non-U.S. equity markets."
- "The model captures the net present value of growth investment opportunities available to investors."
- "The model is most informative when the excess of the earnings yield over the Treasury bond yield is close to the historical average."

Atkinson thinks that the Yardeni model might address some of the criticisms of the Fed model and bring certain improvements. She will use that model as an alternate approach.

Because different results from various equity market valuation models may provide relevant information, Atkinson will present a third earnings-based approach, namely the P/10-year MA(E) model. Ryan identifies many positive features in that model, including the following:

- "The model controls for inflation."
- "The model is independent of changes in accounting rules."
- "The model controls for business cycle effects on earnings."

When evaluating the equity market in the United States, Atkinson uses the following asset-based models: Tobin's q ratio and equity q ratio. She calculates the equity q ratio of Nonfarm Nonfinancial Corporate Business based on the Federal Reserve data shown in Exhibit 2:

Exhibit 2	Nonfarm Nonfinancial Corporate Business for Fourth Quarter of 2008 (Billions of U.S. Dollars)
Assets at market value or replacement cost	27.3
Assets at book value	23.4
Liabilities	13.3
Equities at market value	9.0

Atkinson notes that the Tobin's q ratio that could be derived from Exhibit 2 is less than 1. She asks Ryan what conclusion could be drawn from such a low ratio if it had been obtained for a specific company.

3. Which conclusion presented by Ryan about the top-down approach and the bottom-up approach is *most likely* correct?

    A. Conclusion 1.
    B. Conclusion 2.
    C. Conclusion 3.

4. Based on Exhibit 1, which of the components of economic growth has contributed *most* to GDP growth during the 1970–1989 time period?

    A. Labor input.
    B. Capital stock.
    C. Total factor productivity.

5. Which of the following criticisms expressed by Ryan about the use of historical data is the *least* valid?

    A. In a context of hyperinflation, the approach may not be appropriate.
    B. The companies' growth rates may not match GDP growth for long periods.
    C. Government-implemented measures may not be taken into account in any of the growth factors.

6. Which of the following advantages listed by Ryan with respect to the earnings-based approach studied by Atkinson is *most likely* correct? The model:

    A. can be used for non-U.S. equity markets.
    B. captures the net present value of growth investment opportunities available to investors.
    C. is most informative when the excess of the earnings yield over the Treasury bond yield is close to the historical average.

7. The *most likely* improvement from using the Yardeni model instead of the Fed model is that the Yardeni model captures:

    A. a pure equity risk premium.
    B. a pure default risk premium.
    C. the effect of long-term earnings growth on equity market values.

8. Which of the following features of the P/10-year MA(E) model as stated by Ryan is *least likely* to be correct? The model:

    A. controls for inflation.
    B. is independent of changes in accounting rules.
    C. controls for business cycle effects on earnings.

Practice Problems for Reading 19

9. Based on the data shown in Exhibit 2, the equity q ratio is closest to:
   A. 0.6429.
   B. 0.8168.
   C. 0.8911.

10. The *best* conclusion that Ryan can provide to Atkinson regarding the calculated value for Tobin's q ratio is that, based on comparing it to an equilibrium value of 1:
    A. the replacement cost of assets is understated.
    B. the company appears to be overvalued in the marketplace.
    C. the company appears to be undervalued in the marketplace.

The following information relates to Questions 11–16

Egon Carmichael, CFA, is a senior analyst at Supranational Investment Management (Supranational), a firm specializing in global investment analysis. He is meeting with Nicolas Schmidt, a potential client representing a life insurance company, to discuss a report prepared by Supranational on the U.S. equity market. The report contains valuations of the U.S. equity market based on two approaches: the justified P/E model and the Fed model.

When Carmichael informs Schmidt that Supranational applies the neoclassical approach to growth accounting, Schmidt makes the following statements about what he considers to be some limitations of that approach:

Statement 1 The growth in total factor productivity is not directly observable.

Statement 2 The growth factors must be stated in nominal (i.e., not inflation-adjusted) terms.

Statement 3 The total output may not grow at a rate faster than predicted by the growth in capital stock and in labor force.

For use in estimating the justified P/E based on the Gordon constant growth model, Carmichael develops the assumptions displayed in Exhibit 1.

Exhibit 1 Justified P/E Ratio for the U.S. Equity Market: Assumptions

Required real rate of return	5.0%
Inflation-adjusted dividend growth rate	2.5%

Using the assumptions in Exhibit 1, Carmichael's estimate of the justified P/E ratio for the U.S. equity market is 13.2. Schmidt asks Carmichael, "All else equal, what would cause the justified P/E for the U.S. equity market to fall?"

Supranational's report concludes that the U.S. equity market is currently undervalued, based on the Fed model. Schmidt asks Carmichael, "Which of the following scenarios would result in the Fed model most likely indicating that the U.S. equity market is overvalued?"

Scenario 1 The S&P 500 forward earnings yield is 4.5 percent, and the 10-year T-note yield is 4.75 percent.

Scenario 2 The S&P 500 forward earnings yield is 4.5 percent, the 10-year T-note yield is 4.0 percent, and the average difference between the S&P 500 forward earnings yield and the 10-year T-note over the last 20 years has been 0.25 percent.

Scenario 3 The long-term inflation rate is expected to be 2 percent, and the long-term average earnings growth is expected to be 1 percent real.

Schmidt points out that the Fed model has been the subject of criticism and recommends that Carmichael use the Yardeni model to value the U.S. equity market. Before employing the Yardeni model, Carmichael asks Schmidt to identify criticisms of the Fed model that are addressed by the Yardeni model.

Finally, Carmichael presents a third earnings-based approach, the P/10-year MA(E) model, and describes many positive features of that model.

Schmidt mentions that the international life insurance company that he represents might be interested in the equity forecasts produced by Supranational. He says that his company's objective is to accumulate sufficient assets to fulfill the firm's obligations under its long-term insurance and annuity contracts. For competitive reasons, the company wants to quickly detect significant cyclical turns in equity markets and to minimize tracking errors with respect to the equity index. Schmidt asks Carmichael to identify the forecasting approach that is most appropriate.

11. Which of the statements expressed by Schmidt about the neoclassical approach to growth accounting is correct?
    A. Statement 1.
    B. Statement 2.
    C. Statement 3.

12. Carmichael's *most appropriate* response to Schmidt's question about the justified P/E ratio is:
    A. lower volatility of the U.S. equity market.
    B. higher inflation-adjusted dividend growth rate.
    C. higher correlation of U.S. equity market with international equity markets.

13. Carmichael's *most appropriate* response to Schmidt's question about the Fed model is:
    A. Scenario 1.
    B. Scenario 2.
    C. Scenario 3.

14. In response to Carmichael's question about which criticisms of the Fed model are addressed by the Yardeni model, Schmidt's *most appropriate* response is that the Yardeni model does take account of the criticism that the Fed model:
    A. assumes that investors value earnings rather than dividends.
    B. ignores long-term earnings growth opportunities available to shareholders.
    C. assumes that the required rate of return on equity equals the Treasury bill rate.

15. Which of the following features is *least* applicable to the third earnings-based approach presented by Carmichael? The model:
    A. controls for inflation.
    B. is independent of changes in accounting rules.
    C. controls for business cycle effects on earnings.

16. Carmichael's *best* answer to Schmidt's question about a recommended forecasting approach is to use:
    A. a top-down approach.
    B. a bottom-up approach.
    C. both top-down and bottom-up approaches.

SOLUTIONS FOR READING 19

1. **A.** Using the Gordon growth model we have:

   $$V_0 = \frac{D_0(1+g)}{r-g}$$

   Here:

   $D_0 = 450$

   $g = 5.5\%$

   $r = 7.5\%$

   so that:

   $$V_0 = \frac{450(1+0.055)}{0.075 - 0.055}$$
   $$= 23{,}738$$

   B. One variable needed in the H-model is the initial growth rate of the dividend, and another is the number of years during which the dividend growth rate declines from its initial value to the long-term sustainable growth rate. In contrast, such a variable is not present in the Gordon growth model because a single dividend rate applies from the date of valuation to perpetuity.

   C. The Fed model predicts that stocks are overvalued if the forward earnings yield on the equity index (here 6 percent) is less than the yield on Treasury bonds (here 7 percent). Therefore, in Emerge Country, stocks are overvalued.

   The Fed model has three important limitations. It:
   - ignores the equity risk premium;
   - ignores earnings growth; and
   - compares a real variable to a nominal variable.

   D. Industry analysis fits in the middle of both top-down approach and bottom-up approach.

   In the top-down approach, when entering industry analysis, the market analysis has already been completed, so that the analyst knows which equity markets will outperform (compared to bonds or real estate, for example). So what remains to be done is to determine the equity market sectors that are expected to be top performers in each of the already identified best-performing equity markets.

   In the bottom-up approach, when entering industry analysis, the company analysis has already been completed, so the analyst knows which individual securities will outperform. What remains to be done is to aggregate the expected returns of those securities within each industry to identify the industries that are expected to be the best performers.

2. **A.** Using Equation 3, we have:

   Percentage growth in GDP = Growth in total factor productivity
   + (Output of elasticity of capital) × (Growth in capital stock)
   + (1 − Output of elasticity of capital) × (Growth in labor input)
   = 0.6% + (0.3 × 3.5%) + (0.7 × 0.4%)
   = 1.93%

B. Measure 1 Lowering the retirement age will reduce the growth in labor participation and therefore the growth in labor input until a new steady-state labor force participation rate is attained. Subsequent growth in labor input should then track underlying population growth.

   Measure 2 Lowering the subsidies to higher education will most likely reduce future technical innovation and therefore reduce growth in total factor productivity. The effect may be slow at the beginning, but will increase gradually for a period that will extend well beyond the five years of reduction in subsidies.

C. Top-down and bottom-up forecasts frequently differ from each other. In these cases, the reconciling and revision process of the forecasts can:
   - help the analyst better understand the market consensus, and
   - reveal a gap that gives rise to significant market opportunities.

   In spite of the optimistic bias observed by Murray, the bottom-up approach a) may provide the opportunity to identify attractively priced securities irrespective of the attractiveness of the sectors and b) may be a better fit for the investors who focus on a market niche.

D. The denominators of the Tobin's q ratio and of the equity q ratio include the replacement cost of company assets. It is difficult to obtain those replacement costs for two reasons: a) there may be no liquid markets for the assets, and b) intangible assets are often difficult to value.

3. A is correct. It has been shown that bottom-up forecasts are often more optimistic than top-down forecasts (not the other way around). This may be because analysts rely on management's assessment of future probability.

4. C is correct. The contributions from total factor productivity are 2.5 percent and 2.8 percent, respectively, for the periods 1970–1989 and 1990–2009. The corresponding contributions from labor input are 1.8% (= 0.6 × 3.0%) and 2.76% (= 0.6 × 4.6%), and the corresponding contributions from capital stock are 1.92% (= 0.4 × 4.8%) and 1.76% (= 0.4 × 4.4%).

5. C is correct. Government-implemented measures are among the inputs that have an impact on the economy and therefore on the historical data that the analyst uses. It rests upon the analyst to establish whether these measures will continue in the future when he projects economic growth.

6. A is correct. The Fed model, although developed in the United States, can be applied to the valuation of non-U.S. equity markets.

7. C is correct. The Yardeni model incorporates the effect on equity market value of long-term earnings growth.

8. B is correct. The P/10-year MA(E) model is dependent of changes in accounting rules because it averages earnings over 10 years. Therefore, the feature is not applicable to the model.

9. A is correct. The equity q ratio is equal to

   Market value of equities /(Replacement cost of assets – Liabilities)

   = 9.0/(27.3 – 13.3)

   = 0.6429

10. C is correct. A Tobin's q value of less than 1, when 1 is used as a comparison point, indicates that the company is undervalued in the marketplace because it indicates an opportunity to buy assets at a price below their replacement cost.

Solutions for Reading 19

11. A is correct. It is true that the growth in total productivity is not directly observable. That growth is obtained by using the following data: growth in real output, growth in capital stock, and growth in labor input.

12. C is correct. A higher correlation of the U.S. equity market with international equity markets would increase the risk of the U.S. equity market and thus increase the required return (r) on that market. Increasing r would reduce the justified P/E ratio:

$$\frac{P_0}{E_1} = \frac{D_0(1+g)/E_1}{r-g}$$

13. A is correct. It would be true that the Fed model predicts that U.S. stocks are overvalued if the forward earnings yield on the S&P 500 (4.5 percent in this scenario 1) is less than the yield on U.S. Treasury bonds (4.75 percent in this scenario 1).

14. B is correct. A criticism of the Fed model that the Yardeni model does address is that the Fed model does not take account of long-term earnings growth. The Yardeni model includes a long-term earnings growth variable.

15. B is correct. The P/10-year MA(E) model is dependent of changes in accounting rules because it averages earnings over 10 years. Therefore, the feature is not applicable to the model.

16. C is correct. On the one hand, because the insurance company wants to minimize tracking errors with respect to the equity indexes, Carmichael should recommend the top-down approach because the forecast does not need to focus on individual security selection. On the other hand, because the insurance company wants to detect quickly any significant turn in equity markets, Carmichael should recommend the bottom-up approach because the bottom-up approach can be effective in anticipating cyclical turning points.

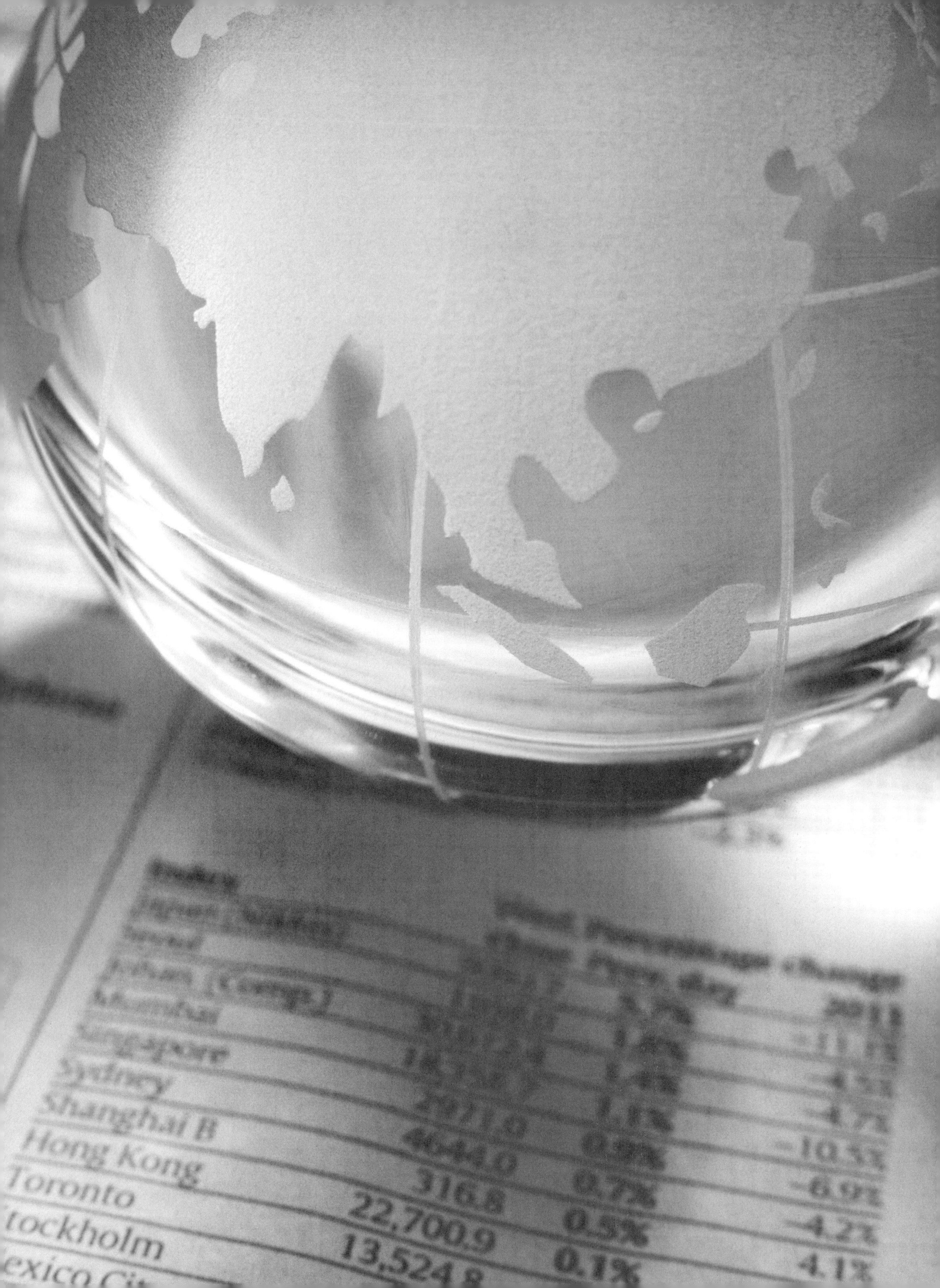

READING
20

Dreaming with BRICs: The Path to 2050

by Dominic Wilson and Roopa Purushothaman

LEARNING OUTCOMES

Mastery	The candidate should be able to:
☐	**a** compare the economic potential of emerging markets such as Brazil, Russia, India, and China (BRICs) to that of developed markets, in terms of economic size and growth, demographics and per capita income, growth in global spending, and trends in real exchange rates;
☐	**b** explain why certain developing economies may have high returns on capital, rising productivity, and appreciating currencies;
☐	**c** explain the importance of technological progress, employment growth, and growth in capital stock in estimating the economic potential of an emerging market;
☐	**d** discuss the conditions necessary for sustained economic growth, including the core factors of macroeconomic stability, institutional efficiency, open trade, and worker education;
☐	**e** evaluate the investment rationale for allocating part of a well-diversified portfolio to emerging markets in countries with above average economic potential.

INTRODUCTION   1

The world economy has changed a lot over the past 50 years. Over the next 50, the changes could be at least as dramatic.

We have highlighted the importance of thinking about the developing world in our recent global research, focusing on key features of development and globalisation that we think are important to investors with a long-term perspective. A major theme of this work has been that, over the next few decades, the growth generated by the large developing countries, particularly the BRICs (Brazil, Russia, India, and China) could become a much larger force in the world economy than it is now—and much larger than many investors currently expect.

Many thanks to Jim O'Neill, Paulo Leme, Sandra Lawson, Warren Pearson and our regional economists for their contributions to this paper.

"Dreaming with BRICs: The Path to 2050," by Dominic Wilson and Roopa Purushothaman, reprinted from *Global Economics Paper Number 99*. Copyright © 2003. Reprinted with permission of The Goldman Sachs Group, Inc.

NOTE: This reading is presented as an example of how economic analysis can serve as the basis for building an emerging markets investment strategy; the inclusion of this reading does not represent an endorsement of the authors' specific conclusions.

In this reading, we gauge just how large a force the BRICs could become over the next 50 years. We do this not simply by extrapolating from current growth rates, but by setting out clear assumptions about how the process of growth and development works and applying a formal framework to generate long-term forecasts. We look at our BRICs projections relative to long-term projections for the G6 (U.S., Japan, U.K., Germany, France, and Italy).[1]

Using the latest demographic projections and a model of capital accumulation and productivity growth, we map out GDP growth, income per capita and currency movements in the BRICs economies until 2050. This allows us to paint a picture of how the world economy might change over the decades ahead.

The results of the exercise are startling. They suggest that if things go right, the BRICs could become a very important source of new global spending in the not too distant future. Exhibit 1 shows that India's economy, for instance, could be larger than Japan's by 2032, and China's larger than the U.S. by 2041 (and larger than everyone else as early as 2016). The BRICs economies taken together could be larger than the G6 by 2039.

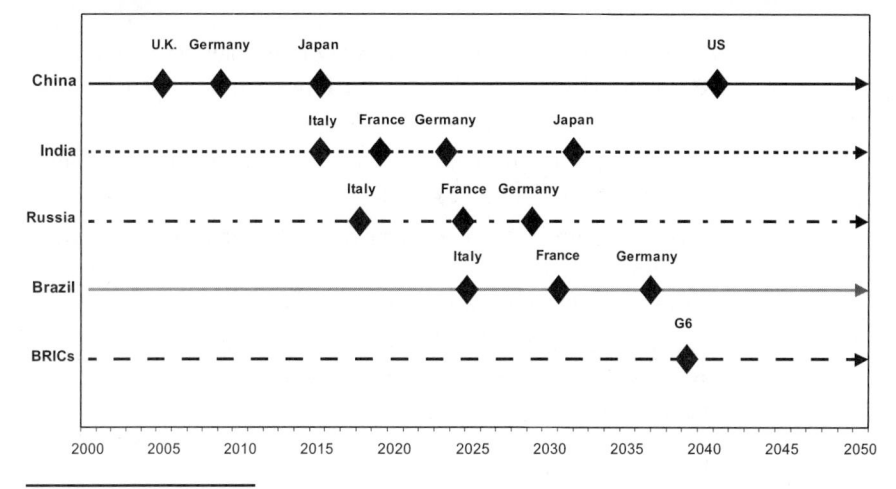

Exhibit 1 Overtaking the G6: When BRICs' US$GDP Would Exceed G6

GS BRICs Model Projections. See reading for details and assumptions.
Note: Diamonds indicate when BRICs' US$GDP exceeds US$GDP in the G6.

Our projections are optimistic, in the sense that they assume reasonably successful development. But they are economically sensible, internally consistent and provide a clear benchmark against which investors can set their expectations. There is a good chance that the right conditions in one or another economy will not fall into place and the projections will not be realized. If the BRICs pursue sound policies, however, the world we envisage here might turn out to be a reality, not just a dream.

The projections leave us in no doubt that the progress of the BRICs will be critical to how the world economy evolves. If these economies can fulfill their potential for growth, they could become a dominant force in generating spending growth over the next few decades.

---

[1] Any decision to limit the sample of countries is to some extent arbitrary. In focusing on the G6 (rather than the G7 or a broader grouping), we decided to limit our focus to those developed economies with GDP currently over US$1 trillion. This means that Canada and some of the other larger developed economies are not included. Adding these economies to the analysis would not materially change the conclusions.

A DRAMATICALLY DIFFERENT WORLD

We start with some key conclusions that describe the way the world might change over the next 50 years. The big assumption underlying all of these projections is that the BRICs maintain growth-supportive policy settings. The figures below illustrate these points. Our conclusions fall under five main topics: 1) economic size; 2) economic growth; 3) incomes and demographics; 4) global demand patterns; and 5) currency movements.

Economic Size

- In less than 40 years, the BRICs' economies together could be larger than the G6 in U.S. dollar terms. By 2025 they could account for over half the size of the G6. Currently they are worth less than 15%.

- In U.S. dollar terms, China could overtake Germany in the next four years, Japan by 2015 and the U.S. by 2039. India's economy could be larger than all but the U.S. and China in 30 years. Russia would overtake Germany, France, Italy and the U.K.

- Of the current G6 (U.S., Japan, Germany, France, Italy, U.K.) only the U.S. and Japan may be among the six largest economies in U.S. dollar terms in 2050.

Economic Growth

- India has the potential to show the fastest growth over the next 30 and 50 years. Growth could be higher than 5% over the next 30 years and close to 5% as late as 2050 if development proceeds successfully.

- Overall, growth for the BRICs is likely to slow significantly over this time frame. By 2050, only India on our projections would be recording growth rates significantly above 3%.

Incomes and Demographics

- Despite much faster growth, individuals in the BRICs are still likely to be poorer on average than individuals in the G6 economies by 2050. Russia is the exception, essentially catching up with the poorer of the G6 in terms of income per capita by 2050. China's per capita income could be similar to where the developed economies are now (about US$30,000 per capita). By 2030, China's income per capita could be roughly what Korea's is today. In the U.S., income per capita by 2050 could reach roughly $80,000.

Figure 1A — BRICs Have a Larger US$GDP than the G6 in Less than 40 Years

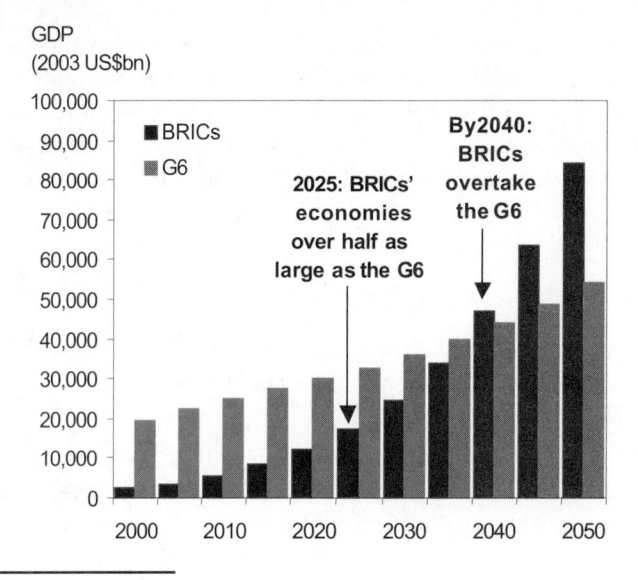

GDP (2003 US$bn)

Annotations:
- 2025: BRICs' economies over half as large as the G6
- By 2040: BRICs overtake the G6

GS BRICs Model Projections. See reading for details and assumptions.

Figure 1B — BRICs' Share of GDP Rises

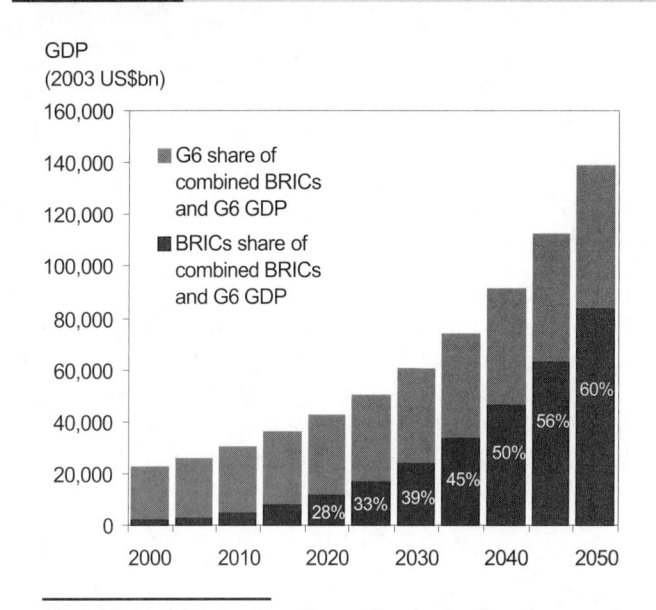

GDP (2003 US$bn)

Legend:
- G6 share of combined BRICs and G6 GDP
- BRICs share of combined BRICs and G6 GDP

BRICs share: 28% (2020), 33% (2025), 39% (2030), 45% (2035), 50% (2040), 56% (2045), 60% (2050)

GS BRICs Model Projections. See reading for details and assumptions.

A Dramatically Different World

Figure 1C — The Largest Economies in 2050

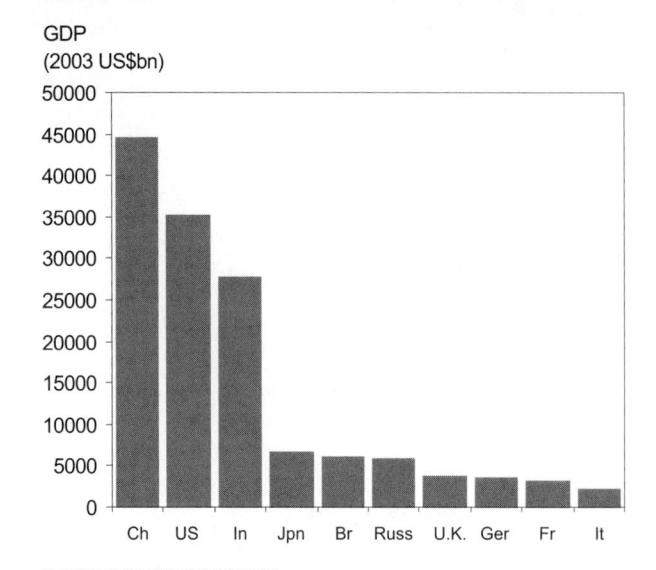

GDP (2003 US$bn), bars for: Ch ~44,500; US ~35,200; In ~27,800; Jpn ~6,700; Br ~6,100; Russ ~5,900; U.K. ~3,800; Ger ~3,600; Fr ~3,100; It ~2,200.

GS BRICs Model Projections. See reading for details and assumptions.

Figure 2A — China Overtakes the G3; India Is Close Behind

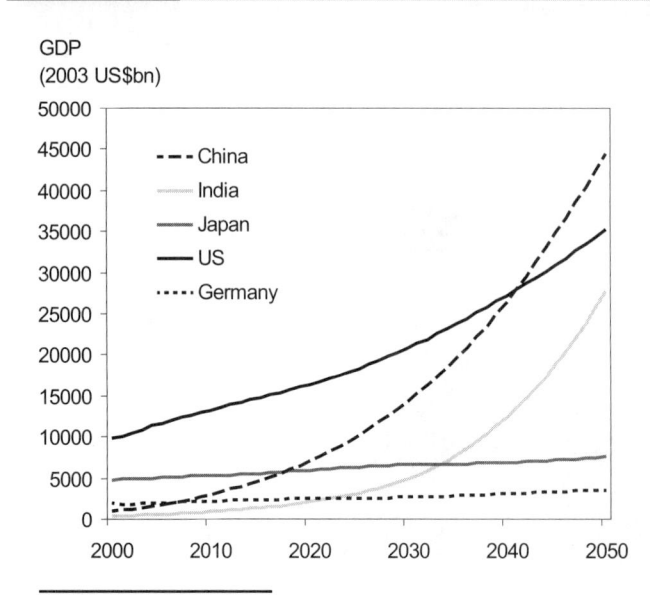

GDP (2003 US$bn), 2000–2050 projections for China, India, Japan, US, Germany.

GS BRICs Model Projections. See reading for details and assumptions.

Figure 2B — India Shows Most Rapid Growth Potential of the BRICs

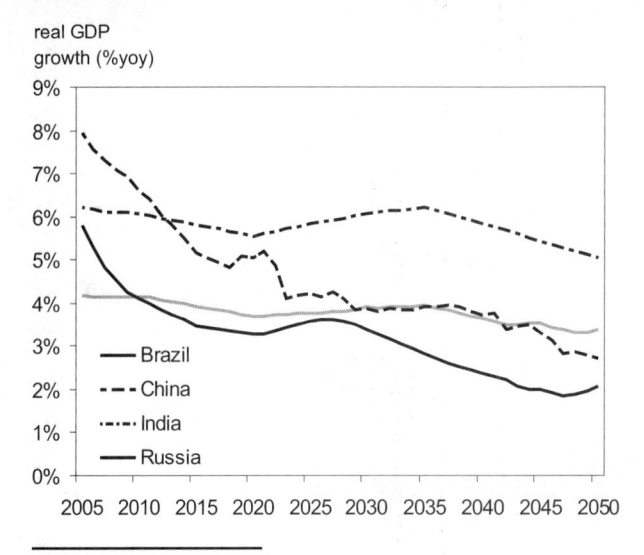

real GDP growth (%yoy); x-axis 2005–2050; series: Brazil, China, India, Russia.

GS BRICs Model Projections. See reading for details and assumptions.

Figure 2C — Incremental Demand from the BRICs Could Eventually Quadruple G6 Demand

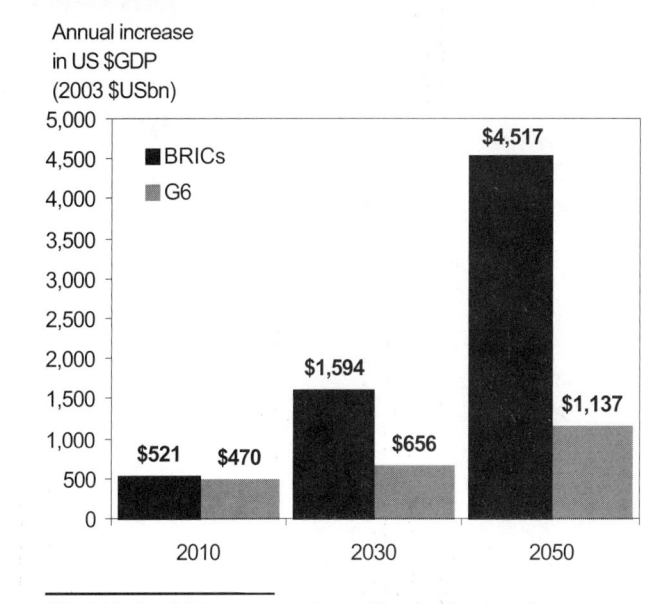

Annual increase in US $GDP (2003 $USbn):

Year	BRICs	G6
2010	$521	$470
2030	$1,594	$656
2050	$4,517	$1,137

GS BRICs Model Projections. See reading for details and assumptions.

- Demographics play an important role in the way the world will change. Even within the BRICs, demographic impacts vary greatly. The decline in working-age population is generally projected to take place later than in the developed economies, but will be steeper in Russia and China than India and Brazil.

| Figure 3 | BRICs' Exchange Rates Could Appreciate by Close to 300% |

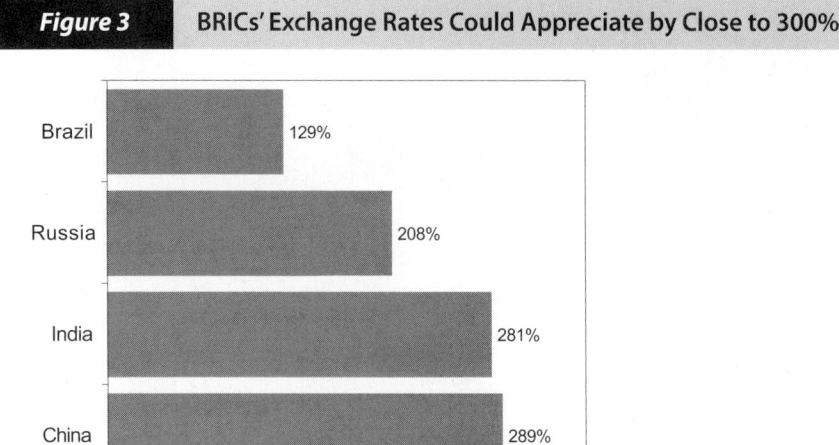

- Brazil: 129%
- Russia: 208%
- India: 281%
- China: 289%

Real exchange rate appreciation (%)

GS BRICs Model Projections. See reading for details and assumptions.

Global Demand Patterns

- As early as 2009, the annual increase in U.S. dollar spending from the BRICs could be greater than that from the G6 and more than twice as much in dollar terms as it is now. By 2025 the annual increase in U.S. dollar spending from the BRICs could be twice that of the G6, and four times higher by 2050.

Currency Movements

- Rising exchange rates could contribute a significant amount to the rise in U.S. dollar GDP in the BRICs. About 1/3 of the increase in U.S. dollar GDP from the BRICs over the period may come from rising currencies, with the other 2/3 from faster growth.
- The BRICs' real exchange rates could appreciate by up to 300% over the next 50 years (an average of 2.5% a year). China's currency could double in value in ten years' time if growth continued and the exchange rate were allowed to float freely.

HOW COUNTRIES GET RICHER

Our predictions may seem dramatic. But over a period of a few decades, the world economy can change a lot. Looking back 30 or 50 years illustrates that point. Fifty years ago, Japan and Germany were struggling to emerge from reconstruction. Thirty years ago, Korea was just beginning to emerge from its position as a low-income nation. And even over the last decade, China's importance to the world economy has increased substantially.

History also illustrates that any kind of long-term projection is subject to a great deal of uncertainty. The further ahead into the future you look, the more uncertain things become. Predictions that the USSR (or Japan) would overtake the U.S. as the dominant economic power turned out to be badly off the mark.

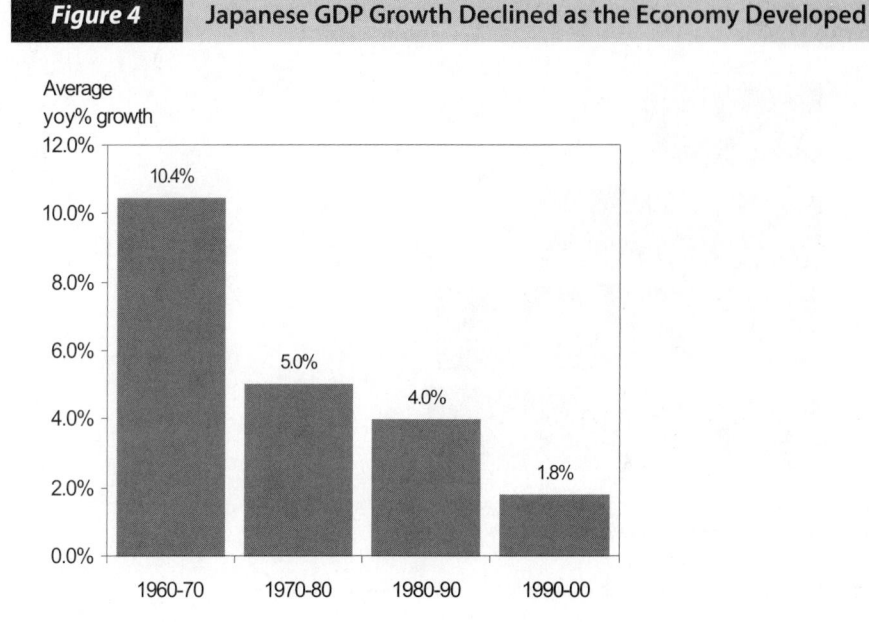

Figure 4   Japanese GDP Growth Declined as the Economy Developed

- 1960–70: 10.4%
- 1970–80: 5.0%
- 1980–90: 4.0%
- 1990–00: 1.8%

(Average yoy% growth)

While this makes modeling these kinds of shifts difficult, it is still essential. Over 80% of the value generated by the world's major equity markets will come from earnings delivered more than 10 years away. Developing strategies to position for growth may take several years and require significant forward planning. The best option is to provide a sensible framework, based on clear assumptions.

As developing economies grow, they have the potential to post higher growth rates as they catch up with the developed world. This potential comes from two sources. The first is that developing economies have less capital (per worker) than developed economies (in the language of simple growth models they are further from their "steady states"). Returns on capital are higher and a given investment rate results in higher growth in the capital stock. The second is that developing countries may be able to use technologies available in more developed countries to "catch up" with developed country techniques.

Figure 5   Higher Income per Capita Moves Exchange Rates Closer to PPP

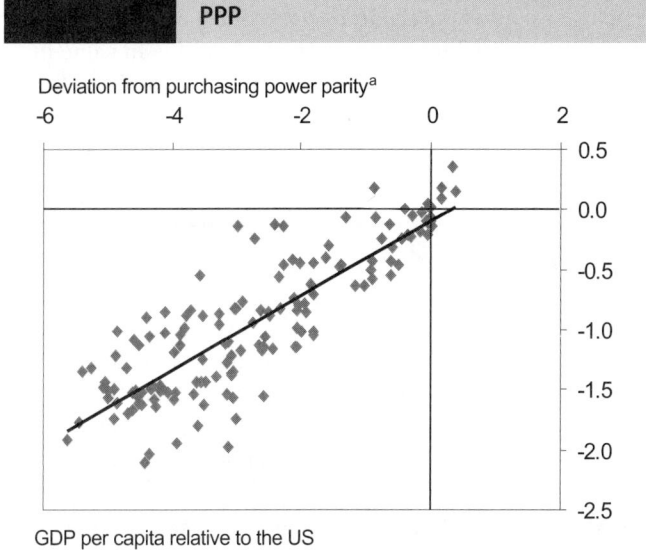

(Scatter plot: Deviation from purchasing power parity[a] vs. GDP per capita relative to the US)

[a]Expressed in logs.

As countries develop, these forces fade and growth rates tend to slow towards developed country levels. In Japan and Germany, very rapid growth in the 1960s and 1970s gave way to more moderate growth in the 1980s and 1990s. This is why simple extrapolation gives silly answers over long time frames. As a crude example, assuming that China's GDP growth continued to grow at its current 8% per year over the next three decades would lead to the prediction that China's economy would be three times larger than the U.S. by 2030 in U.S. dollar terms and 25 times larger by 2050.

Countries also grow richer on the back of appreciating currencies. Currencies tend to rise as higher productivity leads economies to converge on Purchasing Power Parity (PPP) exchange rates. There is a clear tendency for countries with higher income per capita to have exchange rates closer to PPP. The BRICs economies all have exchange rates that are a long way below PPP rates. These large differences between PPP and actual exchange rates come about because productivity levels are much lower in developing economies. As they develop and productivity rises, there will be a tendency for their currencies to rise towards PPP. The idea that countries experiencing higher productivity growth tend to appreciate is an important part of both our GSDEER and GSDEEMER models of equilibrium exchange rates.

BREAKING DOWN GROWTH

To translate these two processes into actual projections, we need to develop a model. The model we use is described in more detail in Appendix 20A, but the intuition behind it is quite simple. Growth accounting divides GDP growth into three components:

- Growth in employment;
- Growth in the capital stock; and
- Technical progress (or total-factor productivity (TFP) growth).[2]

We model each component explicitly. We use the U.S. Census Bureau's demographic projections to forecast employment growth over the long term, assuming that the proportion of the working age population that works stays roughly stable. We use assumptions about the investment rate to map out the path that the capital stock will take over time. And we model TFP growth as a process of catch-up on the developed economies, by assuming that the larger the income gap between the BRICs and the developed economies, the greater the potential for catch-up and stronger TFP growth.

We then use the projections of productivity growth from this exercise to map out the path of the real exchange rate. As in our GSDEER framework, we assume that if an economy experiences higher productivity growth than the U.S., its equilibrium exchange rate will tend to appreciate.

By varying the assumptions about investment, demographics or the speed of catch-up, we can generate different paths for annual GDP, GDP growth, GDP per capita (in local currency or U.S. dollars), productivity growth and the real exchange rate.

Because both the growth and currency projections are long-term projections, we ignore the impact of the economic cycle. Effectively, the projections can be interpreted as growth in the trend (or potential growth) of the economy and the currencies' path as an equilibrium path. Where economies peg their exchange rates (as in China), it is even more important to view the exchange rate projections as an equilibrium real rate. In practice, real exchange rate appreciation might come about through a combination of nominal appreciation and higher inflation, with different mixes having

---

[2] We do not explicitly allow for increases in human capital (education), which are implicitly picked up in the technical progress/TFP term in our model.

different implications. We abstract from inflation, expressing all of our projections in real terms (either 2003 local currency or 2003 U.S. dollars).[3]

Generally speaking, the structure of the models is identical across the four economies. We make two minor alterations. We assume that the "convergence speed" of TFP in Brazil and India is slower than in Russia and China for the first twenty years, largely because of lower education levels and poorer infrastructure (more on these factors below), but gradually rises from 2020 onwards (as these structural problems are addressed) so that all of the BRICs are "running" at the same convergence speed. We also assume that China's investment rate gradually declines from its current levels of around 36% to 30% (close to the Asian average) by 2015.

We use GS forecasts until 2004 and begin the simulations in 2005.

5 A MORE DETAILED LOOK AT THE BRICS' POTENTIAL

We have already highlighted some of the most striking results, though there are many other intriguing aspects. The tables and figures that follow set out the key features of the projections, summarising them in 5-year blocks. They show average GDP growth rates, income per capita in U.S. dollars, the real exchange rate and the main demographic trends.

Table 1 BRICs Real GDP Growth: 5-Year Period Averages

%	Brazil	China	India	Russia
2000–2005	2.7	8.0	5.3	5.9
2005–2010	4.2	7.2	6.1	4.8
2010–2015	4.1	5.9	5.9	3.8
2015–2020	3.8	5.0	5.7	3.4
2020–2025	3.7	4.6	5.7	3.4
2025–2030	3.8	4.1	5.9	3.5
2030–2035	3.9	3.9	6.1	3.1
2035–2040	3.8	3.9	6.0	2.6
2040–2045	3.6	3.5	5.6	2.2
2045–2050	3.4	2.9	5.2	1.9

GS BRICs Model Projections. See reading for details and assumptions.

---

[3] Higher inflation in the BRICs would raise nominal GDP forecasts in local currencies and nominal exchange rates, but would not change the forecasts of real GDP or of U.S. dollar GDP under the standard assumption that higher inflation would translate into an offsetting depreciation in the currency.

A More Detailed Look at The BRICs' Potential

Figure 6 — Working Age Population Projected to Decline

working age population = share of population aged 15-60

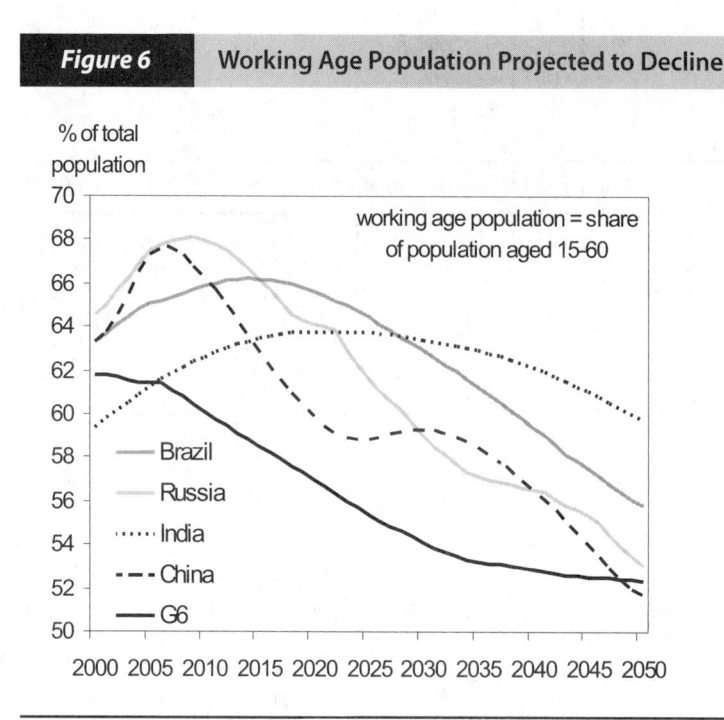

In each economy, as development occurs, growth tends to slow and the exchange rate appreciates. Both rising currencies and faster growth raise U.S. dollar GDP per capita gradually and the gap between the BRICs and developed economies narrows slowly.

The impact of demographics varies, with labour force growth contributing relatively more to growth in India and Brazil and detracting from growth in Russia, where the U.S. Census projections show the labour force shrinking quite rapidly. Where labour force and population growth is rapid, income per capita tends to rise more slowly as higher investment is needed just to keep up with population growth.

To illustrate the shift in economic gravity, we also make comparisons with the G6. To do that, we use a less sophisticated version of the same model to project G6 growth. We assume a common 2% labour productivity growth rate across the G6, so differences in projected GDP growth are purely a function of demographics (and real exchange rates remain roughly stable). A shrinking working age population appears to be the biggest issue in Japan and Italy, whose growth rates are lower than the others, and the smallest issue in the U.S., which maintains the fastest growth.

Table 2 — Projected US$GDP

2003 $USbn	Brazil	China	India	Russia	France	Germany	Italy	Japan	U.K.	U.S.	BRICs Total	G6 Total
2000	762	1,078	469	391	1,311	1,875	1,078	4,176	1,437	9,825	2,700	19,702
2005	468	1,724	604	534	1,489	2,011	1,236	4,427	1,688	11,697	3,330	22,548
2010	668	2,998	929	847	1,622	2,212	1,337	4,601	1,876	13,271	5,441	24,919
2015	962	4,754	1,411	1,232	1,767	2,386	1,447	4,858	2,089	14,786	8,349	27,332
2020	1,333	7,070	2,104	1,741	1,930	2,524	1,563	5,221	2,285	16,415	12,248	29,928
2025	1,695	10,213	3,174	2,264	2,095	2,604	1,625	5,567	2,456	18,340	17,345	32,687
2030	2,189	14,312	4,935	2,980	2,267	2,697	1,671	5,810	2,649	20,833	24,415	35,927
2035	2,871	19,605	7,854	3,734	2,445	2,903	1,708	5,882	2,901	23,828	34,064	39,668

(continued)

Table 2 Continued

2003 $USbn	Brazil	China	India	Russia	France	Germany	Italy	Japan	U.K.	U.S.	BRICs Total	G6 Total
2040	3,740	26,439	12,367	4,467	2,668	3,147	1,788	6,039	3,201	27,229	47,013	44,072
2045	4,794	34,799	18,847	5,156	2,898	3,381	1,912	6,297	3,496	30,956	63,596	48,940
2050	6,074	44,453	27,803	5,870	3,148	3,603	2,061	6,673	3,782	35,165	84,201	54,433

GS BRICs Model Projections. See reading for details and assumptions.

Table 3 Projected US$GDP Per Capita

2003 US$	Brazil	China	India	Russia	France	Germany	Italy	Japan	U.K.	U.S.
2000	4,338	854	468	2,675	22,078	22,814	18,677	32,960	24,142	34,797
2005	2,512	1,324	559	3,718	24,547	24,402	21,277	34,744	27,920	39,552
2010	3,417	2,233	804	5,948	26,314	26,877	23,018	36,172	30,611	42,926
2015	4,664	3,428	1,149	8,736	28,338	29,111	25,086	38,626	33,594	45,835
2020	6,302	4,965	1,662	12,527	30,723	31,000	27,239	42,359	36,234	48,849
2025	7,781	7,051	2,331	16,652	33,203	32,299	28,894	46,391	38,479	52,450
2030	9,823	9,809	3,473	22,427	35,876	33,898	30,177	49,944	41,194	57,263
2035	12,682	13,434	5,327	28,749	38,779	37,087	31,402	52,313	44,985	63,017
2040	16,370	18,209	8,124	35,314	42,601	40,966	33,583	55,721	49,658	69,431
2045	20,926	24,192	12,046	42,081	46,795	44,940	36,859	60,454	54,386	76,228
2050	26,592	31,357	17,366	49,646	51,594	48,952	40,901	66,805	59,122	83,710

GS BRICs Model Projections. See reading for details and assumptions.

Table 4 Projected US$GDP Per Capita Growth: 5-Year Averages

Average %yoy	Brazil	China	India	Russia	France	Germany	Italy	Japan	U.K.	U.S.
2000–2005	−9.8	9.2	3.7	7.0	2.2	1.4	2.7	1.1	3.0	2.6
2005–2010	6.3	11.2	7.5	10.3	1.5	2.0	1.6	0.9	1.9	1.7
2010–2015	6.4	9.2	7.4	8.1	1.5	1.6	1.7	1.2	1.9	1.3
2015–2020	6.2	7.8	7.2	7.5	1.6	1.3	1.7	1.8	1.6	1.3
2020–2025	4.6	7.3	7.4	6.1	1.6	0.9	1.2	1.8	1.2	1.4
2025–2030	4.7	6.9	8.2	6.2	1.6	0.9	0.9	1.5	1.3	1.7
2030–2035	5.2	6.5	8.9	5.2	1.6	1.7	0.8	1.0	1.7	1.9
2035–2040	5.3	6.3	8.9	4.3	1.9	2.0	1.3	1.2	2.0	2.0
2040–2045	5.0	5.9	8.3	3.6	1.9	1.9	1.8	1.6	1.8	1.9
2045–2050	4.9	5.4	7.6	3.4	2.0	1.8	2.1	2.0	1.7	1.9

GS BRICs Model Projections. See reading for details and assumptions.

A More Detailed Look at The BRICs' Potential

Our G6 projections allow us to compare the paths of GDP and GDP per capita in the BRICs with that of the more advanced economies in a common currency. The shift in GDP relative to the G6 takes place steadily over the period, but is most dramatic in the first 30 years. The BRICs overtake the G6 through higher real growth and through the appreciation of BRICs' currencies. About 1/3 of the increase in U.S. dollar GDP from the BRICs over the period may come from rising currencies, with the other 2/3 from faster growth.

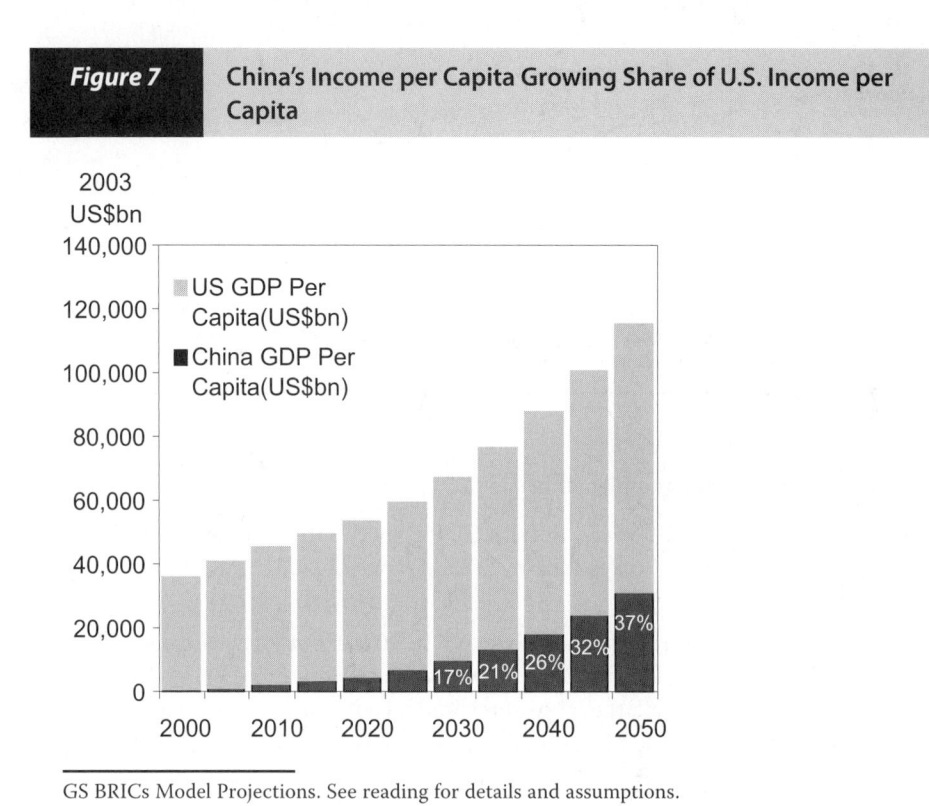

Figure 7 China's Income per Capita Growing Share of U.S. Income per Capita

GS BRICs Model Projections. See reading for details and assumptions.

We also look explicitly at where new demand growth in the world will come from. While it takes some time for the level of GDP in the BRICs to approach the G6, their share of new demand *growth* rises much more rapidly. Because it is incremental demand that generally drives returns, this measure may be particularly useful to assess the extent of opportunities in these markets. We measure that new demand growth as the change in U.S. dollar spending power in the various economies, so again it incorporates both growth and currency effects. On these measures, the BRICs come to dominate the G6 as a source of growth in spending power within 10 years.

| Figure 8 | Projected Population Growth Rates |

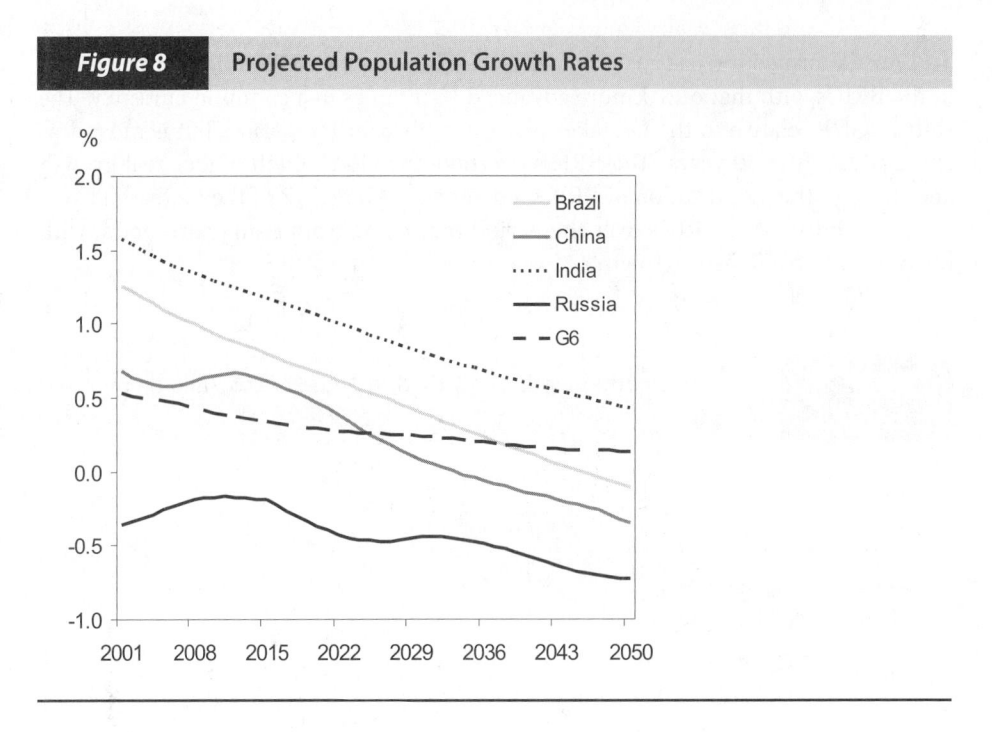

Taking each of the economies in brief:

- **Brazil**. Over the next 50 years, Brazil's GDP growth rate averages 3.6%. The size of Brazil's economy overtakes Italy by 2025; France by 2031; U.K. and Germany by 2036.

- **China**. China's GDP growth rate falls to 5% in 2020 from its 8.1% growth rate projected for 2003. By the mid-2040s, growth slows to around 3.5%. Even so, high investment rates, a large labor force and steady convergence would mean China becomes the world's largest economy by 2041.

- **India**. While growth in the G6, Brazil, Russia and China is expected to slow significantly over the next 50 years, India's growth rate remains above 5% throughout the period. India's GDP outstrips that of Japan by 2032. With the only population out of the BRICs that continues to grow throughout the next 50 years, India has the potential to raise its U.S. dollar income per capita in 2050 to 35 times current levels. Still, India's income per capita will be significantly lower than any of the countries we look at.

- **Russia**. Russia's growth projections are hampered by a shrinking population (an assumption that may be too negative). But strong convergence rates work to Russia's benefit, and by 2050, the country's GDP per capita is by far the highest in the group, and comparable to the G6. Russia's economy overtakes Italy in 2018; France in 2024; U.K. in 2027 and Germany in 2028.

Although we focus on the BRICs, as the four largest developing economies, we do not mean to suggest that development elsewhere is not important. In Box 1, we look at what our approach says for South Africa and the African region and other larger developing economies could also become important.

A More Detailed Look at The BRICs' Potential

BOX 1 SOUTH AFRICA AND THE CHALLENGE FOR THE AFRICAN CONTINENT

With Asia, Europe and Latin America represented in the BRICs profile, some readers will notice Africa's absence. The BRICs are chosen because they are the four largest developing economies currently. Still, it is interesting and important to look beyond at the potential for Africa, and particularly South Africa, the largest economy in the region, to play a part in the same kind of process.

We have already published a 10-year outlook on South Africa using detailed econometric work to project the same components of growth (employment growth, capital stock growth and technical progress) that underpin our methodology here (see *Global Economics Paper #93, South Africa Growth and Unemployment: A Ten-Year Outlook*). The study showed that South Africa could achieve 5% growth over the next decade if the right policies were put in place. The emphasis on getting the conditions for growth right is one that is important for the BRICs also.

To provide comparison, we applied our projection methods for the BRICs to South Africa. The method is simpler than that in our paper on South Africa, but does provide a longer-term outlook. The table sets out the main results in terms of growth.

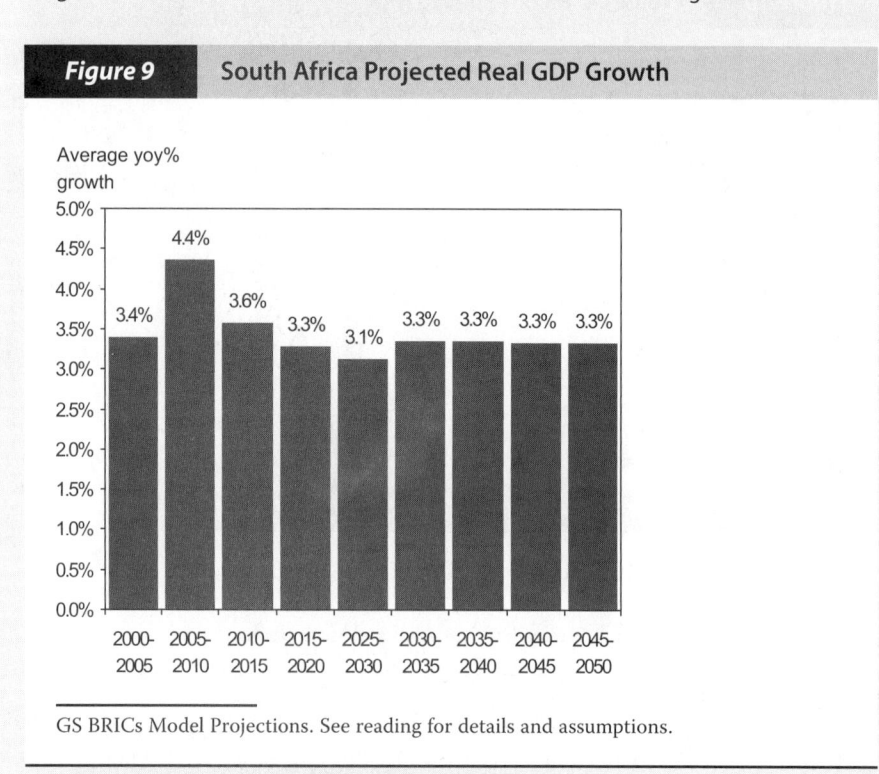

Figure 9 South Africa Projected Real GDP Growth

Period	Average yoy% growth
2000-2005	3.4%
2005-2010	4.4%
2010-2015	3.6%
2015-2020	3.3%
2025-2030	3.1%
2030-2035	3.3%
2035-2040	3.3%
2040-2045	3.3%
2045-2050	3.3%

GS BRICs Model Projections. See reading for details and assumptions.

Projected growth over the next decade is a little lower than the 5% projected in our more detailed study (around 4% here), but the main thrust of the outlook is similar. The differences arise largely because the demographic projections we assume much sharper shrinkage in the labour force (around 1% per year) than did the more detailed exercise. Both in South Africa, and in the region more generally, the challenge of AIDS and the impact it will have on labour force and population dynamics is an important risk and challenge that has no direct counterpart elsewhere.

Table 5	Projected US$GDP Levels				
2003 US$bn	South Africa	Brazil	China	India	Russia
2000	83	762	1078	469	391
2010	147	668	2998	929	847
2020	267	1333	7070	2104	1741
2030	447	2189	14312	4935	2980
2040	739	3740	26439	12367	4467
2050	1174	6074	44453	27803	5870

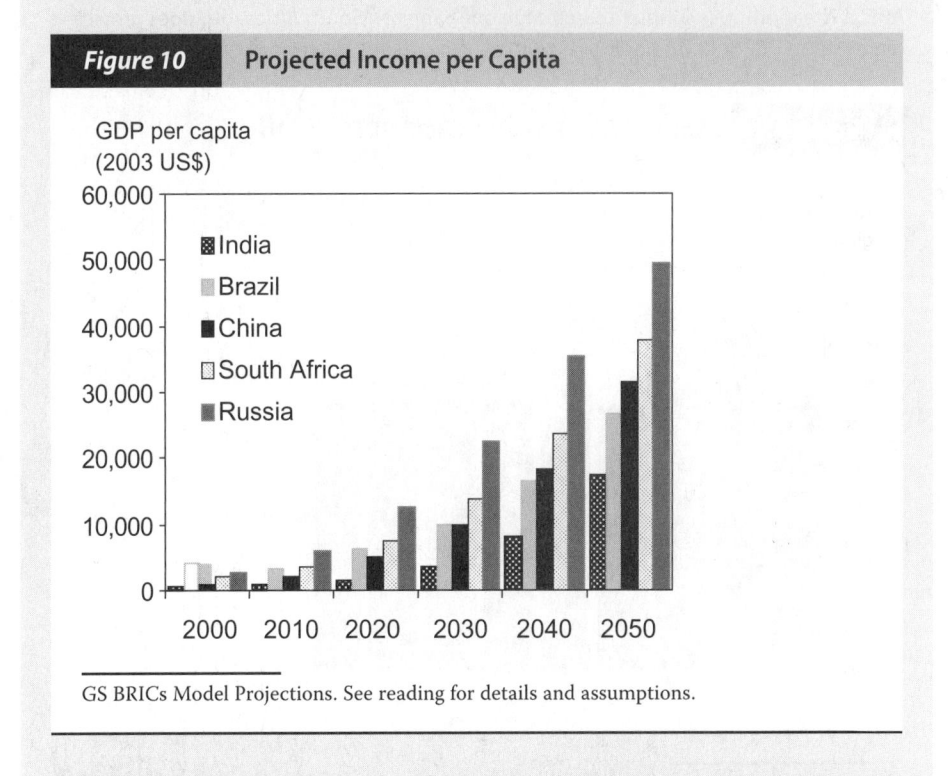

GS BRICs Model Projections. See reading for details and assumptions.

Figure 10 Projected Income per Capita

GS BRICs Model Projections. See reading for details and assumptions.

Our longer-term projections show South Africa growing at an average rate of around 3.5% over the next 50 years, comparable to our predictions for Russia and Brazil. With declining population growth rates, per capita incomes under these projections would rise significantly more rapidly. We find under these projections that South Africa's economy would be significantly smaller than the BRICs in 2050 (around US$1.2bn compared to US$5.9bn for Russia, the smallest of the BRICs economies), though its projected GDP *per capita* would actually be higher.

6 ARE THE RESULTS PLAUSIBLE?

The projection of a substantial shift in the generation of growth towards the BRICs is dramatic. Is it plausible?

We have looked at three main ways to cross check the forecasts, all of which give us broad comfort with the results.

First, the forecasts for GDP growth in the next 10 years are not out of line with the IMF's assumptions of potential growth in these economies (roughly 5% for Russia, 4% for Brazil, 8% for China, 5–6% for India). With the exception of Brazil, our projected growth rates are also close to recent performance. Brazil's performance would have to improve quite significantly relative to the past.

Second, although the implied changes in GDP and currencies may look dramatic on an absolute basis, they are significantly less spectacular than what some economies actually achieved over the last few decades. In Japan, between 1955 and 1985 real GDP increased by nearly 8 times (from initial levels of income per capita not unlike some of the BRICs) and real industrial production increased tenfold. Between 1970 and 1995—the yen appreciated by over 300% in nominal terms against the U.S. dollar. In the more recent past, Korea's GDP in 2000 increased by nearly 9 times between 1970 and 2000. Next to these experiences our projections look quite tame. Although the projections assume that economies remain on a steady development track, they do not assume "miracle-economy" growth.

As a final check on our estimates, we applied an entirely different approach to generate long-term growth projections based on cross-country econometric research. We took a well-known existing econometric model from Levine and Renelt (LR) that explains average GDP growth over the next thirty years as a function of initial income per capita, investment rates, population growth and secondary school enrollments.[4]

Table 6   Comparing Our Projections with the Levine-Renelt Model

30-Year Average Real GDP Growth	Our Projections	Levine-Renelt Model
Brazil	3.7	3.3
Russia	3.9	3.5
India	5.8	5.3
China	5.6	5.8

Although the technique employed is very different and a year-by-year path cannot be generated, the model has close parallels to our own approach. Initial income per capita drives our productivity catch-up, investment drives capital accumulation, and the level of education can be thought of as helping to determine the speed of convergence. Projections using the LR equation are not identical to our own, but close enough to reassure us that we are making sensible assumptions. Our own models are a bit more optimistic about growth prospects in general, but not by much.

7 A LOOK BACK IN TIME—WHAT WOULD WE HAVE SAID IN 1960?

We mentioned earlier that the world has changed a lot in the last fifty years. One further check on the plausibility of our projections is to go back in time, apply the same methods that we have used here and look at how our projections of GDP growth then would have compared with subsequent reality.

---

[4] Levine, Ross & Renelt, David, 1992. "A Sensitivity Analysis of Cross-Country Growth Regression," American Economic Review, Vol. 82 (4) pp. 942–63.

To do that, we looked at a set of 11 developed and developing countries (U.S., U.K., Germany, France, Italy, Japan, Brazil, Argentina, India, Korea and Hong Kong) starting in 1960 and projecting their GDP growth for the following 40 years (data availability meant we could not easily do a full 50 year projection).

We applied the same methodology, modeling capital stock growth as a function of the starting level of capital and investment and technical progress as a catch-up process on the U.S. Because we did not have demographic projections for 1960 (as we do now for the next fifty years), we used actual population data for the period as the basis for our labour force growth assumptions (effectively assuming that this part of the exercise was predicted perfectly).

The results of that exercise are generally encouraging. In general, the projected average growth rates over the period are surprisingly close to the actual outcomes. For the more developed countries, where the growth path has been steadier (France, Germany, U.K., U.S., Italy) the differences between projected and actual growth rates are small.

BOX 2 THE CONDITIONS FOR GROWTH

A set of core factors—macroeconomic stability, institutional capacity, openness and education—can set the stage for growth. Robert Barro's influential work on the determinants of growth found that growth is enhanced by higher schooling and life expectancy, lower fertility, lower government consumption, better maintenance of the rule of law, lower inflation and improvements in the terms of trade. These core policies are linked: institutional capacity is required to implement stable macroeconomic policies, macro stability is crucial to trade, and without price stability a country rarely has much success in liberalizing and expanding trade. We briefly view some of the most recent findings on these ingredients here:

Macro Stability. An unstable macro environment can hamper growth by distorting prices and incentives. Inflation hinders growth by discouraging saving and investment. Accordingly, a key focus is price stability, achieved through fiscal deficit reduction, tighter monetary policy and exchange-rate realignment. Within the BRICs, macroeconomic indicators reflecting policy divergence show wide swings: through the 1990s, Brazil averaged an inflation rate of 548% and a government deficit of 21.2% of GDP, against China's average inflation rate of 8% and government deficit of 2.3% of GDP.

Institutions. Institutions affect the "efficiency" of an economy much in the same way as technology does: more efficient institutions allow an economy to produce the same output with fewer inputs: Bad institutions lower incentives to invest, to work and to save. "Institutions" in this broad sense include the legal system, functioning markets, health and education systems, financial institutions and the government bureaucracy. Recent research argues that poor political and economic policies are only symptoms of longer-run institutional factors—a line of reasoning that could help explain the disappointing results of developing countries' adoption of macroeconomic policy reforms in the 1990s.

Openness. Openness to trade and FDI can provide access to imported inputs, new technology and larger markets. Empirical studies of trade and growth fall into three buckets. First, country studies document the economic and political consequences of import-substitution policies and export promoting policies. Second, much work uses cross-section or panel data to examine the cross-country relationship between openness and growth. This has produced mixed evidence, but in general it demonstrates a positive relationship between openness and growth. Third, sector, industry and plant-level studies investigate the effects of trade policy on employment, profits, productivity and output at a micro-economic level. There appears to be a greater consensus here than in the cross-country work about the productivity-enhancing effects of trade liberalization.

Education. As economies grow rapidly, they may face shortages of skilled workers, meaning that more years of schooling are a prerequisite for the next stage of economic development. Enrollment rates have increased dramatically over the past 30 years, on average over 5% per year, particularly in higher education (around 14%). Among the BRICs, India receives low marks for education indicators, particularly at the primary and secondary levels. Many cross-country studies have found positive and statistically significant correlations between schooling and growth rates of per capita GDP—on the order of 0.3% faster annual growth over a 30-year period from an additional one year of schooling.

For the developing countries (and Japan, which in 1960 was a developing country that was significantly poorer than Argentina) the range of outcomes is wider. For those countries where policy settings were not particularly growth-supportive—India, Brazil and Argentina—actual growth fell below what we would have projected. But for the Asian economies that had an unusually favourable growth experience, our method would have underpredicted actual growth performance in some cases quite significantly.

Overall, the results highlight that our method of projection seems broadly sensible. For the BRICs to meet our projections over the next fifty years, they do not need "miracle" performance—though it is important that they stay on the right track in maintaining broadly favourable conditions for growth.

ENSURING THE CONDITIONS FOR GROWTH — 8

This historical exercise highlights a critical point. For our projections to be close to the truth it is important that the BRICs remain on a steady growth track and keep the conditions in place that will allow that to happen. That is harder than it sounds and is the main reason why there is a good chance that the projections might not be realised. Of the BRICs, Brazil has not been growing in line with projections and may have the most immediate obstacles to this kind of growth. It provides a good illustration of the importance of getting the necessary conditions in place (see Box 3).

Research points to a wide range of conditions that are critical to ensuring solid growth performance and increasingly recognises that getting the right institutions as well as the right policies is important.[5] These are the things that the BRICs must get right (or keep getting right) if the kinds of paths we describe are to be close to the truth. The main ingredients (more detailed discussion of the evidence is provided in the box) are:

- **Sound macroeconomic policies and a stable macroeconomic background.** Low inflation, supportive government policy, sound public finances and a well-managed exchange rate can all help to promote growth. Each of the BRICs has been through periods of macroeconomic instability in the last few decades and some face significant macroeconomic challenges still. Brazil for instance has suffered greatly from the precariousness of the public finances and the foreign borrowing that it brought about.
- **Strong and stable political institutions.** Political uncertainty and instability discourages investment and damages growth. Each of the BRICs is likely to face considerable (and different) challenges in political development over the next few decades. For some (Russia most obviously), the task of institution-building has been a major issue in recent growth performance.
- **Openness.** Openness to trade and foreign direct investment has generally been an important part of successful development. The openness of the BRICs varies, but India is still relatively closed on many measures.

---

5 Because of this, the catch-up process is often described as a process of "conditional convergence" where the tendency for less developed economies to grow more rapidly is only evident after controlling for these conditions.

- **High levels of education.** Higher levels of education are generally helpful in contributing to more rapid growth and catch-up. The LR growth estimates above are based on a strong connection between secondary schooling and growth potential. Of the BRICs, India has the most work to do in expanding education.

BOX 3 BRAZIL: CHALLENGES IN SETTING THE CONDITIONS FOR SUSTAINED GROWTH

Of the BRICs, Brazil is the only one where recent growth experience has been significantly lower than our projected growth rates. This suggests that more needs to be done to unlock sustained higher growth in Brazil than is the case elsewhere and that our convergence assumptions for Brazil (though already lower than in China and Russia) may still prove too optimistic without deeper structural reforms.

Over the last 50 years, Brazil's real GDP growth rate amounted to 5.3%, but Figure 11 shows that growth has been declining sharply since the debt crisis of the 1980s. Following a growth surge between the late 1960s and the early 1970s on the back of economic liberalization, growth rates fell—in part because of a series of external shocks combined with poor policy response amidst a political transition from a military regime to a democracy.

Over the last decade, real GDP growth amounted to 2.9%, compared to an average of 5.3% since 1950. The excessive reliance on external financing and domestic public debt during the oil crisis and during the Real plan has rendered this adjustment effort particularly difficult, in part explaining the marked drop in growth rates.

The adjustment process has also reduced investment, which contributed to a depreciation of the capital stock, particularly in infrastructure, with important consequences for productivity. Even so, temporary surges in external financing or statistical rebounds may push growth higher temporarily, but for Brazil to break the historical downward trend in GDP growth and attain the kind of path set out in our projections here will take more.

The Lula Administration is making some progress. Macro stabilization is a key precondition of successful reform and is now clearly underway. The result of that stabilization is likely to be an improvement in growth over the next year or two that is reflected in our current forecasts of about 3.5% a year. On its own, though, stabilization will be insufficient to raise and sustain Brazil's growth rate to the kinds of levels that are set out in the projections in this paper. If that goal is to be achieved, substantial structural reforms will also be needed.

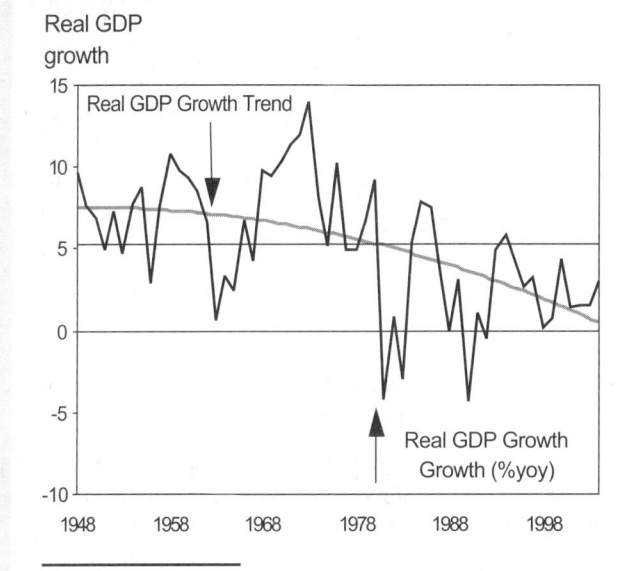

Figure 11 Brazil's Trend GDP Growth Rate Is Declining

GS BRICs Model Projections. See reading for details and assumptions.

How Different Assumptions Would Change Things

> Comparing Brazil with China and the other Asian economies gives a sense of the relatively larger obstacles that Brazil currently faces.
>
> - **Brazil is much less open to trade.** The tradable goods sector in China is almost eight times larger than in Brazil, when measured by imports plus exports.
> - **Investment and savings are lower.** Savings and investment ratios are around 18–19% of GDP compared to an investment rate of 36% of GDP in China and an Asian average of around 30%.
> - **Public and foreign debt are much higher.** Without a deeper fiscal adjustment and lower debt to GDP ratio (currently at 57.7% of GDP on a net basis and 78.2% of GDP on a gross basis), the private sector is almost completely crowded out from credit markets. China's net foreign debt and public debt are both significantly smaller.
>
> Unless significant progress is made in removing or reducing these obstacles, the projections set out here (which still show much lower growth than Brazil's post-war average) are unlikely to be achievable and the slide in trend growth could continue.

Figure 12 How Our Model Fares in Gauging Growth 1960–2000

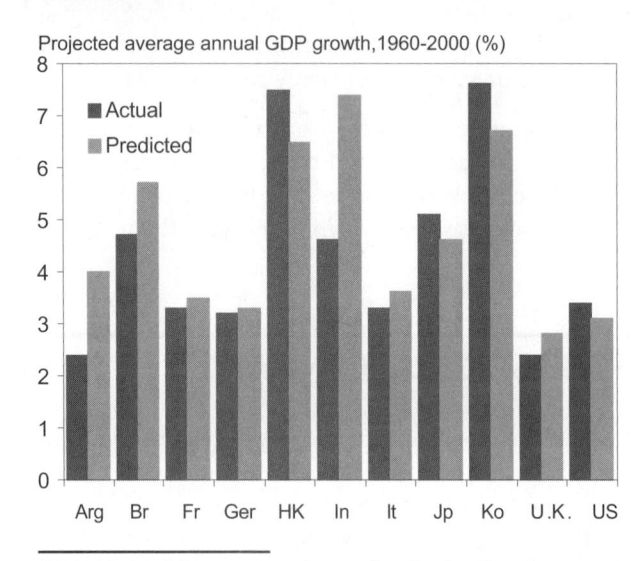

GS BRICs Model Projections. See reading for details and assumptions.

HOW DIFFERENT ASSUMPTIONS WOULD CHANGE THINGS — 9

In our models, the effect of these conditions for growth can be thought of as operating through our assumptions about the investment rate and the rate of catch-up in TFP with the developed economies. If the BRICs economies fail to deliver the kinds of conditions that are broadly necessary for sustained growth, our assumptions about investment and convergence will prove too optimistic. For Brazil and India, in particular, if they succeed more quickly than we expect, investment rates might actually be higher than our projections and convergence more rapid.

To illustrate in a simple way the point that the assumptions that we have made—and the underlying conditions that determine them—are important, we show briefly what happens if we change them:

- **Catch-up.** Because the convergence rate captures a broad range of factors that determine the ability to "catch up," altering it can make a significant difference to projections. For example, if we lower China's "convergence rate" by a third, our projections of average GDP growth rate over the 50-year period fall to 4.3% from 4.8% and our projected 2050 US$GDP level drops by 39%. In our baseline model, rates of convergence are generally slower for India and Brazil than for China and Russia. If we raised our convergence rates in India and Brazil to those of China and Russia, India's 2000–2030 average GDP growth rate would rise to 7.4%, against 5.8% originally. Brazil's GDP growth rate would rise as well: to 4.3% from 3.7%.

- **Investment.** The assumed investment rates are less important, but substantial differences from our assumptions would certainly alter the main conclusions. Lowering our assumptions of China's investment rate by 5 percentage points slightly lowers China's average 2000–2030 GDP growth rate to 5.5% from 5.7%. Cutting 5 percentage points off of investment rates across the BRICs would reduce their GDP levels on average by around 13% by 2050.

- **Demographics.** The demographic assumptions may also turn out to be incorrect. For instance, Russia's demographics might not turn out to be as negative as the U.S. census projections, and declining fertility and rising mortality may turn out to have been a temporary feature of the transition from communism. Shifting demographic trends might also be partly offset by attempts to raise participation or to extend working ages, neither of which we currently capture.

Sensitivity to these kinds of assumptions clearly means that there is significant uncertainty around our projections. The advantage of the framework that we have developed is that we now have the tools to look at these and other questions in much more detail. We also have a clear baseline against which to measure them.

10 IMPLICATIONS OF THE BRICS' ASCENDANCY

Each of the BRICs faces very significant challenges in keeping development on track. This means that there is a good chance that our projections are not met, either through bad policy or bad luck.

Despite the challenges, we think the prospect is worth taking seriously. After all, three of these markets—China, India and Russia—have already been at the top of the growth charts in recent years. They may stay there.

If the BRICs *do* come anywhere close to meeting the projections set out here, the implications for the pattern of growth and economic activity could be very large indeed. Parts of this story—the opportunities in China, for instance—are well understood. But we suspect that many other parts—the potential for India and the other markets and the interplay of aging in the developed economies with growth in the developing ones—may not be.

We will be using the tools developed here to look in detail at different kinds of scenarios and to flesh out the links between our growth projections and investment opportunities, but we set out some brief conclusions here:

- The relative importance of the BRICs as an engine of new demand growth and spending power may shift more dramatically and quickly than expected under the right conditions. Higher growth in these economies could offset the impact of greying populations and slower growth in today's advanced economies.

Implications of the BRICs' Ascendancy

Figure 13 — GDP Size and Relative Income per Capita Levels Will Diverge over Time

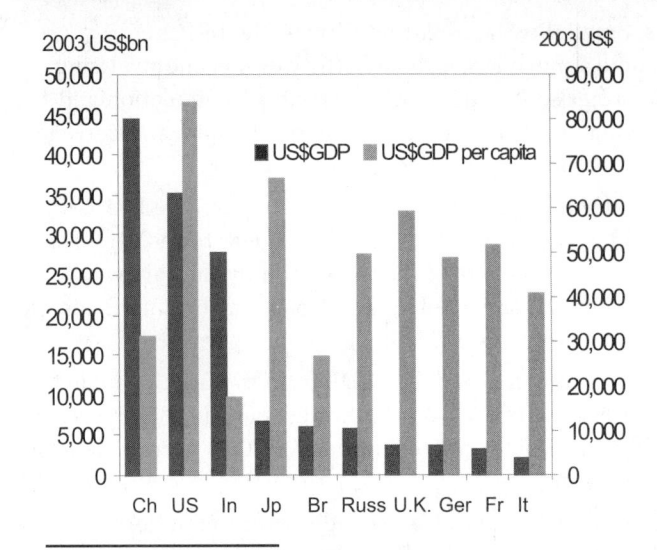

GS BRICs Model Projections. See reading for details and assumptions.

- Higher growth may lead to higher returns and increased demand for capital in these markets—and for the means to finance it. The weight of the BRICs in investment portfolios could rise sharply. The pattern of capital flows might move further in their favour and major currency realignments would take place.

- Rising incomes may also see these economies move through the "sweet spot" of growth for different kinds of products, as local spending patterns change. This could be an important determinant of demand and pricing patterns for a range of commodities.

- As the advanced economies become a shrinking part of the world economy, the accompanying shifts in spending could provide significant opportunities for many of today's global companies. Being invested in and involved in the right markets—and particularly the right emerging markets—may become an increasingly important strategic choice for many firms.

- The list of the world's ten largest economies may look quite different in fifty years' time. The largest economies in the world (by GDP) may also no longer be the richest (by income per capita) making strategic choices for firms more complex.

- Regional neighbours could benefit from the growth opportunities from the BRICs. With three out of the four largest economies in 2050 potentially residing in Asia, we could see important geopolitical shifts towards the Asian region. China's growth is already having a significant impact on the opportunities for the rest of Asia. Sustained strong growth in the other BRICs economies might have similar impacts on their major trading partners.

Are you ready?

SUMMARY

- Over the next 50 years, Brazil, Russia, India and China—the BRICs economies—could become a much larger force in the world economy. Using the latest demographic projections and a model of capital accumulation and productivity growth, we map out GDP growth, income per capita and currency movements in the BRICs economies until 2050.

- The results are startling. If things go right, in less than 40 years, the BRICs economies together could be larger than the G6 in U.S. dollar terms. By 2025 they could account for over half the size of the G6. Currently they are worth less than 15%. Of the current G6, only the U.S. and Japan may be among the six largest economies in U.S. dollar terms in 2050.

- About two-thirds of the increase in U.S. dollar GDP from the BRICs should come from higher real growth, with the balance through currency appreciation. The BRICs' real exchange rates could appreciate by up to 300% over the next 50 years (an average of 2.5% a year).

- The shift in GDP relative to the G6 takes place steadily over the period, but is most dramatic in the first 30 years. Growth for the BRICs is likely to slow significantly toward the end of the period, with only India seeing growth rates significantly above 3% by 2050. And individuals in the BRICs are still likely to be poorer on average than individuals in the G6 economies, with the exception of Russia. China's per capita income could be roughly what the developed economies are now (about U.S.$30,000 per capita).

- As early as 2009, the annual increase in U.S. dollar spending from the BRICs could be greater than that from the G6 and more than twice as much in dollar terms as it is now. By 2025 the annual increase in U.S. dollar spending from the BRICs could be twice that of the G6, and four times higher by 2050.

- The key assumption underlying our projections is that the BRICs maintain policies and develop institutions that are supportive of growth. Each of the BRICs faces significant challenges in keeping development on track. This means that there is a good chance that our projections are not met, either through bad policy or bad luck. But if the BRICs come anywhere close to meeting the projections set out here, the implications for the pattern of growth and economic activity could be large.

- The relative importance of the BRICs as an engine of new demand growth and spending power may shift more dramatically and quickly than expected. Higher growth in these economies could offset the impact of greying populations and slower growth in the advanced economies.

- Higher growth may lead to higher returns and increased demand for capital. The weight of the BRICs in investment portfolios could rise sharply. Capital flows might move further in their favour, prompting major currency realignments.

- Rising incomes may also see these economies move through the "sweet spot" of growth for different kinds of products, as local spending patterns change. This could be an important determinant of demand and pricing patterns for a range of commodities.

- As today's advanced economies become a shrinking part of the world economy, the accompanying shifts in spending could provide significant opportunities for global companies. Being invested in and involved in the right markets—particularly the right emerging markets—may become an increasingly important strategic choice.

- The list of the world's ten largest economies may look quite different in 2050. The largest economies in the world (by GDP) may no longer be the richest (by income per capita), making strategic choices for firms more complex.

APPENDIX 20A

A Long-Term Model of Growth and Exchange Rates

Growth Model

We provide detail on the underlying assumptions of our models. The model relies on a simple formulation of the overall level of GDP (Y) in terms of a) labour (L) b) the capital stock (K) and c) the level of "technical progress" (A) or Total Factor Productivity (TFP).

We assume that GDP is a simple (Cobb-Douglas) function of these three ingredients:

$$Y = AK^{\alpha}L^{1-\alpha}$$

where α is the share of income that accrues to capital.

We then need to describe the process by which each of the different components (labor, the capital stock and TFP) change over time.

- For L, we simply use the projections of the working age population (15–60) from the U.S. Census Bureau.
- For K, we take the initial capital stock, assume an investment rate (investment as a % of GDP) and a depreciation rate to calculate the growth in the capital stock:

$$K_{t+1} = K_t(1-\delta) + \left(\frac{I_t}{Y_t}\right)Y_t$$

- For A, the description of technical progress, we assume that technology changes as part of a process of catch-up with the most developed countries. The speed of convergence is assumed to depend on income per capita, with the assumption that as the developing economies get closer to the income levels of the more developed economies, their TFP growth rate slows. Developing countries can have faster growth in this area because there is room to "catch up" with developed countries:

$$\frac{A_t}{A_{t-1}} = 1.3\% - \beta \ln\left(\frac{Incomepercapita_{DC}}{Incomepercapita_{US}}\right)$$

where β is a measure of how fast convergence takes place and 1.3% is our assumed long-term TFP growth rate for the U.S.

The assumptions needed to generate the forecasts are summarized below:

- Labor force and population, from the U.S. Census Bureau projections.
- Depreciation rate (δ) assumed to be 4% as in the World Bank capital stock estimates.
- Investment rate assumptions based on recent history, for Brazil (19%), for India (22%) for Russia (25%) for China (36% until 2010, declining to 30% thereafter).
- Income share of capital assumed to be 1/3, a standard assumption (α) from historical evidence.

- U.S. long-run TFP growth assumed to be 1.33%, implying steady-state labour productivity growth of 2%—our long-run estimate.
- Convergence speed for TFP (β) assumed to be 1.5%, within the range of estimates from academic research.

Exchange Rate Model

Our model of real exchange rates is then calculated from the predictions of labour productivity growth. Specifically, we assume that a 1% productivity differential in favour of economy A relative to the U.S. will raise its equilibrium real exchange rate against the U.S. dollar by 1%, where our long-run assumption for U.S. productivity growth is again 2%.

$$\Delta \ln(e) = \Delta \ln\left(\frac{Y}{L}\right) - 0.02$$

This assumption that the relationship is one-for-one underpins our GSDEER models, and the coefficient on relative productivity terms in our GSDEEMER models is generally also clustered around 1. We make the simplifying assumption that over the long term, only productivity differentials play a large role in determining real exchange rates.

APPENDIX 20B

Our Projections in Detail

Table B1 Projected US$GDP

2003 US$bn	BRICs				G6						BRICs	G6
	Brazil	China	India	Russia	France	Germany	Italy	Japan	U.K.	U.S.		
2000	762	1,078	469	391	1,311	1,875	1,078	4,176	1,437	9,825	2,700	19,702
2001	601	1,157	466	383	1,321	1,855	1,093	4,032	1,425	10,082	2,607	19,808
2002	491	1,252	474	379	1,346	1,866	1,114	4,358	1,498	10,446	2,595	20,628
2003	461	1,353	511	430	1,387	1,900	1,155	4,366	1,565	10,879	2,754	21,253
2004	435	1,529	554	476	1,455	1,966	1,212	4,366	1,647	11,351	2,994	21,998
2005	468	1,724	604	534	1,489	2,011	1,236	4,427	1,688	11,697	3,330	22,548
2006	502	1,936	659	594	1,520	2,059	1,257	4,498	1,728	12,041	3,691	23,104
2007	539	2,169	718	654	1,547	2,102	1,277	4,536	1,762	12,348	4,079	23,572
2008	579	2,422	782	716	1,572	2,141	1,297	4,556	1,797	12,656	4,499	24,019
2009	622	2,699	853	780	1,597	2,178	1,317	4,573	1,836	12,966	4,953	24,466
2010	668	2,998	929	847	1,622	2,212	1,337	4,601	1,876	13,271	5,441	24,919
2011	718	3,316	1,011	917	1,649	2,246	1,358	4,638	1,918	13,580	5,962	25,389
2012	771	3,650	1,100	990	1,677	2,282	1,381	4,683	1,960	13,883	6,512	25,866
2013	828	4,002	1,196	1,068	1,706	2,317	1,403	4,736	2,004	14,184	7,094	26,349
2014	888	4,371	1,299	1,149	1,736	2,352	1,425	4,795	2,046	14,486	7,707	26,840
2015	952	4,754	1,411	1,232	1,767	2,386	1,447	4,858	2,089	14,786	8,349	27,332

Table B1 Continued

2003 US$bn	\multicolumn{4}{c	}{BRICs}	\multicolumn{6}{c	}{G6}	BRICs	G6
	Brazil	China	India	Russia	France	Germany	Italy	Japan	U.K.	U.S.		
2016	1,019	5,156	1,531	1,322	1,799	2,418	1,469	4,925	2,130	15,106	9,028	27,847
2017	1,091	5,585	1,659	1,417	1,832	2,448	1,492	4,999	2,170	15,427	9,752	28,367
2018	1,167	6,041	1,797	1,518	1,865	2,476	1,513	5,074	2,209	15,750	10,524	28,887
2019	1,248	6,538	1,945	1,626	1,897	2,502	1,534	5,146	2,247	16,083	11,357	29,410
2020	1,333	7,070	2,104	1,741	1,930	2,524	1,553	5,221	2,285	16,415	12,248	29,928
2021	1,397	7,646	2,278	1,829	1,963	2,544	1,571	5,297	2,321	16,765	13,150	30,462
2022	1,465	8,250	2,470	1,924	1,996	2,562	1,588	5,372	2,355	17,133	14,109	31,006
2023	1,537	8,863	2,682	2,028	2,029	2,577	1,603	5,443	2,389	17,518	15,110	31,559
2024	1,613	9,517	2,916	2,141	2,062	2,591	1,615	5,509	2,422	17,918	16,187	32,117
2025	1,695	10,213	3,174	2,264	2,095	2,604	1,625	5,567	2,456	18,340	17,345	32,687
2026	1,781	10,947	3,459	2,395	2,128	2,619	1,634	5,641	2,491	18,803	18,582	33,316
2027	1,873	11,732	3,774	2,533	2,163	2,634	1,644	5,696	2,528	19,293	19,913	33,958
2028	1,971	12,555	4,123	2,679	2,198	2,652	1,653	5,740	2,567	19,801	21,327	34,611
2029	2,076	13,409	4,508	2,828	2,233	2,672	1,662	5,778	2,607	20,319	22,821	35,271
2030	2,189	14,312	4,935	2,980	2,267	2,697	1,671	5,810	2,649	20,833	24,415	35,927
2031	2,308	15,260	5,407	3,131	2,300	2,727	1,678	5,835	2,692	21,371	26,107	36,603
2032	2,436	16,264	5,930	3,283	2,333	2,763	1,686	5,851	2,740	21,946	27,911	37,319
2033	2,572	17,317	6,508	3,434	2,367	2,806	1,692	5,861	2,791	22,554	29,830	38,072
2034	2,716	18,428	7,147	3,585	2,404	2,854	1,699	5,869	2,845	23,187	31,877	38,858
2035	2,871	19,605	7,854	3,734	2,445	2,903	1,708	5,882	2,901	23,828	34,064	39,668
2036	3,033	20,845	8,621	3,881	2,490	2,953	1,719	5,902	2,961	24,492	36,380	40,516
2037	3,201	22,152	9,453	4,028	2,535	3,002	1,733	5,930	3,023	25,168	38,833	41,389
2038	3,374	23,522	10,352	4,175	2,580	3,051	1,748	5,961	3,085	25,852	41,423	42,276
2039	3,554	24,949	11,322	4,321	2,625	3,100	1,767	5,998	3,144	26,542	44,147	43,175
2040	3,740	26,439	12,367	4,467	2,668	3,147	1,788	6,039	3,201	27,229	47,013	44,072
2041	3,932	28,003	13,490	4,613	2,711	3,192	1,810	6,086	3,258	27,929	50,038	44,987
2042	4,128	29,589	14,696	4,756	2,754	3,238	1,834	6,136	3,317	28,654	53,171	45,933
2043	4,336	31,257	15,989	4,891	2,801	3,285	1,859	6,187	3,377	29,399	56,473	46,908
2044	4,560	33,003	17,371	5,022	2,849	3,333	1,885	6,239	3,437	30,170	59,955	47,913
2045	4,794	34,799	18,847	5,156	2,898	3,381	1,912	6,297	3,496	30,956	63,596	48,940
2046	5,031	36,636	20,421	5,289	2,946	3,428	1,941	6,362	3,554	31,761	67,378	49,993
2047	5,276	38,490	22,099	5,417	2,995	3,473	1,971	6,431	3,611	32,592	71,281	51,074
2048	5,527	40,420	23,886	5,552	3,045	3,516	2,001	6,506	3,668	33,437	75,385	52,173
2049	5,789	42,408	25,785	5,701	3,097	3,559	2,031	6,586	3,725	34,297	79,684	53,296
2050	6,074	44,453	27,803	5,870	3,148	3,603	2,061	6,673	3,782	35,165	84,201	54,433

GS BRICs Model Projections. See reading for details and assumptions.

Table B2 Projected US$GDP Per Capita

2003 US$	BRICs				G6					
	Brazil	China	India	Russia	France	Germany	Italy	Japan	U.K.	U.S.
2000	4,338	854	468	2,675	22,078	22,814	18,677	32,960	24,142	34,797
2001	3,381	910	457	2,633	22,143	22,545	18,895	31,775	23,860	35,373
2002	2,726	979	458	2,611	22,461	22,659	19,224	34,297	25,003	36,312
2003	2,530	1,051	486	2,976	23,047	23,059	19,920	34,322	26,042	37,470
2004	2,364	1,181	520	3,305	24,080	23,856	20,881	34,290	27,333	38,735
2005	2,512	1,324	559	3,718	24,547	24,402	21,277	34,744	27,920	39,552
2006	2,668	1,478	602	4,142	24,968	24,986	21,629	35,292	28,509	40,346
2007	2,835	1,646	647	4,570	25,321	25,512	21,960	35,587	28,986	41,004
2008	3,015	1,827	695	5,013	25,650	25,998	22,300	35,751	29,492	41,655
2009	3,209	2,023	748	5,470	25,975	26,452	22,649	35,917	30,043	42,304
2010	3,417	2,233	804	5,948	26,314	26,877	23,018	36,172	30,611	42,926
2011	3,640	2,453	864	6,453	26,682	27,312	23,407	36,516	31,201	43,550
2012	3,875	2,682	929	6,981	27,069	27,767	23,816	36,942	31,808	44,142
2013	4,124	2,922	998	7,540	27,470	28,224	24,234	37,442	32,413	44,715
2014	4,387	3,171	1,071	8,126	27,892	28,674	24,656	38,016	33,007	45,283
2015	4,664	3,428	1,149	8,736	28,338	29,111	25,086	38,626	33,594	45,835
2016	4,957	3,696	1,233	9,389	28,807	29,534	25,522	39,292	34,161	46,440
2017	5,266	3,981	1,321	10,092	29,282	29,936	25,964	40,032	34,700	47,035
2018	5,594	4,283	1,416	10,845	29,762	30,321	26,407	40,795	35,218	47,630
2019	5,939	4,613	1,516	11,655	30,242	30,678	26,833	41,561	35,731	48,247
2020	6,302	4,965	1,622	12,527	30,723	31,000	27,239	42,359	36,234	48,849
2021	6,562	5,346	1,739	13,212	31,211	31,296	27,628	43,186	36,709	49,496
2022	6,838	5,747	1,867	13,959	31,709	31,572	27,995	44,023	37,154	50,182
2023	7,133	6,153	2,007	14,777	32,208	31,824	28,335	44,845	37,593	50,902
2024	7,447	6,587	2,161	15,674	32,701	32,058	28,628	45,648	38,031	51,652
2025	7,781	7,051	2,331	16,652	33,203	32,299	28,894	46,391	38,479	52,450
2026	8,136	7,542	2,517	17,697	33,718	32,555	29,152	47,287	38,958	53,348
2027	8,514	8,068	2,723	18,809	34,251	32,830	29,413	48,037	39,466	54,306
2028	8,919	8,621	2,949	19,983	34,796	33,135	29,671	48,709	40,013	55,297
2029	9,352	9,198	3,199	21,194	35,339	33,483	29,922	49,350	40,585	56,294
2030	9,823	9,809	3,473	22,427	35,876	33,898	30,177	49,944	41,194	57,263
2031	10,320	10,454	3,776	23,674	36,406	34,378	30,417	50,483	41,823	58,281
2032	10,852	11,138	4,110	24,926	36,938	34,938	30,657	50,966	42,534	59,384
2033	11,421	11,859	4,477	26,191	37,493	35,605	30,884	51,400	43,301	60,560
2034	12,030	12,623	4,882	27,470	38,101	36,332	31,126	51,826	44,124	61,786
2035	12,682	13,434	5,327	28,749	38,779	37,087	31,402	52,313	44,985	63,017
2036	13,364	14,293	5,808	30,030	39,518	37,857	31,730	52,868	45,898	64,292
2037	14,075	15,201	6,326	31,323	40,278	38,628	32,116	53,499	46,858	65,581
2038	14,813	16,157	6,884	32,636	41,049	39,408	32,548	54,180	47,827	66,875
2039	15,576	17,159	7,482	33,966	41,834	40,195	33,036	54,924	48,758	68,165

Appendix 20B

Table B2 *Continued*

2003 US$	BRICs				G6					
	Brazil	China	India	Russia	France	Germany	Italy	Japan	U.K.	U.S.
2040	16,370	18,209	8,124	35,314	42,601	40,966	33,583	55,721	49,658	69,431
2041	17,191	19,315	8,810	36,684	43,363	41,727	34,169	56,591	50,569	70,713
2042	18,037	20,443	9,544	38,057	44,151	42,499	34,787	57,507	51,509	72,040
2043	18,935	21,635	10,326	39,386	44,998	43,291	35,442	58,448	52,470	73,401
2044	19,904	22,892	11,160	40,706	45,893	44,110	36,133	59,419	53,434	74,805
2045	20,926	24,192	12,046	42,081	46,795	44,940	36,859	60,454	54,386	76,228
2046	21,964	25,530	12,988	43,463	47,706	45,759	37,627	61,583	55,331	77,680
2047	23,040	26,891	13,988	44,832	48,640	46,559	38,430	62,774	56,275	79,171
2048	24,152	28,321	15,050	46,280	49,601	47,346	39,237	64,035	57,211	80,677
2049	25,318	29,810	16,174	47,871	50,589	48,142	40,061	65,376	58,169	82,196
2050	26,592	31,357	17,366	49,646	51,594	48,952	40,901	66,805	59,122	83,710

GS BRICs Model Projections. See reading for details and assumptions.

Table B3 Projected Real GDP Growth

%yoy	BRICs				G6[a]					
	Brazil	China	India	Russia	France	Germany	Italy	Japan	U.K.	U.S.
2000	4.2	8.0	5.4	10.0	4.2	2.9	3.3	2.8	3.1	3.8
2001	1.5	7.3	4.2	5.0	2.1	0.6	1.7	0.4	2.1	0.3
2002	1.5	8.2	4.7	4.3	1.2	0.2	0.4	0.1	1.9	2.4
2003	1.1	8.1	5.6	6.1	0.5	0.0	0.6	2.7	1.8	2.7
2004	3.5	8.4	5.9	4.4	2.9	1.9	2.4	1.7	2.9	3.5
2005	4.2	7.9	6.2	5.8	2.3	2.3	2.0	1.4	2.4	3.1
2006	4.1	7.6	6.2	5.3	2.1	2.4	1.7	1.6	2.4	2.9
2007	4.1	7.3	6.1	4.8	1.8	2.1	1.6	0.8	2.0	2.6
2008	4.1	7.1	6.1	4.5	1.6	1.9	1.5	0.4	2.0	2.5
2009	4.2	6.9	6.1	4.3	1.6	1.7	1.5	0.4	2.2	2.5
2010	4.2	6.6	6.1	4.1	1.6	1.5	1.6	0.6	2.2	2.4
2011	4.1	6.4	6.0	4.0	1.7	1.6	1.6	0.8	2.2	2.3
2012	4.1	6.0	6.0	3.8	1.7	1.6	1.6	1.0	2.2	2.2
2013	4.0	5.8	5.9	3.7	1.7	1.6	1.6	1.1	2.2	2.2
2014	4.0	5.5	5.9	3.6	1.8	1.5	1.6	1.3	2.1	2.1
2015	3.9	5.2	5.8	3.5	1.8	1.4	1.6	1.3	2.1	2.1
2016	3.9	5.1	5.8	3.4	1.8	1.3	1.5	1.4	2.0	2.2
2017	3.8	4.9	5.7	3.4	1.8	1.2	1.5	1.5	1.9	2.1
2018	3.8	4.8	5.7	3.3	1.8	1.2	1.5	1.5	1.8	2.1
2019	3.7	5.1	5.6	3.3	1.8	1.0	1.4	1.4	1.7	2.1

(continued)

Table B3 Continued

%yoy	BRICs				G6[a]					
	Brazil	China	India	Russia	France	Germany	Italy	Japan	U.K.	U.S.
2020	3.7	5.0	5.5	3.3	1.7	0.9	1.3	1.4	1.7	2.1
2021	3.7	5.2	5.6	3.3	1.7	0.8	1.2	1.5	1.6	2.1
2022	3.7	4.9	5.7	3.3	1.7	0.7	1.0	1.4	1.5	2.2
2023	3.7	4.1	5.7	3.4	1.7	0.6	0.9	1.3	1.4	2.2
2024	3.8	4.2	5.8	3.5	1.6	0.5	0.7	1.2	1.4	2.3
2025	3.8	4.2	5.8	3.6	1.6	0.5	0.6	1.0	1.4	2.4
2026	3.8	4.1	5.9	3.6	1.6	0.6	0.6	1.3	1.4	2.5
2027	3.8	4.3	5.9	3.6	1.6	0.6	0.6	1.0	1.5	2.6
2028	3.8	4.1	6.0	3.6	1.6	0.7	0.6	0.8	1.5	2.6
2029	3.8	3.9	6.0	3.5	1.6	0.8	0.5	0.7	1.6	2.6
2030	3.9	3.9	6.1	3.4	1.5	0.9	0.5	0.6	1.6	2.5
2031	3.9	3.8	6.1	3.3	1.5	1.1	0.5	0.4	1.6	2.6
2032	3.9	3.9	6.1	3.1	1.4	1.3	0.4	0.3	1.8	2.7
2033	3.9	3.8	6.2	3.0	1.5	1.6	0.4	0.2	1.9	2.8
2034	3.9	3.8	6.2	2.9	1.6	1.7	0.4	0.1	1.9	2.8
2035	3.9	3.9	6.2	2.8	1.7	1.7	0.5	0.2	2.0	2.8
2036	3.9	3.9	6.1	2.7	1.8	1.7	0.6	0.3	2.0	2.8
2037	3.8	3.9	6.1	2.6	1.8	1.7	0.8	0.5	2.1	2.8
2038	3.8	3.9	6.0	2.5	1.8	1.6	0.9	0.5	2.1	2.7
2039	3.7	3.8	5.9	2.5	1.8	1.6	1.0	0.6	1.9	2.7
2040	3.6	3.7	5.8	2.4	1.7	1.5	1.2	0.7	1.8	2.6
2041	3.6	3.8	5.8	2.3	1.6	1.4	1.3	0.8	1.8	2.6
2042	3.5	3.4	5.7	2.2	1.6	1.4	1.3	0.8	1.8	2.6
2043	3.5	3.5	5.6	2.1	1.7	1.4	1.4	0.8	1.8	2.6
2044	3.6	3.5	5.5	2.0	1.7	1.5	1.4	0.8	1.8	2.6
2045	3.5	3.3	5.4	2.0	1.7	1.4	1.5	0.9	1.7	2.6
2046	3.4	3.1	5.4	1.9	1.7	1.4	1.5	1.0	1.7	2.6
2047	3.4	2.8	5.3	1.8	1.7	1.3	1.5	1.1	1.6	2.6
2048	3.3	2.9	5.2	1.9	1.7	1.2	1.5	1.2	1.6	2.6
2049	3.3	2.8	5.1	2.0	1.7	1.2	1.5	1.2	1.6	2.6
2050	3.4	2.7	5.1	2.1	1.7	1.2	1.5	1.3	1.5	2.5

[a]Indicative projections made only on the model assumptions described in the text. Not GS official forecasts.
GS BRICs Model Projections. See reading for details and assumptions.

APPENDIX 20C

Demographic Projections: The Cohort Component Method

We have used U.S. census population estimates, which are based on the cohort component population projection method, which follows each cohort of people of the same age throughout its lifetime according to mortality, fertility and migration.

First, fertility rates are projected and applied to the female population in childbearing ages to estimate the number of births every year (see Figure C1). Second, each cohort of children born is also followed through time by exposing it to projected mortality rates. Finally, the component method takes into account any in-migrants who are incorporated into the population and out-migrants who leave the population. Migrants are added to or subtracted from the population at each specific age.

In setting levels for mortality and fertility, available data on past trends provide guidance. For mortality, information concerning programs of public health are taken into account. For fertility, factors such as trends in age at marriage; the proportion of women using contraception; the strength of family planning programs; and any foreseen changes in women's educational attainment or in their labor force participation are factored into the analysis. Assumptions about future migration are more speculative than assumptions about fertility and mortality. The future path of international migration is set on the basis of past international migration estimates as well as the policy stance of countries regarding future international migration flows.

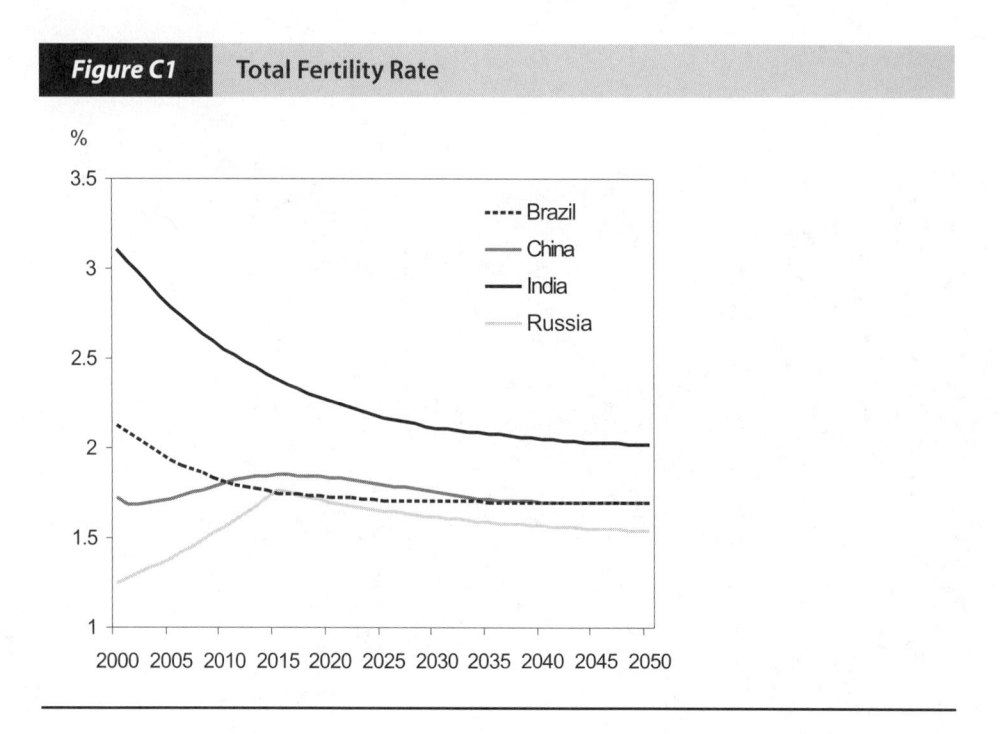

Figure C1 **Total Fertility Rate**

Indices			
Tokyo (Nikkei)			
Seoul			
Jakarta (Comp.)			
Mumbai			
Singapore	18,156.7	1.4%	-4.5%
Sydney	3,971.0	1.1%	-4.7%
Shanghai B	4,644.0	0.9%	-10.5%
Hong Kong	316.8	0.7%	-6.9%
Toronto	22,700.9	0.5%	-4.2%
Stockholm	13,524.8	0.1%	4.1%
Mexico City			

PORTFOLIO MANAGEMENT
STUDY SESSION

8

Asset Allocation

After developing capital market expectations, the next task in the investment management process is determining the strategic asset allocation. Here the manager combines the investment policy statement with capital market expectations to determine target asset class weights. Maximum and minimum permissible asset class weights are often specified as a risk-control mechanism. The investor may consider both single-period and multi-period perspectives when evaluating the return and risk characteristics of potential asset allocations. A single-period perspective has the advantage of simplicity. A multi-period perspective can address the liquidity and tax considerations that arise from rebalancing portfolios through time. Such a perspective can also address serial correlation (long- and short-term dependencies) in returns, but is more costly to implement.

READING ASSIGNMENTS

Reading 21 *Asset Allocation*
Managing Investment Portfolios: A Dynamic Process, Third Edition, John L. Maginn, CFA, Donald L. Tuttle, CFA, Jerald E. Pinto, CFA, and Dennis W. McLeavey, CFA, editors

Reading 22 *The Case for International Diversification*
Global Investments, Sixth Edition, by Bruno Solnik and Dennis McLeavey, CFA

Singapore
Sydney
Shanghai B
Hong Kong
Toronto
316.8
22,700.9
0.5%
-4.2%
0.1%
4.1%

READING 21

Asset Allocation

by William F. Sharpe, Peng Chen, CFA, Jerald E. Pinto, CFA, and Dennis W. McLeavey, CFA

LEARNING OUTCOMES

Mastery	The candidate should be able to:
☐	**a** explain the function of strategic asset allocation in portfolio management and discuss its role in relation to specifying and controlling the investor's exposures to systematic risk;
☐	**b** compare strategic and tactical asset allocation;
☐	**c** discuss the importance of asset allocation for portfolio performance;
☐	**d** contrast the asset-only and asset/liability management (ALM) approaches to asset allocation and discuss the investor circumstances in which they are commonly used;
☐	**e** explain the advantage of dynamic over static asset allocation and discuss the trade-offs of complexity and cost;
☐	**f** explain how loss aversion, mental accounting, and fear of regret may influence asset allocation policy;
☐	**g** evaluate return and risk objectives in relation to strategic asset allocation;
☐	**h** evaluate whether an asset class or set of asset classes has been appropriately specified;
☐	**i** select and justify an appropriate set of asset classes for an investor;
☐	**j** evaluate the theoretical and practical effects of including additional asset classes in an asset allocation;
☐	**k** explain the major steps involved in establishing an appropriate asset allocation;
☐	**l** discuss the strengths and limitations of the following approaches to asset allocation: mean–variance, resampled efficient frontier, Black–Litterman, Monte Carlo simulation, ALM, and experience based;
☐	**m** discuss the structure of the minimum-variance frontier with a constraint against short sales;
☐	**n** formulate and justify a strategic asset allocation, given an investment policy statement and capital market expectations;

Managing Investment Portfolios: A Dynamic Process, Third Edition, John L. Maginn, CFA, Donald L. Tuttle, CFA, Jerald E. Pinto, CFA, and Dennis W. McLeavey, CFA, editors. Copyright © 2007 by CFA Institute.

Mastery	The candidate should be able to:
☐	**o** compare the considerations that affect asset allocation for individual investors versus institutional investors and critique a proposed asset allocation in light of those considerations;
☐	**p** formulate and justify tactical asset allocation (TAA) adjustments to strategic asset class weights, given a TAA strategy and expectational data.

1 INTRODUCTION

For investors, selecting the types of assets for a portfolio and allocating funds among different asset classes are major decisions. A 70/30 stock/bond portfolio has a different expected return, risk, and cash flow pattern than a 30/70 stock/bond portfolio. Which asset allocation is more appropriate for a particular investor will depend on how well the allocation's characteristics match up with the investment objectives and circumstances described in the investor's investment policy statement (IPS). This reading covers the principles of determining an appropriate asset allocation for an investment client. The questions we will address include the following:

- How does asset allocation function in controlling risk?
- What are the major approaches to asset allocation and the strengths and weaknesses of each?
- How should asset classes be defined, and how can one evaluate the benefits from including additional asset classes?
- What are the pitfalls in asset allocation according to practice?
- What are the current choices in optimization?
- How may a portfolio manager use prior investment experience in selecting an asset allocation?
- What are the special considerations in determining an asset allocation for individual and institutional investors?

We have organized this reading as follows: Sections 2 and 3 orient the reader about the role of asset allocation. As the discussion points out, two types of asset allocation—strategic and tactical—have developed into distinct disciplines. Sections 4 through 7 explain the strategic asset allocation process from the selection of asset classes to optimization and implementation, and Sections 8 and 9 focus on strategic asset allocation for individual and institutional investors, respectively. Finally, Section 10 presents tactical asset allocation.

2 WHAT IS ASSET ALLOCATION?

Asset allocation is a process and a result. Strategic asset allocation, the focus of the first part of this reading, is an integrative element of the planning step in portfolio management. In **strategic asset allocation**, an investor's return objectives, risk tolerance, and investment constraints are integrated with long-run capital market expectations to establish exposures to IPS-permissible asset classes. The aim is to satisfy the investor's investment objectives and constraints. Thus strategic asset allocation

What Is Asset Allocation?

can be viewed as a process with certain well-defined steps. Performing those steps produces a set of portfolio weights for asset classes; we call this set of weights the strategic asset allocation (or the **policy portfolio**).[1] Thus "strategic asset allocation" may refer to either a process or its end result.

A second major type of asset allocation is **tactical asset allocation** (TAA), which involves making short-term adjustments to asset-class weights based on short-term expected relative performance among asset classes. We can better understand the contrasts between strategic and tactical asset allocation if we first cover some basic notions concerning strategic asset allocation.

Exhibit 1 gives an example of a strategic asset allocation or policy portfolio. Frequently, the policy portfolio is specified as target percentages for each asset class and a range of permissible values, as shown in the exhibit. Stating a range of permissible values is a risk management device. Because allocations outside the range may have substantially different risk characteristics from the policy portfolio, the portfolio must be rebalanced if an asset-class weight moves outside the permissible range. (The setting of such ranges is discussed in the reading on monitoring and rebalancing.)

Exhibit 1 A Strategic Asset Allocation (Policy Portfolio)

Asset Class	Target Allocation	Permissible Range
1. Domestic equities	50%	46–54%
2. International equities	10	9–11
3. Cash equivalents	2	0–5
4. Domestic intermediate-term bonds	25	22–28
5. Domestic long-term bonds	8	6–10
6. International bonds	5	3–7

Strategic asset allocation is the first element of the portfolio management process to focus on selecting investments. It is a bridge to the execution step of portfolio management but at the broad level of asset classes. Strategic asset allocation is a starting point for portfolio construction and a step of the portfolio management process on which many investors expend considerable thought and effort. Institutional and individual investors often consider it a central element of the investment process. Why do they do so? What role does strategic asset allocation play in relation to risk? We address these questions next.

2.1 The Role of Strategic Asset Allocation in Relation to Systematic Risk

A continuing debate surrounds strategic asset allocation's relative importance, compared with security selection and timing, for producing investment results in practice. Irrespective of that debate (addressed in a subsequent section), strategic asset allocation fulfills an important role as a discipline for aligning a portfolio's risk profile with the investor's objectives.

For the investor, strategic asset allocation is pivotal in executing investment plans. Economically, why is this so? Why should the allocation of funds to asset classes command so much attention among professional investors?

---

[1] The term "policy portfolio" sometimes refers to a strategic asset allocation that ignores an investor's liabilities. The term need not have that connotation, and we do not use it that way in this reading.

A keystone of investment analysis is that systematic risk is rewarded. In the long run, investors expect compensation for bearing risk that they cannot diversify away. Such risk is inherent in the economic system and may relate, for example, to real business activity or to inflation. In the long run, a diversified portfolio's mean returns are reliably related to its systematic risk exposures. Conversely, measuring portfolio risk begins with an evaluation of the portfolio's systematic risk, because systematic risk usually accounts for most of a portfolio's change in value in the long run. Groups of assets of the same type (e.g., debt claims) that are relatively homogeneous (e.g., domestic intermediate-term bonds) should predictably reflect exposures to a certain set of systematic factors. Distinct (and well-differentiated) groups of assets should have distinct exposures to factors and/or exposures to different factors. These observations suggest a key economic role of strategic asset allocation: *The strategic asset allocation specifies the investor's desired exposures to systematic risk.*[2]

Adopting and implementing a strategic asset allocation is an effective way to exercise control over systematic risk exposures. As Example 1 illustrates, less disciplined approaches may offer investment managers incentives to take risks that conflict with the investor's interests.

Example 1

Making Asset Allocation a "Horse Race"

Sanjiv Singh is chief investment officer (CIO) of The Canadian Endowment for the Fine Arts. CEFA has a strategic asset allocation with a weight of 60 percent in equities and 40 percent in bonds. William Smith, a trustee of the endowment, recently suggested to Singh that CEFA replace its strategic asset allocation with a "horse race" or "equal balanced managers" system. According to this approach, as explained by Smith, the trustees would decide only on an asset-class-mix benchmark. For example, the trustees might specify a benchmark with weights of 50 percent on the S&P/TSX Composite Index for Canadian equities, 10 percent on the MSCI Europe Index, and 40 percent on the RBC Capital Markets Canadian Bond Market Index. According to Smith, the trustees could then hire a number of outside investment managers, initially giving them equal amounts of money to manage. The managers would be expected to hold the three component asset classes of the benchmark, but each manager would have substantial freedom to diverge from the 50/10/40 benchmark weights according to his or her judgment. At CEFA's annual review, the trustees would compare each manager's performance with the benchmark and with each other, based on mean returns earned. Managers that performed relatively well would be given more money to manage, at the expense of managers that performed relatively poorly (who might be fired).

Explain the relative merits of strategic asset allocation and the horse race system as approaches to controlling CEFA's systematic risk exposures.

Solution:

Strategic asset allocation is superior to the horse race system as a method for controlling the endowment's systematic risk exposures. Using strategic asset allocation, the trustees maintain maximum control over the risk exposures of the endowment's funds. The policy portfolio reflects what the trustees believe is the best asset mix for CEFA to achieve its return objectives given its risk tolerance.

---

[2] We might say *net* exposures to risk in the sense of netting out the risk exposures of the investor's liabilities (if any).

What Is Asset Allocation?

> In contrast, the horse race system creates incentives for the investment managers to take on a higher level of risk than is appropriate for the endowment. The managers have the incentive to greatly overweight the highest-expected-return asset class in order to finish first in the race, particularly if they are lagging other managers. The resulting portfolio will tend to be less diversified and have higher risk than the policy portfolio.

Strategic asset allocation provides an important set of benchmarks for an investor. It indicates the appropriate asset mix to be held under long-term or "normal" conditions. It also suggests the investor's long-run or "average" level of risk tolerance. The investor may also want to consider reacting to shorter-term forecasts as discussed in the next section.

2.2 Strategic versus Tactical Asset Allocation

Having introduced the basic themes of strategic asset allocation, we are in a position to understand the contrasts between strategic asset allocation and tactical asset allocation.

Strategic asset allocation sets an investor's desired long-term exposures to systematic risk. We have emphasized that the expectations involved in strategic asset allocation are long term. "Long term" has different interpretations for different investors, but five years is a reasonable minimum reference point. Tactical asset allocation involves making short-term adjustments to asset-class weights based on short-term predictions of relative performance among asset classes. TAA can subsume a range of approaches, from occasional and ad hoc adjustments to frequent and model-based adjustments. In practice, TAA often refers to investment disciplines involving short-term (such as quarterly or monthly) adjustments to the proportions invested in equities, bonds, and cash.[3] Taking as the benchmark the policy portfolio invested in passively managed indexes for the asset classes, TAA creates active risk (variability of active returns—i.e., portfolio returns minus benchmark returns). In exchange for active risk, the manager using TAA hopes to earn positive active returns that sufficiently reward the investor after deducting expenses. TAA is an active investment strategy choice that has evolved into a distinct professional money management discipline. This reading discusses strategic asset allocation first, then tactical asset allocation (in Section 10).

Strategic asset allocations are reviewed periodically or when an investor's needs and circumstances change significantly. Among institutional investors, regular annual reviews are now commonplace. Ad hoc reviews and changes to strategic asset allocation in response to the news items of the moment may lead to less thoughtful decisions. Example 2 describes the nature of the capital market expectations involved in strategic asset allocation.

Example 2

Expectations and the Policy Portfolio

John Stevenson is an analyst reporting to CIO Sanjiv Singh. Stevenson strongly believes that domestic equities will underperform international equities during the next six months. He has presented to Singh a detailed analysis in support of his view. Both asset classes are part of the endowment's policy portfolio. Stevenson

---

[3] The discipline is often called "global tactical asset allocation" when executed for asset classes in many country markets.

> suggests that Singh ask CEFA's trustees to convene a special meeting before the regularly scheduled strategic asset allocation review for the purpose of revising downward the weight of domestic equities in the endowment's policy portfolio. Based on the information provided, is such a special meeting appropriate?
>
> **Solution:**
>
> No. The policy portfolio should be revised only to account for changes in the investor's *long-term* capital market forecasts, not to reflect short-term forecasts. If the endowment expected domestic equities to underperform international equities during the next six months, with no implications for long-term relationships, the policy portfolio should not change.

2.3 The Empirical Debate on the Importance of Asset Allocation

In a prior section, we observed that strategic asset allocation plays a pivotal role in establishing exactly the systematic risk exposures that an investor wants. Because of its planning and risk management functions, strategic asset allocation clearly deserves the thought and attention it receives in practice. One might also ask, how important is strategic asset allocation relative to other investment decisions in determining investment results in practice? This empirical question has obvious relevance for budgeting resources effectively.

Not surprisingly, how we interpret and measure "importance" affects any conclusions. A classic and frequently cited empirical study is Brinson, Hood, and Beebower (1986). These authors interpreted the importance of asset allocation as *the fraction of the variation in returns over time* attributable to asset allocation, based on regression analysis. In a regression, total variation is the sum of squared deviations from the mean, and the fraction of total variation accounted for by the regression is the coefficient of determination or *R*-squared. This approach takes the perspective of a single portfolio over time. Brinson et al. concluded that asset allocation explained an average 93.6 percent of the variation of returns over time for 91 large U.S. defined benefit pension plans. The range was 75.5 percent to 98.6 percent, and the study period was 1974–83. A pension fund's policy portfolio was assumed to be the average asset allocation during the study period. On average, timing and security selection explained 100 − 93.6 = 6.4 percent.[4] Furthermore, the contributions of timing and security selection to active returns were on average negative, suggesting that resources invested in these activities were not rewarded on average. Two similar studies followed: Brinson, Singer, and Beebower (1991) updated the average percent of variation explained to 91.5 percent for U.S. plans for the period 1977–87, and Blake, Lehmann, and Timmermann (1999) investigated asset allocation in the United Kingdom. Examining more than 300 medium-size to large actively managed U.K. defined-benefit pension schemes for the period 1986–94, Blake et al. concluded that asset allocation accounted for approximately 99.5 percent of the variation in plan total returns. These studies' results concerning the relative importance of strategic asset allocation reflect at least in part pension funds' typical investment emphasis. Pension funds frequently emphasize strategic asset allocation. We expect asset allocation to explain a high proportion of a given fund's returns over time if that fund's discipline is to consistently adhere to

---

[4] In this study, timing was defined as altering the investment mix weights away from the policy allocation. Security selection refers to selecting individual securities within an asset class.

its strategic asset allocation and limit the scope of security selection (i.e., limit deviations of security holdings in an asset class relative to weights of securities in the asset class's passive benchmarks).

An alternative perspective is asset allocation's importance in explaining the *cross-sectional variation of returns*—that is, the proportion of the variation *among* funds' performance explained by funds' different asset allocations. In other words, to what degree do differences in asset allocation explain differences in rates of return over time for a group of investors?

The degree of diversity among asset allocations must affect the cross-sectional importance of asset allocation that we will find after the fact. For example, if all balanced funds continuously rebalance to a 60/40 stock/bond allocation, then asset allocation will explain precisely none of their return differences. If the investor group is quite diverse in its asset allocations and does not engage in active management, then asset allocation will explain a substantial amount of cross-sectional differences in return; but if that group were composed of very active investors, asset allocation would explain relatively less. Ibbotson and Kaplan (2000) found that asset allocation explained about 40 percent of the cross-sectional variation in mutual fund returns, using 10 years of data (April 1988 to March 1998) for 94 U.S. balanced mutual funds. The remaining 60 percent was explained by factors such as asset-class timing, style within asset classes, security selection, and fees.[5] The cross-sectional percentage of variation explained, 40 percent, was much lower than the median time-series result, 87.6 percent, for the mutual funds. Forty percent, however, is sufficiently large to suggest that those investors in practice significantly differentiate themselves from peers through asset allocation. In other results, Ibbotson et al. concluded as did earlier researchers that after expenses, the sample pension funds and balanced funds were not adding value through timing and security selection.

The research discussed above was empirical—that is, focused on actual performance records. By contrast, Kritzman and Page (2003) explored asset allocation versus security selection in terms of the hypothetical potential to affect terminal wealth. What should investors emphasize if they are skillful, asset allocation or security selection? What should they avoid if they lack skill? The authors found that active security selection led to greater potential dispersion in final wealth than did varying asset allocation. They thus concluded that skillful investors have the potential to earn higher incremental returns through security selection than through asset allocation. Skill as a security selector may be highly valuable. Kritzman and Page also note that security selection's potentially higher incremental returns come at the cost of greater risk; thus not only the investor's skill but his risk aversion must be considered.

What are the practical messages of these studies? Investors need to keep in mind their own specific risk and return objectives and establish a strategic asset allocation that is expected to satisfy both. Sidestepping strategic asset allocation finds no support in the empirical or normative literature. When investors decide whether and to what degree they will engage in active investment approaches, they must objectively assess not only the supply of opportunities (the informational efficiency of markets) but the costs and the skills and information they bring to the task relative to all other market participants. A note of caution consistent with the empirical part of the literature discussed: Because investors in the aggregate are the market and costs do not net out across investors, the return on the average actively managed dollar should be less than the return on the average passively managed dollar, after costs (Sharpe 1991).

---

[5] However the authors did not examine these other components' individual contributions to cross-sectional explanatory power.

3 ASSET ALLOCATION AND THE INVESTOR'S RISK AND RETURN OBJECTIVES

An investor's risk and return objectives may be described in a number of distinct ways, both quantitative and qualitative. The approach we choose in characterizing those objectives determines the type of analysis we perform, the way we model return and risk, and, ultimately, our recommendations. The next subsection outlines the major choice that we face in overall approach. The focus then moves to concepts that will help us to accurately describe an investor's return and risk preferences and the behavioral considerations that may play a role in setting objectives.

3.1 Asset-Only and Asset/Liability Management Approaches to Strategic Asset Allocation

As discussed in the reading on managing institutional portfolios, insurers, defined benefit (DB) pension plans, and certain other institutional investors face streams of significant future liabilities. Controlling the risk related to funding future liabilities is a key investment objective for such investors, who frequently take an asset/liability management approach to strategic asset allocation.

In the context of determining a strategic asset allocation, the **asset/liability management** (ALM) **approach** involves explicitly modeling liabilities and adopting the optimal asset allocation in relationship to funding liabilities.[6] For example, a DB pension plan may want to maximize the future risk-adjusted value of pension surplus (the value of pension assets minus the present value of pension liabilities).[7] Investors other than those with significant future liabilities may adopt an ALM approach by treating future needs (such as for income) as if they were liabilities; we call those needs "quasi-liabilities." Ziemba (2003) discusses this approach for individual investors; the method he describes involves setting penalties for failing to meet annual income needs and specifying a numerical value for the investor's risk tolerance.[8]

In contrast to ALM, an **asset-only** (AO) **approach** to strategic asset allocation does not explicitly involve modeling liabilities. In an AO approach, any impact of the investor's liabilities on policy portfolio selection is indirect (e.g., through the level of the return requirement). Compared with ALM, an AO approach affords much less precision in controlling risk related to the funding of liabilities.

One example of an AO approach to strategic asset allocation is the Black–Litterman (1991, 1992) model. This model takes a global market-value-weighted asset allocation (the "market equilibrium portfolio") as the default strategic asset allocation for investors. The approach then incorporates a procedure for deviating from market capitalization weights in directions that reflect an investor's views on asset classes' expected returns as well as the strength of those views. For example, the weights in a globally diversified index provide a starting point for the investor's policy portfolio weights irrespective of the investor's liabilities (if any). In a later section, we illustrate a simple AO mean–variance approach to strategic asset allocation. However, mean–variance analysis has also been used in ALM approaches to strategic asset allocation, as we will illustrate later.[9]

---

[6] A **liability** is a financial obligation.
[7] See Sharpe (1990).
[8] The objective function is to maximize the expected value of [Final wealth − (Accumulated penalized shortfalls/Risk tolerance)]. The solution approach is a technique known as stochastic programming.
[9] Examples include the mean–variance surplus optimizations of Leibowitz and Henriksson (1988) and Sharpe and Tint (1990); Leibowitz and Henriksson (1989), which incorporates shortfall constraints; and Elton and Gruber (1992), which focuses on the mean and variance of period-by-period changes in net worth.

In a subsequent section we will discuss ALM approaches to asset allocation in more detail. ALM strategies run from those that seek to minimize risk with respect to net worth or surplus (assets minus liabilities) to those that deliberately bear surplus risk in exchange for higher expected surplus, analogous to the trade-off of absolute risk for absolute mean return in an AO approach. We may also describe ALM approaches as either static or dynamic.

To take the risk dimension first, the earliest-developed ALM approaches were at the risk-minimizing end of the spectrum. These strategies are cash flow matching (also known as exact matching) and immunization (also known as duration matching). A **cash flow matching** approach structures investments in bonds to match (offset) future liabilities or quasi-liabilities. When feasible, cash flow matching minimizes risk relative to funding liabilities. An **immunization** approach structures investments in bonds to match (offset) the weighted-average duration of liabilities.[10] Because duration is a first-order approximation of interest rate risk, immunization involves more risk than does cash flow matching with respect to funding liabilities. To improve the risk-control characteristics of an immunization approach relative to shifts in the yield curve, portfolio managers often match the convexity as well as the duration of liabilities. Highly risk-averse approaches such as immunization remain important for investors such as banks and life insurers. ALM approaches permitting higher risk levels include those specifying the satisfaction of liabilities as constraints under which the best asset allocation will be chosen, as well as those incorporating an objective function that includes a penalty for failing to satisfy liabilities.

The second dimension concerns static versus dynamic approaches, and the contrast between them is important for understanding current practice in ALM investing. A **dynamic approach** recognizes that an investor's asset allocation and actual asset returns and liabilities in a given period affect the optimal decision that will be available next period. The asset allocation is further linked to the optimal investment decisions available at all future time periods. In contrast, a **static approach** does not consider links between optimal decisions at different time periods, somewhat analogous to a driver who tries to make the best decision as she arrives at each new street without looking further ahead. This advantage of dynamic over static asset allocation applies both to AO and ALM perspectives. With the ready availability of computing power, institutional investors that adopt an ALM approach to strategic asset allocation frequently choose a dynamic rather than a static approach. A dynamic approach, however, is more complex and costly to model and implement.[11] Nonetheless, investors with significant future liabilities often find a dynamic approach to be worth the cost.

How do the recommended strategic asset allocations resulting from AO and ALM approaches differ? The ALM approach to strategic asset allocation characteristically results in a higher allocation to fixed-income instruments than an AO approach. Fixed-income instruments have prespecified interest and principal payments that typically represent legal obligations of the issuer. Because of the nature of their cash flows, fixed-income instruments are well suited to offsetting future obligations.

What types of investors gravitate to an ALM approach? In general, the ALM approach tends to be favored when:

- the investor has below-average risk tolerance;
- the penalties for not meeting the liabilities or quasi-liabilities are very high;
- the market value of liabilities or quasi-liabilities are interest rate sensitive;

---

[10] Besides matching the weighted-average duration of liabilities, the investments in bonds must satisfy other conditions, including having the same present value as the liabilities being immunized. See Fabozzi (2004b) Chapter 4 and Waring (2004a) for more information on these techniques.

[11] Among the complexities of dynamic ALM modeling are the random components of liabilities in many cases (e.g., pension benefits). Monte Carlo simulation is used in dynamic ALM modeling with multivariate risks.

- risk taken in the investment portfolio limits the investor's ability to profitably take risk in other activities;
- legal and regulatory requirements and incentives favor holding fixed-income securities; and
- tax incentives favor holding fixed-income securities.[12]

Exhibit 2 reflects practical experience with the concerns and typical asset allocation approaches of the various investor types covered in earlier readings.

Exhibit 2 Characteristic Liability Concerns of Various Investors

Type of Investor	Type of Liability (Quasi-Liability)	Penalty for Not Meeting	Asset Allocation Approach in Practice
Individual	Taxes, mortgage payments (living expenses, wealth accumulation targets)	Varies	AO most common ALM
Pension plans (defined benefit)	Pension benefits	High, legal and regulatory	ALM AO
Pension plans (defined contribution)	(Retirement needs)	Varies	Integrated with individual's asset allocation approach
Foundations and endowments	Spending commitments, capital project commitments	High	AO ALM
Life insurance companies	Death proceeds, annuity payments, return guarantees on investment products	Very high, legal and regulatory	ALM
Non-life insurance companies	Property and liability claims	Very high, legal and regulatory	ALM
Banks	Deposits	Very high, legal and regulatory	ALM

Both AO and ALM approaches have appropriate roles in strategic asset allocation depending on the investor's circumstances and needs.

3.2 Return Objectives and Strategic Asset Allocation

Investors have both qualitative and quantitative investment objectives. Qualitative return objectives describe the investor's fundamental goals, such as to achieve returns that will:

- provide an adequate retirement income (for an individual currently in the workforce);
- maintain a fund's real purchasing power after distributions (for many endowments and foundations);
- adequately fund liabilities (for investors such as pension plans and insurance companies); or

---

[12] An ALM approach may incorporate equities, however. For example, after assuring the funding of liabilities, the investor might optimally invest some part of excess assets in equities. For a topical discussion on the variety of approaches to ALM, see Denmark (2005).

Asset Allocation and The Investor's Risk and Return Objectives

- exceed the rate of inflation in the long term (from the prospectus of an inflation-protected bond fund).

We can often concretely determine whether a qualitative objective has been satisfied. For example, we can determine whether a university endowment's investment program has preserved real purchasing power after distributions by reference to the endowment's asset values and a published cost-of-higher-education inflation index. But investors also benefit by formulating quantitative (numerical) goals that reflect the return and risk levels perceived to be appropriate for achieving the qualitative objectives. In an AO approach, the concern is for absolute returns and absolute risk. In an ALM approach, it is for net returns (net of the return or growth rate of liabilities) and risk with respect to funding liabilities. Given a set of capital market expectations, numerical objectives offer great practical help in determining specific asset allocations for final consideration.

Because strategic asset allocation involves meeting an investor's long-term needs, precise statements of numerical return objectives must take account of the effects of compounding.

Consider a foundation's simple additive return objective equal to the spending rate plus the expected inflation rate. This objective aims to preserve the portfolio's real purchasing power after making distributions. If the spending rate is 5 percent and expected inflation is 4 percent, for example, the return requirement would be stated as 9 percent, using an additive return objective. To expect to preserve purchasing power, however, the fund must earn $(1.05)(1.04) - 1.0 = 0.092$ or 9.2 percent, 20 basis points higher than the additive return requirement. The higher the spending and inflation rates, the higher the discrepancy between the additive objective and the need. Through compounding, the practical effect of this divergence increases the greater the number of periods. Further, if we specify that the cost of earning investment returns is 0.30 percent of beginning assets, then we need to earn $(1.05)(1.04)(1.003) - 1.0 = 0.0953$ or 9.53 percent to preserve the portfolio's purchasing power after distributions. We would then have a return objective of 9.53 percent.[13] Thus a careful specification of the numerical return objective should reflect the costs of earning investment returns and inflation as well as their compound effects through time.

Example 3

CEFA's Return Objective

CEFA's trustees have established a policy that calls for annually spending 4 percent of the prior 12-quarter moving average of the portfolio's market value. The trustees have asked Singh to revise the statement of CEFA's return objective to reflect the 4 percent spending rate, a forecast of 2 percent in the long-run inflation rate represented by the consumer price index (CPI), and a 40-basis-point cost of earning investment returns.

Singh makes the following calculation: $(1.04)(1.02)(1.004) - 1 = 0.065$ or 6.5 percent. He drafts the following statement for the trustees to consider:

"The investment objective of the Canadian Endowment for the Fine Arts is to maintain the endowment's real purchasing power after distributions. To attain this objective, the targeted annual rate of return is 6.5 percent, reflecting a spending rate of 4 percent, an expected inflation rate of 2 percent, and a 40-basis-point cost of earning investment returns."

---

[13] Some entities count investment management expenses in spending and the spending rate. If it were explicitly stated that the spending rate of 5 percent included the cost of earning investment returns, then the return objective would be $(1.05)(1.04) - 1.0 = 9.2\%$.

The reading on managing institutional investor portfolios notes that an additive formulation of a return objective can serve as a starting point. Because additive formulations provide an intuitive wording of a return objective, such formulations are common in actual investment policy statements. The differences between additive and multiplicative formulations can be essentially negligible for low levels of spending rates and inflation. Nevertheless, portfolio managers should prefer the multiplicative formulation for strategic asset allocation purposes; managers should also observe the distinction between compound and arithmetic mean rates of growth.

If an investor's return requirement is based on the compound rate of return needed to achieve a goal, the corresponding arithmetic mean one-period return needed to achieve that goal will be higher than the return requirement stated as a compound rate of return. The differences between the arithmetic mean and compound rate of growth (geometric mean) are approximately 13, 50, and 113 basis points for portfolio standard deviations of returns of 5 percent, 10 percent, and 15 percent, respectively.[14] Thus if an investor requires an 8 percent compound growth rate to reach an investment objective, with a 5 percent standard deviation of portfolio returns the investor will need to achieve an 8.13 percent arithmetic mean return to achieve his or her goal. The main point is that if the investor states an arithmetic mean annual return objective based on a compound growth rate calculation, the investor's return objective should reflect an appropriate upward adjustment from the compound growth rate.

Often an investor's time horizon is multistage, reflecting periods with foreseeably distinct needs. For example, an individual investor's retirement often marks the end of an accumulation stage. Multistage horizons present a challenge to strategic asset allocation. A dynamic model most accurately captures the effects of a multistage time horizon on strategic asset allocation. Using a static asset allocation model (such as the mean–variance model), however, we can incorporate multistage effects approximately. For example, we can reflect an investor's average return and risk requirements (for the remaining stages) in the return and risk objectives that guide the strategic asset allocation. The investor should be ready to update the strategic asset allocation to reflect significant shifts in return and risk requirements with the passage of time.

3.3 Risk Objectives and Strategic Asset Allocation

In addition to the investor's return objectives, the investor's risk tolerance enters into creating a policy portfolio. As with return objectives, both qualitative and quantitative risk objectives are important.

Many practitioners will qualitatively evaluate an investor's risk tolerance as below average, average, or above average, based on the investor's willingness and ability to take risk. To apply a quantitative approach to asset allocation, however, we must quantify an investor's attitude to risk. The most precise way to do so is to measure the investor's numerical risk aversion, R_A. Numerical risk aversion can be measured in an interview or questionnaire in which the investor expresses preferences among sets of choices involving risky and certain returns. Risk aversion is the inverse of risk tolerance: A lower value of risk aversion means a higher tolerance for risk. To give approximate guidelines for the scale we will use, an R_A of 6 to 8 represents a high degree of risk aversion (i.e., a low risk tolerance), while an R_A of 1 to 2 represents a relatively low degree of risk aversion (i.e., a high risk tolerance).[15] A mean–variance investor will evaluate an asset allocation (mix) m using Equation 1:

$$U_m = E(R_m) - 0.005 R_A \sigma_m^2 \tag{1}$$

---

[14] These numbers are based on the following approximate relationship: $R_G \approx E(R) - 0.5\sigma^2$, where R_G is the compound growth rate, $E(R)$ is the arithmetic mean return, σ^2 is the variance of return, and all the terms are stated in decimal form rather than percent.

[15] See Ziemba (2003, p. 6). An R_A of zero represents indifference to risk (risk neutrality).

Asset Allocation and The Investor's Risk and Return Objectives

where

U_m = the investor's expected utility for asset mix m

$E(R_m)$ = expected return for mix m

R_A = the investor's risk aversion

σ_m^2 = variance of return for mix m

In Equation 1, $E(R_m)$ and σ_m are expressed as percentages rather than as decimals.[16]

We can interpret the investor's expected utility for asset mix m, U_m, as the asset mix's risk-adjusted expected return for the particular investor. The quantity $0.005 R_A \sigma_m^2$ is a risk penalty that is subtracted from the allocation's expected return to adjust it for risk. The risk penalty's size depends on the investor's risk aversion, R_A, and on the standard deviation of the asset mix, σ_m. The more risk averse the investor, the greater the penalty subtracted from expected return. To illustrate the expression "risk-adjusted expected return," suppose that a moderately risk-averse investor ($R_A = 4$) is choosing between the strategic asset allocations given in Exhibit 3. For that investor,

$$U_m = E(R_m) - 0.005 R_A \sigma_m^2$$
$$= E(R_m) - 0.005(4)\sigma_m^2$$
$$= E(R_m) - 0.02\sigma_m^2$$

Exhibit 3 Strategic Asset Allocation Choices

	Investor's Forecasts	
Allocation	Expected Return	Standard Deviation of Return
A	9.7%	15%
B	7.0	10

The risk-adjusted expected return of Asset Allocation A is $U_A = E(R_A) - 0.02\sigma_A^2 = 9.7\% - 0.02(15.0\%)^2 = 9.7\% - 4.5\% = 5.2\%$ that of Asset Allocation B is $U_B = E(R_A) - 0.02\sigma_A^2 = 7\% - 0.02(10\%)^2 = 7\% - 2\% = 5.0\%$. The investor should prefer A to B because of A's higher risk-adjusted expected return.

Another way an investor can quantify his risk tolerance is in terms of an acceptable level of volatility as measured by standard deviation of return. For example, an investor who is uncomfortable with the volatility associated with a standard deviation of return of 12 percent or higher could eliminate Asset Allocation A from consideration.

Still another way for an investor to quantify risk is in terms of **shortfall risk**, the risk that a portfolio's value will fall below some minimum acceptable level during a stated time horizon. The risks that a retiree's assets will fall below the amount needed to supply an adequate retirement income, or that a defined-benefit plan's assets will be less than the present value of plan liabilities, are examples of shortfall risk. When shortfall risk is an important concern for an investor, an appropriate shortfall risk objective improves the description of the investor's attitude to risk. Shortfall risk is

---

[16] See Bodie, Kane, and Marcus (2004, p. 168) for this expression. A standard expression for a mean–variance investor's expected utility is $U_m = E(R_m) - 0.50 R_A \sigma_m^2$, where expected return and standard deviation are stated in decimal form and 0.5 is a scaling factor. Dividing 0.5 by 100 to get 0.005 in the text expression ensures that we can express expected return and standard deviation as percentages.

one example of the larger concept of **downside risk** (risk relating to losses or worse than expected outcomes only). Downside risk concepts include not only shortfall risk but concepts such as **semivariance** and **target semivariance** that also may be applied in asset allocation and are discussed in statistical textbooks (as well as defined in the glossary).

The oldest shortfall risk criterion is Roy's safety-first criterion. Roy's safety-first criterion states that the optimal portfolio minimizes the probability over a stated time horizon that portfolio return, R_P, will fall below some threshold level R_L that the investor insists on meeting or exceeding. The safety-first optimal portfolio *maximizes* the safety-first ratio (SFRatio):

$$\text{SFRatio} = \frac{E(R_P) - R_L}{\sigma_P} \qquad (2)$$

Equation 2 gives the distance from the expected return to the shortfall level in the numerator. The denominator converts the result into units of the portfolio's standard deviation of return. If a portfolio's expected return were many standard deviations above the threshold return, the chance that the threshold would be breached would be relatively small.[17] There are two steps in choosing among risky portfolios using Roy's criterion (assuming normality):

1. Calculate each portfolio's SFRatio.
2. Choose the portfolio with the highest SFRatio.

If there is an asset offering a risk-free return for the time horizon being considered, and if R_L is less than or equal to that risk-free rate, then it is safety-first optimal to be fully invested in the risk-free asset. Holding the risk-free asset in this case eliminates the chance that the threshold return is not met. Example 4 illustrates a use of Roy's safety-first criterion.

Example 4

Applying Roy's Safety-First Criterion in Asset Allocation

An investment advisor is counseling Aimeé Goddard, a client who recently inherited €1,200,000 and has above-average risk tolerance (R_A = 2). Because Goddard is young and one of her purposes is to fund a comfortable retirement, she wants to earn returns that will outpace inflation in the long term. Goddard expects to liquidate €60,000 of the portfolio in 12 months, however, to make the down payment on a house. If that need arises, she states that it is important for her to be able to take out the €60,000 without invading the initial capital of €1,200,000. Exhibit 4 shows three alternative strategic asset allocations.

Address the following questions:

1. Based only on Goddard's risk-adjusted expected returns for the asset allocations, which asset allocation would she prefer?

2. Given Goddard's desire not to invade the €1,200,000 principal, what is the shortfall level, R_L?

---

[17] The expression does not depend on the normal distribution; it holds under the same general conditions as Chebyshev's inequality (see Elton, Gruber, Brown, and Goetzmann, 2003). We can associate a precise probability of not meeting the return with a given level of this expression, however, if we assume the normal distribution. Note too that if we substitute the risk-free rate R_F for R_L, we obtain the Sharpe ratio. The highest-Sharpe-ratio portfolio is the one that minimizes the probability of a return below the risk-free rate.

Asset Allocation and The Investor's Risk and Return Objectives

Exhibit 4 **Strategic Asset Allocation Choices for Goddard**

	Investor's Forecasts	
Asset Allocation	Expected Return	Standard Deviation of Return
A	10.00%	20%
B	7.00	10
C	5.25	5

3. According to Roy's safety-first criterion, which of the three allocations is the best?
4. Recommend a strategic asset allocation for Goddard.

Solution to 1:

Using Equation 1,

$$U_m = E(R_m) - 0.005 R_A \sigma_m^2$$
$$= E(R_m) - 0.005(2)\sigma_m^2$$
$$= E(R_m) - 0.01\sigma_m^2$$

So Goddard's risk-adjusted returns for Asset Allocations A, B, and C are as follows:

$$U_A = E(R_A) - 0.01\sigma_A^2 = 10.0\% - 0.01(20\%)^2 = 10.0\% - 4.0\% = 6.0\%$$
$$U_B = E(R_B) - 0.01\sigma_B^2 = 7.0\% - 0.01(10\%)^2 = 7.0\% - 1.0\% = 6.0\%$$
$$U_C = E(R_C) - 0.01\sigma_C^2 = 5.25\% - 0.01(5\%)^2 = 5.25\% - 0.25\% = 5.0\%$$

Goddard would be indifferent between A and B based only on their common perceived risk-adjusted expected return of 6 percent.

Solution to 2:

Because €60,000/€1,200,000 is 5.0 percent, for any return less than 5.0 percent Goddard will need to invade principal if she liquidates €60,000. So R_L = 5 percent.

Solution to 3:

To decide which of the three allocations is safety-first optimal, we need to calculate the ratio $[E(R_p) - R_L]/\sigma_p$:

Allocation A: (10 − 5)/20 = 0.25

Allocation B: (7 − 5)/10 = 0.20

Allocation C: (5.25 − 5)/5 = 0.05

Allocation A, with the largest ratio (0.25), is the best alternative according to Roy's safety-first criterion.

Solution to 4:

Both A and B have the same perceived risk-adjusted expected return, but Allocation A is superior according to Roy's safety-first criterion: Allocation A has a smaller probability of not meeting the threshold 5 percent return than Allocation B. Therefore, A would be the recommended strategic asset allocation.

In Example 4 we used a shortfall risk constraint to identify the asset allocation with the *smallest* probability of not meeting a threshold return level. We could calculate that, in Example 4, the selected asset allocation (Asset Allocation A) has a probability of about 40 percent of not meeting a 5 percent return threshold, under a normality assumption. This result suggests another shortfall risk approach. An investor could also specify a given maximum probability of not meeting a return threshold. That probability can be translated into a standard deviation test, if we assume a normal distribution of portfolio returns. For example, suppose that a 2.5 percent probability of failing to meet a return threshold is acceptable. Given a normal distribution of returns, the probability of a return that is more than two standard deviations below the expected return is approximately 2.5 percent. Therefore, if we subtract two standard deviations from a portfolio's expected return and the resulting number is above the client's return threshold, the resulting portfolio passes that shortfall risk test. If the resulting number falls below the client's threshold, the portfolio does not pass that shortfall risk test. Shortfall probability levels of 5 percent and 10 percent translate into 1.65 and 1.28 standard deviations below the mean, respectively, under a normality assumption.

Shortfall risk in relation to liabilities is a key focus of ALM approaches to asset allocation. An AO approach can also easily incorporate shortfall risk in a variety of ways. Besides specifying a shortfall-risk-related objective such as Roy's safety-first criterion, an investor can optimize using a one-sided, downside risk concept rather than a symmetric one such as variance, or by adding a shortfall risk constraint to an optimization based on variance.

3.4 Behavioral Influences on Asset Allocation

Standard finance views investors as rational decision-makers and is based on the axioms of economic utility theory. Behavioral finance, grounded in psychology, focuses on describing individuals' observed economic behavior. By far the majority of research in asset allocation has been in the context of standard finance. Advisors of individual investors in particular, however, may better understand their clients' investment goals, needs, and reactions to proposed asset allocations if they become familiar with behavioral finance tenets such as loss aversion, mental accounting, and regret avoidance.

Behavioral finance asserts that most investors worry more about avoiding losses than acquiring gains. According to behavioral finance, most individuals are risk-seekers when faced with the prospect of a substantial loss.[18] If the advisor establishes that a client is loss averse, one approach may be to incorporate an appropriate shortfall risk constraint or objective in the asset allocation decision. Managing assets with such a constraint or objective should reduce the chance that the client finds himself facing the prospect of a substantial loss. An ALM approach may be appropriate for such clients as well.

If the investor displays mental accounting the investor will place his total wealth into separate accounts and buckets. Each bucket is associated with a different level of risk tolerance depending on a purpose the investor associates with it, such as speculation or building a fund for college expenses. Such an investor looks at his portfolio narrowly in pieces rather than as one fund. The money's source may affect how an individual invests: An investor may be more likely to invest in a risky venture with cash that is drawn from a windfall gain rather than from salary. The standard finance approach to asset allocation involves determining an optimal asset allocation for the total portfolio, typically reflecting an overall, blended measure of a client's risk tolerance. That asset

---

[18] This discussion reflects the insights of the area of behavioral finance theory known as **prospect theory**. The term "prospect theory" comes from the analysis of decision making under risk in terms of choices among prospects. For more details, see the reading on managing individual investor portfolios and see Tversky (1990).

allocation would generally be different than the overall asset allocation implied by summing the asset allocations an investor would choose for each bucket individually, and it could be perceived as inappropriate by the client.

Some writers have suggested meeting mental accounting on its own terms by adopting a multistrategy or goal-based asset allocation procedure.[19] For example, Brunel (2003) recommends an asset allocation framework in which asset allocations are developed for four buckets individually: liquidity, income, capital preservation, and growth. In principle, the number and kind of buckets could be adapted to the needs of each client individually, although at greater cost. A multistrategy approach has greater complexity than the standard finance approach of developing one strategic asset allocation for the client, because it involves many optimizations rather than just one. Furthermore, developing a set of asset allocations for stand-alone portfolios ignores the correlations between assets across portfolios; the resulting overall asset allocation may fail to use risk efficiently. Advisors may need to discuss the advantages of adopting a broad frame of reference in asset allocation.

Behavioral finance asserts that investors are sensitive to regret, the pain that comes when a decision turns out to have been a bad one. The fear of regret may play a role in actual asset allocation decisions in at least two ways. First, it may be a psychological factor promoting diversification.[20] Second, regret avoidance may limit divergence from peers' average asset allocation if the investor is sensitive to peer comparisons.[21]

Example 5

Behavioral Biases in Asset Allocation

Joseph Gowers, CFA, is a financial planner serving high-net-worth individuals. He is discussing strategic asset allocation with May Smith. Smith is 30 years old and in good health. With her formal education behind her, she has begun a promising career in management. She describes herself as ambitious and ready to take calculated risks. She intends to retire at age 60. She also supplies the following facts and comments:

- Smith has no substantial debts and has $150,000 saved from salary and bonuses.
- Smith's $150,000 portfolio is currently invested 80 percent in equity mutual funds and 20 percent in bond mutual funds.
- Besides a checking account to meet her regular expenses, Smith keeps a "rainy day" fund of $25,000 in a separate checking account at her bank. She views both accounts as separate from her investment portfolio because the accounts are for current and potential liquidity needs.
- As a result of an inheritance, she will receive $3,000,000 very shortly. The inheritance was the motivation for seeking professional investment counsel.
- Smith's plan was to set aside $500,000 of the $3,000,000 inheritance for speculative common stock investments and invest the balance of $2,500,000 conservatively in short-term tax-exempt bonds.

---

[19] See Shefrin and Statman (2000), Brunel (2003), and Nevins (2004).
[20] For example, Harry M. Markowitz was quoted in Zweig (1998) as follows concerning investing for retirement: "I should have computed the historical covariances of the asset classes and drawn an efficient frontier. Instead, I visualized my grief if the stock market went way up and I wasn't in it—or if it went way down and I was completely in it. My intention was to minimize my future regret. So I split my contribution fifty-fifty between bonds and equities."
[21] Regret avoidance may also play a role in the implementation of a strategic asset allocation—for example, in some investors' desire to establish the positions in risky asset classes gradually.

- Smith views a $500,000 speculative stock investment as her chance to "score big."
- Smith views the $2,500,000 she intended to invest conservatively as permanently securing a comfortable retirement; she considers the investment of that money the single most important economic decision she will ever make.
- Smith has told Gowers that she is extremely unlikely ever to inherit a meaningful amount of money again and would forever be disappointed if she suffered a serious loss to the $2,500,000.

Based only on the above information, address the following:

1. Compare the consistency of the risk tolerance implied by Smith's current asset allocation with that implied by the asset allocation that would result if Smith's $3,000,000 inheritance were invested according to her plan.
2. Discuss the behavioral biases in Smith's approach to investing her inheritance.
3. Evaluate whether Smith's intended approach is likely to make efficient use of risk by incorporating information about correlations.

Solution to 1:

Ignoring the $25,000 rainy day fund, Smith currently has an aggressive 80/20 stock/bond asset allocation. Stocks represent $120,000 and bonds represent $30,000. Post-inheritance, her expected investable portfolio is $150,000 + $3,000,000 = $3,150,000. If her intended post-inheritance investments are executed, her allocation to stocks will be ($120,000 + $500,000)/$3,150,000 = 0.197, or 19.7 percent. Her bond allocation will be ($30,000 + $2,500,000)/$3,150,000 = 0.803, or 80.3 percent. This asset allocation is far more conservative than her current one. It appears that the risk tolerance level is inconsistent between her current and intended asset allocations.

Solution to 2:

Smith's approach reflects mental accounting, specifically setting up separate buckets for wealth, each serving a specific purpose and each invested independently. She views $500,000 as targeted for growth and $2,500,000 as targeted for capital preservation. A second bias in her intended asset allocation is regret avoidance; she is focused on the disappointment that will result if she does not preserve a once-in-a-lifetime inheritance.

Solution to 3:

Smith's asset allocation is a mental-accounting approach rather than one that optimizes the overall asset allocation taking account of correlations between assets. Her approach is unlikely to result in an efficient strategic asset allocation.

4. THE SELECTION OF ASSET CLASSES

An asset class is a group of assets with similar attributes. The selection of asset classes as inputs to a strategic asset allocation is an important decision, with long-term effects on a portfolio's returns and risk. The selection must be from the set of asset classes permitted by the investment policy statement (the IPS-permissible asset classes). In

The Selection of Asset Classes

practice, the set of IPS-permissible asset classes has considerable variation, reflecting regulatory and other constraints that affect the portfolio. For example, banks and life insurance companies are frequently subject to regulatory restrictions limiting investment in common equity. Before turning to asset-class selection, however, we must discuss how to effectively specify an asset class. For investors subject to regulation, such specifications may be ready-made. Many investors, however, can increase their control over risk by specifying asset classes skillfully.

4.1 Criteria for Specifying Asset Classes

A basic principle is that asset-class specification should support the purposes of strategic asset allocation. For example, if a manager lumps together very different investments such as real estate property and common equities into an asset class called "equities," asset allocation becomes less effective in diversifying and controlling risk. Furthermore, the investor needs a logical framework for examining the not-infrequent claims by sponsors of new investment products that their product is a new asset class rather than an investment strategy. If the product is accepted as an asset class, it will become a part of strategic asset allocations and tend to be more widely held than otherwise. Below we give five criteria that will help in effectively specifying asset classes:

- *Assets within an asset class should be relatively homogeneous.* Assets within an asset class should have similar attributes. In the example just given, defining equities to include both real estate and common stock would result in a nonhomogeneous asset class.

- *Asset classes should be mutually exclusive.* Overlapping asset classes will reduce the effectiveness of strategic asset allocation in controlling risk and also introduce problems in developing asset-class return expectations. For example, if one asset class for a U.S. investor is domestic common equities, then world equities ex-U.S. is more appropriate as an asset class than world equities including U.S. equities.

- *Asset classes should be diversifying.* For risk-control purposes, an included asset class should not have extremely high expected correlations with other asset classes or with a linear combination of the other asset classes. Otherwise the included asset class will be effectively redundant in a portfolio because it will duplicate risk exposures already present. In general, a pairwise correlation above 0.95 is undesirable.

The criticism of relying on pairwise correlations is that an asset class may be highly correlated with some linear combination of other asset classes even when the pairwise correlations are not high.[22] Kritzman (1999) proposed a criterion to assess a proposed asset class's diversifying qualities that is superior to relying on pairwise correlations: For each current asset class, find the linear combination of the other asset classes that minimizes tracking risk with the proposed asset class. (Tracking risk is defined as the square root of the average squared differences between the asset class's returns and the combination's returns.) Similarly find the minimum tracking risk combination of current asset classes for the proposed asset class and qualitatively judge whether it is

---

[22] We can illustrate this assertion as follows. Suppose the returns to three assets are denoted by X, Y, and Z, respectively, and we are considering making Asset Z available for investment. We are unaware of the fact that Z is an exact linear combination of X and Y (i.e., $Z = aX + bY$, where a and b are constants and not both zero). Because a weighted combination of X and Y replicates Z, Asset Z is redundant. We observe that Z has a moderate pairwise correlation of 0.5 with X as well as with Y (furthermore, assume a moderate −0.5 correlation between X and Y). The stated correlations, although not particularly large, are consistent with Z being a redundant asset in the sense mentioned. See Gujarati (2003, pp. 359–60) for details.

sufficiently high based on the current asset classes' tracking risk levels. For example, if the tracking risks for existing asset classes are 18 percent, 12 percent, and 8 percent, a proposed asset class with a 15 percent tracking risk should be diversifying.

- *The asset classes as a group should make up a preponderance of world investable wealth.* From the perspective of portfolio theory, selecting an asset allocation from a group of asset classes satisfying this criterion should tend to increase expected return for a given level of risk. Furthermore, including more markets expands the opportunities for applying active investment strategies, assuming the decision to invest actively has been made.

- *The asset class should have the capacity to absorb a significant fraction of the investor's portfolio without seriously affecting the portfolio's liquidity.*[23] Practically, most investors will want to be able to reset or rebalance to a strategic asset allocation without moving asset-class prices or incurring high transaction costs.

Traditional asset classes include the following:

- *Domestic common equity.* Market capitalization sometimes has been used as a criterion to distinguish among *large-cap, mid-cap,* and *small-cap domestic common equity* as asset classes.

- *Domestic fixed income.* Maturity sometimes has been used to distinguish among *intermediate-term* and *long-term domestic bonds* as asset classes. Recently, inflation protection has been used to distinguish between *nominal bonds* and *inflation-protected bonds* as asset classes.

- *Non-domestic (international) common equity.* Developed market status sometimes has been used to distinguish between *developed market equity* and *emerging market equity.*

- *Non-domestic fixed income.* Developed market status sometimes has been used to distinguish between *developed market fixed income* and *emerging market fixed income.*

- *Real estate.* The term *alternative investments* is now frequently used to refer to all risky asset classes excluding the four listed above. Alternative investments include real estate, private equity, natural resources, commodities, currencies, and the investment strategies represented by hedge funds. The usage is convenient, but such groups should be broken out as separate asset classes alongside real estate because alternative assets are far from homogeneous.

- *Cash and cash equivalents.* Later in this reading, we will explore why a manager sometimes will initially exclude cash and cash equivalents when choosing the optimal asset allocation.

In addition to regulatory constraints, if any, we must examine tax concerns to determine what asset classes to use in strategic asset allocation. Tax-exempt bonds, where available, generally play no role in strategic asset allocation for tax-exempt institutional investors because these bonds' pricing and yields reflect demand from taxable investors. For high-net-worth individuals and taxable institutional investors such as banks and non–life insurers, however, tax-exempt bonds are an appropriate fixed-income asset class, when they are available to the investor. Other considerations besides taxes may also be important. Some assets such as private equity play no role for investors of modest means or with limited due diligence capabilities.

---

[23] The statement of this criterion follows Kritzman (1999) closely.

The Selection of Asset Classes

Example 6

Are Inflation-Protected Bonds an Asset Class?

Bonds with payments linked to inflation indexes (inflation-protected or inflation-indexed bonds) were probably first issued by the Commonwealth of Massachusetts in 1780 and in modern times by Finland (1945), followed by Israel and Iceland in the 1950s, Brazil, Chile, and Colombia in the 1960s, Argentina and the United Kingdom in the 1970s, Australia and Mexico in the 1980s, and Canada, Sweden, New Zealand, the United States, and Turkey more recently.[a]

U.S. Treasury Inflation-Indexed Securities (usually called TIPS) were introduced in 1997. TIPS have a so-called capital-indexed design. That design provides for a fixed real coupon rate with the principal adjusted for inflation or deflation (however, the U.S. Treasury guarantees full payment of the original face value regardless of whatever deflation may occur). Inflation is measured by changes in the U.S. Consumer Price Index (CPI).

Consider the following reasons that have been put forward in support of viewing TIPS as a separate asset class:

Reason A TIPS returns of all maturities (10 years to 30 years) are strongly correlated with each other (Roll 2004).

Reason B TIPS have a low correlation with nominal bonds and equities. From 1997 to 2003, long-term TIPS had correlations with long-term nominal bonds in the range of 0.5 to 0.8 (Roll 2004).

Reason C The economics of TIPS is distinct from the economics of nominal bonds. Volatility of TIPS depends on volatility of real interest rates, whereas the volatility of conventional bonds depends on the volatility of nominal rates. Because it reflects the volatility of inflation, the volatility of nominal rates is generally greater than the volatility of real rates.

Reason D TIPS offer investors inflation and deflation protections that complement those of nominal bonds, whether fixed or floating coupon, as Exhibit 5 illustrates.

Exhibit 5 Protection against Inflation and Deflation

	Coupon	Principal
Nominal fixed-coupon bonds	Deflation protected	Deflation protected
	Inflation unprotected	Inflation unprotected
Nominal floating-coupon bonds	Deflation unprotected	Deflation protected
	Inflation protected	Inflation unprotected
TIPS	Deflation unprotected	Deflation protected (partial)
	Inflation protected	Inflation protected

Reason E To the extent the CPI reflects employment costs, TIPS can be effective in hedging pension benefits that incorporate salary increases.

Appraise the validity of each of Reasons A through E above.

> **Solution:**
>
> All the reasons are valid.
>
> **A.** High within-group correlations are consistent with the criterion that assets within an asset class should be relatively homogeneous.
>
> **B.** These levels of correlation are consistent with the criterion that asset classes should be diversifying.
>
> **C.** This economic argument provides one rationale to explain the level of historical correlations given in B. Differing economics provides some confidence that the observed level of correlations is not an anomaly.
>
> **D.** This argument also makes sense. TIPS permit increased flexibility in meeting investor goals affected by inflation or deflation.[b]
>
> **E.** This point identifies a concrete application of the point made in D and is thus also a valid argument.
>
> ---
> [a] See Shiller (2003) for the early history of such bonds.
> [b] Put another way, TIPS help *complete the market*, a finance expression indicating that the existence of TIPS increases the available set of payoff patterns.

4.2 The Inclusion of International Assets (Developed and Emerging Markets)

In the prior section, we stated that asset classes as a group should make up a preponderance of world investable wealth. According to that criterion, nondomestic (international) assets have a place in the lineup of *permissible* asset classes for many investors. This section addresses the further question of justifying *investment* in a specific class of international assets.

An objective criterion based on mean–variance analysis can help an investor decide whether he can improve on his existing portfolio by adding a positive holding in nondomestic equities or bonds or any other asset class. Suppose an investor holds a portfolio p with expected or mean return $E(R_p)$ and standard deviation of return σ_p. The investor then gains the opportunity to add another asset class to his portfolio. Can the investor achieve a mean–variance improvement by expanding his portfolio to include a positive position in the asset class? To answer this question, we need three inputs:

- the Sharpe ratio of the asset class;
- the Sharpe ratio of the existing portfolio; and
- the correlation between the asset class's return and portfolio p's return, $\text{Corr}(R_{new}, R_p)$.

Adding the asset class (denoted *new*) to the portfolio is optimal if the following condition is met:[24]

$$\frac{E(R_{new}) - R_F}{\sigma_{new}} > \left(\frac{E(R_p) - R_F}{\sigma_p}\right) \text{Corr}(R_{new}, R_p) \qquad (3)$$

This expression says that in order for the investor to gain by adding the asset class, that asset class's Sharpe ratio must exceed the product of the existing portfolio's Sharpe ratio and the correlation of the asset class's rate of return with the current portfolio's

---
[24] See Blume (1984) and Elton, Gruber, and Rentzler (1987).

The Selection of Asset Classes

rate of return. If Equation 3 holds, the investor can combine the new investment with his or her prior holdings to achieve a superior efficient frontier of risky assets (one in which the tangency portfolio has a higher Sharpe ratio).[25] Note that although the expression may indicate that we can effect a mean–variance improvement at the margin by adding a positive amount of a new asset, it offers no information about how much of the new asset to add.

> **Example 7**
>
> ### A Foundation Decides to Add an Asset Class
>
> Wilhelm Schmidt is CIO of a German charitable foundation invested in European equities and bonds. The portfolio has a Sharpe ratio of 0.15. Schmidt is considering adding U.S. equities to the existing portfolio. U.S. equities, as represented by the Russell 3000 Index, have a predicted Sharpe ratio of 0.18; the predicted correlation with existing portfolio is 0.7. Explain whether the foundation should add U.S. equities to its existing portfolio.
>
> ### Solution:
>
> (Sharpe ratio of existing portfolio) × (Correlation of U.S. stocks with the existing portfolio) = (0.15)(0.70) = 0.105. The foundation should add U.S. equities if their predicted Sharpe ratio exceeds 0.105. Because Schmidt predicts a Sharpe ratio of 0.18 for U.S. equities, the foundation should add them to the existing portfolio.

In Example 7, even if the correlation between the foundation's existing portfolio and U.S. equities were + 1.0, so that adding U.S. equities had no potential risk-reduction benefits, Equation 3 would indicate that the class should be added because the condition for adding the asset class would be satisfied, because 0.18 > 0.15(1.0). For any portfolio, we can always effect a mean–variance improvement at the margin by adding an investment with a higher Sharpe ratio than the existing portfolio. This result is intuitive: The higher-Sharpe-ratio investment will mean–variance dominate the existing portfolio in a pairwise comparison. Prior to using the Equation 3 criterion, the investor should check whether distribution of the proposed asset class's returns is pronouncedly non-normal. If it is, the criterion is not applicable.

When investing in international assets, investors should consider the following special issues:

- *Currency risk*. Currency risk is a distinctive issue for international investment. Exchange rate fluctuations affect both the total return and volatility of return of any nondomestic investment. Investors in nondomestic markets must form expectations about exchange rates if they decide not to hedge currency exposures. Currency risk as measured by standard deviation may average half the risk of the corresponding stock market and twice the risk of the corresponding bond market.[26]

- *Increased correlations in times of stress*. Investors should be aware that correlations across international markets tend to increase in times of market breaks or crashes.[27]

---

[25] Of course, the condition is an inequality. We use "equation" to refer to all numbered formulas or conditions for simplicity.
[26] See Solnik and McLeavey (2004, pp. 471–472).
[27] Increased market volatility during such times will by itself tend to produce upwardly biased estimated correlations; after correcting for that bias, however, evidence remains that correlations increase during times of stress. See Solnik and McLeavey (2004) Chapter 9.

- *Emerging market concerns.* Among the concerns are limited free float of shares (shares available in the marketplace), limitations on the amount of nondomestic ownership, the quality of company information, and pronounced non-normality of returns (an issue of concern in using a mean–variance approach to choose an asset allocation).

Many researchers believe U.S. investors underinvest in nondomestic markets, a phenomenon called home country bias. One explanation suggested for this tendency is investors' relative lack of familiarity with nondomestic markets. Indexing to an asset class, however, provides an efficient way to deal with any lack of familiarity.

4.3 Alternative Investments

At the beginning of the 1990s, real estate was the other major asset class besides fixed income and equity that investors would list as an asset class for the investable portfolio. Many investors now group real estate along with a range of disparate nontraditional investments, such as private equity and hedge funds of all descriptions, as alternative investments. Exhibit 6 gives historical data on the mean returns, volatilities, and correlations of four traditional asset classes (from a U.S. perspective) and four alternative asset classes: private equity, real estate, natural resources, and hedge funds. The statistics for alternative asset classes show distinct relationships within the group and between the individual alternative asset classes and traditional asset classes. For example, the correlations of real estate with private equity, natural resources, and hedge funds were 0.32, –0.46, and –0.18, respectively. Real estate had a correlation of 0.02 with U.S. equity; the correlations of U.S. equity with private equity, natural resources, and hedge funds were 0.18, 0.43, and 0.68, respectively. These data suggest that "alternative investments" is a label of convenience for a quite heterogeneous array of investments that may more appropriately be treated as distinct asset classes. The highest correlation of an alternative asset class with a traditional asset class, 0.68 for hedge funds with U.S. equity, was still well below the level (1.0) at which no diversification benefits would exist. In summary, at least these data suggest potentially meaningful diversification benefits from exposure to alternative asset classes. One concern for many investors, however, is the availability of resources to directly or indirectly research investment in these groups. Information for publicly traded equities and bonds is more widely available than for private equity, for example, and indexed investment vehicles for alternative asset groups are often lacking. Thus some investors may face an internal resource constraint limiting investment in alternative assets. Furthermore, the fees and related expenses incurred in many alternative investments are often relatively steep.

Exhibit 6 Mean Returns, Volatilities, and Correlations: U.S. Traditional and Alternative Asset Classes, 1981–2003

	Mean Return	Volatility	1	2	3	4	5	6	7	8
1. U.S. equity	12.3%	15.4%	1.00							
2. Ex-U.S. equity	9.9	18.8	0.71	1.00						
3. U.S. fixed income	10.1	6.7	0.25	0.12	1.00					
4. Ex-U.S. fixed income	9.9	5.9	0.22	0.30	0.74	1.00				
5. Private equity	15.7	15.3	0.18	0.40	–0.23	0.13	1.00			

Exhibit 6 Continued

	Mean Return	Volatility	Correlation 1	2	3	4	5	6	7	8
6. Real estate	7.8	5.5	0.02	0.34	−0.05	0.21	0.32	1.00		
7. Natural resources	15.3	10.3	0.43	0.38	0.09	0.08	0.34	−0.46	1.00	
8. Hedge funds	17.4	7.2	0.68	0.55	0.22	0.19	0.20	−0.18	0.46	1.00

Note: Natural Resources series covers the 1987–2003 period.
Source: UBS Global Asset Management.

THE STEPS IN ASSET ALLOCATION

In establishing a strategic asset allocation, an investment manager must specify a set of asset-class weights to produce a portfolio that satisfies the return and risk objectives and constraints as stated in the investment policy statement. With the specification and listing of the IPS-permissible asset classes in hand, our focus is on understanding the process for establishing and maintaining an appropriate asset allocation. Most organizations undertake this process regularly in **asset allocation reviews**. This section outlines the steps to follow during the review process.[28]

The procedure outlined includes liabilities in the analysis. An asset-only approach can be considered a special case in which liabilities equal zero.

Exhibit 7 shows the major steps. Boxes on the left, labeled C1, C2, and C3, are concerned primarily with the capital markets. Those on the right are investor specific (I1, I2, and I3). Those in the middle (M1, M2, and M3) bring together aspects of the capital markets and the investor's circumstances to determine the investor's asset mix and its performance. The asset allocation review process begins at the top of the diagram and proceeds downward. Then the outcomes (M3) provide feedback to both the capital-market- and investor-related steps at the next asset allocation review.

---

[28] The steps laid out in Exhibit 7 roughly follow the portfolio construction, monitoring, and revision process laid out in Exhibit 1-1 in Chapter 1 of *Managing Investment Portfolios: A Dynamic Process*. The process in Exhibit 7 is truncated, however, because it terminates with the asset allocation decision, implementation, and evaluation rather than proceeding to the optimization of each of the subportfolios (e.g., of fixed income, equity, real estate, and so on).

Exhibit 7 Major Steps in Asset Allocation

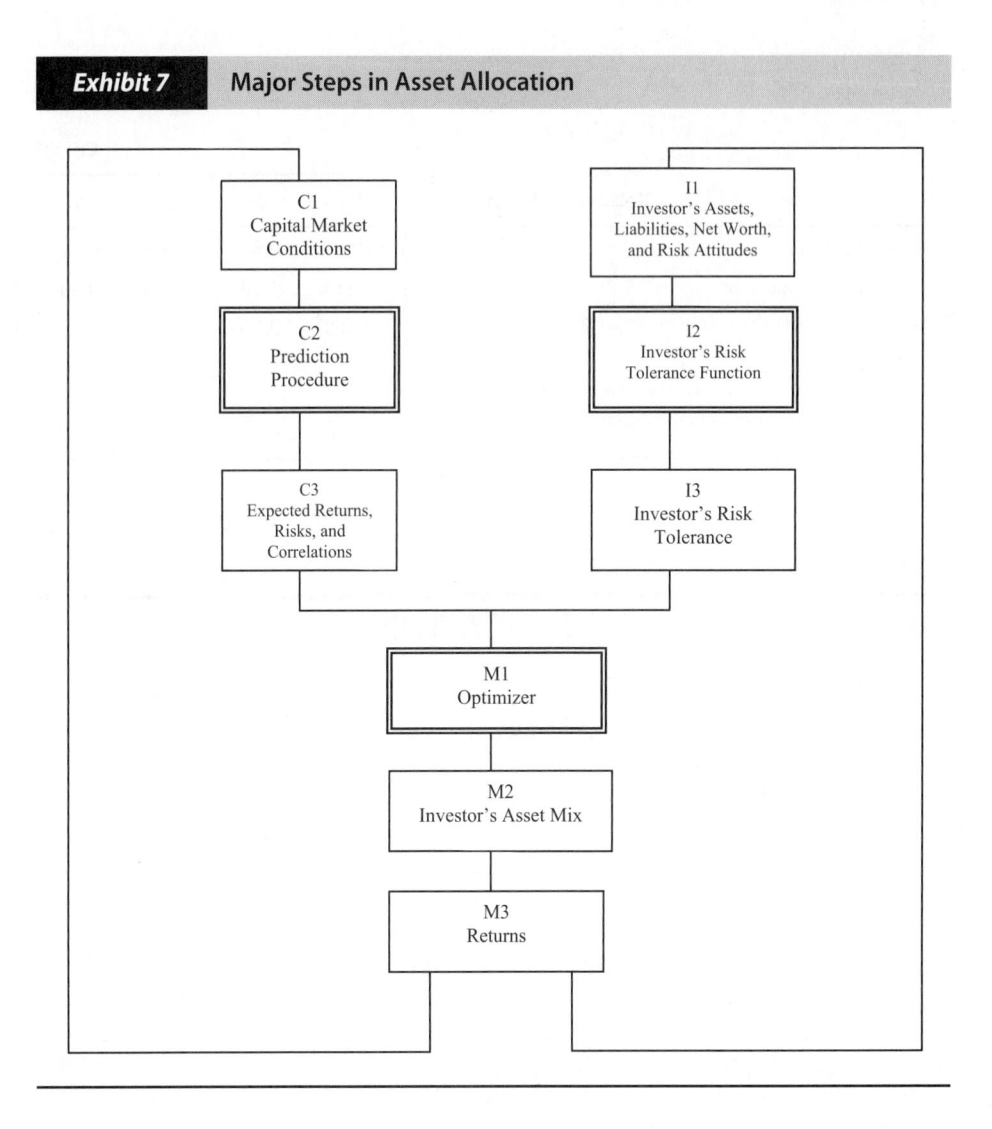

```
        ┌─────────────────┐              ┌─────────────────────┐
        │       C1        │              │         I1          │
        │ Capital Market  │              │ Investor's Assets,  │
        │   Conditions    │              │ Liabilities, Net Worth,│
        └────────┬────────┘              │  and Risk Attitudes │
                 │                       └──────────┬──────────┘
        ┌────────┴────────┐              ┌──────────┴──────────┐
        │       C2        │              │         I2          │
        │   Prediction    │              │  Investor's Risk    │
        │   Procedure     │              │ Tolerance Function  │
        └────────┬────────┘              └──────────┬──────────┘
        ┌────────┴────────┐              ┌──────────┴──────────┐
        │       C3        │              │         I3          │
        │Expected Returns,│              │   Investor's Risk   │
        │   Risks, and    │              │     Tolerance       │
        │  Correlations   │              │                     │
        └────────┬────────┘              └──────────┬──────────┘
                 │                                  │
                 └──────────────┬───────────────────┘
                       ┌────────┴────────┐
                       │       M1        │
                       │    Optimizer    │
                       └────────┬────────┘
                       ┌────────┴────────┐
                       │       M2        │
                       │Investor's Asset Mix│
                       └────────┬────────┘
                       ┌────────┴────────┐
                       │       M3        │
                       │     Returns     │
                       └─────────────────┘
```

Box I1 shows factors that determine risk tolerance—the current values of assets and, if applicable, liabilities (or quasi-liabilities); net worth (assets minus liabilities); and the investor's innate attitude to risk (conservatism).

Net worth generally influences an investor's current tolerance for risk, shown in box I3.[29] We can portray the relationship between the investor's circumstances (box I1) and risk tolerance (box I3) with a **risk tolerance function**. It is shown in box I2 and can be thought of as the nature of the investor's tolerance to risk over various levels of portfolio outcomes. (We could also speak of a risk-aversion function, because risk tolerance and risk aversion are opposite sides of the same coin.)

Box C1 shows the current state of the capital markets. Information such as current and historical asset prices, past and projected asset cash flows, and the yield curve provide major inputs for predicting the expected returns and risks of various asset classes and the correlations among their returns (shown in box C3). If liabilities are relevant, their risks, expected future values, and correlations with various asset classes must also be predicted. Some prediction procedure must be used to translate capital market conditions (box C1) into these estimates of asset and liability returns (box C3); it is shown in box C2. The reading on capital market expectations discusses capital market inputs and prediction procedures in detail.

---

[29] Even when the investor's risk tolerance function is such that changes in net worth do not change his or her risk tolerance, we can still show a link between box I1 and box I3 because new circumstances (or even the process of aging) may alter an investor's risk attitudes.

Given an investor's risk tolerance (box I3) and predictions concerning expected returns, risks, and correlations (box C3), we can use an **optimizer** to determine the most appropriate asset allocation or asset mix (box M2). Depending on such factors as the number of assets and the investor's approach, the optimizer (shown in box M1) could be a simple rule of thumb, a mathematical function, or a full-scale optimization program.

Box M3 shows actual returns. Given the investor's asset mix at the *beginning* of a period (box M2), the asset returns during the period (box M3) plus any cash contributions and minus any cash withdrawals determine the values of the investor's assets at the beginning of the *next* period. New accruals of liabilities and pay-downs of old liabilities must also be considered. Changes in capital markets (including returns on fixed-income obligations) are likely to affect the values of the liabilities as well. Returns in one period thus influence the investor's assets, liabilities, and net worth at the beginning of the next period, as shown by the feedback loop from box M3 to box I1. Returns during a period also constitute part of the overall capital market conditions at the beginning of the next period. This relationship is shown by the feedback loop from box M3 to box C1. These loops illustrate that the process is continuous, with decisions and outcomes in one review period affecting the decisions in the next one.

From period to period, any (or all) of the items in boxes C1, C3, I1, I3, M2, and M3 may change. However, the items in boxes C2, I2, and M1 should remain fixed, because they contain decision rules (procedures). Thus the investor's risk tolerance (box I3) may change, but the risk tolerance *function* (box I2) should not. Predictions concerning returns (box C3) may change, but not the *procedure* (box C2) for making such predictions. The optimal asset mix (box M2) may change, but not the *optimizer* (box M1) that determines it. To emphasize the relative permanence of the contents of these boxes, they have been drawn with double lines.

The process illustrated in Exhibit 7 pertains to both strategic asset allocation reviews and tactical asset allocation if the investor chooses to actively manage asset allocation. For tactical asset allocation, the focus is on the impact of capital market conditions on short-term capital market expectations (box C3), possibly resulting in short-term asset allocation adjustments. The main attention is on the prediction procedure (C1) in a competitive marketplace. By contrast, a strategic asset allocation considers only the effects, if any, of capital market conditions on long-term capital market expectations.

When all the steps discussed in the previous section are performed with careful analysis (formal or informal), the process may be called integrated asset allocation. This term is intended to indicate that all major aspects have been included in a consistent manner. If liabilities are relevant, they are integrated into the analysis. If they are not, the procedure still integrates aspects of capital markets, the investor's circumstances and preferences, and the like. Moreover, each review is based on conditions at the time—those in the capital markets and those of the investor. Thus the process is dynamic as well as integrated.

In the next section, we discuss the optimizer (box M1): the procedure we use to select an asset allocation for an investor.

OPTIMIZATION

A critical step in strategic asset allocation is the procedure we use for converting the inputs to a specific recommended strategic asset allocation. Much of the research by practitioners and academics alike has focused on developing and refining a variety of procedures. Many of the most important established procedures have a quantitative flavor, reflecting not only the advances of modern portfolio theory but also the need for many institutional investors to document relatively objective procedures. Some investment advisors, particularly those serving an individual investor clientele, may use a qualitative approach based on experience. In fact, nearly all professional investors apply judgment in making recommendations. In the following, we examine the major procedures in use today, beginning with one of the most well established.

6.1 The Mean–Variance Approach

Mean–variance analysis provided the first, and still important, quantitative approach to strategic asset allocation. As with all approaches that we will discuss, a strategic asset allocation suggested by mean–variance analysis should be subjected to professional judgment before adoption.

6.1.1 *The Efficient Frontier*

According to mean–variance theory, in determining a strategic asset allocation an investor should choose from among the efficient portfolios consistent with that investor's risk tolerance. Efficient portfolios make efficient use of risk; they offer the maximum expected return for their level of variance or standard deviation of return.

Efficient portfolios plot graphically on the **efficient frontier**, which is part of the **minimum-variance frontier** (MVF). Each portfolio on the minimum-variance frontier represents the portfolio with the smallest variance of return for its level of expected return. The graph of a minimum-variance frontier has a turning point (its leftmost point) that represents the **global minimum-variance** (GMV) **portfolio**. The GMV portfolio has the smallest variance of all minimum-variance portfolios. The portion of the minimum-variance frontier beginning with and continuing above the GMV portfolio is the efficient frontier. Exhibit 8 illustrates these concepts using standard deviation (the positive square root of variance) for the *x*-axis because the units of standard deviation are easy to interpret.

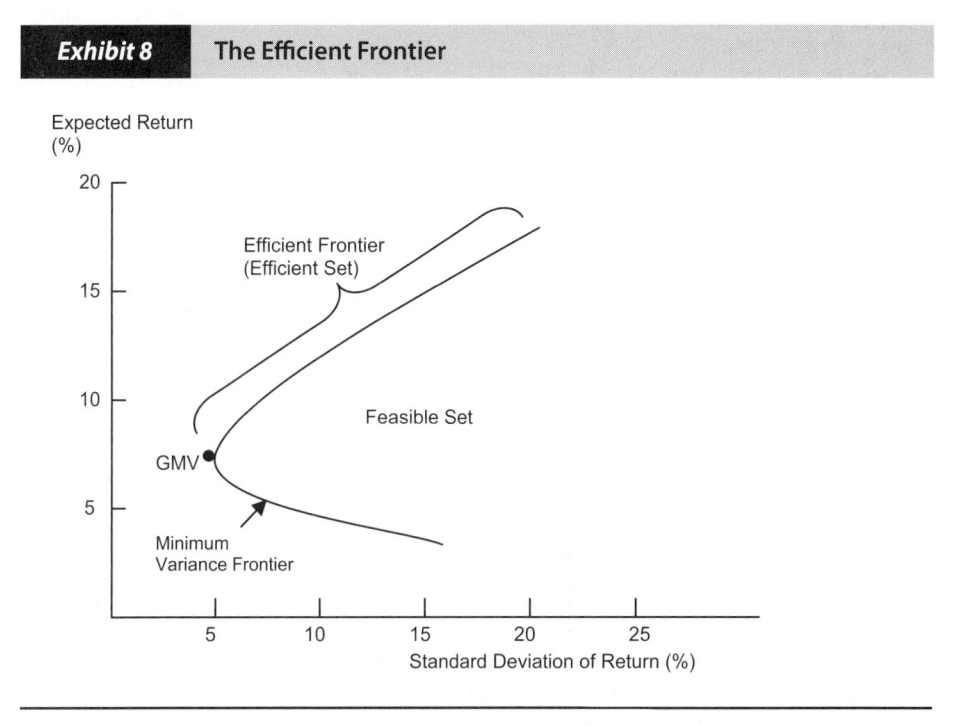

Exhibit 8 The Efficient Frontier

Optimization

Once we have identified an efficient portfolio with the desired combination of expected return and variance, we must determine that portfolio's asset-class weights. To do so, we use mean–variance optimization (MVO).[30] There is a structure to minimum-variance frontiers and consequently to the solutions given by optimizers. Understanding that structure not only makes us more-informed users of optimizers but can also be helpful in practice.

The Unconstrained MVF The simplest optimization places no constraints on asset-class weights except that the weights sum to 1. We call this form an **unconstrained optimization**, yielding the unconstrained minimum-variance frontier. In this case, the Black (1972) two-fund theorem states that the asset weights of any minimum-variance portfolio are a linear combination of the asset weights of any other two minimum-variance portfolios. In an unconstrained optimization, therefore, we need only determine the weights of two minimumvariance portfolios to know the weights of any other minimum-variance portfolio.

For example, in a three-asset-class optimization, if we determine that one minimum-variance portfolio has weights (80%, 15%, 5%) with an expected return of 10.5 percent and that a second has weights (40%, 40%, 20%) with an expected return of 7.4 percent, we can trace out the entire minimum-variance frontier.[31] To find the weights of the minimum-variance portfolio with an expected return of 9.57 percent, for example, we specify the equation

$$9.57 = 10.5w + 7.4(1 - w)$$

where w is the weight in the 10.5%-expected-return portfolio and $(1 - w)$ is the weight in the 7.4%-expected-return portfolio. We find that $w = 0.70$ and $(1 - w) = 0.30$. For each asset class, we use 0.70 and 0.30 to take a weighted average of the asset class's weights in the two minimum-variance portfolios; doing so gives us the weight of the asset class in the 9.57%-expected-return portfolio:

Weight of Asset Class 1: 0.70(80%) + 0.30(40%) = 68.00%

Weight of Asset Class 2: 0.70(15%) + 0.30(40%) = 22.50%

Weight of Asset Class 3: 0.70(5%) + 0.30(20%) = 9.50%

We check that 68% + 22.5% + 9.5% = 100%. To summarize, after determining the asset-class weights and expected returns of two minimum-variance portfolios, we took a desired expected return level (9.57 percent), which we set equal to a weighted average of the expected returns on the two portfolios. This equation had a unique solution, giving two weights (0.70 and 0.30). We applied those two weights to the known asset-class weights of the two minimum-variance portfolios to find the weights of the 9.57%-expected-return portfolio (68.0%, 22.5%, 9.5%).

The Sign-Constrained MVF: The Case Most Relevant to Strategic Asset Allocation The Black theorem is helpful background for the case of optimization that is most relevant to practice, MVO, including the constraints that the asset-class weights be non-negative and sum to 1. We call this approach a **sign-constrained optimization** because it excludes negative weights, and its result is the sign-constrained minimum-variance frontier. A negative weight would imply that the asset class is to be sold short. In a

---

[30] MVOs come in many varieties. Besides special-purpose software, Microsoft Excel with the Solver add-in is a powerful tool for computing the minimum-variance frontier as described in a variety of books and web-available sources. For example, see Benninga (2000) for financial modeling with Excel.

[31] The expression (80%, 15%, 5%) is a compact way of indicating that the weights on the first, second, and third asset classes are 80 percent, 15 percent, and 5 percent, respectively.

strategic asset allocation context, an allocation with a negative asset-class weight would generally be irrelevant. Accordingly, we focus on sign-constrained optimization. In addition to satisfying non-negativity constraints, the structure we describe here also applies when we place an upper limit on one or more asset-class weights.

The constraint against short sales restricts choice. By the nature of a sign-constrained optimization, each asset class in a minimum-variance portfolio is held in either positive weight or zero weight. But an asset class with a zero weight in one minimum-variance portfolio may appear with a positive weight in another minimum-variance portfolio at a different expected return level. This observation leads to the concept of corner portfolios.

Adjacent **corner portfolios** define a segment of the minimum-variance frontier within which 1) portfolios hold identical assets and 2) the rate of change of asset weights in moving from one portfolio to another is constant. As the minimum-variance frontier passes through a corner portfolio, an asset weight either changes from zero to positive or from positive to zero. The GMV portfolio, however, is included as a corner portfolio irrespective of its asset weights.

Corner portfolios allow us to create other minimum-variance portfolios. For example, suppose we have a corner portfolio with an expected return of 8 percent and an adjacent corner portfolio with expected return of 10 percent. The asset weights of *any* minimum-variance portfolio with expected return between 8 and 10 percent is a positive weighted average of the asset weights in the 8%- and 10%-expected-return corner portfolios. *In a sign-constrained optimization, the asset weights of any minimum-variance portfolio are a positive linear combination of the corresponding weights in the two adjacent corner portfolios that bracket it in terms of expected return (or standard deviation of return).* The foregoing statement is the key observation about the structure of a sign-constrained optimization; we may call it the **corner portfolio theorem**. Corner portfolios are generally relatively few in number. Knowing the composition of the corner portfolios allows us to compute the weights of any portfolio on the minimum-variance frontier.

We can illustrate these concepts using the data in Exhibit 9, which gives hypothetical inputs to a sign-constrained optimization. A U.K. institutional investor is developing a strategic asset allocation among six asset classes: domestic (U.K.) equities, international (ex-U.K.) equities, domestic intermediate-term and long-term bonds, international bonds, and real estate. The investor cannot sell securities short or buy on margin. Later we illustrate the effects of changing the expectations for the asset classes in Exhibit 9.

Exhibit 9 U.K. Institutional Investor Capital Market Expectations

Asset Class	Expected Return	Standard Deviation	1	2	3	4	5	6
1. U.K. equities	10.0%	15%	1.00					
2. Ex-U.K. equities	8.0	12	0.76	1.00				
3. Intermediate bonds	4.0	7	0.35	0.04	1.00			
4. Long-term bonds	4.5	8	0.50	0.30	0.87	1.00		
5. International bonds	5.0	9	0.24	0.36	0.62	0.52	1.00	
6. Real estate	7.0	10	0.30	0.25	−0.05	−0.02	0.20	1.00

Exhibit 10 illustrates the efficient frontier based on the expectations in Exhibit 9. Only the efficient portion of the minimum-variance frontier is relevant for the investor's asset allocation decision.

Optimization

Exhibit 10 — An Efficient Frontier Showing Corner Portfolios

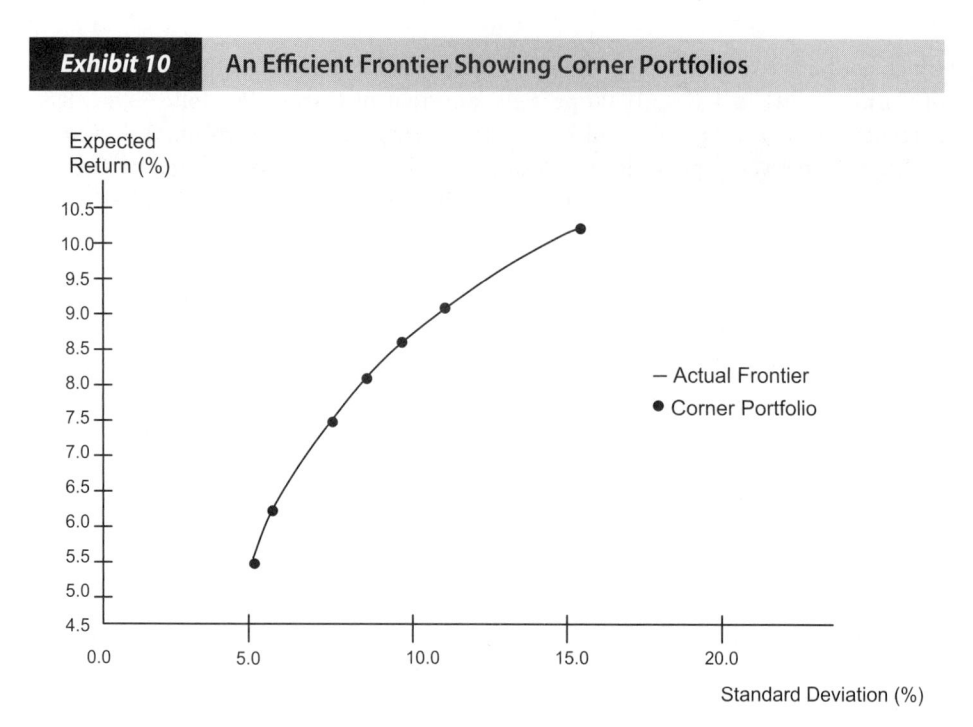

Exhibit 10 shows that in this case, seven corner portfolios provide the information needed to trace the efficient frontier. Exhibit 11 provides information on their composition.[32] We also report the corner portfolios' expected returns and standard deviations of returns, as well as their Sharpe ratios (a measure of risk-adjusted performance) assuming a 2 percent risk-free rate.

Exhibit 11 — U.K. Institutional Investor Corner Portfolios

Corner Portfolio Number	Expected Return	Standard Deviation	Sharpe Ratio	Asset Class (Portfolio Weight) 1	2	3	4	5	6
1	10.00%	15.00%	0.53	100.00%	0.00%	0.00%	0.00%	0.00%	0.00%
2	8.86	11.04	0.62	61.90	0.00	0.00	0.00	0.00	38.10
3	8.35	9.8	0.65	40.31	13.85	0.00	0.00	0.00	45.83
4	7.94	8.99	0.66	32.53	14.30	0.00	0.00	8.74	44.44
5	7.30	7.82	0.68	19.93	21.09	16.85	0.00	0.00	42.13
6	6.13	5.94	0.70	0.00	26.61	37.81	0.00	0.00	35.58
7	5.33	5.37	0.62	0.00	13.01	59.94	0.00	0.00	27.06

Corner Portfolio 1 represents a portfolio 100 percent invested in the highest-expected-return asset class, U.K. equities. The highest-expected-return asset class generally appears as the first corner portfolio. Moving along the efficient frontier from Corner Portfolio 1 to lower levels of expected return, we reach Corner Portfolio 2,

---

[32] Various algorithms are available for computing the weights of the corner portfolios and the sign-constrained minimum-variance frontier more generally. The first was Markowitz's (1959) critical line algorithm; see Sharpe (2000) and www.stanford.edu/~wfsharpe/ for details. We thank Michael Kishinevsky for providing us with a spreadsheet based on the critical-line algorithm that reports corner portfolio weights.

which contains real estate. Any efficient portfolio with expected return between that of Corner Portfolio 1 (i.e., 10.00 percent) and that of Corner Portfolio 2 (i.e., 8.86 percent) holds U.K. equities and real estate, because Corner Portfolio 2 does, and such an "in-between" portfolio would be a weighted average of Corner Portfolio 1 and Corner Portfolio 2. Corner Portfolio 3, with an expected return of 8.35 percent, contains ex-U.K. equities in addition to U.K. equities and real estate. Therefore, any efficient portfolio with expected return between that of Corner Portfolio 2 (i.e., 8.86 percent) and that of Corner Portfolio 3 (i.e., 8.35 percent) holds U.K. equities, ex-U.K. equities, and real estate, because Corner Portfolio 3 does. Each pair of adjacent corner portfolios defines a segment of the efficient frontier that relates to a specific interval for expected returns, and within the segment we find the efficient portfolio for a given level of expected return as a weighted average of the two corner portfolios defining the segment. Corner Portfolio 7 is the GMV portfolio. In any listing of the corner portfolios of an efficient frontier, we always include the GMV portfolio as the last portfolio.

Suppose we want to find the composition of the efficient portfolio with an 8 percent expected return. First we identify the adjacent corner portfolios as Portfolio 3, with an 8.35 percent expected return, and Portfolio 4, with a 7.94 percent expected return. The arithmetic in using the corner portfolio theorem follows a pattern familiar from the Black theorem example:

$$8.0 = 8.35w + 7.94(1 - w)$$

We find that $w = 0.146$ and $(1 - w) = 0.854$. The 8.35%-expected-return corner portfolio has weights (40.31%, 13.85%, 0%, 0%, 0%, 45.83%) and the 7.94%-expected-return corner portfolio has weights (32.53%, 14.30%, 0%, 0%, 8.74%, 44.44%). An efficient portfolio with an 8 percent expected return will have weights of 0.146 × (40.31%, 13.85%, 0%, 0%, 0%, 45.83%) + 0.854 × (32.53%, 14.30%, 0%, 0%, 8.74%, 44.44%) = (33.67%, 14.23%, 0%, 0%, 7.46%, 44.64%).[33] The 8%-expected-return efficient portfolio includes U.K. equities (33.67 percent), ex-U.K. equities (14.23 percent), international bonds (7.46 percent), and real estate (44.64 percent); intermediate and long-term bonds are not in the portfolio.

What is the standard deviation of return on the 8%-expected-return efficient portfolio? We know that it must lie between 9.80 percent (the standard deviation of the 8.35%-expected-return corner portfolio) and 8.99 percent (the standard deviation of the 7.94%-expected-return corner portfolio). Using the correlations from Exhibit 9, we could compute the standard deviation exactly using expressions for portfolio variance given in any investment text. We can also find the approximate standard deviation of the 8%-expected-return efficient portfolio by taking a weighted average of the adjacent corner portfolios' standard deviations of 9.80 percent and 8.99 percent, using the weights of 0.146 and 0.854 computed earlier: 0.146(9.80) + 0.854(8.99) = 9.11 percent. The efficient frontier bows out toward the left as shown in Exhibit 10, reflecting less-than-perfect positive correlation between corner portfolios. As a result, the actual standard deviation of the 8%-expected-return efficient portfolio will be slightly less than 9.11 percent. The linear approximation just illustrated provides a quick approximation (and upper limit) for the standard deviation; we also can apply this approximation in other cases in which we calculate efficient portfolios using the corner portfolio theorem.

---

[33] The compact notation 0.146 × (40.31%, 13.85%, 0%, 0%, 0%, 45.83%) means that we multiply each element in the parenthetical list (vector) by 0.146.

Optimization

> **Example 8**
>
> ## Identifying Asset-Class Weights in Efficient Portfolios
>
> Using the information given in Exhibit 11, answer the following questions:
>
> 1. What is the maximum weight of long-term bonds in any portfolio on the efficient frontier?
> 2. What are the asset-class weights in an efficient portfolio with an expected return of 7 percent?
> 3. Which asset class is most important in the 7%-expected-return efficient portfolio?
> 4. Explain your answer to Part 3.
>
> ### Solution to 1:
>
> The maximum weight of long-term bonds is 0 percent because long-term bonds do not appear with a positive weight in any of the corner portfolios, and any efficient portfolio can be represented as a weighted average of corner portfolios.
>
> ### Solution to 2:
>
> First we identify the adjacent corner portfolios as Corner Portfolio 5 (with a 7.30 percent expected return) and Corner Portfolio 6 (with a 6.13 percent expected return). From the corner portfolio theorem, it follows that
>
> $$7.0 = 7.30w + 6.13(1 - w)$$
>
> We find that $w = 0.744$ and $(1 - w) = 0.256$. The detailed arithmetic follows:
>
> | | |
> |---|---|
> | Weight of U.K. equities | 0.744(19.93%) + 0.256(0%) = 14.83% |
> | Weight of ex-U.K. equities | 0.744(21.09%) + 0.256(26.61%) = 22.50% |
> | Weight of intermediate bonds | 0.744(16.85%) + 0.256(37.81%) = 22.22% |
> | Weight of long-term bonds | 0.744(0%) + 0.256(0%) = 0% |
> | Weight of international bonds | 0.744(0%) + 0.256(0%) = 0% |
> | Weight of real estate | 0.744(42.13%) + 0.256(35.58%) = 40.45% |
>
> As an arithmetic check, 14.83% + 22.50% + 22.22% + 0% + 0% + 40.45% = 100%.
>
> ### Solution to 3:
>
> Real estate (Asset Class 6) with a weight of more than 40 percent appears as the dominant holding in the 7%-expected-return efficient portfolio.
>
> ### Solution to 4:
>
> Real estate is the first or second most important holding in all but the first corner portfolio. Because of its forecasted low correlations with other asset classes (including negative correlations with domestic bonds), real estate brings strong risk-reduction benefits, given this investor's estimates for the MVO inputs. Identifying the asset classes in the GMV portfolio gives a useful indication of the asset classes whose combination of standard deviations and correlations effectively diversify risk. Here those classes are ex-U.K. equities, intermediate-term bonds, and real estate.

As mentioned earlier, investors sometimes place an upper limit on one or more asset-class weights in addition to constraining asset-class weights to be nonnegative. For example, the sign-constrained efficient portfolios represented by Exhibit 11 and discussed in Example 8 have relatively high weights on real estate. If the investor were uncomfortable with a weight on real estate above 15 percent, we could rerun the optimization with a new constraint limiting real estate holdings to no more than 15 percent. The result would be the efficient frontier subject to the new set of constraints, and again it would be represented by a set of corner portfolios.

6.1.2 The Importance of the Quality of Inputs

A limitation of the mean–variance approach is that its recommended asset allocations are highly sensitive to small changes in inputs and, therefore, to estimation error. In its impact on the results of a mean–variance approach to asset allocation, estimation error in expected returns has been estimated to be roughly 10 times as important as estimation error in variances and 20 times as important as estimation error in covariances.[34] Best and Grauer (1991) demonstrate that a small increase in the expected return of one of the portfolio's assets can force half of the assets from the portfolio. Thus *the most important inputs in mean–variance optimization are the expected returns.* Unfortunately, mean returns are also the most difficult input to estimate.

The following example illustrates the extreme weights that may result from MVO and shows the limitations of using unadjusted historical return distribution parameter estimates as inputs. Exhibit 12 presents the historical average annual return, standard deviation, and correlation coefficients across five equity markets from 1992 to 2003. Using these as inputs for MVO, Exhibit 13 presents the resulting optimal allocations along the frontier. The y-axis shows the asset-class weights in a particular portfolio on the efficient frontier. The x-axis runs from 0 to 100 percent and identifies the efficient portfolio by standard deviation: The position of 0 represents the standard deviation of the GMV portfolio and the position of 100 the standard deviation of the highest-mean-return asset class, the Dow Jones Global Index (DJGI) Americas, which is the rightmost point on the efficient frontier without short sales. The position of 50 percent is the midpoint in terms of standard deviations between the GMV portfolio and DJGI Americas. We see that the efficient frontier is dominated by two asset classes: U.K. equity for very low risk efficient portfolios (towards 0 on the x-axis) and Americas equity for moderate and high risk efficient portfolios (towards 100 on the x-axis). Neither Europe ex-U.K. equity nor Japan equity enter into any efficient portfolio.

Exhibit 12 Historical Average Annual Return, Standard Deviation, and Correlation Coefficients: 1992–2003[a]

	Average Return	Standard Deviation	Corr. w/ DJGI Americas TR	Corr. w/ DJGI Asia Pacific Ex-Japan TR	Corr. w/ DJGI Europe Ex-U.K.	Corr. w/ DJGI Japan TR USD	Corr. w/ DJGI U.K. TR USD
DJGI Americas TR	11.87%	18.83%	1.000	0.641	0.747	0.393	0.778
DJGI Asia Pacific ex-Japan TR	11.21	37.03	0.641	1.000	0.584	0.444	0.599
DJGI Europe ex-U.K.	11.04	21.58	0.747	0.584	1.000	0.369	0.768
DJGI Japan TR USD	3.19	33.66	0.393	0.444	0.369	1.000	0.351
DJGI U.K. TR USD	9.58	17.41	0.778	0.599	0.768	0.351	1.000

[a] Correlations are calculated using monthly data.
Note: TR = total return, USD = in U.S. dollar terms.

---

[34] See Ziemba (2003, p. 12).

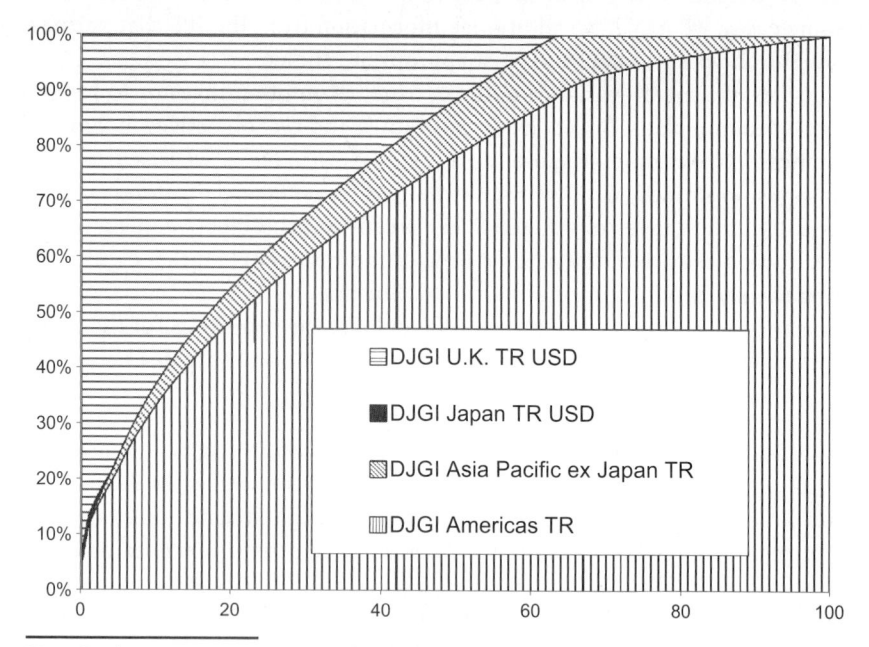

Optimization

Exhibit 13 Efficient Portfolio Weights Using Raw Historical Mean Returns

Note: On the *x*-axis, zero represents the GMV portfolio's standard deviation and 100 represents the highest-mean-return asset class's standard deviation. The *y*-axis shows asset-class weights. The in-figure legend is a key to regions, starting from the topmost at the zero-SD point; Asia Pacific ex-Japan appears only near zero on the *x*-axis.

Practically, the investor should conduct sensitivity analysis with an emphasis on the effects of different expected return estimates. Another approach, which we present later, involves using the concept of the resampled efficient frontier. Using any approach, we need to apply professional judgment in evaluating results. The reading on capital market expectations provides more information on formulating quality capital market expectations.

6.1.3 Selecting an Efficient Portfolio

In his IPS, the investor formulates risk and return objectives. The risk objective reflects the investor's risk tolerance (his capacity to accept risk as a function of both his willingness and ability). If the investor is sensitive to volatility of returns, the investor may quantify his risk objective as a capacity to accept no greater than a 9 percent average standard deviation of return, for example. Given this type of information, how might an investor use MVO to select an asset allocation?

Let us use the data in Exhibit 11 and the results of Example 8 to frame our discussion. Suppose the investor's return objective is 7 percent a year. The 7%-expected-return efficient portfolio identified in Example 8 has a standard deviation of return of less than 7.82 percent (7.82 is the standard deviation of Corner Portfolio 5 that lies above it), so it satisfies the risk objective. The 7%-expected-return efficient portfolio also has the highest Sharpe ratio among the risk-objective-consistent portfolios that satisfy the investor's return objective. Another efficient portfolio to consider is that represented by the fourth corner portfolio with an expected return of 7.94 percent and a standard deviation (8.99 percent) just within the allowable range. That portfolio includes exposure to an additional asset class, international bonds, as do the other efficient portfolios with expected returns above 7.30 percent up to and including 7.94 percent. Indeed, efficient portfolios with expected returns ranging from 7.00 percent to

7.94 percent are all consistent with the stated risk and return objectives, and we could compute the weights of any of those portfolios using the information from Exhibit 11. In some cases, we may have additional information from the IPS that permits us to narrow the choices or select the most appropriate choice.

The results of a mean–variance optimizer may prompt an investor to revise his saving and spending plans, or reconsider his return and risk objectives in light of his circumstances. For example, suppose the investor's return objective was 8.25 percent in the case just examined, with all else unchanged. No efficient portfolio exists that is consistent with the investor's stated 8.25 percent return objective, his risk objective of a standard deviation of 9 percent or less, and his capital market expectations, suggesting the need for a review as indicated. But first, because of the sensitivity of MVO to errors in the inputs, the investor should test the robustness of the efficient frontier asset-class allocations to small changes in the point estimates for expected returns, standard deviations, and expected correlations.

Cash Equivalents and Capital Market Theory Before continuing to our next strategic asset allocation example, we need to address the role of cash equivalents in asset allocation. Practice varies concerning cash equivalents (e.g., Treasury bills) as an asset class to be included in MVO. From a multiperiod perspective, T-bills exhibit a time series of returns with variability, as do equities, and can be included as a risky asset class with positive standard deviation and nonzero correlations with other asset classes. Optimizers linked to historical return databases always include a series such as T-bills as a risky asset class. From a single-period perspective, buying and holding a T-bill to maturity provides a certain return in nominal terms—a return, therefore, that has zero standard deviation and zero correlations with other asset classes.[35] Capital market theory associated with concepts such as the capital asset pricing model, capital allocation line, and capital market line originally took a single-period perspective, which is retained in this reading. The multiperiod perspective in MVO, however, has roughly equal standing in practice.[36] From the context, it will be obvious which perspective is being taken. The term "risk-free rate" suggests a single-period perspective; a reported positive standard deviation for cash equivalents suggests a multiperiod perspective.

When we assume a nominally risk-free asset and take a single-period perspective, mean–variance theory points to choosing the asset allocation represented by the perceived tangency portfolio *if the investor can borrow or lend at the risk-free rate*. (Borrowing in this context means using margin to buy risky assets, resulting in a negative weight on the risk-free asset.) The tangency portfolio is the perceived highest-Sharpe-ratio efficient portfolio. The investor would then use margin to leverage the position in the tangency portfolio to achieve a higher expected return than the tangency portfolio, or split money between the tangency portfolio and the risk-free asset to achieve a lower risk position than the tangency portfolio. The investor's portfolio would fall on the **capital allocation line**, which describes the combinations of expected return and standard deviation of return available to an investor from combining his or her optimal portfolio of risky assets with the risk-free asset. Many investors, however, face restrictions against buying risky assets on margin. Even without a formal constraint against using margin, a negative position in cash equivalents may be inconsistent with an investor's liquidity needs. Leveraging the tangency portfolio may be practically irrelevant for many investors.

---

[35] An inflation-indexed discount instrument, if available, would serve a similar role in an analysis performed in real terms.
[36] Note that treating cash equivalents as risky does not overcome the limitations of MVO as a static approach.

Optimization

We can illustrate the issue using our example of an investor with a 7 percent return objective. The perceived highest-Sharpe-ratio efficient portfolio in our example, the tangency portfolio, is close to Corner Portfolio 6 in Exhibit 11, assuming a 2 percent risk-free rate (see the column on Sharpe ratios in that exhibit). However, Corner Portfolio 6, with an expected return of 6.13, does not satisfy the investor's return objective. By assumption, the investor cannot use margin. Therefore, the investor cannot use the tangency portfolio to meet his or her return objective. Instead, the investor should choose a portfolio to the right of the tangency point on the efficient frontier.

For a different investor, if the tangency portfolio's expected return exceeds the return objective, the investor might combine the tangency portfolio and the 2%-risk-free asset to achieve an optimal portfolio. Thus the investor might first check the tangency portfolio's expected return to see whether it exceeds his or her return objective. If so, combining the tangency portfolio with the risk-free asset may be optimal.

Suppose an investor has a short-term liquidity need that is funded appropriately using cash equivalents. Pragmatically, the investor might set aside an amount equal to the present value of the need, then separately determine an appropriate efficient allocation for the balance of his or her wealth. If the money set aside for the liquidity need earns 1.5 percent annually, for example, we use a 1.5 percent discount rate to determine present value.

To illustrate, suppose an investor sets aside 7.5 percent of assets in cash equivalents to meet a one-year-ahead liquidity need. The investor can then perform an MVO over risky assets as in Exhibit 11 and apply that allocation to the 92.5 percent balance of his or her total funds. For example, if the investor's total wealth is $2,000,000 and the investor needs $150,000 (7.5 percent of $2,000,000) to meet the future liquidity need (i.e., $150,000 is the present value of that need), a 65 percent allocation to equities and 35 percent allocation to bonds will require 0.65($2,000,000 − $150,000) = $1,202,500 and 0.35($2,000,000 − $150,000) = $647,500, respectively. We "take off the table" the cash equivalents targeted to meet the liquidity requirement in this example. Hence, the return objective (which generally relates to longer-term horizons) must be determined against the remaining asset base of $2,000,000 − $150,000 = $1,850,000. (The investor may still allocate some part of that remaining asset base to cash equivalents.)

In Example 9, a different investor formulates different expectations about the asset classes in Exhibit 9. Note that a change in inputs produces eight corner portfolios rather than seven.

Example 9

A Strategic Asset Allocation for Ian Thomas

Ian Thomas is a 53-year-old comptroller for a City of London broker. In excellent health and planning to retire in 12 years, Thomas expects pension income from two sources to supply approximately 60 percent of his annual retirement income needs.

The trustees of one of Thomas's favorite charities have approached him for a £150,000 gift that would permit construction to begin on a new building. With his two children now established independently; a home free and clear of debt; an annual salary of £170,000; and a net worth of £2,750,000 from savings, investment, and inheritance, Thomas considers himself financially secure. Because of his prospect for a substantial pension, he feels well positioned to make a £150,000 gift to the charity. He has notified the trustees that he will make the £150,000 gift in six months (in a new tax year). Thomas intends to fund the gift entirely from his savings; the charity has requested that the gift be in cash or cash equivalents rather than other securities. His £2,750,000 net worth amount includes the £240,000 value of his home. To the extent he undertakes additional real estate investment, he will include the £240,000 as part of the total real estate allocation; he holds the balance of his net worth in securities.

Advised by a financial planner, Thomas has created an IPS. Thomas generally feels comfortable taking thought-out risks and is optimistic about his own and the economy's future. Thomas has shown a definite bias towards equities in his prior investing. Working with his advisor, he has agreed on a set of capital market expectations.[37] The current risk-free rate is 2 percent. Thomas has access to a six-month bank deposit that earns 2 percent.

The following summarizes some key information about Thomas:

Objectives

- *Return objective.* The return objective is to earn an average 8.5 percent annual return.[38]
- *Risk objectives.* Given his substantial assets and the length of the first stage of his time horizon, Thomas has above-average willingness and ability to take risk, quantified as a capacity to accept a standard deviation of return of 18 percent or less.

Constraints

- *Liquidity requirements.* Thomas has minimal liquidity requirements outside the planned £150,000 gift.
- *Time horizon.* His investment horizon is multistage, with the first stage being the 12 years remaining to retirement and the second being his retirement years.
- *Tax considerations.* Thomas holds £2,510,000 of securities in taxable accounts.[39]

Thomas states that he does not want to borrow (use margin) to purchase risky assets. No substantive relevant legal and regulatory factors or unique circumstances affect his decisions.

The IPS specifies that Mr. Thomas's assets "... shall be diversified to minimize the risk of large losses within any one asset class, investment type, geographic location, or maturity date, which could seriously impair Mr. Thomas's ability to meet his long-term investment objectives." It further states that investment results will be evaluated based on absolute risk-adjusted performance and performance relative to benchmarks given elsewhere in the IPS. Exhibit 14 lists Thomas's capital market expectations (in nominal terms), and Exhibit 15 gives results from the sign-constrained MVO based on the inputs in Exhibit 14.

Exhibit 14 Thomas's Capital Market Expectations

Asset Class	Expected Return	Standard Deviation	1	2	3	4	5	6
1. U.K. equities	11.00%	20.0%	1.00					
2. Ex-U.K. equities	9.00	18.0	0.76	1.00				
3. Intermediate bonds	4.00	7.0	0.35	0.04	1.00			
4. Long-term bonds	4.75	8.0	0.50	0.30	0.87	1.00		
5. International bonds	5.00	9.5	0.24	0.36	0.62	0.52	1.00	
6. Real estate	7.00	14.0	0.35	0.25	0.11	0.07	0.12	1.00

---

[37] In relation to the institutional investor's forecasts in Exhibit 9, Thomas's forecasts for the standard deviations of equities, including real estate, are higher; real estate's correlations with intermediate and long-term bonds are also higher, reducing real estate's diversification potential.

[38] We do not present the cash flow considerations that underlie Thomas's return objective, but the return objective is determined on his wealth excluding the cash equivalents set aside to cover his liquidity requirement.

[39] £2,750,000 (net worth) – £240,000 (value of home) = £2,510,000 (securities in taxable accounts).

Optimization

Exhibit 15: Corner Portfolios Based on Thomas's Capital Market Expectations

Corner Portfolio Number	Expected Return	Standard Deviation	Sharpe Ratio	Asset Class (Portfolio Weight)					
				1	2	3	4	5	6
1	11.00%	20.00%	0.45	100.00%	0.00%	0.00%	0.00%	0.00%	0.00%
2	10.09	16.84	0.48	77.35	0.00	0.00	0.00	0.00	22.65
3	9.67	15.57	0.49	63.56	6.25	0.00	0.00	0.00	30.19
4	7.92	11.08	0.53	36.19	4.05	0.00	0.00	30.48	29.28
5	6.47	8.21	0.54	11.41	8.29	0.00	31.31	22.36	26.63
6	5.73	7.04	0.53	0.00	17.60	40.67	11.99	6.77	22.96
7	5.43	6.66	0.52	0.00	16.16	60.78	0.00	3.52	19.54
8	4.83	6.33	0.45	0.00	8.34	77.04	0.00	1.17	13.45

Note: Risk-free rate = 2 percent.

1. Based on mean–variance analysis, perform the following tasks:
   A. Determine the strategic asset allocation that is most appropriate for Thomas.
   B. Justify your answer to Part A.
   C. State the amount of net new investment or disinvestment in real estate.
2. Appraise the effectiveness of ex-U.K. equities in diversifying risk given Thomas's expectations.
3. Identify the corner portfolio most likely to be the tangency portfolio and explain its appropriateness for Thomas in selecting an optimal strategic asset allocation.

To make his risk preferences more precise, Thomas undergoes an interview in which he is asked to express preferences among sets of choices involving risky and certain returns. As a result, Thomas's measured risk aversion, R_A, is ascertained to equal 3.

4. Determine the most appropriate asset allocation for Thomas given his measured risk aversion and his return objective, if Thomas had to choose only one portfolio from the eight corner portfolios given in Exhibit 15. Contrast that asset allocation to the strategic asset allocation chosen as optimal in Part 1A.

Solution to 1A:

The efficient portfolio that satisfies Thomas's return and risk objectives must lie on the portion of the efficient frontier represented between Corner Portfolio 3 (with 9.67 expected return) and Corner Portfolio 4 (with 7.92 percent expected return). Based only on the information given and the IPS, the recommended portfolio is the one that just meets his 8.5 percent return objective. From the corner portfolio theorem, it follows that

$$8.50 = 9.67w + 7.92(1 - w)$$

We find that the weight on Corner Portfolio 3 is $w = 0.331$ and the weight on Corner Portfolio 4 is $(1 - w) = 0.669$. Therefore,

Weight of U.K. equities	0.331(63.56%) + 0.669(36.19%) = 45.25%
Weight of ex-U.K. equities	0.331(6.25%) + 0.669(4.05%) = 4.78%
Weight of intermediate bonds	0.331(0%) + 0.669(0%) = 0%
Weight of long-term bonds	0.331(0%) + 0.669(0%) = 0%
Weight of international bonds	0.331(0%) + 0.669(30.48%) = 20.39%
Weight of real estate	0.331(30.19%) + 0.669(29.28%) = 29.58%

As an arithmetic check, 45.25% + 4.78% + 0% + 0% + 20.39% + 29.58% = 100%.

Solution to 1B:

The recommended portfolio:

- is efficient (i.e., it lies on the efficient frontier);
- is expected to satisfy his return requirement;
- is expected to meet his risk objective;
- has the highest expected Sharpe ratio among the efficient portfolios that meet his return objective; and
- is the most consistent with the IPS statement concerning minimizing losses within any one investment type.

The standard deviation of the recommended asset allocation must be less than that of the third corner portfolio, 15.57, demonstrating that the portfolio meets his risk objective. [More precisely, the standard deviation of the recommendation is slightly less than 0.331(15.57) + 0.669(11.08) = 12.57, the linear approximation.] Thomas is also concerned with absolute risk-adjusted performance. We see from Exhibit 15 that the Sharpe ratio increases as we move from Corner Portfolios 1 through 5, and the recommended portfolio is closer to Corner Portfolio 5 than any other efficient portfolio satisfying Thomas's return objective.

Solution to 1C:

The amount Thomas needs to set aside today is the present value of £150,000 at 2 percent for one-half of one year: (£150,000)/(1.02)$^{0.5}$ = £148,522. The recommended portfolio has a pound allocation to real estate of 29.58% × (£2,750,000 − £148,522) = £769,517. Netting the value of his home, £240,000, the recommended net new investment in real estate is £529,517.

Solution to 2:

Despite the fact that ex-U.K. equities have the second-highest standard deviation of return (18 percent), ex-U.K. equities appear with substantial weight in the efficient portfolio that has the smallest standard deviation of return, the GMV portfolio, as well as in other expected low-risk, efficient portfolios. Thus ex-U.K. equities appear to be an effective risk diversifier.

Solution to 3:

The tangency portfolio is the efficient portfolio with the highest Sharpe ratio. Corner Portfolio 5, with the highest Sharpe ratio (0.54) among the corner portfolios, is most likely to be the tangency portfolio. Because it has an expected return below Thomas's return objective, however, and Thomas does not want to use margin, he can ignore that portfolio in determining his strategic asset allocation.

Solution to 4:

We determine the risk-adjusted expected returns of the corner portfolios using the expression for risk-adjusted expected return of asset mix m, U_m, where $E(R_m)$ is the mix's expected return, R_A is Thomas's measured risk aversion, and σ_m^2 is the mix's variance of return:

$$U_m = E(R_m) - 0.005 R_A \sigma_m^2$$
$$= E(R_m) - 0.005(3)\sigma_m^2$$
$$= E(R_m) - 0.015 \sigma_m^2$$

Optimization

Corner Portfolio 1 $U_1 = 11.00 - (0.015)(20.00)^2 = 5.0$

Corner Portfolio 2 $U_2 = 10.09 - (0.015)(16.84)^2 = 5.8$

Corner Portfolio 3 $U_3 = 9.67 - (0.015)(15.57)^2 = 6.0$

Corner Portfolio 4 $U_4 = 7.92 - (0.015)(11.08)^2 = 6.1$

Corner Portfolio 5 $U_5 = 6.47 - (0.015)(8.21)^2 = 5.5$

Corner Portfolio 6 $U_6 = 5.73 - (0.015)(7.04)^2 = 5.0$

Corner Portfolio 7 $U_7 = 5.43 - (0.015)(6.66)^2 = 4.8$

Corner Portfolio 8 $U_8 = 4.83 - (0.015)(6.33)^2 = 4.2$

The corner portfolio with the highest risk-adjusted expected return is Corner Portfolio 4. It does not meet Thomas's 8.5 percent return objective, however. Corner Portfolio 3, with an expected return of 9.67 percent, has the highest risk-adjusted expected return among the corner portfolios that meet his return objective. *If we limit the choices to the eight corner portfolios*, Corner Portfolio 3 is optimal; the strategic asset allocation it represents has approximate weights of 64 percent in U.K. equities, 6 percent in ex-U.K. equities, and 30 percent in real estate.

Note that the strategic asset allocation chosen as optimal in Part 1A lies between Corner Portfolio 3 and Corner Portfolio 4. To evaluate the risk-adjusted expected return of the strategic asset allocation selected in Part 1A, we could use the linear approximation of 12.57 for its standard deviation mentioned in the solution to Part 1B: $8.50 - (0.015)(12.57)^2 = 6.13$. Because the approximation 12.57 is a slight overestimate, the portfolio's risk-adjusted expected return is somewhat above 6.13. The strategic asset allocation selected in Part 1A has a very slightly higher risk-adjusted expected return than either Corner Portfolio 3 or 4 (which is 6.08 to two decimal places).

In Example 9, Part 1A, the recommended strategic asset allocation was an efficient portfolio that was expected to *just* meet the return objective. With different capital market expectations and risk-free rates, however, that will not always be the case. For example, the expected return of the highest-Sharpe-ratio efficient portfolio (the tangency portfolio) may exceed the return objective, and if so, it may be optimal for the investor to hold the highest-Sharpe-ratio efficient portfolio in combination with the risk-free asset (as suggested in a capital allocation line analysis). On the other hand, as in Example 10, the highest-Sharpe-ratio efficient portfolio's expected return may be below the return objective. Assuming that margin is not allowed, in such cases the highest-Sharpe-ratio portfolio is not optimal for the investor.

Example 10

A Strategic Asset Allocation for CEFA

CIO Sanjiv Singh is considering the recommendation for CEFA's policy portfolio that he will present at the next meeting of the endowment's trustees. CEFA was established to provide funding to museums in their acquisitions programs as well as to make grants to foster education and research into the fine arts. Its portfolio currently has a value of C$80,000,000. Although CEFA's long time horizon implies an above-average ability to take risk, its trustees are conservative. Reflecting their below-average willingness to take risk, the trustees have set a relatively conservative spending rate of 4 percent and have expressed a concern about downside risk. Overall, they have characterized CEFA's risk tolerance as average. The following summarizes some key information about CEFA:

Objectives

The overall investment objective of the Canadian Endowment for the Fine Arts is to maintain the endowment's real purchasing power after distributions.

Return Objectives:

1. CEFA's assets shall be invested to maximize returns for the level of risk taken.
2. CEFA's assets shall be invested with the objective of earning an average 6.5 percent annual return, reflecting a spending rate of 4 percent, an expected inflation rate of 2 percent, and a 40-basis-point cost of earning investment returns.[40]

Risk Objectives:

1. CEFA's portfolio should be structured to maintain diversification levels that are consistent with prudent investment practices.
2. CEFA has a capacity to accept a standard deviation of return of 12 percent or less.
3. CEFA's portfolio should be constructed with consideration of minimizing the probability that the annual portfolio return will fall below CEFA's spending rate.

CEFA has minimal liquidity needs. The IPS further specifies the following permissible asset classes:

- Canadian equities;
- ex-Canada equities;
- Canadian bonds (traditional);
- government of Canada real return bonds (GCRRB);
- international bonds;
- money market instruments rated at least Prime-1 by Moody's Investors Service, A-1 + by Standard & Poor's, or R-1 (middle) by Dominion Bond Rating Service.

Exhibit 16 gives Singh's capital market forecasts, which the trustees have approved. Cognizant of the sensitivity of mean–variance analysis to expected return estimates, Singh will present to the trustees his approach in developing the Canadian equity expected return estimate of 9.5 percent. Singh employed a variation of the Gordon growth model expression as given in Grinold and Kroner (2002):

Exhibit 16 CEFA's Capital Market Expectations

Asset Class	Expected Return (%)	Standard Deviation (%)	1	2	3	4	5
1. Canadian equities	9.50	18	1.00				
2. Ex-Canada equities	7.40	15	0.65	1.00			
3. Canadian bonds	3.80	7	0.25	0.40	1.00		
4. GCRRB	2.70	6	−0.15	0.30	0.75	1.00	
5. International bonds	4.00	9	0.20	0.45	0.60	0.50	1.00

---

40 The calculation is (1.04)(1.02)(1.004) − 1 = 0.065 or 6.5 percent.

Optimization

$$r \approx \frac{D}{P} - \Delta S + i + g + \Delta PE$$

where r is the expected rate of return on equity, D/P is the expected dividend yield (expected per-share dividend, D, divided by price per share, P), ΔS is the expected percent change in number of shares outstanding, i is the expected inflation rate, g is the expected real earnings (not earnings per share) growth rate, and ΔPE is the per-period percent change in the P/E multiple. ΔS is negative in the case of net positive share repurchases, so $-\Delta S$ is the "repurchase yield." The term $D/P - \Delta S$ represents the income return, $i + g$ represents the earnings growth return, and ΔPE represents the repricing return.

Singh forecasts a 2.25 percent dividend yield on Canadian equities, based on the S&P/Toronto Stock Exchange Composite Index and a repurchase yield of 1 percent. He forecasts the long-run inflation rate at 2 percent per year. Singh's forecast of real earnings growth is 4 percent, based on a 1-percentage-point premium for corporate growth over his expected Canadian GDP growth rate of 3.0 percent. Singh forecasts a very minor expansion in P/E multiples of 0.25 percent. Thus his expected return prediction is

$$r \approx 2.25\% - (-1.0\%) + 2.0\% + 4.0\% + 0.25\% = 9.5\%$$

Using a similar process Singh developed forecasts for international (ex-Canada) equities. A consultant developed other forecasts for Singh using economic forecasts and approaches that Singh approved. Singh uses the T-bill yield of 2.3 percent for the risk-free rate.

Exhibit 17 gives results from the sign-constrained MVO based on the inputs in Exhibit 16.

Exhibit 17 Corner Portfolios Based on CEFA's Capital Market Expectations

Corner Portfolio Number	Expected Return	Standard Deviation	Sharpe Ratio	1	2	3	4	5
1	9.50%	18.00%	0.400	100.00%	0.00%	0.00%	0.00%	0.00%
2	8.90	15.98	0.413	71.52	28.48	0.00	0.00	0.00
3	8.61	15.20	0.415	67.63	26.30	0.00	0.00	6.07
4	7.24	11.65	0.424	49.46	16.55	23.05	0.00	10.93
5	5.61	7.89	0.419	39.85	1.01	0.00	47.75	11.38
6	5.49	7.65	0.417	38.86	0.00	0.00	50.00	11.14
7	3.61	5.39	0.244	12.94	0.00	0.00	84.60	2.45

Asset Class (Portfolio Weight) shown in columns 1–5.

Note: Risk-free rate = 2.3 percent.

In consultation with the trustees, Singh has adopted Roy's safety-first criterion for implementing the shortfall risk objective. The safety-first criterion aims to minimize the probability that the portfolio return falls below a threshold level R_L; the safety-first optimal portfolio maximizes the ratio $[E(R_p) - R_L]/\sigma_p$. The higher this ratio for a portfolio, the smaller the probability that the portfolio's return will fall below the threshold level at a given time horizon.

1. Determine and justify the overall most appropriate strategic asset allocation for CEFA using mean–variance analysis.

   A trustee has suggested that CEFA adopt the sole objective of minimizing the level of standard deviation of return subject to meeting its return objective.

2. Determine the most appropriate strategic asset allocation if CEFA adopts the trustee's suggested objective.

Solution to 1:

Note that we need not consider the portion of the efficient frontier beginning at and extending below Corner Portfolio 5, because the portfolios on it do not satisfy CEFA's 6.5 percent return objective.

Corner Portfolio 4 meets CEFA's return objective and risk objectives. It also appears to be the approximate tangency portfolio, with a higher expected Sharpe ratio than neighboring corner portfolios. This asset allocation appears to be optimal for CEFA; it involves an allocation of approximately 49 percent to Canadian equities, 17 percent to ex-Canadian equities, 23 percent to Canadian bonds, and 11 percent to international bonds. The IPS states a concern for shortfall risk below the spending rate. To evaluate the downside risk of Corner Portfolio 4 according to Roy's safety-first criterion, we compute (7.24% − 4%) / 11.65% = 0.28. Corner Portfolio 4's standard deviation is near the maximum acceptable to CEFA, so the trustees would not consider higher-standard-deviation portfolios. They might consider lower-standard-deviation portfolios that meet CEFA's return objective, however.

Thus another portfolio that we might consider is the portfolio that minimizes standard deviation subject to meeting the return objective. To minimize risk *without lowering the Sharpe ratio*, we can combine the tangency portfolio with T-bills to choose a portfolio on CEFA's capital allocation line. (We would lower the Sharpe ratio if we combined Corner Portfolio 4 with Corner Portfolio 5.)

The tangency portfolio (Corner Portfolio 4) has an expected return of 7.24 percent, and the risk-free asset (T-bills) has a nominally certain return of 2.3 percent. Thus to establish the allocation to Corner Portfolio 4 and T-bills, we solve

$$6.50 = 7.24w + 2.3(1 - w)$$

We find that the weight on Corner Portfolio 4 is $w = 0.85$ and the weight on T-bills is $(1 - w) = 0.15$. Therefore, the optimal allocation that minimizes risk is

Weight of Canadian equities	0.85(49.46%) =	42.04%
Weight of ex-Canada equities	0.85(16.55%) =	14.07%
Weight of Canadian bonds	0.85(23.05%) =	19.59%
Weight of international bonds	0.85(10.93%) =	9.29%
Weight of T-bills		15.0%

As an arithmetic check, 42.04% + 14.07% + 19.59% + 9.29% + 15.0% = 100%, ignoring rounding. This portfolio has an expected return of 6.5 percent and a standard deviation of return of 9.9 percent (0.85 × the tangency's portfolio's standard deviation = 0.85 × 11.65% = 9.90%). As mentioned, it has the same Sharpe ratio as Corner Portfolio 4. The deciding factor is shortfall risk. To evaluate this asset allocation's shortfall risk, we compute (6.5 − 4) / 9.9 = 0.25. Because 0.25 is below the value of 0.28 for Corner Portfolio 4, Corner Portfolio 4 (the tangency portfolio) gives the recommended asset allocation for CEFA.

Solution to 2:

If the trustee's suggestion were accepted, the portfolio 15 percent invested in T-bills and 85 percent invested in Corner Portfolio 4 (discussed in Part 1) would be optimal for CEFA; that asset allocation meets CEFA's return objective with minimum standard deviation of return.

6.1.4 *Extensions to the Mean–Variance Approach*

The mean–variance approach has proven readily adaptable to incorporate a number of concerns suggested by practice. Exhibit 18 reviews some of these variations on the model under three groupings.

Exhibit 18   Selected Extensions to the Mean–Variance Approach

Concern	Adaptation	Source
A. Downside risk	1. Mean–semivariance	Markowitz (1959)
	2. MVO with shortfall constraint	Leibowitz and Henriksson (1989)

Optimization

Exhibit 18 Continued

Concern	Adaptation	Source
	3. MV surplus optimization	Leibowitz and Henriksson (1988)
		Sharpe and Tint (1990)
		Elton and Gruber (1992)
	4. Safety-first criterion	Roy (1952)
B. Tracking risk relative to benchmark	5. MVO with constraints on asset weights relative to benchmark	Ad hoc practice
	6. Mean–tracking error (MTE) optimization[a]	Roll (1992)
	7. Mean–variance–tracking error (MVTE) optimization[b]	Chow (1995)
C. Changing correlations in times of stress	9. MVO with adjusted correlation matrix	Chow et al. (1999)

[a]This approach optimizes mean return against tracking error (tracking risk) rather than variance.
[b]This approach adds a tracking risk penalty to the MV objective function.

6.2 The Resampled Efficient Frontier

Experience with MVO has often shown that the composition of efficient portfolios is very sensitive to small changes in inputs. Because forecasting returns, volatilities, and correlations is so difficult and subject to substantial estimation error, what confidence can we have that MVO will suggest the best asset allocations for investors?

Generally, we have little confidence in the results of a single MVO. In practice, professional investors often rerun an optimization many times using a range of inputs around their point estimates to gauge the results' sensitivity to variation in the inputs. The focus, as mentioned earlier, should be on mean return inputs. Although sensitivity analysis is certainly useful, it is ad hoc. Some researchers have sought to address the problem of MVO's input sensitivity by taking a statistical view of efficiency. Jobson and Korkie (1981) first suggested a statistical perspective, and Michaud (1989, 1998) and Jorion (1992) developed it further.

The Michaud approach to asset allocation is based on a simulation exercise using MVO and a data set of historical returns. Using the sample values of asset classes' means, variances, and covariances as the assumed true population parameters, the simulation generates sets of simulated returns and, for each such set (simulation trial), MVO produces the portfolio weights of a specified number of mean–variance efficient portfolios (which may be called *simulated efficient portfolios*). Information in the simulated efficient portfolios resulting from the simulation trials is integrated into one frontier called the resampled efficient frontier.[41] Generally, a simulated efficient portfolio with a mean return, for example, of 7.8 percent would not match up exactly by mean return with a simulated efficient portfolio from another simulation trial. Numbering simulated efficient portfolios by return rank from lowest to highest, one approach to this problem of integration is to associate simulated efficient portfolios of equivalent return rank. Michaud defines a **resampled efficient portfolio** for a given return rank as the portfolio defined by the average weights on each asset class

---

41 The term "resampled" refers to the use of simulation.

for simulated efficient portfolios with that return rank. For example, the fifth-ranked resampled efficient portfolio is defined by the average weight on each of the asset classes for the fifth-ranked simulated efficient portfolios in the individual simulation trials. Averaging weights in this fashion preserves the property that portfolio weights sum to 1, but has been challenged on other grounds.[42] The set of resampled efficient portfolios represents the **resampled efficient frontier**.[43]

The portfolios resulting from the resampled efficient frontier approach tend to be more diversified and more stable through time than those on a conventional mean–variance efficient frontier developed from a single optimization. If at least one draw from an asset class's assumed distribution of returns is sufficiently favorable to the asset class so that it appears in a simulated efficient portfolio, the asset class will be represented in the resampled efficient frontier. This observation explains the fact that most or all asset classes are typically represented in the resampled efficient frontier. On the other hand, the resampled efficient frontier approach has been questioned on grounds such as the lack of a theoretical underpinning for the method and the relevance of historical return frequency data to current asset market values and equilibrium.[44]

6.3 The Black–Litterman Approach

Fischer Black and Robert Litterman developed another quantitative approach to dealing with the problem of estimation error, which we recall is most serious when it concerns expected returns. Two versions of the Black–Litterman approach exist:

- *Unconstrained Black–Litterman* (UBL) *model*. Taking the weights of asset classes in a global benchmark such as MSCI World as a neutral starting point, the asset weights are adjusted to reflect the investor's views on the expected returns of asset classes according to a Bayesian procedure that considers the strength of the investor's beliefs. We call this unconstrained Black–Litterman model, or UBL model, because the procedure does not allow non-negativity constraints on the asset-class weights.

- *Black–Litterman* (BL) *model*. This approach reverse engineers the expected returns implicit in a diversified market portfolio (a process known as **reverse optimization**) and combines them with the investor's own views on expected returns in a systematic way that takes into account the investor's confidence in his or her views.[45] These view-adjusted expected return forecasts are then used in a MVO with a constraint against short sales and possibly other constraints.

The UBL model is a direct method for selecting an asset allocation. It usually results in small or moderate deviations from the asset-class weights in the benchmark in intuitive ways reflecting the investor's different-from-benchmark expectations. Because the UBL model is anchored to a well-diversified global portfolio, it ensures that the strategic asset allocation recommendation is well diversified. In practice, the UBL model is an improvement on simple MVO because the absence of constraints against short sales in the UBL model usually does not result in unintuitive portfolios (e.g., portfolios with large short positions in asset classes), a common result in unconstrained MVO.

Nevertheless, investors often formally want to recognize such constraints in optimization. As a result, the second version of the Black–Litterman approach, the

---

[42] See Scherer (2002).
[43] Resampled efficiency is a U.S. patent–protected procedure with worldwide patents pending. New Frontier Advisors, LLC, is the exclusive worldwide licensee.
[44] See Scherer (2002) for a review and critique of the field.
[45] The notion of using reverse optimization to infer expected returns was first described in Sharpe (1974). See Sharpe (1985), pp. 59–60 for further details.

Optimization

BL model, is probably more important in practice, and will be the chief focus of this section. Although the BL model could be considered a tool for developing capital market expectations for the range of asset classes in a global index such as MSCI World, employed with MVO with short sale constraints it also may be viewed as an asset allocation process with two desirable qualities:

- The resulting asset allocation is well diversified.
- The resulting asset allocation incorporates the investor's views on asset-class returns, if any, as well as the strength of those views.

In the language of the model, a view is an investor forecast on an asset class's return, whether stated in absolute or relative terms. (For instance, "Canadian equities will earn 8 percent per year" is an absolute view, and "Canadian equities will outperform U.S. equities by 1 percent per year" is a relative view.) With each view, the investor also provides the information related to the confidence he has in the view.

A practical goal of the BL model is to create stable, mean–variance-efficient portfolios which overcome the problem of expected return sensitivity. The set of expected asset-class returns used in the BL model blends equilibrium returns and the investor's views, if he or she has any. The equilibrium returns are the set of returns that makes the efficient frontier pass through the market weight portfolio. They can be interpreted as the long-run returns provided by the capital markets. The equilibrium returns represent the information that is built into capital market prices and thus reflects the "average" investor's expectations. A major advantage of this approach is that its starting point is a diversified portfolio with market capitalization portfolio weights, which is optimal for an uninformed investor using the mean–variance approach. Exhibit 19 shows the steps in the BL model.

Exhibit 19 Steps in the BL Model

Step	Description	Purpose
1	Define equilibrium market weights and covariance matrix for all asset classes	Inputs for calculating equilibrium expected returns
2	Back-solve equilibrium expected returns	Form the neutral starting point for formulating expected returns
3	Express views and confidence for each view	Reflect the investor's expectations for various asset classes; the confidence level assigned to each view determines the weight placed on it
4	Calculate the view-adjusted market equilibrium returns	Form the expected return that reflects both market equilibrium and views
5	Run mean–variance optimization	Obtain efficient frontier and portfolios

In Section 6.1.2 on the importance of inputs to mean–variance optimization, we presented a case in which we applied MVO to five equity classes using raw historical statistics as our expectations for the future. The resulting efficient portfolios were concentrated in two assets, U.K. equity and Americas equity. In the balance of this section, we show that the BL model results in better diversified portfolios using the same data as a starting point.[46]

The first step in the BL model is to calculate the equilibrium returns, because the model uses those returns as a neutral starting point. Because we cannot observe

---

46 We do not show the mathematics of the Black–Litterman model. See Idzorek (2002) for an introduction.

equilibrium returns, we must estimate them based on the capital market weights of asset classes and the asset-class covariance matrix. The estimation process can be thought of as a "back-solving" of the mean–variance optimization. In the traditional MVO, the investor uses expected returns and the covariance matrix to derive the optimal portfolio allocations. In the BL model, the investor assumes the market-capitalization weights are optimal (given no special insights) and then uses those weights and the covariance matrix to solve for the expected returns. By the nature of the procedure, these are the expected returns that would make the portfolio represented by the capital market weights mean–variance efficient.

To pick up the example using five equity markets, the first task is to calculate the assets' capitalization weights. Exhibit 20 presents the equity market weights of five major markets across the world reported by Dow Jones Global Index at the end of 2003.

Exhibit 20 DJGI Market Weights, December 2003

	DJGI Americas	DJGI Asia Pacific Ex-Japan	DJGI Europe/ Africa Ex-U.K. and South Africa	DJGI Japan	DJGI U.K.
Dollar weight	$12,362,002	$1,269,324	$3,703,025	$2,238,885	$2,161,903
Percentage weight	56.9%	5.8%	17.0%	10.3%	9.9%

Example 11 shows the selection of an asset allocation that is consistent with the Black–Litterman approach.

> **Example 11**
>
> ### An Asset Allocation for an Investor with No Views
>
> John Merz is not a professional investor and is reticent in expressing any opinion about future asset returns. Merz has average risk tolerance.
>
> 1. If Merz were constrained to invest only in the five asset classes given in Exhibit 20, what would be his optimal asset allocation?
> 2. How would your answer to Part 1 change if Merz had below-average risk tolerance?
>
> ### Solution to 1:
>
> According to the Black–Litterman approach, Merz should invest in the five asset classes in the proportional market-value weights given in Exhibit 20, approximately:
>
> - 57 percent DJGI Americas;
> - 6 percent DJGI Asia Pacific ex-Japan;
> - 17 percent DGJI Europe/Africa ex-U.K. and South Africa;
> - 10 percent DJGI Japan; and
> - 10 percent DJGI U.K.
>
> ### Solution to 2:
>
> Following the Black–Litterman approach, Merz would still hold the five asset classes in market-value weights because he holds no views on the asset classes. He would combine that portfolio with the risk-free asset to lower the overall risk, however.

Optimization

We use the capitalization weights combined with the covariance matrix (computable with data given for correlations and standard deviations in Exhibit 12 in Section 6.1.2). We combine the covariance matrix with the capitalization weights in Exhibit 20 to find equilibrium expected returns, shown in Exhibit 21.[47]

Exhibit 21: Historical Average and Market Equilibrium Returns, 1992–2003

	Historical Average Return (H)	Standard Deviation	Equilibrium Return (E)	E – H
DJGI Americas TR	11.87%	18.83%	9.49%	−2.38%
DJGI Asia Pacific ex-Japan TR	11.21	37.03	12.66	1.45
DJGI Europe/Africa ex-U.K. and S. Africa TR	11.04	21.58	9.58	−1.46
DJGI Japan TR USD	3.19	33.66	9.91	6.72
DJGI U.K. TR USD	9.58	17.41	8.39	−1.19

Exhibit 22 shows the efficient frontier with the equilibrium returns based on the back-solved equilibrium returns. Notice that the efficient frontier passes through the portfolio with market-value weights. Exhibit 23 shows that all five assets enter in efficient portfolios at some level of standard deviation of return, in contrast to the MVO using historical mean returns shown in Exhibit 13. The efficient allocations along the frontier are also much more diversified compared with those resulting from the MVO using historical mean returns. This observation is key, because the investor will use these equilibrium returns as a starting point for mean return estimates.

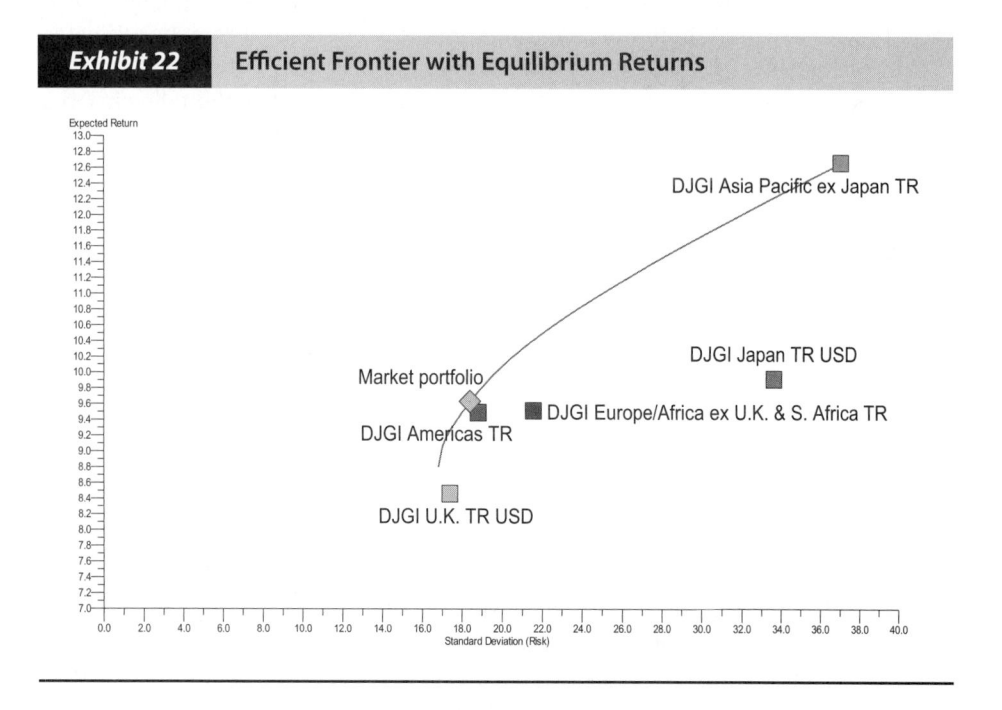

Exhibit 22: Efficient Frontier with Equilibrium Returns

---

[47] The equilibrium return vector (Π) can be calculated using the formula $\Pi = \delta \Sigma w$, where δ is the risk-aversion level of the market portfolio, Σ is the covariance matrix, and w is the vector of market weights.

Exhibit 23 Efficient Portfolio Weights with Equilibrium Returns

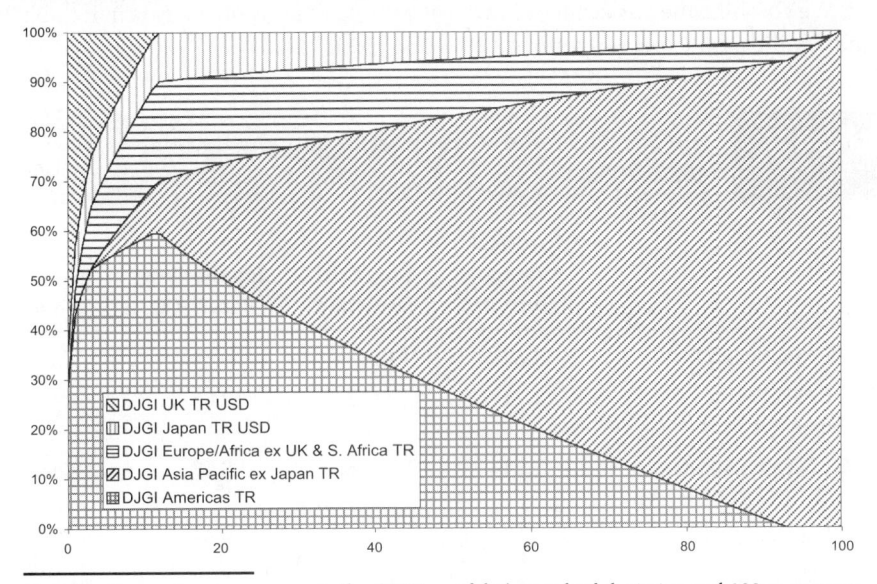

Note: On the *x*-axis, zero represents the GMV portfolio's standard deviation and 100 represents the highest-mean-return asset class's standard deviation. The *y*-axis shows asset-class weights. The in-figure legend is a key to regions, starting from the topmost at the zero-SD point.

Incorporating equilibrium returns has two major advantages. First, combining the investor's views with equilibrium returns helps dampen the effect of any extreme views the investor holds that could otherwise dominate the optimization. The result is generally better-diversified portfolios than those produced from a MVO based only on the investor's views, regardless of the source of those views. Second, anchoring the estimates to equilibrium returns ensures greater consistency across the estimates.

Having established the equilibrium returns, the next step is to express market views and confidence for those views. Suppose the investor has the following two relative views:

- U.K. equity return will be the same as the return on "European equity" (shorthand for DJGI Europe/Africa ex-U.K. and South Africa). Exhibit 21 shows that this view contrasts with an underperformance of 1.46 percent (9.58 – 11.04) for U.K. equities during the 1992–2003 period.

- Asian equity will outperform Japanese equity by 2 percent. From Exhibit 21 we see that this view contrasts with an outperformance of 8.02 percent (11.21 – 3.19) during the 1992–2003 period.

We express the confidence levels for these views as variances. The smaller the variance, the greater the precision of one's view, and the greater one's confidence. We assume the variance for both views is 0.001, which would represent a high level of confidence.

Exhibit 24 presents historical, equilibrium, and Black–Litterman view-adjusted returns. The equilibrium returns are based on current market prices and so reflect investors' expectations about the future. Looking backward, we see that Asian equities outperformed Japan equities by a huge 8.02 percent. Looking forward, the market weights imply a much smaller difference, 2.75 percent (12.66 – 9.91).

Optimization

Exhibit 24: Expected Asset-Class Returns: Black–Litterman and Raw Historical

	Historical Average Return, 1992–2003 (H)	Equilibrium Return (E)	Black–Litterman: Equilibrium with Views (V)	V – H	V – E
DJGI Americas TR	11.87%	9.49%	9.54%	−2.33%	0.05%
DJGI Asia Pacific ex-Japan TR	11.21	12.66	11.99	0.78	−0.66
DJGI Europe/Africa ex-U.K. and S. Africa TR	11.04	9.58	8.81	−2.23	−0.77
DJGI Japan TR USD	3.19	9.91	10.98	7.79	1.07
DJGI U.K. TR USD	9.58	8.39	8.75	−0.83	0.36

The investor's two precise views are intuitively reflected in the Black–Litterman view-adjusted returns. Europe is expected to outperform U.K. equity by 1.19 percent (9.58 − 8.39) according to equilibrium returns. After imposing the view that U.K.'s equity return will equal the European equity return, the expected return difference is only 0.06 percent (8.81 − 8.75). Similarly, after imposing the second view, Asian equity now is expected to outperform Japanese equity by only 1.01 percent, in contrast to the 2.75 percent equilibrium difference. Although neither of the two views concerns DJGI Americas, the Black–Litterman value of DJGI Americas at 9.54 percent is different from the equilibrium return at 9.49 percent. Ripple effects through all return estimates are typical of the Black–Litterman process.

The Black–Litterman view-adjusted returns yield the efficient frontier shown in Exhibit 25. The market portfolio lies close to but no longer exactly on the efficient frontier.

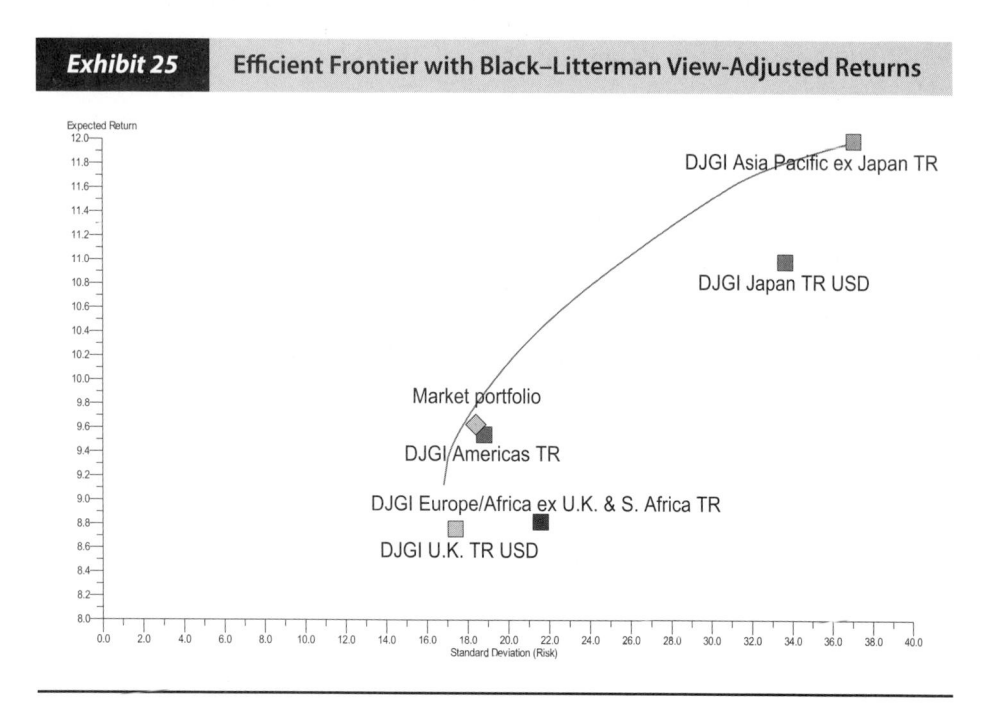

Exhibit 25: Efficient Frontier with Black–Litterman View-Adjusted Returns

Exhibit 26 shows the portfolio weights of efficient portfolios moving upward on the efficient frontier from the GMV portfolio. The view on Japan relative to Asia was more favorable than equilibrium (Exhibit 23) and thus much higher weights for Japan (and smaller weights for Asia) appear in Exhibit 26 than in Exhibit 23. The favorable view on the United Kingdom relative to Europe has caused Europe to drop out of the efficient frontier. Thus differences in efficient portfolio weights relative to equilibrium reflect the investor's views in the intuitively expected directions.

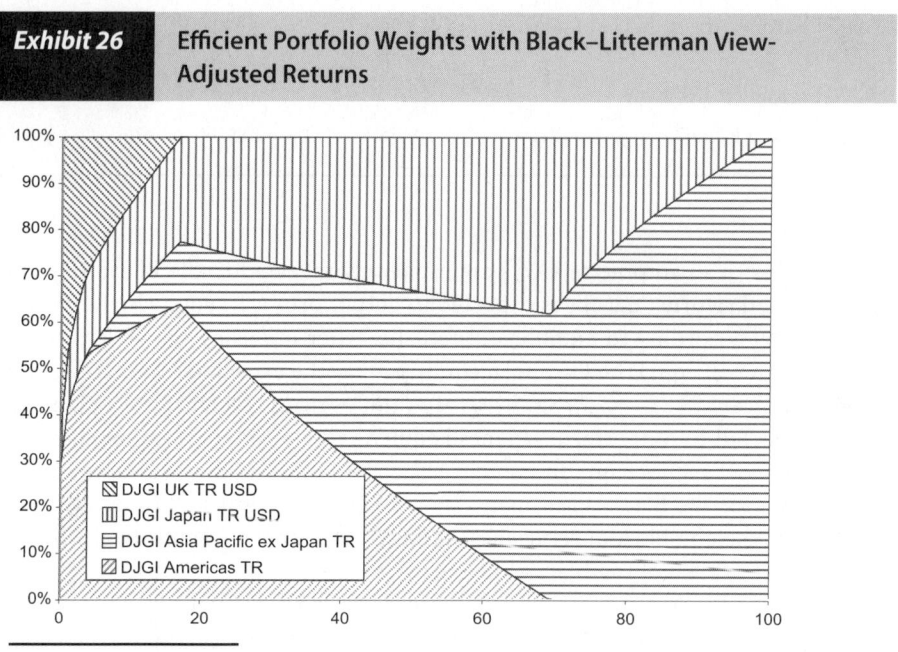

Exhibit 26 Efficient Portfolio Weights with Black–Litterman View-Adjusted Returns

Note: On the *x*-axis, zero represents the GMV portfolio's standard deviation and 100 represents the highest-mean-return asset class's standard deviation. The *y*-axis shows asset-class weights. The in-figure legend is a key to regions, starting from the topmost at the zero-SD point.

Comparing Exhibit 26 with Exhibit 13 (repeated below), we see that the efficient frontier using Black–Litterman view-adjusted returns represents much better-diversified portfolios than does the efficient frontier that results from using raw historical mean returns.

In our example, we used an unadjusted covariance matrix of historical returns for simplicity. This approach does not represent best practice, because historical covariances reflect sampling error as well as events unique to the historical time period used. Litterman and Winkelmann (1998) outlined the method they prefer for estimating the covariance matrix of returns, as well as several alternative methods of estimation. Qian and Gorman (2001) have extended the BL model, enabling investors to express views on volatilities and correlations in order to derive a conditional estimate of the covariance matrix of returns. They asserted that the conditional covariance matrix stabilizes the results of MVO.

Optimization

Exhibit 13	Efficient Portfolio Weights Using Raw Historical Mean Returns (Repeated)

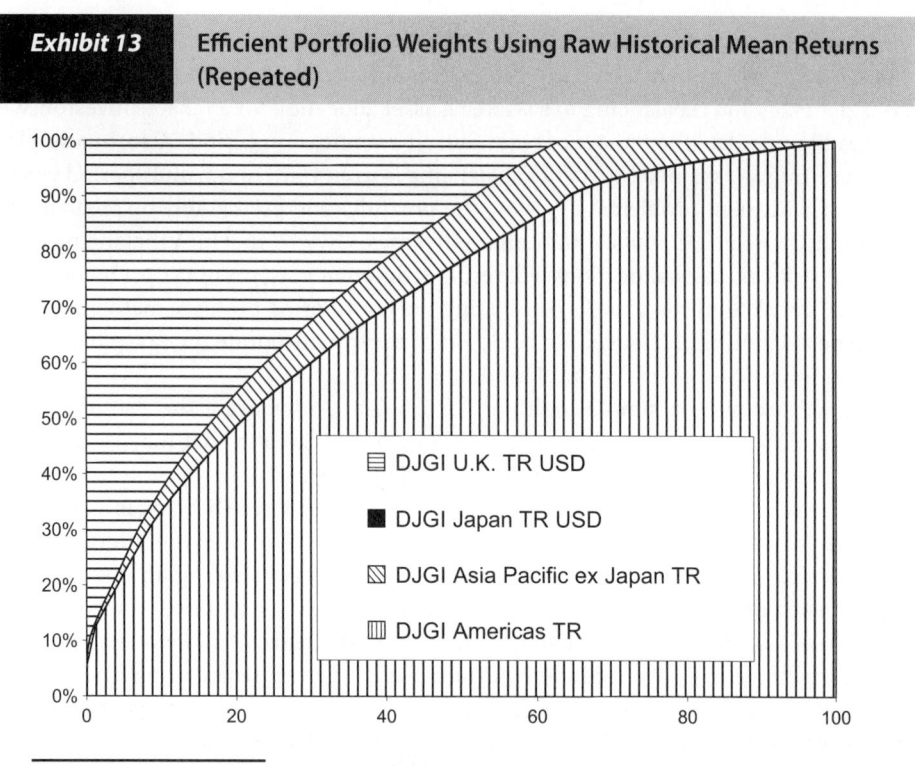

Note: On the *x*-axis, zero represents the GMV portfolio's standard deviation and 100 represents the highest-mean-return asset class's standard deviation. Asia Pacific ex-Japan appears only near zero on the *x*-axis. The *y*-axis shows asset-class weights. The in-figure legend is a key to regions, starting from the topmost at the zero-SD point; Asia Pacific ex-Japan appears only near 0 level on the *x*-axis.

Based on practical experience with the model, Bevan and Winkelmann (1998) and He and Litterman (1999) reported that the Black–Litterman model helps overcome the problem of unintuitive, highly concentrated, input-sensitive portfolios that has been associated with MVO. According to Lee (2000), the BL model largely mitigates the problem of estimation error-maximization by spreading any such errors throughout the entire set of expected returns. Thus this approach represents a significant alternative among the quantitative tools an investment advisor may use in developing a strategic asset allocation.

6.4 Monte Carlo Simulation

Monte Carlo simulation, a computer-based technique, has become an essential tool in many areas of investments. In its application to strategic asset allocation, Monte Carlo simulation involves the calculation and statistical description of the outcomes resulting in a particular strategic asset allocation under random scenarios for investment returns, inflation, and other relevant variables. The method provides information about the range of possible investment results from a given asset allocation over the course of the investor's time horizon, as well as the likelihood that each result will occur.

Monte Carlo simulation contrasts to and complements MVO. Standard MVO is an analytical methodology based on calculus. By contrast, Monte Carlo simulation is a statistical tool. Monte Carlo simulation imitates (simulates) an asset allocation's real-world operation in an investments laboratory, where the investment advisor incorporates his best understanding of the set of relevant variables and their statistical properties.

Using Monte Carlo simulation, an investment manager can effectively grapple with a range of practical issues that are difficult or impossible to formulate analytically. Consider taxes and rebalancing to a strategic asset allocation for a taxable investor. We can readily calculate the impact of taxes during a single time period. Also, in a single-period setting as assumed by MVO, rebalancing is irrelevant. In the multiperiod world of most investment problems, however, the portfolio will predictably be rebalanced, triggering the realization of capital gains and losses. Given a specific rebalancing rule, different strategic asset allocations will result in different patterns of tax payments (and different transaction costs too). Formulating the multiperiod problem mathematically would be a daunting challenge. We could more easily incorporate the tax-rebalancing interaction in a Monte Carlo simulation.

We will examine a simple multiperiod problem to illustrate the use of Monte Carlo simulation, evaluating the range of outcomes for wealth that may result from a strategic asset allocation (and not incorporating taxes).

The value of wealth at the terminal point of an investor's time horizon is a criterion for choosing among asset allocations. Future wealth incorporates the interaction of risk and return. The need for Monte Carlo simulation in evaluating an asset allocation depends on whether there are cash flows into or out of the portfolio over time. For a given asset allocation with no cash flows, the sequence of returns is irrelevant; ending wealth will be path independent (unrelated to the sequence or path of returns through time). We could find expected terminal wealth and percentiles of terminal wealth analytically.[48] Investors save to and spend from their portfolios, however, so the more typical case is that terminal wealth is path dependent (the sequence of returns matters) because of the interaction of cash flows with returns earned. With terminal wealth path dependent, an analytical approach is not feasible but Monte Carlo simulation is. Example 12 applies Monte Carlo simulation to evaluate a strategic asset allocation of an investor who regularly withdraws from his portfolio.

Example 12

Monte Carlo Simulation for a Retirement Portfolio with a Proposed Asset Allocation

Edward Renshaw has sought the advice of an investment advisor concerning his retirement portfolio. At the end of 2003, he is 65 years old and holds a portfolio valued at $1,000,000. Renshaw would like to withdraw $50,000 a year to supplement the corporate pension he has begun to receive. Given his health and family history, Renshaw believes he should plan for a retirement lasting 20 years. He is also concerned about passing along to his two children at least the portfolio's current value when he dies. Consulting with his advisor, Renshaw has expressed this desire quantitatively: He wants the median value of his bequest to his children to be worth no less than his portfolio's current value of $1,000,000. The median is the most likely outcome. The asset allocation of his retirement portfolio is currently 50/50 U.S. equities/U.S. intermediate-term government bonds. Renshaw and his advisor have decided on the following set of capital market expectations:

- U.S. equities: expected return 12.4 percent, standard deviation 20.4 percent;
- U.S. intermediate-term government bonds: expected return 5.6 percent, standard deviation 5.7 percent;

---

[48] Making a plausible statistical assumption such as a lognormal distribution for ending wealth.

Optimization

- predicted correlation between U.S. equities and U.S. intermediate-term government bond: 0.042; and
- long-term inflation rate: 3.1 percent.

With the current asset allocation, the expected return on Renshaw's retirement portfolio is 8.9 percent with a standard deviation of 10.6 percent. Exhibit 27 gives the results of the Monte Carlo simulation.[49]

Based on the information given, address the following:

1. Justify the choice of presenting ending wealth in terms of real rather than nominal wealth in Exhibit 27.

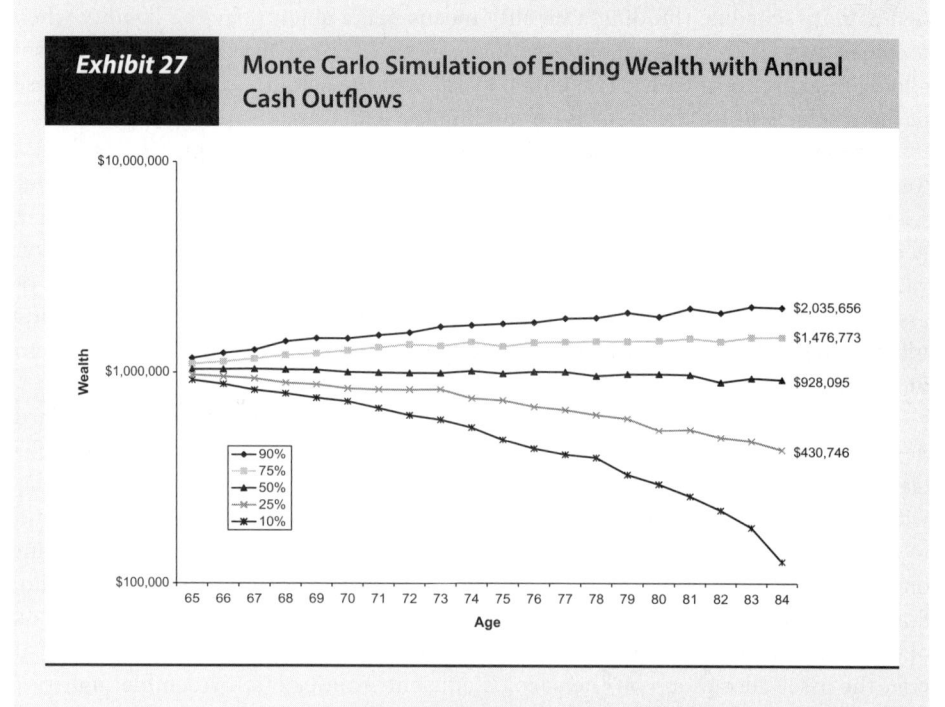

Exhibit 27 Monte Carlo Simulation of Ending Wealth with Annual Cash Outflows

[Chart: Wealth (log scale) vs. Age (65–84), showing percentile lines:
- 90%: $2,035,656
- 75%: $1,476,773
- 50%: $928,095
- 25%: $430,746
- 10%: (lowest line, declining to near $100,000)]

2. Is the current asset allocation expected to satisfy Renshaw's investment objective?

Solution to 1:

Renshaw wants the median value of his bequest to his children to "be worth no less than his portfolio's current value of $1,000,000." We need to state future amounts in terms of today's values (i.e., in real dollars) to assess their worth relative to $1,000,000. Exhibit 27 thus gives the results of the Monte Carlo simulation in real dollar terms.

Solution to 2:

From Exhibit 27 we see that the median terminal value of the retirement portfolio in real dollars is less than the initial value of $1,000,000. Therefore, the most likely bequest is less than the amount Renshaw has specified that he wants. The current asset allocation is not expected to satisfy all his investment objectives.

---

[49] Note that the y-axis in this figure is a logarithmic scale. The quantity $1,000,000 is the same distance from $100,000 as $10,000,000 is from $1,000,000, because $1,000,000 is 10 times $100,000 just as $10,000,000 is 10 times $1,000,000. $100,000 is 10^5 and $1,000,000 is 10^6. In Exhibit 27, a distance halfway between the $100,000 and $1,000,000 hatch marks is $10^{5.5}$ = $316,228.

An investor seeking an advisor's help often has an existing portfolio, and we can use a Monte Carlo simulation to evaluate it relative to the investor's goals. We can run the simulation at the individual security level or the asset-class level. The risk–return characteristics at the asset-class level are more stable than at the individual security level. Consequently, to evaluate a strategic asset allocation over a long time horizon, Monte Carlo simulation at the asset-class level is usually more appropriate.

6.5 Asset/Liability Management

Up to this point we have discussed optimization in the context of an asset-only approach to asset allocation. In many cases, however, an asset portfolio is meant to fund a specified liability schedule (funding a liability means being able to pay the liability when it comes due). Such cases call for an ALM approach. Using an ALM approach, asset allocation must consider the risk characteristics of the liabilities in addition to those of the assets, because the focus is on funding the liabilities.

For many years, mean–variance analysis in its various developments has been a tool of choice for developing asset allocation policy. Earlier we presented the efficient frontier. That efficient frontier is more precisely the "asset-only" efficient frontier, because it fails to consider liabilities. **Net worth** (the difference between the market value of assets and liabilities), also called **surplus**, summarizes the interaction of assets and liabilities in a single variable. The ALM perspective focuses on the **surplus efficient frontier**. Mean–variance surplus optimization extends traditional MVO to incorporate the investor's liabilities.

Exhibit 28 shows a surplus efficient frontier. The x-axis represents the standard deviation and the y-axis gives expected values. The leftmost point on the surplus efficient frontier is the minimum surplus variance (MSV) portfolio, the efficient portfolio with the least risk from an ALM perspective. The MSV portfolio might correspond to a cash flow matching strategy or an immunization strategy. The rightmost point on the surplus efficient frontier represents the highest-expected-surplus portfolio. Similar to traditional MVO, the highest-expected-surplus portfolio typically consists of 100 percent in the highest-expected-return asset class. In fact, at high levels of risk, the asset allocations on the surplus efficient frontier often resemble high-risk asset-only efficient portfolios. Exhibit 28 plots the investor's liability as a point with positive standard deviation but negative expected value (because the investor owes the liability and so effectively has a short position).

The investor must choose a policy portfolio on the surplus efficient frontier. Investors with low risk tolerance may choose to bear minimal expected surplus risk and thus select the MSV portfolio. Other investors might choose to bear some greater amount of surplus risk with the expectation of greater ending surplus. Understanding "beta" to loosely mean compensated risk, we can call this choice the surplus beta decision. If we evaluate surplus risk relative to the risk of the MSV portfolio, we can measure the surplus beta decision in terms of the increment of risk accepted above the risk of the MSV portfolio.[50]

---

[50] See Barton Waring (2004b) for more details on this type of analysis.

Optimization

Exhibit 28   Surplus Efficient Frontier

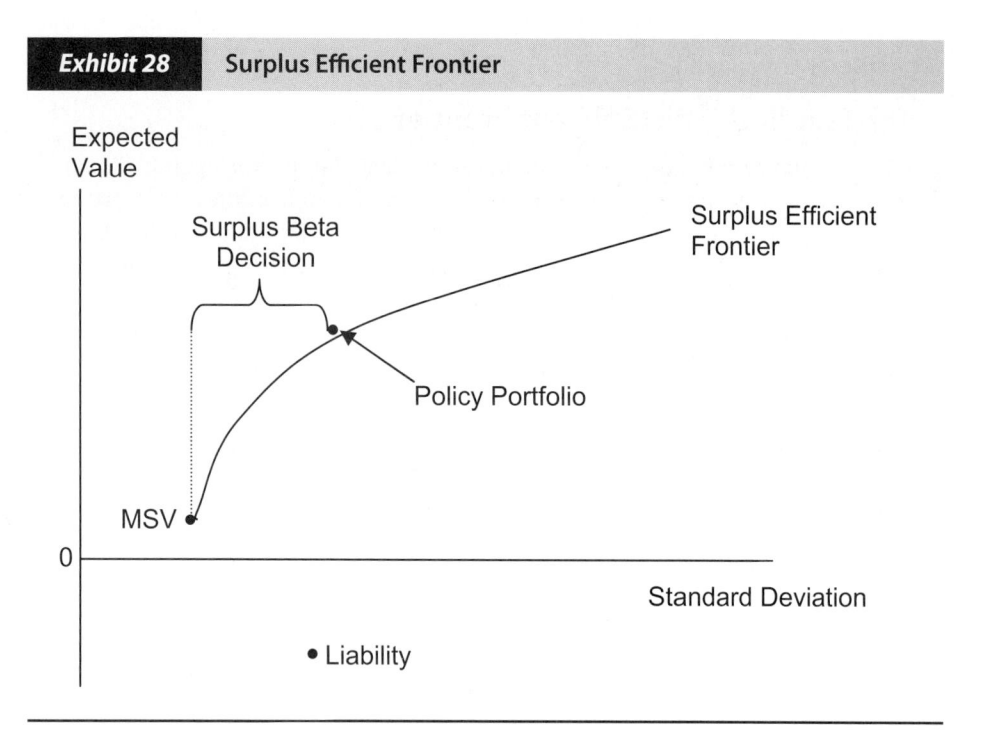

[Figure: Surplus Efficient Frontier chart showing Expected Value vs. Standard Deviation, with MSV, Surplus Beta Decision, Policy Portfolio labeled on the frontier curve, and Liability point below the x-axis.]

The estimation error problems of traditional MVO also apply to surplus optimization. The techniques that help mitigate these problems in traditional MVO, such as resampling and the Black–Litterman model, can be used in this context as well.

6.5.1 An ALM Example: A Defined-Benefit Pension Plan

For a DB pension plan, net worth is called pension surplus. The funding ratio, calculated by dividing the value of pension assets by the present value of pension liabilities, measures the relative size of pension assets compared with pension liabilities.[51] Some countries state requirements pertaining to pension plan contributions in terms of the **funding ratio**.

- If the funding ratio exceeds 100 percent, then the pension fund is overfunded.
- If the funding ratio is less than 100 percent, then the pension fund is underfunded.
- If the funding ratio equals 100 percent, then the pension fund is exactly fully funded.

Effectively managing a pension fund's surplus is often taken to be the plan sponsor's goal. If surplus is positive, the sponsor can finance future liability accruals, at least in part, by drawing on the surplus. If the present value of liabilities exceeds the value of assets (i.e., a negative surplus or unfunded liability exists), however, the sponsor must make up the asset shortfall through future contributions from the sponsor's assets or investment earnings. Surplus increases with plan contributions and investment earnings and decreases with plan withdrawals or investment losses. A pension plan's surplus is thus a logical variable for optimization.

Example 13 illustrates a variation on the surplus efficient frontier that appears not infrequently; in that example, the efficient frontier is stated in terms of the funding ratio.

---

51 The funding ratio has also been referred to as the funded ratio or **funded status**.

Example 13

The Funding Ratio Efficient Frontier

George Thomadakis is chief pension officer of Alaia Manufacturing, Inc. (ALA), which has a very young workforce. The duration of plan liabilities is estimated at 18 years. The plan has $250 million in assets and $250 million in liabilities as measured by the projected benefit obligation (PBO). Using capital market expectations approved by the plan's trustees, and a mean–variance surplus optimization approach, Thomadakis has graphed the PBO funding ratio efficient frontier as shown in Exhibit 29 for a forthcoming strategic asset allocation review.

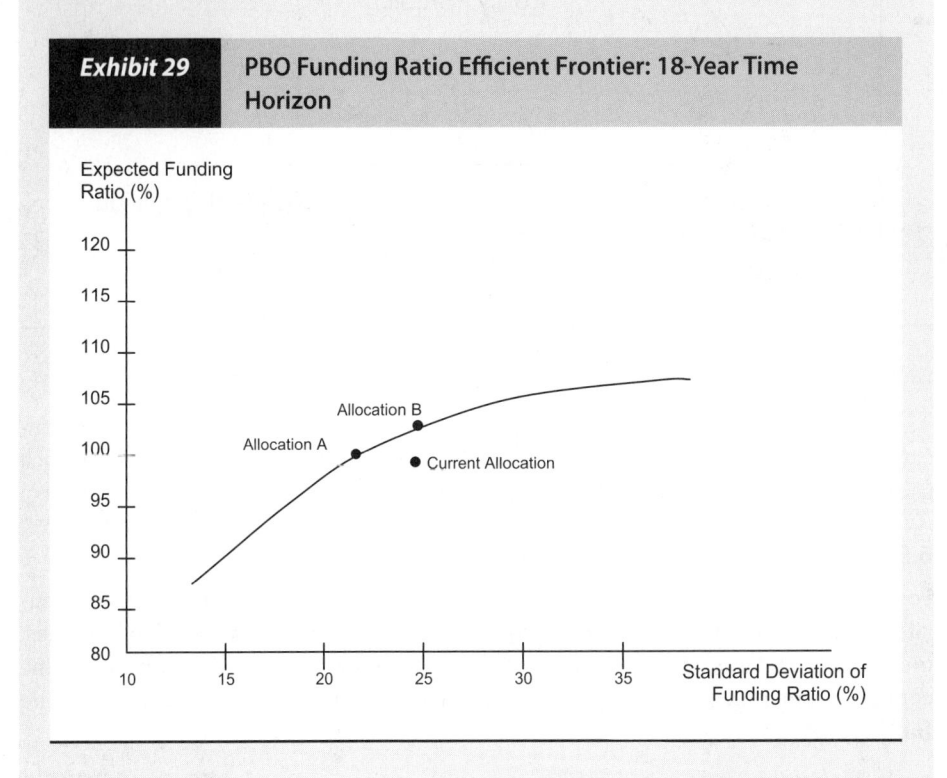

Exhibit 29 PBO Funding Ratio Efficient Frontier: 18-Year Time Horizon

Thomadakis will recommend that the plan's trustees replace the current strategic asset allocation with either Asset Allocation A or Asset Allocation B, shown in Exhibit 29. Justify his recommendation.

Solution:

The current strategic asset allocation is expected to maintain a 100 percent funding ratio with expected volatility of 25 percent a year at an 18-year time horizon. Allocation A is expected to result in the same 100 percent funding ratio as the current strategic asset allocation but with less risk (the standard deviation of A is approximately 22 percent, below the current allocation's 25 percent level). Allocation B is expected to result in a higher than 100 percent funding ratio with the same risk as the current asset allocation. Both A and B lie on the efficient frontier, but the current asset allocation is not efficient. Thus both A and B are superior to the current asset allocation; in deciding between the two, the trustees must determine whether lower risk or a higher expected funding ratio is more important.

Optimization

Continuing with the example of the ALA pension plan, suppose that the expected return on plan assets and plan liabilities are 7.8 percent and 5 percent, respectively. A liability return is the change in value of a liability, just as an asset return is the change in value of an asset.

- The forecast of pension assets at a one-year horizon is ($250,000,000) × 107.8% = $269,500,000.
- The forecast of pension liabilities is $250,000,000 × 105% = $262,500,000.
- The forecast of surplus is $269,500,000 − $262,500,000 = $7,000,000, which we could also compute directly as $250,000,000 × (7.8% − 5%).
- The forecast of the funding ratio is $269,500,000/$262,500,000 = 1.027, or 102.7 percent.
- Making projections for underfunded and overfunded pension follows the same computational pattern.

Now consider how we would evaluate a proposal that the ALA pension adopt a 60/40 stock/bond asset allocation. Continuing with the facts presented in Example 13, now assume that the return on the pension liability tracks the return on U.S. government long-term bonds and that the IPS permits investment in:

- domestic stocks (proxied by the S&P 500);
- developed market stocks (proxied by the MSCI EAFE Index);
- U.S. government long-term bonds; and
- cash equivalents (proxied by U.S. 30-day T-bills).

Exhibit 30 provides the capital market expectations.

Exhibit 30 Capital Market Expectations

	Expected Return	Standard Deviation	Corr. w/ S&P 500 TR	Corr. w/ MSCI EAFE TR	Corr. w/ U.S. LT Govt. TR	Corr. w/ U.S. 30-Day T-Bill TR
S&P 500 TR	10%	20%	1.00			
MSCI EAFE TR	10	25	0.59	1.00		
U.S. LT Govt TR	5	10	0.12	0.08	1.00	
U.S. 30-Day T-Bill TR	3	3	−0.03	−0.11	0.23	1.00

The capital market expectations given in Exhibit 30 produce the surplus efficient frontier shown in Exhibit 31. The 60/40 stock/bond policy mix portfolio more precisely consists of 30 percent S&P 500, 30 percent international stocks, 30 percent U.S. long-term government bonds, and 10 percent T-bills. Example 14 evaluates this asset allocation from an ALM perspective.

Exhibit 31 Surplus Efficient Frontier: Evaluating a 60/40 Stock/Bond Mix

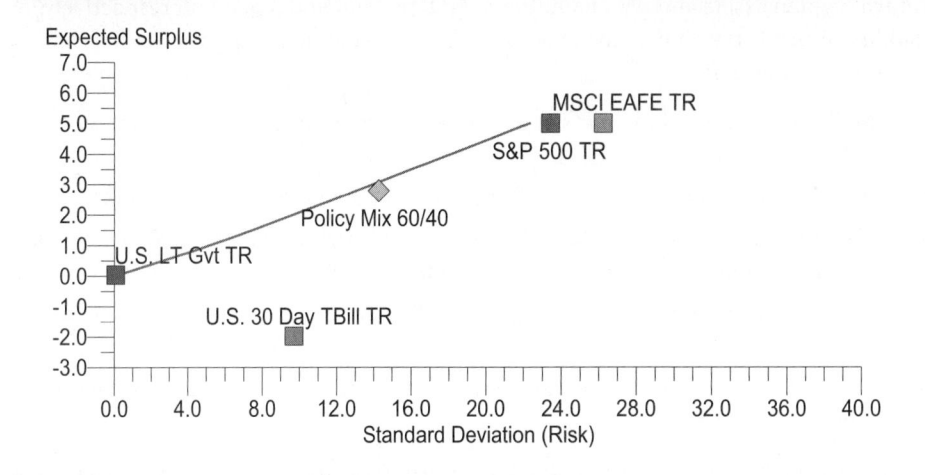

Example 14

The Surplus Efficient Frontier

Exhibit 32 shows the asset-class weights in the efficient portfolios running from the MSV portfolio to the highest-expected-return surplus efficient portfolio for the ALA pension fund.

1. Appraise the surplus efficiency of the proposed 60/40 policy mix.
2. Justify the absence of T-bills in surplus efficient portfolios for the ALA pension.

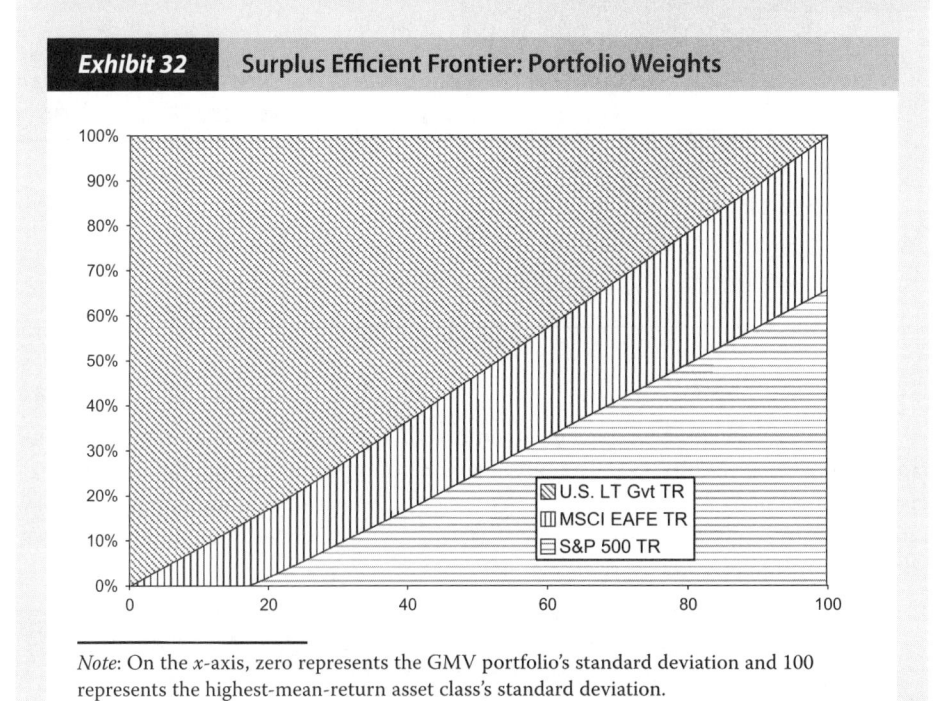

Exhibit 32 Surplus Efficient Frontier: Portfolio Weights

Note: On the x-axis, zero represents the GMV portfolio's standard deviation and 100 represents the highest-mean-return asset class's standard deviation.

Optimization

Solution to 1:

The 60/40 asset allocation is almost but not exactly surplus efficient: It lies just below the surplus efficient frontier. The proposed 60/40 asset allocation includes a 10 percent weighting in T-bills. As Exhibit 32 shows, U.S. T-bills do not enter into any surplus efficient portfolio; including T-bills in the policy mix accounts at least in part for the 60/40 portfolio not appearing on the surplus efficient frontier.

Solution to 2:

According to Exhibit 32, no surplus efficient portfolio includes T-bills. The pension liability behaves as a long-term bond, by assumption. Intuitively, if we can invest in long-term bonds, we can completely negate surplus risk. By itself, holding long-term bonds is riskier than holding T-bills, but relative to the pension liability, T-bills are riskier. The MSV portfolio is 100 percent long-term bonds. If we want to move from the MSV portfolio to higher-expected-surplus portfolios, we logically require equities with a 10 percent expected return, not T-bills.

Example 15

Interpreting the Surplus Efficient Frontier

Thomadakis is interested in the performance of the 60/40 asset allocation if pension assets were $200,000,000 rather than $250,000,000. With plan assets at that level, the funding ratio would be 80 percent ($200,000,000/$250,000,000), so the plan would be underfunded. Exhibit 33 depicts the surplus efficient frontier in that case.

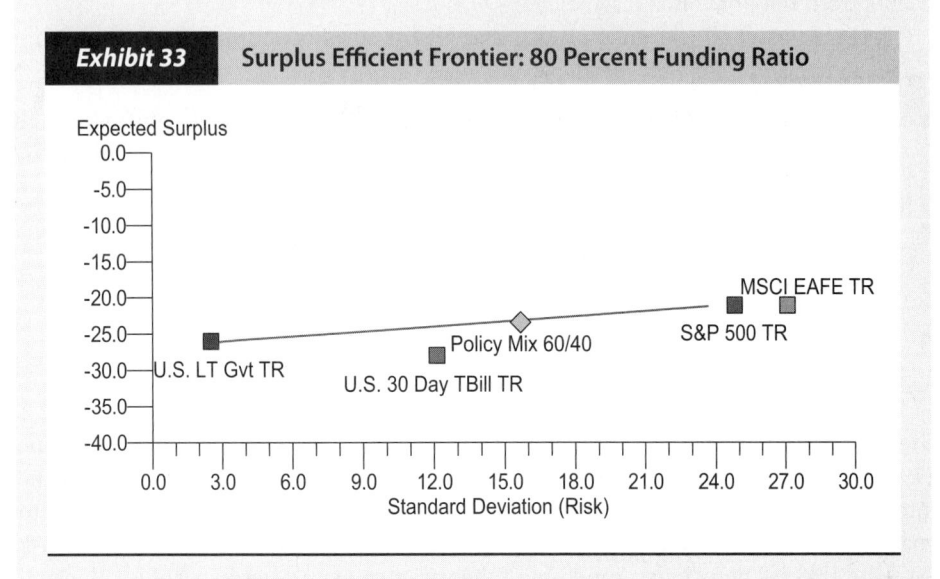

Exhibit 33   Surplus Efficient Frontier: 80 Percent Funding Ratio

Based on Exhibit 33, address the following:

1. Contrast the position of the surplus efficient frontier with an 80 percent funding ratio to its position with a 100 percent funding ratio.
2. Appraise the surplus efficiency of the 60/40 strategic asset allocation.

> **Solution to 1:**
>
> The MSV portfolio's expected surplus is now negative, and the MSV portfolio has positive risk rather than zero risk. All surplus efficient portfolios have negative expected surplus. Because the plan is currently only 80 percent funded, one year's expected positive asset returns are expected to be insufficient to make up the funding shortfall whatever the risk assumed. (This fact implies that the pension plan sponsor will probably need to make additional contributions in the future to help make up the funding shortfall.) The MSV portfolio has positive risk because a $200,000,000, 100 percent position in long-term bonds cannot completely offset the liability, which is effectively a $250,000,000 short position in long-term bonds.
>
> **Solution to 2:**
>
> The 60/40 allocation appears to be surplus efficient at an 80 percent funding ratio because it lies on the surplus efficient frontier.

6.5.2 Asset/Liability Modeling with Simulation

Managers often use Monte Carlo simulation together with surplus optimization (or sometimes standard mean–variance optimization) to provide more detailed insight on the performance of asset allocations under consideration. Simulation is particularly important for investors with long time horizons, because the MVO or surplus optimization is essentially a one-period model. Monte Carlo simulation can help to confirm that the recommended allocations provide sufficient diversification and to evaluate the probability of funding shortfalls (requiring contributions), the likelihood of breaching return thresholds, and the growth of assets with and without disbursements from the portfolio.

A simple asset allocation approach that blends surplus optimization with Monte Carlo simulation follows these steps:[52]

- Determine the surplus efficient frontier and select a limited set of efficient portfolios, ranging from the MSV portfolio to higher-surplus-risk portfolios, to examine further.

- Conduct a Monte Carlo simulation for each proposed asset allocation and evaluate which allocations, if any, satisfy the investor's return and risk objectives.

- Choose the most appropriate allocation that satisfies those objectives.

Below we elaborate on the steps.

Step 1 The first step in the three-step ALM employs the model presented in Sharpe (1990).[53] The objective function is to maximize the risk-adjusted future value of the surplus (or net worth). Formally, in a mean–variance context, doing so amounts to maximizing the difference between the expected change in future surplus and a risk penalty. The risk penalty is a function of the variance of changes in surplus value and the investor's risk tolerance (or risk aversion).

$$U_m^{\text{ALM}} = E(\text{SR}_m) - 0.005 R_A \sigma^2(\text{SR}_m) \tag{4}$$

---

[52] The approach illustrated reflects the input of R. Charles Tschampion, CFA.
[53] We state the expression consistently with Equation 1.

Optimization

where

U_m^{ALM} = the surplus objective function's expected value for a particular asset mix m, for a particular investor with the specified risk aversion

$E(SR_m)$ = expected surplus return for asset mix m, with surplus return defined as (change in asset value − change in liability value)/(initial asset value)

$\sigma^2(SR_m)$ = variance of the surplus return for the asset mix m[54]

R_A = risk-aversion level

In Equation 4, $E(SR)$ and $\sigma(SR)$ are expressed as percentages rather than as decimals. A set of proposed efficient portfolios may be found by incrementing the risk-aversion parameter from 0 (highest expected surplus asset allocation) upwards; we might also include the immunizing or cash flow matching portfolio as a traditional risk-minimizing choice.[55]

Suppose an insurance company with a risk-aversion level of 6 is deciding between the two asset allocations shown in Exhibit 34.

Exhibit 34 Expectation Concerning Surplus Return

Asset Allocation	Expected Surplus Return	Standard Deviation of Surplus Return
A	5.0%	12%
B	0.5	8

Investor's Forecasts

With a risk aversion of 6, the insurer has objective function

$$U_m^{ALM} = E(SR_m) - 0.005 R_A \sigma^2(SR_m)$$
$$= E(SR_m) - 0.005(6)\sigma^2(SR_m)$$
$$= E(SR_m) - 0.03\sigma^2(SR_m)$$

For Asset Allocation A,

$$U_A^{ALM} = E(SR_A) - 0.03\sigma^2(SR_A) = 5.0 - 0.03(12)^2 = 5 - 4.32 = 0.68$$

For Asset Allocation B,

$$U_B^{ALM} = E(SR_B) - 0.03\sigma^2(SR_B) = 0.5 - 0.03(8)^2 = 0.5 - 1.92 = -1.42$$

Because 0.68 is greater than −1.42, the insurer should prefer Allocation A.

Step 2 Before conducting a Monte Carlo simulation, we need to project pension payments and specify the rule for making contributions. Exhibit 35 is an example of a projection of pension payments that could enter into a Monte Carlo simulation.

---

[54] Given the return on assets (AR) and the return on liabilities (LR), with A_0 and L_0 the market value of assets and liabilities, we could calculate surplus variance using
$$\sigma^2(SR) = \sigma^2(AR) + \sigma^2(LR) \times (L_0/A_0)^2 - 2\rho(AR, LR) \times \sigma(AR) \times \sigma(LR) \times (L_0/A_0).$$

[55] In practice, a restriction against short sales of an asset class would make the procedure more complex.

Exhibit 35 Projected Pension Payments

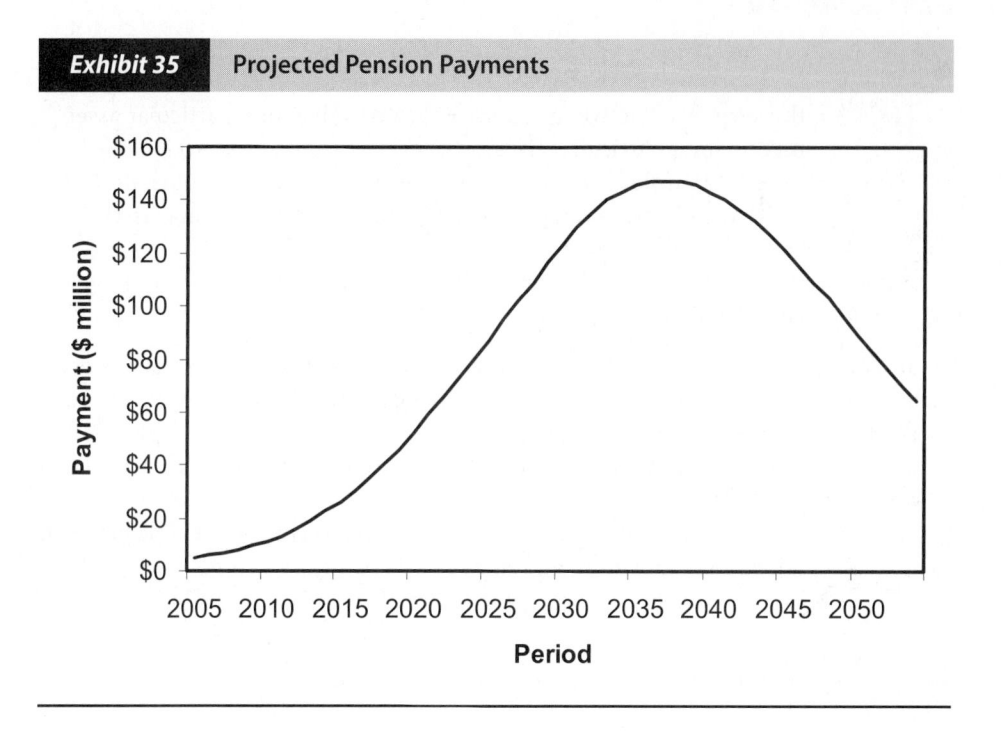

The Monte Carlo simulation produces a frequency distribution for the future values of the asset mix, plan liabilities, and net worth or surplus. In a broad sense, the second step is a process of simulating how a particular asset allocation may perform in funding liabilities given the investor's capital market expectations.

Simulated results for portfolio returns are typically reported in inflation-adjusted terms and represent the probability of achieving actual real return levels for different time periods. Projected benefit payments are also reported in today's dollars. Therefore, all simulations regarding ending wealth values have been adjusted for inflation.

Step 3 This step may involve the investor's professional judgment as well as quantitative criteria. One example of quantitative criteria is as follows:

1. Median funded ratio after 20 years equals at least 100 percent.
2. No more than a 10 percent probability of a funded ratio less than 90 percent in any one year.
3. Subject to the above, to minimize the present value of pension contributions.

Employing a systematic process such as that given will help in selecting a strategic asset allocation that appropriately balances risk and return.

6.6 Experience-Based Approaches

Quantitative approaches to optimization are a mainstay of strategic asset allocation because they add discipline to the process. When professionally executed and interpreted, such approaches have been found to be useful in practice. Many investment advisors, however—particularly those serving individual clients—rely on tradition, experience, and rules of thumb in making strategic asset allocation recommendations. Although these approaches appear to be ad hoc, their thrust often is consistent with financial theory when examined carefully. Furthermore, they may inexpensively suggest asset allocations that have worked well for clients in the broad experience of many investment advisors. In this section, we describe some of the most common experience-based approaches and ideas concerning asset allocation.

Optimization

1. *A 60/40 stock/bond asset allocation is appropriate or at least a starting point for an average investor's asset allocation.* From periods predating modern portfolio theory to the present, this asset allocation has been suggested as a neutral (neither highly aggressive nor conservative) asset allocation for an average investor.[56] The equities allocation is viewed as supplying a long-term growth foundation, the fixed-income allocation as supplying risk-reduction benefits. If the stock and bond allocations are themselves diversified, an overall diversified portfolio should result.

2. *The allocation to bonds should increase with increasing risk aversion.* We can illustrate this idea with the example of the Vanguard LifeStrategy® Funds, which offer four choices of relatively fixed asset allocations stated to be appropriate for investors with different risk tolerances, investment objectives, and time horizons, as shown in Exhibit 36.[57]

Exhibit 36 Asset Allocation of the Vanguard LifeStrategy Funds

LifeStrategy Fund (Risk Profile)	Stocks	Bonds	Short-Term Fixed Income
Income Fund (conservative)	20%	60%	20%
Conservative Growth Fund (moderate)	40	40	20
Moderate Growth Fund (moderately aggressive)	60	40	0
Growth Fund (aggressive)	80	20	0

An increased allocation to fixed income on average should tend to lower the portfolio's interim volatility over the investor's time horizon. Conservative investors highly value low volatility.

3. *Investors with longer time horizons should increase their allocation to stocks.* One idea behind this rule of thumb is that stocks are less risky to hold in the long run than the short run, based on past data. This idea, known as time diversification, is widely believed by individual and institutional investors alike. Theoreticians who have explored the concept have found that conclusions depend on the assumptions made—for example, concerning utility functions and the time series properties (independence/non-independence) of returns, among other assumptions.[58]

4. *A rule of thumb for the percentage allocation to equities is 100 minus the age of the investor.* This rule of thumb implies that young investors should adopt more aggressive asset allocations than older investors. For example, it would recommend a 70/30 stock bond allocation for a 30-year-old investor. Exhibit 37 offers an example of this principle, if not the above rule of thumb precisely.

---

[56] As one example, Mellon Capital Management's *Capital Communications* (Summer 2000) describes a 60/40 stock/bond mix as the neutral asset allocation for "normal" market conditions.
[57] Vanguard provides a questionnaire for investors to assess their risk tolerance.
[58] See Ross (1999) for an analysis of the critique on time diversification begun by Samuelson (1963).

| Exhibit 37 | Life-Cycle Investment Guide to Asset Allocation |

Investor Age Range	Stocks	Real Estate	Bonds	Cash
20s	65%	10%	20%	5%
30s to 40s	55	10	30	5
50s	45	12	38	5
60+	25	15	50	10

Source: Malkiel (2004).

For young investors, an aggressive portfolio may be more appropriate because they have a longer time frame to make up any losses as markets fluctuate, and because young investors have a lifetime of earnings from employment ahead of them. For many investors, the present value of those future earnings may be relatively low risk and uncorrelated with stock market returns, justifying higher risk in their financial portfolio. We return to this subject in a later section.

The investment practitioner should be familiar with the entire range of asset allocation approaches, including the widely held ideas discussed above.

7 IMPLEMENTING THE STRATEGIC ASSET ALLOCATION

Strategic asset allocation is part of the *planning* step in portfolio management, and in this reading we have focused on how to choose an appropriate strategic asset allocation. Managers also must be familiar with the implementation choices such decisions will create, however. In the following we briefly discuss those choices.

7.1 Implementation Choices

For each asset class specified in the investor's strategic asset allocation, the investor will need to select an investment approach. At the broadest level, the choice is among:

- passive investing;
- active investing;
- semi-active investing or enhanced indexing; or,
- some combination of the above.

A second choice concerns the instruments used to execute a chosen investment approach.

- A passive position can be implemented through:
  - a tracking portfolio of cash market securities—whether self-managed, a separately managed account, an exchange-traded fund, or a mutual fund—designed to replicate the returns to a broad investable index representing that asset class;
  - a derivatives-based portfolio consisting of a cash position plus a long position in a swap in which the returns to an index representing that asset class is received; or
  - a derivatives-based portfolio consisting of a cash position plus a long position in index futures for the asset class.

Implementing the Strategic Asset Allocation

- Active investing can be implemented through:
  - a portfolio of cash market securities that reflects the investor's perceived special insights and skill and that also makes no attempt to track any asset-class index's performance, or
  - a derivatives-based position (such as cash plus a long swap) to provide commodity-like exposure to the asset class plus a market-neutral long–short position to reflect active investment ideas.
- Semiactive investing can be implemented through (among other methods):
  - a tracking portfolio of cash market securities that permits some under- or overweighting of securities relative to the asset-class index but with controlled tracking risk, or
  - a derivatives-based position in the asset-class plus controlled active risk in the cash position (such as actively managing its duration).

The IPS will often specify particular indexes or benchmarks for each asset class. Such a specification is useful not only for performance evaluation but for guiding passive investment, if that approach is chosen.

The selection of investment approaches for asset classes specified in the strategic asset allocation is an early-stage planning decision. The factors that may affect this decision include the investor's return requirements and risk objective; the perception of informational efficiency (availability of profitable active investment opportunities); the investor's self-perception of investment skill; costs; and peer practice.

7.2 Currency Risk Management Decisions

Whether using passive or active investing, if any money is allocated to a nondomestic asset class, the investor's portfolio will be exposed to **currency risk**—the volatility of the home-currency value of nondomestic assets that is related to fluctuations in exchange rates. Therefore, the investor must decide what part of the net exposures to currencies to hedge (eliminate). The hedging decision affects the expected return and volatility characteristics of the portfolio. Hedging can be managed passively, i.e., not incorporating views on currency returns, or managed actively, when the investor has definite forecasts about currency returns and the desire to exploit them tactically. The asset allocation and hedging decisions can be optimized jointly, but in practice the currency risk hedging decision is frequently subordinated to the asset allocation decision—that is, currency exposures are optimized or selected subsequent to determination of the asset allocation. Often, this type of subordination accompanies delegation of the currency management function to a currency overlay manager—a specialist in currency risk management operating in currency forward and other derivatives markets to establish desired currency exposures. If asset returns and currency returns are correlated, however, there will be efficiency losses relative to joint optimization.[59] In many cases, the IPS will give instructions on policy with respect to currency hedging.

7.3 Rebalancing to the Strategic Asset Allocation

What does "rebalancing" mean? We should distinguish between 1) changes to the policy portfolio itself because of changes in the investor's investment objectives and constraints, or because of changes in his or her long-term capital market expectations and 2) adjusting the actual portfolio to the strategic asset allocation because asset

---

[59] See Clarke and Kritzman (1996) and references therein for technical details and Solnik and McLeavey (2004) for a general introduction to currency risk management.

price changes have moved portfolio weights away from the target weights beyond tolerance limits. Although "rebalancing" is used sometimes to refer to the first type of adjustments, in industry practice rebalancing usually refers to 2) and thus we should know some basic facts about it in that sense.[60]

Rebalancing may be done on a calendar basis (such as quarterly) or on a percentage-of-portfolio basis. Percentage-of-portfolio rebalancing occurs when an asset-class weight first passes through a rebalancing threshold (also called a trigger point). For example, in Exhibit 1 we stated the target allocation to equities as 50 percent with a permissible range of 46 percent to 54 percent. The endpoints 46 percent and 54 percent are rebalancing thresholds. When a threshold is breached, the asset-class weight may be rebalanced all the way back to the target weight (50 percent), or to some point between the target weight and the threshold that has been passed, according to the discipline the investor has established. A variety of approaches exist for setting the thresholds. Although some investors set them in an ad hoc fashion, disciplined approaches exist that consider the investor's risk tolerance, the asset's volatility correlations with other asset classes, and transaction costs.[61] The percentage-of-portfolio approach done in a disciplined fashion provides a tighter control over risk than calendar-basis rebalancing. The reading on monitoring and rebalancing provides more information on these topics.

8 STRATEGIC ASSET ALLOCATION FOR INDIVIDUAL INVESTORS

What characteristics of individual investors distinguish them from other investors in ways that may affect the strategic asset allocation decision? Individual investors are taxable and must focus on after-tax returns. Tax status distinguishes individual investors from tax-exempt investors (such as endowments) and even other taxable investors such as banks, which are often subject to different tax schedules than individual investors. Other, inherent rather than external, differences exist, however. Asset allocation for individual investors must account for:

- the part of wealth flowing from current and future labor income, and the changing mix of financial and labor-income-related wealth as a person ages and eventually retires;
- any correlation of current and future labor income with financial asset returns; and
- the possibility of outliving one's resources.

As discussed in a prior section, psychological factors may also play a role. Behavioral finance points to a variety of issues that individual investors and their advisors face when determining the asset allocation. In the next sections, however, we focus on the three concerns mentioned above.

8.1 Human Capital

An individual investor's ability and willingness to bear risk depends on:

- personality makeup;
- current and future needs; and

---

60 Perold and Sharpe (1988) called such a rebalancing approach a constant-mix strategy. We discuss the Perold–Sharpe theory of adjusting asset mix between a risky and a safe asset class in the reading on monitoring and rebalancing.
61 See Masters (2003) for an example.

Strategic Asset Allocation for Individual Investors

- current and anticipated future financial situation, considering all sources of income.

As Malkiel (2004) states in *A Random Walk Down Wall Street*, "The risks you can afford to take depend on your total financial situation, including the types and sources of your income exclusive of investment income." Earning ability is important in determining capacity for risk. People with high earning ability can take more risk because they can more readily recoup financial losses than lower-earning individuals.[62] A person's earning ability is captured by the concept of human capital.

Human capital, the present value of expected future labor income, is not readily tradable. In addition to human capital, an individual has **financial capital**, which consists of more readily tradable assets such as stocks, bonds, and real estate. Human capital is often an investor's single largest asset. Young investors generally have far more human capital than financial capital. With little time to save and invest, their financial capital may be very small. But young investors have a long work life in front of them, and the present value of expected future earnings is often substantial.

The following example illustrates the importance of human capital at young ages and its declining importance as retirement approaches. Our hypothetical investor is 25 years old, makes $50,000 per year, and has $100,000 of current investments with a 5 percent annual real return. Human capital is estimated using Equation 5:

$$\text{Human capital}(t) = \sum_{j=t}^{T} \frac{I_j}{(1+r)^{(j-t)}} \tag{5}$$

where

t = current age
I_j = expected earnings at age j
T = life expectancy
r = discount rate[63]

We then follow the growth of human and financial capital until retirement at age 65. Exhibits 38 and 39 illustrate the magnitudes and relative proportions of financial capital and human capital for a hypothetical investor from age 25 to age 65.

---

[62] Educational attainments and working experience are the two most significant factors in determining a person's earning ability.

[63] The discount rate should be adjusted to the risk level of the person's labor income. For simplicity, we assume it is 3 percent after inflation.

Exhibit 38 Financial Capital and Human Capital Trends as Investor Ages

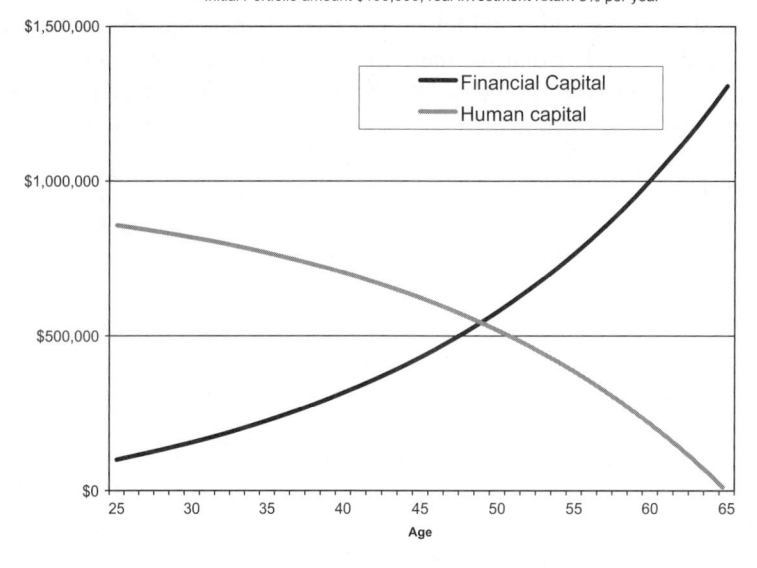

Age 25, income $50,000, income increases with inflation, real discount rate for future income & Mortality 5%
Initial Portfolio amount $100,000; real investment return 5% per year

Exhibit 39 Financial Capital and Human Capital Relative to Total Wealth

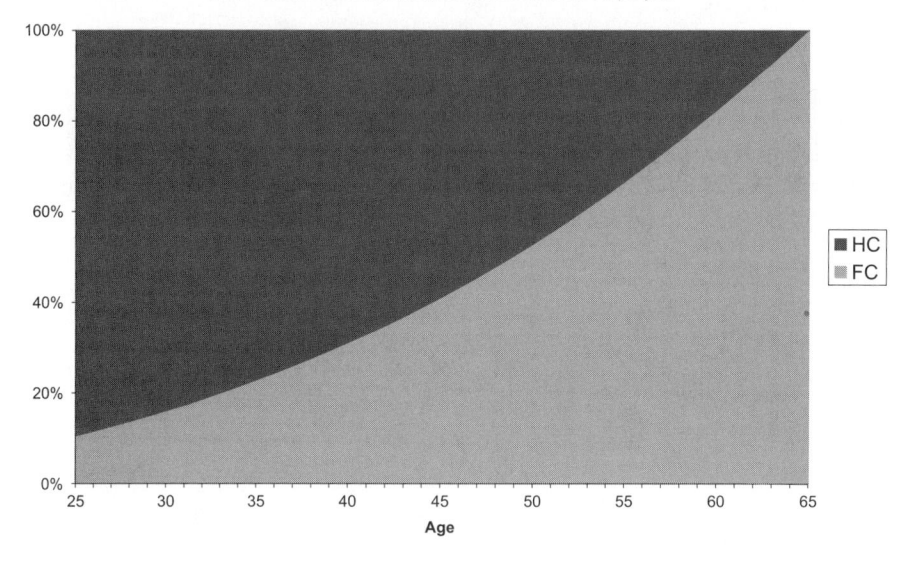

Age 25, income $50,000, income increases with inflation, real discount rate for future income & Mortality 5%
Initial Portfolio amount $100,000; real investment return 5% per year

From Exhibit 38 we observe that when the investor is 25 years old, his human capital far outweighs his financial capital. Human capital is estimated to be approximately $900,000 and represents about 90 percent of the total wealth (human plus financial capital), while financial capital is only $100,000. As the investor gets older, the investor will continue to make savings contributions and earn positive returns, so his or her financial capital will increase. At age 65, human capital decreases to zero, while the financial portfolio peaks above $1 million.[64]

---

[64] In this example, we ignore any corporate or governmental retirement benefits after retirement.

Strategic Asset Allocation for Individual Investors

Human capital's importance is often underestimated. Using the 1992 Survey of Consumer Finances, Lee and Hanna (1995) estimated that the ratio of financial assets to total wealth including human capital was 1.3 percent for the median household in the United States—for half of the households, financial assets represented less than 1.3 percent of total wealth. For 75 percent of households, financial assets represented less than 5.7 percent of total wealth, while for 90 percent of households it was 17.4 percent or less. Thus for most households studied, wealth was chiefly in the form of human capital.

Asset Allocation and Human Capital Strategic asset allocation concerns the asset mix for financial capital. Nevertheless, for individual investors, strategic asset allocation must also consider human capital as Merton (2003) has emphasized. When our perspective incorporates human capital, we see the logic in the traditional professional advice on asset allocation for individuals: that the appropriate strategic asset allocation varies with age or life cycle.

According to theory, asset allocation advice crucially depends on whether labor income and human capital are both considered. Ignoring human capital, individuals should optimally maintain constant portfolio weights throughout their life given certain assumptions, including assumptions about the investor's risk aversion (Samuelson 1969, Merton 1969).[65] When we do take labor income into account, individuals appear to optimally change their asset allocation in ways related to their life cycle and characteristics of their labor income. In *Strategic Asset Allocation: Portfolio Choice for Long-Term Investors* (2002), Campbell and Viceira reached several intuitive theoretical conclusions:

1. Investors with safe labor income (thus safe human capital) will invest more of their financial portfolio into equities. A tenured professor is an example of a person with safe labor income; an at-will employee in a downsizing company is an example of a person with risky labor income.
2. Investors with labor income that is highly positively correlated with stock markets should tend to choose an asset allocation with less exposure to stocks. A stockbroker with commission income is an example of a person who has that type of labor income.
3. The ability to adjust labor supply (high labor flexibility) tends to increase an investor's optimal allocation to equities.

Concerning the second point above, Davis and Willen (2000) estimated the correlation between labor income and equity market returns in the U.S., using the Current Occupation Survey (a U.S. government survey that randomly samples about 60,000 U.S. households each month). They found that the correlation typically lies in the interval from –0.10 to 0.20. The typical investor need not worry about his or her human capital being highly correlated with the stock market. For some investors (e.g., stockbrokers), however, the correlation of labor income with stock market returns is a definite concern for asset allocation.

Labor flexibility, the third point, relates to an individual's ability to adjust how long and how much he or she works. Bodie, Merton, and Samuelson (1992), like Campbell and Viceira, concluded that investors with a higher degree of labor flexibility should take more risk in their investment portfolios. The intuition is that labor flexibility can function as a kind of insurance against adverse investment outcomes; for example, working longer hours or retiring later can help offset investment losses. Younger investors typically have such flexibility. Hanna and Chen (1997) took account of human capital in using simulation to explore the optimal asset allocation for individual investors

---

[65] The investor must be assumed to have what is known as constant relative risk aversion (CRRA). See Elton, Gruber, Brown, and Goetzmann (2003) for a description of CRRA.

with varying time horizons. Assuming human capital is risk free (which increases the capacity for bearing risk), they concluded that for most investors with long horizons, an all-equity portfolio is optimal.

A concrete illustration will help us understand the life-cycle-relatedness of an individual's asset allocation. We present a simple case in which future labor income is certain—that is, human capital is a risk-free asset. Later we comment on the effects of risky human capital on asset allocation.

Assume that only two asset classes are available: stocks and bonds. The investor can invest financial capital (FC) in these two financial assets; human capital (HC) constitutes the balance of wealth and has effectively bond-like investment characteristics. If the investor's inherent risk appetites remain constant through time, the investor's optimal allocation of total wealth between the risky and risk-free assets will remain constant during his lifetime, all else equal.

Continuing with our investor from Exhibit 38, we assume that a 50/50 stock/bond strategic asset allocation for total wealth (financial and human capital) is optimal. Now compare the appropriate asset allocation for the investor at 25, 55, and 65 years old. Without considering human capital, the investor would optimally maintain a 50/50 stock/bond strategic asset allocation throughout his life.

Taking human capital into account, however, the 25-year-old investor should choose a 100 percent stock asset allocation for his financial capital because he already has 95 percent of his total wealth (represented by his human capital) effectively invested in bonds. Investing 100 percent of his financial capital in stocks is the closest he can get his total portfolio to the target 50/50 asset allocation without using leverage (borrowing money to buy stocks). As shown in Exhibit 40, at age 55, his total wealth consists of 50 percent financial capital and 50 percent human capital. With that split, his optimal strategic asset allocation for financial capital is 100 percent stocks, because he thereby achieves the target 50/50 allocation for his total wealth. After age 55, the allocation to stocks declines, reaching 50 percent at retirement at age 65 when human capital effectively reaches zero.

Exhibit 40 Changing Optimal Asset Allocations from Age 25 through Retirement

	Age 25 FC: 5% Total Wealth HC: 95% Total Wealth	Age 55 FC: 50% Total Wealth HC: 50% Total Wealth	Age 65 FC: 100% Total Wealth HC: 0% Total Wealth
Overall asset allocation maintaining a fixed 50/50 strategic asset allocation for FC	FC: 50/50 Stocks/Bonds HC: 100% Bonds **Overall AA: 2.5/97.5 Stocks/Bonds**	FC: 50/50 Stocks/Bonds HC: 100% Bonds **Overall AA: 25/75 Stocks/Bonds**	FC: 50/50 Stocks/Bonds HC: n/a **Overall AA: 50/50 Stocks/Bonds**
Recommended FC asset allocation considering human capital	FC: 100/0 Stocks/Bonds HC: 100% Bonds Overall AA: 5/95 Stocks/Bonds	FC: 100/0 Stocks/Bonds HC: 100% Bonds Overall AA: 50/50 Stocks/Bonds	FC: 50/50 Stocks/Bonds HC: n/a Overall AA: 50/50 Stocks/Bonds

Note: FC is financial capital, HC is human capital.

In this simple example, we have illustrated that an investor would logically allocate more to stocks as a young person than as an old person. The result comes from the declining proportion of total wealth represented by human capital as the investor ages and the assumed risk characteristics of human capital. Although investment advisors frequently suggest that individuals follow a life-cycle-related asset allocation strategy, empirical studies suggest that only a small minority of investors actually adjust their asset allocations accordingly.[66]

In the above example we assumed human capital is risk free. In reality, for most individuals future labor income is neither certain nor safe. Most people face the risk of losing their job or being laid off. Uncertainty in labor income makes human capital a risky asset. How do we incorporate risky human capital into asset allocation?

We first need to establish the risk and return characteristics of the individual's human capital. Risky human capital may have two components: a component correlated with stock market returns and a component uncorrelated with stock market returns. The two types affect the asset allocation decision differently.

When the investor's labor income is risky but not correlated with the stock market, the investor's optimal strategic asset allocation over time follows by and large the same pattern as the case where the investor's human capital is risk free—so long as the risk of human capital (i.e., income variance over time) is small. This effect occurs because the investor's human capital does not add to his or her stock market exposure. When the risk of uncorrelated human capital is substantial, however, the investor's optimal allocation to stocks is less than it would be otherwise, all else equal.

By contrast, when a large part of an investor's human capital is correlated with the stock market, the appropriate strategic asset allocation involves a much higher allocation to bonds at young ages. For example, some large part of an equity portfolio manager's human capital is positively correlated with stock market returns. Portfolio managers earn more and have greater job security when the stock market does well. This investor should prefer an asset allocation with reduced exposure to stocks because part of the investor's human capital is implicitly invested in the stock market. Nevertheless, because the share of wealth represented by human capital declines with age, the correlated-human-capital factor favoring bonds should become less important as the portfolio manager approaches retirement. Contrary to the risk-free human capital case, the appropriate allocation to stocks at this later life stage may be greater than when the portfolio manager is younger.

In summary, to effectively incorporate human capital in developing the appropriate asset allocation, an individual's investment advisor must determine 1) whether the investor's human capital is risk-free or risky and 2) whether the human capital's risk is highly correlated with the stock market. Advisors should keep in mind the following themes:

- Investors should invest financial capital assets in such a way as to diversify and balance out their human capital.

- A young investor with relatively safe human capital assets and/or greater flexibility of labor supply has an appropriate strategic asset allocation with a higher weight on risky assets such as stocks than an older investor. The allocation to stocks should decrease as the investor ages. When the investor's human capital is risky but uncorrelated with the stock market, the optimal allocation to stocks may be less but still decreases with age.

- An investor with human capital that has high correlation with stock market returns should reduce the allocation to risky assets for financial assets and increase the allocation to financial assets that are less correlated with the stock market.[67]

---

[66] For example, see Ameriks and Zeldes (2001).
[67] For example, alternative assets with low correlation to the stock market (commodities, hedge funds, etc.) can be very attractive for these investors.

8.2 Other Considerations in Asset Allocation for Individual Investors

The human lifespan is finite but uncertain. As human beings we face both mortality risk and longevity risk.

Mortality risk is the risk of loss of human capital if an investor dies prematurely. Of course, it is the investor's family that bears the effects of mortality risk. Life insurance has long been used to hedge this risk. Mortality risk may suggest the holding of a liquidity reserve fund but otherwise plays no explicit role in strategic asset allocation.

Longevity risk is the risk that the investor will outlive his or her assets in retirement. In the United States, 65-year-old women have about an 81 percent chance of living to age 80; for men, the chance is 68 percent. When combined with the life expectancy of a spouse, the odds reach about 91 percent that at least one person in a married couple aged 65 will live to age 80. For a broader sense of the potential longevity risk, Exhibit 41 illustrates survival probabilities of 65-year-olds in the United States. The "joint" column shows the probability that at least one person in a married couple will survive to age 80, 85, 90, 95, and 100. The next column shows the probability that an individual will survive to the various ages. For married couples, in more than 78 percent of the cases, at least one spouse will still be alive at age 85.

Exhibit 41 Probability of 65-Year-Olds Living to Various Ages (U.S. Data)

Age	Joint	Individual	Male	Female
80	90.6%	74.0%	68.0%	80.6%
85	78.4	56.8	49.3	65.3
90	57.0	36.3	29.5	44.5
95	30.9	17.6	13.4	23.0
100	11.5	6.0	4.2	8.6

Source: 1996 U.S. Annuity 2000 Mortality Table (Society of Actuaries).

Like mortality risk, longevity risk is independent of financial market risk. In contrast to mortality risk, however, the investor bears longevity risk directly. Longevity risk is also related to income needs and so logically should be directly related to asset allocation, unlike mortality risk. But many investment retirement plans ignore longevity risk. For example, many such approaches assume that the investor needs to plan only to age 85. Although 85 years is approximately the life expectancy for a 65-year-old individual in many countries, life expectancy is only an average. Approximately half of U.S. investors currently age 65 will live past age 85; for a married couple, the odds of one spouse surviving beyond age 85 are more than 78 percent. If investors use an 85-year life expectancy to plan their retirement income needs, many of them will outlive their personal retirement resources (other than government and corporate pensions).

Longevity risk cannot be completely managed through asset allocation. One reaction to this risk might be to bear greater investment risk in an effort to earn higher long-term returns. If the investor can tolerate additional risk, this approach may be appropriate. Such a strategy reduces longevity risk only in expectation, however; the higher mean return may not be realized and the investor may still outlive his resources.

In fact, exposure to longevity risk offers no potential reward, and investors should be willing to pay a premium to transfer it just as they transfer property and liability exposures through homeowners insurance.[68] Transferring longevity risk in whole or in

---

[68] Living a long life is desirable from many aspects; we are only focusing on the financial aspect of longevity.

part to an insurer through an annuity contract may be rational. Insurers can profitably accept longevity risks by 1) spreading the risks among a large group of annuitants and 2) making careful and conservative assumptions about the rate of return earned on their assets. A life annuity type of instrument should be considered for many retirement plans. A **life annuity** guarantees a monthly income to the annuitant for the rest of his life. Life annuities may have one of three forms:[69] In a **fixed annuity**, the periodic income payments are constant in amount; in a **variable annuity**, the payments vary depending on an underlying investment portfolio's returns; and an **equity-indexed annuity** provides a guarantee of a minimum fixed payment plus some participation in stock market gains, if any. In an asset allocation, we would include the value of a fixed annuity as a risk-free asset and that of a variable annuity as a risky holding (looking through to the underlying portfolio's composition for a more precise classification). An equity-indexed annuity resembles a risk-free asset plus a call option on stock returns. Purchasing an annuity, however, is a product choice quite distinct from the strategic asset allocation decision.

Example 16

Critique of an Asset Allocation Approach for Individual Clients

Ridenour Associates is an investment management firm focused on high-net-worth individuals.

As a preliminary step to asset allocation, twice a year Ridenour develops three or four economic scenarios in-house. The senior staff assigns probabilities and generates return forecasts for domestic stocks, domestic bonds, and cash equivalents (the only asset types the firm uses); then expected values are computed for each asset category.

The staff develops a table containing a range of possible strategic asset allocations. Each allocation selected for the table has the highest three-year expected return among those allocations expected to have a 90 percent probability of achieving a specific minimum annual return. In consultation with the client, the Ridenour portfolio manager will choose one or two minimum return thresholds and then discuss the associated recommended asset allocations. If one or both recommended allocations appear to satisfy the client's other return and risk objectives, then a selection will be made from those choices. Ridenour repeats this process approximately every six months, when new allocations are developed. Exhibit 42 shows the current list.

Exhibit 42 Ridenour Associates' Recommended Asset Allocations (1 June 2005)

Minimum Annual Return Threshold (90% Probability)	Anticipated 3-Year Compound Annual Return	Recommended Asset Allocation		
		Cash	Bonds	Stocks
−6%	12.0	10%	30%	60%
−4	11.0	20	40	40

(continued)

---

69 See Rejda (2005).

Exhibit 42 Continued

Minimum Annual Return Threshold (90% Probability)	Anticipated 3-Year Compound Annual Return	Recommended Asset Allocation		
		Cash	Bonds	Stocks
−2	10.0	30	40	30
0	9.0	50	30	20
2	8.5	60	30	10
4	8.0	70	20	10
6	7.5	80	15	5

Discuss the strengths and weaknesses of Ridenour's asset allocation approach.

Solution:

Ridenour's approach has the following strengths and weaknesses:

Strengths

- The process is explicit and relatively straightforward.
- It offers clients a fairly wide range of choice across the risk–return spectrum, and permits allocations to be selected and varied according to client needs and preferences.
- It forces client interaction to take place at least twice a year, providing recurring opportunity for discussion, education, and updating.

Weaknesses

- Ridenour's approach employs only three classes of domestic securities. It excludes tax-exempt bonds from consideration, although in certain countries such bonds may play a role in the portfolios of high-net-worth investors, who generally are subject to high tax rates. The process also excludes asset classes such as international securities that may offer diversification benefits.
- The approach fails to give differentiated attention to human capital considerations. Young wealthy clients may want their exposure to equities to exceed the 60 percent maximum Ridenour allows.
- The three-year time horizon for assessing asset allocations is artificial. The horizon must be chosen with reference to each client's needs and circumstances. In addition, twice-a-year revision of three-year forecasts may result in excessive trading and high transaction costs.

9   STRATEGIC ASSET ALLOCATION FOR INSTITUTIONAL INVESTORS

The basic principles of optimization do not vary depending on the type of investor we are considering. The results and recommendations can only be as good as our inputs and model choices, however. In recommending a strategic asset allocation, we should seek a comprehensive picture of the investor's characteristics and choose our models and inputs appropriately. The following sections introduce institutional investors' characteristics and concerns as they affect strategic asset allocation. We discuss five major kinds of institutional investors: defined-benefit plans, foundations, endowments, insurance companies, and banks.

9.1 Defined-Benefit Plans

Pension plan sponsors use a variety of methods to select an asset allocation, with a strong focus on ALM techniques. Whatever approach they choose, plan sponsors typically face a range of constraints motivated by regulatory and liquidity concerns.

1. **Regulatory constraints.** The United States, the United Kingdom, Canada, the Netherlands, and Australia generally rely on the prudent person concept rather than limitations on asset-class holdings in their oversight of pension investing.[70] Nevertheless, the restriction on Canadian pension funds' holding of non-Canadian investments valued at cost to no more than 30 percent of assets is an example of a regulatory *maximum*. Denmark requires pension funds to have 60 percent at a *minimum* invested in domestic debt. Another example of a regulatory constraint is a set of "basket clauses," which place percentage limits for the aggregate holdings of certain illiquid or alternative investments (venture capital, hedge funds, emerging market securities, etc.). Regulatory constraints are intended to promote safety and diversification and to discourage conflicts of interest (e.g., by limitations on self-investment).
2. **Liquidity constraints.** A fund may have sufficiently high liquidity requirements that it must limit its percentage of illiquid assets (e.g., private debt, private equity, or real estate).

Just as for any other investor, a strategic asset allocation for a pension fund should meet the investor's return objective and be consistent with the fund's risk tolerance. In a prior section, we used defined-benefit plans to illustrate an ALM approach to asset allocation. From an ALM perspective, the following are desirable characteristics for an asset allocation:

- The risk of funding shortfalls is acceptable.
- The anticipated volatility of the pension surplus is acceptable. Low pension surplus volatility is generally associated with asset allocations whose duration approximately matches the duration of pension liabilities, because pension liabilities behave similarly to bonds as concerns interest rate sensitivity.
- The anticipated volatility of the contributions is acceptable.

An asset-only approach to a pension fund's strategic asset allocation was traditionally, and remains, a choice in professional investment practice. From an asset-only perspective, a reasonable starting point is the efficient asset allocation with the lowest standard deviation of return that meets the specified return objective of the pension fund.

In either an ALM or AO approach, if pension liabilities are fixed in nominal terms, inflation is not a concern. Otherwise, the advisor needs to consider how much inflation protection the asset allocation is expected to afford. Many pension sponsors attempt to use investments such as equities that represent real claims on the economy to at least partially offset the pension plan's exposure to higher wage and salary costs from inflation and productivity gains. Pensions in Australia, Canada, the United Kingdom, and the United States traditionally have given stocks a major role.

---

[70] See Davis (1995). A percentage limitation on investment in the sponsoring company's stock is common in these countries, however.

In certain continental European countries and in Japan, however, bond investments have traditionally played the major role, consistent with a risk-averse ALM concept of pension investing. Exhibits 43 and 44 show these country differences.

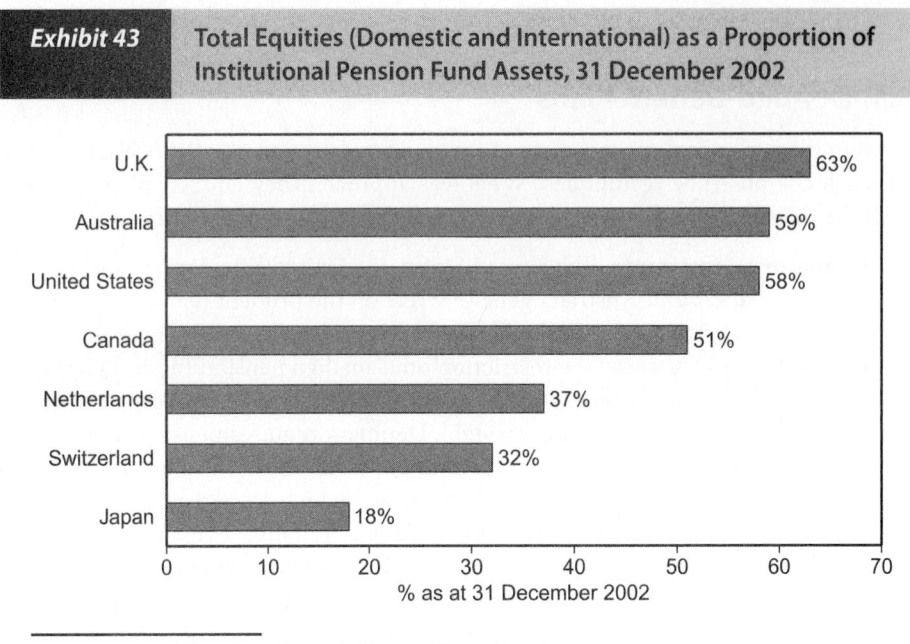

Exhibit 43 Total Equities (Domestic and International) as a Proportion of Institutional Pension Fund Assets, 31 December 2002

Country	% as at 31 December 2002
U.K.	63%
Australia	59%
United States	58%
Canada	51%
Netherlands	37%
Switzerland	32%
Japan	18%

Source: Memorandum (March 2004), Watson Wyatt Canada.

Exhibit 44 Total Bonds (Domestic and International) as a Proportion of Institutional Pension Fund Assets, 31 December 2002

Country	% as at 31 December 2002
Japan	76%
Netherlands	44%
Switzerland	39%
Canada	36%
UK	32%
United States	29%
Australia	20%

Source: Memorandum (March 2004), Watson Wyatt Canada.

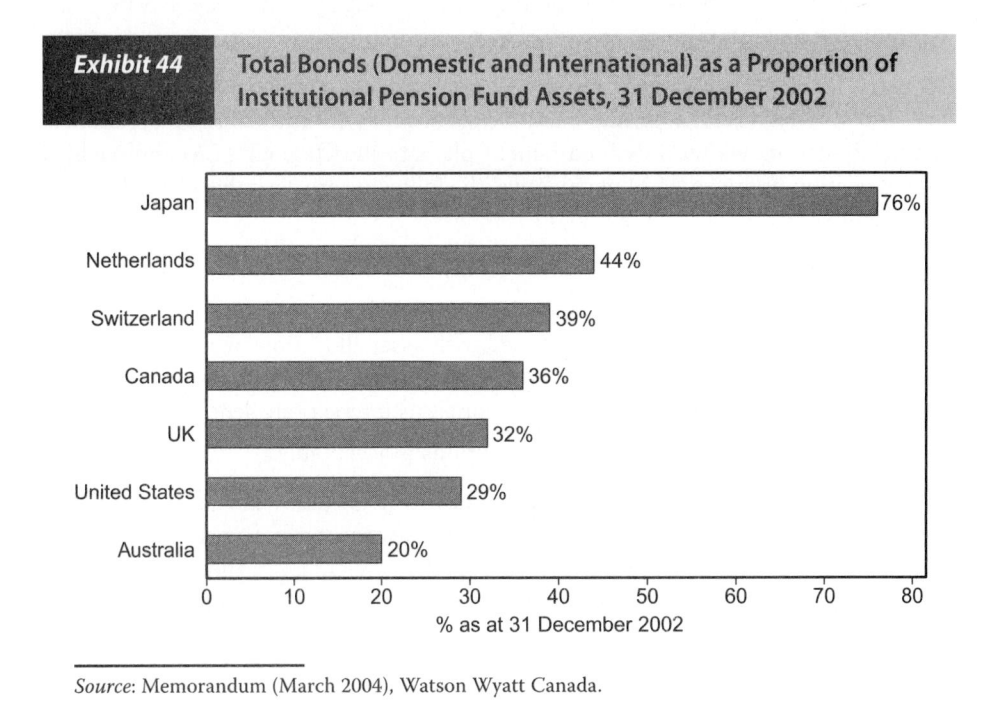

Exhibit 45 shows pension asset allocations in Canada and the United States, two countries where pension plans on average have an equity bias. The greater allocation to non-Canadian equities in Canada is logical, because Canadian equity markets total less than one-tenth the size of U.S. markets. In the United Kingdom, which also has an equities orientation in pension asset allocation, real estate investment has tended to play a substantially larger role than in Canada or the United States.

| Exhibit 45 | Asset Allocations of Canadian and U.S. Pension Funds, 31 December 2002 |

	Canadian Pension Funds[a]	U.S. Pension Funds
Domestic equities	25%	49%
Nondomestic equities	26	9
Domestic bonds	33	28
Nondomestic bonds	3	1
Real estate	4	3
Cash	2	6
Other	5	4
Alternatives	2	–
Total	100%	100%

[a]These data are for the top 100 pension funds in Canada and exclude the Canada Pension Plan (CPP) and the Québec Pension Plan (QPP). These funds account for approximately 65 percent of the market excluding CPP and QPP.
Source: Memorandum (March 2004), Watson Wyatt Canada.

Example 17 illustrates how to evaluate a set of allocations in light of a pension plan's risk and return objectives.

Example 17

Asset Allocation for the ASEC Defined-Benefit Pension Plan

George Fletcher, CFA, is chief financial officer of Apex Sports Equipment Corporation (ASEC), based in the United States. ASEC is a small company, and all of its revenues are domestic. ASEC also has a relatively young staff, and its defined-benefit pension plan currently has no retirees. The duration of the plan's liabilities is 20 years, and the discount rate applied to these liabilities is 7.5 percent for actuarial valuation purposes. The plan has $100 million in assets and a $5 million surplus. ASEC's pension plan has above-average risk tolerance. Fletcher has concluded that ASEC's current total annual return objective of 9 percent is appropriate—above-average risk tolerance makes it reasonable to attempt to achieve more than the return requirement of 7.5 percent. Exhibit 46 presents the existing asset allocation of ASEC's pension fund.

| Exhibit 46 | Original ASEC Strategic Asset Allocation |

Asset Class	Allocation
Large-cap U.S. equities	50%
Small-cap U.S. equities	10
U.S. 30-day Treasury bills	10
U.S. intermediate-term bonds (5-year duration)	20
U.S. long-term bonds (20-year duration)	10
Total	100%

(continued)

Exhibit 46 Continued

Asset Class	Allocation
Risk-free rate	5.0%
Expected total portfolio return (annual)	9.0%
Standard deviation (annual)	13.0%
Sharpe ratio	0.31

The ASEC pension oversight committee now requests that Fletcher research additional asset classes to include in the strategic asset allocation. The board tells him not to consider U.S. venture capital or real estate at this time. Fletcher conducts his research and concludes that both developed and emerging international markets offer diversification benefits. He constructs the four possible asset allocations shown in Exhibit 47.

Exhibit 47 Proposed Strategic Asset Allocations for ASEC

	Allocation			
Asset Class	A	B	C	D
Large-cap U.S. equities		35%	35%	50%
Small-cap U.S. equities		15	10	10
International developed market equities		15	10	
International emerging market equities		5	5	
U.S. 30-day Treasury bills		15		20
U.S. intermediate-term bonds (5-year duration)		15		20
U.S. long-term bonds (20-year duration)	100%		40	
Expected return (annual)	7.0%	9.5%	9.0%	8.5%
Standard deviation (annual)	8.0%	13.5%	11.5%	12.0%
Sharpe ratio	0.25	0.33	0.35	0.29

Based on the above information, recommend and justify two of these four asset allocations in Exhibit 47 for final consideration. The selections must:

- meet the pension plan's return objective;
- be consistent with the pension plan's risk tolerance;
- improve on the original asset allocation's expected risk-adjusted performance;
- have acceptable surplus volatility (the risk caused by a mismatch between plan assets and plan liabilities); and
- provide inflation protection.

Strategic Asset Allocation for Institutional Investors

> **Solution:**
>
> Justification exists for recommending either Asset Allocation B or Asset Allocation C as best for achieving the objectives simultaneously. The justification for choosing B or C might address the following points.
>
> i. *Meets the return objective.* The board's return objective is 9 percent. Only Allocations B and C have expected returns satisfying this long-term return objective.
>
> ii. *Consistent with risk tolerance.* As judged by the standard deviation of return compared with that of the original asset allocation, all four allocations in Exhibit 47 are acceptable.
>
> iii. *Risk-adjusted performance.* The Sharpe ratio is a common barometer of risk-adjusted performance; it estimates an investment's or portfolio's expected excess return per unit of risk. Asset Allocation C has a higher Sharpe ratio than that of the original portfolio (0.35 versus 0.31) and the highest Sharpe ratio of any allocation shown in Exhibit 47. Allocation B is the only other alternative with a higher Sharpe ratio than the original asset allocation. The difference between the Sharpe ratios for B and C is small.
>
> iv. *Acceptable surplus volatility.* Allocations A and C include long-term U.S. bonds with 20-year duration, which may make these allocations more closely match the stated duration of ASEC's liabilities (20 years) than the other allocations do. Closely matching the duration of assets and liabilities should reduce pension-surplus volatility. Therefore, some may view a strategy of matching bonds with 20-year duration to the 20-year-duration liabilities as appropriate because it may minimize surplus volatility.
>
> v. *Inflation protection.* Ongoing pension liabilities contain uncertainty in both the amount and timing of the cash outlay, because of factors such as varying future inflation and interest rates. In this context, Allocation A, which consists of 100 percent bonds, is not diversified and offers no protection against the risk that inflation will increase plan liabilities through inflation-related wage and benefit increases. Allocation C, which consists 40 percent in 20-year duration bonds and 60 percent in equities, is a better choice than A. Allocation B, which is 70 percent invested in a diversified portfolio of U.S. and non-U.S. equities, may provide even more protection than Allocation C against the erosion of values.
>
> In summary, the above considerations clearly point to a selection from Asset Allocation B or C.

9.2 Foundations and Endowments

We can consider foundations and endowments together, because they frequently share many characteristics as generally tax-exempt long-term investors with various spending commitments. These investors must generate a high long-term rate of return in order to provide a substantial spending flow as well as to compensate for inflation. For endowments that support institutions such as universities, the relevant inflation rates have generally exceeded those of the overall economy. Historically, fixed-income investments such as bonds or cash have not provided meaningful returns above inflation. In order to generate the high returns necessary to fund meaningful spending distributions, most endowments invest predominantly in equities or equity-like investments. Equities have been viewed as supplying the long-term growth bias, with bonds playing a role in diversification.[71]

Fiduciaries of endowments and foundations should focus on developing and adhering to appropriate long-term investment and asset allocation policies. Low-cost, easy-to-monitor, passive investment strategies are often their primary approach to implementing a strategic asset allocation. The institution's investment policy and approach should be understood and embraced by the organization's governing body to ensure steady and disciplined execution of the program through the markets' cycles and vicissitudes.

Because of limited resources to fund the costs and complexities of due diligence, small endowments have a constrained investment opportunity set compared with large endowments. Furthermore, the constrained opportunity set may preclude participation in high-return opportunities in some alternative asset classes. The National Association of College and University Business Officers reports that on 30 June 2004, endowments with more than $1 billion of assets were on average more than 28 percent invested in alternative assets. In comparison, endowments with between $50 million and $100 million were on average less than 7 percent invested in alternative assets. These small endowments had an average 22 percent allocation to fixed-income assets, compared with the 15 percent held by large endowments.[72]

Example 18 reviews the construction of an investment policy statement for a foundation and addresses the formulation of an appropriate strategic asset allocation in light of the IPS.

Example 18

Asset Allocation for the Help for Students Foundation

The Help for Students Foundation (HFS) exists to provide full scholarships to U.S. universities for gifted high school graduates who otherwise would be denied access to higher education. Additional facts concerning the organization are as follows:

- Per-student full scholarship costs, which have been rising rapidly for many years, were $30,000 this year and are expected to grow at least 4 percent annually for the indefinite future.

- The market value of HFS's investment assets is $300 million, currently allocated as shown below:
    - 35 percent to long-maturity U.S. Treasury bonds;
    - 10 percent to a diversified portfolio of corporate bond issues;
    - 10 percent to U.S. bank certificates of deposit (CDs); and
    - 45 percent to large-cap, income-oriented U.S. stocks.

- HFS's entire annual administrative costs are paid for by supporters' donations.

- An amount equal to 5 percent of the year-end market value of HFS's investment portfolio must be spent annually in order to preserve the foundation's existing tax-exempt status under U.S. law.

---

[71] Swensen (2000, p. 54) provides a clear statement of this viewpoint.
[72] See www.ncccs.cc.nc.us/Resource_Development/docs/Endowment%20study/02_SummaryofFindings.pdf.

The IPS currently governing trustee actions, unchanged since its adoption in the early 1960s, reads as follows:

> The Foundation's purpose is to provide university educations for as many deserving individuals as possible for as long as possible. Accordingly, investment emphasis should be on the production of income and the minimization of market risk. Because all expenses are in U.S. dollars, only domestic securities should be owned. It is the Trustees' duty to preserve and protect HFS's assets while maximizing its grant-making ability and maintaining its tax-exempt status.

After a long period in which board membership was unchanged, new and younger trustees are now replacing retiring members. As a result, many aspects of HFS's operations are under review, including the principles and guidelines that have shaped past investment decision making. Referring to the above facts, address the following tasks:

1. Identify four shortcomings of the existing IPS and explain why these policy aspects should be reviewed.
2. Create a new IPS for the foundation. In your response, be specific and complete with respect to investment objectives and constraints.
3. Using the policy created in Part 2 above, revise HFS's existing asset allocation and justify the resulting asset mix. You must choose from the following asset classes in constructing your response (calculations are not required).

Asset Class	Expected Total Return
Cash equivalents	4%
Medium- and long-term government bonds	7
Real estate	8
Large- and small-cap U.S. equities	10
International equities (EAFE)	12

Solution to 1:

Shortcomings of HFS's existing IPS, and an explanation of why these policy aspects should be reviewed, are as follows:

- The statement's "emphasis . . . on the production of income and the minimization of market risk" is inappropriate. The return objective should focus on total (expected) return rather than on its components. Furthermore, the return focus should be on enhancing either real total return or nominal return to include protection of purchasing power. Either maximization of return for a given level of (nondiversifiable) risk or minimization of risk for a given level of return is a more appropriate objective statement than the current one.
- The existing IPS does not specify important constraints normally included, such as time horizon, liquidity, tax considerations, legal and regulatory considerations, and unique needs.
- It is unclear whether the IPS of the early 1960s has been subjected to periodic review. The new statement should be reviewed at regular intervals (e.g., annually), and this review requirement should be specific in the IPS.

- It is unclear whether the four asset classes in which the foundation is now invested represent the only classes considered. In any event, the asset-mix policy should permit inclusion of more asset classes, including alternative investments.
- The IPS should specify the limits within which HFS's manager(s) may tactically allocate assets.
- The limitation of holding "only domestic securities" because "all expenses are in U.S. dollars" is inappropriate. At a minimum, non-U.S. investment, with some form of currency exchange risk hedge, should be considered when the return–risk tradeoff for these securities exceeds that on domestic securities.

Solution to 2:

A statement such as the following is appropriate:

Objectives

- **Return requirement.** In order to maintain its ability to provide inflation-adjusted scholarships and its tax-exempt status, HFS requires a real rate of return of 5 percent. The appropriate definition of inflation in this context is the 4 percent rate at which full scholarship cost per student is expected to increase.
- **Risk tolerance.** Given its very long time horizon, HFS has the ability to take moderate risk, with associated volatility in returns, in order to maintain purchasing power, as long as no undue volatility is introduced into the flow of resources to cover near-term scholarship payments.

Constraints

- **Liquidity requirements.** Given the size of HFS's assets and the predictable nature of its annual cash outflows, its liquidity needs can be easily ascertained and met. A systematic plan for future needs can be constructed and appropriate portfolio investment built to meet these planned needs.
- **Time horizon.** The foundation has a potentially infinite time horizon. A three-to-five year cycle of investment policy planning with reviews should be put into place.
- **Tax considerations.** Maintenance of HFS's tax-exempt status, including the 5 percent minimum spending requirement, should receive ongoing attention. The foundation's tax status should be examined and reviewed annually in connection with its annual audit report.
- **Legal and regulatory considerations.** Foundation trustees and others involved in investment decision making should understand and obey applicable state law and adhere to the prudent person standard.
- **Unique circumstances.** There are no significant circumstances not already considered under objectives and other constraints.

Solution to 3:

In designing a revised asset allocation, the board should assume long-term historical risk and correlation measures for each of the five asset classes. Some adjustments may be necessary, however, such as for the positive risk and correlation bias of real estate resulting from the use of appraisal value in calculating real estate returns.

> Given the answers to Parts 1 and 2 and the expected returns given in the statement of Part 1, increased investment in common stock, including large- and small-cap domestic equities and international equities, and in real estate (for its inflation hedging and diversification attributes) is warranted. Bank CDs should be minimized or eliminated; with no pressing liquidity needs, HFS can minimize its cash equivalent holdings. One appropriate allocation that includes both the current target (required) and possible future range (not required) is as follows:
>
> | Asset Class | Future Range | Current Target |
> | --- | --- | --- |
> | Cash equivalents | 0–5% | 2% |
> | Medium- and long-term (U.S.) Government bonds | 20–35 | 30 |
> | Real estate | 0–10 | 8 |
> | Large- and small-cap U.S. equities | 30–50 | 40 |
> | International equities (EAFE) | 5–20 | 20 |
>
> Equity securities make up 60 percent of the total in this allocation, an appropriate mix given the relatively moderate spread between fixed-income and equity expected returns.

9.3 Insurance Companies

An insurer's strategic asset allocation must complement and coordinate with the insurer's operating policy. Investment portfolio policy thus seeks to achieve the most appropriate mix of assets 1) to counterbalance the risks inherent in the mix of insurance products involved and 2) to achieve the stated return objectives. The insurer must consider numerous factors in arriving at the appropriate mix, the most important of which are asset/liability management concerns, regulatory influences, time horizons, and tax considerations.

Insurers are taxable enterprises, in contrast to defined-benefit pension plans, endowments, and most foundations. Therefore, insurers focus on after-tax return and risk. Like defined-benefit plans, however, insurers face contractual liabilities to insureds. As a result, an ALM approach to strategic asset allocation is generally chosen. ALM considerations include yield, duration, convexity, key rate sensitivity, value at risk, and the effects of asset risk on capital requirements given the spread of risk-based capital regulation.[73] Public policy frequently views insurance portfolios as quasi trust funds, further stressing the importance of managing risk.

We have discussed the ALM approach to strategic asset allocation in earlier sections; however, portfolio segmentation is a distinctive feature of life insurers' investment activities that we have not addressed previously. **Portfolio segmentation** is the creation of subportfolios within the general account portfolio, according to the product mix for each individual company. In this approach, the insurer groups liabilities according to the product line of business or segment. (Some insurers segment by individual product line; others group similar lines according to such characteristics as duration.) Portfolios are then constructed by segment in such a way that the most appropriate securities fund each product segment. An asset type's appropriateness is measured on at least three bases: expected return, interest rate risk (duration), and

---

[73] Value at risk is an estimate of the loss that we expect to be exceeded with a given level of probability over a specified time period.

credit risk characteristics. Each of these factors is evaluated relative to the competitive, actuarial, and statutory characteristics of the product line(s) being funded. Each segment has its own return objective, risk parameters, and liquidity characteristics.

Most life insurance companies in the United States and Canada have adopted some form of portfolio segmentation. Prior to segmentation, the return on invested assets in the general account was required to be allocated proportionately to various lines of insurance business (whole life, annuities, group, and so on).[74] Compared with that method, portfolio segmentation offers the following advantages:

- provides a focus for meeting return objectives by product line;
- provides a simple way to allocate investment income by line of business;
- provides more-accurate measurement of profitability by line of business. For example, the insurer can judge whether its returns cover the returns it offers on products with investment features such as annuities and guaranteed investment contracts (GICs);[75]
- aids in managing interest rate risk and/or duration mismatch by product line; and
- assists regulators and senior management in assessing the suitability of investments.

The portfolio segmentation approach establishes multiple asset allocations that are each appropriate for the product lines associated with the segments. Most life insurance companies have found that too many segments create span of control and suboptimization problems. Thus, most companies use relatively few segments. Furthermore, the optimization of the total portfolio is the ultimate controlling factor for determining the asset allocation for each segment and the portfolio as a whole.

Another development affecting insurers has been the expansion of their opportunity set. Exhibit 48 illustrates the evolution of the asset classes in which life insurers invest. Compared with the past, insurers now make use of a much wider array of investment vehicles. The individual entries in Exhibit 48 deserve comment.

Exhibit 48 Assets in Which Life Insurance Companies Invest

Traditional	Contemporary
Bonds	Bonds
Domestic	Domestic
(Aaa/AAA–Baa/BBB)	● Aaa/AAA–Ba/BB quality
	● Junk bonds
	● Residential mortgage backed
	● Commercial mortgage backed
	● Asset backed

---

[74] Allocation has generally been on the basis of the ratio of each line's reserves to total reserves. Companies use one of two methods for determining the investment yield by line of business. The investment year method credits the cash available for investment from a particular line of business with the new money rate (average yield for new investments in that year). The portfolio method allocates return to line of business on the basis of the cumulative investment return of the entire portfolio (not distinguishing among years). Statutorily, all general account assets of a life insurance company back all liabilities. For reporting purposes only, however, insurers can divide their general account portfolios into segments by line of business.

[75] A **guaranteed investment contract** is a debt instrument issued by insurers, usually in large denominations, that pays a guaranteed, generally fixed interest rate for a specified time period.

Exhibit 48   Continued

Traditional	Contemporary
	• Collateralized bond obligations
	• Collateralized loan obligations
	Nondomestic
	• Hedged
	• Unhedged
Mortgage loans: residential	Mortgage loans: commercial and residential
Stocks: common and preferred	Common and preferred stocks: domestic and international
Equity real estate	Equity real estate
Other: venture capital	Venture capital
	Hedge funds
	Derivative investments
	• Futures
	• Options
	• Interest rate swaps

Source: Mutual of Omaha Companies.

Fixed-income investments constitute the majority holding of most life and non-life insurers. Casualty insurance companies traditionally maintain a bond portfolio to offset insurance reserves, with capital and surplus funds invested largely in common stocks. As previously mentioned, insurance companies are sensitive to cash flow volatility and reinvestment risk, and fixed-income investments are made with these concerns in mind, as well as the expected compensation for bearing these risks. Insurance companies traditionally have been buyers of investment-grade bonds (Baa/BBB or higher), with emphasis on Baa/BBB and A quality bonds. Many insurers, especially large companies, occasionally purchase bonds of Ba/BB quality or below. Because of the importance of private placement bonds in life insurance company portfolios, credit analysis has long been considered one of the industry's strengths.

In recent years, many insurance companies have included some exposure to high-yield, below-investment-grade (junk) bonds. Further, historical default rates support an expectation for the realization of a significant net yield advantage over U.S. Treasuries from a diversified portfolio of junk bonds over the holding period. This projected advantage, typically anywhere from 300 to 600 basis points (net), is well in excess of the spreads over Treasuries available from Baa/BBB securities and even mortgage loans. In the United States, there are generally regulatory constraints on junk bond holdings. For example, in New York, regulations limit junk bonds to 20 percent of assets for those insurance companies doing business in that state. Also, the default rates on junk bonds, which exceeded 10 percent in the early 1990s and again in the early 2000s, have tempered some of the life insurance industry's enthusiasm for this asset class.

In addition to credit quality, insurers must also consider bonds' taxability. In the United States, bonds issued by states and municipalities are generally exempt from taxation at the federal level (state bonds are also exempt from state taxes, and municipal bonds from municipal and state taxes, in general). For tax reasons, non-life insurers have often been major purchasers of such tax-exempt bonds.

For a life insurance company, the selection of bond maturities is substantially dictated by its need to manage the interest rate risk exposure arising from asset/liability duration mismatch. Consequently, life insurers typically structure the bond portfolio's maturity schedule in line with the estimated liability cash outflows, at least in the short and intermediate term.

Insurers hold equity investments for several reasons. Life insurers market a variety of products such as variable annuities and variable life insurance policies that may be linked to equity investments. Insurers then hold equity investments in the separate account(s) associated with those products. Another important function of the investment operation is to provide growth of surplus to support the expansion in insurance volume; common stocks, equity investments in real estate, and venture capital have been the investment alternatives most widely used to achieve surplus growth. Surplus adequacy is a growing concern for the life insurance industry. Companies are looking at more-aggressive capital appreciation-oriented strategies as well as financial leverage to supplement the narrowing contributions to surplus from the newer product lines. At the same time, concerns regarding valuation risk (discussed earlier) have led most life insurers to limit common stock holdings (at market value) as a percentage of surplus rather than as a percentage of assets as specified in the statutes.

Insurers (particularly life insurers) generally maintain limited liquidity reserves; most life insurers depend on their fixed-income portfolio's maturity schedule and their ability to control interest rate risk to assure that surrenders and/or policy loans can be funded with little or no loss of principal income. Casualty insurers, especially those with relatively short duration liabilities, tend to have higher liquidity requirements than other insurers.

Example 19 provides an example of an asset allocation for a stock life insurer (a life insurer organized as a corporation owned by shareholders).

9.4 Banks

Banks are financial intermediaries with a traditional focus on taking deposits and lending money. As such, they are taxable investors with predominantly short- and intermediate-term liabilities.

Although we can view a bank's strategic asset allocation from the perspective of all bank assets including loans, real estate (including bank premises) and so forth, a bank's securities portfolio is subject to a distinct set of regulations and is traditionally treated separately.

As discussed in the reading on managing institutional investor portfolios, a bank's securities portfolio plays an important role in 1) managing the balance sheet's overall interest rate risk, 2) managing liquidity (assuring adequate cash is available to meet liabilities), 3) producing income, and 4) managing credit risk. The first concern is the most important and dictates an ALM approach to asset allocation. Banks' portfolios of loans and leases are generally not very liquid and may carry substantial credit risk. Therefore, a bank's securities portfolio plays a balancing role in providing a ready source of liquidity and in offsetting loan-portfolio credit risk.

Example 19

An Asset Allocation for a Stock Life Insurer

ABC Life is a hypothetical stock life insurer. The following asset allocation would not be unusual for a stock life insurer. The allocation reflects regulatory constraints operative in the United States.

Strategic Asset Allocation for Institutional Investors

Asset Class	Target	Permissible Range
Cash equivalents	2%	1–5%
Public bonds	35	30–40
Government	2	0–5
Corporate	15	10–20
Mortgage backed	8	4–12
Residential	5	2–8
Commercial	3	0–6
Asset backed	5	2–8
International	5	2–8
Private placement bonds	32	27–37
Corporate	20	15–25
Asset backed	10	5–15
International	2	0–4
Public common stocks	10	5–15
Large cap	5	2–8
Small cap	3	1–5
International	2	0–4
Private equity	5	0–10
Venture capital	2	0–4
Buyout	3	0–5
Commercial mortgage loans	10	5–15
Apartment	4	2–6
Industrial	3	1–5
Office	3	1–5
Retail mortgage loans	2	0–5
Real estate	4	0–6
Commercial	4	0–6
Residential	0	0–0
International	0	0–0
Land	0	0–0

As with the portfolios of insurers, public policy usually views bank portfolios as quasi public trust funds. Thus banks typically face detailed regulatory restrictions on maximum holdings of asset types, often stated as a percentage of capital. In turn, the risk of assets affects banks' costs through the operation of risk-based capital rules.

Example 20

An Asset Allocation for a Commercial Bank

William Bank is a hypothetical U.S. commercial bank. Although a more detailed breakdown of asset classes would be more realistic, the asset allocation presented below shows the typical emphasis on high-credit-quality debt instruments.

The target percentages are stated as a percentage of the securities portfolio, for consistency with the presentation elsewhere, but regulatory guidelines are as a percentage of capital (capital stock and surplus plus undivided profits).

Investment Portfolio Asset Type	Target	Regulatory Guideline
U.S. Treasury bonds	10%	no limitation
Agency obligations	65	no limitation
Tax-exempt general obligations	3	no limitation
Tax-exempt other	5	<4% of capital, >Baa/BBB
Corporate bonds	12	<10% of capital, >Baa/BBB
Money-market preferred stock	5	<15% of capital

10. TACTICAL ASSET ALLOCATION[76]

Tactical asset allocation (TAA) involves deliberately underweighting or overweighting asset classes relative to their target weights in the policy portfolio in an attempt to add value. TAA is active management at the asset-class level. Thus in a top-down perspective, TAA would follow the strategic asset allocation decision and stand one level above decisions about how to manage money within an asset class. TAA can be conducted independently of the within-class investment decisions by using derivative securities, a cost-efficient means for changing asset-class exposures. In that case, TAA can be described as an overlay strategy.

TAA is based on short-term expectations and perceived disequilibria. We know from prior discussion that strategic asset allocation reflects the investor's long-term capital market expectations. That concept is logical because strategic asset allocation concerns meeting the investor's long-term objectives. The investor's short-term views may well differ from his long-term views, however. TAA involves tactical bets to exploit those differences. Economically speaking, it seeks to exploit transitory deviations of asset-class values from their expected long-term relationships. An investor may make occasional tactical weight adjustments in some circumstances or may have an ongoing and more systematic program of tactical adjustments. Both can be described as tactical asset allocation. TAA can be managed in-house or delegated to one of the many professional investment managers who run TAA programs.

TAA is frequently based on the following three principles:

1. *Market prices tell explicitly what returns are available.* Cash yields reveal the immediate nominal return accorded short-term investors. The yield to maturity of T-bills is the nominal reward for holding them to maturity. Thus, at least for this and similar pure discount instruments, investors have *objective knowledge* of prospective returns. Although prices yield less direct information about prospective return for other asset classes, we can at least make educated estimates. For example, we could use dividend yield plus growth rate to estimate the return to equities. Inevitably, reality will not quite match these expectations. Nevertheless history suggests that simple objective measures provide a useful, objective guide to future rewards.

---

[76] This section was contributed by Robert D. Arnott.

Tactical Asset Allocation

As an illustration, Exhibit 49 demonstrates one method for constructing return expectations (many others are in industry use as well). Almost any investment we might choose has three components to return: income, growth in income, and changing valuation levels (changes in the value that the market assigns to each dollar of income). For the last 77 years, U.S. stocks delivered a real return, over and above inflation, of nearly 7 percent. This return consisted of 4.2 percent from yield, a growth rate in dividends that was 1.2 percent above the rate of inflation, and 1.5 percent from a tripling in the price/dividend ratio (a 70 percent decline in dividend yields). Looking to the future, can we count on continued expansion in the price/dividend ratio? Doing so would be dangerous, because the ratio could as easily go the other way. Can we count on 4.2 percent from income? Not when the current market yield is 1.8 percent as of this writing. This method thus suggests a 3 percent real return as one possible starting point for expectations of U.S. equity returns.

Exhibit 49 Long-Term Return Attribution for U.S. Equities

	January 1926–September 2003	As of September 2003
Average dividend yield	4.2%	1.8%
Growth in real dividends	1.2	1.2
Change in valuation levels[a]	1.5	0.0
Real stock return	6.9	3.0
Less average real bond yield	2.1	2.4
Less bond valuation change[b]	−0.3	0.0
Real bond return	1.8	2.4
Return differential	5.1	0.6

[a]Yields went from 5.1 percent to 1.6 percent, representing a 1.5 percent annual increase in the price/dividend valuation level.
[b]Bond yields fell during this period, and real yields on reinvestment were also poor during much of this span.

2. *Relative expected returns reflect relative risk perceptions.* When investors perceive more risk, they demand payment for assuming it. If expected equity returns are particularly high compared with bond expected returns, the market is clearly according a substantial risk premium to stocks. It does so when investors in general are uneasy with the outlook for stocks. In the 20 years following the deepest point of the Great Depression of the 1920s, equity dividend yields were significantly higher than the yields on bonds. Apprehensive of a replay of the depression, stockholders demanded a compensatory premium. Ultimately, the markets rewarded those investors willing to bear equity risk. Conversely, as recently as 1981, demoralized U.S. bond investors priced those securities to reflect their unprecedented volatility amid fears of rebounding inflation.

In the mid- to late-1990s, investors embraced the concept that stocks had little risk when measured over the long-term, which lowered their perception of equity risk. Many investors greatly increased their stock holdings without regard to their investment time horizons. As stock prices rose and the risk premium of stocks declined, so the prospects of future rewards from stocks declined as well. The subsequent bursting of the stock market bubble in March 2000 was merely the effect of the market reestablishing an appropriate risk premium for what is still the riskier asset class.

Exhibit 50 illustrates the link between risk and reward in U.S. markets for the last 30 years. It shows how the risk premium that is delivered for investing in stocks rather than bonds varies through time, in line with the relative volatility of stocks over bonds. The volatility is calculated as the mean absolute deviation of global stock total returns divided by the mean absolute deviation of global bond total returns during the prior five years.

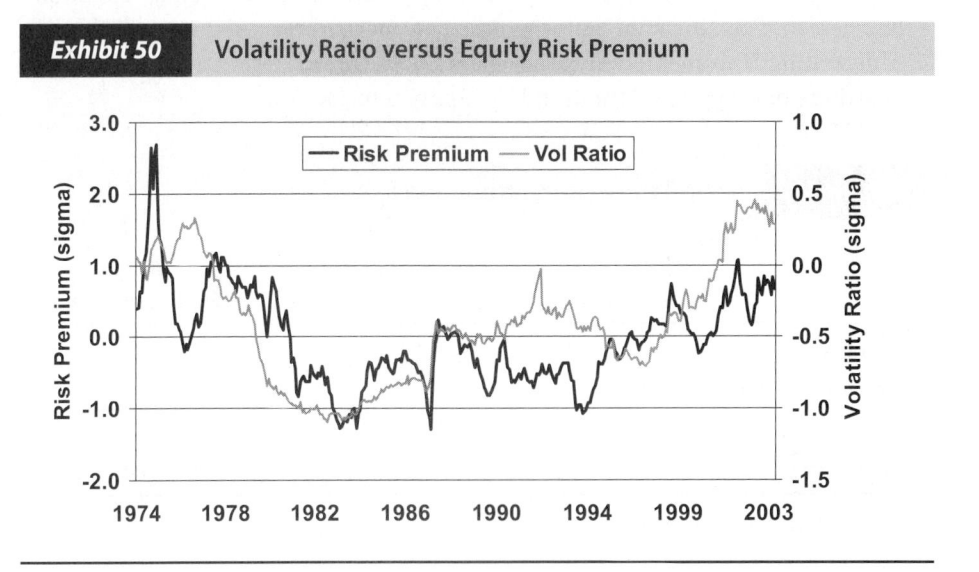

Exhibit 50   Volatility Ratio versus Equity Risk Premium

In 1988, the global equity risk premium dipped below normal levels and remained low for most of the next decade. At the same time, the global volatility ratio rose, and these two measures diverged until the volatility and risk premium again converged in the mid-1990s. In the long term, these measures tend to track one another. In the short term, they provide information when they diverge.

If relative expected returns reflect relative risk perceptions and those perceptions do not have a solid economic basis, overweighting the out-of-favor asset class can be fruitful. To illustrate such an analysis, the period just subsequent to the end of 2003 saw the volatility ratio rise in line with, albeit somewhat faster than, the equity risk premium. This implies that the equity risk premium, although still high by historical standards, may be at least partially explained by a higher than usual volatility ratio, and hence it is not as bullish an indicator for equities as it would be otherwise. The equity risk premium is best viewed in the context of the relative risk of global markets, not in isolation.

3. *Markets are rational and mean reverting.* If the TAA manager can identify departures from equilibrium in the relative pricing of asset classes, the manager may try to exploit them with knowledge that departures from equilibrium compress a proverbial spring that drives the system back towards balance. If 6 percent bonds produce zero return over a certain year (by declining in price enough to offset the coupon), they then offer a higher yield in subsequent years to a prospective holder. Because this process is inherently finite, these bonds, short of default, will eventually produce their promised returns. Bond price changes, moving cyclically, exhibit negative annual serial correlation, a characteristic prized by contrarian tactical asset allocators.

Tactical Asset Allocation

In the same way, differences between expected return on equities and realized return persist over time, but only if earnings growth estimates are inaccurate. They typically are inaccurate, of course, but the law of large numbers provides more confidence in estimating returns of asset classes than individual securities. Similarly, aggregated reported earnings are more meaningful than earnings reported on a company-by-company basis, because the most egregious earnings manipulations are tempered by results from more-truthful peers. Similar to bond yield for bonds, earnings yields on stocks provide an effective (if approximate) valuation measure of future stock returns.

The above three principles address the returns that an investor may expect the markets to deliver when they function rationally and tend toward fair value. The suggested tactical asset allocation decisions were contrarian in nature. The tactical asset allocator should be aware that if a rule for trading leads to superior performance, investors on the losing side of the trades may eventually stop playing; market prices will then adjust to reflect changes in supply and demand, and a trading rule may cease to work. Furthermore, the tactical asset allocator should be aware that deviations from fair value based on historical analysis could persist if the economic environment has changed. Factors such as:

- changes in assets' underlying risk attributes;
- changes in central bank policy;
- changes in expected inflation; and
- position in the business cycle

need to be considered in evaluating relative valuations, because they can either mark changes in return regimes or otherwise explain current pricing. A U.S. TAA manager (managing a mix of U.S. stocks, U.S. bonds, and cash) might specify one weighting of relative value and business cycle variables during periods of expansionary Federal Reserve policy (indicated by Fed discount rate decreases) and another weighting during periods of restrictive Fed policy. Fed policy changes could mark periods in which the relationships between stocks and bonds differ. Besides relative value and business cycle variables, some TAA managers use technical/sentiment variables in assessing future asset-class prospects. Price momentum is an example of a technical/sentiment indicator. It is not contradictory that an asset could exhibit momentum at a short time horizon and mean reversion at another, longer, time horizon.

Risk and costs deserve close attention. TAA may decrease or increase the absolute risk level of the investor's overall portfolio, depending on manager skill, the type of TAA discipline involved, and the direction of markets during the time period considered. Relative to the strategic asset allocation, however, TAA is a source of tracking risk. To manage that risk, in practice, TAA managers often are limited to making adjustments within given bands or tactical ranges around target asset-class weights. As an example, the tactical range could be the target weight ± 5 percent or ± 10 percent of portfolio value. With a ± 10 percent tactical range and a 60 percent target for equities, the TAA manager could weight equities within a range of 50 percent to 70 percent. At least one study has found that within-asset-class active management is a much greater source of risk relative to the strategic asset allocation than the selection of tactical weights.[77]

TAA must overcome a transaction-costs barrier to be advantageous. The potential benefits of any tactical adjustment must be examined on an after-costs basis.

Example 21 illustrates in a simplified setting the basic mechanics of a TAA program. Example 22 presents several more advanced concepts.

---

[77] See Ammann and Zimmerman (2001).

Example 21

Global Tactical Asset Allocation Adjustments

Georgina Henry is chief investment officer of the Glenmore University Endowment (GUE) based in Canada. GUE's strategic asset allocation is as follows, where percentages refer to proportions of the total portfolio.

Global equities		70%
Canadian equities	30%	
U.S. equities	30	
European equities	10	
Global fixed income		30%
Canadian bonds	20	
U.S. bonds	10	

Exhibit 51 gives Henry's asset class expectations.

Exhibit 51 Total Return Expectations for Asset Classes

Asset Class	Long-Term	Short-Term
Global equities	A	B
Canadian equities	10%	12%
U.S. equities	8	8
European equities	7	7
Global fixed income	C	D
Canadian bonds	5%	6%
U.S. bonds	5	3

GUE runs a top-down global tactical asset allocation program that first looks at the overall allocation between global equities and global fixed income, and then at the asset allocation within global equities and global fixed income. Assume that the risk characteristics of asset classes are constant.

1. Calculate the long-term and short-term return expectations for global equities (*A* and *B*, respectively) and global fixed income (*C* and *D*, respectively).

2. Determine and justify the changes in portfolio weights (relative to the policy portfolio target weights) that would result from a global tactical asset allocation program.

Solution to 1:

Canadian equities, U.S. equities, and European equities represent respectively 30%/70% = 0.4286, 30%/70% = 0.4286, and 10%/70% = 0.1429 of global equities. Therefore, for global equities,

$$A = (0.4286 \times 10\%) + (0.4286 \times 8\%) + (0.1429 \times 7\%) = 8.7143\%, \text{ or } 8.71\%$$

$$B = (0.4286 \times 12\%) + (0.4286 \times 8\%) + (0.1429 \times 7\%) = 9.5714\%, \text{ or } 9.57\%$$

Tactical Asset Allocation

Global equities' short-term expected return at 9.57 percent is above the long-term expectation of 8.71 percent because Canadian equities are expected in the short term to outperform their long-term expected return. Canadian bonds and U.S. bonds represent respectively 20%/30% = 0.6667 and 10%/30% = 0.3333 of global fixed income. Therefore, for global fixed income,

$C = (0.6667 \times 5\%) + (0.3333 \times 5\%) = 5\%$

$D = (0.6667 \times 6\%) + (0.3333 \times 3\%) = 5\%$

Global fixed income's short-term expected return at 5 percent equals its long-term expectation. Within global fixed income, however, Canadian bonds are expected short-term at 6 percent to outperform their long-term expected return while U.S. bonds are expected short term at 3 percent to underperform their long-term expected return.

Solution to 2:

The results in Part 1 suggest three actions:

- Because global equities appear undervalued compared with global fixed income in the short term, increase the weight on global equities from 70 percent and decrease the weight on global fixed income from 30 percent. The justification is that the short-term expected return on global equities is higher than its long-term expectation, while the short-term expected return on global fixed income is unchanged from its long-term expectation.

- Within global equities, overweight Canadian equities versus their target weight of 30 percent and decrease the weight on U.S. and European equities. Although the short-term expected returns on U.S. and European equities are unchanged from their long-term expectations, Canadian equities are expected to outperform short term.

- Within the new global fixed-income allocation, overweight Canadian bonds and underweight U.S. bonds, reflecting their short-term expected performance.

Example 22

A Tactical Asset Allocation Decision

William Davenport is the chief investment officer of an endowment that is invested 45 percent in U.S. equities, 15 percent in non-U.S. developed market equities, and 40 percent in U.S. Treasury Inflation-Indexed Securities (often called TIPS). The endowment annually reviews its strategic asset allocation. Its IPS authorizes tactical ranges of ± 10 percent in each asset class. Based on his own past observations and his reading of the investment literature, Davenport believes the following:

- U.S. monthly equity returns are less sensitive to the U.S. business contractions than monthly equity returns in European markets and Japan. That is, in U.S. recessions, U.S. equities' returns may actually be relatively better than equity market returns in Europe and Japan.

- An increase in the yield of a 1-year Treasury note indicates a decrease in the probability of a recession in one year's time.

> Based on a decrease in the yield of U.S. 1-year T-notes, Davenport has suggested a 55/5/40 U.S. equities/developed market equities/TIPS tactical asset allocation.
>
> 1. Evaluate whether the recommended tactical asset allocation is feasible.
> 2. Appraise the logic of the recommendation.
> 3. Evaluate the additional information that should be considered before adopting Davenport's recommendation.
>
> **Solution to 1:**
>
> Davenport's TAA suggestion is just within the tactical ranges allowed by the endowment's IPS. Therefore, the suggestion is feasible.
>
> **Solution to 2:**
>
> If Davenport's beliefs are correct, the decrease in the T-note yield indicates an increase in the probability of a U.S. recession in one year. If a recession occurs, he expects U.S. stocks to outperform non-U.S. equities. Therefore, shifting funds from non-U.S. to U.S. equities is logical.
>
> **Solution to 3:**
>
> The following information should be assessed:
>
> - The costs of the tactical adjustment in relation to the expected benefits.
> - The increase in tracking risk and the change in expected absolute risk in relation to the expected benefits.
> - The economic logic of Davenport's beliefs. If they have an economic logic, it is more likely that relationships based on past observations will hold for the future.
> - The strength of the expected relationships. Davenport is suggesting making the maximum permissible allocation to U.S. equities. After the adjustment, the portfolio may be less well diversified than previously. Is the size of the bet justified?
> - The presence of any factor such as a change in the risk attributes of assets that may make past relationships fail to hold in the future.

SUMMARY

Portfolio management involves steps of planning, execution, and feedback. In the planning step, strategic asset allocation plays a pivotal, top-level role in converting the investor's objectives, constraints, and long-term capital market expectations into an appropriate portfolio. Tactical asset allocation is a major discipline for attempting to capitalize on perceived disequilibria among asset-class relative values. In this reading we have presented and illustrated the fundamentals of both disciplines.

- Strategic asset allocation is the allocation of funds among different asset classes so as to satisfy an investor's long-term objectives and constraints.
- The strategic asset allocation specifies the investor's desired exposures to systematic risk.
- Tactical asset allocation involves making short-term adjustments to asset-class weights based on short-term predictions of relative performance among asset classes.

Summary

- Asset allocation appears to explain a large fraction in the variation of returns over time for a given portfolio. The proportion of the cross-sectional variation of portfolios' returns explained by portfolios' different asset allocations appears to be smaller but still very substantial.

- There are two major approaches to strategic asset allocation: asset-only and asset/liability management. The asset-only approach does not take explicit account of the investor's liabilities, if any. The asset/liability management approach involves explicitly modeling the investor's liabilities and adopting the asset allocation that is optimal in relation to funding liabilities.

- A dynamic approach to asset allocation has the advantage over a static approach in that it takes into account the links between the asset allocations chosen at different periods. The disadvantages of a dynamic approach are its greater cost and complexity.

- The specification of a numerical return objective should account for the costs of earning investment returns and inflation as well as their compound effects through time. A multiplicative return objective takes compounding into account and is the most precise; an additive objective does not and thus will underestimate the return needed, despite providing a quick approximation. For instance, if the spending rate is 5 percent, the inflation rate 3 percent, and the costs of earning investment returns 0.30 percent, the multiplicative objective is (1.05)(1.03)(1.003) − 1 = 0.0847, or 8.47 percent; the corresponding additive objective is 0.05 + 0.03 + 0.003 = 0.083, or 8.3 percent.

- The asset classes chosen for strategic asset allocation should satisfy the following five criteria: 1) Assets within an asset class should be relatively homogeneous, 2) asset classes should be mutually exclusive, 3) asset classes should be diversifying, 4) the asset classes as a group should make up a preponderance of world investable wealth, and 5) the asset class should have the capacity to absorb a significant fraction of the investor's portfolio without seriously affecting the portfolio's liquidity.

- After the preliminaries of specifying and listing IPS-permissible asset classes, asset allocation involves a series of steps on the capital markets side and the investor side. On the capital markets side, the steps are to 1) observe capital market conditions; 2) formulate a prediction procedure; and 3) obtain expected returns, risks, and correlations from the prediction procedure based on capital market conditions. On the investor side, the steps are to 1) observe the investor's assets, liabilities, net worth, and risk attitudes; 2) formulate the investor's risk tolerance function; and 3) obtain the investor's risk tolerance. The optimization approach (optimizer) is specified and the investor's asset mix is determined using the optimizer, using the investor's capital market expectations and risk tolerance as inputs. Finally returns are observed, which provides feedback for the next asset allocation review.

- The mean–variance approach to asset allocation involves selecting the efficient portfolio that best satisfies the investor's risk and return objectives and constraints.

- Simulation and mean–variance analysis are used to develop the resampled efficient frontier. Because the procedure takes account of estimation error, the resampled efficient portfolios on the frontier may be more diversified and stable over time than conventional mean–variance efficient portfolios. The resampled efficient frontier is used as if it were a conventional efficient frontier to select the portfolio that best satisfies the investor's needs.

- The Black–Litterman approach with a constraint against short sales reverse-engineers the expected returns implicit in a diversified market portfolio; it combines those expected returns with the investor's own views (if any) in a systematic way that takes into account the investor's confidence in his or her views.

- Monte Carlo simulation is used to evaluate a proposed asset allocation's multiperiod performance. Important real-life complications such as cash inflows and outflows, taxes, and transaction costs can be modeled in a Monte Carlo simulation.

- The ALM approach to strategic asset allocation focuses on optimizing with respect to net worth or surplus (the value of assets minus the present value of liabilities). In its mean–variance implementation, ALM involves selecting a portfolio from the surplus efficient frontier; Monte Carlo simulation is helpful in evaluating the range of outcomes of a surplus efficient portfolio in funding liabilities over the investor's time horizon.

- Experience-based approaches include the ideas that a 60/40 stock/bond allocation is appropriate for the average investor; that the allocation to bonds should increase with the investor's risk aversion; that the allocation to stocks should increase with the investor's time horizon; and that younger investors should allocate more to stocks than older investors.

- In a mean–variance approach to asset allocation, a non-negativity constraint on asset-class weights is specified. A small number of portfolios called corner portfolios completely describe the resulting efficient frontier. We can find the weights of any portfolio on the minimum-variance frontier (and efficient frontier) using the two corner portfolios that bracket it in terms of expected return. This result allows us to easily identify the composition of any efficient portfolio.

- Strategic asset allocation for individual investors should consider both their financial capital and their human capital (the present value of their expected future labor income). Human capital as a share of total capital tends to decline as an individual approaches retirement. Consequently, if an investor's human capital is risk free or low risk and uncorrelated with his financial capital, his optimal allocation to stocks tends to decline as he approaches retirement, all else equal. To the extent the investor's human capital is positively correlated with stocks, the investor's allocation to stocks will be less than otherwise. Individual investors have a focus on after-tax returns.

- Defined-benefit pension plans, life insurance companies, non-life insurance companies, and banks face high penalties for not meeting liabilities. Insurance companies and banks take an ALM approach to investing; DB pension plans frequently do also, or at least take ALM considerations into account. By contrast, foundations and endowments tend to take an asset-only approach to investing. Of the investors listed, life and non-life insurance companies and banks are taxable and have a focus on after-tax returns.

PRACTICE PROBLEMS FOR READING 21

1. Paula Williams is chair of the Investment Committee of the Robinson Furniture Manufacturing (RFM) defined-benefit pension plan. The committee has established the strategic asset allocation given in Exhibit 1. The RFM pension liability can be modeled approximately as a short position in a long-term bond. The expected return on a long-term bond is 4.5 percent.

Exhibit 1   RFM Policy Portfolio

Asset Class	Target Allocation	Permissible Range
1. Domestic equities	40%	30–50%
2. International equities	10	5–15
3. Domestic long-term bonds	25	20–30
4. Inflation-protected bonds	25	20–30

Exhibit 2   Policy Portfolio: Statistics

Measure	
Expected return	8%
Standard deviation of return	12%
Sharpe ratio	0.40
Probability portfolio return is below 4.5% over one year	0.10

   A. Contrast the appropriateness of using indexed investments versus a single security to represent domestic and international equities in the RFM policy portfolio, given the economic role of strategic asset allocation.

   B. Discuss the effects of the following implementation choices on the measured importance of RFM's policy portfolio:

   i. rebalancing to the policy mix.

   ii. investing actively within an asset class or indexing to asset.

   iii. adopting a policy portfolio that is much different from those of peers.

   An institutional analyst makes a presentation to the Investment Committee showing promising past results from an investment program based on the following two variables, measured quarterly:

   X = (Earnings yield − Real short-term bond yield)
       − Past average difference

   Y = Change in OECD (Organization for Economic Cooperation and Development) leading indicators

The analyst proposes that the weightings of domestic and international equities be adjusted quarterly within a band of ±10 percentage points of their target portfolio weights based on the values of X and Y.

C. Identify the type of investment program being suggested and critique the proposal.

The Investment Committee of RFM hears a second analyst presentation. This analyst recommends that the committee adopt a dynamic ALM approach to choosing its strategic asset allocation.

D. Justify the analyst's recommendation, explain the differences between a static and a dynamic ALM approach to asset allocation, and explain an advantage and a disadvantage of the dynamic approach.

E. Identify the risk-minimizing strategic asset allocation from an ALM perspective.

The following information relates to Questions 2–4

Exhibit 3 Forecasts

	Investor's Forecasts	
Asset Allocation	Expected Return	Standard Deviation of Return
A	11.5%	18%
B	8	14
C	6	10

2. On the scale discussed in the reading, Robert Langland's risk aversion (R_A) is 5. Recommend an asset allocation for him.

3. The Garrett Foundation would like to choose an asset allocation that minimizes the probability of returns below its annual spending rate of 3.5 percent. Recommend an asset allocation for the foundation.

4. William Ernst needs to spend 5 percent from his portfolio annually. He anticipates that inflation will be 2.4 percent annually. Ernst incurs expenses of 60 basis points a year in investing his portfolio. Which asset allocations satisfy Ernst's return requirement?

5. Critique the following specifications of asset classes:
   A. U.S. equities, world equities, U.S. bonds.
   B. Canadian equities, Canadian bonds, alternative assets.
   C. Small-cap U.S. equities, large-cap U.S. equities, real estate, private equity, ex-U.S. developed market equities, emerging market equities, ex-U.S. bonds.

6. The Ingo Fund is a Swedish foundation currently invested in Swedish equities and government bonds. The portfolio has a Sharpe ratio of 0.40. The fund is considering adding U.S. real estate to its portfolio. U.S. real estate as represented by the NACREIF (National Council of Real Estate Investment Fiduciaries) Index has a predicted Sharpe ratio of 0.12; the predicted correlation with the existing portfolio is 0.35. Based solely on the above information, determine whether the Ingo Fund should add U.S. real estate to its portfolio.

7. Contrast the elements in the strategic asset allocation process that are relatively stable to those that frequently change.

Practice Problems for Reading 21

8. Compare and contrast the global minimum variance portfolio with the minimum surplus variance portfolio.

9. Claudine Robert is treasurer and vice chair of the Investment Committee of Le Fonds de Recherche des Maladies du Coeur (FRMC), a French foundation with €95,000,000 in assets that supports medical research relating to heart diseases and treatments. For the annual asset allocation review, Robert has prepared the set of capital market expectations shown in Exhibit 4.

Exhibit 4 Capital Market Expectations

Asset Class	Expected Return	Standard Deviation	Correlation 1	2	3	4
1. French equities	8.6%	20%	1.00			
2. Ex-France equities	6.7	15	0.65	1.00		
3. French bonds	4.1	10	0.34	0.25	1.00	
4. Real estate	5.0	12	0.50	0.35	0.17	1.00

Based on these capital market expectations, Robert has developed the analysis shown in Exhibit 5.

Exhibit 5 Corner Portfolios

Portfolio	Expected Return	Standard Deviation	Sharpe Ratio	Asset Class (Portfolio Weight) 1	2	3	4
1	8.60%	20.00%	0.330	100.00%	0.00%	0.00%	0.00%
2	7.91	16.78	0.352	63.53	36.47	0.00	0.00
3	7.55	15.48	0.358	53.22	37.23	0.00	9.55
4	5.03	8.42	0.360	0.00	24.70	43.30	32.00
5	4.69	8.15	0.329	0.00	10.90	55.56	33.53

Note: Risk-free rate = 2 percent.

Robert also has noted the following facts:

- FRMC's spending rate is 3.5 percent, the expected long-term expected inflation rate is 2.25 percent, and the cost of earning investment returns has averaged 43.6 basis points annually.
- FRMC has a multiplicative return requirement based on the spending rate, the expected inflation rate, and the cost of earning investment returns.
- FRMC is not permitted to borrow to purchase risky assets.

A. Describe how corner portfolios arise and explain how to use them in strategic asset allocation.

B. Compute FRMC's return requirement (in percent, to two decimal places) and contrast it to an additive return requirement based on the same inputs.

C. Recommend the strategic asset allocation that Robert should present for approval at the asset allocation review.

The following information relates to Questions 10–11

- In Exhibit 6, plots are based on applying portfolio weights to true return parameters (mean returns, variances of returns, and correlations).
- In Exhibit 7, each of the three series of points (e.g., 1, 2, 3, 4, 5 is a series) represents one simulated efficient frontier from one simulation trial.

Exhibit 6

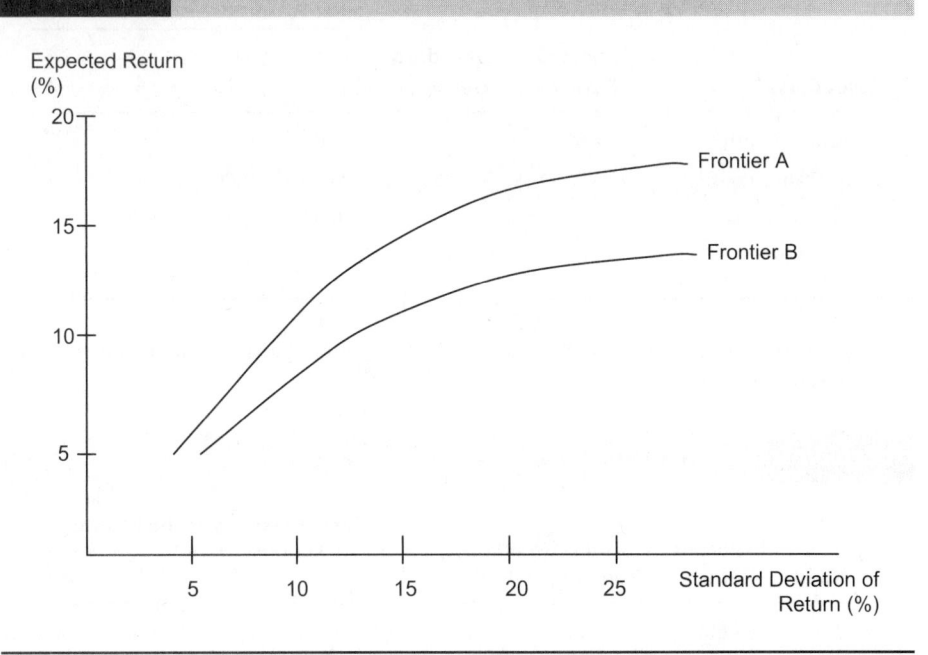

Plot of Expected Return (%) vs. Standard Deviation of Return (%) showing two curves: Frontier A (upper) and Frontier B (lower).

Exhibit 7

Scatter plot of Expected Return vs. Standard Deviation of Return showing three series of points labeled 1–5, 1′–5′, and 1″–5″.

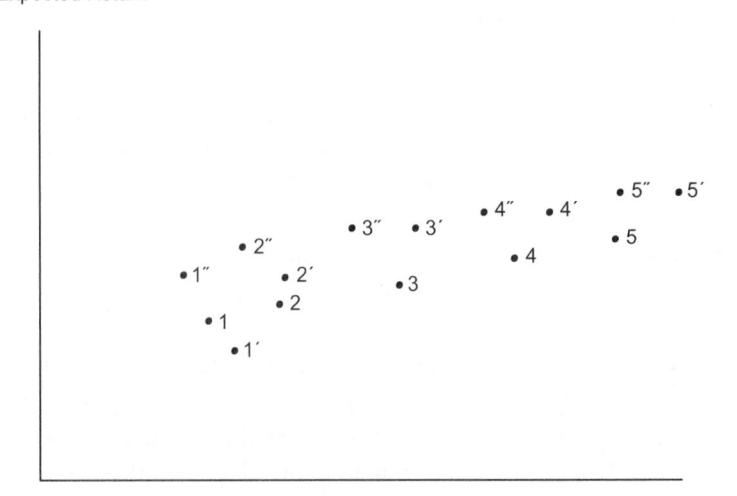

Practice Problems for Reading 21

10. **A.** In Exhibit 6, if Frontier B is a mean–variance efficient frontier in which the efficient portfolios' portfolio weights reflect perfect knowledge of the true return parameters, discuss whether Frontier A could be:

    i. the conventional mean–variance efficient frontier.

    ii. the resampled efficient frontier.

    B. Identify and explain the set of inputs to which mean–variance optimization is most sensitive.

11. **A.** Identify the scatter of points in Exhibit 7.

    B. Describe how to compute a resampled efficient frontier from the scatter of points shown in Exhibit 7.

12. John Stevenson retired at the end of 2002 at age 65. His $1,000,000 portfolio is invested 70 percent in common stocks and 30 percent in bonds. He anticipates liquidating $50,000 a year from the portfolio during retirement. Exhibit 8 gives the results of a Monte Carlo simulation showing the performance of the 70/30 asset allocation (net of the planned liquidations) in real dollar terms given Stevenson's capital market expectations.

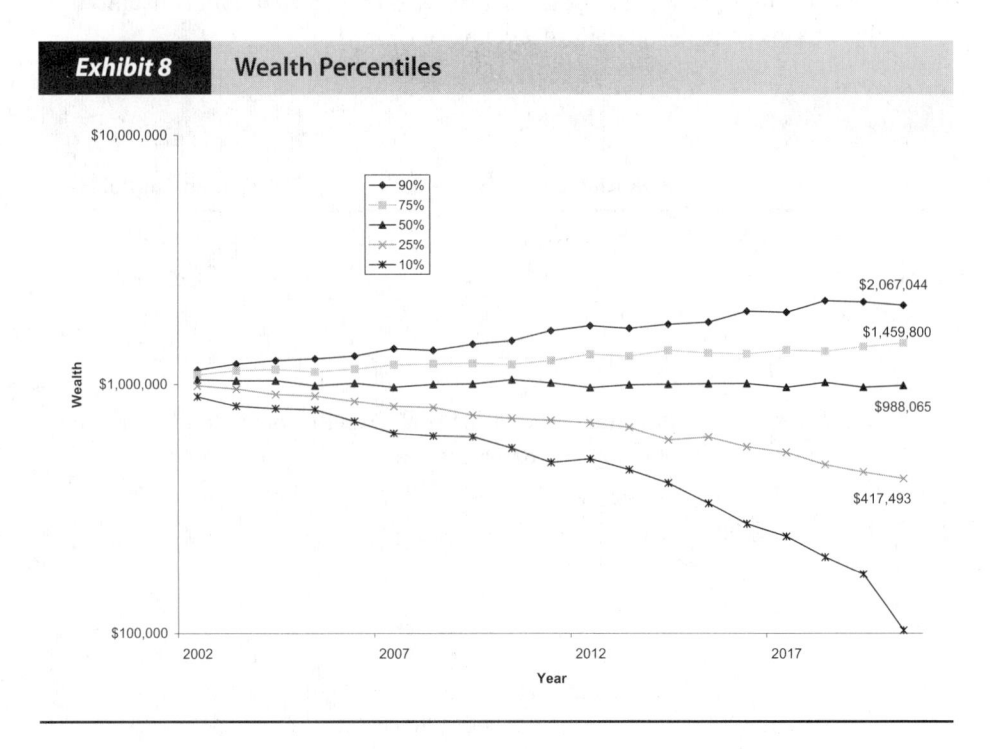

Exhibit 8 Wealth Percentiles

[Chart showing wealth percentiles from 2002 to beyond 2017, with ending values: 90% = $2,067,044; 75% = $1,459,800; 50% = $988,065; 25% = $417,493; 10% trending toward $100,000]

Stevenson wants his portfolio value (in real dollars) to be at least $630,000 when he turns 75 in 2012. He requires a 90 percent probability of meeting this goal. Determine whether Stevenson's current asset allocation promises to satisfy that requirement.

13. The Inner Life Insurance Company (ILIC) is considering the asset allocation shown in Exhibit 9. ILIC has risk aversion (R_A) of 5 using the scale presented in the text.

    A. Recommend an asset allocation for ILIC.

    B. Recommend a statistical method that ILIC should use to obtain information about a proposed asset allocation's performance over time, given its forecasts concerning liabilities and its capital market expectations.

Exhibit 9	Investor's Forecasts	
Asset Allocation	Expected Surplus Return	Standard Deviation of Surplus Return
A	6.5%	14%
B	4	10
C	0	2

14. For the following types of investors, appraise the importance of using the specified asset class for strategic asset allocation.

   A. Long-term bonds for a life insurer and for a young investor.

   B. Common stock for a bank and for a young investor.

   C. Domestic tax-exempt bonds for an endowment and for a mid-career professional.

   D. Private equity for a major foundation and for a young investor.

15. Exhibit 10 shows William Smith's financial and human capital in constant dollars terms at 30, 50, and 65 years of age.

Exhibit 10	Financial and Human Capital	
Age	Financial Capital ($)	Human Capital ($)
30	100,000	2,100,000
50	900,000	1,300,000
65	2,000,000	200,000

Smith's target asset allocation for total wealth is 60/40 stocks/bonds. Assume that his human capital is approximately risk free and uncorrelated with stock returns. Determine Smith's optimal asset allocation for stocks and bonds in his financial portfolio at the following ages:

   A. 30.

   B. 50.

   C. 65.

   D. Discuss whether your conclusions in Parts A, B, and C are consistent with experience-based approaches to asset allocation.

16. Wendy Willet is chief investment officer of the Allright University Endowment (AUE) based in the United States. The strategic asset allocation of AUE is as follows, where percentages refer to proportions of the total portfolio:

Global equities		60%
U.S. equities	30%	
Ex-U.S. equities	30%	
Global fixed income		40%
U.S. bonds	30%	
Ex-U.S. bonds	10%	

Exhibit 11 gives Willet's expectations.

Practice Problems for Reading 21

Exhibit 11	Expected Return for Asset Classes		
Asset Class		Long-Term	Short-Term
Global equities		A	B
U.S. equities		8%	14%
Ex-U.S. equities		10	10
Global fixed income		C	D
U.S. bonds		6%	8%
Ex-U.S. bonds		5	4

AUE runs a top-down global tactical asset allocation program that looks first at the overall allocation between global equities and global fixed income, then at the asset allocation within global equities and global fixed income. Assume that the asset classes' risk characteristics are constant.

A. Calculate the long-term and short-term expectations for global equities (A and B, respectively) and global fixed income (C and D, respectively).

B. Determine and justify the changes in portfolio weights (in relation to the policy portfolio target weights) that would result from a global tactical asset allocation program.

17. Hugh Donovan is chief financial officer of LightSpeed Connections (LSC), a rapidly growing U.S technology company with a traditional defined-benefit pension plan. Because of LSC's young workforce, Donovan believes the pension plan has no liquidity needs and can thus invest aggressively to maximize pension assets. He also believes that Treasury bills and bonds, yielding 5.4 percent and 6.1 percent respectively, have no place in a portfolio with such a long time horizon. His strategy, which has produced excellent returns for the past two years, is to invest the portfolio as follows:

- 50 percent in a concentrated pool (15 to 20 stocks) of initial public offerings (IPOs) in technology and internet companies, managed internally by Donovan;
- 25 percent in a small-cap growth fund;
- 10 percent in a venture capital fund;
- 10 percent in an S&P 500 index fund; and
- 5 percent in an international equity fund.

Working with LSC's Investment Committee, the firm's president, Eileen Jeffries, has produced a formal investment policy statement, which reads as follows:

> The LSC Pension Plan's return objective should focus on real total returns that will fund its long-term obligations on an inflation-adjusted basis. The "time-to-maturity" of the corporate workforce is a key element for any defined pension plan; given our young workforce, LSC's Plan has a long investment horizon and more time available for wealth compounding to occur. Therefore, the Plan can pursue an aggressive investment course and focus on the higher return potential of capital growth. Under present U.S. tax laws, pension portfolio income and capital gains are not taxed. The portfolio should focus primarily on investments in businesses directly related to our main business to leverage our knowledge base.

Jeffries takes an asset-only approach to strategic asset allocation. He is considering three alternative allocations, shown in Exhibit 12 along with the portfolio's current asset allocation.

Exhibit 12 Alternative Asset Allocations and Current Portfolio

Asset	Portfolio A	Portfolio B	Portfolio C	Current Portfolio
S&P 500 Index	25%	16%	35%	10%
IPO/tech portfolio	20	40	10	50
Small-cap growth fund	26	10	19	25
International equity fund	0	16	15	5
Venture capital fund	10	5	5	10
Money market fund	7	7	2	0
Corporate bond fund	12	6	14	0
Total	100%	100%	100%	100%
Expected return	16.6%	22.1%	13.3%	26.2%
Standard deviation	26.7%	38.4%	19.8%	55.2%

Select and justify the portfolio that is most appropriate for LSC's pension plan.

18. Bontemps International (BI) is a financially healthy, rapidly growing import/export company with a young workforce. Information regarding the company's ERISA-qualified defined-benefit pension plan appears in Exhibits 13 and 14.

In accordance with BI policy, the plan discounts its liabilities at the market interest rate for bonds of the same duration.

Last year the surplus declined, although the actual investment return at 10 percent was 100 basis points more than the board's stated long-term objective. Anticipating the board's desire to avoid a repetition of last year's shrinkage in the surplus, BI's chief financial officer, Giselle Donovan, wants to recommend an alternative portfolio for board consideration. Donovan is considering the portfolios shown in Exhibit 15.

Recommend one of the portfolios (A through F) for the board's consideration and justify the choice.

Exhibit 13

Asset Class	Percent Allocation	Prior-Year Total Return
Large-cap U.S. equities	35%	10.0%
Small-cap U.S. equities	10	12.0
International equities	5	7.0
Total equities	50	
U.S. Treasury bills (1-year duration)	10	4.5
U.S. intermediate bonds and mortgage-backed securities (4-year duration)	39	1.0
U.S. long-term bonds (10-year duration)	1	19.0%[a]
Total fixed income	50%	
Total	100%	10.0%

[a] Income element 7.0%; gain element 12.0%.

Practice Problems for Reading 21

Exhibit 14

Present value of plan liabilities	$298 million
Market value of plan assets	$300 million
Surplus	$2 million
Duration of liabilities	10 years
Actuarial return assumption	7.0%
BI board's long-term total return objective	9.0%

Exhibit 15   Portfolio Alternatives

	A	B	C	D	E	F	Current Portfolio
Domestic large-cap equities	0%	25%	30%	0%	30%	30%	35%
Domestic small-cap equities	0	15	20	0	5	20	10
International equities	0	20	20	0	20	20	5
Subtotal equity	0%	60%	70%	0%	55%	70%	50%
Treasury bills (1-year duration)	100	20	5	0	0	0	10
Intermediate bonds (4-year duration)	0	20	20	0	0	0	39
Long bonds (10-year duration)	0	0	5	100	45	30	1
Subtotal fixed income	100%	40%	30%	100%	45%	30%	50%
Total	100%	100%	100%	100%	100%	100%	100%
Expected annual return	5.5%	9.4%	10.0%	7.1%	9.3%	10.2%	9.0%
Return volatility	0.0	10.3	13.0	0.0	10.3	14.0	10.0
Surplus volatility	11.0	7.0	11.0	0.0	5.5	7.5	8.0

19. The Medical Research Foundation (MRF) has just learned that it will receive a $45 million cash gift in three months. The gift will greatly increase the size of the foundation's endowment from its current $10 million. The foundation's grant-making (spending) policy has been to pay out virtually all of its annual net investment income. Because MRF's investment approach has been conservative, the endowment portfolio now consists almost entirely of fixed-income assets. The finance committee understands that these actions are causing the real value of foundation assets and the real value of future grants to decline because of inflation effects. Until now, the finance committee has believed it had no alternative to these actions, given the large immediate cash needs of the research programs being funded and the size of the foundation's capital base. The foundation's annual grants must at least equal 5 percent of its assets' market value to maintain its U.S. tax-exempt status, a requirement that is expected to continue indefinitely. No additional gifts or fundraising activity are expected for the foreseeable future.

Given the change in circumstances that the cash gift will make, the finance committee wishes to develop new grant-making and investment policies. Annual spending must at least meet the 5 percent of market value requirement, but the committee is unsure how much higher spending can or should be. The committee wants to pay out as much as possible because of the critical nature of the research being funded; however, it understands that preserving the real value of the foundation's assets is equally important in order to preserve its future grant-making capabilities. You have been asked to assist the committee in developing appropriate policies. Exhibit 16 summarizes the capital markets data.

Recommend and justify a long-term asset allocation.

Exhibit 16   Capital Markets Annualized Return Data

Asset	1926–1992 Average	1993–2000 Consensus Forecast
U.S. Treasury bills	3.7%	4.2%
Intermediate-term U.S. T-bonds	5.2	5.8
Long-term U.S. T-bonds	4.8	7.7
U.S. corporate bonds (AAA)	5.5	8.7
Non-U.S. bonds (AAA)	N/A	8.4
U.S. common stocks (large cap)	10.3	9.0
U.S. common stocks (small cap)	12.2	12.0
Non-U.S. common stocks (all)	N/A	10.1
Venture capital	N/A	15.5
Real estate	N/A	8.5
U.S. inflation	3.1%	3.5%

SOLUTIONS FOR READING 21

1. **A.** The economic role of strategic asset allocation is to supply the investor's desired exposures to systematic risk. A single company's shares have substantial idiosyncratic or nonsystematic risk. By contrast, an indexed investment is a highly diversified portfolio with negligible nonsystematic risk. Representing an equity asset class with an indexed investment far better fulfills the purposes of strategic asset allocation.

   B.
   i. The more frequently RFM rebalances to its strategic asset allocation, the more important strategic asset allocation will appear in a time-series sense as in Brinson, Hood, and Beebower (1986).

   ii. If RFM chooses to index, the measured time-series importance of strategic asset allocation will increase, but it will decrease if RFM actively manages within asset classes, all else equal. This effect will occur because the percent of total variation explained by security selection will increase. Active management will also tend to decrease the measured cross-sectional importance of asset allocation.

   iii. By itself, choosing a policy portfolio that is distinct from one's peers should not affect asset allocation's measured importance in a time-series sense. It will tend to differentiate RFM's returns from those of its peers, however, and tend to make asset allocation appear important in a cross-sectional sense.

   C. The institutional analyst is proposing a tactical asset allocation program because it involves making short-term adjustments to asset-class weights based on short-term expected relative performance differences between domestic and international equities. A problem with the TAA program is that the band of asset weights within which the proposed TAA would operate is too wide in relation to the permissible range for international equities determined by the Investment Policy Committee.

   D. A major concern of a DB pension plan is funding the pension liability. An ALM approach more directly and precisely addresses that concern than an asset-only approach to strategic asset allocation. A dynamic ALM approach considers the interperiod linkages of optimal investment decisions. By contrast, a static approach does not account for such linkages. A single-period mean–variance surplus optimization model is an example of a static ALM model. An advantage of a dynamic ALM approach is that it takes account of interperiod linkages; a disadvantage is that it is more costly and complex to implement than a static approach.

   E. Because the RFM pension liability can be modeled approximately as a short position in a long-term bond, the risk-minimizing strategic asset allocation is 100 percent invested in long-term bonds.

2. Using Equation 1,

   $$U_m = E(R_m) - 0.005 R_A \sigma_m^2$$
   $$= E(R_m) - 0.005(5)\sigma_m^2$$
   $$= E(R_m) - 0.025\sigma_m^2$$

   Therefore, for Allocation A,
   $U_A = E(R_A) - 0.025\sigma_A^2 = 11.5 - 0.025(18)^2 = 11.5 - 8.1 = 3.4$ percent;

   Allocation B, $U_B = E(R_B) - 0.025\sigma_B^2 = 8 - 0.025(14)^2 = 8 - 4.9 = 3.1$ percent;

and for Allocation C,
$$U_C = E(R_C) - 0.025\sigma_C^2 = 6 - 0.025(10)^2 = 6 - 2.5 = 3.5 \text{ percent}$$

Asset Allocation C appears best because it affords Lagland the highest risk-adjusted expected return.

3. We can use Roy's safety-first criterion with a return threshold (R_L) of 3.5 percent to decide which of the three allocations best meets the Garrett Foundation's objective. The asset allocation with the highest ratio $[E(R_p) - R_L]/\sigma_p$ is the one that minimizes the probability of not meeting the return threshold.

   Allocation A: 0.444 = (11.5 − 3.5) / 18
   Allocation B: 0.321 = (8 − 3.5) / 14
   Allocation C: 0.250 = (6 − 3.5) / 10

   Allocation A, with the largest ratio (0.444), is the foundation's best alternative according to Roy's safety-first criterion.

4. Because (1.05)(1.024)(1.006) − 1 = 0.082 or 8.2 percent, only Asset Allocation A with an expected return of 11.5 percent promises to satisfy Ernst's return requirement.

5. **A.** U.S. equities form a major part of world equities, so the specification does not meet the criterion that asset classes should be mutually exclusive. A possible additional criticism is that the asset classes may be nonhomogeneous. Narrower asset-class specifications may help control systematic risk.

   B. Alternative assets need to be subdivided further for asset allocation purposes because they are not homogeneous as a group. A further possible criticism is that the asset classes do not make up a preponderance of world wealth because Canadian markets are only a small fraction of world wealth (the text mentions that Canadian equity markets are one-tenth as large as U.S. equity markets).

   C. With the addition of U.S. fixed-income asset classes, this asset-class set should meet all the stated criteria. The specification between small- and large-cap stocks is frequently encountered because they are well differentiated; however, the argument could be made that mid-cap stocks should be added (or the limits of "small-cap" and "large-cap" defined to cover "mid-cap") to better cover investable wealth.

6. According to Equation 3, the new asset class's Sharpe ratio must exceed the quantity (Sharpe ratio of existing portfolio) × (Correlation of U.S. real estate with the existing portfolio) = 0.40(0.35) = 0.14 for it to be optimal to add the new asset class. Thus the foundation should add U.S. real estate if its predicted Sharpe ratio exceeds 0.14. Because the fund predicts a Sharpe ratio of 0.12 for U.S. real estate, the foundation should not add that asset class to the existing portfolio.

7. The relatively constant elements in the asset allocation process are the prediction procedure, the investor's risk tolerance function, and the optimizer. Most of the investor's expertise goes into formulating these stable elements. The prediction procedure represents the investor's perception of best process for developing capital market expectations. The investor's risk tolerance function represents a quantification of his risk attitudes. The optimizer is the procedure for producing the best asset allocation. By contrast, the other elements of the process are inputs or outputs that are regularly revised.

Solutions for Reading 21

8. The global minimum-variance portfolio has the smallest variance among all portfolios on the minimum-variance frontier. The concept is important in a mean–variance asset-only approach to asset allocation. By contrast, the minimum surplus variance portfolio concept is important in a mean–variance surplus optimization approach that focuses on surplus or net worth. The minimum surplus variance portfolio has minimum variance of surplus among all portfolios on the surplus efficient frontier.

9. **A.** Corner portfolios arise from a mean–variance optimization in which asset-class weights are constrained to be nonnegative. The global minimum-variance portfolio is always included as a corner portfolio. Corner portfolios are minimum-variance portfolios in which an asset weight changes from zero to positive or from positive to zero along the minimum-variance frontier. The usefulness of corner portfolios comes from the fact that, although few in number, they can be used to find the composition of any minimum-variance portfolio.

   B. FRMC's return requirement is $(1.035)(1.0225)(1.00436) - 1.0 = 0.06290$ or 6.29 percent a year. This result contrasts to an additive return requirement of $3.5\% + 2.25\% + 0.436\% = 6.19\%$, which is lower.

   C. The highest Sharpe-ratio-efficient portfolio is close to Corner Portfolio 4. Corner Portfolio 4's expected return of 5.03 percent, however, does not satisfy FRMC's return objective of 6.29 percent. The efficient portfolio that just satisfies FRMC's return requirement must lie between Corner Portfolio 4 and Corner Portfolio 3, which has an expected return of 7.55 percent. The portfolio thus identified will have the highest Sharpe ratio among those efficient portfolios satisfying FRMC's return requirement.

   From the corner portfolio theorem, it follows that

   $$6.29 = 7.55w + 5.03(1 - w)$$

   We find that the weight on Corner Portfolio 3 is $w = 0.500$ and the weight on Corner Portfolio 4 is $(1 - w) = 0.500$. Therefore,

Weight of French equities	$0.5(53.22\%) + 0.5(0.00\%) = 26.61\%$
Weight of ex-France equities	$0.5(37.23\%) + 0.5(24.70\%) = 30.97\%$
Weight of French bonds	$0.5(0\%) + 0.5(43.30\%) = 21.65\%$
Weight of real estate	$0.5(9.55\%) + 0.5(32.00\%) = 20.78\%$

   As an arithmetic check, $26.61\% + 30.97\% + 21.65\% + 20.78\% = 100\%$.

10. **A.** **i.** No. A conventional mean–variance efficient frontier is calculated using estimates of return distribution parameters. By assumption, the weights in Frontier B do not reflect estimation error, so the resulting efficient frontier must be superior to the conventional efficient frontier using estimates (in fact, it must be the best attainable). A frontier is superior to another frontier if it lies above it.

    ii. No. An efficient frontier reflecting the true return parameters must lie above the resampled efficient frontier. Resampled efficiency addresses estimation error by averaging portfolio weights across different simulations but cannot completely remove its impact.

    B. The results of MVO, in particular the composition of efficient portfolios, are most sensitive to expected return inputs. As discussed in the text, estimation error in expected returns has been estimated to be roughly 10 times as important as estimation error in variances and 20 times as important as estimation in covariances.

11. **A.** The scatter of points in Exhibit 7 can be called a statistical equivalence region because these points represent possible efficient portfolios that could result from sampling based on the same underlying return parameters.

   B. For each series of points, the numbering represents a rank order by mean return. The first point in the resampled efficient frontier is found by averaging the portfolio weights of assets in 1, 1′, and 1″; the second by averaging 2, 2′, and 2″; and so forth to the highest mean return resampled efficient portfolio (averaging the weights of 5, 5′, and 5″).

12. According to the Monte Carlo simulation, the current asset allocation is not expected to satisfy Stevenson's requirement. The y-axis in Exhibit 8 is a logarithmic scale. Because $\log_{10}(630{,}000) = 5.8$ while $\log_{10}(100{,}000) = 5$ and $\log_{10}(1{,}000{,}000) = 6$, \$630,000 would be a point eight-tenths of the distance between the \$100,000 and \$1,000,000 hatch marks. Note that the relevant line is the 10% one, because 90 percent of outcomes lie above it, and that in the year 2012 (10 years from 2002) the 10% line clearly is less than that "eight-tenths" point. Thus Stevenson cannot expect that portfolio value (in real dollars) to be at least \$630,000 with a probability of 90 percent at age 75.

13. **A.** We use Equation 4

$$U_m^{ALM} = E(SR_m) - 0.005 R_A \sigma^2(SR_m)$$
$$= E(SR_m) - 0.005(5)\sigma^2(SR_m)$$
$$= E(SR_m) - 0.025\sigma^2(SR_m)$$

   For Allocation A,

$$U_A^{ALM} = E(SR_A) - 0.025\sigma^2(SR_A) = 6.5 - 0.025(14)^2$$
$$= 6.5 - 4.90 = 1.60$$

   For Allocation B,

$$U_B^{ALM} = E(SR_B) - 0.025\sigma^2(SR_B) = 4.0 - 0.025(10)^2 = 4.0 - 2.50$$
$$= 1.50$$

   For Allocation C,

$$U_C^{ALM} = E(SR_C) - 0.025\sigma^2(SR_C) = 0.0 - 0.025(2)^2 = 0.0 - 0.10$$
$$= -0.10$$

   ILIC should prefer Asset Allocation A because it has the highest risk-adjusted expected return.

   B. ILIC can use Monte Carlo simulation to obtain information concerning an asset allocation over time, as described in the text.

14. **A.** Long-term bond holdings are important for life insurers because of their ALM emphasis and the long-term nature of their liabilities. In contrast, individual investors do not have ALM concerns to the same degree, in general. As discussed in the reading as well, because of the importance of human capital in relation to financial capital during youth, for many young investors equity investments will be very large relative to fixed-income holdings. In conclusion, long-term bonds are generally more important in strategic asset allocation for life insurers than for young investors.

Solutions for Reading 21

B. Banks are generally restricted by regulations in their holdings of common stock. Overall, common stock plays a minimal role in banks' securities portfolio. By contrast, because of human capital considerations mentioned in the solution to Part A, common stock investments tend to be very important for young investors (with the possible exception of those investors whose employment income is linked to equity market returns).

C. Because endowments are tax exempt, tax-exempt bonds play no role in their strategic asset allocation. In contrast, tax-exempt bonds sometimes play a substantive role for individual investors in high tax brackets, such as many mid-career professionals.

D. Private equity may play a role in the strategic asset allocation of substantial investors, both institutional and individual. A major foundation is much more likely to have the resources to research and invest in private companies than young investors and to play a role in strategic asset allocation.

15. A. At age 30, the closest Smith can get to his optimal 60/40 asset allocation is to invest 100 percent of his financial assets in stocks, a 100/0 stock/bond mix. Then his effective asset allocation for total wealth is $100,000/$2,200,000 = 4.55 percent stocks and 95.45 percent bonds.

B. At age 50, the closest Smith can get to his optimal 60/40 asset allocation is to invest 100 percent of his financial assets in stocks, 100/0 stock/bond mix. Then his effective asset allocation for total wealth is $900,000/$2,200,000 = 40.91 percent stocks and 59.09 percent bonds.

C. At age 65, Smith can attain his optimal 60/40 asset allocation by holding 0.60 × $2,200,000 = $1,320,000 in stocks for an asset allocation of $1,320,000/$2,000,000 = 66 percent stocks and 34 percent bonds, considering financial capital only.

D. At ages 30, 50, and 65, Smith's financial asset allocations were determined to be 100/0, 100/0, and 66/34, respectively. The results are consistent with the experience-based principle that for most individual investors, the allocation to stocks should be relatively large early in life and smaller later in life.

16. A. U.S. equities, and ex-U.S. equities represent respectively 30%/60% = 0.5 and 30%/60% = 0.5 of global equities. Therefore, for global equities,

$$A = (0.5 \times 8\%) + (0.5\% \times 10\%) = 9\%$$

$$B = (0.5 \times 14\%) + (0.5\% \times 10\%) = 12\%$$

Global equities' short-term expected return at 12 percent is above the long-term expectation of 9 percent because U.S. equities are expected in the short-term to outperform their long-term expected return.

U.S. bonds and ex-U.S. bonds represent respectively 30%/40% = 0.75 and 10%/40% = 0.25 of global fixed income. Therefore, for global fixed income,

$$C = (0.75 \times 6\%) + (0.25\% \times 5\%) = 5.75\%$$

$$D = (0.75 \times 8\%) + (0.25\% \times 4\%) = 7\%$$

Global fixed income's short-term expected return at 7 percent is above its long-term expectation of 5.75 percent. However within global fixed income U.S. bonds are expected short term at 8 percent to outperform their long term expected return while ex-U.S. bonds are expected short term at 4 percent to underperform their long-term expected return.

B. The results in Part A suggest three actions:

- In absolute terms, the global equities' short-term expected return is 300 basis points above its expected long-term value of 9 percent; in relative terms, that is equivalent to a 12%/9% − 1.0 = 33% higher expected return. For global fixed income, the absolute and relative expected return differences are 125 basis points and 22 percent, respectively. Because global equities appear more undervalued than global bonds, increase the weight on global equities from 60 percent and decrease the weight on global fixed income from 40 percent.

- Within global equities, overweight U.S. equities versus their target weight of 30 percent and decrease the weight on ex-U.S. equities from 30 percent. Although the short-term expected return on ex-U.S. equities is the same as the long-term expectation, U.S. equities are expected to outperform their long-term expected return by 600 basis points in the short term.

- Within the new global fixed-income allocation, overweight U.S. bonds and underweight ex-U.S. bonds, reflecting their short-term expected performance.

17. Portfolio C is the only appropriate choice. It is well diversified across all asset classes with minimal IPO/technology exposure, and only 34 percent of the portfolio exposed to the riskier asset classes in total (IPO/Tech, small-cap growth, and venture capital). IPO/Tech assets may be highly correlated with the plan sponsor's underlying business, thereby exposing both the company and the plan beneficiaries to excessive risk in the event of a sharp downturn in the company's business. Portfolio C has a Sharpe ratio higher than that of the current portfolio; Portfolio C's Sharpe ratio is lower than, but in line with, those of Portfolios A and B. Portfolio C is better diversified across asset classes and substantially less volatile. Finally, Portfolio C has minimal reserves, which is appropriate given the plan's long time horizon and minimal liquidity needs.

18. To avoid a repetition of last year's shrinkage in the plan's surplus, BI's board must consider both surplus management and the level of total return produced. As such, Donovan should recommend that the board consider Portfolio E minimizes surplus volatility while meeting the board's expected return objective of 9 percent. Its absolute volatility is only slightly more than that of the current portfolio (which offers a lower rate of return) and equals that of Portfolio B (which offers a slightly higher expected return but also higher surplus volatility). Adopting Portfolio E would minimize surplus volatility without significantly increasing absolute risk or sacrificing expected return.

19. The real return from the recommended allocation should meet the minimum required return identified in the IPS. The allocation philosophy will reflect the Foundation's return objective, above-average risk tolerance, low liquidity requirements, and tax-exempt status. In general the portfolio allocation should include the following:

- An allocation to fixed-income instruments of less than 50 percent, because real returns of bonds are forecasted to be lower than those of stocks. Bonds will be included primarily for diversification and risk reduction. The ongoing cash flow from the bond portfolio should easily provide for all normal working capital needs.

Solutions for Reading 21

- An allocation to equities greater than 50 percent. A number of factors support a high allocation to equities: historical and expected real returns are high, the horizon is long, risk tolerance is above average, and taxes are not a consideration.

- Within the equity universe, large-cap, small-cap, international stocks and venture capital should be considered. Diversifying within the equity universe will contribute to risk reduction, and total return could be enhanced.

- Real estate should be included in the portfolio as an alternative to stocks and bonds. It will provide diversification as well as inflation protection in the long term.

An example of an appropriate modestly aggressive allocation is shown below:

Asset Class	7-Year Forecast of Real Returns	Recommended Allocation	Real Return Contribution
Cash (U.S.):			
T-bills	0.7%	0%	—
Bonds			
Intermediate	2.3	5	0.115%
Long treasury	4.2	10	0.420
Corporate	5.2	10	0.520
International	4.9	10	0.490
Stocks			
Large cap	5.5	30	1.650
Small cap	8.5	10	0.850
International	6.6	10	0.660
Venture capital	12.0	5	0.600
Real estate	5.0	10	0.500
Total expected real return		100%	5.805%

Singapore
Sydney
Shanghai B
Hong Kong
Toronto
316.8
0.7%
-6.9%
22,700.9
0.5%
-4.2%
13,524.8
0.1%
4.1%

READING
22

The Case for International Diversification

by Bruno Solnik and Dennis McLeavey, CFA

LEARNING OUTCOMES	
Mastery	The candidate should be able to:
☐	a discuss the implications of international diversification for domestic equity and fixed-income portfolios, based on the traditional assumptions of low correlations across international markets;
☐	b distinguish between the asset return and currency return for an international security;
☐	c evaluate the contribution of currency risk to the volatility of an international security position;
☐	d discuss the impact of international diversification on the efficient frontier;
☐	e evaluate the potential performance and risk-reduction benefits of adding bonds to a globally diversified stock portfolio;
☐	f explain why currency risk should not be a significant barrier to international investment;
☐	g critique the traditional case against international diversification;
☐	h discuss the barriers to international investments and their impact on international investors;
☐	i distinguish between global investing and international diversification and discuss the growing importance of global industry factors as a determinant of risk and performance;
☐	j discuss the basic case for investing in emerging markets, as well as the risks and restrictions often associated with such investments.

International portfolio investment has long been a tradition in many European countries, but it is a more recent practice in North America.[1] There is now a strong trend toward international diversification in all countries, however, especially among U.S. institutional investors, such as corporate and public pension funds. In the early 1970s, U.S. pension funds basically held no foreign assets; the percentage of foreign assets approached 20 percent of total assets by 2006. British institutional investors hold

---

[1] The terminology varies across countries. Americans use the word *international* to refer to non-U.S. investments and *global* to refer to U.S. plus non-U.S. investments. Other English-speaking nationals tend to use the word *foreign* to refer to nondomestic investments and *international* to refer to domestic plus foreign investments. We use the U.S. terminology.

Global Investments, Sixth Edition, by Bruno Solnik and Dennis McLeavey, CFA. Copyright © 2009 by Pearson Education. Reprinted with permission of Pearson Education, publishing as Prentice Hall.

more than 25 percent of their assets in non-British securities. Some Dutch pension funds have more than half of their assets invested abroad. Recently, private investors have joined the trend toward global investment.

Indeed, the mere size of foreign markets justifies international diversification, even for U.S. investors. At the end of 2006, the world stock market capitalization was around $25 trillion. The U.S. stock market accounted for roughly half of the world market. The growth of the world stock market since the early 1970s has been remarkable. In 1974, the New York Stock Exchange was the only significant market in the world, representing 60 percent of a world market capitalization of less than $1 trillion.[2] As shown in Exhibit 1, the size of the world market multiplied by a factor of 50 in the next 32 years, and the share of U.S. equity moved from 60 percent to less than 30 percent in 1988 and back to 40 percent by the end of 2006. The Asia–Pacific region, which made up one-third of the world stock market in the early 1990s, shrank to 25 percent at the end of 2006. Europe makes up one-third of the world market. The world market capitalization of bonds, domestic and international, was around $66 trillion at the end of 2006. U.S. dollar bonds accounted for roughly 45 percent of the world bond market, while yen bonds accounted for somewhat less than 20 percent and bonds denominated in European currencies accounted for some 30 percent.

In a fully efficient, integrated, global capital market, buying the world market portfolio would be the natural passive strategy. In theory, an American investor should hold half of the portfolio in international securities. But, even if one does not believe in a perfect, integrated world market, the case for diversifying in international securities is strong. The basic argument in favor of international diversification is that foreign investments allow investors to reduce the total risk of the portfolio, while offering additional profit potential. By expanding the investment opportunity set, international diversification helps to improve the risk-adjusted performance of a portfolio.

Exhibit 1 Stock Market Capitalization Developed Markets to 2000; All Markets from 2002

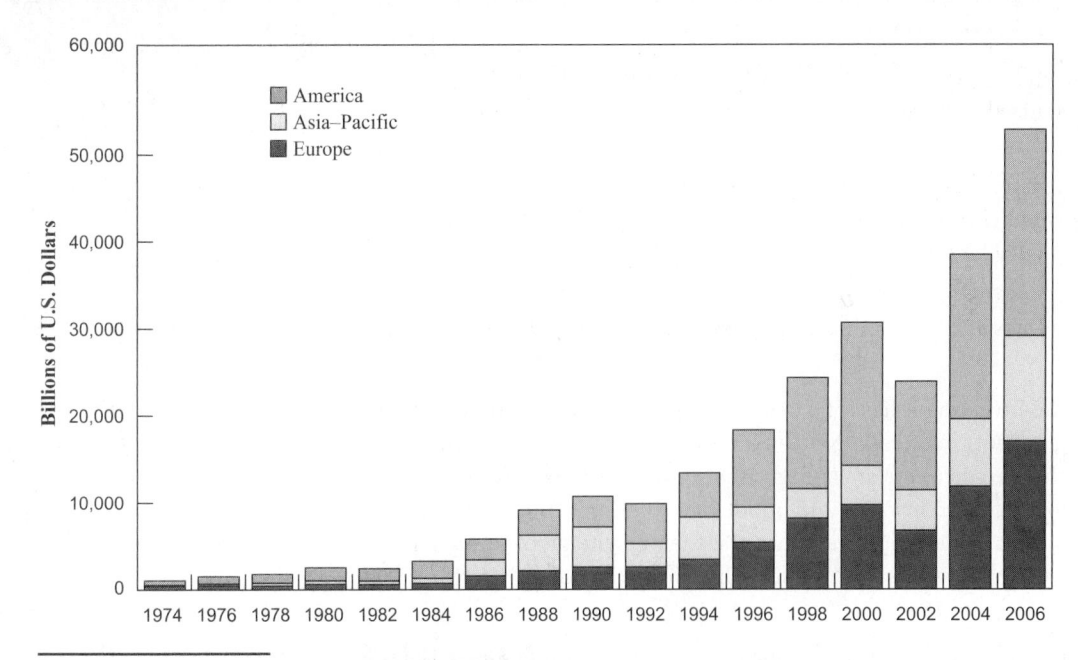

Source: Data from World Federation of Stock Exchanges.

---

[2] At that time, Solnik (1974) presented the case for international diversification to U.S. pension plans that had zero overseas investments.

Domestic securities tend to move up and down together because they are similarly affected by domestic conditions, such as monetary announcements, movements in interest rates, budget deficits, and national growth. This creates a definite positive correlation among nearly all stocks traded in the same national equity market. The correlation applies equally to bonds; bond prices on the same national market are very strongly correlated. Investors have searched for methods to spread their risks and diversify away the national market risk. In their variety, foreign capital markets provide good potential for diversification beyond domestic instruments and markets.

This reading presents the advantages and disadvantages of international investing. It focuses on equity investments but also refers to bond investments. The first section presents the traditional case for international diversification. However, this case has been criticized recently because of an increase in international correlations, especially in periods of high market volatility. The second section reviews these criticisms. The third section revisits the benefits of a global approach in light of the recent changes in the global economic landscape. The last section presents the case for investing in emerging markets.

THE TRADITIONAL CASE FOR INTERNATIONAL DIVERSIFICATION

There are two motivations for global investment. All else being equal, a low international correlation allows reduction of the volatility, or total risk, of a global portfolio. A low international correlation also provides profit opportunities for an active investor: Because markets do not move up or down together, an expert investor can hope to adjust the international asset allocation of the global portfolio toward markets with superior expected returns. This should lead to a superior risk-adjusted performance. On the other hand, barriers to international investments also exist. Hence, we will discuss risk reduction through attractive correlations, superior expected returns, and trends in barriers.

Risk Reduction through Attractive Correlations

The objective of risk diversification is to reduce the total risk of a portfolio. Of course, one hopes simultaneously to achieve high expected returns, as discussed in the next section. The total risk of most stock markets is larger than that of the U.S. market when the dollar is used as the base currency. In part, this is caused by currency risk, which adds to the risk of a foreign investment, even though the volatility of national markets is often comparable when measured in their local currency.[3] Nevertheless, the addition of more risky foreign assets to a purely domestic portfolio still reduces its total risk as long as the correlation of the foreign assets with the domestic market is not large. This can be shown mathematically.

Let's consider a portfolio partly invested in domestic assets (e.g., a U.S. stock index for a U.S. investor) and partly invested in foreign assets (e.g., a French stock index). The proportions invested in each asset class is denoted w_d for domestic assets and w_f for foreign assets; they sum to 100 percent. The returns are denoted R_p for the portfolio, R_d for the domestic assets, and R_f for the foreign assets. All returns are measured in the base currency (e.g., the U.S. dollar for a U.S. investor). So, the return on foreign assets is subject to currency risk. The domestic and foreign assets have standard

---

[3] Similarly, the volatility of the U.S. stock market would look larger than that of the French stock market when returns are measured in euros.

deviations denoted σ_d and σ_f, respectively. The total risk of the portfolio is its standard deviation σ_p. The correlation between the two asset classes is denoted $\rho_{d,f}$. Remember that the variance of the portfolio is the square of its standard deviation, and that the covariance between the two asset classes is given by

$$\text{cov}_{d,f} = \rho_{d,f}\sigma_d\sigma_f$$

First, note that the expected return on the portfolio is simply equal to the average expected return on the two asset classes:

$$E(R_p) = w_d E(R_d) + w_f E(R_f) \tag{1}$$

A well-known mathematical result is that the variance of the portfolio is equal to

$$\sigma_p^2 = w_d^2\sigma_d^2 + w_f^2\sigma_f^2 + 2w_d w_f \text{cov}_{d,f}$$

or

$$\sigma_p^2 = w_d^2\sigma_d^2 + w_f^2\sigma_f^2 + 2w_d w_f \rho_{d,f}\sigma_d\sigma_f$$

The standard deviation is simply equal to the square root:

$$\sigma_p = \left(w_d^2\sigma_d^2 + w_f^2\sigma_f^2 + 2w_d w_f \rho_{d,f}\sigma_d\sigma_f\right)^{1/2} \tag{2}$$

The portfolio's total risk σ_p will always be *less* than the average of the two standard deviations: $w_d\sigma_d + w_f\sigma_f$. The only case in which it will be equal is when the correlation[4] is exactly equal to 1.0 (perfect correlation between the two assets). Otherwise diversification benefits will show, and the lower the correlation, the bigger the risk reduction (see Example 1).

Currency Considerations

The return and risk of an asset depend on the currency used. For example, the return and risk of a French asset will be different if measured in the euro or in the dollar. The dollar value of the asset is equal to its euro value multiplied by the exchange rate (number of dollars per euro):

$$V^\$ = V \times S$$

where V and $V^\$$ are, respectively, the values in the local currency (euro) and in the dollar, and S is the exchange rate (number of dollars per euro). The rate of return in dollars from time 0 to time 1 is given by

$$r^\$ = \frac{V_1^\$ - V_0^\$}{V_0^\$} = \frac{V_1 S_1 - V_0 S_0}{V_0 S_0} = \frac{V_1 - V_0}{V_0} + \frac{S_1 - S_0}{S_0} + \frac{V_1 - V_0}{V_0} \times \frac{S_1 - S_0}{S_0}$$

$$r^\$ = r + s + (r \times s)$$

where r is the return in local currency, $r^\$$ is the return in dollars, and s is the percentage exchange rate movement.[5]

---

[4] A correlation coefficient between two random variables lies between +1.0 and −1.0. A coefficient of 1.0 means that the two markets go up and down in identical cycles, whereas a coefficient of −1.0 means that they are exactly countercyclical. For more details, see DeFusco et al. (2001).
[5] If a dividend or coupon is paid in period 1, it will be included in V_1.

The Traditional Case For International Diversification

Example 1

International Risk Diversification Benefits

Assume that the domestic and foreign assets have standard deviations of σ_d = 15 percent and σ_f = 17 percent, respectively, with a correlation of $\rho_{d,f}$ = 0.4.

1. What is the standard deviation of a portfolio equally invested in domestic and foreign assets?
2. What is the standard deviation of a portfolio with a 40 percent investment in the foreign asset?
3. What is the standard deviation of a portfolio equally invested in domestic and foreign assets if the correlation is 0.5? What if the correlation is 0.8?

Solution to 1:

The variance of the total portfolio equally invested ($w_d = w_f$ = 50%) in both assets, σ_p^2, is given by

$$\sigma_p^2 = 0.5^2 \left[\sigma_d^2 + \sigma_f^2 + \left(2\rho_{df}\sigma_d\sigma_f\right)\right]$$

$$\sigma_p^2 = 0.5^2 \left[225 + 289 + \left(2 \times 0.4 \times 255\right)\right] = 179.5$$

Hence, the standard deviation σ_p is given by $\sqrt{179.5}$, or 13.4 percent, which is significantly less than that of the domestic asset. Since one can diversify in several foreign markets, the total risk of the portfolio could be further reduced.

Solution to 2:

The risk reduction depends on the percentage invested in each asset. A portfolio invested 60 percent in the domestic asset and 40 percent in the foreign asset has a variance given by

$$\sigma_p^2 = \left(0.6^2 \times \sigma_d^2\right) + \left(0.4^2 \times \sigma_f^2\right) + \left(2 \times 0.4 \times 0.6 \times \rho_{d,f}\sigma_d\sigma_f\right)$$

$$= 176.2$$

The standard deviation is σ_p = 13.27 percent, and this is the lowest-risk portfolio.

Solution to 3:

The risk reduction also depends on the level of correlation. If the correlation is 0.5 instead of 0.4, the risk of the portfolio equally invested becomes σ_p = 13.87 percent. If the correlation is 0.8, the risk of the portfolio equally invested becomes σ_p = 15.18 percent. The risk of the portfolio increases with the level of correlation.

For example, if the return on a French asset is 5 percent in euros and the euro appreciates by 1 percent, the return in dollars is 6.05 percent. This is slightly different from the sum of the euro return and of the currency movement, because the currency appreciation applies not only to the original capital, but also to the capital gain. This cross product is equal to 5% × 1% = 0.05 percent.

It is easy to compare the risks of an asset measured in different currencies. To simplify notations, it is usually assumed that the cross product $r \times s$ is small relative to r and s and can be ignored for risk calculations. Hence, the variance of the dollar return is simply equal to the variance of the sum of the local currency return and the exchange rate movement:

$$\text{var}(r^\$) = \text{var}(r + s) = \text{var}(r) + \text{var}(s) + 2\text{cov}(r,s)$$

or

$$\sigma_f^2 = \sigma^2 + \sigma_s^2 + 2\rho\sigma\sigma_s$$

where σ_f^2 is the variance of the foreign asset measured in dollars, σ^2 is its variance in local currency, σ_s^2 is the variance of the exchange rate (number of dollars per local currency), and ρ is the correlation between the asset return, in local currency, and the exchange rate movement. As the correlation is never greater than 1.0, the asset and currency risks are not additive, and we have

$$\sigma_f \leq \sigma + \sigma_s$$

The difference between σ_f and σ is called the contribution of currency risk (see Example 2).

In this reading, we assume that we measure all returns and risk in the currency of the investor, namely, the U.S. dollar. The issue of currency hedging is discussed in other readings.

Example 2

Currency Risk Contribution

Suppose that we have a foreign investment with the following characteristics:

$$\sigma = 15.5\% \quad \sigma_s = 7\% \quad \rho = 0$$

What is the risk in domestic currency and the contribution of currency risk?

Solution:

We have

$$\sigma_f^2 = \sigma^2 + \sigma_s^2 + 0 = (15.5)^2 + (7.0)^2 = 289.25$$

Hence, the standard deviation σ_f is given by $\sqrt{289.25}$, or 17 percent. Note that this number is well below the sum of the risk of the asset measured in the local currency ($\sigma = 15.5\%$) and the risk of the currency ($\sigma_s = 7\%$). Currency risk increases the asset risk only from 15.5 percent in the local currency to 17 percent in domestic currency. Hence, the difference between σ_f and σ is the contribution of currency risk, here $\sigma_f - \sigma = 1.5$ percent.

Efficient Portfolios

A portfolio is mean–variance efficient if it has the highest level of expected return for a given level of risk.[6] The set of all *efficient portfolios* is called the *efficient frontier*. The simple calculation for two assets is illustrated in Example 3.

Of course, one can invest in many different domestic and international assets. Combining all domestic stocks in an efficient mean–variance fashion, we derive the domestic efficient frontier represented in Exhibit 3. Combining all domestic and international stocks in an efficient mean–variance fashion, we derive the global mean–variance-efficient frontier represented on the same exhibit. The global efficient frontier is to the left of the domestic efficient frontier, showing the increased return opportunities and risk diversification benefits brought by the enlarged investment

---

[6] See DeFusco et al. (2007).

The Traditional Case For International Diversification

universe. For example, portfolio A is on the domestic efficient frontier. Portfolio B on the global efficient frontier has the same return but less risk than portfolio A; portfolio C on the global efficient frontier has the same risk but more return than portfolio A.

Example 3

Risk–Return Trade-off of Internationally Diversified Portfolios

Assume that the domestic and foreign assets have standard deviations of $\sigma_d = 15$ percent and $\sigma_f = 17$ percent, respectively, with a correlation of $\rho_{d,f} = 0.4$. The expected returns of the domestic and foreign assets are equal, respectively, to $E(R_d) = 10$ percent and $E(R_f) = 12$ percent. Draw the set of all portfolios combining these two assets with positive weights in a risk–return graph.

Solution:

We can use Equations 1 and 2 to derive the set of portfolios invested in various proportions in the two assets. Their representation in a risk–return graph is given in Exhibit 2, in which D and F represent the domestic and foreign assets, respectively.

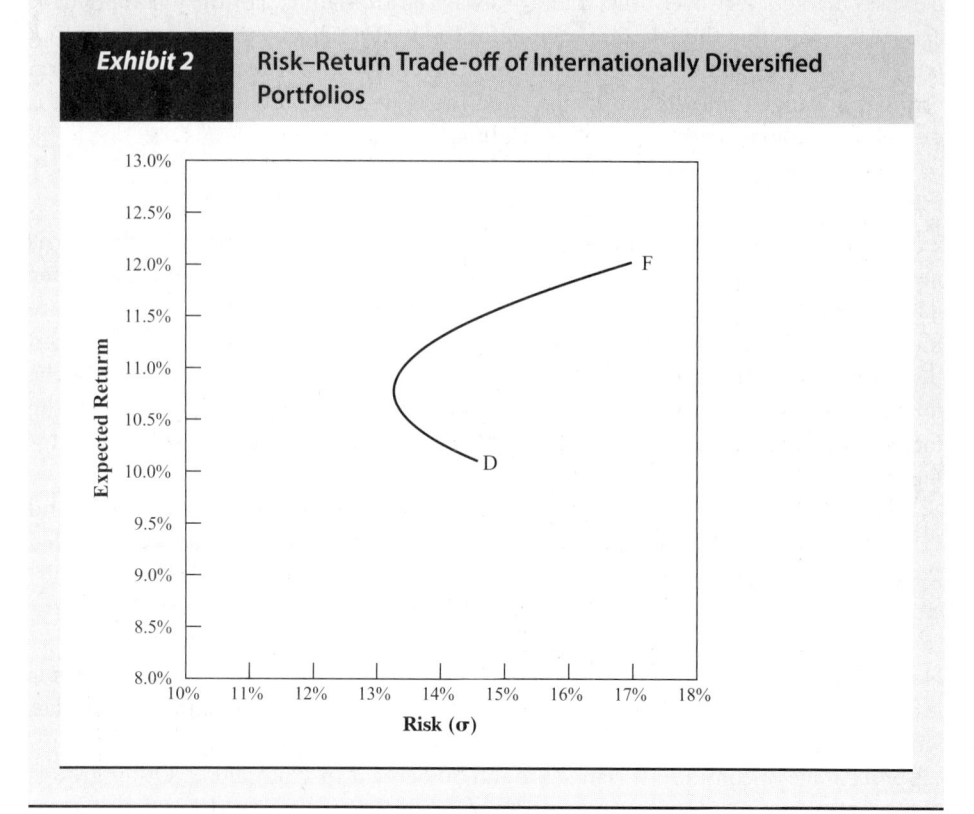

Exhibit 2 Risk–Return Trade-off of Internationally Diversified Portfolios

A prerequisite for this argument is that the various capital markets of the world have somewhat independent price behaviors. If the Paris Bourse and the London Stock Exchange moved in parallel with the U.S. market, diversification opportunities would not exist. So, we start by an empirical investigation of the level of international correlation.

Exhibit 3   Risk–Return Trade-off of Internationally Diversified versus Domestic-Only Portfolios

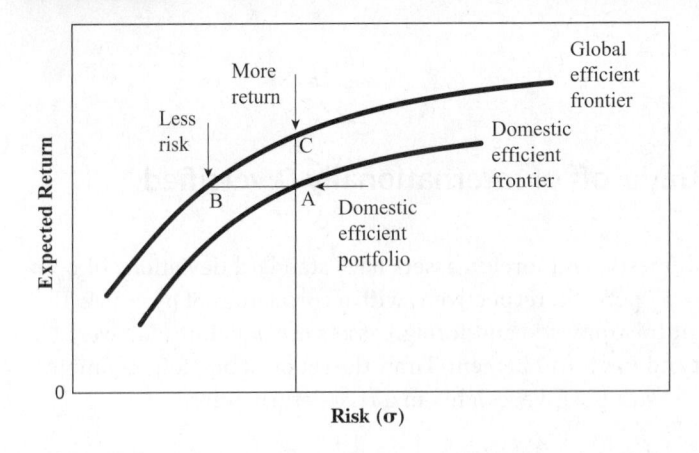

The correlations between various stock and bond markets are systematically monitored by major international money managers. Although the correlation coefficients between markets vary over time, they are always far from unity. For the portfolio manager, this means that there is ample room for successful risk diversification. Following is a discussion of some recently estimated correlations, as illustration. Correlation estimates change somewhat over time, and the issue of stability in the correlation is discussed in the next sections of this reading.

Equity

Exhibit 4 gives the correlations across selected national stock markets with returns measured in two different currencies over the 10-year period from May 1997 to May 2007. The bottom left part of the matrix gives the correlation when all returns are measured in U.S. dollars. The top right part of the matrix gives the correlation when the foreign investments are fully hedged against currency risk; in other words, the foreign currency is assumed to be sold forward for an amount equal to that of the foreign stock investment. Let's first examine the correlations when no currency hedging is undertaken (U.S. dollar returns).

For example, Exhibit 4 indicates that the correlation between the Japanese and U.S. stock markets is 0.43. The square of this correlation coefficient, usually called R-square or R^2, indicates the percentage of common variance between the two markets. Note that the R-square is simply the square of the correlation ρ. Here only 19 percent ($R^2 = 0.44^2$) of stock price movements are common to the Japanese and U.S. markets.[7] Note that on average, the common variance between the U.S. and other markets is less than 50 percent (average ρ on the order of 0.7). The correlation of the U.S. market with Canada and major European markets is stronger than with Japan, with a typical percentage of common variance around 50 percent (ρ around 0.7). Other groups of countries are also highly correlated, indicating strong regional links. Germany and France tend to have high correlations because their economies are interrelated. Conversely, Japan shows little correlation with European or U.S. markets. This result confirms that the Japanese business cycle has been somewhat disconnected from the rest of the world.

---

7 An R^2 of 19 percent may be interpreted as follows: 19 percent of the Japanese stock price movements are the result of influences common to the U.S. stock market. In other words, 81 percent of the price movements are independent of U.S. market influences.

The Traditional Case For International Diversification

Exhibit 4 Correlation of Stock Markets, 1997–2007 Monthly Returns in U.S. Dollars (Bottom Left) and Currency Hedged (Top Right)

	United States	Canada	United Kingdom	France	Germany	Italy	Switzerland	Japan	Hong Kong	Europe	EAFE	World	Emerging Markets
United States	1.00	0.73	0.74	0.71	0.73	0.55	0.66	0.41	0.51	0.77	0.77	0.91	0.67
Canada	0.72	1.00	0.60	0.65	0.61	0.51	0.56	0.47	0.54	0.67	0.70	0.77	0.70
United Kingdom	0.73	0.62	1.00	0.76	0.72	0.66	0.73	0.40	0.46	0.86	0.83	0.82	0.59
France	0.70	0.66	0.77	1.00	0.87	0.78	0.77	0.45	0.39	0.91	0.88	0.83	0.59
Germany	0.73	0.63	0.73	0.86	1.00	0.72	0.71	0.42	0.39	0.88	0.85	0.83	0.61
Italy	0.52	0.51	0.62	0.78	0.71	1.00	0.65	0.36	0.26	0.80	0.75	0.68	0.50
Switzerland	0.57	0.51	0.70	0.72	0.64	0.62	1.00	0.45	0.37	0.81	0.80	0.76	0.54
Japan	0.43	0.50	0.40	0.35	0.30	0.23	0.40	1.00	0.31	0.47	0.66	0.56	0.56
Hong Kong	0.51	0.55	0.48	0.41	0.41	0.28	0.37	0.43	1.00	0.45	0.50	0.54	0.66
Europe	0.76	0.69	0.86	0.91	0.88	0.78	0.78	0.40	0.48	1.00	0.92	0.88	0.65
EAFE	0.76	0.74	0.83	0.85	0.81	0.70	0.76	0.65	0.57	0.90	1.00	0.90	0.72
World	0.91	0.78	0.81	0.81	0.81	0.64	0.69	0.56	0.57	0.87	0.90	1.00	0.74
Emerging Markets	0.66	0.72	0.58	0.60	0.62	0.49	0.47	0.52	0.68	0.65	0.73	0.74	1.00

329

The last four rows and columns in Exhibit 4 give the correlation of each national market with four international indexes calculated by Morgan Stanley Capital International. The first three indexes refer to developed stock markets. The Europe index is made up of stock markets from Europe. The Europe, Australasia, and Far East (EAFE) index is the non-U.S. world index and is made up of stock markets from those parts of the world. The World index is a market capitalization–weighted index of all the major stock markets of the world. The Emerging Markets index is a cap-weighted index of emerging stock markets. The correlation of the U.S. market with the EAFE index is 0.76. Therefore, the overall common variance between U.S. and non-U.S. stock indexes is 58 percent ($R^2 = 0.76^2 = 58\%$). This implies that any well-diversified portfolio of non-U.S. stocks provides an attractive risk-diversification vehicle for a domestic U.S. portfolio. The same conclusion, that foreign stocks provide attractive risk-diversification benefits to a domestic stock portfolio, holds true from any other national viewpoint.

The correlation of the U.S. stock market with the world index is much larger ($R^2 = 0.91^2 = 83\%$) than it is for the EAFE index. But this should not be surprising, since the U.S. market accounts for a significant share of the world market.

In general, the low correlation across countries offers risk diversification and return opportunities. It allows naive investors to spread risk, since some foreign markets are likely to go up when others go down. This also provides opportunities for expert international investors to time the markets by buying those markets that they expect to go up and neglecting the bearish ones.

The degree of independence of a stock market is directly linked to the independence of a nation's economy and governmental policies. To some extent, common world factors affect expected cash flows of all firms and therefore their stock prices. However, purely national or regional factors seem to play an important role in asset prices, leading to sizable differences in the degrees of independence between markets. It is clear that constraints and regulations imposed by national governments, technological specialization, independent fiscal and monetary policies, and cultural and sociological differences all contribute to the degree of a capital market's independence. On the other hand, when there are closer economic and government policies, as among the euro countries, one observes more commonality in capital market behavior. In any case, the covariation between markets is still far from unity, leaving ample opportunities for risk diversification.

The last row/column of Exhibit 4 reports the correlation with a diversified index of emerging markets. Emerging markets present a positive but rather low correlation with developed markets; the correlation with the U.S. stock market is 0.66. The case for diversifying into emerging markets is discussed in the last section of this reading.

Let's now examine the correlation across stock markets when full currency hedging is undertaken. The correlation coefficients in the top right part of the matrix are very similar to the U.S. dollar correlations. For example, the correlation between the U.S. and Japanese markets decreases slightly to 0.41, but some other correlations are slightly higher. There is little difference between stock market correlations when we look at hedged and unhedged returns.

Bonds

Similar conclusions can be reached for bonds, as can be seen in Exhibit 5, which is presented in a fashion similar to that of Exhibit 4, but for a different time period. Let's first look at the correlation of the various bond markets when returns are all expressed in U.S. dollars (the bottom left part of the exhibit). For example, the correlation of U.S. dollar returns of U.S. and French bonds is only 0.38, or an average percentage of common variance of less than 15 percent (the square of 0.38). The correlation of U.S. bonds with every foreign bond market is below 0.50. Canadian dollar bonds are most strongly correlated with U.S. dollar bonds. In general, long-term return variations are not highly correlated across countries.

Exhibit 5 Correlation of Bond Markets, January 1992–January 2002 Monthly Returns in U.S. Dollars (Bottom Left) and Currency Hedged (Top Right)

	United States	Canada	United Kingdom	France	Germany	Italy	Switzerland	Netherlands	Japan	U.S. Equity
United States	1.00	0.64	0.51	0.49	0.55	0.33	0.37	0.57	0.23	0.19
Canada	0.49	1.00	0.47	0.37	0.36	0.28	0.23	0.38	0.16	0.26
United Kingdom	0.49	0.30	1.00	0.68	0.74	0.50	0.51	0.75	0.05	0.19
France	0.38	0.11	0.61	1.00	0.85	0.71	0.63	0.83	0.09	0.09
Germany	0.40	0.13	0.62	0.92	1.00	0.58	0.68	0.94	0.25	0.07
Italy	0.27	0.23	0.54	0.61	0.53	1.00	0.34	0.57	0.08	0.21
Switzerland	0.32	0.05	0.50	0.88	0.89	0.43	1.00	0.71	0.24	−0.05
Netherlands	0.40	0.14	0.59	0.96	0.96	0.55	0.90	1.00	0.24	0.12
Japan	0.17	0.06	0.23	0.42	0.46	0.12	0.50	0.48	1.00	−0.09
U.S. Equity	0.19	0.41	0.17	−0.01	0.00	0.08	−0.14	0.01	0.11	1.00

Regional blocs do appear. European bond markets tend to be quite correlated. This is especially true of countries from the Eurozone, because a common currency was progressively introduced over the period under study. The Eurozone bond markets now exhibit a correlation close to 1.0 for government bonds.

The general observation is that national monetary/budget policies are not fully synchronized. For example, the growing U.S. budget deficit in the mid-1980s, associated with high U.S. interest rates and a rapid weakening of the dollar, was not matched in other countries. The relative independence of national monetary/budget policies, influencing both currency and interest rate movements, leads to a surprisingly low correlation of U.S. dollar returns on the U.S. and foreign bond markets. Hence, foreign bonds allow investors to diversify the risks associated with domestic monetary/budget policies.

Finally, the last asset class in Exhibit 5 is U.S. equity. The correlation of foreign bonds with the U.S. stock market is quite small. This is not surprising, given the independence between U.S. and foreign national economic and monetary policies. Foreign bonds offer excellent diversification benefits to a U.S. stock portfolio manager.

Let us now examine the correlation across bond markets when full currency hedging is undertaken. The correlation coefficients in the top right part of the matrix are somewhat different from the U.S. dollar correlations. This is because there exists a correlation between currency movements and bond yield movements (and hence bond returns). For example, some countries practice a "leaning against the wind" policy, whereby they raise their interest rates to defend their currencies. So the correlation of two national bond markets would be different if we look at hedged returns or at currency-adjusted returns.

Leads and Lags

So far, we have talked about the contemporaneous correlation across markets taking place when an event or factor affects two or more markets simultaneously. Some investigators have attempted to find leads or lags between markets. For example, they studied whether a bear market in February on Wall Street would lead to a drop in prices on other national markets in March. No evidence of a systematic delayed reaction of one national market to another has ever been found, except for daily returns, as outlined later. The existence of such simple market inefficiencies is, indeed, unlikely, because it would be easy to exploit them to make an abnormal profit.

One must take into account the time differences around the world, however, before assessing whether a given national market leads or lags other markets. The stock exchanges in New York and Tokyo are not open at the same time. If important news hits New York prices on a Tuesday, it will affect Tokyo prices on Wednesday. If important news hits London prices on a Tuesday, it will affect New York prices the same day, because New York generally lags London by five hours. Indeed, when it is Tuesday noon in New York, it is already Tuesday 17:00 (or 5 p.m.) local time in London and Wednesday 02:00 (or 2 a.m.) in Tokyo.[8] The opening and closing times of the three major stock markets are depicted in Exhibit 6, in which the trading hours are indicated using both the universal GMT (Greenwich Mean Time) and the American EST (Eastern Standard Time). It can be seen that New York and Tokyo official trading hours never overlap. London and New York trading hours generally overlap for two hours. If the markets are efficient, international news should affect all markets around the globe simultaneously, with markets closed at that hour reflecting the news immediately on opening. For example, if important news is revealed after noon EST, it can be impounded in Japanese and British stock prices only the next day; because

---

[8] Europe and the United States, but not Asia, change time during the summer (daylight savings time in the United States), but not necessarily on the same date.

The Traditional Case For International Diversification

of the time differences involved, we should not be surprised to find a lagging correlation of Tokyo and London with New York when returns are measured from closing price to closing price. This lagged correlation can be explained by the difference in time zones, not by some international market inefficiency that could be exploited to make a profit. This effect gets drastically reduced when looking at correlation of longer-period return, for example, monthly returns.

Exhibit 6 Stock Exchange Trade Hours in Greenwich Mean Time (GMT) and Eastern Standard Time (EST) Clocks

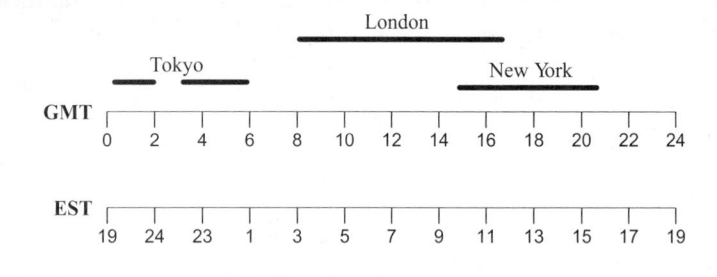

```
                    London
           Tokyo              New York
GMT  |--|--|--|--|--|--|--|--|--|--|--|--|
     0  2  4  6  8  10 12 14 16 18 20 22 24

EST  |--|--|--|--|--|--|--|--|--|--|--|--|
     19 24 23 1  3  5  7  9  11 13 15 17 19
```

Portfolio Return Performance

We have devoted so much attention to the risk-reduction benefits of international investment because risk diversification is the most established and frequently invoked argument in favor of foreign investment, justifying foreign investment even to the naive investor. However, risk reduction is not the sole motive for international investment. Indeed, mere risk reduction could more easily be achieved by simply investing part of one's assets in domestic risk-free bills. Unfortunately, although the inclusion of risk-free bills lowers the portfolio risk, it also lowers expected return. In the traditional framework of the capital asset pricing model (CAPM), the expected return on a security is equal to the risk-free rate plus a risk premium. In an efficient market, reducing the risk level of a portfolio by adding less-risky investments implies reducing its expected return. International diversification, however, implies no reduction in expected return. Such diversification lowers risk by eliminating nonsystematic volatility without sacrificing expected return. A traditional way to evaluate a portfolio's risk-adjusted performance is to evaluate its *Sharpe ratio*. This is the ratio of the return on a portfolio, in excess of the risk-free rate, divided by its standard deviation (see Example 4). Money managers attempt to maximize this Sharpe ratio, which gives the excess return per unit of risk. Global investing should increase the Sharpe ratio because of the reduction in risk. Investing in foreign assets allows a reduction in portfolio risk (the denominator of the Sharpe ratio) without necessarily sacrificing expected return (the numerator of the Sharpe ratio). Both domestic and foreign investors can see their Sharpe ratio increase if they diversify away from purely local assets. As long as the expected returns on domestic and foreign assets are comparable, both types of investors would benefit from international risk reduction compared to a portfolio of purely local assets. The second argument for an increase in the Sharpe ratio is that more profitable investments are possible in an enlarged investment universe. Higher expected returns may arise from faster-growing economies and firms located around the world, or simply from currency gains. These advantages can be obtained by optimizing the global asset allocation.

Example 4

International Diversification and the Sharpe Ratio

Assume that the domestic and foreign assets have standard deviations of $\sigma_d = 15$ percent and $\sigma_f = 17$ percent, respectively, with a correlation of $\rho_{d,f} = 0.4$. The risk-free rate is equal to 4 percent in both countries.

1. The expected returns of the domestic and foreign assets are both equal to 10 percent: $E(R_d) = E(R_f) = 10$ percent. Calculate the Sharpe ratios for the domestic asset, the foreign asset, and an internationally diversified portfolio equally invested in the domestic and foreign assets. What do you conclude?

2. Assume now that the expected return on the foreign asset is higher than on the domestic asset, $E(R_d) = 10$ percent but $E(R_f) = 12$ percent. Calculate the Sharpe ratio for an internationally diversified portfolio equally invested in the domestic and foreign assets, and compare your findings to those in Part 1.

Solution to 1:

The domestic asset has an expected return of 10 percent and a standard deviation of 15 percent. For this asset,

$$\text{Sharpe ratio} = \frac{E(R) - \text{Risk-free rate}}{\sigma} = \frac{10\% - 4\%}{15\%} = 0.4$$

The foreign asset has a Sharpe ratio of $\frac{10\% - 4\%}{17\%} = 0.353$

A portfolio equally invested in the domestic and foreign asset has an expected return of 10 percent and a standard deviation σ_p given by

$$\sigma_p^2 = 0.5^2 \left[\sigma_d^2 + \sigma_f^2 + \left(2\rho_{d,f}\sigma_d\sigma_f\right) \right]$$

$$\sigma_p^2 = 0.5^2 \left[225 + 289 + (2 \times 0.4 \times 255) \right] = 179.5$$

Hence, the standard deviation σ_p is given by $\sqrt{179.5}$, or 13.4 percent. The Sharpe ratio of the portfolio is equal to

$$\text{Sharpe ratio} = \frac{E(R_p) - \text{Risk-free rate}}{\sigma_p} = \frac{10\% - 4\%}{13.4\%} = 0.448$$

The foreign asset has a lower Sharpe ratio than the domestic asset because it has the same expected return but a larger standard deviation. However, the equally weighted portfolio benefits from risk diversification and a lower standard deviation. Hence, its Sharpe ratio is better than the ratios of both the domestic and the foreign assets.

Solution to 2:

A portfolio equally invested in the domestic and foreign asset has an expected return of 11 percent (0.5 × 10% + 0.5 × 12% = 11%). Hence, the Sharpe ratio is equal to (11% − 4%) / 13.4% = 0.522. The portfolio's Sharpe ratio is now better than that of the domestic asset (0.4), both because of risk-diversification benefits and because of the superior expected return of the foreign asset [new Sharpe ratio of (12% − 4%) / 17% = 0.471].

The Traditional Case For International Diversification

An Ex Post Example

It is easy to derive the global asset allocation that would have been optimal from a risk–return viewpoint over some past period, but the results depend on the period selected. To illustrate such an analysis, Exhibit 7 shows optimal global stock allocations for different risk levels and for a U.S. investor, as reported by Odier and Solnik (1993). This is the efficient frontier based on returns for the period 1980–1990. No investment constraints other than no short selling are applied; results do not reflect any currency hedging. The mean annual return is given on the Y axis, and the asset volatility (standard deviation) is given on the X axis. Each asset or portfolio is represented by one point on the graph (a few selected markets are plotted on the graph). The U.S. stock market has a risk of 16.2 percent and an annualized total return of 13.3 percent. Other stock markets are more volatile, partly because of currency risk. By combining the various national stock markets, we get diversified portfolios whose returns and risks can be calculated, because we know the returns and covariances of all the assets. Investors select asset allocations that lie on the efficient frontier depicted in Exhibit 7. The best achievable risk-return trade-offs—the optimal asset allocations—lie on the efficient frontier.

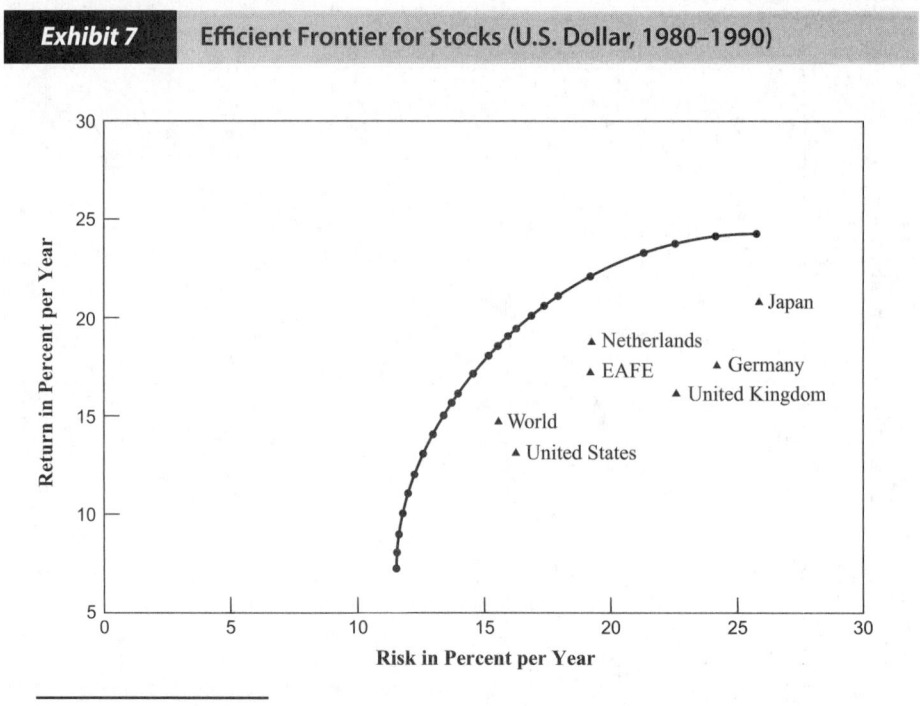

Exhibit 7 Efficient Frontier for Stocks (U.S. Dollar, 1980–1990)

Source: P. Odier and B. Solnik. Adapted from "Lessons for International Asset Allocation," *Financial Analysts Journal*, March/April 1993. Copyright © 2007 CFA Institute. All Rights Reserved.

As Exhibit 7 shows, international diversification of a pure U.S. stock portfolio would greatly enhance returns without a large increase in risk. A global stock portfolio with the same risk level as the purely U.S. stock portfolio (16.2% per year) would achieve an annualized total return above 19 percent, compared with 13.3 percent for the U.S. portfolio.

Can bonds help improve the risk-adjusted performance of globally diversified portfolios? The question here is not whether investors should prefer portfolios made up solely of bonds or solely of stocks, but whether bonds should be added to a stock portfolio in a global investment strategy. Exhibit 8 gives the efficient frontier for a global asset allocation allowing for bonds and stocks, foreign and domestic. To keep the exhibit readable, we did not plot individual bond and stock markets, but only the U.S. bond and stock indexes, as well as the world stock index. Their relative positions are consistent with theory. U.S. bonds have a lower risk and a lower return. Over the long run, riskier stock investments are compensated by a risk premium. The global asset allocations on the efficient frontier strongly dominate U.S. investments. The global efficient asset allocation with a return equal to that of the U.S. stock market (13.3% per year) has a risk equal to only half that of the U.S. stock market. Conversely, a global efficient allocation with the same risk as the U.S. stock market outperforms the U.S. stock market by 8 percent per year. Similarly, any domestic U.S. stock/bond strategy is strongly dominated by a global stock/bond strategy. A domestic portfolio of U.S. stocks and bonds tends to have half the return of that on a global efficient allocation with the same risk level. Adding foreign bonds in a global asset allocation can be attractive from a risk–return viewpoint because of their low correlation with domestic bond and stock investments, as outlined previously.

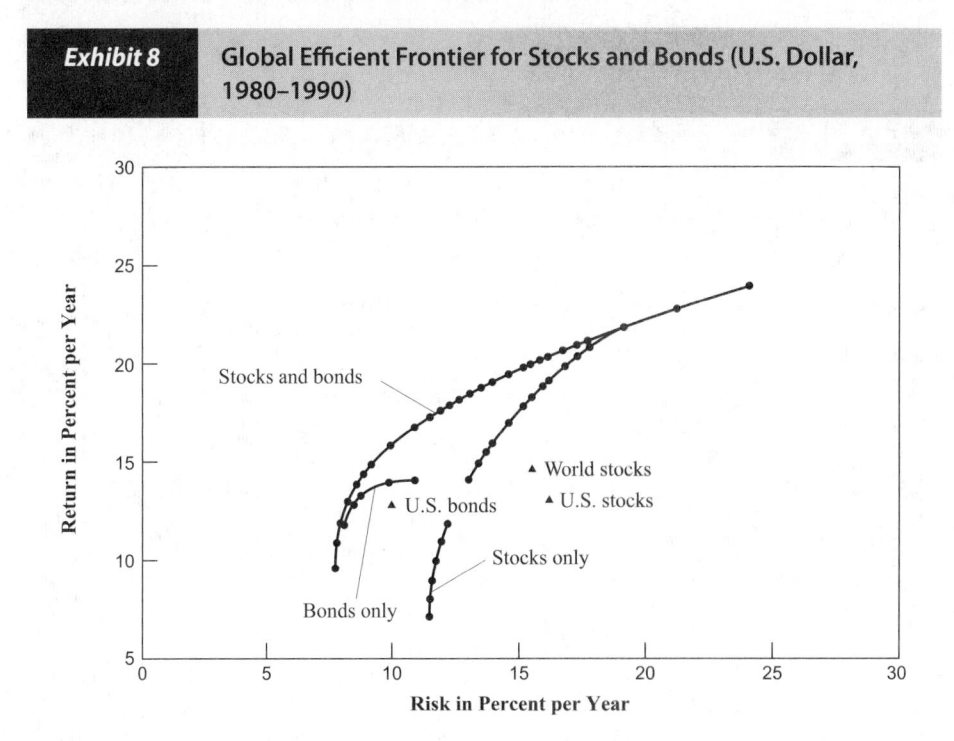

Exhibit 8 Global Efficient Frontier for Stocks and Bonds (U.S. Dollar, 1980–1990)

Source: P. Odier and B. Solnik. Adapted from "Lessons for International Asset Allocation," *Financial Analysts Journal*, March/April 1993. Copyright © 2007 CFA Institute. All Rights Reserved.

Exhibit 8 also shows the global efficient frontier for stocks only (same as Exhibit 7) as well as the efficient international frontier for bonds only. Clearly, stocks offer a strong contribution to a bond portfolio in terms of risk–return trade-off; the bond-only efficient frontier is also dominated by a global strategy.

Exhibit 9 shows the efficient frontier for Japanese, German, and British investors. All calculations are performed in the respective national currencies. Conclusions similar to those developed earlier can be reached when we take the viewpoint of investors from different countries of the world. The benefits of global investing can hold from all national viewpoints simultaneously. The expanded investment universe (from domestic to global) offers potentials for risk diversification and return improvement, and hence an improvement in the Sharpe ratio for all investors.

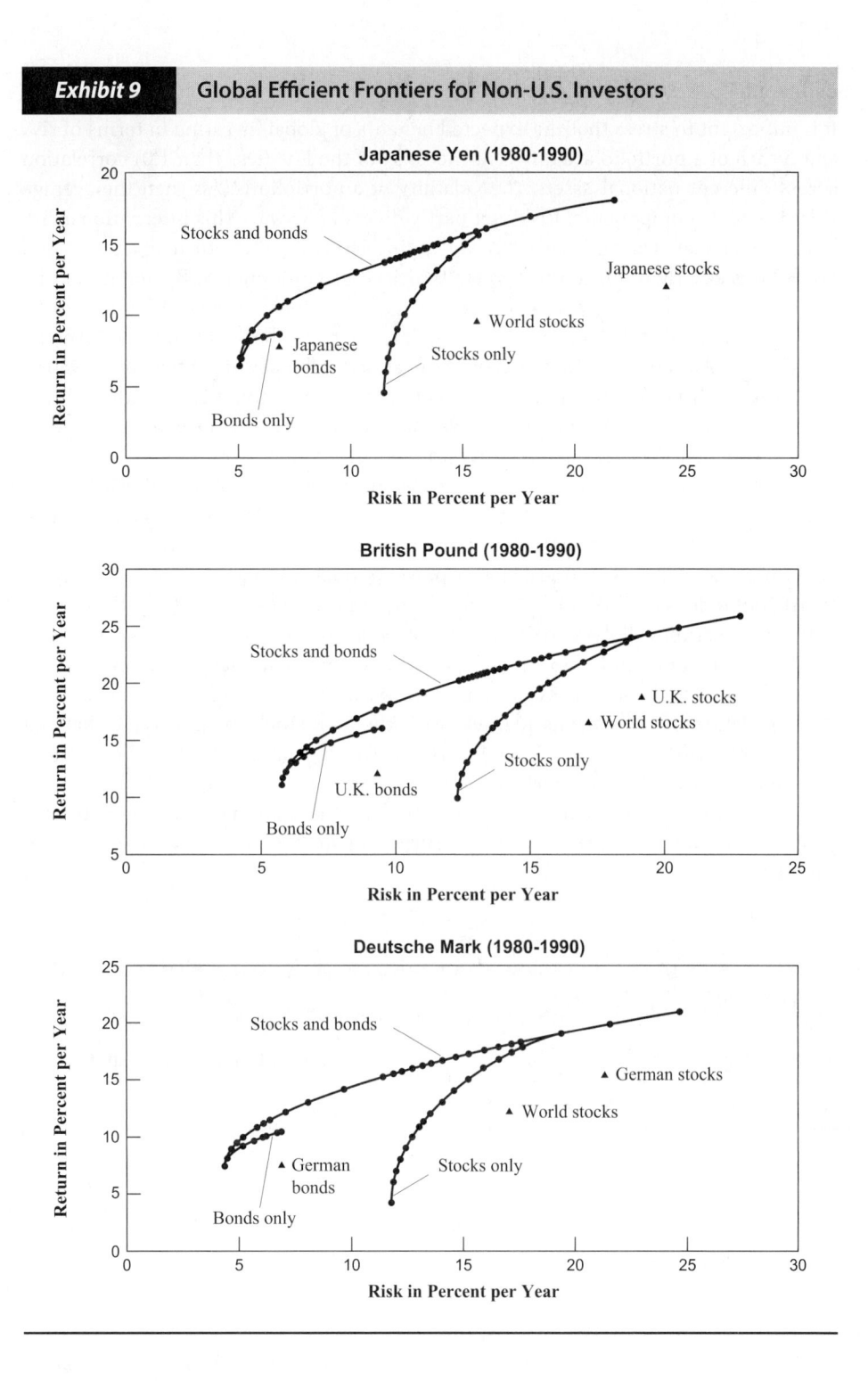

The Traditional Case For International Diversification

Exhibit 9   Global Efficient Frontiers for Non-U.S. Investors

[Three charts showing efficient frontiers: Japanese Yen (1980–1990), British Pound (1980–1990), and Deutsche Mark (1980–1990), plotting Return in Percent per Year against Risk in Percent per Year, with curves for "Stocks and bonds" and "Stocks only," and reference points for domestic bonds, domestic stocks, and world stocks.]

The potential profits are large, but optimizing them requires some forecasting skills. A major question is how much of the potential can be achieved through superior management skills. Even if only 20 percent of the profits could be reaped, global-asset allocation would seem to be very valuable in risk–return terms. It is, of course, quite difficult to know in advance what these optimal asset allocations will be. Therefore, all we can conclude is that the opportunities for increased risk-adjusted returns are sizable and that the performance gap between optimal global asset allocations and a simple world index fund is potentially quite wide. Whether any money manager has sufficient expertise to realize most, or even part, of this performance differential is yet another question.

Different Market Environments

It is important to stress that the expected benefits of global investing in terms of risk and return of a portfolio are different. Because of the low (less than 1.0) correlation across different national assets, the volatility of a portfolio is *less* than the average volatility of its components. Risks get partly diversified away. This international risk reduction appears from any currency viewpoint. However, the return on a diversified portfolio is exactly *equal* to the average return of its components. By definition, the return on the world index is the average return of all national markets. In other words, some countries will outperform the world index, whereas others will underperform the world index. Although international diversification has looked attractive from 1980 to 1990 from both a risk and a return viewpoint for a U.S. investor, this is not the case for a Japanese investor, whose national stock market had higher returns than the world index. Over that decade, Japanese investors benefited only from the risk reduction provided by a passive global portfolio, such as the world index. Again, this illustrates the mathematics of the world index, whose return is exactly the weighted average of its components. It is unlikely that any single market will under- or overperform the other markets in all time periods. Hence, passive global diversification is wise in terms of risk, but it does not provide a "free lunch" in terms of return. Similarly, the ex post optimal allocation will depend on the period under study.

This is illustrated in Exhibit 10, which gives the mean annual return (in U.S. dollars) on major stock markets in successive five-year periods. Exhibit 10 also provides the correlation of the various markets with the U.S. stock market. Note that the 1990–2000 period saw a reversal of performance for Japanese investors. The Japanese stock market strongly underperformed the world index. International diversification was very attractive for Japanese investors. The fact that national stock markets have different long-term performances is not surprising and could justify an active asset allocation strategy.

Exhibit 10 Mean Return and Correlation of Selected Markets with the U.S. Equity Market Five-Year Periods from 1971 to 2005, in U.S. Dollars

	Mean Return (in % per Year)				Correlation with U.S. Equity		
5-Year Period	United States	Japan	Europe	EAFE	Japan	Europe	EAFE
1971–1975	1.4	22.1	5.5	9.80	0.40	0.61	0.59
1976–1980	12.3	20.7	12.2	17.0	0.12	0.28	0.36
1981–1985	15.0	19.3	16.3	16.8	0.32	0.49	0.46
1986–1990	12.7	20.6	18.2	18.7	0.25	0.64	0.44
1991–1995	16.9	5.6	12.9	10.1	0.22	0.65	0.47
1996–2000	18.4	−4.6	16.0	7.6	0.48	0.62	0.66
2001–2005	−0.2	6.4	4.0	4.8	0.40	0.87	0.85

Forward-Looking Optimization

Although ex post exercises yield some interesting general lessons, portfolio management needs to be forward looking. An adequate global asset allocation should be based on market forecasts, not on past returns. Several factors can help formulate expectations.

In the long run, the performance of stock markets can be explained by national economic factors. The difference in performance between the U.S., Europe, and Japan equity markets reported in Exhibit 10 is largely the result of differences in real growth

The Traditional Case For International Diversification

rates. This can be seen in Exhibit 11, which gives the mean annual growth rate in GDP for successive 10-year periods for the United States, Japan, Europe, and the average of all OECD countries. For example, real growth was much higher in Japan than in the United States in the 1970s and 1980s, and much lower in the 1990s. The stock markets' performance followed the same pattern.

Exhibit 11 Real Growth Rate (GDP Growth) of Selected Regions' Ten-Year Periods from 1971 to 2000

GDP Growth	United States (%)	Japan (%)	Europe (%)	OECD (%)
1971–1980	2.76	4.51	2.95	3.13
1981–1990	2.48	4.15	2.34	2.71
1991–2000	3.40	1.30	2.50	2.30

Economic flexibility is also an important factor in investment performance, which may explain differences between past and future performances among emerging countries. Wage and employment rigidity is bad for the national economy. In countries such as France, Canada, and Sweden, corporations have a difficult time adjusting to slowing activity; on the other hand, they do not take full advantage of growth opportunities because they are reluctant to hire new employees, whom they cannot fire if activity slows.

Economic forecasting is a useful exercise, but it should be stressed that scenarios that are widely expected to take place should already be impounded in current asset prices. For example, if a Country X is widely expected to experience higher economic growth than other countries, that fact should be reflected in higher stock prices in Country X. If future growth develops according to expectations, there is no reason to have higher future returns for stocks of Country X. So, investors forecasting economic growth rates must take into account the market consensus about future growth rates.

It should be stressed that there is no guarantee that the past will repeat itself. Indeed, over any given period, one national market is bound to outperform the other, and if an investor had perfect foresight, the best strategy would be to invest solely in the top-performing market, or even in the top-performing security in that market. But because of the great uncertainty of forecasts, it is always better to spread risk in the fund by diversifying globally across markets with comparable expected returns. This ensures a favorable risk–return trade-off or, in the jargon of theory, higher risk-adjusted expected returns. If managers believe that they have some relative forecasting ability, they will engage in active investment strategies that reap the benefits of international risk diversification while focusing on preferred markets. For example, a U.S. investor may concentrate on U.S. and European stocks if she is bullish on those markets and may avoid Japan for political or currency reasons.

Some emerging economies offer attractive investment opportunities. The local risks (volatility, liquidity, political environment) are higher, as illustrated by numerous crises, but the expected profit is large. Furthermore, those risks get partly diversified away in a global portfolio. Hence, emerging markets and alternative investments can have a positive contribution in terms of risk–return trade-offs.

Currency Risk Not a Barrier to International Investment

Currency fluctuations affect both the total return and the volatility of any foreign currency–denominated investment. From time to time, in fact, the effects of currency fluctuations on the investment return may exceed that of capital gain or income, especially over short periods of time. Empirical studies indicate that currency risk, as measured by the standard deviation of the exchange rate movement, is smaller than the risk of the corresponding stock market (roughly half). On the other hand, currency risk is often larger than the risk (in local currency) of the corresponding bond market (roughly twice). In a global portfolio, the depreciation of one currency is often offset by the appreciation of another. Indeed, several points are worth mentioning regarding currency risk.

First, market and currency risks are not additive. This would be true only if the two were perfectly correlated. In fact, there is only a weak, and sometimes negative, correlation between currency and market movements. This point was stressed in the previous section. In Example 2, the exchange rate standard deviation is 7 percent compared with a local-currency standard deviation of 15.5 percent for the foreign stock. However, the contribution of currency risk to total risk is only 1.5 percentage points. So, currency risk adds only some 10 percent (1.5 percent as a fraction of 15.5 percent) to the risk of a foreign asset. This is a typical figure.

The correlation between changes in the exchange rate and the asset price is an important element in assessing the contribution of currency risk. The lower the correlation, the smaller the contribution of currency risk to total risk.

Second, the exchange risk of an investment may be hedged for major currencies by selling futures or forward currency contracts, buying put currency options, or even borrowing foreign currency to finance the investment. So, currency risk can easily be eliminated in international investment strategies. But currencies can also provide some attractive profit opportunities.

Third, the contribution of currency risk should be measured for the total portfolio rather than for individual markets or securities, because part of that risk gets diversified away by the mix of currencies represented in the portfolio. As stressed by Jorion (1989), the contribution of currency risk to the total risk of a portfolio that includes only a small proportion of foreign assets (say, 5 percent) is insignificant. The contribution of currency risk is larger if one holds the world market portfolio and, hence, a large share of foreign assets. Actually holding some foreign-currency assets can provide some diversification to domestic fiscal and monetary risks. A lax domestic monetary policy can be bad for domestic asset prices and lead to a home-currency depreciation. Foreign currencies help diversify that risk.

Fourth, the contribution of currency risk decreases with the length of the investment horizon. Exchange rates tend to revert to fundamentals over the long run (mean reversion). Hence, an investor with a long time horizon should care less about currency risk than should an investor who is concerned about monthly fluctuations in the portfolio's value. Froot (1993) shows that currency risk can disappear over very long term horizons (over one or several decades).

2. THE CASE AGAINST INTERNATIONAL DIVERSIFICATION

Several impediments to international portfolio investing are often mentioned. First, the case for international diversification presented earlier has been attacked on the basis that it strongly overstates the risk benefits of international investing. Second, skeptics also look at the historical performance of their domestic market relative to other foreign markets. Third, there are numerous physical barriers to international investing.

The Case Against International Diversification

Increase in Correlations

It is often argued that the benefits of international diversification are overstated because markets tend to be more synchronized than suggested previously. There is no reason for the correlation between two equity markets to remain constant over a long period of time. Indeed, it has been observed that international correlations have trended upward over the past decade. It has also been observed that international correlation increases in periods of high market volatility.

Correlations Have Increased over Time

Economies and financial markets are becoming increasingly integrated, leading to an increase in international correlation of asset prices. Economic and financial globalization observed at the turn of the millennium can be witnessed in many areas.

- Capital markets are being deregulated and opened to foreign players. Markets that used to be segmented are moving toward global integration.

- Capital mobility has increased, especially among developed countries. International capital flows have dramatically increased since the 1950s. The success of international investing means that foreign institutional investors, such as pension funds, are now major players on most domestic markets.

- National economies are opening up to free trade, in part under the pressure of the World Trade Organization and of regional agreements such as NAFTA, ASEAN, and the European Union. Hence, national economies are becoming more synchronized.

- As the economic environment becomes global, corporations become increasingly global in their operations. They achieve this global strategy through increased exports, international organic growth, and foreign acquisitions. A simple indicator is provided by the amount of cross-border mergers and acquisitions (M&As) shown in Exhibit 12. The amount of cross-border M&As has risen dramatically in the past twenty years. Cross-border M&As were few in the early 1990s, but they have become an increasing proportion of total M&As. While the economic slowdown and bear equity market of the early 2000s have slowed down M&As, the share of cross-border M&As among total M&As has steadily risen since 2003.

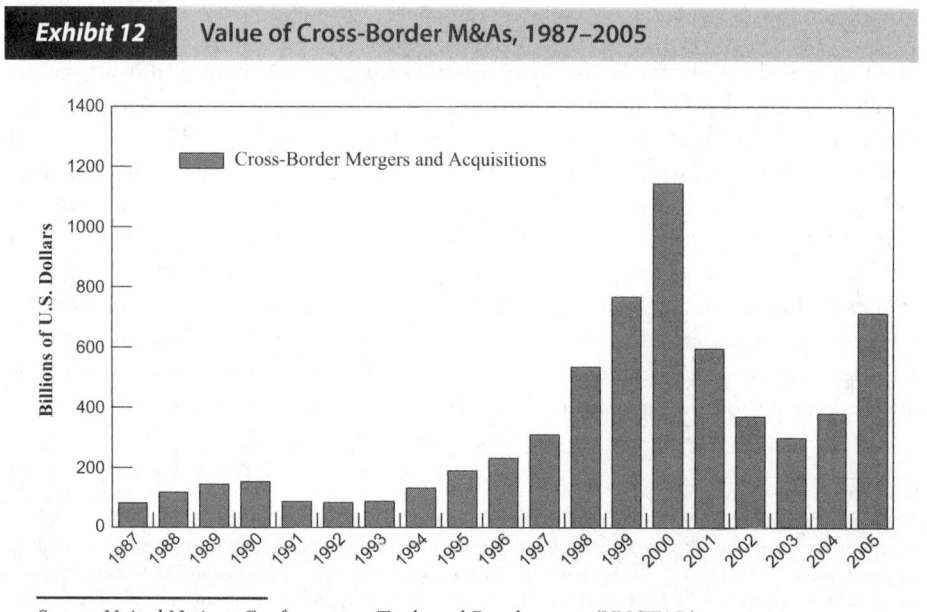

Exhibit 12   Value of Cross-Border M&As, 1987–2005

Source: United Nations Conference on Trade and Development (UNCTAD).

As corporations become more global, it is not surprising to see the correlation between their stock prices increase. The legal nationality of a corporation becomes less important. As a firm competes globally and derives a significant part of its cash flows from abroad, its value is affected by global factors, not primarily by the location of its headquarters. Hence, it is not surprising to find that country factors become less important and that the correlation among national stock markets tends to increase.

International correlations move over time, as can be seen in Exhibit 10. Correlation is high in periods when global shocks affect all countries (e.g., the oil shock of the early 1970s) and lower in other periods. However, Exhibit 10 suggests that the correlation between the U.S. and other stock markets has been trending upward since 1975.

Goetzmann, Li, and Rouwenhorst (2001) examined the correlation structure of the major world equity markets from the late nineteenth century until the end of 2000. They found that correlations varied considerably through time, with peaks in the late nineteenth century, the Great Depression, and the late twentieth century. They concluded that the current diversification benefits to global investing were relatively low compared with the rest of capital market history, because correlation was at a high point.

Correlation Increases When Markets Are Volatile

A major criticism addressed to the mean–variance framework used to present the case for international diversification is that it assumes "normality." In statistical terms, all returns are supposed to have a "joint multivariate normal distribution." In real life, returns are not exactly drawn from normal probability tables with constant correlations across assets. Three deviations from market "normality" are most often mentioned:

- Distributions of returns tend to have fat tails (leptokurtic distribution). In other words, the occurrence of large positive or negative returns is more frequent than expected under normal distributions.[9]

- Market volatility varies over time, but volatility is "contagious." In other words, high volatility in the U.S. stock market tends to be associated with high volatility in foreign stock markets, as well as in other financial markets (bond, currency).

- The correlation across markets increases dramatically in periods of high volatility, for example, during major market events such as the October 1987 crash.

The fact that there are fat tails or that volatility tends to move up or down together on all markets is not a direct attack on global risk diversification. It simply says that a static mean–variance analysis is a simplified view of the world and that more sophisticated quantitative methods could be used; it does not negate the advantage of international risk reduction. Correlation moves over time[10] for obvious reasons. There are tranquil periods during which domestic factors dominate and markets are not strongly correlated across countries. There are times during which global shocks affect simultaneously all economies and business cycles move in sync. The oil shock of 1974 provides an example, as shown in Exhibit 10, and the correlation measured from 1971 to 1975 was much higher than in the next five years. The correlation estimated over a long period of time is simply an average over these various market cycles.

---

[9] See, for example, Longin (1996).
[10] Longin and Solnik (1995) studied the eight major stock markets from 1960 to 1990, using a GARCH methodology. They rejected the hypothesis that correlation is constant and found a modest but significant increase in international correlation over this 30-year period. Goetzmann, Li, and Rouwenhorst (2001) studied the correlation of the stock markets of France, Germany, the United Kingdom, and the United States from 1870 to 2000. They split the data into six periods based on historical events such as world wars. They found that the correlation structure differed significantly among many of the six time periods.

The Case Against International Diversification

For reasons mentioned previously, correlation of developed stock markets tends to increase slowly over time. But what is really troubling is that correlation seems to increase dramatically in periods of crises, so that the benefits of international risk diversification disappear when they are most needed. This phenomenon is sometimes referred to as *correlation breakdown*.

If all markets crash when your domestic market is crashing, there is little risk benefit to being internationally diversified. While it might be beneficial in "normal" times, it becomes useless in the exceptional times when there is a huge loss on domestic investments. And remember that fat tails mean that the occurrence of such crashes is more frequent than expected under "normality."

This concept is illustrated in Exhibit 13, which is reproduced from Bookstaber (1997). In one day of October 1987, the U.S. stock market crashed by some 20 percent, or about 20 times its historical daily standard deviation. The British, Japanese, and German markets dropped between 8 and 15 times their normal standard deviations. Other bond and currency market indicators also witnessed large declines.

Exhibit 13 1987 U.S. Stock Market Crash One-Day Movement in Units of "Normal" Daily Standard Deviations

Currency	Risk Factor	Movement (Standard Deviations)
USD	DV 0.01–10 Yr	−8
USD	2s–10s Spread	4
USD	Swaps to Bonds Spread	7
USD	S&P 500	−20
JPY	Nikkei	−15
JPY	JPY/$	4
GBP	DV 0.01–10 Yr	−5
GBP	FTSE 100	−13
GBP	GBP/$	3
DEM	DV 0.01–10 Yr	−4
DEM	DAX	−8

Source: Bookstaber (1997).

Implications of such correlation breakdowns extend well beyond international portfolio diversification. If they occur, correlation breakdowns would render very inefficient any hedging operations based on correlations, or betas, estimated over long-term historical data.

Past Performance Is a Good Indicator of Future Performance

Another criticism of international investing is country-specific, as it is typically formulated by investors whose markets have enjoyed a prolonged period of good performance. Skeptics point to the fact that, in recent periods, their domestic markets have generated greater returns than most other markets, and hence that there is no need for international investments in the future. As can be seen in Exhibit 10, the Japanese equity market had a superb performance relative to the rest of the world in the 1970s and 1980s. International investing was not in favor in Japan in 1990. A similar attitude has been adopted recently in the United States: U.S. equity yielded greater returns than overseas equity markets, especially Japan, in the 1990s and early 2000s. After a few years of poor performance of their foreign investments relative to domestic equities, U.S. investors were less inclined toward international investing.[11] But that has changed again since 2000, as the U.S. equity market has been strongly outperformed by international markets.

Simply extrapolating past performance to forecast future expected returns is questionable. It is unlikely that one country will always outperform all others, just as one domestic sector is unlikely to continually outperform all other domestic sectors. It could be that one economy is deemed to be more efficient than others, but this should be reflected in higher equity prices. Let's assume, for example, that the U.S. economy is indeed more flexible and competitive than all others in the foreseeable future. In a global context, in which foreign investors extensively invest in the United States and vice versa, this forecast should be discounted today in higher U.S. equity prices. If investors share the vision that the U.S. economy will be superior to other economies forever, that forecast should be reflected immediately into higher U.S. stock prices today, not by higher future returns forever. Future outperformance of U.S. stocks must be caused by "surprise," the unexpected news that the U.S. economy is doing even better than expected. To justify continuing outperformance in the future, we must go from positive surprise to positive surprise.

Barriers to International Investments

The relative size of foreign capital markets would justify extensive foreign investment by investors of any nationality. Empirical studies build a strong case for international diversification. However, international investment, although rapidly growing, is still not widespread in several countries and is certainly far from what it should be according to the world market portfolio weights. This conservative behavior may be explained by the prevalence of potential barriers to foreign investment.

Familiarity with Foreign Markets

Culture differences are a major impediment to foreign investment. Investors are often unfamiliar with foreign cultures and markets. They feel uneasy about the way business is done in other countries: the trading procedures, the way reports are presented, different languages, different time zones, and so on. Many investors, especially Americans, feel more comfortable investing in domestic corporations. In turn, these local corporations provide some international exposure through their exports, foreign subsidiaries, or acquisitions of foreign corporations. Foreign markets and corporations are perceived as more risky simply because they are unfamiliar.

Political Risk

Some countries run the risk of being politically unstable. Many emerging markets have periodically suffered from political, economic, or monetary crises that badly affected the value of local investments. For example, a currency crisis could curtail the dollar value of local investments. Simply looking at a statistical measure of risk based on recent-past stock-price behavior can be misleading and underestimate the risk of a crisis. A statistician would say that the distribution of return on such investments is not "normal" and that the standard deviation of return is not a good proxy of the risk borne.

---

[11] See, for example, Joel Chernoff, "International Investments May Not Decrease Risk after All," *Pensions and Investments*, January 7, 2002.

Market Efficiency

A first question in market efficiency is that of *liquidity*. Some markets are very small; others have many issues traded in large volume. Of course, some issues on the major markets, as well as some of the smaller national markets, trade on little volume. Large institutional investors may wish to be careful and invest only a small part of their portfolios in these small-capitalization, less-liquid shares. Indeed, it may be difficult to get out of some national markets on a large scale. An excellent performance on a local index may not translate into a similarly good performance on a specific portfolio because of the share price drop when liquidating the portfolio. Another liquidity risk is the imposition of capital controls on foreign portfolio investments. Such capital control prevents the sale of a portfolio of foreign assets and the repatriation of proceeds. This has never happened on any of the major capital markets of the world; the cost of such a political decision would be very high for any government because it would reduce its borrowing capacity on the international capital market. However, it is a definite risk for investments in many emerging countries. Such capital controls may be imposed in an extreme financial or political crisis, and international money managers need to carefully monitor a few high-risk countries.

In some countries, especially emerging countries, corporations do not provide *timely and reliable information* on their activity and prospects. Foreign investors tend to avoid such corporations. The rapid growth in international investing has put intense pressure on these corporations to live up to the transparency that is the norm in major developed markets.

Another issue in market efficiency is *price manipulation* and *insider trading*. If foreign markets were too affected by these problems, a manager would probably not run the risk of investing in these markets to benefit the domestic speculators. Many studies have established that all major stock markets are nearly efficient in the usual sense. Some countries, however, have historically been quite lax in terms of price manipulation, insider trading, and corporate governance. In some countries, majority stockholders can take advantage of their controlling interest to the detriment of minority stockholders.[12] The globalization of financial markets leads to a rapid improvement in national regulations to control this type of behavior. Some U.S. pension plans, notably CalPERS, have been very active in inciting corporations worldwide to improve their corporate governance.

Regulations

In some countries, regulations constrain the amount of foreign investment that can be undertaken by local investors. For example, institutional investors are sometimes constrained on the proportion of foreign assets they can hold in their portfolios. Such quotas can be found in some European countries and even among U.S. public pension plans.

Some countries limit the amount of foreign ownership in their national corporations. This is typically the case for emerging countries, which tend to limit foreign ownership to a maximum percentage of the capital of each firm. This is also the case for some developed countries. For example, Swiss corporations tend to issue special shares to foreign owners, and these shares trade at a premium over those available solely to Swiss nationals. Again, the trend is toward progressive removal of these constraints. For example, the European Union prohibits any ownership discrimination among its members. Such constraints are rarely found for bond investments. All governments are happy to have foreign investors subscribe to their bond issues, financing their budget deficit. Conversely, they often force their national institutional investors to hold domestic bonds. This limits the scope of international investing by these institutional investors.

---

[12] See, for example, the case of Italy in Zingales (1994).

Transaction Costs

The transaction costs of international investments can be higher than those of domestic investments. It is difficult to calculate the average transaction cost on a typical trade. A first component of transaction costs is the brokerage commission, and it varies in the way it is charged (fixed or negotiable commission, variable schedule, or part of the bid–ask spread). However, brokerage commissions on stocks tend to be low in the United States (typically 0.10% for large transactions) and higher in some foreign countries (ranging from 0.10% to 1.0%). In a few countries, commissions are fixed, and a stamp tax applies. However, the deregulation of capital markets is lowering these commissions worldwide. A large component of transaction costs is the price impact of a trade. For example, a large buy order will raise the price. This is a function of the size of the order. Liquidity can be limited on many national stock markets, inducing high transaction costs. However, this effect is present in any country. For example, transaction costs on the NASDAQ can be large, because of the limited liquidity on most issues.

It is even more difficult to quote a so-called average commission for bonds. On most of the major bond markets (including the international bond market), prices are quoted net, so that the commissions have to be inferred from the bid–ask spread, which depends on the volume of transactions on a specific bond. In general, commissions on bonds tend to be very low on all markets.

Custody costs tend to add to the costs of international investments. Custody costs tend to be higher for international investments because here, investors engage in a two-level custodial arrangement, in which a master custodian deals with a network of subcustodians in every country. Higher costs are also incurred because of the necessity of a multicurrency system of accounting, reporting, and cash flow collection. Some countries have a very inexpensive and efficient centralized custodial system with a single clearinghouse, and local costs tend to be less than in the United States. However, the need for the international network may raise the annual cost to more than 0.10 percent of assets.

Management fees charged by international money managers tend to be higher than those charged by domestic money managers. This is justified by the higher costs borne by the money managers for various services:

- international database subscriptions;
- data collection;
- research;
- the international accounting system;
- communication costs (international telephone, computer links, and travel).

Management fees for foreign portfolios typically run a few basis points higher than fees on similar domestic portfolios. Some investors believe that they can limit costs by simply buying foreign firms listed on their domestic markets (called American Depositary Receipts, or ADRs, in the United States). Although this may be a practical alternative for the private investor, it is a questionable strategy for larger investors. A growing number of companies have multiple listings, but these companies tend to be large multinational firms that provide fewer foreign diversification benefits than a typical foreign firm. Also, the foreign share price of a corporation (e.g., the U.S. dollar ADR price of a French firm) is often determined by its domestic market price adjusted by the exchange rate. When a large order to buy an ADR is received, brokers will generally arbitrage between the prices in New York and the local market. This means that on most ADRs, the execution will be made at a high price compared with the local price (adjusted for the exchange rate). The commission seems low, but the market impact on the price tends to be high. It is often in the best interest of a large customer to deal on the primary market, where there is the largest transaction volume for the shares. However, there are significant exceptions. Several Dutch and British companies have a very large transaction volume on U.S. markets.

Taxes

Withholding taxes exist on most stock markets. The country where a corporation is headquartered generally withholds an income tax on the dividends paid by the corporation. This tax can usually be reclaimed after several months; this time lag creates an opportunity cost. In a very few cases, part of the tax is completely lost, according to the tax treaty between the two countries. Alternatively, a taxable investor may claim the amount as a tax credit in his home country, but this is not possible for a nontaxable investor, such as a pension plan. However, the withholding tax (generally 15%) applies only to the dividend yield. For a yield of 2 percent, a total loss of withholding tax on common stocks would imply a 0.30 percent reduction in performance. There are also a few countries (e.g., Australia and France) where investors benefit from some tax credit for the tax that the local corporation has paid on its profits distributed as dividends. This tax credit is usually not available to nonresidents. Withholding taxes have been progressively eliminated on bonds.

Currency Risk

As discussed, currency risk can be a major cause of the higher volatility of foreign assets, but is often overstated. Furthermore, it is a risk that need not be borne, because it can be hedged with derivatives. Nevertheless, currency hedging leads to additional administrative and trading costs.

Conclusions

Altogether, foreign investment may not seem more costly for a resident from a high-cost country, such as Switzerland, but it is clearly more expensive for a U.S. resident. For a U.S. investor, a ballpark estimate of the increase in total costs (management fee, taxes, commissions, custody) is on the order of 0.10 percent to 0.50 percent for stocks and 0 percent to 0.20 percent for bonds. The difference would be less for a passively managed fund. These figures are still small compared with the risk–return advantage of foreign investment, as presented in the first part of this reading. However, they could explain why an investor would want to overweigh the domestic component of the portfolio compared with the world market portfolio weights. Information and transaction costs, differential taxes, and sometimes political or transfer risk give a comparative advantage to the domestic investor on the home market. This does not imply that foreign investment should be avoided altogether.

THE CASE FOR INTERNATIONAL DIVERSIFICATION REVISITED

Many of the barriers to global investing are disappearing because of the market liberalization induced by global investors. For example, on many days, trading by foreign investors on European equity markets dominates trading by local investors. The global equity landscape has changed dramatically in past decades. Some of the attacks on global diversification are faulty because they are based on poor statistical analysis. More importantly, the scope of international investing has changed, and investors should adapt accordingly.

Pitfalls in Estimating Correlation During Volatile Periods

In the presence of positive correlation between two markets, we would expect that a large market drop (rise) in one country be associated with a large market drop (rise) in the other country, even if the correlation remains constant. The question is whether the simultaneous movements are so large that they indicate that correlation is truly increasing in crisis periods. Before concluding on the basis of casual observations, we need to address some econometric issues in correlation estimation. The correlation coefficient is a complex parameter whose statistical properties are not well understood. The conclusion of a correlation breakdown is derived by estimating the correlation in periods of high volatility of returns. This is called *conditioning* correlation on high volatility. Unfortunately, many authors have shown that this is a biased sampling estimate of the true correlation.[13] An example can illustrate this argument. Suppose that two markets have a constant joint-normal distribution of returns with a constant correlation of 0.50. Let's now estimate what would be the sampling correlation if we focus only on volatile observations. For example, suppose that we split the sample in two fractiles (50%) based on the absolute return of one market. The first sample is made of "small" returns, the second of "large" returns (positive or negative). Under the assumption of normality with constant correlation, the estimated *conditional correlation* of small returns is 0.21 and the conditional correlation of large returns is 0.62, even though the true correlation is constant and equal to 0.50. This result can easily be replicated by a simulation on a spreadsheet. If we focus only on the 5 percent most volatile observations, the estimated correlation jumps to 0.81. Still, the true market correlation has not changed. So, the apparent shift in correlation is spurious.

Loretan and English (2000) use a correct statistical procedure to study the correlation of equities, bonds, and foreign exchange during various periods of market turbulence. They conclude that "a significant portion of shifts of correlations over time—including those that occurred in the fall of 1998—may reflect nothing more than the predictable effect of differences in sample volatilities on measured correlation, rather than breaks in the data-generating process for asset returns." In other words, the apparent observation that correlation increases in periods of market turbulence is simply an observation that market volatility has increased, but the true correlation remains constant. Forbes and Rigobon (2002) also study numerous crisis periods, including the October 1987 stock market crash. They conclude that "tests for contagion based on cross-market correlation coefficient are problematic due to the bias introduced by changing volatility in market returns (i.e. heteroskedasticity)." They propose an adjustment for this heteroskedasticity bias and find that correlation does not increase significantly in periods of crisis. To summarize, the conclusion that correlation increases in periods of crisis seems to be simply a statistical bias due to faulty econometrics.

Previous results are based on the volatility of asset returns, with no distinction made between bear and bull markets. Longin and Solnik (2001) find that measured correlations behave as expected under the theory of constant correlation in the presence of large positive shocks, but tend to increase in the presence of large negative shocks. So, there still is some evidence that the international correlation of equity markets increases in periods of market distress, but the evidence is not as strong as suggested by some practitioners. Simply graphing the conditional correlation estimated over moving windows of 52 weeks or 200 days can be very misleading, because correlation estimates are biased upward or downward, depending on the volatility of market returns. This bias begs for correction. In reality, the true correlation is much more stable than implied by a casual visual inspection of the graph. Furthermore, Ang and Bekaert (2002) introduce an asset allocation model with different correlation regimes

---

[13] See Boyer, Gibson, and Loretan (1999); Loretan and English (2000); and Forbes and Rigobon (2002).

(normal and volatile periods), and they show that the existence of increased correlation in bear markets has only a small influence on the optimal global asset allocation.

To compute a correlation coefficient, one resorts to a time-series estimation over a rather long period, assuming that the distribution of returns stays the same over the estimation period. Overlapping data have been used to study the changes in correlations; this is a poor method to study changes in correlation over time. An alternative is to look at the cross-sectional dispersion of country market returns at any given point of time. If the markets move quite independently, there should be a large dispersion of returns across national markets in any given day, week, or month. Conversely, if the markets move together, all returns should be closely bunched together. Solnik and Roulet (2000) suggest the cross-sectional standard deviation of returns as a simple measure of dispersion to study the correlation of markets.

Expanded Investment Universe and Performance Opportunities

International correlation among developed equity markets is expected to increase over time for reasons outlined earlier. Economies and markets are becoming increasingly integrated, as corporations pursue global strategies. However, the secular increase can only be slow. In some periods, global factors dominate, but this temporary phenomenon should not be confused with a secular trend. The rise and demise of the technology, media, and telecommunications sector in the late 1990s was a worldwide phenomenon. Business cycles are increasingly synchronized, but there still exist vast regional and national differences. To take the late 1990s as an example, most of Asia was in a prolonged recession while the United States was booming. Even within the European Union, the economic performance differs widely among countries. The three leading economies, France, Germany, and the United Kingdom, demonstrated big differences in the timing and intensity of their economic growth.

As major markets become intertwined, new investment opportunities emerge. In the early 1960s, there were only a couple of developed equity markets in the world. Countries like France, Germany, or Japan could be regarded as risky taken in isolation, but they provided diversification benefits to a U.S. or British investor. At the time, they had all the characteristics of emerging markets. Markets in Italy, Spain, Scandinavia, or Hong Kong progressively emerged a few years later. Many national stock markets, which were viewed as "outlandish" thirty years ago, have become "mainstream." But new markets are emerging. Associated with the slow increase in correlation of developed markets is the expansion of the investment universe. This is a natural evolutionary process. As stressed by Goetzmann, Li, and Rouwenhorst (2001), periods of globalization imply both an increase in correlation among developed markets and the emergence of new markets. The investment opportunity set enlarges, thereby offering additional international diversification benefits.

The question of global investing also should be put in a broader context. Although stock markets have become more mature and integrated, the investment universe has greatly expanded beyond equity. The case for global diversification now applies to a wide range of asset classes beyond foreign stock markets. These include emerging stock markets, foreign bonds, and alternative investments such as high-yield bonds, currency, global real estate, private equity, and various arbitrage strategies.

Global Investing Rather than International Diversification

In the 1990s, the traditional approach to international diversification was based on the premise that country factors were the dominant factors affecting all stocks of a country. Investors were diversifying across country factors, and each stock was assigned to a country based on the location of its headquarters. The investment process was to adopt a two-step process:

- First, decide on a country allocation
- Second, select securities within countries

Today we can observe that companies compete in global industries and have extensive foreign operations. This simple process breaks down in a world where the nationality of a firm becomes fuzzy and industries cut across countries.

Global Industry Factors

With increased globalization, industry factors are growing in importance, while country factors see their influence reduced. Numerous studies[14] show that industry factors have a growing influence on stock returns relative to country-specific factors. For example, Exhibit 14 displays the pure factor return correlation that considers the country and industry effects independent of each other. The lower the correlation, the larger the risk–benefit diversification. In the early 1990s, countries were less correlated than industries, and country diversification brought great risk diversification benefits. It is clear that there is still benefit from country diversification in the 2000s, but that the benefits from industry diversification, in the form of declining correlation, have become prominent. Increasingly, corporations are focusing on their core business in worldwide fashion rather than spreading domestically across many business lines. For example, Ford, DaimlerChrysler, Renault, and Toyota belong to the same car manufacturing industry and are, to some extent, affected by the same industry factor. All of them have activities in many countries. For example, Daimler-Benz, a German firm, acquired Chrysler, an American firm, while Renault, a French firm, linked with Nissan, a Japanese firm. Ford has many subsidiaries and brand names worldwide.

Regional and Country Factors

But regional factors are still present. When car sales are buoyant in France, there is a much bigger impact on Renault than on Ford. Diermeier and Solnik (2001) showed that the stock valuation of corporations reflects the geographical distribution of their activities. For example, a corporation like Toyota, which has extensive activities in Japan and in the United States, is strongly influenced by both country factors. So, the picture is quite complex because from a market valuation perspective, we cannot simply use the location of the corporation's headquarters to define its nationality. When we talk about country factors, we should take into account the geographical distribution of activities. The more international the corporation is, the less it is sensitive to purely domestic country factors. This is illustrated in Example 5.

---

[14] See Cavaglia, Brightman, and Aked (2000); Baca, Garbe, and Weiss (2000); and Gérard, Hillion, and de Roon (2002).

Exhibit 14 Average Correlation of Countries and of Industries

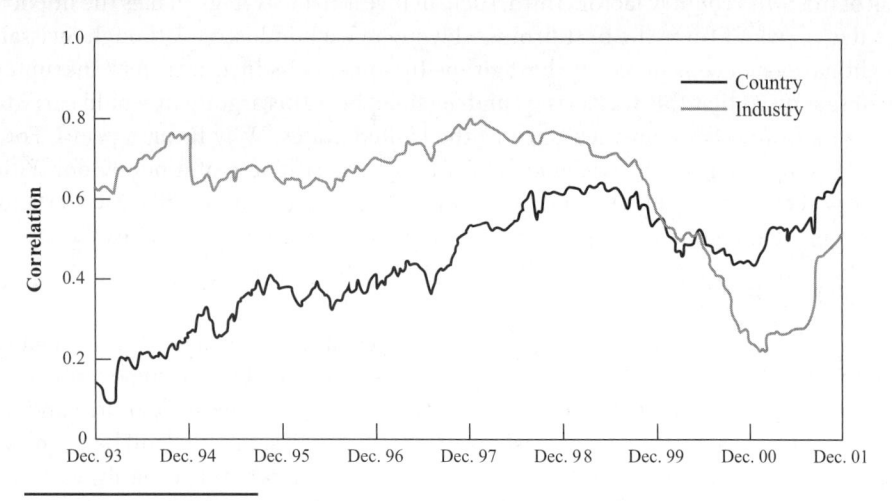

Source: UBS Global Asset Management.

Example 5

Country and Industry Exposures

Ford and Honda are two companies in the car manufacturing industry, deriving, respectively, 19 percent and 9 percent of their revenues in Europe. Lehman* and Nomura are two companies in the financial services industry, deriving, respectively, 7 percent and 42 percent of their revenues in Europe.

You are bullish about the European economy and neutral about the Japanese and U.S. economies. You are bullish about the financial services industry. Which stock would you overweight in your portfolio?

Solution:

You should overweight Nomura. It is a Japanese company but with extensive operations in Europe (42% of revenues), which will enable it to capitalize on European economic growth. Lehman is also in the financial services industry but has small operations in Europe.

*Barclays has acquired Lehman Brothers and will maintain the family of Lehman Brothers indices and the associated index calculation, publication, and analytical infrastructure and tools.

Why Still Diversify Internationally?

Even if industry factors have become increasingly important and corporations are becoming more international, it would be wrong to assume that investing purely at home is a wise strategy from a risk viewpoint. A question sometimes asked is, "Since domestic companies are engaging in international activities, why not simply gain the risk diversification benefits in my portfolio by simply holding domestic companies?" This is not a good strategy because country factors still have a significant influence, and because a purely domestic portfolio is poorly diversified. Let us take the example of a Swiss investor who holds only Swiss equity. The portfolio is, to some extent, international, but it carries a lot of specific, or idiosyncratic, risk. First, some industries are not present among Swiss corporations. Second, the portfolio is still very exposed to the risk of the Swiss country factor. Third, such an investment strategy makes the implicit bet that a Swiss firm is the best firm worldwide in each industry. Although Swissair might have been considered the best airline by some Swiss investors, its bankruptcy in 2001 showed that this was a risky, undiversified bet. This argument would carry to investors from other countries, such as the United States. Why favor, a priori, Ford or GM rather than BMW or Peugeot? Although the riskiness of a purely domestic strategy seems obvious if we take the viewpoint of a small country like Switzerland, the conceptual argument extends to large countries like the United States.

Global Investing

In a way, the investment world is more complex than it was years ago with segmented national equity markets. It will probably be years before we have a single, fully integrated, global equity market. In this light, the analysis of the individual firm and its diversity becomes more critical. To some extent, the analysis should still be country-specific: Country factors are still significant and many firms are still primarily domestic in their activities. It must also be industry-specific and firm-specific.

Globalization gives more importance to industries and individual companies and less to countries. It implies that investors should be more global in their investment approach, from research to portfolio construction. Even for a purely domestic portfolio, analysts must research the global product market of the domestic companies and their international competition. In global portfolio construction, a cross-country, cross-industry approach is required to capture the full risk benefits of international diversification, and this is rarely practiced. More fundamentally, it seems increasingly harder to justify a "nationalistic" approach to equity investment, with a separation of domestic versus foreign investments. In a world where financial markets have become very integrated across borders and where corporations pursue global strategies, investment managers should respond with truly global financial analysis and portfolio construction. Industries cut across national boundaries, and factors that affect stock pricing are global. The question is no longer "Should I put 20 percent of my assets abroad?" but rather "How can I afford not to be global in all aspects of my investment management approach?"

4 THE CASE FOR EMERGING MARKETS

The Basic Case

Emerging economies offer attractive investment opportunities. The local risks (volatility, liquidity, and political risk) are higher, as illustrated by numerous crises, but the expected profit is large. Exhibit 15 plots the value of the MSCI indexes of developed stock markets ("World") and of emerging stock markets ("Emerging") over the period December 1987 to December 2006. Although the higher volatility of emerging markets is apparent, they also had a significantly larger return over the long run. Both indexes are based at 100 at the end of 1987. Although the higher volatility of emerging markets is apparent, they also had a significantly larger return over the long run. While most emerging markets were still in their infancy, they had an excellent performance in the early 1980s. As shown in Exhibit 15, the excellent performance continued until the mid-1990s. The Emerging index rose from 100 in December 1987 to approximately 700 in September 1994, while the World index rose to only 180. In late 1994, Mexico suffered a severe financial crisis that partly spread to other equity markets in Latin America: The Emerging index dropped to 520 within six months (loss of 25%), but

The Case For Emerging Markets

it quickly recovered and reached a new peak in July 1997 at about 720. In late 1997, several emerging Asian countries got into severe currency and economic troubles: The Emerging index dropped to 320 by August 1998 (a yearly loss of some 50%). By March 2000, the Emerging index was up again around 680 (a gain of over 200%). But emerging markets followed the world bear market after 2000 and dropped again. The rebound from 2002 to mid-2007 has been spectacular. From 1987 to May 2007, the geometric mean returns in U.S. dollars are 8.9 percent per year for the World index and 14.5 percent per year for the Emerging index; however, the volatility (annualized standard deviation) is 13.8 percent for the World index and 22.6 percent for the Emerging index.

Exhibit 15   Performance of World Developed Markets and Emerging Markets

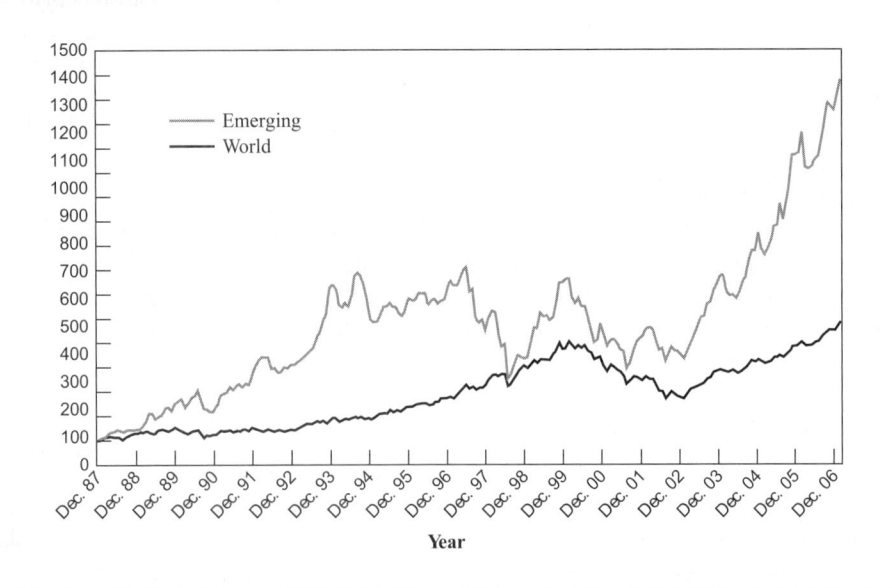

Emerging markets also present a positive but moderate correlation with developed markets; the correlation with the world index of developed markets from 1987 to 2007 was 0.64, and R^2 of only 41 percent. Because of the low correlation[15] between emerging and developed markets, the risks of investing in emerging markets get partly diversified away in a global portfolio. Hence, emerging markets can have a positive contribution in terms of risk–return trade-offs. Let's review the main factors affecting expected returns and risks that should be taken into account when including emerging markets in a global asset allocation.

Volatility, Correlations, and Currency Risk

Volatility

The volatility of emerging markets is much larger than that of developed markets (see Bekaert, Erb, Harvey, and Viskanta [1998]). Furthermore, the distribution of returns is not symmetric, and the probability of a shock (a large price movement) is higher

---

[15] The correlation, however, is still generally positive. One should not be surprised to find that in some periods when developed markets drop, emerging markets also drop, and by a large amount because of their high volatility. This happened in 2000. In other periods, an appreciation of emerging markets can offset a loss in developed markets.

than would be the case if the distribution of returns were normal. This finding implies that the standard deviation is not a sufficient measure of market risk. Investment risk in emerging economies often comes from the possibility of a crisis.

The development of many emerging markets stems from the winds of political reform and liberalization. This is clearly the case in Central Europe since the fall of communism. This is also the case in China with its economic reforms. Problems can easily materialize, however. Some emerging countries do not have a fully stable political and social situation. The explosive social transformation brought about by rapid, and sometimes anarchic, economic growth can lead to serious imbalances, causing social and political unrest. For example, some Chinese cities have industrialized very rapidly, while rural regions became more aware of their poverty.

The infrastructure can limit growth. Thailand and China, for example, have stretched the limit of their existing road infrastructures. Education structures are often insufficient to train a large number of workers and managers in modern international techniques. Multilateral development banks have made education a priority, but improvements are very slow, as local teachers must first be trained but are then tempted to leave the education system after their training. The quality of goods produced may be below international standards because of a lack of training and quality standards different from those required in developed countries.

Corruption is a rampant problem everywhere but may be more so in some emerging countries. Family ownership tends to favor family and friends at the detriment of other stockholders, especially foreign ones. Links between politicians and companies' managers sometimes go beyond what would be in the best interest of stockholders. The banking sector is sometimes poorly regulated, unsupervised, undercapitalized for the lending risks assumed, and lacking in the sophistication required by modern financial operations.

Correlation

International correlation tends to increase in periods of crises, and emerging markets are subject to periodic large crises. Patel and Sankar (1998) find that crises on emerging markets tend to be more prolonged than crises on developed markets, and tend to spread to all emerging markets in the region. It is often the case, however, that a crisis affecting one emerging country does not spread to other emerging countries, especially outside its region. This is the case when the crisis is caused primarily by domestic political problems; many examples can be found in the recent past. An emerging market boom or crisis does not necessarily spread to developed markets, explaining the rather low correlation between developed and emerging markets. Spread depends on whether the factors creating the boom or crisis are primarily local or global.

Currency Risk

Another observation is the correlation between stock and currency returns. Developed markets sometimes exhibit a negative correlation with the value of their currencies. Namely, the local stock market tends to appreciate when the value of the local currency depreciates; the argument is based on an improvement in the international competitiveness of the local firms. This is not the case for emerging stock markets. Both the stock market and the currency are affected by the state of the economy. In periods of crisis, both drop significantly. For example, the Korean won lost more than 50 percent of its value in 1997, and the Seoul stock market also dropped. Both went up significantly in 1998, when the Korean situation showed some encouraging signs. Numerous similar examples could be found in Asia or Latin America. This positive correlation means that foreign investors suffer doubly from currency risk in emerging markets.

Portfolio Return Performance

Emerging markets have a vocation to become developed markets. To emerge, an equity market has to move from an embryonic stage to that of a truly active market attracting international investors. If successful, the market will grow, become more mature, and reach the stage of becoming a developed market. This process should lead to high returns. Clearly, a major argument for investing in emerging economies is their prospective economic growth. Portfolio managers want to find countries that will exhibit in the future the type of growth witnessed by Japan between the 1960s and the 1980s. Most analysts expect emerging economies to grow at a higher rate than developed nations, given the liberalization of international trade. Arguments frequently mentioned are lower labor costs, lower level of unionization and social rigidities, delocalization of production by high-cost developed countries, and rapid growth in domestic demand. The arrival of foreign capital helps those countries develop at a rapid pace and to compete on the world goods market. The transition to a more democratic political system with less corruption, more efficient regulation of the financial industry and other sectors, promotion of free enterprise, and application of the rule of law should strongly benefit local stock markets. Some specific factors could also affect the local stock markets. For example, pension funds have recently been created in many Latin American countries and are likely to invest heavily in their local stock markets. Many countries are pursuing an active program of privatization, and more local firms are attracted by the financing potential of stock markets. Under pressure from international investors, emerging markets are becoming more efficient, providing more rigorous research on companies and progressively applying stricter standards of market supervision. Accounting standards that conform with international accounting standards (IFRS) have been adopted in most countries and are being progressively implemented. Most of these markets have automated their trading and settlement procedures, using computer software tested on developed markets. High returns can be expected in emerging economies that are successful in achieving this transition.

Investability of Emerging Markets

Foreign investors face restrictions when investing on many emerging markets. Although many emerging countries are very liberal toward foreign capital, investability is somewhat restricted in other countries. Restrictions can take many forms:

- *Foreign ownership* can be limited to a maximum percentage of the equity capital of companies listed on the emerging market. This limit can be zero for "strategic" companies, and a fixed percentage for all other companies.[16]

- *Free float* is often small because the local government is the primary owner of many companies. Even though the total market cap of a company looks large, the float available to foreign or domestic private investing is limited.

- *Repatriation of income or capital* can be somewhat constrained. Such capital flows have been liberalized in most emerging countries, but controls are periodically applied in periods of severe crisis. For example, this happened in Malaysia during the 1997 crisis.

- *Discriminatory taxes* are sometimes applied to foreign investors, although this is becoming exceptional.

---

[16] Similar restrictions apply, to a much smaller extent, in developed markets. For example, U.S. companies in the defense or transportation industries have foreign ownership constraints.

- *Foreign currency restrictions* are sometimes applied. For example, China applied a dual-currency system for residents and for foreign investors.
- *Authorized investors* are the only investors allowed to invest in some emerging countries (e.g., India and Taiwan). These authorized foreign investors are typically institutional investors, not private ones.

The pace of liberalization of emerging markets is rapid, and investability regulations are undergoing continual change. However, there is always the risk of an imposition of constraints in periods of crisis.

Another major problem with investing in emerging markets is the lack of *liquidity*. Any sizable transaction can have a very large price impact. So, there could be a significant performance difference between a "paper" portfolio, such as a passive index, and an actual portfolio.

Providers of emerging-market stock indexes have tried to reflect the investability of markets by constructing "investable" or "free" indexes. In building global emerging-market indexes, foreign ownership restrictions and free float strongly affect the weight of a given emerging country in the index.

Segmentation versus Integration Issue

In integrated markets, assets with identical risk should command identical return, regardless of location. In segmented markets, the expected returns on similar assets from different countries should not be related. In practice, emerging markets are somewhat segmented from the international market. Segmented asset pricing is attractive to the global investor. It implies that assets are mispriced relative to their "international" value. Harvey (1995) and Erb, Harvey, and Viskanta (1998) found evidence to reject the hypothesis that emerging stock markets are priced as if they were integrated in the world market. Returns on local companies are strongly influenced by domestic variables rather than by global variables, and domestic risk is priced, not global risks. As emerging markets are increasingly liberalized, this conclusion is likely to change. In a segmented market, expected asset return should be proportional to local risks. The local volatility is much higher than the contribution of the asset to the world market risk (its beta), which is what should matter in integrated asset pricing. So, expected returns in segmented markets should also be higher.

Despite all the problems of emerging economies, which create higher investment risks, emerging stock markets are an attractive asset allocation opportunity. Again, the idea is that investors should be willing to buy emerging markets, which are inherently very volatile, because some of them are likely to produce very high returns. Altogether, the contribution of emerging markets to the total risk of the global portfolio is not very large because of their low correlation with developed markets.

SUMMARY

- International investing reduces risk because the correlations between country markets are less than 1.0. For a two-asset portfolio of domestic and foreign assets, the expected portfolio return is the weighted average of the domestic expected return and the foreign expected return. The standard deviation is the square root of the quantity: the weight squared times the variance of the domestic asset plus the weight squared times the variance of the foreign asset plus twice the product of the weights times the correlation times the standard deviations of the two assets.

Summary

- The domestic rate of return on a foreign asset is the rate of return of that asset in the foreign currency plus the rate of return on the exchange rate plus the product of the rate of return in the foreign currency times the rate of return on the exchange rate. The variance of the domestic rate of return is approximately the variance of the local return plus the variance of the exchange rate return plus twice the covariance of the local return and exchange rate return.
- International diversification provides an efficient frontier that dominates the domestic-only efficient frontier because the domestic-only frontier is more constrained.
- The factors causing equity market correlations across countries to be relatively low are the independence of different nations' economies and government policies, technological specialization, independent fiscal and monetary policies, and cultural and sociological differences.
- The factors causing bond market correlations across countries to be relatively low are the differences in national monetary and budgetary policies.
- No evidence has been found of a systematic delayed reaction of one national market to another, except for daily returns as a result of time differences around the world.
- An increased Sharpe ratio from international investing is possible because of risk reduction and the increase in profitable investment opportunities in an enlarged investment universe.
- Currency risk may only slightly magnify the volatility of foreign currency—denominated investments, because market and currency risks are not additive, exchange risk can be hedged, the contribution of currency risk should be measured for the total portfolio, and the contribution of currency risk decreases with the time horizon. Currency risk is relatively more important for bond investments than equity investments.
- The increase in correlations between national markets reduces diversification benefits. This increase is due to such factors as deregulation, capital mobility, free trade, and the globalization of corporations.
- The country-specific argument against international diversification arises during periods when the domestic market does better than most other markets, leading some to say that there is no need for international investments in the future because the domestic market is outperforming.
- The potential physical barriers to international investing include lack of familiarity with foreign markets, political risk, lack of market efficiency, regulations, transaction costs, taxes, and currency risks.
- The pitfall in estimating correlations during volatile periods is that correlations conditioned on part of a sample are biased. The apparent observation that correlation increases in periods of market turbulence can simply be an observation that market turbulence has increased but the true correlation has remained constant.
- International performance opportunities have increased over time because many markets are moving from the emerging to the developing category.
- International diversification refers to diversifying internationally because correlations between country markets are less than 1.0. As the industry factor becomes more important relative to the country factor, global investing refers to investing in the best companies, wherever they are located in the world, and recognizing that these companies will also be investing worldwide.
- Compared with developed markets, emerging markets exhibit higher volatility than developed markets, with asymmetric return distributions and increasing

international correlations in times of crises, but they also exhibit higher return opportunities because of the early growth stages of their economies.

- In contrast to developed economies, emerging markets exhibit positive correlations between the local stock market and the currency; that is, when they do poorly, both the local stock market and the currency do poorly together.
- The investability in emerging markets is constrained by various regulations and liquidity problems.
- Emerging markets tend to be somewhat segmented, and mispricing is evident.

PRACTICE PROBLEMS FOR READING 22

1. The standard deviation of a foreign asset in local currency is σ = 8.5 percent, and the standard deviation of the exchange rate is σ_s = 5.5 percent.

   A. If the correlation between the asset return, in local currency, and the exchange rate movement is ρ = 0, calculate the amount of risk that can be attributed to currency risk.

   B. If the correlation between the asset return, in local currency, and the exchange rate movement is ρ = 0.25, calculate the amount of risk that can be attributed to currency risk.

   C. If the correlation between the asset return, in local currency, and the exchange rate movement is ρ = −0.45, calculate the amount of risk that can be attributed to currency risk.

   D. What is the impact of the level of correlation between the asset return in local currency and the exchange rate movement on the risk of a foreign asset measured in dollars?

2. Assume that the domestic volatility (standard deviation) of the German stock market (in euros) is 18.2 percent. The volatility of the euro against the U.S. dollar is 11.7 percent.

   A. What would the dollar volatility of the German stock market be for a U.S. investor if the correlation between the stock market returns and exchange rate movements were zero?

   B. Suppose the dollar volatility of the German stock market is 20.4 percent. What can you conclude about the correlation between German stock market movements and exchange rate movements?

3. Assume that the domestic volatility (standard deviation) of the German bond market (in euros) is 5.5 percent. The volatility of the euro against the U.S. dollar is 11.7 percent.

   A. What would the dollar volatility of the German market be for a U.S. investor if the correlation between the bond market returns and exchange rate movements were zero?

   B. Suppose the dollar volatility of the German bond market is 13.6 percent. What can you conclude about the correlation between German bond market movements and exchange rate movements? What might explain this correlation?

4. Indicate whether the following statement is correct, and explain your reasoning: "The best diversification vehicle is an asset with high volatility and low correlation with the portfolio."

5. Consider the correlations (in U.S. dollars) of worldwide bond markets presented in Exhibit 5. Explain the reasons for the correlations observed between the United States and other countries, and indicate the motivations for diversifying a U.S. dollar bond portfolio into foreign-currency bonds.

6. What factors can be used to explain differences in the long-run performance of equity markets of different countries?

7. Is currency risk a barrier to international investment?

Practice Problems and Solutions: 1–8 taken from *Global Investments*, Sixth Edition, by Bruno Solnik and Dennis McLeavey, CFA, and *Solutions Manual* to accompany *Global Investments*, Sixth Edition, by Bruno Solnik and Dennis McLeavey, CFA. Copyright © 2009 by Pearson Education. Reprinted with permission of Pearson Education, publishing as Prentice Hall. All other problems and solutions copyright © CFA Institute.

8. Despite strong arguments in favor of international diversification, international portfolio investment is still not widespread in many countries. One reason for this is the presence of barriers to international investment. List and explain the various barriers to international investment.

The following information relates to Questions 9–14

The Dorian Foundation, a U.S.-based not-for-profit charitable organization, currently has all of its assets invested in domestic securities. The trustees of the Foundation have just been informed that it will receive a large gift from one of its patrons. The trustees instruct Marie Collier, a consultant to the Foundation, to assess the desirability of investing the proceeds of the gift in international securities. If the entire proceeds from the gift are invested in international securities, the portfolio will be 10 percent international securities and 90 percent domestic securities.

In preparation for her presentation to the trustees, Collier collects the data in Exhibit 1.

Exhibit 1 Current Portfolio and Non-U.S. Country Equity Return Expectations

Variable	Country A	Country B
Standard deviation of country equity return in local currency	11.62%	10.27%
Standard deviation of exchange rate between local currency and US$	8.48%	7.35%
Correlation between country equity return, in local currency, and exchange rate	0.30	0.10
Correlation between country equity return and the Foundation's current portfolio return, both measured in US$	0.60	0.55
Standard deviation of country equity return in US$		13.21%

Note: Standard deviation of the Foundation's current domestic portfolio returns in US$ = 10.45%

Collier points out that exchange rate volatility can have a significant impact on the expected returns and potential diversification benefits to a U.S.-based investor such as the Foundation. She cautions that an analyst must consider the effects of exchange rate volatility on asset return volatility within a particular market as well as across markets. She notes that if the correlation between Country B's equity return and the exchange rate declines from 0.10 to –0.20, the standard deviation of Country B's equity return (measured in US$) will fall to 11.37 percent. Collier states, "Thus, the impact of a change in correlation (from 0.10 to –0.20) is that the currency risk contribution to the standard deviation of Country B's equity return (measured in US$) will be negative."

Collier notes that although currency fluctuations are an important factor in international investing, the Foundation must also consider the following attributes associated with international investing:

Attribute 1   The contribution of currency risk to portfolio standard deviation decreases as a function of the investment horizon.

Attribute 2   Correlations among country returns increase when markets become more volatile.

Practice Problems for Reading 22

Collier presents evidence that international investing provides diversification benefits that would improve the Sharpe ratio of the Foundation's portfolio.

Dana Lambert, a trustee of the Foundation, asks Collier two questions about international investing and the portfolio's expected Sharpe ratio:

Question 1   "With respect to international investing, is there anything other than diversification that will improve the portfolio's expected Sharpe ratio?"

Question 2   "Are there strategies other than international investing that would also improve the portfolio's expected Sharpe ratio?"

Collier responds, "Yes to both your questions. First, in addition to diversification, international investing also provides a larger investment universe, which can improve the expected Sharpe ratio. Second, another investment strategy that would improve the expected Sharpe ratio is to increase the portfolio's holding of risk-free securities."

Collier concludes her presentation with a discussion of investing in emerging markets. William Armitage, a trustee of the Foundation, asks Collier to discuss how return volatility and currency risk associated with emerging markets will impact risk–return characteristics of the portfolio. Collier responds as follows:

Return Volatility: While the volatility of emerging markets is larger than that of developed countries, the standard deviation is a sufficient measure of market risk.

Current Risk: Emerging equity markets often exhibit a positive correlation with the value of their currencies resulting in foreign investors suffering doubly from currency risk in emerging markets.

9. If the entire proceeds of the gift are invested in Country B, then based on the information provided in Exhibit 1, the standard deviation of the Foundation's new portfolio is *closest* to:
   A. 9.63%.
   B. 10.19%.
   C. 10.44%.

10. Based on the data in Exhibit 1, the standard deviation of Country A's equity return measured in US$ is *closest* to:
    A. 9.81%.
    B. 16.31%.
    C. 18.03%.

11. If other things are unchanged, Collier's statement about the impact on currency risk of a change in the correlation between Country B's equity return and the exchange rate from 0.10 to −0.20 is:
    A. correct.
    B. incorrect, because the currency risk contribution to the standard deviation of Country B's US$ equity return will be 1.10%.
    C. incorrect, because the currency risk contribution to the standard deviation of Country B's US$ equity return will be 1.84%.

12. Is Collier correct with respect to the two attributes of international investing?

	Attribute 1	Attribute 2
A.	No	No
B.	No	Yes
C.	Yes	Yes

13. Are Collier's statements in response to Lambert's questions regarding the Sharpe ratio correct?

	Response to Question 1	Response to Question 2
A.	No	No
B.	Yes	No
C.	Yes	Yes

14. Collier's responses to Armitage's inquiry about return volatility and currency risk of emerging markets are *most likely*:

	Return Volatility	Currency Risk
A.	Correct	Correct
B.	Correct	Incorrect
C.	Incorrect	Correct

SOLUTIONS FOR READING 22

1. **A.** $\sigma_f^2 = \sigma^2 + \sigma_s^2 + 2\rho\sigma\sigma_s = (8.5)^2 + (5.5)^2 + 2(0)(8.5)(5.5) = 102.5$

   $\sigma_f = 10.12\%$

   Contribution of currency risk = 10.12 − 8.5 = 1.62%

   B. $\sigma_f^2 = \sigma^2 + \sigma_s^2 + 2\rho\sigma\sigma_s = (8.5)^2 + (5.5)^2 + 2(0.25)(8.5)(5.5)$

   $= 125.9$

   $\sigma_f = 11.22\%$

   Contribution of currency risk = 11.22 − 8.5 = 2.72%

   C. $\sigma_f^2 = \sigma^2 + \sigma_s^2 + 2\rho\sigma\sigma_s = (8.5)^2 + (5.5)^2 + 2(-0.45)(8.5)(5.5)$

   $= 60.4$

   $\sigma_f = 7.77\%$

   Contribution of currency risk = 7.77 − 8.5 = − 0.73%

   D. When the correlation between the asset return, in local currency, and the exchange rate movement is low enough, currency risk may actually reduce the asset risk measured in dollars. However, in cases in which the correlation is zero or positive, asset risk in dollars is higher than asset risk in local currency because of currency risk.

2. **A.** If the correlation between stock market returns and exchange rate movements were equal to zero, the dollar volatility of the German stock market would be

   $\sigma_f^2 = \sigma^2 + \sigma_s^2 + 2\rho\sigma\sigma_s = (18.2)^2 + (11.7)^2 + 2(0)(18.2)(11.7)$

   $= 468.13$

   $\sigma_f = 21.64\%$

   B. Because the actual dollar volatility is only 20.4 percent, we conclude that the correlation between stock market returns and exchange rate movements is negative.

3. **A.** If the correlation between bond market returns and exchange rate movements were equal to zero, the dollar volatility of the German bond market would be

   $\sigma_f^2 = \sigma^2 + \sigma_s^2 + 2\rho\sigma\sigma_s = (5.5)^2 + (11.7)^2 + 2(0)(5.5)(11.7)$

   $= 167.14$

   $\sigma_f = 12.93\%$

   B. Because the actual dollar volatility is 13.6 percent, we conclude that the correlation between bond market returns and exchange rate movements is positive. When the euro gets weaker, U.S. investors lose on the exchange rate and also on bond market returns measured in euros. This can be explained by the idea that a weak currency usually goes with rising interest rates (and negative bond market return).

4. The best diversification vehicle is an asset whose value gets significantly higher when the rest of the portfolio's value is low, and thereby partially offsets the loss of other assets. The best vehicle is an asset with a negative correlation (so

it goes up when the portfolio goes down) and high volatility (large upswings when the portfolio goes down). Thus the statement is correct.

5. A review of the correlations in Exhibit 5 indicates that correlations of the U.S bond market with foreign bond markets are well below 0.50, when measured in dollar terms. These low correlations can be attributed to the fact that national monetary/budget policies are not fully synchronized. The conclusions reached regarding the risk-reducing benefits of low correlations in global equity markets also apply to global bond markets. Foreign bonds are therefore a good vehicle of diversification and can significantly reduce the volatility of the portfolio. This makes foreign bonds attractive to a U.S. investor, despite foreign exchange risk.

6. In general, over the long run, the performance of stock markets is closely tied to national economic factors. For example, in the case of Japan, real average annual GDP growth was 4.51 percent from 1971 to 1980, and 4.15 percent from 1981 to 1990 (see Exhibit 11). These real GDP growth rates dominated growth rates for the United States, Europe, and the Organization for Economic Cooperation and Development (OECD) for the same periods. This is reflected in stock market performance numbers presented in Exhibit 10. For the period from 1971 to 1990, the average annual mean return for Japanese stocks was 20.68 percent, much higher than stock returns in the United States and Europe. From 1991 to 2000, it was the United States that had the highest real GDP growth rates and best-performing stock market.

   Economic flexibility is another important factor. Countries such as France, Canada, and Sweden have suffered from wage and employment rigidities not typically faced in many emerging countries. This economic flexibility is likely to reflect itself in stock market performance in the long run. Many countries are improving their global competitiveness, which should be reflected in market valuation.

7. Currency fluctuations have an impact on the total return and volatility of foreign currency–denominated investments. However, there are at least four reasons why currency risk is not a barrier to international investment:

   - Market and currency risks are not additive. This is because the correlation between currency and market movements is quite weak and sometimes negative. Consequently, the contribution of currency risk to the risk of a foreign investment is quite small.
   - Currency risk can be hedged away by selling currency futures or forward contracts.
   - If foreign assets represent a small portion of the portfolio, then the contribution of currency risk is insignificant (Jorion, 1989). Also, if the portfolio consists of multiple currencies, some portion of the risk is diversified away.
   - Currency risk decreases with the length of the investment horizon, because exchange rates tend to revert to fundamentals.

8. There are a number of barriers to international investment, including the following:

   - *Familiarity with foreign markets.* Many investors are not familiar with business customs overseas and are therefore inclined to invest in domestic companies.
   - *Political risk.* This is a major concern, especially in emerging markets in which political and economic instability have had a debilitating impact on security prices in local-currency and dollar terms.

Solutions for Reading 22

- *Market efficiency.* Liquidity risk is a major concern for investors venturing overseas because it limits the ability of large investors to change asset allocations without signaling their actions to the rest of the market. Capital controls are another source of liquidity risk because such controls limit the repatriation of funds to the home country. In many countries, market efficiency is limited by the fact that companies do not provide accurate and timely information. Price manipulation and insider trading also limit market efficiency and benefit local investors at the expense of foreign investors.

- *Regulations.* Certain countries have regulations that inhibit foreign investment by limiting the amount of overseas investment by local investors. Other countries limit the amount of foreign ownership in domestic firms. These regulations generally limit the scope of international investment.

- *Transactions costs.* Transactions costs tend to be higher for international investments relative to domestic investments. The higher transactions costs for international investments are due to higher brokerage commissions and market impact, custody costs, and higher portfolio management fees.

- *Taxes.* Taxes have a relatively small impact on the international investment decision. Withholding taxes on dividends are typically reclaimed after a few months, but this represents an opportunity cost because funds are tied up.

- *Currency risk.* Although currency risk can be hedged, it does lead to additional administrative and trading costs and thus adds to the overall cost of international investment.

9. B is correct. The standard deviation of the new portfolio is calculated using the following formula:

$$\sigma_p = \left[(W_{U.S.})^2(\sigma_{U.S.})^2 + (W_B)^2(\sigma_B)^2 + 2\rho_{B,U.S.}W_{U.S.}W_B\sigma_{U.S.}\sigma_B\right]^{1/2}$$

$$\sigma_p = \left[(0.90)^2(0.1045)^2 + (0.10)^2(0.1321)^2 + (2 \times 0.55 \times 0.9 \times 0.1 \times 0.1045 \times 0.1321)\right]^{1/2}$$

$$= 10.19\%$$

where:

$W_{U.S.}$ = proportion of portfolio invested in U.S. securities after the receipt of the proceeds of the gift to the fund are invested in Country B,
$\sigma_{U.S.}$ = standard deviation of the Foundation's current portfolio return in US$,
W_B = of portfolio invested in Country B securities after the receipt of the proceeds of the gift to the fund are invested in Country B,
σ_B = standard deviation of Country B's equity return in US$, and
$\rho_{B,U.S.}$ = correlation between Country B's equity return and U.S. equity return measured in US$.

10. B is correct. The standard deviation of the foreign equity return measured in US$, σ_p, is calculated as:

$$\left[\sigma^2 + \sigma_s^2 + 2\rho(\sigma)(\sigma_s)\right]^{0.5} = \left[(11.62)^2 + (8.48)^2 + 2(0.30)(11.62)(8.48)\right]^{0.5} = 16.31\%$$

where:

σ_f^2 = variance of foreign asset measured in domestic currency (in this case US$),
σ^2 = variance of foreign asset in local currency,
σ_s^2 = variance of the exchange rate, and
ρ = correlation between the asset return, in local currency, and the exchange rate movement.

11. B is correct. Collier's statement is incorrect because the currency risk contribution to the standard deviation of Country B's US$ equity return will be 1.10%. The currency risk contribution to the standard deviation of Country B equity measured in US$ is calculated as:

σ of Country B's equity return (measured in US$) − σ of Country B's equity (in local currency) = (11.37% − 10.27%) = 1.10%

Where:

σ of Country B's equity return (measured in US$)

$$= \left[\sigma^2 + \sigma_s^2 + 2\rho(\sigma)(\sigma_s)\right]^{0.5} = \left[(10.27)^2 + (7.35)^2 + (2 \times -0.2 \times 10.27 \times 7.35)\right]^{0.5} = 11.37\%$$

12. C is correct. Both of the attributes of international investing are factually correct. The contribution of currency risk decreases as a function of the investment horizon, and correlations increase when markets become more volatile.

13. B is correct. International investing provides a larger investment universe where more profitable investments are possible. More profitable investments can increase the Sharpe ratio. However, Collier's second response is incorrect. Increasing the portfolio's holdings of risk-free securities will not improve the Sharpe ratio because, in an efficient market, increasing holdings of risk-free securities will cause both risk and return to fall in proportion, and the Sharpe ratio therefore does not change.

14. C is correct. Collier's comment about volatility is incorrect. The volatility of emerging markets is greater than developed markets but the distribution of returns is not symmetric. Therefore the standard deviation is *not* a sufficient measure of market risk; Collier's comment about currency risk is correct. Emerging markets often exhibit positive correlations with the value of their currencies resulting in foreign investors suffering doubly from currency risk in emerging markets.

Glossary

10-year moving average price/earnings A price-to-earnings ratio in which the numerator (in a U.S. context) is defined as the real S&P 500 price index and the denominator as the moving average of the preceding 10 years of real reported earnings on the S&P 500.

AUM fee A fee based on assets under management; an ad valorem fee.

Absolute-return vehicles Investments that have no direct benchmark portfolios.

Accounting risk The risk associated with accounting standards that vary from country to country or with any uncertainty about how certain transactions should be recorded.

Accreting swap A swap where the notional amount increases over the life of the swap.

Accumulated benefit obligation (ABO) The present value of pension benefits, assuming the pension plan terminated immediately such that it had to provide retirement income to all beneficiaries for their years of service up to that date.

Accumulated service Years of service of a pension plan participant as of a specified date.

Active management An approach to investing in which the portfolio manager seeks to outperform a given benchmark portfolio.

Active return The portfolio's return in excess of the return on the portfolio's benchmark.

Active risk A synonym for tracking risk.

Active-lives The portion of a pension fund's liabilities associated with active workers.

Active/immunization combination A portfolio with two component portfolios: an immunized portfolio which provides an assured return over the planning horizon and a second portfolio that uses an active high-return/high-risk strategy.

Active/passive combination Allocation of the core component of a portfolio to a passive strategy and the balance to an active component.

Actual extreme events A type of scenario analysis used in stress testing. It involves evaluating how a portfolio would have performed given movements in interest rates, exchange rates, stock prices, or commodity prices at magnitudes such as occurred during past extreme market events (e.g., the stock market crash of October 1987).

Ad valorem fees Fees that are calculated by multiplying a percentage by the value of assets managed; also called assets under management (AUM) fees.

Adaptive markets hypothesis (also AMH) A hypothesis that applies principles of evolution—such as competition, adaptation, and natural selection—to financial markets in an attempt to reconcile efficient market theories with behavioral alternatives.

Adverse selection risk The risk associated with information asymmetry; in the context of trading, the risk of trading with a more informed trader.

Algorithmic trading Automated electronic trading subject to quantitative rules and user-specified benchmarks and constraints.

Allocation/selection interaction return A measure of the joint effect of weights assigned to both sectors and individual securities; the difference between the weight of the portfolio in a given sector and the portfolio's benchmark for that sector, times the difference between the portfolio's and the benchmark's returns in that sector, summed across all sectors.

Alpha Excess risk-adjusted return.

Alpha and beta separation An approach to portfolio construction that views investing to earn alpha and investing to establish systematic risk exposures as tasks that can and should be pursued separately.

Alpha research Research related to capturing excess risk-adjusted returns by a particular strategy; a way investment research is organized in some investment management firms.

Alternative investments Groups of investments with risk and return characteristics that differ markedly from those of traditional stock and bond investments.

Amortizing swap A swap where the notional amount declines over the life of the swap.

Anchoring and adjustment An information-processing bias in which the use of a psychological heuristic influences the way people estimate probabilities.

Anchoring and adjustment bias An information-processing bias in which the use of a psychological heuristic influences the way people estimate probabilities.

Anchoring trap The tendency of the mind to give disproportionate weight to the first information it receives on a topic.

Angel investor An accredited individual investing chiefly in seed and early-stage companies.

Anomalies Apparent deviations from market efficiency.

Ask price (or ask, offer price, offer) The price at which a dealer will sell a specified quantity of a security.

Ask size The quantity associated with the ask price.

Asset allocation reviews A periodic review of the appropriateness of a portfolio's asset allocation.

Asset covariance matrix The covariance matrix for the asset classes or markets under consideration.

Asset swap A swap, typically involving a bond, in which fixed bond payments are swapped for payments based on a floating rate.

Asset-only (AO) approach In the context of determining a strategic asset allocation, an approach that focuses on the characteristics of the assets without explicitly modeling the liabilities.

Asset/liability management The management of financial risks created by the interaction of assets and liabilities.

Asset/liability management (ALM) approach In the context of determining a strategic asset allocation, an asset/liability management approach involves explicitly modeling liabilities and adopting the allocation of assets that is optimal in relationship to funding liabilities.

Assurity of completion In the context of trading, confidence that trades will settle without problems under all market conditions.

Assurity of the contract In the context of trading, confidence that the parties to trades will be held to fulfilling their obligations.

Asynchronism A discrepancy in the dating of observations that occurs because stale (out-of-date) data may be used in the absence of current data.

Automated trading Any form of trading that is not manual, including trading based on algorithms.

Availability bias An information-processing bias in which people take a heuristic approach to estimating the probability of an outcome based on how easily the outcome comes to mind.

Average effective spread A measure of the liquidity of a security's market. The mean effective spread (sometimes dollar weighted) over all transactions in the stock in the period under study.

Back office Administrative functions at an investment firm such as those pertaining to transaction processing, record keeping, and regulatory compliance.

Back-to-back transaction A transaction where a dealer enters into offsetting transactions with different parties, effectively serving as a go-between.

Backtesting A method for gaining information about a model using past data. As used in reference to VAR, it is the process of comparing the number of violations of VAR thresholds over a time period with the figure implied by the user-selected probability level.

Backwardation A condition in the futures markets in which the benefits of holding an asset exceed the costs, leaving the futures price less than the spot price.

Balance of payments An accounting of all cash flows between residents and nonresidents of a country.

Bancassurance The sale of insurance by banks.

Barbell portfolio A portfolio made up of short and long maturities relative to the investment horizon date and interim coupon payments.

Base-rate neglect A type of representativeness bias in which the base rate or probability of the categorization is not adequately considered.

Basis The difference between the cash price and the futures price.

Basis point value (BPV) Also called *present value of a basis point* or *price value of a basis point* (PVBP), the change in the bond price for a 1 basis point change in yield.

Basis risk The risk that the basis will change in an unpredictable way.

Batch auction markets Auction markets where multilateral trading occurs at a single price at a prespecified point in time.

Bayes' formula A mathematical rule explaining how existing probability beliefs should be changed given new information; it is essentially an application of conditional probabilities.

Bear spread An option strategy that involves selling a put with a lower exercise price and buying a put with a higher exercise price. It can also be executed with calls.

Behavioral finance An approach to finance based on the observation that psychological variables affect and often distort individuals' investment decision making.

Behavioral finance macro A focus on market level behavior that considers market anomalies that distinguish markets from the efficient markets of traditional finance.

Behavioral finance micro A focus on individual level behavior that examines the behavioral biases that distinguish individual investors from the rational decision makers of traditional finance.

Best efforts order A type of order that gives the trader's agent discretion to execute the order only when the agent judges market conditions to be favorable.

Beta A measure of the sensitivity of a given investment or portfolio to movements in the overall market.

Beta research Research related to systematic (market) risk and return; a way investment research is organized in some investment management firms.

Bid (or bid price) The price at which a dealer will buy a specified quantity of a security.

Bid price The price at which a dealer will buy a specified quantity of a security.

Bid size The quantity associated with the bid price.

Bid–ask spread The difference between the current bid price and the current ask price of a security.

Binary credit options Options that provide payoffs contingent on the occurrence of a specified negative credit event.

Block order An order to sell or buy in a quantity that is large relative to the liquidity ordinarily available from dealers in the security or in other markets.

Bond-yield-plus-risk-premium method An approach to estimating the required return on equity which specifies that required return as a bond yield plus a risk premium.

Bottom-up Focusing on company-specific fundamentals or factors such as revenues, earnings, cash flow, or new product development.

Bounded rationality The notion that people have informational and cognitive limitations when making decisions and do not necessarily optimize when arriving at their decisions.

Box spread An option strategy that combines a bull spread and a bear spread having two different exercise prices, which produces a risk-free payoff of the difference in the exercise prices.

Broad market indexes An index that is intended to measure the performance of an entire asset class. For example, the S&P 500 Index, Wilshire 5000, and Russell 3000 indexes for U.S. common stocks.

Broker An agent of a trader in executing trades.

Brokered markets Markets in which transactions are largely effected through a search-brokerage mechanism away from public markets.

Bubbles Episodes in which asset market prices move to extremely high levels in relation to estimated intrinsic value.

Buffering With respect to style index construction, rules for maintaining the style assignment of a stock consistent with a previous assignment when the stock has not clearly moved to a new style.

Build-up approach Synonym for the risk premium approach.

Bull spread An option strategy that involves buying a call with a lower exercise price and selling a call with a higher exercise price. It can also be executed with puts.

Bullet portfolio A portfolio made up of maturities that are very close to the investment horizon.

Business cycle Fluctuations in GDP in relation to long-term trend growth, usually lasting 9–11 years.

Business risk The equity risk that comes from the nature of the firm's operating activities.

Butterfly spread An option strategy that combines two bull or bear spreads and has three exercise prices.

Buy side Investment management companies and other investors that use the services of brokerages.

Buy-side traders Professional traders that are employed by investment managers and institutional investors.

Calendar rebalancing Rebalancing a portfolio to target weights on a periodic basis; for example, monthly, quarterly, semi-annually, or annually.

Calendar-and-percentage-of-portfolio rebalancing Monitoring a portfolio at regular frequencies, such as quarterly. Rebalancing decisions are then made based upon percentage-of-portfolio principles.

Calmar ratio The compound annualized rate of return over a specified time period divided by the absolute value of maximum drawdown over the same time period.

Cap A combination of interest rate call options designed to hedge a borrower against rate increases on a floating-rate loan.

Cap rate With respect to options, the exercise interest rate for a cap.

Capital adequacy ratio A measure of the adequacy of capital in relation to assets.

Capital allocation line A graph line that describes the combinations of expected return and standard deviation of return available to an investor from combining an optimal portfolio of risky assets with a risk-free asset.

Capital flows forecasting approach An exchange rate forecasting approach that focuses on expected capital flows, particularly long-term flows such as equity investment and foreign direct investment.

Capital market expectations (CME) Expectations concerning the risk and return prospects of asset classes.

Caplet Each component call option in a cap.

Carried interest A private equity fund manager's incentive fee; the share of the private equity fund's profits that the fund manager is due once the fund has returned the outside investors' capital.

Carry Another term for owning an asset, typically used to refer to commodities. (See also *carry market*).

Carry market A situation where the forward price is such that the return on a cash-and-carry is the risk-free rate.

Cash balance plan A defined-benefit plan whose benefits are displayed in individual recordkeeping accounts.

Cash flow at risk A variation of VAR that measures the risk to a company's cash flow, instead of its market value; the minimum cash flow loss expected to be exceeded with a given probability over a specified time period.

Cash flow matching An asset/liability management approach that provides the future funding of a liability stream from the coupon and matured principal payments of the portfolio. A type of dedication strategy.

Cell-matching technique (stratified sampling) A portfolio construction technique used in indexing that divides the benchmark index into cells related to the risk factors affecting the index and samples from index securities belonging to those cells.

Certainty equivalent The maximum sum of money a person would pay to participate or the minimum sum of money a person would accept to not participate in an opportunity.

Chain-linking A process for combining periodic returns to produce an overall time-weighted rate of return.

Cheapest-to-deliver A bond in which the amount received for delivering the bond is largest compared with the amount paid in the market for the bond.

Civil law A legal system derived from Roman law, in which judges apply general, abstract rules or concepts to particular cases. In civil systems, law is developed primarily through legislative statutes or executive action.

Claw-back provision With respect to the compensation of private equity fund managers, a provision that specifies that money from the fund manager be returned to investors if, at the end of a fund's life, investors have not received back their capital contributions and contractual share of profits.

Closed-book markets Markets in which a trader does not have real-time access to all quotes in a security.

Closeout netting In a bankruptcy, a process by which multiple obligations between two counterparties are consolidated into a single overall value owed by one of the counterparties to the other.

Cobb-Douglas model A production function (model for economic output) based on factors of labor and capital that exhibits constant returns to scale.

Cobb-Douglas production function A production function (model for economic output) based on factors of labor and capital that exhibits constant returns to scale.

Cognitive dissonance The mental discomfort that occurs when new information conflicts with previously held beliefs or cognitions.

Cognitive errors Behavioral biases resulting from faulty reasoning; cognitive errors stem from basic statistical, information processing, or memory errors.

Collar An option strategy involving the purchase of a put and sale of a call in which the holder of an asset gains protection below a certain level, the exercise price of the put, and pays for it by giving up gains above a certain level, the exercise price of the call. Collars also can be used to provide protection against rising interest rates on a floating-rate loan by giving up gains from lower interest rates.

Collateral return (or collateral yield) The component of the return on a commodity futures contract that comes from the assumption that the full value of the underlying futures contract is invested to earn the risk-free interest rate.

Collateralized debt obligation A securitized pool of fixed-income assets.

Combination matching (or horizon matching) A cash flow matching technique; a portfolio is duration-matched with a set of liabilities with the added constraint that it also be cash-flow matched in the first few years, usually the first five years.

Commingled real estate funds (CREFs) Professionally managed vehicles for substantial commingled (i.e., pooled) investment in real estate properties.

Commitment period The period of time over which committed funds are advanced to a private equity fund.

Commodities Articles of commerce such as agricultural goods, metals, and petroleum; tangible assets that are typically relatively homogeneous in nature.

Commodity spread Offsetting long and short positions in closely related commodities. (See also *crack spread* and *crush spread*).

Commodity trading advisors Registered advisors to managed futures funds.

Common law A legal system which draws abstract rules from specific cases. In common law systems, law is developed primarily through decisions of the courts.

Community property regime A marital property regime under which each spouse has an indivisible one-half interest in property received during marriage.

Completeness fund A portfolio that, when added to active managers' positions, establishes an overall portfolio with approximately the same risk exposures as the investor's overall equity benchmark.

Confidence band With reference to a quality control chart for performance evaluation, a range in which the manager's value-added returns are anticipated to fall a specified percentage of the time.

Confidence interval An interval that has a given probability of containing the parameter it is intended to estimate.

Confirmation bias A belief perseverance bias in which people tend to look for and notice what confirms their beliefs, to ignore or undervalue what contradicts their beliefs, and to misinterpret information as support for their beliefs.

Confirming evidence trap The bias that leads individuals to give greater weight to information that supports an existing or preferred point of view than to evidence that contradicts it.

Conjunction fallacy An inappropriate combining of probabilities of independent events to support a belief. In fact, the probability of two independent events occurring in conjunction is never greater than the probability of either event occurring alone; the probability of two independent events occurring together is equal to the multiplication of the probabilities of the independent events.

Conservatism bias A belief perseverance bias in which people maintain their prior views or forecasts by inadequately incorporating new information.

Consistent growth A growth investment substyle that focuses on companies with consistent growth having a long history of unit-sales growth, superior profitability, and predictable earnings.

Constant returns to scale A characteristic of a production function such that a given percentage increase in capital stock and labor input results in an equal percentage increase in output.

Contango A condition in the futures markets in which the costs of holding an asset exceed the benefits, leaving the futures price more than the spot price.

Contingent immunization A fixed-income strategy in which immunization serves as a fall-back strategy if the actively managed portfolio does not grow at a certain rate.

Continuous auction markets Auction markets where orders can be executed at any time during the trading day.

Contrarian A value investment substyle focusing on stocks that have been beset by problems.

Controlled foreign corporation A company located outside a taxpayer's home country and in which the taxpayer has a controlling interest as defined under the home country law.

Convenience yield The nonmonetary return offered by an asset when the asset is in short supply, often associated with assets with seasonal production processes.

Conversion factor An adjustment used to facilitate delivery on bond futures contracts in which any of a number of bonds with different characteristics are eligible for delivery.

Convexity A measure of how interest rate sensitivity changes with a change in interest rates.

Convexity adjustment An estimate of the change in price that is not explained by duration.

Cooling degree-day The greater of i) 65 degrees Fahrenheit minus the average daily temperature, and ii) zero.

Core capital The amount of capital required to fund spending to maintain a given lifestyle, fund goals, and provide adequate reserves for unexpected commitments.

Core-plus A fixed-income mandate that permits the portfolio manager to add instruments with relatively high return potential to core holdings of investment-grade debt.

Core–satellite A way of thinking about allocating money that seeks to define each investment's place in the portfolio in relation to specific investment goals or roles.

Core-satellite portfolio A portfolio in which certain investments (often indexed or semiactive) are viewed as the core and the balance are viewed as satellite investments fulfilling specific roles.

Corner portfolio Adjacent corner portfolios define a segment of the minimum-variance frontier within which portfolios hold identical assets and the rate of change of asset weights in moving from one portfolio to another is constant.

Corner portfolio theorem In a sign-constrained mean–variance optimization, the result that the asset weights of any minimum-variance portfolio are a positive linear combination of the corresponding weights in the two adjacent corner portfolios that bracket it in terms of expected return (or standard deviation of return).

Corporate governance The system of internal controls and procedures used to define and protect the rights and responsibilities of various stakeholders.

Corporate venturing Investments by companies in promising young companies in the same or a related industry.

Country beta A measure of the sensitivity of a specified variable (e.g., yield) to a change in the comparable variable in another country.

Covered call An option strategy involving the holding of an asset and sale of a call on the asset.

Crack spread The difference between the price of crude oil futures and that of equivalent amounts of heating oil and gasoline.

Credit VAR A variation of VAR related to credit risk; it reflects the minimum loss due to credit exposure with a given probability during a period of time.

Credit default swap A swap used to transfer credit risk to another party. A protection buyer pays the protection seller in return for the right to receive a payment from the seller in the event of a specified credit event.

Credit derivative A contract in which one party has the right to claim a payment from another party in the event that a specific credit event occurs over the life of the contract.

Credit event An event affecting the credit risk of a security or counterparty.

Credit forwards A type of credit derivative with payoffs based on bond values or credit spreads.

Credit method When the residence country reduces its taxpayers' domestic tax liability by the amount of taxes paid to a foreign country that exercises source jurisdiction.

Credit protection seller With respect to a credit derivative, the party that accepts the credit risk of the underlying financial asset.

Credit risk (or default risk) The risk of loss caused by a counterparty's or debtor's failure to make a timely payment or by the change in value of a financial instrument based on changes in default risk.

Credit spread forward A forward contract used to transfer credit risk to another party; a forward contract on a yield spread.

Credit spread option An option based on the yield spread between two securities that is used to transfer credit risk.

Credit spread risk The risk that the spread between the rate for a risky bond and the rate for a default risk-free bond may vary after the purchase of the risky bond.

Credited rates Rates of interest credited to a policyholder's reserve account.

Cross hedging With respect to hedging bond investments using futures, hedging when the bond to be hedged is not identical to the bond underlying the futures contract. With respect to currency hedging, a hedging technique that uses two currencies other than the home currency.

Cross-default provision A provision stipulating that if a borrower defaults on any outstanding credit obligations, the borrower is considered to be in default on all obligations.

Crush spread The difference between the price of a quantity of soybeans and that of the soybean meal and oil that can be produced by those soybeans.

Currency return The percentage change in the spot exchange rate stated in terms of home currency per unit of foreign currency.

Currency risk The risk associated with the uncertainty about the exchange rate at which proceeds in the foreign currency can be converted into the investor's home currency.

Currency swap A swap in which the parties make payments based on the difference in debt payments in different currencies.

Currency-hedged instruments Investment in nondomestic assets in which currency exposures are neutralized.

Current credit risk (or jump-to-default risk) The risk of credit-related events happening in the immediate future; it relates to the risk that a payment currently due will not be paid.

Cushion spread The difference between the minimum acceptable return and the higher possible immunized rate.

Custom security-based benchmark A custom benchmark created by weighting a manager's research universe using the manager's unique weighting approach.

Cyclical stocks The shares of companies whose earnings have above-average sensitivity to the business cycle.

Day traders Traders that rapidly buy and sell stocks in the hope that the stocks will continue to rise or fall in value for the seconds or minutes they are prepared to hold a position. Day traders hold a position open somewhat longer than a scalper but closing all positions at the end of the day.

Dealer (or market maker) A business entity that is ready to buy an asset for inventory or sell an asset from inventory to provide the other side of an order.

Decision price (also called arrival price or strike price) The prevailing price when the decision to trade is made.

Decision risk The risk of changing strategies at the point of maximum loss.

Deduction method When the residence country allows taxpayers to reduce their taxable income by the amount of taxes paid to foreign governments in respect of foreign-source income.

Deemed dispositions Tax treatment that assumes property is sold. It is sometimes seen as an alternative to estate or inheritance tax.

Deemed distribution When shareholders of a controlled foreign corporation are taxed as if the earnings were distributed to shareholders, even though no distribution has been made.

Default risk The risk of loss if an issuer or counterparty does not fulfill its contractual obligations.

Default risk premium Compensation for the possibility that the issue of a debt instrument will fail to make a promised payment at the contracted time and in the contracted amount.

Default swap A contract in which the swap buyer pays a regular premium; in exchange, if a default in a specified bond occurs, the swap seller pays the buyer the loss due to the default.

Defaultable debt Debt with some meaningful amount of credit risk.

Deferred swap A swap with terms specified today, but for which swap payments begin at a later date than for an ordinary swap.

Defined-benefit plan A pension plan that specifies the plan sponsor's obligations in terms of the benefit to plan participants.

Defined-contribution plan A pension plan that specifies the sponsor's obligations in terms of contributions to the pension fund rather than benefits to plan participants.

Deflation A decrease in the general level of prices; an increase in the purchasing power of a unit of currency.

Delay costs (or slippage) Implicit trading costs that arise from the inability to complete desired trades immediately due to order size or market liquidity.

Delivery option The feature of a futures contract giving the short the right to make decisions about what, when, and where to deliver.

Delta The relationship between the option price and the underlying price, which reflects the sensitivity of the price of the option to changes in the price of the underlying.

Delta hedge An option strategy in which a position in an asset is converted to a risk-free position with a position in a specific number of options. The number of options per unit of the underlying changes through time, and the position must be revised to maintain the hedge.

Delta-normal method A measure of VAR equivalent to the analytical method but that refers to the use of delta to estimate the option's price sensitivity.

Demand deposit A deposit that can be drawn upon without prior notice, such as a checking account.

Demutualizing The process of converting an insurance company from mutual form to stock.

Descriptive statistics Methods for effectively summarizing data to describe important aspects of a dataset.

Diff swap A swap in which payments are based on the difference in floating interest rates on a given notional amount denominated in a single currency.

Differential returns Returns that deviate from a manager's benchmark.

Diffusion index An index that measures how many indicators are pointing up and how many are pointing down.

Direct commodity investment Commodity investment that involves cash market purchase of physical commodities or exposure to changes in spot market values via derivatives, such as futures.

Direct market access Platforms sponsored by brokers that permit buy-side traders to directly access equities, fixed income, futures, and foreign exchange markets, clearing via the broker.

Direct quotation Quotation in terms of domestic currency/foreign currency.

Discounted cash flow models (DCF models) Valuation models that express the idea that an asset's value is the present value of its (expected) cash flows.

Discretionary trust A trust structure in which the trustee determines whether and how much to distribute in the sole discretion of the trustee.

Disintermediation To withdraw funds from financial intermediaries for placement with other financial intermediaries offering a higher return or yield. Or, to withdraw funds from a financial intermediary for the purposes of direct investment, such as withdrawing from a mutual fund to make direct stock investments.

Disposition effect As a result of loss aversion, an emotional bias whereby investors are reluctant to dispose of losers. This results in an inefficient and gradual adjustment to deterioration in fundamental value.

Distressed debt arbitrage A distressed securities investment discipline that involves purchasing the traded bonds of bankrupt companies and selling the common equity short.

Distressed securities Securities of companies that are in financial distress or near bankruptcy; the name given to various investment disciplines employing securities of companies in distress.

Diversification effect In reference to VAR across several portfolios (for example, across an entire firm), this effect equals the difference between the sum of the individual VARs and total VAR.

Dividend recapitalization A method by which a buyout fund can realize the value of a holding; involves the issuance of debt by the holding to finance a special dividend to owners.

Dollar duration A measure of the change in portfolio value for a 100 bps change in market yields.

Double inflection utility function A utility function that changes based on levels of wealth.

Downgrade risk The risk that one of the major rating agencies will lower its rating for an issuer, based on its specified rating criteria.

Downside deviation A measure of volatility using only rate of return data points below the investor's minimum acceptable return.

Downside risk Risk of loss or negative return.

Due diligence Investigation and analysis in support of an investment action or recommendation, such as the scrutiny of operations and management and the verification of material facts.

Duration A measure of the approximate sensitivity of a security to a change in interest rates (i.e., a measure of interest rate risk).

Dynamic approach With respect to strategic asset allocation, an approach that accounts for links between optimal decisions at different points in time.

ESG risk The risk to a company's market valuation resulting from environmental, social, and governance factors.

Earnings at risk (EAR) A variation of VAR that reflects the risk of a company's earnings instead of its market value.

Earnings momentum A growth investment substyle that focuses on companies with earnings momentum (high quarterly year-over-year earnings growth).

Econometrics The application of quantitative modeling and analysis grounded in economic theory to the analysis of economic data.

Economic exposure The risk associated with changes in the relative attractiveness of products and services offered for sale, arising out of the competitive effects of changes in exchange rates.

Economic indicators Economic statistics provided by government and established private organizations that contain information on an economy's recent past activity or its current or future position in the business cycle.

Economic surplus The market value of assets minus the present value of liabilities.

Effective duration Duration adjusted to account for embedded options.

Effective spread Two times the distance between the actual execution price and the midpoint of the market quote at the time an order is entered; a measure of execution costs that captures the effects of price improvement and market impact.

Efficient frontier The graph of the set of portfolios that maximize expected return for their level of risk (standard deviation of return); the part of the minimum-variance frontier beginning with the global minimum-variance portfolio and continuing above it.

Electronic communications networks (ECNs) Computer-based auctions that operate continuously within the day using a specified set of rules to execute orders.

Emerging market debt The sovereign debt of nondeveloped countries.

Emotional biases Behavioral biases resulting from reasoning influenced by feelings; emotional biases stem from impulse or intuition.

Endogenous variable A variable whose values are determined within the system.

Endowment bias An emotional bias in which people value an asset more when they hold rights to it than when they do not.

Endowments Long-term funds generally owned by operating nonprofit institutions such as universities and colleges, museums, hospitals, and other organizations involved in charitable activities.

Enhanced derivatives products companies (or special purpose vehicles) A type of subsidiary separate from an entity's other activities and not liable for the parent's debts. They are often used by derivatives dealers to control exposure to ratings downgrades.

Enterprise risk management An overall assessment of a company's risk position. A centralized approach to risk management sometimes called firmwide risk management.

Equal probability rebalancing Rebalancing in which the manager specifies a corridor for each asset class as a common multiple of the standard deviation of the asset class's returns. Rebalancing to the target proportions occurs when any asset class weight moves outside its corridor.

Equal weighted In an equal-weighted index, each stock in the index is weighted equally.

Equitized Given equity market systematic risk exposure.

Equity q The ratio of a company's equity market capitalization divided by net worth measured at replacement cost.

Equity risk premium Compensation for the additional risk of equity compared with debt.

Equity-indexed annuity A type of life annuity that provides a guarantee of a minimum fixed payment plus some participation in stock market gains, if any.

Estate All of the property a person owns or controls; may consist of financial assets, tangible personal assets, immovable property, or intellectual property.

Estate planning The process of preparing for the disposition of one's estate (e.g., the transfer of property) upon death and during one's lifetime.

Eurozone The region of countries using the euro as a currency.

Ex post alpha (or Jensen's alpha) The average return achieved in a portfolio in excess of what would have been predicted by CAPM given the portfolio's risk level; an after-the-fact measure of excess risk-adjusted return.

Excess capital An investor's capital over and above that which is necessary to fund their lifestyle and reserves.

Excess currency return The expected currency return in excess of the forward premium or discount.

Exchange A regulated venue for the trading of investment instruments.

Exchange fund A fund into which several investors place their different share holdings in exchange for shares in the diversified fund itself.

Glossary

Execution uncertainty Uncertainty pertaining to the timing of execution, or if execution will even occur at all.

Exemption method When the residence country imposes no tax on foreign-source income by providing taxpayers with an exemption, in effect having only one jurisdiction impose tax.

Exogenous shocks Events from outside the economic system that affect its course. These could be short-lived political events, changes in government policy, or natural disasters, for example.

Exogenous variable A variable whose values are determined outside the system.

Externality Those consequences of a transaction (or process) that do not fall on the parties to the transaction (or process).

Factor covariance matrix The covariance matrix of factors.

Factor push A simple stress test that involves pushing prices and risk factors of an underlying model in the most disadvantageous way to estimate the impact of factor extremes on the portfolio's value.

Factor sensitivities (also called factor betas or factor loadings) In a multifactor model, the responsiveness of the dependent variable to factor movements.

Factor-model-based benchmark A benchmark that is created by relating one or more systematic sources of returns (factors or exposures) to returns of the benchmark.

Fallen angels Debt that has crossed the threshold from investment grade to high yield.

Fed model An equity valuation model that relates the earnings yield on the S&P 500 to the yield to maturity on 10-year U.S. Treasury bonds.

Federal funds rate The interest rate on overnight loans of reserves (deposits) between U.S. Federal Reserve System member banks.

Fee cap A limit on the total fee paid regardless of performance.

Fiduciary A person or entity standing in a special relation of trust and responsibility with respect to other parties.

Financial capital As used in the text, an individual investor's investable wealth; total wealth minus human capital. Consists of assets that can be traded such as cash, stocks, bonds, and real estate.

Financial equilibrium models Models describing relationships between expected return and risk in which supply and demand are in balance.

Financial risk Risks derived from events in the external financial markets, such as changes in equity prices, interest rates, or currency exchange rates.

Fiscal policy Government activity concerning taxation and governmental spending.

Fixed annuity A type of life annuity in which periodic payments are fixed in amount.

Fixed trust A trust structure in which distributions to beneficiaries are prescribed in the trust document to occur at certain times or in certain amounts.

Fixed-rate payer The party to an interest rate swap that is obligated to make periodic payments at a fixed rate.

Flexible-premium variable life (or variable universal life) A type of life insurance policy that combines the flexibility of universal life with the investment choice flexibility of variable life.

Floating supply of shares (or free float) The number of shares outstanding that are actually available to investors.

Floating-rate payer The party to an interest rate swap that is obligated to make periodic payments based on a benchmark floating rate.

Floor A combination of interest rate options designed to provide protection against interest rate decreases.

Floor broker An agent of the broker who, for certain exchanges, physically represents the trade on the exchange floor.

Floorlet Each component put option in a floor.

Forced heirship rules Legal ownership principles whereby children have the right to a fixed share of a parent's estate.

Formal tools Established research methods amenable to precise definition and independent replication of results.

Forward curve The set of forward or futures prices with different expiration dates on a given date for a given asset.

Forward discount (or forward premium) The forward rate less the spot rate, divided by the spot rate; called the forward discount if negative, and forward premium if positive.

Forward hedging Hedging that involves the use of a forward contract between the foreign asset's currency and the home currency.

Forward strip Another name for the *forward curve*.

Foundations Typically, grant-making institutions funded by gifts and investment assets.

Fourth market A term occasionally used for direct trading of securities between institutional investors; the fourth market would include trading on electronic crossing networks.

Framing An information-processing bias in which a person answers a question differently based on the way in which it is asked (framed).

Framing bias An information-processing bias in which a person answers a question differently based on the way in which it is asked (framed).

Front office The revenue generating functions at an investment firm such as those pertaining to trading and sales.

Front-run To trade ahead of the initiator, exploiting privileged information about the initiator's trading intentions.

Full replication When every issue in an index is represented in the portfolio, and each portfolio position has approximately the same weight in the fund as in the index.

Fully funded plan A pension plan in which the ratio of the value of plan assets to the present value of plan liabilities is 100 percent or greater.

Functional duration (or multifunctional duration) The key rate duration.

Fund of funds A fund that invests in a number of underlying funds.

Fundamental law of active management The relation that the information ratio of a portfolio manager is approximately equal to the information coefficient multiplied by the square root of the investment discipline's breadth (the number of independent, active investment decisions made each year).

Funded status The relationship between the value of a plan's assets and the present value of its liabilities.

Funding ratio A measure of the relative size of pension assets compared to the present value of pension liabilities. Calculated by dividing the value of pension assets by the present value of pension liabilities. Also referred to as the funded ratio or funded status.

Funding risk The risk that liabilities funding long asset positions cannot be rolled over at reasonable cost.

Futures contract An enforceable contract between a buyer (seller) and an established exchange or its clearinghouse in which the buyer (seller) agrees to take (make) delivery of something at a specified price at the end of a designated period of time.

Futures price The price at which the parties to a futures contract agree to exchange the underlying.

Gain-to-loss ratio The ratio of positive returns to negative returns over a specified period of time.

Gamblers' fallacy A misunderstanding of probabilities in which people wrongly project reversal to a long-term mean.

Gamma A numerical measure of the sensitivity of delta to a change in the underlying's value.

Global custodian An entity that effects trade settlement, safekeeping of assets, and the allocation of trades to individual custody accounts.

Global investable market A practical proxy for the world market portfolio consisting of traditional and alternative asset classes with sufficient capacity to absorb meaningful investment.

Global minimum-variance (GMV) portfolio The portfolio on the minimum-variance frontier with smallest variance of return.

Gold standard currency system A currency regime under which currency could be freely converted into gold at established rates.

Gordon (constant) growth model A version of the dividend discount model for common share value that assumes a constant growth rate in dividends.

Government structural policies Government policies that affect the limits of economic growth and incentives within the private sector.

Grinold–Kroner model An expression for the expected return on a share as the sum of an expected income return, an expected nominal earnings growth return, and an expected repricing return.

Growth in total factor productivity A component of trend growth in GDP that results from increased efficiency in using capital inputs; also known as technical progress.

Guaranteed investment contract A debt instrument issued by insurers, usually in large denominations, that pays a guaranteed, generally fixed interest rate for a specified time period.

H-model A variant of the two-stage dividend discount model in which growth begins at a high rate and declines linearly throughout the supernormal growth period until it reaches a normal growth rate that holds in perpetuity.

Hague Conference on Private International Law An intergovernmental organization working toward the convergence of private international law. Its 69 members consist of countries and regional economic integration organizations.

Halo effect An emotional bias that extends a favorable evaluation of some characteristics to other characteristics.

Heating degree-day The greater of i) the average daily temperature minus 65 degree Fahrenheit, and ii) zero.

Hedge funds A historically loosely regulated, pooled investment vehicle that may implement various investment strategies.

Hedge ratio The relationship of the quantity of an asset being hedged to the quantity of the derivative used for hedging.

Hedged return The foreign asset return in local currency terms plus the forward discount (premium).

Hedging A general strategy usually thought of as reducing, if not eliminating, risk.

Herding When a group of investors trade on the same side of the market in the same securities, or when investors ignore their own private information and act as other investors do.

High yield A value investment substyle that focuses on stocks offering high dividend yield with prospects of maintaining or increasing the dividend.

High-water mark A specified net asset value level that a fund must exceed before performance fees are paid to the hedge fund manager.

High-yield investing A distressed securities investment discipline that involves investment in high-yield bonds perceived to be undervalued.

Hindsight bias A bias with selective perception and retention aspects in which people may see past events as having been predictable and reasonable to expect.

Historical simulation method The application of historical price changes to the current portfolio.

Holdings-based style analysis An approach to style analysis that categorizes individual securities by their characteristics and aggregates results to reach a conclusion about the overall style of the portfolio at a given point in time.

Home bias An anomaly by which portfolios exhibit a strong bias in favor of domestic securities in the context of global portfolios.

Human capital (or net employment capital) An implied asset; the present value of expected future labor income.

Hybrid markets Combinations of market types, which offer elements of batch auction markets and continuous auction markets, as well as quote-driven markets.

Hypothetical events A type of scenario analysis used in stress testing that involves the evaluation of performance given events that have never happened in the markets or market outcomes to which we attach a small probability.

Illiquidity premium Compensation for the risk of loss relative to an investment's fair value if an investment needs to be converted to cash quickly.

Illusion of control A bias in which people tend to believe that they can control or influence outcomes when, in fact, they cannot. Illusion of knowledge and self-attribution biases contribute to the overconfidence bias.

Illusion of control bias A bias in which people tend to believe that they can control or influence outcomes when, in fact, they cannot. Illusion of knowledge and self-attribution biases contribute to the overconfidence bias.

Immunization An asset/liability management approach that structures investments in bonds to match (offset) liabilities' weighted-average duration; a type of dedication strategy.

Immunized time horizon The time horizon over which a portfolio's value is immunized; equal to the portfolio duration.

Implementation shortfall The difference between the money return on a notional or paper portfolio and the actual portfolio return.

Implementation shortfall strategy (or arrival price strategy) A strategy that attempts to minimize trading costs as measured by the implementation shortfall method.

Implied yield A measure of the yield on the underlying bond of a futures contract implied by pricing it as though the underlying will be delivered at the futures expiration.

Incremental VAR A measure of the incremental effect of an asset on the VAR of a portfolio by measuring the difference between the portfolio's VAR while including a specified asset and the portfolio's VAR with that asset eliminated.

Indexing A common passive approach to investing that involves holding a portfolio of securities designed to replicate the returns on a specified index of securities.

Glossary

Indifference curve analysis A decision-making approach whereby curves of consumption bundles, among which the decision-maker is indifferent, are constructed to identify and choose the curve within budget constraints that generates the highest utility.

Indirect commodity investment Commodity investment that involves the acquisition of indirect claims on commodities, such as equity in companies specializing in commodity production.

Inferential statistics Methods for making estimates or forecasts about a larger group from a smaller group actually observed.

Inflation An increase in the general level of prices; a decrease in the purchasing power of a unit of currency.

Inflation hedge An asset whose returns are sufficient on average to preserve purchasing power during periods of inflation.

Inflation premium Compensation for expected inflation.

Information coefficient The correlation between forecast and actual returns.

Information ratio The mean excess return of the account over the benchmark (i.e., mean active return) relative to the variability of that excess return (i.e., tracking risk); a measure of risk-adjusted performance.

Information-motivated traders Traders that seek to trade on information that has limited value if not quickly acted upon.

Infrastructure funds Funds that make private investment in public infrastructure projects in return for rights to specified revenue streams over a contracted period.

Initial public offering The initial issuance of common stock registered for public trading by a formerly private corporation.

Input uncertainty Uncertainty concerning whether the inputs are correct.

Inside ask (or market ask) The lowest available ask price.

Inside bid (or market bid) The highest available bid price.

Inside bid–ask spread (also called market bid–ask spread, inside spread, or market spread) Market ask price minus market bid price.

Inside quote (or market quote) Combination of the highest available bid price with the lowest available ask price.

Inside spread (also called market bid–ask spread, inside bid–ask spread, or market spread) Market ask price minus market bid price.

Institutional investors Corporations or other legal entities that ultimately serve as financial intermediaries between individuals and investment markets.

Interest rate management effect With respect to fixed-income attribution analysis, a return component reflecting how well a manager predicts interest rate changes.

Interest rate parity A formula that expresses the equivalence or parity of spot and forward rates, after adjusting for differences in the interest rates.

Interest rate risk Risk related to changes in the level of interest rates.

Interest rate swap A contract between two parties (counterparties) to exchange periodic interest payments based on a specified notional amount of principal.

Interest spread With respect to banks, the average yield on earning assets minus the average percent cost of interest-bearing liabilities.

Internal rate of return The growth rate that will link the ending value of the account to its beginning value plus all intermediate cash flows; money-weighted rate of return is a synonym.

Intestate Having made no valid will; a decedent without a valid will or with a will that does not dispose of their property is considered to have died intestate.

Inventory cycle A cycle measured in terms of fluctuations in inventories, typically lasting 2–4 years.

Inverse floater A floating-rate note or bond in which the coupon is adjusted to move opposite to a benchmark interest rate.

Investment skill The ability to outperform an appropriate benchmark consistently over time.

Investment style A natural grouping of investment disciplines that has some predictive power in explaining the future dispersion in returns across portfolios.

Investment style indexes Indices that represent specific portions of an asset category. For example, subgroups within the U.S. common stock asset category such as large-capitalization growth stocks.

Investor's benchmark The benchmark an investor uses to evaluate performance of a given portfolio or asset class.

Irrevocable trust A trust arrangement wherein the settlor has no ability to revoke the trust relationship.

J factor risk The risk associated with a judge's track record in adjudicating bankruptcies and restructuring.

Joint ownership with right of survivorship Jointly owned; assets held in joint ownership with right of survivorship automatically transfer to the surviving joint owner or owners outside the probate process.

Justified P/E The price-to-earnings ratio that is fair, warranted, or justified on the basis of forecasted fundamentals.

Key rate duration A method of measuring the interest rate sensitivities of a fixed-income instrument or portfolio to shifts in key points along the yield curve.

Lagging economic indicators A set of economic variables whose values correlate with recent past economic activity.

Leading economic indicators A set of economic variables whose values vary with the business cycle but at a fairly consistent time interval before a turn in the business cycle.

Legal/contract risk The possibility of loss arising from the legal system's failure to enforce a contract in which an enterprise has a financial stake; for example, if a contract is voided through litigation.

Leverage-adjusted duration gap A leverage-adjusted measure of the difference between the durations of assets and liabilities which measures a bank's overall interest rate exposure.

Leveraged floating-rate note (leveraged floater) A floating-rate note or bond in which the coupon is adjusted at a multiple of a benchmark interest rate.

Liability As used in the text, a financial obligation.

Life annuity An annuity that guarantees a monthly income to the annuitant for life.

Lifetime gratuitous transfer A lifetime gift made during the lifetime of the donor; also known as *inter vivos* transfers.

Limit order An instruction to execute an order when the best price available is at least as good as the limit price specified in the order.

Linear programming Optimization in which the objective function and constraints are linear.

Liquidity The ability to trade without delay at relatively low cost and in relatively large quantities.

Liquidity risk Any risk of economic loss because of the need to sell relatively less liquid assets to meet liquidity requirements; the risk that a financial instrument cannot be purchased or sold without a significant concession in price because of the market's potential inability to efficiently accommodate the desired trading size.

Liquidity-motivated traders Traders that are motivated to trade based upon reasons other than an information advantage. For example, to release cash proceeds to facilitate the purchase of another security, adjust market exposure, or fund cash needs.

Lock-up period A minimum initial holding period for investments during which no part of the investment can be withdrawn.

Locked up Said of investments that cannot be traded at all for some time.

Logical participation strategies Protocols for breaking up an order for execution over time. Typically used by institutional traders to participate in overall market volumes without being unduly visible.

Longevity risk The risk of outliving one's financial resources.

Loss-aversion bias A bias in which people tend to strongly prefer avoiding losses as opposed to achieving gains.

Low P/E A value investment substyle that focuses on shares selling at low prices relative to current or normal earnings.

M² A measure of what a portfolio would have returned if it had taken on the same total risk as the market index.

Macaulay duration The percentage change in price for a percentage change in yield. The term, named for one of the economists who first derived it, is used to distinguish the calculation from modified duration. (See also *modified duration*).

Macro attribution Performance attribution analysis conducted on the fund sponsor level.

Macro expectations Expectations concerning classes of assets.

Managed futures Pooled investment vehicles, frequently structured as limited partnerships, that invest in futures and options on futures and other instruments.

Manager continuation policies Policies adopted to guide the manager evaluations conducted by fund sponsors. The goal of manager continuation policies is to reduce the costs of manager turnover while systematically acting on indications of future poor performance.

Manager monitoring A formal, documented procedure that assists fund sponsors in consistently collecting information relevant to evaluating the state of their managers' operations; used to identify warning signs of adverse changes in existing managers' organizations.

Manager review A detailed examination of a manager that currently exists within a plan sponsor's program. The manager review closely resembles the manager selection process, in both the information considered and the comprehensiveness of the analysis. The staff should review all phases of the manager's operations, just as if the manager were being initially hired.

Market ask The lowest available ask price.

Market bid The best available bid; highest price any buyer is currently willing to pay.

Market bid–ask spread (also called inside bid–ask spread, inside spread, or market spread) Market ask price minus market bid price.

Market fragmentation A condition whereby a market contains no dominant group of sellers (or buyers) that are large enough to unduly influence the market.

Market impact (or price impact) The effect of the trade on transaction prices.

Market integration The degree to which there are no impediments or barriers to capital mobility across markets.

Market microstructure The market structures and processes that affect how the manager's interest in buying or selling an asset is translated into executed trades (represented by trade prices and volumes).

Market model A regression equation that specifies a linear relationship between the return on a security (or portfolio) and the return on a broad market index.

Market on close order A market order to be executed at the closing of the market.

Market on open order A market order to be executed at the opening of the market.

Market order An instruction to execute an order as soon as possible in the public markets at the best price available.

Market oriented With reference to equity investing, an intermediate grouping for investment disciplines that cannot be clearly categorized as value or growth.

Market quote (or inside quote) Combination of the highest available bid price with the lowest available ask price.

Market risk The risk associated with interest rates, exchange rates, and equity prices.

Market segmentation The degree to which there are some meaningful impediments to capital movement across markets.

Market spread (also called market bid–ask spread, inside spread, or Inside bid–ask spread) Market ask price minus market bid price.

Market-adjusted implementation shortfall The difference between the money return on a notional or paper portfolio and the actual portfolio return, adjusted using beta to remove the effect of the return on the market.

Market-not-held order A variation of the market order designed to give the agent greater discretion than a simple market order would allow. "Not held" means that the floor broker is not required to trade at any specific price or in any specific time interval.

Marking to market A procedure used primarily in futures markets in which the parties to a contract settle the amount owed daily. Also known as the *daily settlement*.

Mass affluent An industry term for a segment of the private wealth marketplace that is not sufficiently wealthy to command certain individualized services.

Matrix prices Prices determined by comparisons to other securities of similar credit risk and maturity; the result of matrix pricing.

Matrix pricing An approach for estimating the prices of thinly traded securities based on the prices of securities with similar attributions, such as similar credit rating, maturity, or economic sector.

Maturity premium Compensation for the increased sensitivity of the market value of debt to a change in market interest rates as maturity is extended.

Maturity variance A measure of how much a given immunized portfolio differs from the ideal immunized portfolio consisting of a single pure discount instrument with maturity equal to the time horizon.

Maximum loss optimization A stress test in which we would try to optimize mathematically the risk variable that would produce the maximum loss.

Mega-cap buy-out funds A class of buyout funds that take public companies private.

Mental accounting bias An information-processing bias in which people treat one sum of money differently from another equal-sized sum based on which mental account the money is assigned to.

Micro attribution   Performance attribution analysis carried out on the investment manager level.

Micro expectations   Expectations concerning individual assets.

Middle-market buy-out funds   A class of buyout funds that purchase private companies whose revenues and profits are too small to access capital from the public equity markets.

Midquote   The halfway point between the market bid and ask prices.

Minimum-variance frontier   The graph of the set of portfolios with smallest variances of return for their levels of expected return.

Missed trade opportunity costs   Unrealized profit/loss arising from the failure to execute a trade in a timely manner.

Model risk   The risk that a model is incorrect or misapplied; in investments, it often refers to valuation models.

Model uncertainty   Uncertainty concerning whether a selected model is correct.

Modified duration   An adjustment of the duration for the level of the yield. Contrast with *Macaulay duration*.

Monetary policy   Government activity concerning interest rates and the money supply.

Money markets   Markets for fixed-income securities with maturities of one year or less.

Money-weighted rate of return   Same as the internal rate of return; the growth rate that will link the ending value of the account to its beginning value plus all intermediate cash flows.

Mortality risk   The risk of loss of human capital in the event of premature death.

Multifactor model   A model that explains a variable in terms of the values of a set of factors.

Multifactor model technique   With respect to construction of an indexed portfolio, a technique that attempts to match the primary risk exposures of the indexed portfolio to those of the index.

Multiperiod Sharpe ratio   A Sharpe ratio based on the investment's multiperiod wealth in excess of the wealth generated by the risk-free investment.

Mutuals   With respect to insurance companies, companies that are owned by their policyholders, who share in the company's surplus earnings.

Natural liquidity   An extensive pool of investors who are aware of and have a potential interest in buying and/or selling a security.

Net employment capital   See human capital.

Net interest margin   With respect to banks, net interest income (interest income minus interest expense) divided by average earning assets.

Net interest spread   With respect to the operations of insurers, the difference between interest earned and interest credited to policyholders.

Net worth   The difference between the market value of assets and liabilities.

Net worth tax or net wealth tax   A tax based on a person's assets, less liabilities.

Nominal default-free bonds   Conventional bonds that have no (or minimal) default risk.

Nominal gross domestic product   (nominal GDP) A money measure of the goods and services produced within a country's borders.

Nominal risk-free interest rate   The sum of the real risk-free interest rate and the inflation premium.

Nominal spread   The spread of a bond or portfolio above the yield of a Treasury of equal maturity.

Nonfinancial risk   Risks that arise from sources other than the external financial markets, such as changes in accounting rules, legal environment, or tax rates.

Nonparametric   Involving minimal probability-distribution assumptions.

Nonstationarity   A property of a data series that reflects more than one set of underlying statistical properties.

Normal portfolio   A portfolio with exposure to sources of systematic risk that are typical for a manager, using the manager's past portfolios as a guide.

Notional amount   The dollar amount used as a scale factor in calculating payments for a forward contract, futures contract, or swap.

Notional principal amount   The amount specified in a swap that forms the basis for calculating payment streams.

Objective function   A quantitative expression of the objective or goal of a process.

Open market operations   The purchase or sale by a central bank of government securities, which are settled using reserves, to influence interest rates and the supply of credit by banks.

Open outcry auction market   Public auction where representatives of buyers and sellers meet at a specified location and place verbal bids and offers.

Operational risk   The risk of loss from failures in a company's systems and procedures (for example, due to computer failures or human failures) or events completely outside of the control of organizations (which would include "acts of God" and terrorist actions).

Opportunistic participation strategies   Passive trading combined with the opportunistic seizing of liquidity.

Optimization   With respect to portfolio construction, a procedure for determining the best portfolios according to some criterion.

Optimizer   A heuristic, formula, algorithm, or program that uses risk, return, correlation, or other variables to determine the most appropriate asset allocation or asset mix for a portfolio.

Option-adjusted spread (OAS)   The current spread over the benchmark yield minus that component of the spread that is attributable to any embedded optionality in the instrument.

Options on futures   (futures options) Options on a designated futures contract.

Options on physicals   With respect to options, exchange-traded option contracts that have cash instruments rather than futures contracts on cash instruments as the underlying.

Order-driven markets   Markets in which transaction prices are established by public limit orders to buy or sell a security at specified prices.

Ordinary life insurance   (also whole life insurance) A type of life insurance policy that involves coverage for the whole of the insured's life.

Orphan equities investing   A distressed securities investment discipline that involves investment in orphan equities that are perceived to be undervalued.

Orphan equity   Investment in the newly issued equity of a company emerging from reorganization.

Output gap   The difference between the value of GDP estimated as if the economy were on its trend growth path (potential output) and the actual value of GDP.

Overall trade balance   The sum of the current account (reflecting exports and imports) and the financial account (consisting of portfolio flows).

Overconfidence bias A bias in which people demonstrate unwarranted faith in their own intuitive reasoning, judgments, and/or cognitive abilities.

Overconfidence trap The tendency of individuals to overestimate the accuracy of their forecasts.

Pairs trade (or pairs arbitrage) A basic long–short trade in which an investor is long and short equal currency amounts of two common stocks in a single industry.

Panel method A method of capital market expectations setting that involves using the viewpoints of a panel of experts.

Partial correlation In multivariate problems, the correlation between two variables after controlling for the effects of the other variables in the system.

Partial fill Execution of a purchase or sale for fewer shares than was stipulated in the order.

Participate (do not initiate) order A variant of the market-not-held order. The broker is deliberately low-key and waits for and responds to the initiatives of more active traders.

Passive management A buy-and-hold approach to investing in which an investor does not make portfolio changes based upon short-term expectations of changing market or security performance.

Passive traders Traders that seek liquidity in their rebalancing transactions, but are much more concerned with the cost of trading.

Payer swaption A swaption that allows the holder to enter into a swap as the fixed-rate payer and floating-rate receiver.

Payment netting A means of settling payments in which the amount owed by the first party to the second is netted with the amount owed by the second party to the first; only the net difference is paid.

Pension funds Funds consisting of assets set aside to support a promise of retirement income.

Pension surplus Pension assets at market value minus the present value of pension liabilities.

Percentage-of-portfolio rebalancing Rebalancing is triggered based on set thresholds stated as a percentage of the portfolio's value.

Percentage-of-volume strategy A logical participation strategy in which trading takes place in proportion to overall market volume (typically at a rate of 5–20 percent) until the order is completed.

Perfect markets Markets without any frictional costs.

Performance appraisal The evaluation of portfolio performance; a quantitative assessment of a manager's investment skill.

Performance attribution A comparison of an account's performance with that of a designated benchmark and the identification and quantification of sources of differential returns.

Performance evaluation The measurement and assessment of the outcomes of investment management decisions.

Performance measurement A component of performance evaluation; the relatively simple procedure of calculating an asset's or portfolio's rate of return.

Performance netting risk For entities that fund more than one strategy and have asymmetric incentive fee arrangements with the portfolio managers, the potential for loss in cases where the net performance of the group of managers generates insufficient fee revenue to fully cover contractual payout obligations to all portfolio managers with positive performance.

Performance-based fee Fees specified by a combination of a base fee plus an incentive fee for performance in excess of a benchmark's.

Periodic auction markets Auction markets where multilateral trading occurs at a single price at a prespecified point in time.

Permanent income hypothesis The hypothesis that consumers' spending behavior is largely determined by their long-run income expectations.

Plan sponsor An enterprise or organization—such as a business, labor union, municipal or state government, or not-for-profit organization—that sets up a pension plan.

Pledging requirement With respect to banks, a required collateral use of assets.

Point estimate A single-valued estimate of a quantity, as opposed to an estimate in terms of a range of values.

Policy portfolio A synonym of strategic asset allocation; the portfolio resulting from strategic asset allocation considered as a process.

Policyholder reserves With respect to an insurance company, an amount representing the estimated payments to policyholders, as determined by actuaries, based on the types and terms of the various insurance policies issued by the company.

Political risk (or geopolitical risk) The risk of war, government collapse, political instability, expropriation, confiscation, or adverse changes in taxation.

Portable Moveable. With reference to a pension plan, one in which a plan participant can move his or her share of plan assets to a new plan, subject to certain rules, vesting schedules, and possible tax penalties and payments.

Portable alpha A strategy involving the combining of multiple positions (e.g., long and short positions) so as to separate the alpha (unsystematic risk) from beta (systematic risk) in an investment.

Portfolio segmentation The creation of subportfolios according to the product mix for individual segments or lines of business.

Portfolio trade (also known as program trade or basket trade) A trade in which a number of securities are traded as a single unit.

Position a trade To take the other side of a trade, acting as a principal with capital at risk.

Post-trade transparency Degree to which completed trades are quickly and accurately reported to the public.

Potential output The value of GDP if the economy were on its trend growth path.

Preferred return With respect to the compensation of private equity fund managers, a hurdle rate.

Premium Regarding life insurance, the asset paid by the policy holder to an insurer who, in turn, has a contractual obligation to pay death benefit proceeds to the beneficiary named in the policy.

Prepackaged bankruptcy A bankruptcy in which the debtor seeks agreement from creditors on the terms of a reorganization before the reorganization filing.

Prepaid swap A contract calling for payment today and delivery of the asset or commodity at multiple specified times in the future.

Present value distribution of cash flows A list showing what proportion of a portfolio's duration is attributable to each future cash flow.

Present value of a basis point (PVBP) The change in the bond price for a 1 basis point change in yield. Also called *basis point value* (BPV).

Pretrade transparency Ability of individuals to quickly, easily, and inexpensively obtain accurate information about quotes and trades.

Price discovery Adjustment of transaction prices to balance supply and demand.

Price improvement Execution at a price that is better than the price quoted at the time of order placement.

Price risk The risk of fluctuations in market price.

Price uncertainty Uncertainty about the price at which an order will execute.

Price value of a basis point (also PVBP) The change in the bond price for a 1 basis point change in yield. Also called *basis point value* (BPV).

Price weighted With respect to index construction, an index in which each security in the index is weighted according to its absolute share price.

Priced risk Risk for which investors demand compensation.

Primary risk factors With respect to valuation, the major influences on pricing.

Prime brokerage A suite of services that is often specified to include support in accounting and reporting, leveraged trade execution, financing, securities lending (related to short-selling activities), and start-up advice (for new entities).

Principal trade A trade with a broker in which the broker commits capital to facilitate the prompt execution of the trader's order to buy or sell.

Private equity Ownership interests in non-publicly-traded companies.

Private equity funds Pooled investment vehicles investing in generally highly illiquid assets; includes venture capital funds and buyout funds.

Private exchange A method for handling undiversified positions with built-in capital gains in which shares that are a component of an index are exchanged for shares of an index mutual fund in a privately arranged transaction with the fund.

Private placement memorandum A document used to raise venture capital financing when funds are raised through an agent.

Probate The legal process to confirm the validity of a will so that executors, heirs, and other interested parties can rely on its authenticity.

Profit-sharing plans A defined-contribution plan in which contributions are based, at least in part, on the plan sponsor's profits.

Projected benefit obligation (PBO) A measure of a pension plan's liability that reflects accumulated service in the same manner as the ABO but also projects future variables, such as compensation increases.

Prospect theory An alternative to expected utility theory, it assigns value to gains and losses (changes in wealth) rather than to final wealth, and probabilities are replaced by decision weights. In prospect theory, the shape of a decision maker's value function is assumed to differ between the domain of gains and the domain of losses.

Protective put An option strategy in which a long position in an asset is combined with a long position in a put.

Proxy hedging Hedging that involves the use of a forward contract between the home currency and a currency that is highly correlated with the foreign asset's currency.

Prudence trap The tendency to temper forecasts so that they do not appear extreme; the tendency to be overly cautious in forecasting.

Public good A good that is not divisible and not excludable (a consumer cannot be denied it).

Purchasing power parity The theory that movements in an exchange rate should offset any difference in the inflation rates between two countries.

Pure sector allocation return A component of attribution analysis that relates relative returns to the manager's sector-weighting decisions. Calculated as the difference between the allocation (weight) of the portfolio to a given sector and the portfolio's benchmark weight for that sector, multiplied by the difference between the sector benchmark's return and the overall portfolio's benchmark return, summed across all sectors.

Quality control charts A graphical means of presenting performance appraisal data; charts illustrating the performance of an actively managed account versus a selected benchmark.

Quality option (or swap option) With respect to Treasury futures, the option of which acceptable Treasury issue to deliver.

Quantitative easing A policy measure in which a central bank buys financial assets to inject a predetermined quantity of money in the financial system.

Quote-driven markets (or dealer markets) Markets that rely on dealers to establish firm prices at which securities can be bought and sold.

Quoted depth The number of shares available for purchase or sale at the quoted bid and ask prices.

Rate duration A fixed-income instrument's or portfolio's sensitivity to a change in key maturity, holding constant all other points along the yield curve.

Ratio spread An option strategy in which a long position in a certain number of options is offset by a short position in a certain number of other options on the same underlying, resulting in a risk-free position.

Rational economic man A self-interested, risk-averse individual who has the ability to make judgments using all available information in order to maximize his/her expected utility.

Re-base With reference to index construction, to change the time period used as the base of the index.

Real estate Interests in land or structures attached to land.

Real estate investment trusts (REITs) Publicly traded equities representing pools of money invested in real estate properties and/or real estate debt.

Real option An option involving decisions related to tangible assets or processes.

Real risk-free interest rate The single-period interest rate for a completely risk-free security if no inflation were expected.

Rebalancing ratio A quantity involved in reestablishing the dollar duration of a portfolio to a desired level, equal to the original dollar duration divided by the new dollar duration.

Recallability trap The tendency of forecasts to be overly influenced by events that have left a strong impression on a person's memory.

Receiver swaption A swaption that allows the holder to enter into a swap as the fixed-rate receiver and floating-rate payer.

Recession A broad-based economic downturn, conventionally defined as two successive quarterly declines in GDP.

Reference entity An entity, such as a bond issuer, specified in a derivatives contract.

Regime A distinct governing set of relationships.

Regret The feeling that an opportunity has been missed; typically an expression of *hindsight bias*.

Regret-aversion bias An emotional bias in which people tend to avoid making decisions that will result in action out of fear that the decision will turn out poorly.

Regulatory risk The risk associated with the uncertainty of how a transaction will be regulated or with the potential for regulations to change.

Reinvestment risk The risk of reinvesting coupon income or principal at a rate less than the original coupon or purchase rate.

Relative economic strength forecasting approach An exchange rate forecasting approach that suggests that a strong pace of economic growth in a country creates attractive investment opportunities, increasing the demand for the country's currency and causing it to appreciate.

Relative strength indicators A price momentum indicator that involves comparing a stock's performance during a specific period either to its own past performance or to the performance of some group of stocks.

Remaindermen Beneficiaries of a trust; having a claim on the residue.

Representativeness bias A belief perseverance bias in which people tend to classify new information based on past experiences and classifications.

Repurchase agreement A contract involving the sale of securities such as Treasury instruments coupled with an agreement to repurchase the same securities at a later date.

Repurchase yield The negative of the expected percent change in number of shares outstanding, in the Grinold–Kroner model.

Resampled efficient frontier The set of resampled efficient portfolios.

Resampled efficient portfolio An efficient portfolio based on simulation.

Residence jurisdiction A framework used by a country to determine the basis for taxing income, based on residency.

Residence–residence conflict When two countries claim residence of the same individual, subjecting the individual's income to taxation by both countries.

Residence–source conflict When tax jurisdiction is claimed by an individual's country of residence and the country where some of their assets are sourced; the most common source of double taxation.

Residue With respect to trusts, the funds remaining in a trust when the last income beneficiary dies.

Retired-lives The portion of a pension fund's liabilities associated with retired workers.

Returns-based benchmarks Benchmarks that are constructed using 1) a series of a manager's account returns and 2) the series of returns on several investment style indexes over the same period. These return series are then submitted to an allocation algorithm that solves for the combination of investment style indexes that most closely tracks the account's returns.

Returns-based style analysis An approach to style analysis that focuses on characteristics of the overall portfolio as revealed by a portfolio's realized returns.

Reverse optimization A technique for reverse engineering the expected returns implicit in a diversified market portfolio.

Revocable trust A trust arrangement wherein the settlor (who originally transfers assets to fund the trust) retains the right to rescind the trust relationship and regain title to the trust assets.

Risk budgeting The establishment of objectives for individuals, groups, or divisions of an organization that takes into account the allocation of an acceptable level of risk.

Risk exposure A source of risk. Also, the state of being exposed or vulnerable to a risk.

Risk premium approach An approach to forecasting the return of a risky asset that views its expected return as the sum of the risk-free rate of interest and one or more risk premiums.

Risk profile A detailed tabulation of the index's risk exposures.

Risk tolerance The capacity to accept risk; the level of risk an investor (or organization) is willing and able to bear.

Risk tolerance function An assessment of an investor's tolerance to risk over various levels of portfolio outcomes.

Roll return (or roll yield) The component of the return on a commodity futures contract that comes from rolling long futures positions forward through time.

Rolling return The moving average of the holding-period returns for a specified period (e.g., a calendar year) that matches the investor's time horizon.

Sample estimator A formula for assigning a unique value (a point estimate) to a population parameter.

Sample-size neglect A type of representativeness bias in which financial market participants incorrectly assume that small sample sizes are representative of populations (or "real" data).

Sandwich spread An option strategy that is equivalent to a short butterfly spread.

Satisfice A combination of "satisfy" and "suffice" describing decisions, actions, and outcomes that may not be optimal, but are adequate.

Savings–investment imbalances forecasting approach An exchange rate forecasting approach that explains currency movements in terms of the effects of domestic savings–investment imbalances on the exchange rate.

Scenario analysis A risk management technique involving the examination of the performance of a portfolio under specified situations. Closely related to *stress testing*.

Secondary offering An offering after the initial public offering of securities.

Sector/quality effect In a fixed-income attribution analysis, a measure of a manager's ability to select the "right" issuing sector and quality group.

Security selection effect In a fixed-income attribution analysis, the residual of the security's total return after other effects are accounted for; a measure of the return due to ability in security selection.

Segmentation With respect to the management of insurance company portfolios, the notional subdivision of the overall portfolio into sub-portfolios each of which is associated with a specified group of insurance contracts.

Self-attribution bias A bias in which people take personal credit for successes and attribute failures to external factors outside the individual's control.

Self-control bias A bias in which people fail to act in pursuit of their long-term, overarching goals because of a lack of self-discipline.

Sell side Broker/dealers that sell securities and make recommendations for various customers, such as investment managers and institutional investors.

Semiactive management (also called enhanced indexing or risk-controlled active management) A variant of active management. In a semiactive portfolio, the manager seeks to outperform a given benchmark with tightly controlled risk relative to the benchmark.

Glossary

Semivariance A measure of downside risk. The average of squared deviations that fall below the mean.

Separate property regime A marital property regime under which each spouse is able to own and control property as an individual.

Settlement date (payment date) The designated date at which the parties to a trade must transact.

Settlement netting risk The risk that a liquidator of a counterparty in default could challenge a netting arrangement so that profitable transactions are realized for the benefit of creditors.

Settlement risk When settling a contract, the risk that one party could be in the process of paying the counterparty while the counterparty is declaring bankruptcy.

Settlor (or grantor) An entity that transfers assets to a trustee, to be held and managed for the benefit of the trust beneficiaries.

Shari'a The law of Islam. In addition to the law of the land, some follow guidance provided by Shari'a or Islamic law.

Sharpe ratio (or reward-to-variability) A measure of risk-adjusted performance that compares excess returns to the total risk of the account, where total risk is measured by the account's standard deviation of returns.

Shortfall risk The risk that portfolio value will fall below some minimum acceptable level during a stated time horizon; the risk of not achieving a specified return target.

Shrinkage estimation Estimation that involves taking a weighted average of a historical estimate of a parameter and some other parameter estimate, where the weights reflect the analyst's relative belief in the estimates.

Shrinkage estimator The formula used in shrinkage estimation of a parameter.

Sign-constrained optimization An optimization that constrains asset class weights to be nonnegative and to sum to 1.

Smart routing The use of algorithms to intelligently route an order to the most liquid venue.

Smoothing rule With respect to spending rates, a rule that averages asset values over a period of time in order to dampen the spending rate's response to asset value fluctuation.

Social proof A bias in which individuals tend to follow the beliefs of a group.

Socially responsible investing (ethical investing) An approach to investing that integrates ethical values and societal concerns with investment decisions.

Soft dollars (also called soft dollar arrangements or soft commissions) The use of commissions to buy services other than execution services.

Sole ownership Owned by one person; assets held in sole ownership are typically considered part of a decedent's estate. The transfer of their ownership is dictated by the decedent's will through the probate process.

Solow residual A measure of the growth in total factor productivity that is based on an economic growth model developed by economist Robert M. Solow.

Sortino ratio A performance appraisal ratio that replaces standard deviation in the Sharpe ratio with downside deviation.

Source jurisdiction A framework used by a country to determine the basis for taxing income or transfers. A country that taxes income as a source within its borders imposes source jurisdiction.

Source–source conflict When two countries claim source jurisdiction of the same asset; both countries may claim that the income is derived from their jurisdiction.

Sovereign risk A form of credit risk in which the borrower is the government of a sovereign nation.

Spot return (or price return) The component of the return on a commodity futures contract that comes from changes in the underlying spot prices via the cost-of-carry model.

Spread duration The sensitivity of a non-Treasury security's price to a widening or narrowing of the spread over Treasuries.

Spread risk Risk related to changes in the spread between Treasuries and non-Treasuries.

Stack and roll A hedging strategy in which an existing stack hedge with maturing futures contracts is replaced by a new stack hedge with longer dated futures contracts.

Stack hedge Hedging a stream of obligations by entering futures contracts with a *single* maturity, with the number of contracts selected so that changes in the *present value* of the future obligations are offset by changes in the value of this "stack" of futures contracts.

Stale price bias Bias that arises from using prices that are stale because of infrequent trading.

Static approach With respect to strategic asset allocation, an approach that does not account for links between optimal decisions in future time periods.

Static spread (or zero-volatility spread) The constant spread above the Treasury spot curve that equates the calculated price of the security to the market price.

Stationary A series of data for which the parameters that describe a return-generating process are stable.

Status quo bias An emotional bias in which people do nothing (i.e., maintain the "status quo") instead of making a change.

Status quo trap The tendency for forecasts to perpetuate recent observations—that is, to predict no change from the recent past.

Sterling ratio The compound annualized rate of return over a specified time period divided by the average yearly maximum drawdown over the same time period less an arbitrary 10 percent.

Stock companies With respect to insurance companies, companies that have issued common equity shares.

Stock index futures Futures contracts on a specified stock index.

Straddle An option strategy involving the purchase of a put and a call with the same exercise price. A straddle is based on the expectation of high volatility of the underlying.

Straight-through processing Systems that simplify transaction processing through the minimization of manual and/or duplicative intervention in the process from trade placement to settlement.

Strangle A variation of a straddle in which the put and call have different exercise prices.

Strap An option strategy involving the purchase of two calls and one put.

Strategic asset allocation 1) The process of allocating money to IPS-permissible asset classes that integrates the investor's return objectives, risk tolerance, and investment constraints with long-run capital market expectations. 2) The result of the above process, also known as the policy portfolio.

Stratified sampling (or representative sampling) A sampling method that guarantees that subpopulations of interest are represented in the sample.

Strike spread A spread used to determine the strike price for the payoff of a credit option.

Strip An option strategy involving the purchase of two puts and one call.

Strip hedge Hedging a stream of obligations by offsetting each individual obligation with a futures contract matching the maturity and quantity of the obligation.

Structural level of unemployment The level of unemployment resulting from scarcity of a factor of production.

Structured note A variation of a floating-rate note that has some type of unusual characteristic such as a leverage factor or in which the rate moves opposite to interest rates.

Style drift Inconsistency in style.

Style index A securities index intended to reflect the average returns to a given style.

Stylized scenario A type of analysis often used in stress testing. It involves simulating the movement in at least one interest rate, exchange rate, stock price, or commodity price relevant to the portfolio.

Sunshine trades Public display of a transaction (usually high-volume) in advance of the actual order.

Surplus The difference between the value of assets and the present value of liabilities. With respect to an insurance company, the net difference between the total assets and total liabilities (equivalent to policyholders' surplus for a mutual insurance company and stockholders' equity for a stock company).

Surplus efficient frontier The graph of the set of portfolios that maximize expected surplus for given levels of standard deviation of surplus.

Survey method A method of capital market expectations setting that involves surveying experts.

Survival probability The probability an individual survives in a given year; used to determine expected cash flow required in retirement.

Survivorship bias Bias that arises in a data series when managers with poor track records exit the business and are dropped from the database whereas managers with good records remain; when a data series as of a given date reflects only entities that have survived to that date.

Swap A contract calling for the exchange of payments over time. Often one payment is fixed in advance and the other is floating, based upon the realization of a price or interest rate.

Swap rate The interest rate applicable to the pay-fixed-rate side of an interest rate swap.

Swap spread The difference between the fixed rate on an interest rate swap and the rate on a Treasury note with equivalent maturity; it reflects the general level of credit risk in the market.

Swap tenor The lifetime of a swap.

Swap term Another name for *swap tenor*.

Swaption An option to enter into a swap.

Symmetric cash flow matching A cash flow matching technique that allows cash flows occurring both before and after the liability date to be used to meet a liability; allows for the short-term borrowing of funds to satisfy a liability prior to the liability due date.

Tactical asset allocation Asset allocation that involves making short-term adjustments to asset class weights based on short-term predictions of relative performance among asset classes.

Tactical rebalancing A variation of calendar rebalancing that specifies less frequent rebalancing when markets appear to be trending and more frequent rebalancing when they are characterized by reversals.

Tail value at risk (or conditional tail expectation) The VAR plus the expected loss in excess of VAR, when such excess loss occurs.

Target covariance matrix A component of shrinkage estimation; allows the analyst to model factors that are believed to influence the data over periods longer than observed in the historical sample.

Target semivariance The average squared deviation below a target value.

Target value The value that the portfolio manager seeks to ensure; the value that the life insurance company has guaranteed the policyholder.

Tax avoidance Developing strategies that minimize tax, while conforming to both the spirit and the letter of the tax codes of jurisdictions with taxing authority.

Tax efficiency The proportion of the expected pretax total return that will be retained after taxes.

Tax evasion The practice of circumventing tax obligations by illegal means such as misreporting or not reporting relevant information to tax authorities.

Tax premium Compensation for the effect of taxes on the after-tax return of an asset.

Tax risk The uncertainty associated with tax laws.

Taylor rule A rule linking a central bank's target short-term interest rate to the rate of growth of the economy and inflation.

Term life insurance A type of life insurance policy that provides coverage for a specified length of time and accumulates little or no cash values.

Territorial tax system A framework used by a country to determine the basis for taxing income or transfers. A country that taxes income as a source within its borders imposes source jurisdiction.

Testamentary gratuitous transfer The bequeathing or transfer of assets upon one's death. From a recipient's perspective, it is called an inheritance.

Testator A person who makes a will.

Theta The change in price of an option associated with a one-day reduction in its time to expiration; the rate at which an option's time value decays.

Tick The smallest possible price movement of a security.

Time deposit A deposit requiring advance notice prior to a withdrawal.

Time to expiration The time remaining in the life of a derivative, typically expressed in years.

Time-series estimators Estimators that are based on lagged values of the variable being forecast; often consist of lagged values of other selected variables.

Time-weighted average price (TWAP) strategy A logical participation strategy that assumes a flat volume profile and trades in proportion to time.

Time-weighted rate of return The compound rate of growth over a stated evaluation period of one unit of money initially invested in the account.

Timing option With respect to certain futures contracts, the option that results from the ability of the short position to decide when in the delivery month actual delivery will take place.

Tobin's q An asset-based valuation measure that is equal to the ratio of the market value of debt and equity to the replacement cost of total assets.

Top-down Proceeding from the macroeconomy, to the economic sector level, to the industry level, to the firm level.

Total factor productivity (TFP) A variable which accounts for that part of Y not directly accounted for by the levels of the production factors (K and L).

Total future liability With respect to defined-benefit pension plans, the present value of accumulated and projected future service benefits, including the effects of projected future compensation increases.

Total rate of return A measure of the increase in the investor's wealth due to both investment income (for example, dividends and interest) and capital gains (both realized and unrealized).

Total return The rate of return taking into account capital appreciation/depreciation and income. Often qualified as follows: **Nominal** returns are unadjusted for inflation; **real** returns are adjusted for inflation; **pretax** returns are returns before taxes; **post-tax** returns are returns after taxes are paid on investment income and realized capital gains.

Total return analysis Analysis of the expected effect of a trade on the portfolio's total return, given an interest rate forecast.

Total return swap A swap in which one party agrees to pay the total return on a security. Often used as a credit derivative, in which the underlying is a bond.

Tracking risk (also called tracking error, tracking error volatility, or active risk) The condition in which the performance of a portfolio does not match the performance of an index that serves as the portfolio's benchmark.

Trade blotter A device for entering and tracking trade executions and orders to trade.

Trade settlement Completion of a trade wherein purchased financial instruments are transferred to the buyer and the buyer transfers money to the seller.

Trading activity In fixed-income attribution analysis, the effect of sales and purchases of bonds over a given period; the total portfolio return minus the other components determining the management effect in an attribution analysis.

Transaction exposure The risk associated with a foreign exchange rate on a specific business transaction such as a purchase or sale.

Translation exposure The risk associated with the conversion of foreign financial statements into domestic currency.

Transparency Availability of timely and accurate market and trade information.

Treasury spot curve The term structure of Treasury zero coupon bonds.

Twist With respect to the yield curve, a movement in contrary directions of interest rates at two maturities; a nonparallel movement in the yield curve.

Type I error With respect to manager selection, keeping (or hiring) managers with zero value-added. (Rejecting the null hypothesis when it is correct).

Type II error With respect to manager selection, firing (or not hiring) managers with positive value-added. (Not rejecting the null hypothesis when it is incorrect).

Unconstrained optimization Optimization that places no constraints on asset class weights except that they sum to 1. May produce negative asset weights, which implies borrowing or shorting of assets.

Underfunded plan A pension plan in which the ratio of the value of plan assets to the present value of plan liabilities is less than 100 percent.

Underlying An asset that trades in a market in which buyers and sellers meet, decide on a price, and the seller then delivers the asset to the buyer and receives payment. The underlying is the asset or other derivative on which a particular derivative is based. The market for the underlying is also referred to as the spot market.

Underwriting (profitability) cycle A cycle affecting the profitability of insurance companies' underwriting operations.

Unhedged return A foreign asset return stated in terms of the investor's home currency.

Unit-linked life insurance (or variable life insurance) A type of ordinary life insurance in which death benefits and cash values are linked to the investment performance of a policyholder-selected pool of investments held in a so-called separate account.

Universal life insurance A type of life insurance policy that provides for premium flexibility, an adjustable face amount of death benefits, and current market interest rates on the savings element.

Unrelated business income With respect to the U.S. tax code, income that is not substantially related to a foundation's charitable purposes.

Unstructured modeling Modeling without a theory on the underlying structure.

Uptick rules Trading rules that specify that a short sale must not be on a downtick relative to the last trade at a different price.

Urgency of the trade The importance of certainty of execution.

Utility The level of relative satisfaction received from the consumption of goods and services.

Utility theory Theory whereby people maximize the present value of utility subject to a present value budget constraint.

Valuation reserve With respect to insurance companies, an allowance, created by a charge against earnings, to provide for losses in the value of the assets.

Value The amount for which one can sell something, or the amount one must pay to acquire something.

Value at risk (VAR) A probability-based measure of loss potential for a company, a fund, a portfolio, a transaction, or a strategy over a specified period of time.

Value weighted (or market-capitalization weighted) With respect to index construction, an index in which each security in the index is weighted according to its market capitalization.

Value-motivated traders Traders that act on value judgments based on careful, sometimes painstaking research. They trade only when the price moves into their value range.

Variable annuity A life annuity in which the periodic payment varies depending on stock prices.

Variable life insurance (or unit-linked life insurance) A type of ordinary life insurance in which death benefits and cash values are linked to the investment performance of a policyholder-selected pool of investments held in a so-called separate account.

Variable prepaid forward A monetization strategy that involves the combination of a collar with a loan against the value of the underlying shares. When the loan comes due, shares are sold to pay off the loan and part of any appreciation is shared with the lender.

Variable universal life (or flexible-premium variable life) A type of life insurance policy that combines the flexibility of universal life with the investment choice flexibility of variable life.

Vega A measure of the sensitivity of an option's price to changes in the underlying's volatility.

Venture capital The equity financing of new or growing private companies.

Venture capital firms Firms representing dedicated pools of capital for providing equity or equity-linked financing to privately held companies.

Venture capital fund A pooled investment vehicle for venture capital investing.

Venture capital trusts An exchange-traded, closed-end vehicle for venture capital investing.

Venture capitalists Specialists who seek to identify companies that have good business opportunities but need financial, managerial, and strategic support.

Vested With respect to pension benefits or assets, said of an unconditional ownership interest.

Vintage year With reference to a private equity fund, the year it closed.

Vintage year effects The effects on returns shared by private equity funds closed in the same year.

Volatility Represented by the Greek letter sigma (σ), the standard deviation of price outcomes associated with an underlying asset.

Volatility clustering The tendency for large (small) swings in prices to be followed by large (small) swings of random direction.

Volume-weighted average price (or VWAP) The average price at which a security is traded during the day, where each trade price is weighted by the fraction of the day's volume associated with the trade.

Volume-weighted average price (VWAP) strategy A logical participation strategy that involves breaking up an order over time according to a prespecified volume profile.

Wealth relative The ending value of one unit of money invested at specified rates of return.

Weather derivative A derivative contract with a payment based on a weather-related measurement, such as heating or cooling degree days.

Whole life insurance (also ordinary life insurance) A type of life insurance policy that involves coverage for the whole of the insured's life.

Wild card option A provision allowing a short futures contract holder to delay delivery of the underlying.

Will (or testament) A document associated with estate planning that outlines the rights others will have over one's property after death.

Within-sector selection return In attribution analysis, a measure of the impact of a manager's security selection decisions relative to the holdings of the sector benchmark.

Worst-case scenario analysis A stress test in which we examine the worst case that we actually expect to occur.

Yardeni model An equity valuation model, more complex than the Fed model, that incorporates the expected growth rate in earnings.

Yield beta A measure of the sensitivity of a bond's yield to a general measure of bond yields in the market that is used to refine the hedge ratio.

Yield curve The relationship between yield and time to maturity.

Yield curve risk Risk related to changes in the shape of the yield curve.

Yield to worst The yield on a callable bond that assumes a bond is called at the earliest opportunity.

Zero-cost collar A transaction in which a position in the underlying is protected by buying a put and selling a call with the premium from the sale of the call offsetting the premium from the purchase of the put. It can also be used to protect a floating-rate borrower against interest rate increases with the premium on a long cap offsetting the premium on a short floor.

Zero-premium collar A hedging strategy involving the simultaneous purchase of puts and sale of call options on a stock. The puts are struck below and the calls are struck above the underlying's market price.

Index

A

accounting standards, in emerging markets, 355
active investing, 271
active risk, 209
additive formulation of return objective, 216
ADRs. *see* American Depositary Receipts
ALM approach. *see* asset/liability management approach
alpha research, 8
alternative investments
  asset allocation with, 228–229
  defined, 214
  smoothed data for, 14–16
American Depositary Receipts (ADRs), 346
anchoring trap, 20–21
annuities, 279
appraisal data, capital market expectations and, 14–16
ARCH time-series models. *see* autoregressive conditional heteroskedasticity time-series models
Argentina
  currency crisis, 75
  growth projections, 188
  inflation-protected bonds, 225
  market integration, 42
  trade partners, 81
arithmetic mean return, geometric vs., 23
ASEAN. *see* Association of Southeast Asian Nations
Asia. *see also* MSCI EAFE (Europe, Australasia, and Far East) Index; *specific countries*
  inflation in, 55
  Pacific region
    economic indicators, 80
    world stock market capitalization, 322
Asian financial crisis (1997)
  and currency values, 96
  as exogenous shock, 72
  and inflation, 55
  international interactions in, 73, 76
asset allocation, 205–319
  asset classes for, 222–229
    alternative investments, 228–229
    inflation-protected bonds, 225–226
    international assets, 226–228
    specifying, 223–224
  defined, 206–207
  importance of, 210–211
  investor objectives for, 212–222
    and asset-only vs. ALM approaches, 212–214
    and investor behavior, 220–222
    return objectives, 214–216
    risk objectives, 216–220
  optimization of, 231–270
    ALM approach, 260–268
    Black–Litterman approach, 250–257
    experience-based approaches, 268–270
    mean–variance approach, 232–249
    Monte Carlo simulation, 257–260
    with resampled efficient frontier, 249–250
  practice problems, 303–312
  solutions to problems, 313–319
  steps in, 229–231
  strategic
    asset-only vs. ALM approaches, 212–214
    implementing, 270–272
    for individual investors, 272–280
    for institutional investors, 280–294
    and investor objectives, 214–220
    and systematic risk, 207–209
    tactical vs., 209–210
  tactical, 294–300
    global adjustments in, 298–299
    investment decisions for, 299–300
    strategic vs., 209–210
asset allocation reviews, 229
asset-based models of equity market, 153–157
asset classes, 222–229
  of alternative investments, 228–229
  forecasting returns of, 86–100
    cash and equivalents, 86–87
    common shares, 90–93
    currencies, 95–96
    defaultable debt, 89
    emerging market bonds, 89
    and exchange rates, 96–100
    and historical capital market expectations, 94–95
    inflation-indexed bonds, 89–90
    nominal default-free bonds, 88
    real estate, 94
  inflation/deflation effects for, 57–58
  of inflation-protected bonds, 225–226
  of international assets, 226–228
  specification criteria for asset allocation, 223–224
asset covariance matrix, 28
asset/liability management (ALM) approach
  asset-only approach vs., 212–214
  for defined-benefit pension plans, 261–264, 281
  and funding ratio efficient frontier, 262
  for insurance companies, 289
  and Monte Carlo simulation, 266–268
  optimizing asset allocation with, 260–268
  and surplus efficient frontier, 264–266
asset-only approach to asset allocation, 212–214
asset-pricing theory, risk premiums in, 49
assets
  correlations of (*see* correlations of assets)
  international, 226–228
  real, 57–58
Association of Southeast Asian Nations (ASEAN), 341
assumptions, about BRICs, 191–192
asynchronism, 17n.8
Australia. *see also* MSCI EAFE (Europe, Australasia, and Far East) Index
  asset allocation in pension plans, 281, 282
  CLI for, 79
  Conference Board index, 81
  equity risk premium, 38
  expected returns for equities/bonds, 24
  inflation-protected bonds, 225
  market integration, 42
  prudent person concept for pension investing, 281
  real GDP growth rate, 31
Austria, 8, 80
automobile industry, international correlation in, 350
autoregressive conditional heteroskedasticity (ARCH) time-series models, 26n.25

B

Bahrain, 73
balance of payments, 75n.65
Bank of Japan, 63, 80
Bank of Thailand, 96
bank reserves, 63
banks
  central, 55, 61, 87
  liabilities for, 214
  strategic asset allocation for, 292–294
behavior, investor, 220–222
behavioral finance, 22
Belgium
  equity risk premium, 38
  Eurozone membership, 8
  expected returns for equities/bonds, 24
  trade partners, 80
benchmarks, unconditioned, 19
Bernstein, Peter L., 10
beta research, 8
biases
  in analyst methods, 18
  data measurement, 14–16
Big Four European countries, CLI for, 79

I-1

Black, Fischer, 250
Black–Litterman approach, 11, 250–257
    asset allocation example, 252
    as asset-only approach, 212
    and efficient portfolio, 255–257
    ICAPM vs., 39
    steps in, 251
    unconstrained model, 250
Bloomberg, 100, 101
BLS. *see* Bureau of Labor Statistics
bonds
    asset allocation in pension plans with, 282
    efficient frontier for international, 335–336
    emerging market, 89
    expected returns, 24, 35
    experience-based allocation with, 269
    inflation/deflation effects for, 57–58
    inflation-indexed, 89–90
    inflation-protected, 225–226
    insurance company investment in, 290–292
    junk, 291
    nominal default-free, 88
    risk reduction with international diversification for, 330–332
    tax-exempt, 224
    transaction costs of, 346
    Treasury
        and Fed model, 34, 146
        junk bond yield vs., 291
        T-bill yield vs., 53
        U.S. dollar, 322
    yield to maturity of, 34
bond-yield-plus-risk-premium method, 37
bond yields
    nominal, 73–74
    real, 88–89
    yield to maturity, 34
    yield to worst, 34n.38
Brazil, inflation-protected bonds in, 225
Brazil, Russia, India, and China (BRICs), 171–201
    changing assumptions about, 191–192
    conditions for growth, 188–191
    economic predictions for, 173–177
    exchange rates, 177
    GDP of, 174–176
    GDP prediction, 180–183, 196–200
    growth accounting model for, 179–180
    and growth rates of developing countries, 177–179
    historical analysis, 187–189
    implications of ascendancy, 192–193
    income per capita prediction, 183, 186
    long-term model of growth and exchange rates, 195–196
    plausibility of predictions, 186–187
    population prediction, 181, 184, 201
    South Africa vs., 185–186
    in world economy, 171–172
Brazilian Institute for Geography and Statistics, 80
Brazil Industrial Production, 80–81
BRICs. *see* Brazil, Russia, India, and China

British Retail Consortium (BRC) survey, 60
bubbles, 30n.31
budget deficits
    and fiscal policy, 64
    and government structural policies, 69–70
build-up approach, 34–38
Bureau of Labor Statistics (BLS), 13
business cycle analysis, 49–65
    factors affecting, 59–65
        business investment, 60–61
        consumer spending, 59–60
        fiscal policy, 64–65
        monetary policy, 61–64
    inflation and deflation in, 54–58
    inventory cycle, 50–51
    market expectations in, 58–59
    and returns for common shares, 93
    stages of business cycle, 51–54
business cycles
    and consumer confidence, 51–53
    defined, 49
    international correlation in, 349
    stages of, 51–54
business investment, in business cycle analysis, 59–61

C

California Public Employees' Retirement System (CalPERS), 345
Canada
    asset allocation in pension plans, 281–283
    bond market correlation, 331
    CLI for, 79
    equity risk premium, 38
    expected returns for equities/bonds, 24
    inflation-protected bonds, 225
    prudent person concept for pension investing, 281
    real GDP growth rate, 31
    stock market correlation, 329
    trade partners, 81
Canadian Endowment for the Fine Arts (CEFA) case study, 208–210, 215, 245–248
capital
    financial, 273, 274, 276
    human, 70, 272–277
capital allocation line, 240
capital asset pricing model (CAPM), 333
capital flows
    and currency returns, 96
    forecasting approach based on, 98, 99
capital market expectations (CME), 5–120
    and ALM approach, 263
    and asset class returns, 94–95
    in business cycle analysis, 58–59
    defined, 6
    economic analysis of, 49–101
        business cycle analysis, 49–65
        and economic forecasting, 77–86
        exogenous shocks in, 71–72
        forecasting asset class returns with, 86–100
        growth trends, 65–70

information sources for, 100–101
international interactions in, 72–77
forecasting of, 13–22
    biases of analyst methods, 18
    conditioning information, 18–19
    correlations in, 19–20
    data measurement errors and biases, 14–16
    economic data, 13–14
    and *ex post* risk, 17–18
    and GNP vs. GDP, 13
    with historical estimates, 16–17
    and model uncertainty, 22
    psychological traps with, 20–22
framework, 7–12
    and expected return estimates, 11–12
    historical analysis in, 10
    and inconsistency of correlation estimates, 12
    information requirements, 8–10
modifying, 94–95
and policy portfolio, 209–210
practice problems, 104–110
setting, 23–48
    with formal tools, 23–46
    and judgment, 48–49
    with survey and panel methods, 47–48
solutions to problems, 111–120
capital markets
    anomalies in, 22
    business cycle effects on, 51, 52
    forecasts of, 42–44
capital market theory, 240–241
CAPM. *see* capital asset pricing model
case studies
    CEFA, 208–210, 215, 245–248
    Ian Thomas, 241–245
cash
    in asset allocation, 224
    forecasts of returns, 86–87
    inflation/deflation effects for, 57–58
cash equivalents
    in asset allocation, 224
    and efficient portfolio for mean–variance approach, 240–241
    forecasts of returns, 86–87
cash flow matching approach, for asset allocation, 213
causality relationships, 20
CEFA case study. *see* Canadian Endowment for the Fine Arts case study
central banks, monetary policy of, 55, 61
central bank watching, 87
Central Europe, emerging markets in, 354. *see also specific countries*
Chebyshev's inequality, 218n.17
checklist approach to economic forecasting, 83–85
Chile
    degree of specialization, 72
    inflation-protected bonds, 225
    market integration, 42
China. *see also* Brazil, Russia, India, and China (BRICs)
    economic experience, 125–127
    economic projections, 174
    and future economic growth, 129–130

Index

historical growth accounting, 126
H-model for estimating P/E, 129–136
justified P/E ratio estimates, 124
macroeconomic linkages, 72
market development, 354
TFP growth, 68
trade partners, 80, 81
China Industrial Production index, 80
Citi Non-U.S. World Government Bond Index, 42
CME. *see* capital market expectations
Cobb-Douglas production function, 124
Colombia, 225
common shares, earnings of, 90–93
competition, government structural policies and, 70
conditional correlation, 348
conditioning correlation, 348
conditioning information, 18–19
Conference Board, 78, 81, 100
confirming evidence trap, 21
Congressional Budget, 101
constant growth model. *see* Gordon growth model
constant returns to scale, 125
consumer confidence, business cycle and, 51–53
consumer income growth, in econometric modeling, 77
consumers, economic growth trends and, 66–67
consumer spending
  and business cycle, 59
  in business cycle analysis, 59–60
  in econometric modeling, 77
  in United Kingdom, 47–48
corner portfolios, 234–238
corner portfolio theorem, 234
correlation breakdown, 343
correlations of assets
  conditional, 348
  conditioning, 348
  in emerging markets, 354
  inconsistency of estimates, 12
  increases in, 341–343
  judgment in estimates, 48
  leads/lags in, 332–333
  and market integration, 341–342
  misinterpretations of, 19–20
  nonlinear, 20
  partial, 20
  in times of stress, 227
  and volatility, 342–343, 348–349
corruption, in emerging market, 354
costs
  custody, 346
  transaction, 346–347
country factors, in global investing, 350–352
country risk, in emerging markets, 74–77
covariance, estimating, 27, 29
covariance matrix
  multifactor model for estimating, 27–30
  shrinkage estimator of, 24–25
  target, 25
CPI. *see* U.S. Consumer Price Index

CPI-U. *see* U.S. Consumer Price Index for All Urban Consumers
cross-sectional variation of returns, asset allocation and, 211
currency(-ies)
  in country risk analysis, 75–76
  devaluing, 63
  forecasts of returns, 95–96
  and investability of emerging markets, 356
  risk reduction for, 324–326
currency risk
  in emerging markets, 354
  and international diversification, 324–326, 339–340, 347, 354
  and strategic asset allocation, 227, 271
current account deficits, 98–99
custody costs, of international investments, 346
cyclical stocks, 91
Cyprus, 8

D

DaimlerChrysler, 350
data measurement, biases and errors in, 14–16
data-mining biases, 18
DB pension plans. *see* defined-benefit pension plans
DCF models. *see* discounted cash flow models
DC pension plans. *see* defined-contribution pension plans
debt
  defaultable, 89
  emerging market, 89
  external, 76
  foreign debt to GDP ratio, 76
  Treasury, 35–36
defaultable debt, 89
default risk premiums, 35
deficits
  budget, 64, 69–70
  current account, 98–99
  twin deficits problem, 70
defined-benefit (DB) pension plans
  ALM approach, 261–264
  asset allocation for, 210–211
  liabilities for, 214
  strategic asset allocation for, 281–285
defined-contribution (DC) pension plans, 214
deflation
  in business cycle analysis, 54–58
  defined, 57
  monetary policy for, 63
Denmark
  CLI for, 79
  equity risk premium, 38
  expected returns for equities/bonds, 24
  real GDP growth rate, 31
descriptive statistics, 23
developed economies
  analysis of emerging vs., 74
  correlation with Emerging Markets index, 353
  justified P/E estimates for, 136–137
developing countries, 177–179. *see also* emerging markets

diffusion index, 79
discounted cash flow (DCF) models, 11, 30–34
discriminatory taxes, in emerging markets, 355
disinflation, 54
diversification, international. *see* international diversification
DJGI. *see* Dow Jones Global Index
DJGI Americas
  annual return, standard deviation, and correlation of, 238
  Black–Litterman view-adjusted returns, 255, 256
  efficient portfolio weights using historical mean returns, 257
  efficient portfolio weights with equilibrium returns, 254
  historical average and market equilibrium returns, 253
  market weights, 252
DJGI Asia Pacific
  annual return, standard deviation, and correlation of, 238
  Black–Litterman view-adjusted returns, 255, 256
  efficient portfolio weights with equilibrium returns, 254
  using historical mean returns, 257
  historical average and market equilibrium returns, 253
  market weights, 252
DJGI Europe, 238
DJGI Europe/Africa
  Black–Litterman view-adjusted returns, 255
  efficient portfolio weights with equilibrium returns, 254
  historical average and market equilibrium returns, 253
  market weights, 252
DJGI Japan
  annual return, standard deviation, and correlation of, 238
  Black–Litterman view-adjusted returns, 255, 256
  efficient portfolio weights with equilibrium returns, 254
  using historical mean returns, 257
  historical average and market equilibrium returns, 253
  market weights, 252
DJGI U.K.
  annual return, standard deviation, and correlation of, 238
  Black–Litterman view-adjusted returns, 255, 256
  efficient portfolio weights with equilibrium returns, 254
  using historical mean returns, 257
  historical average and market equilibrium returns, 253
  market weights, 252
dollar, U.S., 99
domestic common equity, 224
domestic fixed income, 224
domestic investing, risks of, 351–352
Dow Jones Euro Stoxx 5 Index, 136–137

Dow Jones Global Index (DJGI), 252. *see also entries beginning* DJGI
downside risk, asset allocation and, 218
dynamic approach to asset allocation, 213

E
early upswing phase (business cycle), 52, 53, 91
earnings-based models for equity market
  10-year Moving Average Price/Earnings, 150–153
  Fed model, 144–147
    with U.K. data, 145–146
    with U.S. data, 144–145
  Yardeni model, 147–150
Eastern Bloc, historical data from, 136. *see also specific countries*
ECB. *see* European Central Bank
econometric modeling, 77–78, 86
econometrics, 77
economic analysis, 49–101
  business cycle analysis, 49–65
    factors affecting, 59–65
    inflation and deflation in, 54–58
    inventory cycle, 50–51
    market expectations in, 58–59
    stages of business cycle, 51–54
  and economic forecasting, 77–86
    checklist approach, 83–85
    econometric modeling, 77–78
    economic indicators, 78–83
    strengths and weaknesses of forecasting, 85–86
  exogenous shocks in, 71–72
  forecasting asset class returns with, 86–100
    cash and equivalents, 86–87
    common shares, 90–93
    currencies, 95–96
    emerging market bonds, 89
    and forecasting exchange rates, 96–100
    and historical capital market expectations, 94–95
    inflation-indexed bonds, 89–90
    nominal default-free bonds, 88
    real estate, 94
  growth trends, 65–70
    consumer impact on, 66–67
    in GDP, 67–69
    and government structural policies, 69–70
  information sources for, 100–101
  international interactions, 72–77
    in emerging markets, 74–77
    interest rate/exchange rate linkages, 72–74
    macroeconomic linkages, 72
economic data, for CME forecasts, 13–14
economic forecasting, 77–86
  checklist approach, 83–85
  econometric modeling, 77–78
  with economic indicators, 78–83
    for Asia Pacific, 80
    for Europe, 79–80
    for North America, 81–83

    for South America, 80–81
    worldwide, 79
  strengths and weaknesses of forecasting, 85–86
Economic Freedom Index, 75
economic growth
  of BRICs, 188–191, 195–196
  checklist for, 84
  in country risk analysis, 75
  in developing countries, 177–179
  future growth predicted for China, 129–130
  trends in, 49, 65–70
    consumer impact on, 66–67
    for GDP, 67–69
    and government structural policies, 69–70
economic indicators
  advantages and disadvantages of, 86
  for Asia Pacific, 80
  economic forecasting with, 78–83
  for Europe, 79–80
  for North America, 81–83
  for South America, 80–81
  worldwide, 79
Economic Optimism Index, 47–48
economic shocks, 65, 71–72
education, in emerging markets, 354
efficient frontier
  with Black–Litterman view-adjusted returns, 255
  with equilibrium returns, 253
  funding ratio, 262
  and international diversification, 326–327
  for international investments, 335–337
  for mean–variance approach, 232–238
    sign-constrained optimization, 233–238
    unconstrained optimization, 233
  resampled, 249–250
  surplus, 260, 261, 264–266
efficient portfolio
  and Black–Litterman approach, 255–257
  mean–variance, 249
  for mean–variance approach, 239–249
    and cash equivalents/capital market theory, 240–241
    CEFA case study, 245–248
    Ian Thomas case study, 241–245
  resampled, 249–250
  and risk reduction with international diversification, 326–328
emerging market bonds, 89
emerging market debt, 89
emerging markets
  common shares in, 93
  country risk analysis, 74–77
  developed vs. emerging economies, 74
  in economic analysis, 74–77
  international diversification with, 352–356
    about, 352–353
    correlation, 354
    currency risk, 354
    and investability of markets, 355–356
    portfolio return performance, 355

    segmented vs. integrated markets, 356
    volatility, 353–354
  and strategic asset allocation, 228
Emerging Markets index, 329, 330, 352–353
endogenous variables, 19
endowments
  liabilities for, 214
  strategic asset allocation for, 285
Engle, Robert F., 26
Enron, 65
equilibrium
  of inflation premium and real interest rate, 36
  rational belief, 22n.18
equilibrium models, for capital market expectations, 39–44
equilibrium returns, from Black–Litterman model, 251–254
equilibrium return vector, 253n.47
equities
  and asset allocation in pension plans, 281, 282
  correlation with world bond markets, 331
  domestic vs. non-domestic common, 224
  drivers of returns for, 123–124
  expected returns, 24
  inflation/deflation effects for, 57–58
  international, 335
  risk reduction with international diversification for, 328–330
equity–bonds covariance matrix, 27–30
equity-indexed annuities, 279
equity market
  asset-based models, 153–157
  constant growth model, 30–31
  discounted cash flow models, 30–34
  earnings-based models, 144–153
    10-year Moving Average Price/Earnings, 150–153
    Fed model, 144–147
    Yardeni model, 147–150
  forecasts of, 137–143
    market EPS, 141–143
    portfolio suitability of, 139–140
    types of forecasts, 137–138
    using both forecasting approaches, 140–141
  relative value models, 144–157
equity market valuation, 123–169
  drivers of equity returns, 123–124
  forecasts of market, 137–143
  justified P/E estimates, 124–137
    for developed economies, 136–137
    and neoclassical approach to growth accounting, 124–125, 127–128
  practice problems, 161–166
  relative value models, 144–157
  solutions to problems, 167–169
equity q ratio
  and asset-based models, 154–156
  strengths and limitations, 157
equity risk premium
  for capital market expectations, 37–38
  and Fed model, 145

Index

Grinold–Kroner model for forecasting, 33
volatility ratio vs., 296
estimates
  correlation, 12
  covariance, 27, 29
  expected return, 11–12
  historical, 16–17
  justified P/E, 124–137
  point, 23n.19
estimators
  sample, 23–24
  shrinkage, 24–26
  time-series, 26
Estonia, 8
EU. *see* European Union
EU-25 region, CLI for, 79
euro
  exchange rate pegging, 73
  and U.S. dollar, 99
Europe. *see also* MSCI EAFE (Europe, Australasia, and Far East) Index; *specific countries*
  asset allocation in pension plans, 282
  China stock market volatility vs., 133
  economic indicators, 79–80
  GDP growth, 339
  international diversification regulation, 345
  and justified P/E estimates, 131
  mean return, 338
  and neoclassical approach to growth accounting, 127
  stock market correlation, 329, 338
  TFP growth, 68, 69
  and world stock market capitalization, 322
European Central Bank (ECB)
  monetary policy, 64, 98
  open market operations by, 87
European Union (EU)
  CLI, 79
  economic growth projections, 128
  historical growth accounting for, 126
  international diversification rules, 345
  international market correlations, 341
Eurozone, 8
  capital flows forecasting approach, 98
  CLI, 79
  economy valuation, 136
  monetary policy, 64
  open market operations in, 87
Eurozone Harmonized Index of Consumer Prices (HICP), 79
ex ante risk
  for equities, 38
  from *ex post* risk, 17–18
excess corporate growth, 31
Exchange Rate Mechanism, 73
exchange rates
  of BRICs, 177
  forecasts of, 96–100
    capital flows, 98
    government intervention, 100
    purchasing power parity, 97
    relative economic strength, 97
    savings–investment imbalances, 98–99
    USD/euro exchange rate, 99

and interest rates, 72–74, 97
and long-term model of growth for BRICs, 195–196
exogenous economic shocks, 71–72
exogenous variables, 19
expectations, capital market. *see* capital market expectations
expected income return, 33
expected nominal earnings growth return, 33
expected repricing return, 33
expected returns
  estimates of, 11–12
  Gordon growth model, 30–31
  Grinold–Kroner approach, 33
  risk-adjusted, 217
  risk premium approach, 35
  unconditional, 18–19
experience-based approaches, for asset allocation, 268–270
ex post risk
  and forecasts of capital market expectations, 17–18
  and international diversification, 335–337
external accounts, in country risk analysis, 75–76
external debt, in country risk analysis, 76
externalities, 70n.64

F

factor betas, 28
factor covariance matrix, 27–30
factor loadings, 28
factor sensitivities, 28
FDI. *see* foreign direct investment
federal funds rate (fed funds), 61, 86–87
Federal Reserve
  economic data from, 100
  fed funds rate, 62, 86–87
  monetary policy, 98
  monetary policy in recessions, 58–59
  response to financial crisis, 72
Federal Reserve Bank of Philadelphia, 47
fed funds. *see* federal funds rate
Fed model, 34, 144–147
  strengths and limitations, 156
  with U.K. data, 145–146
  with U.S. data, 144–145
financial capital, asset allocation with, 273, 274, 276
financial crises, as exogenous shocks, 72
financial market equilibrium models, 39–44
Finland, 8, 225
fiscal policy
  in business cycle analysis, 53, 64–65
  in country risk analysis, 75
  and government structural policies, 69–70
  and monetary policy, 64–65
fixed annuities, longevity risk management with, 279
fixed-income markets, discounted cash flow models in, 30–34
fixed-income premiums, for capital market expectations, 35–37
Ford Motor Company, 350, 351

forecasts
  asset class returns, 86–100
    cash and equivalents, 86–87
    common shares, 90–93
    currencies, 95–96
    defaultable debt, 89
    emerging market bonds, 89
    and forecasting exchange rates, 96–100
    and historical capital market expectations, 94–95
    inflation-indexed bonds, 89–90
    nominal default-free bonds, 88
    real estate, 94
  capital market expectations, 13–22, 42–44
    and biases of analyst methods, 18
    conditioning information, 18–19
    correlations in, 19–20
    data measurement errors and biases, 14–16
    economic data, 13–14
    and *ex post* risk, 17–18
    and GNP vs. GDP, 13
    with historical estimates, 16–17
    and model uncertainty, 22
    psychological traps with, 20–22
  economic, 77–86
    checklist approach, 83–85
    econometric modeling, 77–78
    economic indicators, 78–83
    strengths and weaknesses of forecasting, 85–86
  equity market, 137–143
    market EPS, 141–143
    portfolio suitability of, 139–140
    types of forecasts, 137–138
    using both forecasting approaches, 140–141
equity risk premium, 33
exchange rates, 96–100
  capital flows, 98
  government intervention, 100
  purchasing power parity, 97
  relative economic strength, 97
  savings–investment imbalances, 98–99
  USD/euro exchange rate, 99
returns, 33–34
foreign debt to GDP ratio, 76
foreign direct investment (FDI), 98
foreign markets, familiarity with, 344
foreign ownership, investability of emerging markets and, 355
foreign trade, business cycle and, 59
formal tools for capital market expectations, 23–46
  discounted cash flow models, 30–34
  financial market equilibrium models, 39–44
  and justification of capital market forecasts, 42–44
  risk premium approach, 34–38
  Singer–Terhaar approach, 39–46
  statistical methods, 23–30
forward justified P/E estimates, 130–131
forward-looking optimization, for international diversification, 338–339

foundations
  addition of asset class by, 227
  liabilities for, 214
  strategic asset allocation for, 285–289
France
  bond market correlations, 331
  BRIC growth rate vs., 184
  Chinese economy vs., 173
  CLI, 79
  Conference Board index, 81
  diversification opportunities, 349
  economic projections, 174
  equity risk premium, 38
  Eurozone membership, 8
  expected returns for equities/bonds, 24
  growth projections, 181, 182, 188, 193, 196–200
  market integration, 42
  real GDP growth rate, 31
  stock market correlations, 329
  trade partners, 80
free float, investability of emerging markets and, 355
free indexes, in emerging markets, 356
French Monthly Business Survey, 80
FTSE 100
  and Fed model with U.K. data, 146
  forecasting approaches for, 137
  formulating CMEs from, 23
funded status, 261n.51
funding ratio, 261, 262

G
G6
  BRIC economies vs., 172–174, 177
  BRIC growth rate vs., 184
  Chinese economy vs., 173
  growth projections, 181, 182, 183, 196–200
G-7
  CLI, 79
  expansion phases in, 93
GDP. see gross domestic product
generalized peso problem, 17n.10
geometric mean return, arithmetic vs., 23
German IFO Business Survey, 80
German Industrial Production index, 79–80
Germany, 81
  bond market correlation, 331
  bond yields, 74
  BRIC growth rate vs., 184
  Chinese economy vs., 173
  CLI, 79
  Conference Board index, 81
  diversification opportunities, 349
  equity risk premium, 38
  Eurozone membership, 8
  expected returns for equities/bonds, 24
  global efficient frontier, 337
  growth rate, 174, 177, 179, 181, 182, 188, 193, 196–200
  inflation forecast, 56–57
  market integration, 42
  real GDP growth rate, 31
  stock market correlation, 329
  trade partners, 81
  and U.S. stock market crash, 343

GIM. see global investable market
global financial crisis (2007-2009), 64
global industry factors, in investing, 350
global investable market (GIM), 39
global investing, 349–352
  global industry factors, 350
  regional and country factors, 350–351
  risk of domestic investing, 351–352
global minimum-variance (GMV) portfolio, 232
GNP. see gross national product
Goldman Sachs, 47
gold standard currency system, 55
Gordon (constant) growth model
  for equity markets, 30–31
  and Fed model, 145
government policy(-ies)
  and business cycle, 59
  and exogenous shocks, 71
  structural, 69–70
government regulations
  and international diversification, 345
  pension investing, 281
Granger, Clive W. J., 26n.25
Great Depression, 295
Greece, 8
Grinold–Kroner model, 32
gross domestic product (GDP)
  of BRICs, 174–176
  in business cycles, 50
  in econometric modeling, 77
  and economic growth trends, 67–69
  foreign debt to GDP ratio, 76
  GNP vs., 13
  growth rate of nominal, 31
  growth rate of real, 31
  prediction for BRICs, 180–183, 196–200
gross national product (GNP), 13
growth accounting
  for BRICs, 179–180
  neoclassical approach to, 124–125, 127–128
guaranteed investment contract, 290
Gulf Cooperation Council, 73

H
hedge funds, 228, 229
hedging, of currency risk, 271
HICP. see Eurozone Harmonized Index of Consumer Prices
historical analysis
  of BRICs, 187–189
  and capital market expectations, 7, 10, 11
  Grinold–Kroner model, 32
historical estimates, capital market expectations from, 16–17
historical statistical approach to formulating CMEs, 23–24
H-model for estimating P/E, 129–136
Honda, 351
Hong Kong
  diversification opportunities, 349
  Economic Freedom Index, 75
  exchange rate pegging, 73
  growth projections, 188
  and SPDR S&P China ETF, 130

stock market correlation, 329
trade partners, 80
household savings rate, 60
human capital
  and government structural policies, 70
  and strategic asset allocation for individual investors, 272–277
Humphrey-Hawkins report, 144

I
ICAPM. see international CAPM-based approach
Iceland, 225
IFRS. see International Financial Reporting Standards
ILGS. see Index-Linked Gilts
illiquidity premium, 35n.43
IMF. see International Monetary Fund
immunization approach to asset allocation, 213
implementation, in strategic asset allocation, 270–272
income
  and consumption, 67
  domestic fixed, 224
  in econometric modeling, 77
  expected return for, 33
  labor, 275
  permanent income hypothesis, 66–67
  repatriation of, 355
income per capita, for BRICs, 183, 186
indexes. see also specific indexes
  diffusion, 79
  in emerging markets, 356
  limitations of data on, 13, 14
Index-Linked Gilts (ILGS), 89
Index of Leading Economic Indicators (LEI), 81–83
India, 174. see also Brazil, Russia, India, and China (BRICs)
individual investors
  CME research, 8
  liabilities for, 214
  strategic asset allocation for, 272–280
    critique of, 279–280
    human capital factors, 272–277
    and mortality/longevity risk, 278–280
individual local market, 41
Indonesia, 80
industry factors, in global investing, 350–352
inferential statistics, 23
inflation
  in business cycle analysis, 54–58
  and defined-benefit pension plans, 281
  and nominal default-free bonds, 88
  and P/E ratios, 93
inflation-indexed bonds, 89–90
inflation premiums, 35–37
inflation-protected bonds, 225–226
inflection point, inventory cycle, 50
information
  for capital market expectations, 7–10
  conditioning, 18–19
  for economic analysis, 100–101
  and international diversification, 345
infrastructure
  in emerging markets, 354
  and government structural policies, 70

Index

initial recovery phase (business cycle), 51, 53
input uncertainty, 22
insider trading, 345
Institute of Supply Management (ISM), 60, 82, 100
institutional investors
　CME research, 8
　strategic asset allocation for, 280–294
　　banks, 292–294
　　defined-benefit plans, 281–285
　　foundations and endowments, 285–289
　　insurance companies, 289–293
insurance companies, strategic asset allocation for, 289–293
integrated markets, 40–42, 356
interest rates
　and exchange rate, 72–74, 97
　long-term real risk-free, 36
　and monetary policy, 61, 63
　neutral level of, 61
　nominal risk-free, 35
　real risk-free, 35, 36
international assets, 226–228
international CAPM-based approach (ICAPM), 39–42
international diversification, 321–366
　about, 321–323
　with emerging markets, 352–356
　　about, 352–353
　　correlation, 354
　　currency risk, 354
　　and investability of markets, 355–356
　　portfolio return performance, 355
　　segmented vs. integrated markets, 356
　　volatility, 353–354
　impediments, 340–347
　　increased correlations, 341–343
　　and past as indicator of future performance, 343–344
　　physical barriers, 344–347
　motivations, 323–340
　　currency risk, 339–340
　　portfolio return performance, 333–339
　　risk reduction, 323–333
　practice problems, 359–362
　recent changes, 348–352
　　correlations in volatile periods, 348–349
　　expansion of investment universe, 349
　　global investing, 349–352
　　solutions to problems, 363–366
International Financial Reporting Standards (IFRS), 355
international interactions in economic analysis, 72–77
　for emerging markets, 74–77
　interest rate/exchange rate linkages, 72–74
　macroeconomic linkages, 72
International Monetary Fund (IMF), 74, 100
inventory cycle, 49–51
inventory/sales ratio, 50–51

investability, of emerging markets, 355–356
investable indexes, 356
investment
　in econometric modeling, 77
　and economic growth, 68–69
　expansion of, 349
　for strategic asset allocation, 270–271
　for tactical asset allocation, 299–300
investment environment, for capital market expectations, 7, 11
investment policy statement (IPS), 222–223
investors
　behavior of, 220–222
　individual
　　CME research, 8
　　liabilities for, 214
　　strategic asset allocation for, 272–280
　institutional
　　CME research, 8
　　strategic asset allocation for, 280–294
　liabilities for, 214
　objectives of, 212–222
　　and asset-only vs. asset/liability management approaches, 212–214
　　and behavior influences on asset allocation, 220–222
　　return objectives, 214–216
　　risk objectives, 216–220
IPS. see investment policy statement
Ireland
　equity risk premium, 38
　Eurozone membership, 8
　expected returns for equities/bonds, 24
ISM. see Institute of Supply Management
Israel, 225
Italy
　bond market correlation, 331
　Chinese economy vs., 173
　CLI, 79
　diversification opportunities, 349
　economic projections, 174
　equity risk premium, 38
　Eurozone membership, 8
　expected returns for equities/bonds, 24
　growth projections, 181, 182, 188, 193, 196–200
　real GDP growth rate, 31
　stock market correlation, 329
　trade partners, 80

J

Japan
　asset allocation in pension plans, 282
　bond market correlation, 331
　China stock market volatility vs., 133
　CLI, 79
　Conference Board index, 81
　diversification, 338, 349
　economic growth, 66, 174, 177, 179, 181, 182, 188, 189, 193, 196–200
　emerging market debt, 89
　equity risk premium, 38
　expected returns for equities/bonds, 24
　GDP growth, 339
　global efficient frontier, 337
　and international investing, 343–344

　and justified P/E estimates, 131
　mean return, 338
　monetary policy, 63
　population growth, 129
　real GDP growth rate, 31
　savings–investment imbalances forecasting approach, 98
　stock market correlation, 328, 329, 338
　TFP growth, 68
　trade partners, 81
　and U.S. stock market crash, 343
JPMorgan, 26
judgment, analyst, 48–49
junk bonds, 291
justified P/E estimates, 124–137
　for China
　　and economic experience, 125–127
　　and future economic growth, 129–130
　　H-model for estimating P/E, 129–136
　for developed economies, 136–137

K

Kuwait, 73

L

labor flexibility, 275–276
labor force, economic growth and, 68
labor income, 275
lagging economic indicators, 78
lags, in correlations of assets, 332–333
late upswing phase (business cycle), 52, 53
Latin America
　debt crisis, 72
　emerging markets, 355
leading economic indicator (LEI), 78
leads, in correlations of assets, 332–333
Lehman Aggregate Bond Index, 42
Lehman Brothers, 351
LEI. see Index of Leading Economic Indicators; leading economic indicator
liabilities. see also asset/liability management (ALM) approach
　defined, 212n.6
　for investors, 214
life annuities, 279
life insurance companies, liabilities for, 214
liquidity
　in country risk analysis, 76
　illiquidity premium, 35n.43
　and international diversification, 345
　and investability of emerging markets, 356
　and pension investing, 281
liquidity risk, international diversification and, 345
Litterman, Robert, 250
Livingston, Joseph, 47
Livingston Survey, 47
locked up investments, 42
London Stock Exchange, 332, 333
long data series, capital market expectations from, 16–17
longevity risk, strategic asset allocation and, 278–280

Long-Term Capital Management (LTCM), 72
long-term real risk-free interest rate, 36
Luxembourg, 8

M

macroeconomics, 72, 137
macro expectations, 6
Malta, 8
market efficiency, diversification and, 345
market environment, diversification and, 338
market EPS, forecasts of, 141–143
market risk, 340
markets
  capital
    anomalies in, 22
    business cycle effects on, 51, 52
    forecasts of, 42–44
  emerging
    common shares in, 93
    country risk analysis, 74–77
    developed vs. emerging economies, 74
    in economic analysis, 74–77
    international diversification with, 352–356
    and strategic asset allocation, 228
  equity
    asset-based models, 153–157
    constant growth model, 30–31
    discounted cash flow models, 30–34
    earnings-based models, 144–153
    forecasts of, 137–143
    relative value models, 144–157
  fixed-income, 30–34
  foreign, 344
  global investable, 39
  integrated, 40–42, 356
  perfect, 40
  segmented, 40–42, 356
Markowitz, Harry M., 221n.20
M&As. *see* mergers and acquisitions
Massachusetts, Commonwealth of, 225
maturity, yield curve and, 53
maturity premiums, 35
mean returns
  arithmetic vs. geometric, 23
  shrinkage estimator of, 26
mean–variance approach, 232–249
  efficient frontier, 232–238
    sign-constrained optimization, 233–238
    unconstrained optimization, 233
  efficient portfolio selection, 239–248
    cash equivalents and capital market theory, 240–241
    CEFA case study, 245–248
    Ian Thomas case study, 241–245
  extensions of, 248–249
  formulating CMEs with, 23
  inputs for, 238–239
mean–variance efficient portfolios, 249
mean–variance optimization (MVO)
  ALM, 266–268
  efficient frontier, 233
  Monte Carlo simulation vs., 257–258
mergers and acquisitions (M&As), cross-border, 341
Mexican peso, 17n.10

Mexico
  CLI, 79
  Conference Board index, 81
  currency crisis, 72
  inflation-protected bonds, 225
  trade partners, 81
microeconomics, 138
micro expectations, 6
Microsoft Excel, mean-variance optimization with, 233n.30
Middle East, oil shocks, 71. *see also specific countries*
minimum surplus variance (MSV), 260
minimum-variance frontier (MVF), 232
model uncertainty, capital market expectations and, 22
monetary policy
  in business cycle analysis, 53, 61–64
    with interest rates at zero, 63
    money supply trends, 63
    and Taylor rule, 62–63
    in U.S. vs. Eurozone, 64
  in country risk analysis, 75
  and fiscal policy, 64–65
  in recessions, 58–59
money managers, forecasting by, 86–87
money supply, trends in, 63
Monte Carlo simulation
  and ALM approach, 266–268
  for optimization of asset allocation, 257–260
mortality risk, strategic asset allocation and, 278–280
MPSR. *see* multiperiod Sharpe ratio
MSCI China Index, 132n.14
MSCI EAFE (Europe, Australasia, and Far East) Index
  capital market expectations, 263
  in capital market forecasts, 42
  mean return, 338
  stock market correlation with, 329, 330, 338
MSCI World index
  and Emerging Markets index, 352–353
  stock market correlation, 329
MSV. *see* minimum surplus variance
multifactor models, for capital market expectations, 26–30
multiperiod Sharpe ratio (MPSR), 44
multiplicative formulation of return objective, 216
multistrategy asset allocation procedure, 221
MVF. *see* minimum-variance frontier
MVO. *see* mean–variance optimization

N

NAFTA. *see* North American Free Trade Agreement
NASDAQ, 346
National Bureau of Statistics (NBS), 80
National Council of Real Estate Investment Fiduciaries (NCREIF), 43
natural resources, 228, 229
NBS. *see* National Bureau of Statistics
NCREIF. *see* National Council of Real Estate Investment Fiduciaries
neoclassical approach to growth accounting, 124–125, 127–128

Netherlands
  bond market correlation, 331
  equity risk premium, 38
  Eurozone membership, 8
  expected returns for equities/bonds, 24
  market integration, 42
  pension plans, 281, 282
  prudent person concept, 281
  real GDP growth rate, 31
  trade partners, 80, 81
  transaction volume on U.S. market, 347
net worth, ALM approach and, 260
neutral level of interest rates, 61
New York Stock Exchange
  dominant position, 322
  leads and lags, 332–333
New Zealand, 225
Nikkei 225 Index, 137
Nissan, 350
nominal bond yields, 73–74
nominal default-free bonds, 88
nominal gross domestic product
  growth rate of, 31
  and money supply, 63
nominal risk-free interest rate, 35
Nomura, 351
non-domestic common equity, 224
non-life insurance companies, liabilities for, 214
nonlinear correlations of assets, 20
nonstationarity, 16
North America, 81–83. *see also specific countries*
North American Free Trade Agreement (NAFTA), 79, 341
Norway
  CLI, 79
  equity risk premium, 38
  expected returns for equities/bonds, 24

O

objectives, investors', 212–222
  in asset-only vs. ALM approaches, 212–214
  behavioral influences on asset allocation, 220–222
  return objectives, 214–216
  risk objectives, 216–220
OECD. *see* Organization for Economic Cooperation and Development
oil shocks, 71
Oman, 73
OPEC. *see* Organization of the Petroleum Exporting Countries
open market operations, 87
optimization
  of asset allocation, 231–270
    ALM approach, 260–268
    Black–Litterman approach, 250–257
    experience-based approaches, 268–270
    mean–variance approach, 232–249
    Monte Carlo simulation, 257–260
    with resampled efficient frontier, 249–250
    sign-constrained, 233–238
    unconstrained, 233
  of international diversification, 338–339
optimizers, 231

Index

Organization for Economic Cooperation and Development (OECD)
  CLI, 79
  economic data from, 100
  GDP growth, 339
Organization of the Petroleum Exporting Countries (OPEC), 71
outcome monitoring, for capital market expectations, 7
output gap, business cycle, 50
overall trade balance, 75n.65
overconfidence trap, 21

P
panel methods, 47–48
partial correlation of assets, 20
passive investing, strategic asset allocation for, 270
past performance, as indicator of future, 343–344
P/E. *see* price to earnings ratio
pension funds
  asset allocation, 210–211
  and international diversification, 345
  Latin America, 355
pension plans
  defined-benefit
    ALM approach, 261–264
    asset allocation for, 210–211
    liabilities for, 214
    strategic asset allocation for, 281–285
  defined-contribution, 214
pension surplus, 261
perfect markets, 40
permanent income hypothesis, 66–67
peso, Mexican, 17n.10
physical barriers to international diversification, 344–347
  currency risk, 347
  familiarity with foreign markets, 344
  market efficiency, 345
  political risk, 344
  regulations, 345
  taxes, 347
  transaction costs, 346–347
PMI. *see* purchasing managers index
point estimates, 23n.19
Poland, 73
policy portfolio, 207. *see also* strategic asset allocation
political corruption, 354
political leadership, 76
political risk, 344
population, of BRICs, 181, 184, 201
population mean, estimating, 16n.7
portfolio return performance
  for emerging markets, 355
  international diversification, 333–339
    ex post example, 335–337
    forward-looking optimization, 338–339
    and market environment, 338
    and Sharpe ratio, 334
portfolios
  corner, 234–238
  efficient
    and Black–Litterman approach, 255–257
    for mean–variance approach, 239–249

    resampled, 249–250
    and risk reduction with international diversification, 326–328
  global minimum-variance, 232
  policy, 207
  segmentation of, 289–290
  suitability of equity market forecasts for, 139–140
  tangency, 241
Portugal, 8
potential output, 50
PPP. *see* Purchasing Power Parity
premiums
  bond-yield-plus-risk-premium method, 37
  default risk, 35
  equity risk, 33, 37–38, 145, 296
  fixed-income, 35–37
  illiquidity, 35n.43
  inflation, 35–37
  maturity, 35
  risk, 11, 34–42, 49
  tax, 35
priced risk, 34
price manipulation, 345
price to earnings ratio (P/E)
  of common shares, 93
  H-model for estimating, 129–136
  justified estimates, 124–137
    for developed economies, 136–137
    and neoclassical approach to growth accounting, 124–125, 127–128
private equity, 228
private sector, government structural policies in, 70
privatization, in emerging markets, 355
productivity, total factor, 67–69
  and BRIC growth accounting, 179–180
  growth in, 67–69
  and neoclassical approach to growth accounting, 124–126
prospect theory, 220n.18
prudence trap, 21
prudent person concept, 281
psychological traps, in capital market expectations, 20–22
public good, 70n.64
public sector, government structural policies in, 70
purchasing managers index (PMI), 60–61
Purchasing Power Parity (PPP)
  and BRIC economies, 179
  and exchange rates, 97

Q
Qatar, 73
quantitative easing, 55, 64

R
rational belief equilibrium, 22n.18
real assets, inflation/deflation effects for, 57–58
real bond yields, 88–89
real estate
  in asset allocation, 224
  forecasts of returns, 94
  inflation/deflation effects for, 57–58
  market integration, 42

  mean returns, volatilities, and correlations, 228, 229
real gross domestic product, growth rate of, 31
real interest rate, inflation premium and, 36
real risk-free interest rate, 35, 36
rebalancing
  of asset allocation, 271–272
  and Monte Carlo simulation, 258
re-basing, of indices, 14
recallability trap, 21
recession phase (business cycle), 52–53
  defined, 50
  earnings in, 91
  and market expectations, 58–59
  yield curve as predictor of, 53
regimes, 16, 17
regional factors, in global investing, 350–351
regression analysis, regime changes and, 17
regret, investor, 221
relative economic strength forecasting approach, 97, 99
relative value models for equity market, 144–157
  asset-based models, 153–157
  earnings-based models, 144–153
    10-year Moving Average Price/Earnings, 150–153
    Fed model, 144–147
    Yardeni model, 147–150
Renault, 350
repatriation, of income and capital, 355
repurchase yield, 32
resampled efficient frontier, 249–250
resampled efficient portfolio, 249–250
rescaling, of appraisal data, 15–16
residuals, 68
return(s)
  cross-sectional variation of, 211
  drivers of, 123–124
  equilibrium, 251–254
  expected
    estimates of, 11–12
    Gordon growth model, 30–31
    Grinold–Kroner approach, 33
    risk premium approach, 35
    unconditional, 18–19
  forecasting, 86–100
    for cash and equivalents, 86–87
    for common shares, 90–93
    for currencies, 95–96
    for defaultable debt, 89
    for emerging market bonds, 89
    and exchange rates, 96–100
    and historical capital market expectations, 94–95
    for inflation-indexed bonds, 89–90
    for nominal default-free bonds, 88
    for real estate, 94
  mean, 23, 26
  portfolio
    and international diversification, 333–339
    for investments in emerging markets, 355
  variation of, 210–211

return objectives, asset allocation and, 214–216
Reuters, 101
reverse optimization, 250
risk
    active, 209
    and ALM approaches to asset allocation, 213
    country, 74–77
    currency
        in emerging markets, 354
        and international diversification, 324–326, 339–340, 347, 354
        and strategic asset allocation, 227, 271
    of domestic investing, 351–352
    downside, 218
    ex ante, 17–18, 38
    ex post, 17–18, 335–337
    and human capital, 277
    and international diversification, 323–333
        for bonds, 330–332
        currency considerations, 324–326
        efficient portfolios, 326–328
        for equities, 328–330
        leads/lags in correlations, 332–333
    liquidity, 345
    longevity, 278–280
    market, 340
    mortality, 278–280
    political, 344
    priced, 34
    shortfall, 217–218, 220
    systematic, 207–209
    and TAA, 297
risk-adjusted expected return, 217
risk aversion, 269
risk-free interest rates, 35, 36
RiskMetrics Group, 26
risk objectives, asset allocation and, 216–220
risk premium approach to capital market expectations, 11, 34–38
    equity risk premiums, 37–38
    fixed-income premiums, 35–37
    general expression, 35
risk premiums
    about, 37
    in asset-pricing theory, 49
    equity, 37–38
    financial market equilibrium models for, 39–42
    fixed-income, 35–37
risk tolerance
    and asset allocation reviews, 230
    and strategic asset allocation, 216–217
Roy's safety-first criterion, 218–219
Russell 2500 Index, 42
Russia, 72. *see also* Brazil, Russia, India, and China (BRICs)

S

safety-first ratio (SFRatio), 218
sales, inventory and, 50–51
sample estimators, 23–24
sampling theory, 16n.7
Saudi Arabia, 73, 80

savings–investment imbalances forecasting approach, 98–99
Scandinavia, 349
Schroder Salomon Smith Barney, 47
segmented markets, 40–42, 356
semiactive investing, 271
semivariance, asset allocation and, 218
Seoul Stock Exchange, 354
September 11 terrorist attacks, 59
SFRatio. *see* safety-first ratio
share repurchases, Grinold–Kroner model for, 32
Sharpe ratio
    for international assets, 226–227
    and international portfolio return performance, 333–334
shortfall risk, 217–218, 220
short-term borrowing, country risk and, 76
shrinkage estimation, 24–26
sign-constrained optimization, 233–238
simulated efficient portfolios, 249
Singapore, 68, 75
Singer–Terhaar approach, 39–46
Slovakia, 8
Slovenia, 8
slowdown phase (business cycle), 52, 53
small-cap stock effect, 18
smoothed data, 14–16
Solow residual, 125
South Africa
    BRICs vs., 185–186
    equity risk premium, 38
    expected returns for equities/bonds, 24
South America, 80–81. *see also specific countries*
South Korea
    Chinese economy vs., 173
    Conference Board index, 81
    currency risk, 354
    economic growth, 177, 188
    trade partners, 80, 81
Soviet Union, 126, 127
S&P 500 Index
    appraisal data on, 15, 16
    capital market expectations from, 263
    in capital market forecasts, 42
    and Fed model, 144, 147
    forecasting approaches for, 137
    Grinold–Kroner analysis, 32
    and justified P/E estimates, 132
    in LEI, 82
    market earnings per share forecasting, 138–140
    and Yardeni model, 147
Spain
    Conference Board index, 81
    diversification opportunities, 349
    equity risk premium, 38
    Eurozone membership, 8
    expected returns for equities/bonds, 24
S&P China BMI Index
    dividend discount model, 134
    H-model, 130
    and justified P/E estimates, 132
    U.S. stock market returns vs., 133
SPDR S&P China ETF, 130
spending. *see* consumer spending

State Street Global Advisors, 130
static approach to asset allocation, 213
stationary time series, 23
statistical methods for setting capital market expectations, 23–30
    multifactor models, 26–30
    sample estimators, 23–24
    shrinkage estimators, 24–26
    time-series estimators, 26
Statistisches Bundesamt Deutschland, 79
status quo trap, 21
stocks
    cyclical, 91
    experience-based allocation approaches, 269
    small-cap stock effect, 18
strategic asset allocation, 206–207
    asset-only vs. ALM approaches, 212–214
    implementing, 270–272
        currency risk management decisions, 271
        investment approach and instrument selection, 270–271
        and rebalancing, 271–272
    for individual investors, 272–280
        critique of, 279–280
        human capital factors, 272–277
        and mortality/longevity risk, 278–280
    for institutional investors, 280–294
        banks, 292–294
        defined-benefit plans, 281–285
        foundations and endowments, 285–289
        insurance companies, 289–293
    and return objectives, 214–216
    and risk objectives, 216–220
    and systematic risk, 207–209
    tactical vs., 209–210
structural level of unemployment, 70
structural policies, government, 69–70
surplus, 260
surplus efficient frontier, 260, 261, 264–266
surplus optimization, 266–268
survey methods, 47–48
survivorship bias, 14
Sweden
    CLI for, 79
    expected returns for equities/bonds, 24
    inflation-protected bonds, 225
    real GDP growth rate, 31
Swissair, 352
Switzerland
    asset allocation in pension plans, 282
    bond market correlation, 331
    CLI for, 79
    country factors v. industry factors, 352
    equity risk premium, 38
    expected returns for equities/bonds, 24
    international diversification regulation, 345
    market integration, 42
    real GDP growth rate, 31
    stock market correlation, 329
    trade partners, 80
systematic risk, 207–209

Index

T

tactical asset allocation (TAA), 294–300
  defined, 207
  global adjustments in, 298–299
  investment decisions for, 299–300
  strategic asset allocation vs., 209–210
tangency portfolio, 241
Tankan Survey, 80
target covariance matrix, 25
target semivariance, 218
taxes
  discriminatory, 355
  and government structural policies, 70
  and insurance company bond investments, 291
  and international diversification, 347
  withholding, 347
tax-exempt bonds, 224
tax premiums, 35
Taylor rule, 62–63
T-bills. see U.S. Treasury bills
T-bonds. see U.S. Treasury bonds
10-year Moving Average Price/Earnings, 150–153, 156
TFP. see total factor productivity
Thailand, 80, 354
Thomas, Ian (case study), 241–245
time differences, correlations of assets and, 332–333
time horizon
  for capital market expectations, 7, 10
  for experience-based allocation approaches, 269–270
  and return objectives of investors, 216
time-period biases, 18
time-series estimators, 26
TIPS. see U.S. Treasury Inflation-Protected Securities
Tobin's q ratio
  and asset-based models, 153–156
  strengths and limitations, 157
Tokyo Stock Exchange, 332–333
total factor productivity (TFP)
  and BRIC growth accounting, 179–180
  growth in, 67–69
  and neoclassical approach to growth accounting, 124–126
Toyota, 350
trade
  and business cycle, 59
  and currency returns, 96
trade balance, overall, 75n.65
transaction costs, 346–347
transcription errors, 14
Turkey, 79, 225
twin deficits problem, 70
two-layer factor approach for modeling covariance, 29

U

UBL model. see unconstrained Black–Litterman model
uncertainty, input and model, 22
unconditional expected returns, 18–19
unconditioned benchmarks, 19
unconstrained Black–Litterman (UBL) model, 250
unconstrained optimization, 233
unemployment, structural level of, 70
unilateral pegging of currency, 72
United Arab Emirates, 73, 80
United Kingdom
  asset allocation, 210, 281, 282
  bond market correlation, 331
  BRC survey, 60
  BRIC growth rate vs., 184
  Chinese economy vs., 173
  CLI, 79
  Conference Board index, 81
  denationalization, 133
  diversification opportunities, 349
  economic growth, 66, 174, 181, 182, 188, 193, 196–200
  equity risk premium, 38
  expected returns for equities/bonds, 24
  Fed model with U.K. data, 145–146
  global efficient frontier, 337
  inflation, 54, 55
  inflation-indexed bonds, 89
  inflation-protected bonds, 225
  market integration, 42
  prudent person concept, 281
  real GDP growth rate, 31
  return on government bonds, 88
  short-term consumer spending, 47–48
  stock market correlation, 329
  TFP growth, 69
  trade partners, 80
  transaction volume on U.S. market, 347
  and U.S. stock market crash, 343
United Nations System of National Accounts (UNSNA), 13
United States
  asset allocation, 210, 211, 281–283
  bond market correlation, 331
  bond yields, 74
  capital flows forecasting approach, 98
  China equity market valuation vs., 132–134
  Chinese economy vs., 173
  CLI, 79
  degree of specialization, 72
  Economic Freedom Index, 75
  economic growth, 126, 128, 174, 181, 182, 188, 193, 196–200
  equity risk premium, 33, 38
  exchange rate linkages with, 73
  expected returns for equities/bonds, 24
  Fed model with U.S. data, 144–145
  GDP growth, 339
  growth accounting in, 127
  inflation, 54, 55
  inflation-indexed bonds, 89
  inflation-protected bonds, 225
  international diversification, 344, 345, 349
  inventory/sales ratio, 50–51
  long-term government bonds, 263
  macroeconomic linkages, 72
  market integration, 42
  mean return, 338
  monetary policy, 63, 64
  P/E ratios, 93
  PMI, 60–61
  prudent person concept, 281
  real GDP growth rate, 31
  recessions, 58–59
  return on government bonds, 88
  stock market correlation, 328–330
  TFP growth, 68–69
  trade partners, 80, 81
  and world stock market capitalization, 322
U.S. Commerce Department, 81
U.S. Consumer Price Index (CPI), 150, 225
U.S. Consumer Price Index for All Urban Consumers (CPI-U), 13, 43
U.S. dollar, 99
U.S. dollar bonds, 322
U.S. Treasury bills (T-bills)
  and capital market expectations, 263
  in capital market forecasts, 43
  nominal risk-free interest rate, 35
  and TAA, 294
  yield curve of T-bonds and, 53
U.S. Treasury bonds (T-bonds)
  and Fed model, 34, 146
  junk bond yield vs., 291
  yield curve of T-bills and, 53
U.S. Treasury debt, maturity premium for, 35–36
U.S. Treasury Inflation-Protected Securities (TIPS), 89, 225–226
U.S. Treasury notes, 147
U.S. Treasury securities, Fed model and, 144–146
University of Michigan Survey, 100
UNSNA. see United Nations System of National Accounts
unstructured modeling, 77n.66
Uruguay, 42

V

valuation. see equity market valuation
Vanguard LifeStrategy® funds, 269
variable annuities, 279
variables, endogenous vs. exogenous, 19
variation, of returns, 210–211
VE Post Venture Capital Index, 43
volatility
  and correlations of international assets, 342–343, 348–349
  of emerging markets, 74
  and historical analysis, 17
  of investing in emerging markets, 353–354
  as measure of risk tolerance, 217
volatility clustering, 26
volatility ratio, 296
Volcker, Paul, 58

W

Wal-Mart Stores, 69
wealth effect, permanent income hypothesis and, 66
Welch, 47
Wen Jiabao, 128
Western Europe, 129. see also specific countries
withholding taxes, 347
World Bank, 74, 100
world economy, BRICs in, 171–172
World Trade Organization, 341
worldwide economic indicators, 79

Y

Yardeni, Edward, 144
Yardeni model, 147–150, 156
yield
  bond
    nominal, 73–74
    real, 88–89
  yield to maturity, 34
  yield to worst, 34n.38
  repurchase, 32
yield curve
  and monetary/fiscal policy, 65
  as predictor of economic growth, 53
yield to maturity (YTM), bond, 34
yield to worst, 34n.38

Z

Zheng, Hu, and Bigstein (ZHB) projections, 128–129